# COMMUNICATION
## MAKING CONNECTIONS

William J. Seiler • Melissa L. Beall

**Third Custom Edition for Kean University**

Taken from:

*Communication: Making Connections,* Seventh Edition
by William J. Seiler and Melissa L. Beall

PEARSON

Custom
Publishing

Cover Art: *One from Many,* by Robin MacDonald-Foley

Taken from:

*Communication: Making Connections,* Seventh Edition
by William J. Seiler and Melissa L. Beall
Copyright © 2008 by Pearson Education, Inc.
Published by Allyn and Bacon
Boston, Massachusetts 02116

Printed in the United States of America

10  9  8  7  6  5  4  3  2  1

ISBN 0-536-46026-4

2007560028

LG/LD

Please visit our web site at *www.pearsoncustom.com*

PEARSON CUSTOM PUBLISHING
501 Boylston Street, Suite 900, Boston, MA 02116
A Pearson Education Company

# Contents

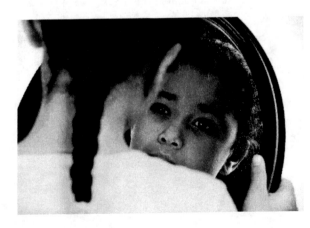

CHAPTER **6** Connecting Listening and Thinking in the Communication Process 138

CHAPTER **7** Selecting a Topic and Connecting to the Audience 162

# CHAPTER 8 Gathering and Using Information   190

# CHAPTER 9 Organizing and Outlining Your Speech   214

# CHAPTER **10** Managing Anxiety and Delivering Your Speech 252

# CHAPTER **11** Informative Speaking 288

# CHAPTER 12 Persuasive Speaking 318

■ **PART THREE** Connecting in Relational Contexts

CHAPTER **13** Interpersonal Communication 352

CHAPTER **14** Developing Relationships 380

# CHAPTER **15** Group and Team Communication  414

# CHAPTER 16  Participating in Groups and Teams  442

# APPENDIX  Employment Interviewing: Preparing for Your Future  467

# APPENDIX B  Making Team Decisions Systematically  B-1

Taken from *Communicating With Creativity and Confidence*, Second Edition
by Gay Lumsden and Donald Lumsden

SPEECH EVALUATION FORM

# Preface

## Why We Don't "Leave Well Enough Alone"

**C**ommunication: Making Connections is about communication and the way it connects us to others in our everyday lives. We wrote in our last edition, "This field is not only interesting—it's useful—something that we can use all of our lives." We believe this is true even more today. Communication in our everyday lives has become more complex because our world is increasingly more diverse and more complex. We are a "wired" society and use technology in its many forms constantly. Given these lifestyle behaviors, we

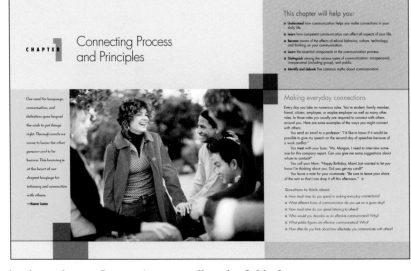

realized that a communication textbook needs to reflect society as well as the field of communication, and we weren't willing to leave well enough alone. Our approach for revising this edition then became: *Nothing—no topic, no illustration, no example, and no exercise—is sacred.* To implement this basic value and reflect the current knowledge of communication studies, we reviewed and revised every aspect of the book. The following summarizes the changes we view as being the most important and hopefully most helpful to students' success in connecting with others in their daily lives.

We are awed, humbled, and gratified that so many instructors chose *Communication: Making Connections* for their students. Our overall theme in this edition, as in the previous editions, remains "showing students how to 'make connections' between communication and their daily lives."

Because we want this book to help students become more competent communicators in a variety of contexts, we continue to emphasize theory and up-to-date research as it relates to practical application and concrete communicative skills. Our purpose is to help students learn about communication principles, public speaking, interpersonal communication, and group communication skills that they can use in the years ahead.

Our goal hasn't changed: to make our book enjoyable, yet comprehensive, practical, readable, and intellectually sound. We make every effort in this edition, as in previous editions, to make practical connections between theory, research, and skills, so that it is challenging but not overwhelming.

# Changes in the Seventh Edition

The seventh edition represents input from many talented and helpful individuals. We listened to not only those who reviewed our text and draft chapters but to the many students and instructors who have used our text. We were also fortunate to have a developmental editor who pushed us to rethink everything we had done in the past. We assure you that the changes, while substantial, do not take away from the strengths that students and instructors said they enjoyed in our previous edition. Here are some of the more obvious changes that we made:

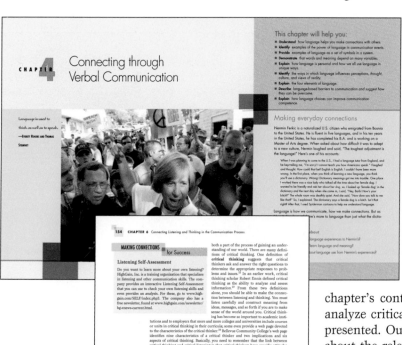

■ **We better integrated the "making connections" theme throughout this edition to ensure that students see and understand the connections communication has to all aspects of their everyday lives.** Almost every chapter has a new opening entitled "Making Everyday Connections." This feature provides students with real communicative situations that are likely to be part of their everyday communication encounters. In addition, the questions posed after each opening situation relate to the chapter's content and require the students to analyze critically the communication situation presented. Our goal is to make students think about the relevance of the content and how it relates to their own lives.

■ **New and updated Making Connections for Success boxes.** Making Connections for Success helps students think critically about communication in their lives. Each box contains skill-building activities and thought-provoking questions to help students become more competent communicators.

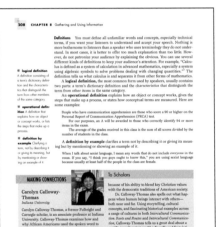

■ **Making Connections to Scholars,** a feature introduced in the sixth edition, is updated to help students know about the people who have made a difference in the way we approach, research, and teach communication concepts. This feature emphasizes the importance of research and creates a personal connection between the students and the scholars in our discipline. In most chapters we highlight the research of some of the most prolific and influential scholars in the communication discipline. It is important for students to know that the concepts we present in the text are based on research conducted by communication scholars.

■ **Making Technology Connections** is a **new feature** that emphasizes the role and importance of technology in our everyday interactions. The feature allows students to see how technology influences communication and how it can both help and hinder competent communication. Students will have hands-on experience as well as reflect on their experiences with technology in everyday communication.

■ **Changes in the book's design improve its appeal and readability.** Many new photos and updated contemporary examples of communication situations bolster existing examples and enhance the relevance of the content. Photos and captions clearly reflect the content and provide relevant examples of communication concepts and principles to help the students learn.

■ **Expanded coverage of gender, cultural diversity, ethics, and critical thinking.** Revised and improved examples are representative of today's students, including nontraditional students. This seventh edition includes up-to-date coverage of gender differences in interpersonal, presentational, and small-group communication; new coverage of critical thinking and listening; and a balanced coverage of cultural and ethical issues throughout the text that provide a better understanding of the communication competencies needed to succeed in a global environment. We expanded critical thinking exercises and added many new thought-provoking questions throughout the text as well as in new end-of-chapter discussion questions.

■ **Part Two, "Connecting in the Public Context," is expanded and revised.** All six chapters in this section include new examples, figures, and illustrations. We adapt situations and topics our students used in our classes and include them as examples throughout the chapters, demonstrating how to develop an idea from topic choice through speech delivery. Brainstorming and organizing ideas through strategies such as mind mapping are covered in new ways. We include discussion of presentations in the classroom and beyond, streamlined the text, and add more explanations and examples. Whenever possible, concepts are illustrated to help students' understanding. In response to requests, we added more suggestions for topic ideas within the chapters as well as in the appendices for Chapters 11 and 12. Many examples demonstrate how competent speakers connect with their listeners.

■ **Using the Internet for Research—new sources and examples in this edition.** Wherever possible, we include numerous Internet sources. Many students, for better or worse, use the Internet as a default option for researching their speeches. Throughout Part Two we offer guidelines for finding, using, and evaluating Internet and other sources. We explain basic strategies for using search engines. Instructors who want to give even greater attention to the Internet can do so with the *Allyn & Bacon Research Guide.* Taken together, these resources provide the most up-to-date, thorough, and helpful coverage of the Internet available with any introductory communication textbook.

■ Our previous editions were considered by many to be a model for other communication texts in the area of technology. **This edition further integrates technology into most chapters and also has an interactive website at www.mycommunicationlab.com.** The website complements the text and allows students to interact more thoroughly with its content. With the addition of Making Technology Connection boxes, easily accessible websites, and technology examples throughout the text, students will learn how technology influences our communication and connections with others, as well as communication concepts.

■ **Updated coverage of online discussion in the small-group chapters.** Students learn how to make the most of an online discussion and why online communication has become a popular means of interaction. The advantages and disadvantages of using online discussions are explained.

■ **Updated to include the most recent research and examples.** When appropriate, we describe research studies and cite the scholars conducting the research. These updates help students understand the relationship between developing research and the concepts in the text.

■ **The updated appendix, "Interviewing: Preparing for Your Future," now includes more information on online job searches, preparation for the employment interview, and other aspects of the employment interview.** This appendix is specifically written for first- or second-year students as they prepare for their future career searches.

Nevertheless, because the appendix addresses many important issues in preparing for and participating in the employment interview, it is useful to all students. The appendix includes one of the best sections on using the Internet for job searches and résumé development of any introductory communication textbook.

■ **Discussion Starters provide springboards for class discussion.** Most end-of-each chapter discussion starters have been revised to build on the Making Connections features. The discussion starters provide another vehicle for students to actively discuss and apply what they have read in each chapter.

# ■ Content Changes in the Seventh Edition

## ■ Part One: Making Connections through Communication (Chapters 1 through 6)

■ Chapters incorporate more examples of our "wired" society and how much technology influences us. We emphasize how communication in its various forms helps us make connections with others. We also include examples beyond the classroom to include the workplace and community.

■ We revised the sections on understanding perception's influence on our communication, perception formation, verbal communication, interpretation, and perception checking.

■ We created a new introduction to self-concept to make it more relevant to everyday-lives of students. We added a new section on personal social identity to illustrate how groups influence who we are and our communication with others. The sections on self-concept development, self-fulfilling prophecy, impression management, and enhancing self were revised. The section on gender expectations was expanded and made more relevant to today's students.

■ The language and listening chapters are significantly updated with current research and examples. We include examples from our own students' experiences with making connections through language and listening. There are more cultural perspectives in the boxed features and illustrations in these chapters. Our examples from literature as well as the Internet give a "real-world" flavor to the explanations and help students think about the similarities and differences between language used for writing and speaking.

## ■ Part Two: Connecting in the Public Context (Chapters 7 through 12)

■ Most examples are updated throughout the section. We ensure that the reader will connect the text concepts both to public communication and interpersonal communicative efforts. We also incorporate famous and not-so-famous communicators.

■ Examples of choosing a topic, gathering and using information, and organizing and outlining ideas are updated. Examples from our own students' speeches are included (with student permission), and show how ideas develop from choosing a speech topic to completing and delivering the speech.

■ More technology examples are included in the text and boxed features, to offer students useful information about using electronic resources in developing their speeches.

■ Ethical perspectives are constantly brought into focus.

■ Examples of speech topics within the chapters and in the chapter appendices include those our students discussed and discarded as well as those they actually selected for their presentations.

### ■■ Part Three: Connecting in Relational Contexts (Chapters 13 through 16 and the Appendix)

■ We updated the introduction on interpersonal communication and relationships to include more on the effects of technology on relationship development.

■ The definition of *interpersonal communication* is revised to bring it more in line with current research.

■ We include a new sub-section within group formation to cover the downside of groups and to develop a new section on entiativity (the perception of being a coherent entity) and its influences on group membership. The section on leadership is revised to incorporate more up-to-date information on leadership styles and their role in today's society.

■ We revised the appendix on interviewing to be as up-to-date as possible, with new sections on electronic job searches, applying online, and emailing résumés to potential employers.

## ■ Pedagogical Aids in the Text

Communication competence is a learned skill. Although natural ability is an asset, any person's capabilities in communication can be improved through (1) an understanding of communicative theories and principles, (2) training in its basic principles, (3) practice, and (4) improving communication competence. This new edition meets students' needs in all four areas by providing:

■ Actively stated and specific learning objectives at the beginning of each chapter that help students focus on what they will learn.

■ Everyday communication situations, Making Everyday Connections, which allow students to think critically about their communication and how they might improve it.

■ Thorough and systematic explanations of basic communication principles.

■ Thought-provoking Making Connections for Success boxes that encourage students' active involvement throughout each chapter.

■ Clear and concrete student-oriented examples, photos, cartoons, and other visual materials that support and expand on key concepts.

■ Lists of Guidelines that help students transform theory into practice.

■ End-of-chapter summaries that highlight key concepts.

■ Discussion starter questions that engage and encourage students to think critically and apply what they have learned.

■ Key terms defined in the margins.

# ■ Organization of the Text

The chapters are arranged to provide a practical and workable approach to teaching the fundamentals of communication. Part One: "Making Connections through Communication" provides the necessary background and basic principles for all communication. Part Two: "Connecting in the Public Context" helps students develop their speaking skills as they learn to select a topic, analyze an audience, gather and use supporting and clarifying materials, organize and outline speech material, deliver a speech with confidence, and effectively inform and persuade an audience. Part Three: "Connecting in Relational Contexts" describes communication in relationships and small groups and teams.

We present the foundations first, following with discussion of public communication skills and interpersonal and group communication. We discuss public communication skills before interpersonal communication because we believe that they are fundamental to all communication. All communication is goal-oriented. Therefore, in order to communicate effectively throughout life—whether socially, on the job, in one-to-one situations, in small groups, or before an audience—a person must be able to communicate with confidence, support and clarify his or her thoughts, organize information, analyze those with whom he or she is communicating, and inform and persuade effectively. This presentation sequence is also based on the recognition that although introductory communication students must master a great deal of basic information before they give a speech, course time constraints necessitate preparing and presenting speeches as early in the term as possible. Introducing public speaking skills first provides more balance between speech presentations and other activities, and alleviates the tendency to focus on speechmaking exclusively at the end of the term.

The broad range of material covered in the introductory communication course offers instructors a variety of ways to teach the course—by emphasizing interpersonal communication or public speaking, or by placing equal emphasis on all types of communication. Each chapter is completely self-contained, allowing the instructor to easily arrange the sequence to meet the demands of his or her specific teaching situation.

# ■ Supplements for the Instructor

## ■■ Print Resources

■ **Instructor's Resource Manual** by Melissa Beall and Marilyn Shaw, both of University of Northern Iowa. Provides nut-and-bolts information about developing an introductory communication course and methods for aiding instruction. The manual includes suggestions for organizing and managing the course; classroom and outside classroom exercises and assignments; resources such as additional readings, games, simulations, and films; a section on evaluating speeches; a section on training and working with part-time instructors and graduate teaching assistants; and finally, a section on the Personalized System of Instruction, an efficient and effective method for teaching the introductory course.

■ **Test Bank** by Kane Madison Klick, University of Nebraska–Lincoln, with Deborah Whitt and Marilyn Shaw. The completely revised test bank contains multiple-choice, true/false, and short-answer questions for each chapter. All questions are referenced by page and chapter number and include an indicator of difficulty.

■ **A&B Public Speaking Transparency Package, Version II** One hundred full-color transparencies created with PowerPoint software provide visual support for classroom lectures and discussions.

■ **The Blockbuster Approach: Teaching Interpersonal Communication with Video,** Third Edition, by Thomas E. Jewell, Bergen Community College. This guide describes commercial videos that instructors can use to illustrate interpersonal concepts and complex interpersonal relationships. Includes sample activities.

■ **New Teachers Guide to Public Speaking,** Third Edition, by Calvin Troup, Duquesne University. This guide helps new instructors to teach effectively the introductory course. It covers topics such as preparing for the term course, planning, evaluating speeches, utilizing the textbook, integrating technology into the classroom, and much more.

■ **Great Ideas for Teaching Speech (GIFTS),** Third Edition, by Raymond Zeuschner, California Polytechnic State University, San Luis Obispo. This instructional booklet provides descriptions of and guidelines for classroom assignments successfully used by experienced public speaking instructors.

■ **A Guide for New Teachers of Introduction to Communication,** Second Edition, by Susanna G. Porter, of Kennesaw State University. This guide helps new teachers provide effective instruction for the introductory communication course.

## ■■ Electronic Resources

■ **MyCommunicationLab.** Where students learn to communicate with confidence. MyCommunicationLab is an interactive and instructive online solution. Designed to supplement a traditional lecture course, or to completely administer an online course, MyCommunicationLab combines multimedia, video, communication activities, research support, tests, and quizzes to make teaching and learning fun! Students benefit from a wealth of video clips that feature student and professional speeches, small-group scenarios, and interpersonal interactions—some with running commentary and critical questions—all geared to help students learn to communicate with confidence. **URL:** www.mycommunicationlab.com (access code required).

■ **Computerized Test Bank.** A computerized version of the printed Test Bank is available with our testing system, TestGen EQ. The fully networkable test-generating software is now available on a multiplatform CD-ROM. The user-friendly interface enables instructors to view, edit, and add questions; transfer questions to tests; and print tests in a variety of fonts. Search and sort features allow instructors to locate questions quickly and arrange then in a preferred order.

■ **PowerPoint Presentation,** prepared by Paul Lakey, Abilene Christian University. This text-specific package consists of a collection of lecture outlines and graphic images keyed to every chapter in the text. Available for download at www.ablongman. com/irc.

■ **Allyn & Bacon Communication Digital Media Archive, Version 3.0,** available on CD-ROM, offers more than two hundred still images, video excerpts, and PowerPoint slides that can be used to enliven classroom presentations.

■ **VideoWorkshop for Introduction to Communication, Version 2.0** (www.ablongman. com/videoworkshop), by Kathryn Dindia, University of Wisconsin. *VideoWorkshop for Introduction to Communication* is a new way to bring video into your course for maximized learning. This total teaching and learning system includes quality video footage on any easy-to-use CD-ROM, plus the Student Learning Guide and the Instructor's Teaching Guide—both with textbook-specific correlation grids. The result? A program that brings textbook concepts to life and helps your students understand, analyze, and apply the objectives of the course. *VideoWorkshop* is available for your students as a value-pack option with this textbook.

## Video Materials

■ **The Allyn & Bacon Communication Video Library.** A collection of communication videos produced by Films for the Humanities and Social Sciences. Topics include, but are not limited to: Business Presentations, Great American Speeches, and Conflict Resolution. Contact your Allyn & Bacon sales representative for ordering information. Some restrictions apply.

■ **A&B Contemporary Classic Speeches DVD.** This exciting supplement includes over 120 minutes of video footage in DVD format. Biographical and historical summaries help students understand the context and motivation behind each speech. May also be packaged with participating A&B texts.

■ **The Allyn & Bacon Student Speeches Video Library.** This collection of communication videos includes videos from the American Forensic Association highlighted award-winning student speeches, classroom-based student speeches, and a collection of videos produced by Film for the Humanities and Sciences. Topics include, but are not excluded to, Business Presentations, Great American Speeches, and Conflict Resolution. See the Communication Video Guide for details and restrictions.

■ **The Allyn & Bacon Public Speaking Video.** This video includes excerpts of classic and contemporary speeches as well as student speeches to illustrate the public speaking process. One speech is delivered two times under different circumstances by the same person to illustrate the difference between effective and non-effective delivery based on appearance, non-verbal, and verbal style. For adopters only. Restrictions apply. See your Allyn & Bacon representative for details.

■ **The Allyn & Bacon Interpersonal Communication Video.** The interpersonal video contains three scenarios that illustrate key concepts in interpersonal communication. A Faculty User's Guide features transcripts and teaching activities. For adopters only. Restrictions apply. See your Allyn & Bacon representative for details.

## ■ Student Supplements

### ■ Print Resources

■ **Personalized System of Instruction (PSI) Study Guide Manual.** This manual provides students with questions and exercises to aid them in studying. To meet their individual needs, instructors can modify this manual designed originally for use at the University of Nebraska–Lincoln. For a sample manual, contact Bill Seiler, Department of Communication Studies, University of Nebraska–Lincoln, Lincoln, Nebraska 68588-0329 or call 402-472-2069. E-mail address is bseiler@unl.edu.

■ **ResearchNavigator.com Guide: Speech Communication.** This updated booklet by Steven L. Epstein of Suffolk County Community College includes tips, resources, and URLs to aid students conducting research on Pearson Education's research website, www.researchnavigator.com. The Research Navigator database (access code required) offers students unlimited access to a collection of more than 25,000 discipline-specific articles from top-tier academic publications and peer-reviewed journals, the *New York Times,* and popular news publications. The guide introduces students to the basics of the Internet and the World Wide Web, includes article search tips and lists journals useful for research in their discipline. The guide includes hundreds of discipline-related web resources and information on how to correctly cite research. The guide is available packaged with new copies of the text.

■ **Study Card for Introduction to Communication.** Colorful, affordable, and packed with useful information, the Study Card makes studying easier, more efficient, and more enjoyable. The Study Card distills course information to the basics, helping students quickly master the fundamentals, review a subject for reinforcement, or prepare for an exam. Students can keep these laminated, durable Study Cards for years to come and pull them out whenever needed for a quick review. Sold separately or packaged with participating A&B texts.

■ **Speech Preparation Workbook,** by Jennifer Dreyer and Gregory H. Patton, of San Diego State University. This workbook takes students through the stages of speech creation—from audience analysis to writing the speech—and includes guidelines, tips, and easy-to-fill-in pages. Sold separately or packaged with participating A&B texts.

■ **Preparing Visual Aids for Presentation,** Fourth Edition, by Dan Cavanaugh. This booklet provides a host of ideas for using today's multimedia tools to improve presentations, including suggestions for planning a presentation, guidelines for designing visual aids and storyboarding, and a walkthrough showing how to prepare a Power-Point display. Sold separately or packaged with participating A&B texts.

■ **Public Speaking in the Multicultural Environment,** Second Edition, by Devorah Lieberman, of Portland State University. This two-chapter essay focuses on speaking and listening to a culturally diverse audience and emphasizes preparation, delivery, and perception of speeches. Sold separately or packaged with participating A&B texts.

■ **The Speech Outline: Outlining to Plan, Organize, and Deliver a Speech: Activities and Exercises,** by Reeze L. Hanson and Sharon Condon, of Haskell Indian Nations University. This brief workbook includes activities, exercises, and answers to help students develop and master the critical skill of outlining. Sold separately or packaged with participating A&B texts.

■ **Pathways to Careers in Communication.** The National Communication Association's booklet provides information about the discipline, its history and importance, information on career possibilities, and other available resources for investigating communication studies. Value packed with any A&B Communication text.

## ■■ Electronic Resources

■ **Introduction to Communication Study Site,** www.abintrocommunication.com. This website includes links to sites with speeches in text, audio, and video formats, as well as links to other valuable websites. The site also contains flashcards and a fully expanded set of practice tests for all major topics.

■ **Allyn & Bacon Communication Studies Web Site,** by Terrence Doyle, Northern Virginia Community College; Tim Borchers, Moorehead State University; and Nan Peck, Northern Virginia Community College. This site includes modules on interpersonal communication, small-group communication, and public speaking. It includes web links, enrichment materials, and interactive activities to enhance students' understanding of key concepts. Access this site at www.ablongman.com/commstudies.

■ **Speech Writer's Workshop CD-ROM, Version 2.0.** This exciting public speaking software includes a *Speech Handbook* with tips for researching and preparing speeches; a *Speech Workshop*, which guides students step-by-step through the speech writing process; a *Topics Dictionary*, which gives students hundreds of ideas for speeches; and the *Documentor* citation database, which helps students format bibliographic entries in either MLA or APA style. Students can purchase this product at no additional cost when value packed with any Allyn & Bacon texts. (Some restrictions apply.)

■ **VideoWorkshop for Introduction to Communication, Version 2.0** (www.ablongman .com/videoworkshop), by Kathryn Dindia, University of Wisconsin. *VideoWorkshop for Introduction to Communication* is more than just video footage you can watch. It's a total learning system. Our complete program includes quality video footage on an easy-to-use dual platform CD-ROM, plus a Student Learning Guide with textbook-specific Correlation Grids. The result? A program that brings textbook concepts to life with ease that helps your students understand, analyze, and apply the objectives of the course. *VideoWorkshop* is available as a value-pack option with this textbook.

# ■ Acknowledgments

Numerous people have contributed to the previous editions as well as this edition of the book. First and foremost are the students who used this book and shared their time and learning experiences with us, the instructors who patiently taught us about communication and life, the colleagues who shared their expertise with us, the many graduate students who worked in our basic speech courses over the years, and the hundreds of undergraduate assistants and assistant supervisory instructors who assisted in the University of Nebraska's Personalized System of Instruction basic communication course during the past 30 years.

A project of large proportion, this edition required the talents and hard work of many people. We extend our appreciation to Dr. Larry Routh, the Director of Career Planning and Placement at the University of Nebraska–Lincoln, for his review and guidance in the writing of the Employment Interview appendix.

Special thanks go to Marilyn Shaw, Instructor of the Introductory Communication course at the University of Northern Iowa for assisting with the Instructor's Manual. We also thank Kane Click, University of Nebraska–Lincoln for his help in revising the test bank. In addition to Marilyn and Kane, many other faculty and graduate students helped us by providing ideas and suggestions too numerous to mention here. Especially: Elissa Arterburn, Diane Badzinski, Karla Bergen, Mary Bort, Dawn Braithwaite, Ann Burnett, John Caughlin, Susan Cusmano, Linda Dickmeyer, Gus Friedrich, Bobbie Harry, Adam Jones, Jack Kay, Jody Koenig Kellas, Emily Lamb, Karen Lee, Ronald Lee, Rob Patterson, Drew McGukin, Carol Morgan, Bill Mullen, Angelia Nunziata, Jack Sargent, Paul Schrodt, Jordan Soliz, Blair Thompson, Shawn Wahl, and Nicole Zumbach.

We offer a special thank you to Deborah Whitt, Wayne State College, Wayne, Nebraska, and Carla L. Sloan, Liberty University, Lynchburg, Virginia, for their insight and thoughtful reviews of specific chapters. We also thank all the undergraduate and graduate students at University of Nebraska–Lincoln and the University of Northern Iowa who provided resources and examples. Finally, we offer thanks to the communication scholars who so graciously agreed to allow us to use their names, information, and photographs in our book: Carolyn Calloway-Thomas, Randy Y. Hirokawa, Mark Knapp, Sandra Petronio, Robert L. Scott, Cynthia Stohl, Karen Tracy, Judith Trent, Bill Wilmot, Andrew Wolvin, and David Zarefsky.

We are also extremely grateful to Hilary Jackson, developmental editor, for her critical guidance, editing, and developmental skills. She made exceptional contributions to our final product. Her goal to improve our text and to ensure that it was the best edition possible, in our humble opinion, was accomplished. We gratefully acknowledge all those at Allyn & Bacon who had a hand in getting our manuscript into book form. We also thank Karon Bowers, Editor-in-Chief, for her continued support (even though she is a huge Texas football fan and will not let us forget that Texas won the National Championship in 2005).

The publishing of any book requires people dedicated to high quality, and this edition of our book is no exception. We thank all those who participated in the review process of the first six editions of the book: Philip M. Backlund, Central Washington University; William Patrick Barlow, Madison Area Technical College; Marty Birkholt, Creighton University; Barbara L. Breaclen, Lane Community College; Scott Britten, Tiffin University; Allan R. Broadhurst, Cape Cod Community College; Michael Bruner, University of North Texas; Diane O. Casagrande, West Chester University; Patricia Comeaux, University of North Carolina at Wilmington; Juanita E. Dailey, University of Rio Grande; Linda Y. Devenish, Ithaca College; Carley H. Dodd, Abilene Christian University; Terrence Doyle, Northern Virginia Community College; Sean M. Dunn, Bridgewater College; Richard C. Emanuel, University of Montevallo; Skip Eno, University of Texas at San Antonio; Jeanine Fassl, University of Wisconsin at Whitewater; Julia Fennell, Community College of Allegheny County, South Campus; Mary C. Forestieri, Lane Community College; Robert E. Frank, Morehead State University; Anne Grissom, Mountain View College; Kelby K. Halone, Clemson University; Ted Hindermarsh, Brigham Young University; Colleen Hogan-Taylor, University of Washington; David D. Hudson, Golden West College; Mary Lee Hummert, University of Kansas; David A. Humphrey, College of DuPage; Stephen K. Hunt, Illinois State University; Karla Kay Jensen, Nebraska Wesleyan University; Kathryn C. Jones, Northern Virginia Community College, Annandale Campus; Thomas J. Knutson, California State University at Sacramento; Charles J. Korn, Northern Virginia Community College; Donald L. Loeffler, Western Carolina University; Louis A. Lucca, La Guardia Community College (CUNY); Mary Y. Mandeville, Oklahoma State University; Corinne E. Morris, Northeast Community College; William L. Mullen, Liberty University; Kay E. Neal, University of Wisconsin, Oshkosh; Nan Peck, Northern Virginia Community College; Sandra E. Presar, West Virginia Wesleyan College; Marlene M. Preston, Virginia Polytechnic Institute and State University; Richard G. Rea, University of Arkansas; Marc E. Routhier, Frostburg State College; Jared Saltzman, Bergen Community College; Marilyn M. Shaw, University of Northern Iowa; Cheri J. Simonds, Illinois State University; Donald B. Simmons, Asbury College; Mary Anne Trasciatti, Hofstra University; Beth Waggenspack, Virginia Polytechnic Institute and State University; Catherine Egley Waggoner, Ohio State University; Gretchen Aggertt Weber, Horry-Georgetown Technical College; Kathie A. Webster, Northwest Missouri State University; Larry A. Weiss, University of Wisconsin at Oshkosh; Cherie C. While, Muskingum Area Technical College; Karen Wolf, Suffolk Community College; David W. Worley, Indiana State University.

Finally, thanks to those who provided analysis of the sixth edition and made recommendations and suggestions for the new edition: David A. Humphrey, College of DuPage; William L. Mullen, Liberty University; Marlene M. Preston, Virginia Polytechnic Institute and State University; Jared Saltzman, Bergen Community College; and Karen Wolf, Suffolk Community College.

# ■ Some Concluding Comments . . . And a Request for Your Thoughts

It is time to ask for *your* help again. As we have in previous editions, we spared no effort to make this new edition the best ever. While we are always striving for perfection, we, however, more often than not, fall short on some things. There is always room for improvement! In this respect, we sincerely request your comments. If there's something you feel can be improved, please let us know. Write, call, fax, or email us at one of the addresses below. We will listen and respond to your comments as quickly as possible. Thank you in advance for your help.

William (Bill) J. Seiler
Department of Communication Studies
University of Nebraska
Lincoln, NE 68588–0329
Phone: 402–472–2069
Fax: 402–472–6921
bseiler@unl.edu

Melissa L. Beall
Department of Communication Studies
University of Northern Iowa
Cedar Falls, IA 50613–0139
Phone: 319–273–9292
Fax: 319–273–7356
Melissa.Beall@uni.edu

# The Authors

**Bill Seiler** is Professor and Chair of the Department of Communication Studies, University of Nebraska–Lincoln, where he has taught since 1972. He is an avid golfer who plays every chance he gets which unfortunately is never enough. (This is his excuse for not playing well.) He loves his Nebraska Huskers and travels to one or two away games each year. He and his college sweetheart, Kathi, celebrated their 40th wedding anniversary on August 6, 2006. They live on a small acreage outside Lincoln with their cat, Jordan. Their two daughters, Dana and Dionne, no longer live at home. Their extended family now includes Dana's husband, Lee, and Dana and Lee's son, Grant.

Bill earned a Bachelor's of Education from the University of Wisconsin at Whitewater, Master of Arts from Kansas State University, and doctorate from Purdue University. He has an adjunct appointment in Teachers College as a professor of Curriculum and Instruction. Dr. Seiler is an experienced educator, consultant, researcher, and author, and has published numerous monographs, articles, and educational materials in the area of communication.

In addition, Dr. Seiler has presented lectures and speeches throughout the Midwest. He has published two other textbooks, *Communication in Business and Professional Organizations* and *Communication for the Contemporary Classroom*. He has also served on editorial boards for several of his discipline's research journals and has held a variety of offices in his discipline's professional associations.

Dr. Seiler received honors as Outstanding Educator of America, Outstanding University and College Teacher by the Nebraska Communication Association, Outstanding Young Alumni and Distinguished Alumni Awards from the University of Wisconsin at Whitewater (the only person to receive both awards in the university's history), and 2002 Boss of the Year Award at the university. He is also listed in the International Who's Who in Education.

Dr. Seiler has been directing the introductory course at the University of Nebraska for over 34 years. He was one of the first people in the nation to use the Personalized System of Instruction (PSI) in a large multiple section basic communication course. Presently, the University of Nebraska teaches over a thousand students a year using the PSI method in the basic communication course.

**Melissa Beall** is a professor in the Communication Studies Department at the University of Northern Iowa (UNI). She is also a member of the teacher education faculty. An avid Husker fan, she always wears red and white on football Saturdays. Dr. Beall earned all three of her degrees from the University of Nebraska–Lincoln and appreciates that she has two "home" states, Iowa and Nebraska. Her expertise includes communication education, listening, intercultural communication, communication and technology, and communication theory, but she considers herself a communication "generalist." She has taught at all levels, pre-kindergarten through adult education, and loves to teach. As a high school teacher in Nebraska, Dr. Beall taught English, theatre, speech, and debate; directed plays; and coached the speech and debate team. She also taught classes at UNL and Doane College–Lincoln. At UNI, she teaches Oral Communication and courses such as Listening, Public Speaking, Critical Thinking in Communication, Communication Education: College Teaching, Communication and Technology, Language and Communication, Intercultural Communication, and Communication Theory.

Dr. Beall's honors include Scottish Rite Distinguished Educator, Nebraska Speech Communication and Theatre Association's Outstanding Young High School Teacher, and the National Communication Association's Marcella E. Oberle Outstanding K–12 Teacher. The National Communication Association, Central States Communication Association, and Western States Communication Association each selected her as Master Teacher. She served on numerous editorial boards, and has presented over five hundred papers, programs, and workshops for professional organizations. Dr. Beall presents technology, listening, and critical thinking workshops for schools, departments, and business organizations. Dr. Beall serves as President of the Iowa Communication Association and Regional Vice President, North America, of three organizations: the World Communication Association, the Pacific and Asian Communication Association, and the International Association of Communication Sciences. She is a past president of the Central States Communication Association and of the International Listening Association. She has served as an officer in many divisions in the National Communication Association. Dr. Beall and her husband, Hugh, travel extensively and love to garden and read.

# CHAPTER 1

# Connecting Process and Principles

"Our need for language, conversation, and definition goes beyond the wish to put things right. Through words we come to know the other person—and to be known. This knowing is at the heart of our deepest longings for intimacy and connection with others."

—HARRIET LERNER

# This chapter will help you:

- **Understand** how communication helps you make connections in your daily life.

- **Learn** how competent communication can affect all aspects of your life.

- **Become** aware of the effects of ethical behavior, culture, technology, and thinking on your communication.

- **Learn** the essential components in the communication process.

- **Distinguish** among the various types of communication: intrapersonal, interpersonal (including group), and public.

- **Identify and debunk** five common myths about communication.

## Making everyday connections

Every day you take on numerous roles. You're student, family member, friend, citizen, employee, or maybe employer as well as many other roles. In those roles you usually are required to connect with others around you. Here are some examples of the ways you might connect with others:

You send an email to a professor: "I'd like to know if it would be possible to give my speech on the second day of speeches because of a work conflict."

You meet with your boss: "Ms. Morgan, I need to interview someone for this company report. Can you give me some suggestions about whom to contact?"

You call your Mom: "Happy Birthday, Mom! Just wanted to let you know I'm thinking about you. Did you get my card?"

You leave a note for your roommate: "Be sure to leave your share of the rent so that I can drop it off this afternoon." ■

**Questions to think about**

- How much time do you spend in making everyday connections?

- What different forms of communication do you use on a given day?

- How much time do you spend listening to others?

- Who would you describe as an effective communicator? Why?

- What public figures are effective communicators? Why?

- How often do you think about how effectively you communicate with others?

We live in a "connected world." Everywhere we look there's someone talking on a cell phone or listening to an iPod or MP3 player. At work and for our studies, we're connected to the Internet. The World Wide Web is *the* source of information on every aspect of our lives from resources for class papers and presentations to chat rooms that allow us to connect with our friends, to MySpace.com that allows us to present ourselves in the ways we choose. In our leisure time, we're connected to the Internet, TV, cell phones, music, or video games. Life is a series of connections, mediated or face-to-face. Despite these connections, we don't really spend much reflective thought about how we make and maintain connections. Communication is something we take for granted. We talk, therefore, we communicate. But just because we can talk, can we *really* communicate effectively? What is competent communication? For our purposes, **communication competence** is the ability to take part in effective communication that is characterized by skills and understandings that enable communicators to exchange messages successfully.

## ■ Communication: Making Connections

Communication helps us to *make connections* with each other and with the world. We communicate with many people in a variety of situations, daily. We listen to professors, employers, co-workers, family members, friends, and many others each hour. Whatever your cultural background, learning style, or geographical location, you'll find that your communication proficiency can mean greater academic success, better relationships, a better job, and greater satisfaction in your life. Communication professors are not the only ones who see how important it is to be able to communicate effectively and make connections with others. In *The Dance of Connection,* psychologist Harriet Lerner says, "The thread that unites my work both as an author and as a psychotherapist is my desire to help people speak wisely and well, sometimes about the most difficult subjects. This includes asking questions, getting a point across, clarifying desires, beliefs, values, and limits. How such communication goes determines whether we want to come home or stay away at the end of the day."[1]

> ■ **communication competence** The ability to take part in effective communication that is characterized by skills and understandings that enable communicators to exchange messages successfully.

When you stop to really think about a typical day in your life, you'll discover that you spend a lot of time *making connections.* And, you'll also realize that communication allows you to make those connections. Communication takes many forms and you, as a communicator, must have a wide range of behaviors to be able to adapt to the variety of situations in which you find yourself. In Making Everyday Connections, we identified only four typical daily communication situations; obviously, there are many others. In this text, we provide a variety of ideas and approaches to help you learn more about the exciting ways that people make connections through communication. This chapter presents the concepts and processes of effective communication in everyday life. We examine the essential components and principles, the types and contexts, and the myths about communication. You will have the opportunity to think about the role of communication in an increasingly multicultural and technological world. We'll provide some hands-on activities and some reflective questions to apply to your personal life and to use communication to *make connections* in all areas of your life.

# ■ What Is Communication?

What is communication? And what do we mean when we say that communication occurs? How do we know when we have communicated effectively? How do we use communication to *make connections* in our lives? The answers to these questions require an understanding of the principles and process of communication as well as some guidelines for achieving success.

We define **communication** as the simultaneous sharing and creating of meaning through human symbolic interaction. (The terms in this definition will be explained in more detail throughout the book.) It might seem obvious but bears repeating: Communication is complex. If it were simple, people would have few difficulties with it, and we would not need to study it! But this complex and challenging process is critical to making connections in all our relationships, from the professional to the romantic and everything in between.

Communication as a discipline has existed for thousands of years. Scholars in ancient Greece and Rome recognized communication as a powerful means of influence. Classical rhetoricians studied the principles of the effective composition and delivery of persuasive speeches. In the Middle Ages in western Europe such religious leaders as St. Augustine developed written and spoken communication such as letter writing and preaching in order to spread the Christian faith. In the Western world, public speaking, storytelling, and debating have been important means of changing public opinion and persuading others to take political action. African, Eastern, and Middle Eastern cultures, too, have long emphasized the importance of effective communication. According to intercultural communication scholars Samovar and Porter, "the Buddha advised his disciples to avoid 'harsh speech.'"[2] Communication colleagues in Japan, Korea, and Malaysia confirm that the study of communication is an

■ **communication**
The simultaneous sharing and creating of meaning through human symbolic action.

## MAKING CONNECTIONS for Success

### What is Communication?

Communication is central to our ideas of a "good" life. Communication is even identified as a way to make the world a better, safer place. In the United States numerous public figures are identified as competent communicators. Presidents Ronald Reagan, Bill Clinton, and Franklin Delano Roosevelt were known as effective communicators. Reagan, upon leaving the presidency reportedly said, "I've been called The Great Communicator. If I am it's because I have great things to communicate." Media figures Oprah Winfrey, Ellen DeGeneres, and Dr. Phil have award-winning talk shows that draw large audiences because each knows how to connect with people. Think about these examples, and then, answer the following questions:

1. What qualities do you think "great communicators" have?
2. What characteristics do the six people identified above have in common?
3. How do you think the ability to communicate effectively made a difference in these public figures' lives?
4. Who are the people in your life whom you consider to be effective communicators? Why are they effective?

Compare and discuss your answers and reasons with others in your class or in your workplace. How many on your list were on the lists of others? Were their reasons similar to yours?

ancient and valued tradition in their cultures. Well-known practitioners of this art include Condoleeza Rice, Hillary Rodham Clinton, Maya Angelou, Toni Morrison, Margaret Thatcher, Abraham Lincoln, Mother Theresa, Eleanor Roosevelt, Oprah Winfrey, Franklin Delano Roosevelt, Ronald Reagan, Bill Clinton, Winston Churchill, Mohandas Gandhi, Martin Luther King, Jr., Mao Tse-tung, and Colin Powell.

Communication refers to the process by which we create and share meanings. **Communications,** however, is the word generally used to denote the delivery systems for mediated and mass communication. People often confuse the two words, but they are quite different. Communication is what you and your friend do when you discuss the next speech assignment. Communications involve ways of disseminating information, as in "The Internet is a vital communications link for students and office workers."

According to this definition, speech communication involves a range of behaviors and occurs in a variety of situations: public and private, business and social, home and school, formal and informal. The diverse situations are all connected by one common thread—*human symbolic interaction,* or people using a symbol system (language) to share thoughts, feelings, beliefs, attitudes, customs, and ideas. As you read this text, you will learn about human symbolic interaction as it occurs within and among individuals, groups, organizations, cultures, and cocultures. You will learn more about the nature of the communication *process:* listening, thinking, speaking in public settings, speaking in small-group settings, and speaking with one, two, or a small number of people in your interpersonal relationships. Your ability to communicate by using speech will be one of the determining factors in your success in the classroom, in the workplace, and in your personal life. Being an effective communicator saves time, makes life more enjoyable, allows people to establish and maintain relationships successfully, and facilitates accomplishing personal goals. The humorist James Thurber may have said it best: "Precision of communication is important, more important than ever, in our era of hair-trigger balances, when a false, or misunderstood word may create as much disaster as a sudden thoughtless act."[3]

# ■ Why Should We Study Communication?

Although you have communicated for many years, you probably have not had the opportunity to learn about communication competence. The ability to communicate might seem natural because unless there are disabilities, most of us readily develop speaking skills. But the ability to *communicate* (not simply to utter words) is learned, and learning to be a competent communicator is a difficult, lifelong project. You can make progress quickly, however, if you work hard to learn the principles and concepts and then apply them in practice situations. Think about your life experiences, then connect the chapter material, class applications, and discussions to your life. These skills will enable you to reap benefits in career development, ethical behavior, and the promotion of positive relationships among people of diverse cultural backgrounds. We live in a time of rapid technological change. Put simply, effective communication is critical to living successfully in today's society.

## ■ Communication and Career Development

Most of us aspire to succeed in our chosen careers. We enter college to better ourselves and to prepare for satisfying jobs. Communication plays an important role in career success. Leaders in education, business, and industry have identified several critical

**■ communications**
Denotes the delivery systems for mediated and mass communication.

life skills that are necessary to function successfully in the workforce, and communication is one of the most valued areas of expertise. For example, several recent studies[4] reinforce what previous research had already demonstrated: Employers want workers at all levels who know how to communicate. The specific recommendations are found in Table 1.1.

In other words, effective workplace communicators can explain ideas clearly and give good directions. Effective communicators are good listeners who work well with others and represent their companies well in small- and large-group settings. Too often, employers believe that these skills are lacking in their employees. Introductory courses in communication, such as the one for which you are reading this text, focus on these skills.

Personnel directors have described their needs in prospective employees as follows: Send me people who know how to speak, listen, and think, and I'll do the rest. I can train people in their specific job responsibilities, as long as they listen well, know how to think, and can express themselves well.[5] In fact, most careers involve contact with others and require the ability to communicate effectively with them. Business and industry often look for the most competent communicators when they hire new employees. So, although some companies provide on-the-job training in communication skills, it is by far most advantageous to develop excellent speaking, listening, and

■ **TABLE 1.1** Top Ten Qualities and Skills Employers Seek

1. Communication skills (verbal and written)
2. Honesty/integrity (ethics) (throughout text)
3. Teamwork skills (see Chapters 15 and 16)
4. Interpersonal skills (see Chapters 13 and 14)
5. Motivation/initiative
6. Strong work ethic
7. Analytical skills (see Chapters 6, 9, 10, 11, 12, 15, and 16)
8. Flexibility/adaptability (see Chapter 10)
9. Computer skills
10. Organizational skills (see Chapters 9,15, and 16)

*Sources:* National Association of Colleges & Employers, *Job Outlook 2003;* 21st Century Workforce Commission, *A Nation of Opportunity: Strategies for Building Tomorrow's 21st Century Workforce* (Washington, D.C.: U.S. Department of Labor, 2003).

Employers want workers who can speak effectively, listen carefully and efficiently, and think critically.

## MAKING CONNECTIONS
### for Success

### Your Communication Effectiveness

In the surveys cited in the text, executives indicated that all employees need to improve their communication skills. The executives also noted that greater flexibility and higher ethical standards should be a focus of career preparation. If a prospective employer asked you the following questions, how would you respond?

1. Are you an effective communicator? Why? Why not?
2. What are five of your communication concerns?
3. What anxieties about communication do you have? (James McCroskey and his colleagues at West Virginia University developed the Perceived Report of Communication Apprehension [PRCA] to help identify the strength of one's communication anxiety. You might wish to look at Dr. McCroskey's

web page—www.jamescmccroskey.com—for more information; try a web search on communication apprehension, and complete a PRCA form found on the Web. We discuss communication apprehension more fully in Chapter 10.)

4. What areas of communication do you need to improve? How do you know you need to work on these areas?
5. Describe one instance in which you found yourself wishing that you were a better listener.
6. What were you doing the last time you found yourself wishing you were a better communicator? What did you mean by the term?
7. In what recent situations did you find yourself wondering how to be more effective in interpersonal relationships?

analytical abilities before applying for the exciting job that could launch or enhance your career.

### ■ Communication and Ethical Behavior

All societies hold certain ethical standards—ideals about what is right and what is wrong—and unethical behavior often carries a penalty. People have been removed from political office, lost their jobs, or been publicly chastised for violating ethical standards and codes. Such behaviors often involve unethical acts related to communication. Financiers have received prison terms for participating in insider trading—using illegally obtained information to make money on the stock market. Sharing such information constitutes an illegal act of communication. Another such behavior is telling lies, whether done to hurt someone else or to protect or enhance one's own position. Though politicians spring to mind as typical offenders in this category, other examples show that the problem is more widespread, for example, enhancing one's résumé to increase the chances of being hired or "borrowing" a friend's old term paper or speech to pass a course.

Sometimes people think they need to find so-called shortcuts to accomplish tasks, whether it be questionable accounting procedures in business, insider trading to keep more money, or stealing ideas to complete a presentation or paper. Technology allows us to find and use all kinds of information. A quick search of the Internet provides numerous sources for A, B, or even C papers for a "minimal cost" and "minimal risks to you." And, while those papers can save time and effort, they can also cost you a passing grade, or even a diploma from your institution.

The Internet has made plagiarism a much greater possibility because of the ease with which people can access information. There are so many sites with so much

## MAKING CONNECTIONS for Success

### Ethical Perspectives

The news has been filled with examples of behaviors that have taken people to court and to serving time for violating accepted societal standards. Martha Stewart spent time in prison for insider trading. Jeff Skilling and the late Ken Lay were sentenced to prison for fraud and conspiracy charges in the Enron investment scandal. James Frey wrote a book on his addictions that he labeled as a memoir. Oprah Winfrey selected the book for her Book Club, but when it came out that Frey's "memoir" was really a work of fiction, Oprah reprimanded him on her TV show. Frey apologized but will likely have a hard time getting a manuscript accepted again. These examples demonstrate some of the risks created when one breaks ethical standards.

1. Where do we get our views of ethics?
2. What are your own views of ethical behaviors?
3. What specific behaviors violate your ethical code to the point that you would have to confront someone if they acted in a certain way?
4. What other examples of ethical violations currently or recently in the news can you identify?
5. Would you ever plagiarize? When? Why? Why not?
6. What policies does your college/university have in place for plagiarism and/or a breach of ethics?
7. What are the penalties for such behavior?

information that people often believe they can access sites, take what they want, and never be caught. Plagiarism, in whatever form and however accessible, is still unethical, and it can result in students failing courses and even being removed from their colleges and universities. In the workplace, plagiarism and other unethical behaviors can result in the loss of one's job or a demotion. In recent years, newspaper reporters have been in the news for fabricating stories and losing their jobs. Ethics and plagiarism are discussed throughout the text and are defined here. **Ethics** refers to an individual's system of moral principles. **Plagiarism** is the use of another person's information, language, or ideas without citing the originator and making it appear that the user is the originator.

Ethical communicators speak responsibly and give credit to any sources that contribute to the message being conveyed. An ethical communicator does not plagiarize and does not lie. Aristotle, a Greek rhetorician (384–322 B.C.), suggested that communication was most powerful when the speaker's character, or *ethos* (ethical appeal), was engaged in presenting the truth.[6] (Chapter 10 further develops this concept.) Quintilian (A.D. ca. 35–ca. 100), another rhetorician, stated (before the days of inclusive language) that communication needed to be presented by "a good man speaking well."[7]

An important distinction to make here is that unethical communication may, in fact, constitute effective communication. If one person persuades another to do something morally wrong, the communication has been effective, but it is not virtuous. Unethical communication should never be condoned, even when it has appeared to succeed. A good deal of critical thinking is needed as we attempt to be effective *and* ethical communicators and as we evaluate others' communication to determine its ethical content.

Today, many colleges and universities offer or even require ethics classes to encourage students to take ethical responsibilities seriously and to remind them that

■ **ethics** An individual's system of moral principles.

■ **plagiarism** The use of another person's information, language, or ideas without citing the originator and making it appear that the user is the originator.

the need for responsible, ethical behavior pervades all aspects of life. Throughout this text, examples of ethical dilemmas and perspectives will help you become aware of the need for ethical communication behaviors.

## ▪▪ Communication and Our Multicultural Society

Job transfers, changes in economic and political conditions, and numerous other factors cause people to move from place to place, often leaving their country of birth to put down roots elsewhere. Many countries are experiencing an increase in this trend. In the United States, for example, what was once a population with a white majority of northern European roots is now a diverse mosaic of people of different ethnic and cultural backgrounds. In this environment, we can all grow to appreciate the distinctions that make each culture unique as well as the interconnectedness shared by all, sometimes described as the "global village." But a great deal of knowledge, flexibility, and sensitivity are necessary if people of diverse cultural backgrounds are to communicate successfully and live well together.

Current demographic trends and projections in the United States make it not an option, but a necessity, to interact successfully with people of all racial, ethnic, cultural and religious heritage. The U.S. Census Bureau reports the following demographic breakdown by race (all ages)[8] and voting registration in 2004[9]:

| Group | Population Numbers | #'s Voting | % Voting |
|---|---|---|---|
| Hispanic Origin (any race) | 32,832,000 | 27,129 | 47.2 |
| White, alone | 196,929,000 | 176,618 | 65.4 |
| Black, not Hispanic | 33,619,000 | 24,910 | 60.0 |
| American Indian, Eskimo, and Aleut (not Hispanic) | 2,059,000 | NR | NR |
| Asian and Pacific Islander, not Hispanic | 10,620,000 | 9,291 | 44.1 |
| (Numbers in thousands) | | | |

This translates to roughly the following percentages: 69 percent of the population is White; 13 percent, Hispanic; 13 percent, Black; 4 percent, Asian and Pacific Islander; and 1 percent, American Indian. Projections from the Census Bureau suggest a significant increase in Hispanic, Black, and Asian numbers in the near future, with a decline or stable percentage for Whites. The changes in "how we look" are already occurring in elementary schools and high schools, as well as college and university classrooms. Language differences complicate communication within many schools. Some kindergarten through twelfth-grade schools on the East and West Coasts and in other such populous areas as Chicago, Cincinnati, Dallas, and St. Louis have students representing fifty to one hundred or more different native languages. College and university classrooms, too, have increasing numbers of students whose first language is not English, and each one's cultural and ethnic background affects the way these students communicate in the classroom, the residence hall, the supermarket, and the workplace.

Language structure itself influences and is influenced by culture. Nonverbal communication behaviors, such as physical stance, eye contact, style of speaking, and so on, are also largely determined by cultural background. It takes a great deal of patience, understanding, and respect to learn to communicate effectively in situations involving different language backgrounds and different social and conversational customs. Thus, it is important to learn all we can about the backgrounds of the people with whom we relate at school, work, or in the community, to consider how our own customs might seem unusual to a person of a different heritage, and to cultivate an open mind and a good sense of humor. These attitudes will facilitate communication and will also enrich our lives.

## ■■ Communication and Our Technological Society

The world seems to be getting smaller, because so many people travel and because mass media brings the world to our living rooms, residence hall rooms, offices, and even our automobiles. Advancements in technology often make it possible for us to experience historic events not only moments after they occur, but sometimes even *while* they occur. Now memorable images brought to us courtesy of modern technology include the horror

## MAKING CONNECTIONS
### for Success

### Communication and Culture

One of the ways in which any society or culture ensures the transmission of cultural traditions and values is in its stories. Many of the stories we read as young children contain life lessons. The stories of Dr. Seuss, for example, always have a moral: *Green Eggs and Ham* teaches us the value of repeatedly presenting ideas in slightly different forms in order to convince others, and *The Lorax* provides reasons we should value our natural resources. Even common folk stories such as "The Three Little Pigs" may demonstrate the value of a work ethic. Other stories provide examples of specific cultural values. Most immigrants to the United States bring their cultures' stories with them. Paul Fleischman's small book *Seedfolks* describes how a neighborhood of people from many different countries of origin learn how to become a community.

1. What are some of the stories you learned, read, or were told as you grew up?
2. What values did the stories convey or emphasize?
3. What stories will you or have you shared with your own children or relatives? Why?

Advancements in technology, such as the satellite communication used here, often make it possible for us to make immediate contact. Messages by way of email, fax, or telephone can be sent to almost any part of the world.

## Being Wired

We live in a "wired" world. Most of us cannot begin to imagine life without the gadgets and the instant access we have to everyone and everything. We can have a Myspace.com site and present what we want to the world. One of your authors recently attended a performance by Ashley Gearing, a 15-year-old singer from western New England, who at age 12 had a Billboard chart hit before she ever had a record label. Some of Ashley's promotional materials included the URL www.myspace.com/AshleyGearing. A visit to that site provides one with examples of Ashley's latest songs from a newly released CD, her appearance schedule, news and notes, and biographical data.

Ashley uses Myspace.com to promote her career and to make connections with others. Many of us use Myspace.com or similar locations to share with others and perhaps to gain new friends. Not all who enter information into these website have innocent purposes in mind. Some criminals lurk on these sites hoping to find someone of whom they can take advantage. Police officers, too, visit these pages to

find criminal perpetrators before it's too late. Some libraries, schools, communities, and families have placed restrictions on time spent and sites visited, because of the unknown factors of the Internet and the ability to hide one's true self and motivations. With that in mind, answer the following questions and share them with friends/classmates to compare your stories.

1. Have you or a friend ever experienced a cyber relationship?
2. How did the relationship develop?
3. What rules did you/your friend follow in establishing and maintaining this relationship?
4. What concerns do you have about this kind of relationship? Why?
5. Did anyone ever attempt to monitor or stop your use of the Internet? How? For what reasons?
6. How is cybercommunication easier or more difficult than face-to-face communication with family and friends?

of 9/11, the Asian tsunami of 2005, the devastation wrought by hurricane Katrina, the War in Iraq, the Lebanese-Israeli conflict, and the May 2006 earthquake that killed thousands in Indonesia. We can communicate with people in almost any part of the world; we can send messages via email, fax, and telephone. We can use digital cameras at our computers or cell phones and visit face to face with people around the globe. We can turn on the television and see and hear what is happening anywhere in the world or even in space. Interviews with world leaders, celebrities, and ordinary people are broadcast on the Web, television, and radio every day. If you happen to be in the right place at the right time, witnessing a news event or simply crossing the path of a reporter looking for a story, your image, words, or voice may be instantaneously transmitted to your community, the nation, or the world.

The way technology has sped the pace of communication adds to the challenge of both presenting and receiving meaningful messages. Flashing images and sound bites can be hard to interpret. The sheer volume of communication presented through electronic media can seem overwhelming. Yet technological developments are exciting in that they increase the avenues through which communication can occur and make the process quick and easy. Those who take time to learn and practice the principles of sound communication will be able to use to the best advantage these technological means of sending and receiving messages. (See Chapter 17, available on the Internet at www.ablongman.com/seiler6e, for more information on mediated and mass communication.)

# ■ Principles of Communication

To appreciate the true nature of communication, it is important to understand four fundamental principles:

1. Communication is a process.
2. Communication is a system.
3. Communication is both interactional and transactional.
4. Communication can be intentional or unintentional.

These principles are readily applicable to life beyond the classroom (and they improve interactions within the classroom as well). No doubt, situations from your personal life—family relationships, work experiences, or your participation in sports teams, music groups, social clubs, or political or community action organizations—will come to mind as we discuss the dynamics of communication. An understanding of these principles should make a difference in your life, building greater understanding and cooperation into relationships at any level.

## ■ Communication Is a Process

Communication is considered a **process,** because it involves a series of actions that has no beginning or end and is constantly changing.[10] It is not an object that you can hold to examine or dissect. It is like the weather, which changes constantly.[11] Sometimes the weather is warm, sunny, and dry; at other times, it is cool, cloudy, and wet. The weather is a result of complex interrelationships among variables, such as high and low pressure systems, the position of the earth, and ocean currents, that can never be exactly duplicated. Similarly, communication is an ongoing, constantly changing process.

Communication also involves variables that can never be duplicated. The interrelationships among people, environments, skills, attitudes, status, experiences, and feelings all determine communication at any given moment. Think about a relationship you developed with someone recently. How did it occur? It may have happened by chance (striking up a conversation with someone you met while walking to class), or it may have been a prearranged meeting (a business meeting with a prospective client). No two relationships are developed in the same way. And like the weather, some relationships are warm and others are cool.

Communication is both ever-changing and capable of effecting change. Saying something that you wish you hadn't said is an excellent example of this principle. No matter how hard you try to take back your comment, you cannot. It has made its impact and has, in all likelihood, affected your relationship with another person in some way. The change might not be immediate or significant, but it does take place as a result of your communication.

Furthermore, the communication and the changes it produces might not have a clearly identifiable beginning or end. Certain events led up to it, and as we noted, results of the communication will follow in its wake. Communication generally is not characterized by abrupt endings and beginnings; rather, it takes place within a flow. If you were to stop in mid-conversation and walk away, that conversation would still have an effect on you; it would not end. You would carry away some new information or at least a general impression, whether positive or negative. If you understand that

■ **process** Series of actions that has no beginning or end and is constantly changing.

communication is a process, you will be able to see how events and relationships constantly change and yet also have continuity.

## Communication Is a System

Simply stated, a **system** is a combination of parts interdependently acting to form a whole. The human body is an excellent example of a system. All parts of the body are interdependent and work together to form one complex system. If something is not functioning correctly, some response usually occurs either to correct what has gone wrong or to warn that something is going wrong. When you have a headache, it affects not only your head but also the rest of your body, including the thinking process and emotions. You may find that you have trouble seeing and even walking. You may not wish to eat, because your head pain seems to have taken over your body. If you have a severe headache, you may have trouble thinking clearly because of the pounding in your head. You may also have difficulty explaining something to your co-workers or friends. Because each part of the system is connected, your ability to think clearly, speak clearly, or listen effectively leads to ineffective communication.

Systems also exist in the workplace, in the family, and in the classroom. If your supervisor had a fight at home, that event may affect the supervisor's relationship with the workers; the supervisor may be irritable and snap at you and others. Although you don't know what has caused the irritability, it does affect all who must deal with it. In other words, the supervisor's domestic squabble has an impact not only on the home system but also on the system at work. In a similar sense, the communication process is a system and occurs only when the necessary components interact. If components of communication malfunction or are absent, communication is prevented or ineffective.

## Communication Is Both Interactional and Transactional

The interactional and transactional aspects of communication are closely related and should be considered together. **Interaction** is an exchange of communication in which people take turns sending and receiving messages. It is similar to playing catch. Someone throws a ball. Another person catches it and throws it back. Each throw and each catch is a separate action. It is, however, necessary for the ball to get to the other person before it can be thrown back. Figure 1.1 illustrates this interaction. In interaction, there is a distinct time delay between each message being sent. An example of communication as an interaction is a phone conversation between two people. Person A speaks and Person B listens, then Person B speaks and Person A listens, and so on. Each message is a separate action. Even though there is a reaction to each message being sent, the reaction and message are not simultaneous.

Most face-to-face communication does not occur as a series of distinctly separate actions. Thus, the term **transaction** is used to extend the concept of interaction to include simultaneous actions. Persons involved in transaction engage in sending (encoding) and receiving (decoding) messages at the same time (see Figure 1.2). For example, when you and your friends talk, teachers communicate to their students, or supervisors talk to their employees, they not only send information but also receive information at the same time. Each person is sending and receiving messages simultaneously. This does not necessarily mean that they are talking at the same time; it does mean, however, that two-way communication is taking place. If you fail to look

■ **system**
Combination of parts interdependently acting to form a whole.

■ **interaction**
Exchange of communication in which communicators take turns sending and receiving messages.

■ **transaction**
Exchange of communication in which the communicators act simultaneously, that is, encoding and decoding occur at the same time.

■ **FIGURE 1.1**  Communication as Interaction

Interaction is a series of distinctly separate actions, or turn taking. That is, Person A communicates (message 1) to Person B, then B communicates (message 2) to A, then A communicates to B, and so on.

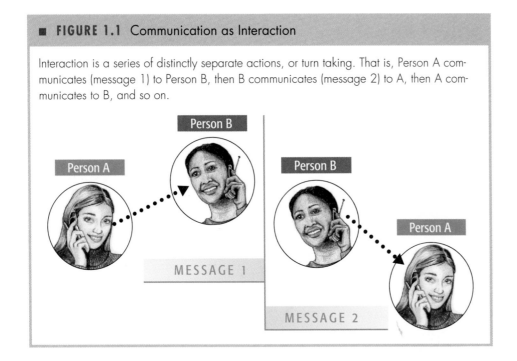

your friend in the eye because you're thinking about something else, your friend may wonder what you're hiding. You are distracted, your friend thinks you're hiding something, and each of you is simultaneously sending and receiving messages. In addition, neither of you is communicating effectively because of your own interpretation of events.

Without simultaneous actions, face-to-face communication would be impossible or extremely limited, like sending a letter to someone and then having to wait a week or two for a response. In face-to-face communication, each person affects the other and shares in the process simultaneously. Thus, communication transaction can be seen as the simultaneous exchange by which we share our reality with others. The principle of transaction is more fully depicted in Figure 1.2.

■ **FIGURE 1.2**  Communication as Transaction

In a transaction, each person communicates simultaneously. That is, both Person A and Person B are communicating at the same time. This does not mean that they are both speaking at once. Instead, each is aware of and reacting to the other. The sender is also a receiver, and the receiver is also a sender. Each is actively involved in what is happening.

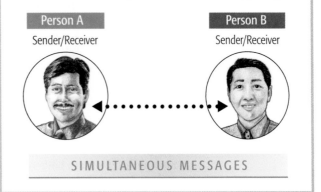

## ▪▪ Communication Can Be Intentional or Unintentional

When one person communicates with another, he or she intends that specific messages with specific purposes and meanings be received. Communication can occur, however, regardless of whether it is intended. **Intentional communication** is a

■ **intentional communication** A message that is purposely sent to a specific receiver.

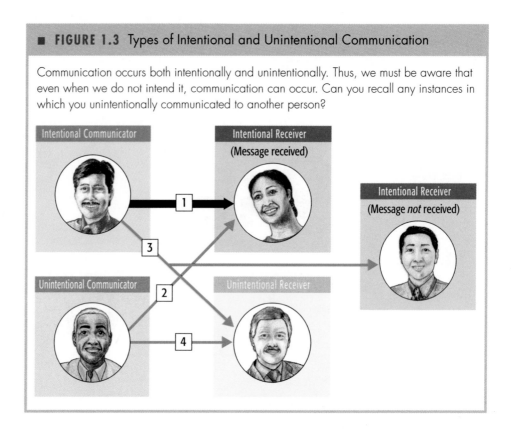

### ■ FIGURE 1.3 Types of Intentional and Unintentional Communication

Communication occurs both intentionally and unintentionally. Thus, we must be aware that even when we do not intend it, communication can occur. Can you recall any instances in which you unintentionally communicated to another person?

message that is purposely sent to a specific receiver. **Unintentional communication** is a message that is not intended to be sent or was not intended for the individual who received it. On the basis of intent or lack of intent, four possible communication situations can occur, as shown in Figure 1.3. This is shown by Arrow 1 and is generally the way communication takes place. Arrow 2 indicates a situation in which a person unintentionally communicates something to someone who is intentionally trying to receive a message or messages. This situation occurs every time someone reads more into a communication act than was intended by the source. For example, when a student in a quiet classroom gets up to sharpen a pencil, the eyes of other students immediately focus on the moving student, who might have no specific intention of communicating anything. The movement, however, provides an opportunity for observers to attribute varying meanings to the message. For instance, one person might believe that the moving student is trying to flirt with her, another might think he is trying to call attention to himself, and the instructor might think he is trying to disrupt the classroom. Despite the student's lack of intention to communicate anything, others have read meaning into his behavior, and he may have to deal with their interpretations.

Arrow 3 illustrates the opposite situation. Here the source intends to send a message, but the person for whom the message is intended is not consciously or intentionally receiving it. Such a situation happens in the classroom when students daydream while the instructor is lecturing.

Arrow 4 shows that communication can be unintentional for both the source and the receiver and can occur without anyone intentionally sending or receiving a

■ **unintentional communication** A message that is not intended to be sent or is not intended for the person who receives it.

message. Communication that is not intended or that is at least not consciously sent and received is usually nonverbal. Nonverbal communication is any information that is expressed without words. For example, the clothing a person wears might not be worn to communicate any specific message, and persons observing the clothing might not intentionally or consciously receive any message through it, but they do see it. Thus, communication occurs even though neither the person nor the observer has any intention of communicating. Think of a time when you received a message that was not intended for you and you were upset by your interpretation. Why were you upset?

# ■ Essential Components of Communication

Although there is no exhaustive list of the myriad components of communication, eight of the most basic elements are worth examining in detail:

1. Source/Sender
2. Message
3. Interference/Noise
4. Channel
5. Receiver
6. Feedback
7. Environment
8. Context

Figure 1.4 illustrates how these components interact when two people are communicating, yet it depicts each element's movement and interdependence on the other elements only in a limited way. During actual communication, these components are

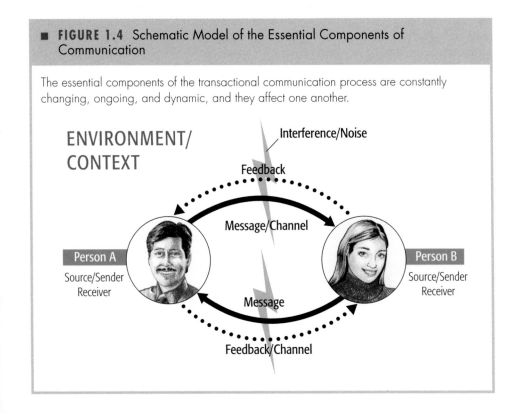

■ **FIGURE 1.4** Schematic Model of the Essential Components of Communication

The essential components of the transactional communication process are constantly changing, ongoing, and dynamic, and they affect one another.

ENVIRONMENT/
CONTEXT

Interference/Noise

Feedback

Message/Channel

Person A
Source/Sender
Receiver

Person B
Source/Sender
Receiver

Message

Feedback/Channel

## MAKING CONNECTIONS for Success

### Communication Principles in the Workplace

Erin is a server at a local restaurant. She receives $3.15 per hour plus her tips. It's important for her to connect with her customers. If she has a bad day and lets it affect her verbal and nonverbal communication, it will likely also affect the amount of tips she receives. Even when she is tired, she has to smile and act friendly and perhaps even energetic when she's with her customers.

1. How is Erin's physical or emotional state likely to affect her communication? How must she change if she wants good tips?
2. Why should Erin change her behavior? Is it ethical to do so?
3. What principles of communication do you find in this example?
4. Compare some of your own workplace situations with others in class. How did you see communication principles in these examples?

constantly in flux as the communicators react to each other. The model also shows that communication is a process, that the components work together as a system, that interaction and transaction are both possible modes of communication, and that intentional and unintentional communication can occur—thus illustrating the principles of communication that we have already discussed.

Now that you can see how these elements relate during communication, we will discuss each one separately.

### ■ Source/Sender

The **source** is the creator of the message. Because communication usually involves more than one person, more than one source of communication can exist at one time. In the model in Figure 1.4, both persons function as a source. Likewise, both the teacher and the students in a classroom can function as sources, sending messages simultaneously to one another—teacher to students, students to teacher, and students to students.

The communication source performs four roles: He or she determines the meaning of what is to be communicated, encodes the meaning into a message, sends the message, and perceives and reacts to a listener's response to the message. Person A, when acting as source, also brings into play the communicative skills, knowledge, attitudes, and sociocultural background that make him or her a unique individual. No two communicators are identical in their abilities to communicate, nor do they see others, events, or situations in exactly the same way. The greater the differences between Person A and Person B, the more effort and skill it will take for Person A to effectively communicate with Person B. Respecting another person's views, even when they differ from one's own, is the first step to communicating well in such situations.

**Determining Meanings.** The meaning behind the message determines how you'll create the message. Your word choices and tone of voice and other nonverbal behaviors will help indicate your meaning to those with whom you communicate, and require careful choices on your part. When you tell your friends that you received an A on the presentation in your communication class, you have to choose the ultimate meaning you wish to convey. Do you want them to congratulate you? Do you want them to think you're smart? Do you want them to know you worked hard? Or, do you wish to let them know that the hard work was worth the effort? Or, perhaps you just want to express your pleasure on receiving a good grade. How do you choose words and behavior to do that?

**Encoding.** Once a source has chosen a meaning, she or he **encodes** it. In other words, a source translates the thoughts or feelings into words, sounds, and physical expressions, which make up the actual message that is to be sent. According to symbolic interactionism, a theory created by sociologist George Mead and his students, the most human and humanizing activity people engage in is talking with one

**source** The creator of messages.

**encoding** Process by which the source translates thoughts or feelings in words, sounds, and physical expressions, which together make up the actual message that is to be sent.

another. It is our conversations with others, our participation in the communication process in social settings, that allow us to construct meaning. According to social interactionism, the meaning we attribute in those interactions is determined by our language choices. Furthermore, symbolic interactionism also explains that we talk to ourselves (intrapersonal communication) as we sort through difficult circumstances, solve problems, and make decisions.

**Sending.**    The source then sends the message, which involves the source's ability to communicate overtly, that is, to use voice and body to express the intended meaning accurately. For example, if your internal meaning is to tell the other person how pleased you are to receive a high grade on your presentation, then you must use words and actions to illustrate what you are feeling and thinking.

**Reacting.**    Finally, a source must interpret the receiver's response to the message. A source's perception of a receiver's response in most communication situations is simultaneous with the response. For example, the person you are telling about the high grade will be sending you messages (smiles, nods of the head, eye contact) as you speak in reaction to what you are saying. If you interpret that response as positive, you will probably continue to tell more about your high grade.

## Message

A **message** is the stimulus produced by the source. Messages are comprised of words, grammar, organization of thoughts, physical appearance, body movement, voice, aspects of the person's personality and self-concept, and personal style. Environment and noise can also shape the message. Any stimulus that affects a receiver is a message from the source, regardless of whether the source intended to send it. Hence, if you ask a frowning friend what is wrong and the friend says, "Oh, nothing," you're sure to believe that there *really is* something wrong. The frown communicates that the words and the actions do not fit together and you're more likely to believe the frown than the words. Your friend may not want to discuss anything with you, but you still attach meaning to all that occurs.

Remember, each message is unique. Even if the same message were to be created over and over again, it would differ in each instance because messages cannot be repeated or received in exactly the same way or in the same context. To illustrate this, imagine reading the headline "The World Has Been Invaded by Small Green People!" in a comic book and then in your local newspaper. Although the words might be the same, the messages conveyed would be quite different.

## Interference/Noise

Anything that changes the meaning of an intended message is called **interference.** It is included in our model because it is present, to one degree or another, in every communication environment.

Interference can be external and physical, such as noise caused by the slamming of a door, someone talking on a cell phone, or the blasting of a stereo. Other examples of external interference include an unpleasant environment, such as a smoke-filled room or a room that is too cool or too hot; an odor, such as that of overly strong perfume; or distracting characteristics of the speaker, such as too much makeup, a speech impediment, talk that is too fast or too slow, mumbling pronunciation, or weird clothing.

Interference can also be internal and psychological. For example, thoughts going through a person's mind can interfere with the reception or creation of a message. A

■ **message** The stimulus that is produced by the source.

■ **interference** Anything that changes the meaning of an intended message.

person who speaks in a loud voice to get someone's attention may create both physical and psychological interference. If the receiver perceives the loudness as anger, the loud voice creates not only a distraction from attending but also a distortion of interpretation. If the receiver responds accordingly, the sender may be quite surprised. Essentially, interference is anything that reduces or distorts the clarity, accuracy, meaning, understanding, or retention of a message.

## Channel

A **channel** is the route by which messages flow between sources and receivers. The usual communication channels are light waves and sound waves, which allow us to see and hear one another. The medium through which the light and sound waves travel, however, may differ. For example, when two people are talking face to face, light and sound waves in the air serve as the channels. If a letter is sent from one person to another, light waves serve as the channel, but the paper and the writing itself serve as the means by which the message is conveyed. Books, films, videotapes, television sets, computers, radios, magazines, newspapers, and pictures are media through which messages may be conveyed.

We also receive communication by smelling, touching, and tasting. We sometimes take these senses for granted, but imagine walking into a bakery and not being able to smell the aroma or taste the flavors. All you have to do is hug someone you care about to recognize how important touch is as a means of communicating. All five senses, therefore, contribute to communication.

## Receiver

Both persons function as receivers in the model depicted in Figure 1.4. A **receiver** analyzes and interprets messages, in effect translating them into meaning. This process is called **decoding.** *You are simultaneously a receiver and a source.* As you listen to another person's message, you react with body movements and facial expressions, and the person sending the message receives the information conveyed by your physical reactions. Like the source, a receiver has several roles: to receive (hear, see, touch, smell, or taste) the message; to attend to the message; to interpret and analyze the message; to store and recall the message; and to respond to the source, message, channel, environment, and noise. In addition, Person B also has communication skills, knowledge, attitudes, and a sociocultural background that differ from those of Person A. The greater the differences between Person A and Person B, the more effort Person B must make to be a competent receiver.

## Feedback

Another component in the communication process is **feedback,** the response to a message that a receiver sends back to a source. Feedback enables a sender to determine whether the communication has been received and understood as intended. To share meaning accurately, the sender must correct faulty messages and misconceptions, repeat missed meanings, and correct responses as necessary.

Feedback is a natural extension of effective receiving. Receivers have the responsibility of attending to, decoding, and determining a message's intended meaning. The next logical step is to provide responses (feedback) that let the sender know that the message was received and understood. It is then up to the sender to decide whether the feedback provides enough information to judge whether the receiver accurately interpreted the message. Thus, feedback serves as a kind of control mech-

■ **channel** The route (such as sound waves or light waves) by which messages flow between sources and receivers.

■ **receiver** The individual who analyzes and interprets the message.

■ **decoding** The process of translating a message into the thoughts or feelings that were communicated.

■ **feedback** The response to a message that the receiver sends to the source.

anism in the communication process. Unfortunately, we too often fail to monitor our own communication and, more important, others' reactions to it, so we are often not heard or are misunderstood. To imagine the consequences, consider what would happen to the temperature in a room if the heater and the thermostat acted independently of each other.

Feedback is an essential component of the communication process, because it is not only a corrective device but also a means by which we learn about ourselves. It helps us adjust to others and assess ourselves. Giving feedback to others is just as important as receiving it, making the communication truly a shared process.

Feedback offers other advantages. A classic study found that when feedback is increased, reception of information is enhanced.[12] The experiment required four groups of students to construct geometric patterns that were described by a teacher under conditions that differed for each group: (1) zero feedback—the teacher's back was turned to the students, and students were not allowed to ask questions or make noise; (2) visible audience feedback—the students could see the teacher's face but could not ask questions; (3) limited verbal feedback—the students were allowed to ask the teacher questions, but the teacher could respond only with yes or no; (4) free feedback—all channels of communication were open, with no limits placed on the type of questions asked of the teacher or the depth of response the teacher could provide. Students provided with no opportunity to receive feedback from the teacher fared poorly, whereas each increasing level of feedback produced better results. This study resulted in two important findings: (1) As the amount of feedback increases, so does the accuracy of communication and (2) as the amount of feedback increases, so does the recipient's confidence in performance.

## ▬ Environment

The **environment,** or atmosphere, refers to the psychological and physical surroundings in which communication occurs. The environment encompasses the attitudes, feelings, perceptions, and relationships of the communicators as well as the characteristics of the location in which communication takes place, for example, the size, color, arrangement, decoration, and temperature of the room.

The environment affects the nature and quality of the communication. For example, it is much easier to carry on an intimate conversation in a private, quiet, and comfortable setting than in a public, noisy, and uncomfortable setting. Most of us find it easier to communicate with someone we know than with someone we do not know. Some environments appear to foster communication, whereas others seem to inhibit it. Consider these contrasting environments:

> The room is clean, painted light blue, and has quiet music playing in the background. Two people, seated in soft, comfortable chairs, are facing each other, smiling, and one is gently touching the other. They show genuine concern for each other. Their communication is open and caring.
>
> The room is dirty, painted dark brown, and has loud music playing in the background. Two people, seated ten feet apart on folding chairs, are staring at each other. They show little respect or concern for each other. Their communication is guarded.

How does the appearance of the room ultimately affect the negative communication? Both effective and ineffective communication are, in part, products of their environments. Effective communication can occur anywhere and under most circumstances, but pleasing, comfortable environments (along with open, trusting relationships) are more likely to produce positive exchanges.

■ **environment** The psychological and physical surroundings in which communication occurs.

### ■■ Context

The broad circumstances or situation in which communication occurs is called the **context.** Communication does not occur in a vacuum. It takes place in informal and formal settings such as between two friends, among five colleagues in a business meeting, or between a rabbi, priest, cleric, or minister and a group of worshippers. The number of people, the type of communication, and the situation in which the communication occurs all lend themselves to the context. Each context affects what we say and how we say it. They also help to determine the type of communication to use.

| GUIDELINES | Understanding Yourself and the Communication Process |
|---|---|

1. Remember that competent communicators do everything they can to help their listeners understand the communication in the way it is intended.
2. Recognize that interference from both external and internal sources may make the communication act difficult to interpret the way you, the sender, intend it.
3. Although you cannot control environmental factors (heat or lack of it, outside noise, dim or too bright lighting), you can control your own speech rate, volume, use of pauses, use of gestures and correct pronunciations, and these factors can help you be more effective.
4. If you carefully choose your words and the way you present your message (encoding), your listeners have a better chance of understanding you.
5. If you observe your listeners (receivers), you will learn how to read their feedback and be able to adapt your message to them.
6. Remember that listening is a critical aspect of the communication process.

## ■ Types of Communication

Type of communication is usually distinguished by the number of people involved, by the purpose of the communication, and by the degree of formality in which it occurs. Each type of communication involves appropriate verbal and nonverbal behaviors. Five types of communication are discussed in this text: intrapersonal, interpersonal, small group, team, and public. We also refer to elements of mass, or mediated, communication here and throughout the text.

### ■■ Intrapersonal Communication

To communicate with others, we must first understand how we communicate with ourselves. This process of understanding information within oneself is called **intrapersonal communication.** As we mature, we learn a lot about ourselves and our surroundings. Much of what we learn is gained from our own experiences. Even though there are many things we are taught by others, there are many things we must learn through our own experiences and can learn no other way. For example, the first time you experience the sensation of warmth coming over your chilled body is a form of intrapersonal communication. If the warmth is coming from a fire, the fire is the source of heat, but that heat is not really known to you until it is felt by your body and is eventually registered in your brain. Your skin senses the heated air and transmits the sensation through your central nervous system to

■ **context** Circumstances or situation in which communication occurs.

■ **intrapersonal communication** The process of understanding information within oneself.

your brain, which records it as warmth. In this sense you are communicating within yourself.

Intrapersonal communication also occurs anytime we evaluate or attempt to understand the interaction that occurs between us and anything that communicates a message to us. We are involved in intrapersonal communication as we receive, attend to, interpret and analyze, store and recall, or respond in some fashion to any message. Thus, communication between two individuals is far more complex than it appears on the surface.

Intrapersonal communication includes diverse internal activities such as thinking, problem solving, conflict resolution, planning, emotion, stress, evaluation, and relationship development. All messages that we create first occur within us. This makes communication a personal event, because we can never divorce ourselves from our interaction with others, no matter how neutral or empathic we may think we are. We say, "I understand your feelings," to someone, but we understand another's feelings only after they are filtered through our own feelings and perceptions. Ultimately, all communication takes place within each of us as we react to communication cues. Intrapersonal communication may occur without the presence of any other type of communication, but all other types of communication cannot occur without it. In fact, intrapersonal communication is occurring almost always, and yet we don't often think about it as a type of communication.

## Interpersonal Communication

**Interpersonal communication** is creating and sharing meaning between persons who are in a relationship. It is similar to intrapersonal communication in that it helps us share information, solve problems, resolve conflicts, understand our perception of self and of others, and establish relationships with others. (In Chapters 13 and 14, interpersonal relationships and our relationships with friends and family members are discussed in more detail.)

A subcomponent of interpersonal communication is dyadic communication. **Dyadic communication** is simply defined as an exchange of information between two people. It includes informal conversations, such as talks with a parent, spouse, child, friend, acquaintance, or stranger, as well as more formal conversations, such as interviews. An **interview** is a carefully planned and executed question-and-answer session designed to exchange desired information between two parties. (Chapter 8 and the Appendix discuss, respectively, information and employment interviews.)

Another subcomponent of interpersonal communication is **small-group communication,** an exchange of information among a relatively small number of people, ideally five to seven, who share a common purpose, such as completing a task, solving a problem, making a decision, or sharing information. (Chapters 15 and 16 discuss the purposes, characteristics, leadership, participation, decision making, problem solving, and evaluation of communication in small groups.)

## Public Communication

In **public communication,** a message is transmitted from one person who speaks to a number of individuals who listen. The most widely used form of public communication is the public speech. We find ourselves on the listening end of a public speech in lecture classes, political rallies, group meetings, convocations, and religious services.

Although there are many similarities between public speaking and other types of communication, there are also some differences. Public speaking almost always is

■ **interpersonal communication** The creating and sharing of meaning between people who are in a relationship.

■ **dyadic communication** An exchange of information between two people.

■ **interview** A carefully planned and executed question-and-answer session designed to exchange desired information between two parties.

■ **small-group communication** An exchange of information among a relatively small number of people, ideally five to seven, who share a common purpose, such as completing a task, solving a problem, making a decision, or sharing information.

■ **public communication** Transmission of a message from one person who speaks to a number of individuals who listen.

more highly structured than the other types. If it is to be done well, it demands much detailed planning and preparation by the speaker. Unlike participants in other types of communication, listeners do not regularly interrupt the speaker with questions or comments. It is the responsibility of the public speaker to anticipate questions that listeners may have and to attempt to answer them.

Public speaking almost always requires a more formal use of language and a more formal delivery style than the other types. The use of jargon, poor grammar, or slang is usually not accepted or tolerated in public speeches. The public speaker must use language precisely and must speak clearly in order to be heard throughout the audience. This may require that the speaker eliminate distracting vocal and physical mannerisms that might be tolerated in other types of communication.

Public speeches are often presented for three purposes: to inform, to persuade, and to entertain. They are also presented to introduce, to pay tribute, to accept, and to welcome. (Chapters 7 through 12 consider public speaking in detail.)

## ▬▬ Mass and Mediated Communication

**Mediated communication** is any communication that is transmitted by some kind of mechanistic means, such as radio, television, telephone, or the Internet; it may be one-on-one communication. **Mass communication,** on the other hand, generally means that someone is communicating with or to a large number of people. Radio, television, newspapers, magazines, books, the World Wide Web, movies, recordings, CD-ROM, and DVD are types of mass communication. They are the means by which messages of some type are directed to a large group (mass) of people. It becomes confusing when we use some form of media to communicate with large numbers or

■ **mediated communication** Any communication transmitted by some kind of mechanistic means, such as radio, television, telephone, or the Internet; it may be one-on-one communication.

■ **mass communication** Communicating with or to a large number of people.

Technology allows us to make connections with each other and with the world. Technology is indeed changing our way of communicating and how we relate with others.

masses of people; and despite the popularity of mass communication, there is very little interaction between the sender and the receiver of the communication.

Technology has advanced so quickly and is so popular that we can purchase relatively inexpensive hardware and software and have global "face-to-face conversations." Digital cameras allow us to share pictures of ourselves, our families, and special events with friends all over the world. Email messages have even become a part of the international space program. The seven astronauts on the ill-fated *Columbia* sent numerous email messages to their families and friends during their shuttle mission. In fact, emails were sent early on the morning of February 1, 2003, just before the shuttle's reentry into the earth's atmosphere. Family members were quoted as saying that they found comfort in the knowledge that their loved ones sent emails describing their love of their work. (For a comprehensive view of the Internet, its technologies, and usage, check this website: www.livinginternet.com.) As technology continues to develop and change, one thing remains consistent: Communication is the process that helps us *make connections.* Communication is a learned tool that helps us in our personal and family lives, our social and work lives, and in our roles as citizens of the world. Many people are concerned that the way we interact with each other on a one-to-one basis will be negatively affected by technology. Therefore, it becomes increasingly important to search for ways to use it positively.

# Misconceptions about Communication

Several misconceptions keep many of us from examining *our* own communication more closely. Notice the emphasis on *our* own! Most of us who have problems communicating tend to look for the fault in places other than ourselves. Becoming aware that these misconceptions exist and that many people accept them as truths should help us to understand why the study of communication is necessary. Here are some of the most common myths that interfere with people's improving their own communication skills.

## Myth 1: Communication Is a Cure-All

The first misconception is the notion that communication has the magical power to solve all of our problems. The act of communicating with others does not carry any guarantees. Obviously, without communication, we cannot solve our problems, but sometimes communication can create more problems than it solves.

You can probably provide several personal experiences that prove this point. Let one of us provide one of our own. Our neighbor is a realtor. She created a flyer for distribution in the neighborhood and asked me to read it and tell her what I thought about it. She had obviously spent a great deal of time on the project. When I looked it over, I told her that I thought the message would not reach what she said was her intended audience. She became quite agitated and said that I was the only one who had anything negative to say. I had taken her message literally, when she really wanted affirmation that she had done a good job. How might I have prevented making her angry?

Communication can help to eliminate or reduce our problems, but it is not a panacea. Communicating itself does not make the difference; the message that is communicated does.

## ■ Myth 2: Quantity Means Quality

We often assume that the more we communicate, the better. People who communicate a great deal are often perceived to be more friendly, competent, and powerful and to have more leadership potential than those who do not. However, quantity of communication is not the same as quality. A mother tells her high-school son that he cannot wear a certain shirt to his older brother's college graduation ceremony. The younger son likes the shirt and feels that it is appropriate and that everyone else wears similar shirts. Neither mother nor son will change their view and they continue to argue. Each becomes more defensive and louder until another family member steps in to stop the argument. In this case, as in the one in the first myth, it isn't the act or the amount of communication but the content of communication that makes the difference.

## ■ Myth 3: Meaning Is in the Words We Use

If your sister tells you that she doesn't feel well, what would that mean to you? That she is sick? That she has a cold? That she has an upset stomach? That her feelings have been hurt? It could mean any number of things, for, without context and more information, the statement is not clear. If she tells you that she has a cold and doesn't feel well, is that message clear? Well, at least it would narrow the choices a little. Confusion may arise because the statement "I don't feel well" is relative; that is, it might not mean the same thing to you that it does to her. Some people use the statement to refer to a minor discomfort, whereas others mean they are more seriously ill. The words themselves could refer to many degrees or types of conditions. Thus, *meanings are in people and not in the words they use.*

The notion that words contain meanings is probably the most serious misconception of all. Words have meaning only when we give them meanings. *No two people share the same meanings for all words, because no two people completely share the same background and experiences.* Thus, the meaning of a word cannot be separated from the person using it.

## ■ Myth 4: We Have a Natural Ability to Communicate

Many people believe that because we are born with the physical and mental equipment needed to communicate, communication must be a natural ability. This simply is not true. The ability to communicate, like almost everything we do, is learned. Most of us possess the physical ability to tie our shoes, but we still have to learn how the strings go together. Similarly, most of us are born with the ability to see, but that does not make us able to read. Reading requires knowledge of the alphabet, the acquisition of vocabulary, and practice. The ability to communicate requires not only that we be capable but also that we understand how human communication works and that we have an opportunity to use that knowledge.

## ■ Myth 5: Communication Is Reversible

All of us sometimes make a blunder in communication. We might think that we can take something back, but that is impossible. Once something is said, it is out there; the listener will have to deal with that message, and the speaker will have to try to explain and compensate for what was said. For example, in a moment of anger, we say something that we regret and later ask the other person to "forget that I even said that." Although the other person may forgive us for speaking in anger, it is not likely that he or she will forget what was said. When we communicate through writing, we can take things back until we let someone else see what we've written. When we send oral messages, others can hear and will respond to what we say, even if we don't really mean to say things the way they come out. It is important, therefore, to carefully organize our thoughts and choose our words before we utter them to others. As you study this textbook and the communication process in class, you will learn more about communication competence.

# ■ Improving Communication Competence

To be competent communicators, we must understand the role of communication in our lives and be aware of the complexity of the communication process and different types of communication. We also need to realize that myths about communication may hinder our ability to develop effective communication.

Throughout this chapter we have referred to the concept of communication competence. We will discuss it throughout the text, provide examples of such competence, and ask you to evaluate your ability to communicate effectively in a variety of situations. Earlier in the text, we described communication competence as the ability to engage in effective communication. Communication competence, however,

The successful career woman, in addition to other qualifications, has developed a broad communication repertoire—a wide range of communication behaviors from which to choose. Competent communicators are able to coordinate several communication tasks simultaneously.

is a concept that various authors have defined in various ways. One noteworthy definition is provided by communication scholars Dan O'Hair, Gustav Friedrich, John Wiemann, and Mary Wiemann, who state that "communication competencies are skills and understandings that enable communication partners to exchange messages appropriately and effectively."[13] This chapter has only introduced the types of skills and understandings necessary to successful communication. One such skill is the ability to select and implement the most appropriate communication behavior for a particular situation. Good communicators have developed a broad communication **repertoire,** a range of communication behaviors from which to choose.[14] Another hallmark of communication competence is the ability to evaluate the effectiveness of a given communication after the fact.[15]

Competence is also characterized by the ability to coordinate several communication tasks simultaneously. For example, a competent communicator will, at the same time, choose a way of conveying a message, consider what the receiver's various responses might be, and plan a way to restate the message if the first attempt is not effective.

■ **repertoire** Wide range of communication behaviors from which effective communicators make choices.

## Communication Principles and Intercultural Competence

In a letter to one of your authors, Korean communication scholar Myung Seok Park asserted, "To coexist peacefully in this world where cultural conflicts are ever intensifying, each person is urgently called upon to inculcate into his or her personal psyche the need for intercultural competence, that is, a special knowledge of foreign cultures, including verbal and nonverbal behavior patterns, cultural values and beliefs (reasoning and thinking patterns), attitudes, and an understanding of the major economic, social, and political variables affecting the conduct of international affairs." Think about Professor Park's challenge and answer the following questions.

1. What does Professor Park believe we should know about other cultures?
2. What reasons does he give for learning more about other cultures?
3. What other reasons are there?
4. What personal experiences have you had that would let you believe that intercultural competence is necessary?

Reprinted by permission of Myung Seok Park

Consider the last time you asked a question or responded to another student or your professor in a classroom. What did you think about before you raised your hand or before you spoke? How did the reactions of your professor or classmates as you spoke affect the way you presented your ideas? What would you do differently the next time? Reflecting on your answers to these questions can help you find ways to become a better communicator.

Through practice and study, you will become comfortable with communicating in a variety of situations. Background knowledge about communication, practical experience, and feedback given in the classroom will help you think on your feet and make better decisions as you communicate. You will also gain confidence and the ability to evaluate your skills as your work in this course progresses.

## Summary

Competent communication is essential in all aspects of our everyday lives. Effective communication enhances our personal, social, and career relationships and allows us to make connections with people from other cultures. The communication process is one that is learned; therefore, we can improve our effectiveness as communicators by applying the guidelines and principles identified in this chapter.

In this course, you will be involved in practical and applied situations involving the various types of communication. Intrapersonal communication occurs when we communicate with ourselves (thinking, making choices, making decisions). Interpersonal communication involves creating and sharing messages with one or more other people. When we work in small groups in the classroom or the workplace, we need to know more about group and team communication. When you give a speech in front of your class, you are a public communicator who considers all aspects of the communication process in order to effectively present your messages to your classmates. Technology is important to most of us, and mediated communication and mass communication demonstrate the role of technology in our lives.

We sometimes mistakenly believe that communication can solve all problems. It cannot, but learning how to be an effective communicator can go a long way toward helping us get along better with the people around us. Merely increasing the amount of communication might lead to more confusion and misunderstanding. Problems stem from communicators, not from the act of communication. Communication is a tool we need to learn to use as effectively as we can. We should strive for *communication competence* if we wish to *make connections* with others.

# Discussion Starters

1. Why is communication regarded as difficult and complex?
2. Whom do you identify as an effective communicator? Why?
3. What is the difference between effective and ineffective communication?
4. Why should you study communication?
5. What is the role of communication in our lives?
6. Explain what it means when we say that communication is a process.
7. How does a system differ from a process?
8. What would happen if there were no feedback?
9. How can feedback motivate you to be more effective?
10. How can feedback deter you from effective communication?
11. What can you do to improve your own communication with people from another culture?
12. How will the Internet change the way we communicate?

# Notes

1. H. Lerner, *The Dance of Connection* (New York: Quill/Harper Collins Publishers 2001), xiv.
2. L. A. Samovar and R. E. Porter, *Communication Between Cultures,* 6th ed. (Belmont, CA: Wadsworth Publishing Co., 2007).
3. J. Thurber, "Friends, Romans, Countrymen, Lend Me Your Ear Muffs," in *Lanterns and Lances* (New York: Harper & Row, 1960), 40.
4. National Association of Colleges & Employers, *Job Outlook 2003;* also, 21st Century Workforce Commission, *A Nation of Opportunity: Strategies for Building Tomorrow's 21st Century Workforce* (Washington, DC: U.S. Department of Labor, 2000); *Spanning the Chasm: Corporate and Academic Cooperation to Improve Work-Force Preparation* (Washington, DC: American Council of Education, 1997); "Survey by the National Association of Colleges and Employers," in Work Week, *Wall Street Journal,* February 8, 2000.
5. Personal conversations with business executives, personnel managers, and recruiters, May 2000, January 2003, and January 2006.
6. Aristotle, *The Rhetoric and Poetics of Aristotle,* trans. W. R. Roberts and I. Bywater (New York: The Modern Library, 1954), 24–25.
7. W. M. Smail, *Quintillian on Education,* Book XII, Chapter 1 (Oxford: Clarendon Press, 1938), 108.
8. U.S. Census Bureau, "Resident Population Estimates of the United States by Sex, Race, and Hispanic Origin: April 1, 1990 to July 1, 1999 with Short-Term Projection to November 1, 2000," www.census.gov/population. Internet release date January 2, 2001, last accessed June 26, 2006.
9. U.S. Census Bureau, U.S. Department of Commerce, "Voting and Registration in the Election of 2004," www.census.gov/population/www/socdemo/voting.html. Issued March 2006, last accessed June 26, 2006.
10. D. K. Berlo, *The Process of Communication* (New York: Holt, Rinehart & Winston, 1960), 23.
11. J. T. Masterson, S. A. Beebe, and N. H. Watson, *Speech Communication Theory and Practice* (New York: Holt, Rinehart & Winston, 1983), 6–7.
12. H. J. Leavitt and R. Mueller, "Some Effects of Feedback on Communication," *Human Relations* 4 (1951): 401–10.
13. D. O'Hair, G. W. Friedrich, J. M. Wiemann, and M. O. Wiemann, *Competent Communication,* 2nd ed. (New York: St. Martin's Press, 1997), 21.
14. B. S. Wood, ed., *Development of Functional Communication Competencies: Grades 7–12* (Urbana, IL: ERIC Clearinghouse on Reading and Communication Skills and Speech Communication Association, 1977), 5.
15. Ibid., 5–6.

# CHAPTER 2

# Connecting Perceptions and Communication

"We don't see things as they are, we see them as we are."

—ANAÏS NIN

# This chapter will help you:

- **Make** the connection between perception and communication competence.

- **Know** what perception is and its effects on our communication.

- **Understand** why perceptions differ from one person to another.

- **Interpret** perceptions as well as improve your communication competence.

# Making everyday connections

Suppose that while you are at the grocery store, another shopper hits you with her cart and then looks at you as if it were your fault that you were in her way. Your past experiences tell you instantly that this person may be hostile and someone who gets angry easily. You may react with anger yourself—give her a dirty look, or express your feelings in another way. But what if after hitting you with the cart she said, "Oh, I'm so sorry, please excuse me?" If you perceived her communication to be genuinely sorry, the chances are good that you would not seek retaliation and might simply say, "That's okay," despite being a bit irritated by her carelessness.

But what if she muttered, "Oh, I'm sorry," but at the same time said it in a tone of voice and provided facial expressions that you perceived to be less than sincere. You likely would react and communicate entirely differently. Your perception of the woman, based on each of the above messages, would influence your reaction to her. ■

## Questions to think about

- Explain perception's role in the above situation.

- What influences our perception of events more, what we see or what is said? Why?

- How might the woman's appearance (e.g., clothes, tattoos, jewelry, ethnic origin) influence or change our perception of the woman's behavior?

- What lessons can we learn about perception and its role in communicating with others?

- How might a competent communicator respond to the above situation?

- Describe a situation or situations in which either your or another person's perception(s) influenced what was communicated.

Perceptions do influence our reactions and our communication. It is virtually impossible for our feelings about things to be the same as others'. We perceive feelings based on communication.

© Jim Toomey, King Features Syndicate.

# ■ Perception and Communication

**Perception** involves selecting, organizing, and interpreting information in order to give personal meaning to the communication we receive. What we perceive about ourselves, others, objects, and events gives meanings to our experiences, and it is these meanings, based on our perception, that we communicate to others. The meanings we give to our experiences almost always originate in us and do not reflect a totally objective account of the experiences themselves. No two people have internalized identical meanings for the same words, messages, or experiences. Communication is indeed personal! In this chapter, we discuss perception and how it is connected to communication. In  Chapter 3, we focus on self-concept.

Perception is at the heart of all communication. It can also be argued that without communication, perceptions could not exist. Thus, the statement that communication is at the heart of all perceptions is equally true. Robert L. Scott, a communication scholar, writes, "Nothing is clear in and of itself but in some context for some persons."[1] A difference between two people's perceptions, for example, does not necessarily make the perception of one person more correct or accurate than that of the other. It does, however, mean that communication between individuals who see things differently may require more understanding, negotiation, persuasion, and tolerance of those differences.

Perception, like communication, is a complex phenomenon. To receive stimuli from our surroundings and to form perceptions requires that we utilize at least one of our five senses: hearing,  touching, smelling,  seeing, and tasting.

Our perceptions of people and events, whether accurate or inaccurate, influence our communication as illustrated in the Making Everyday Connections example at the beginning of the chapter. For example, the woman with the grocery cart may seem hostile, but it could be that she is just having a bad day. And yet, we react to her based on our first assumption. Our views of people, situations, events, or objects are our perceptions and represent our reality of what we see and hear. However, what may be reality for us may not be the same for someone else. For example, when someone says to another person, "I understand how difficult this might be for you," the statement is based on one person's perception of another's communication. It does

■ **perception** The process of selecting, organizing, and interpreting information in order to give personal meaning to the communication we receive.

Border demonstrations illustrate an issue in which perceptions play a major role in what is communicated and how it is received. When different people view an issue in different ways, as in the Mexican/U.S. border controversy, we need to stress understanding, negotiation, persuasion, and tolerance of those differences.

not mean they know exactly what the other person is experiencing. The competent communicator understands the role of perception and its influence on communication and vice versa.

## MAKING CONNECTIONS

### Robert L. Scott
*University of Minnesota*

Robert L. Scott, communication scholar, provides insight into how people use communication to make sense of their worlds. He is best known for his assertion that "rhetoric is epistemic," which suggests that in the process of communicating with others, people create and share new meaning. According to Scott, when we talk with others we say things in ways that create a social meaning. Because we all bring different perceptions, ideas, and experiences into our communication with others, we influence each other. Thus, when individuals see things differently it requires more understanding, negotiation, persuasion, and tolerance on the part of everyone.

### To Scholars

Dr. Scott's contributions have made a difference because he tells us that in order to be effective communicators we must be responsible and ethical to those who open themselves to our attempts to inform and persuade them. According to Scott, we must be willing to listen and to adapt; that is, we must take the interests of others into account if we are to be ethical communicators.

Dr. Scott is an emeritus faculty member at the University of Minnesota. He has published numerous research articles and books, and was named a Distinguished Scholar by the National Communication Association—one of the first ten people in the communication discipline to be given this honor. He also loves to read a variety of books, play the trombone, and engage in intellectual discussions.

# ■ Understanding Perception

Perceiving in and of itself sounds and appears simple enough. After all, we do it every day, and it seems so natural that we hardly give our perceptions a thought. We just do it, think little about it, and move on. But perception is a very complex cognitive process that, if not understood, could lead to a variety of communication misunderstandings, some of which could be quite costly. To perceive our surroundings, we must first be aware of them. Second, we must form our perceptions cognitively, and then, finally we must be able to verbally communicate them.

## ■ Awareness

The first time you walk into a classroom, what do you notice? More than likely your senses are fully or at least partially engaged and you observe who else is in the room. You see and hear other students, some of whom you know from previous classes, others whom you have never seen before. You may see writing on the chalkboard, the teacher, and other aspects of the classroom and those in it. Being aware of what is going on and taking in the sights, sounds, smells, and so on can only occur if you are paying attention to them. Each person, sound, object, or surrounding that we attend to is processed and catalogued by our minds, especially when new or novel. However, we are creatures of habit, and when others behave in routine or predictable ways, we are more likely to gloss over or ignore the details, which can lead to misunderstandings or inaccurate communication.

## ■ Perception Formation

The way our mind filters and sorts information that it receives has a profound effect on how we perceive others, how we talk with them, and how they respond to us. Each of us differs in how we organize and interpret our experiences and thus the way we see the world around us. **Cognitive complexity** is a term used by psychologists to explain how our minds process and store simple to complex information. For example, most children have rather simple information processing systems in which to classify their experiences. When children see another person, they are likely to focus on concrete aspects, such as a person's height (tall or short), attractiveness (pretty or not pretty), or race (same or different), rather than on abstract psychological aspects, such as sincerity, honesty, and so on. Children often do not perceive relationships among multiple perceptions, such as how sincerity may relate to honesty or vice versa. Similarly if a child, for example, sees an animal with four legs for the first time and is told that it is a dog (doggie), because of the child's low level of cognitive complexity, he or she will call every animal with four legs a dog (doggie) until taught otherwise.

Of course, as we mature and become adults, we learn to distinguish between and among different experiences, all of which help to develop our cognitive abilities. The more cognitively complex our ability to process and store information, the more sophisticated our perceptions are. You might notice that a person talks a lot, dresses well, tells good jokes, and is attractive in appearance. At an abstract psychological level you might infer that the behaviors you observe reflect an extroverted, sincere, and self-confident personality. This level of assessment is a sophisticated explanation, because it involves perceptions of why the person acts as he or she does, and it is based solely on concrete observations.

People who have high levels of cognitive complexity are likely to be flexible in interpreting complicated events and situations and are able to integrate new informa-

■ **cognitive complexity** Explains how our minds process and store simple to complex information.

tion into their perceptions. Also, people who are cognitively complex are likely to use "person-centered" messages when communicating with others. These individuals are likely to take multiple considerations into their perspective when communicating with others. For example, those with high degrees of cognitive complexity are able to take into account others' values, beliefs, and emotional needs and incorporate them into their messages. Being able to do this allows those with high levels of cognitive complexity to be effective communicators, because they are able to understand and process multiple perspectives at one time. Individuals who have less complex cognitive abilities, however, are unable to process multiple perspectives and, thus, often ignore information that does not fit their past experiences. They may even throw out their old perceptions completely and replace them with new ones.

## ■■ Verbal Communication

When we think of perception we mostly associate the term with what we see, but we also form perceptions based on the sound of individuals' speech patterns, which includes voice, grammar, and word choices. People's speech patterns create images of age, competency, intelligence, cultural or ethnic background, and gender. For example, a soft-spoken voice might be seen as timid or lacking in confidence, a loud voice as overbearing or controlling, a squeaky voice as annoying, or a deep voice as masculine. We also create images based on accent, speed, fluency, and quality of people's voices. It is not unusual for Americans to think "foreigner" automatically when they hear an unfamiliar accent. How people use their voice creates a variety of images, both positive and negative. Think about how a person's voice influences your perception of their credibility, competency, intelligence, age, or gender.

A college student says, "Okay, I don't understand what you was saying," an athlete being interviewed responds to a question, "We got our butts kicked, like you know," or a store owner says, "We don't got any more of these." How might these statements affect your perception of those making them? If the college student were dressed in a suit and tie, would that change your perception of him? If the athlete were a star player, would that change your perception of her? Would knowing that the store owner just became a citizen of the United States affect your perception of her?

There is a radio commercial that says, "People judge us by the words we use." It's true, people do judge us by the words we use or don't use. Our word choices in spoken and written communication can affect how others perceive us. The more sophisticated vocabulary that we are able to use when we speak or write, the more likely others will perceive us to be intelligent or highly educated. In addition to the words we choose, our pronunciation of the words we use, our accent, and our vocal quality all create images that influence how we are received and reacted to by others. The connection between how and what we communicate and others' perceptions of us cannot be ignored.

The Making Everyday Connections example at the beginning of the chapter illustrates that the way something is said can quickly either reinforce or change the perception of what took place. Our perceptions are formed not only by what we see, but by what we hear. If the tone of the woman's voice in the example is perceived to be sincere and the woman sounds sorry for what happened, then her behavior would more likely be interpreted positively. If, however, the opposite was perceived, then the interpretation could lead to retaliation or at the very least a nasty exchange of words and hand gestures.

We are taught to believe that actions speak louder than words. But do they? We would have to say, it depends! The perceptions that are created by what we see do have a powerful influence, but so do words. If someone you respect tells you that you should avoid going to a certain store because that store doesn't sell quality products, you may avoid that store based on what you were told. You might also tell someone else that you had heard that the store doesn't sell quality products. Your and your friend's image of the store is based on what you were told and not on what you experienced or saw for yourselves. What was told to you about the store was enough for you to form a negative image of the store even though you had never shopped there. We often set expectations based on what we have heard someone say. However, after years of experiences of our own, we find our initial perceptions to be either accurate or inaccurate, which may lead us to modify them. Therefore, the connection between our perceptions and how we communicate and behave cannot be ignored.

# ■ The Nature of Perception

Our lack of awareness of how perception operates can lead us to misunderstand and misjudge others' ideas and behavior. Many people imagine the brain to be similar in operation to a camera or tape recorder; information enters through the eyes or ears and is stored in the brain. Actually, far too much information exists for the brain to absorb at once, so the brain ignores much of it. It accepts a certain amount of information and organizes it into meaningful patterns. It discards a tremendous amount of information. Much of what we know about the way we perceive events, objects, and people seems to involve how we select, organize, and interpret information (see Table 2.1). All of these connections happen in milliseconds. Selecting must always occur first; however, organizing and interpreting do not always occur in exactly the same sequence. For example, it is possible to perceive information, interpret it, and then organize it or to organize it and then interpret it.

## ■ Selection

Because it is impossible to attend to, sense, perceive, retain, and give meaning to every stimulus we encounter, we narrow our focus. A **stimulus** incites or quickens action, feeling, or thought. Although we are exposed to millions of bits of stimuli, or data, at one time, the mind can process only a small fraction of them. On both the unconscious level of the nervous system and the conscious level of directing atten-

■ **stimulus** Something that incites or quickens action, feeling, or thought.

### ■ TABLE 2.1 The Perception Process

| TERM | DEFINITION | EXAMPLE |
|---|---|---|
| *Selection* | Sorting one stimulus from another | Selective exposure<br>Selective attention<br>Selective retention |
| *Organization* | Sorting, organizing, or categorizing | Closure<br>Proximity<br>Similarity |
| *Interpretation* | Assigning meaning to stimuli | Based on past experience<br>Based on new situations<br>Based on opinions of others |

tion, **selection** occurs as the brain sorts one stimulus from another, based on criteria formed by our previous experiences. There are three kinds of selection: selective exposure, selective attention, and selective retention.

**Selective Exposure.**    The deliberate choices we make to experience or to avoid experiencing particular stimuli are referred to as **selective exposure.** For example, you might dislike violent and sexist lyrics in the music you listen to, so you avoid purchasing CDs by certain individuals or groups known for such lyrics. When we choose to communicate with certain individuals instead of others, we are also using selective exposure.

**Selective Attention.**    Focusing on specific stimuli while ignoring or downplaying other stimuli is called **selective attention.** That is, you concentrate on the data you wish to attend to, in order to eliminate or reduce the effects of all extraneous stimuli. This task is often easier said than done. Paying attention to something usually requires decisive effort, but even the best attempts to concentrate can be interrupted by distractions. For example, a book dropped in a quiet classroom, a loud sneeze, background talking, a siren, a baby's cry, a call for help, an odor, or a movement can avert our attention from the task in which we are involved. Continuing to attend to the original task may require extra effort. Similarly, when we converse with someone in a crowded lounge with loud music playing in the background, we focus on each other's words more attentively and ignore the other sounds. This blocking out of all extraneous stimuli to concentrate on the other person is an instance of selective attention. To make sense out of the multitude of stimuli that surround us, we learn to focus on those we find interesting or important and ignore those that are not.

**Selective Retention.**    Because we cannot possibly remember all the stimuli we encounter, we also select the information we will retain. **Selective retention** occurs when we process, store, and retrieve information that we have already selected,

■ **selection** Sorting of one stimulus from another.

■ **selective exposure** The deliberate choices we make to experience or to avoid particular stimuli.

■ **selective attention** Focusing on specific stimuli while ignoring or downplaying other stimuli.

■ **selective retention** Processing, storing, and retrieving of information that we have already selected, organized, and interpreted.

## MAKING CONNECTIONS for Success

### What You Say Can Create Good and Bad Images!

Create a list of two or three one-word descriptions that could create a positive image of a person, e.g., cool. Create a list of two or three one-word descriptions that could create a negative perception of a person, e.g., nerd.

Choosing the descriptive words from each list you created, insert one at a time in the blank space below. Then find two or three people older or younger than yourself and tell them that you are going to describe a person to them and that you want to know how your description would affect their communication with that person should they meet him. Here is the statement for you to insert your "word" description:

"John is (a) _____ ."

You can use your voice to emphasize the word in order to make it sound more realistic!

1. Ask the person to describe the image they have of John based on what you said about him.
2. Ask the person to tell you how the image they formed of John would likely affect their communication should they meet him.
3. What did you learn about communication and perception from this brief exercise that can improve your communication competency?

organized, and interpreted. We are more likely to remember information that agrees with our views and to selectively forget information that does not. Also, after perceiving and selecting certain stimuli, we may retain only a portion of them. For example, how many times have you listened to someone tell you how to do something, and later, after thinking that you had completed the task, found that you had done only a portion of it? Chances are that you retained the pleasant parts of the task and forgot the not-so-pleasant parts. Selection plays an important role in what, why, and how we communicate.

## ▪▬ Organization

To help you understand how we organize stimuli and its effect on communication, consider what happens when you enter a room filled with people. When you first walk in, you begin to sort and organize people into groups or categories. Chances are you will first begin to look for people whom you know; by doing so you are categorizing the people in the room according to those you know and those you don't know. People whom you know and who happen to be nearest to you are those whom you will likely visit first. It is also likely that you will spend more time with those whom you perceive to be like you than with those who are not.

In the crowd, a woman spots a man she has been interested in but whom she has met only briefly at another gathering. As she moves through the crowd toward him, another woman moves next to the man and places her arm around him. He also places his arm around her, and they engage in what seems to be intimate conversation. The first woman quickly moves back into the crowd so as not to be noticed by him and begins talking with another friend, but her mind is still concentrating on the image of the man and the other woman. Her thoughts of him drift off as she tries to involve herself in conversation with her friend. From this example, it is clear that the way we organize the stimuli around us affects our choices concerning with whom we communicate, what we communicate, how we communicate, and why we communicate with others.

We categorize stimuli in our environment in order to make sense of them. This **organization** of data plays an important role in how we perceive and communicate about events, objects, and people.

**Closure.**   Another way to organize the stimuli around us is through **closure.** We tend to fill in missing pieces and to extend lines in order to finish or complete figures. This completion process is called closure. In Figure 2.1, we see a figure—a cow—that doesn't really exist in the printed material. This occurs because we are always trying to make meaningless mater-

▪ **organization**
Categorizing of stimuli in our environment in order to make sense of them.

▪ **closure** Filling in of details so that a partially perceived entity appears to be complete.

▪ **FIGURE 2.1**  Closure: Cow or Incomplete Drawing?

The partial outlines of this shape lead us to fill in the missing lines so that we can make sense of it. This organizing of the visual data allows us to give meaning to the drawing.

ground for successful communication. Finally, stereotypes repeat and reinforce beliefs until they come to be taken as the truth. Stereotypes ultimately perpetuate inaccuracies about people and thus impede communication. Although many stereotypes are negative, there are positive stereotypes as well. For example, to stereotype men as decisive or women as sensitive projects positive images that should be equally applicable to both genders.

Perceptual set and stereotypes both involve selective attention and selective retention. The difference between a stereotype and a perceptual set is that a stereotype uses categories and a perceptual set does not. To illustrate perceptual set, see Figure 2.3. Like most of us, you probably found that saying the color the word was in rather than the name of the color that was written was somewhat difficult to do. For most of us, our brain doesn't process the color the word is in as quickly as the word that is written. The "ABC" example further illustrates how our past experiences condition us to ignore certain information to achieve speed and efficiency when processing information. Most of us see the number 13 as the letter B because that is what we would expect to follow the letter A and to precede the letter C.

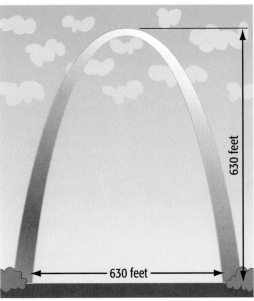

Perceptual set can interfere with communication. For example, some parents communicate with their offspring as if they were still children, even though they are adults. Their perceptual set may be that belief that "they are our children, and they will always be our children." Therefore, the parents are unwilling or unable to communicate with them as adults.

Perceptual set may prevent us from seeing things that differ from what we expect to see and hear or from noticing changes in people and things. Massimo Piattelli-Palmarini, in his book *Inevitable Illusions: How Mistakes of Reason Rule Our Minds,* uses the example of the St. Louis arch to illustrate the point that "the eye sees what it sees, even when we know what we know."[3] He points out that the arch is as wide as it is tall, yet it appears to be taller than it is wide. According to Piattelli-Palmarini, this inability to see the similarity between the arch's height and width demonstrates that our minds are unable to adjust their perceptions even when we know the facts. He says the errors, or illusions, usually occur without our being aware of them. Perceptual set operates in a similar manner. Differences between what we do, what happens to us, and what is innate within us create bias, something that all of us have.[4] Our brains always make sure, or at least try to make sure, that what we see or hear or both see *and* hear represents reality rather than assumptions that may be false. A nineteenth-century humorist, Artemus Ward, put it this way: "It ain't the things we don't know that get us in trouble. It's the things we do know that ain't so." We are all, at times, victims of unconsciously making inaccurate assumptions that can seriously affect our communication.

Perceptual sets, like stereotypes, do not always limit or hinder us. Sometimes they help us make decisions more efficiently. They provide us with expectations of how things, events, or people should be, and they enable us to compare our expectations with the reality of the moment and to respond accordingly. The key is to avoid the assumption that perceptual sets will always be accurate. Many communication

### Seeing Is Believing or Is It?

If you enjoy optical illusions and how they affect our perception, you might enjoy going to this website: www.michaelbach.de/ot/. The site allows you to actually experience the illusion and explains what is happening and why. There are also many other wonderful sites to explore—do a search using *optical illusions* as your key words.

1. What did you learn from the site about perception?
2. How can the site help you become a more competent communicator?

scholars believe that *the greatest single problem with human communication is the assumption that our perceptions are always correct.*[5]

## ■ Attribution Error

It is human nature to attribute, or assign, causes to people's behavior. **Attribution** is the complex process through which we attempt to understand the reasons behind others' behaviors. There are two factors that influence our assumptions about our own and others' behavior: the *situation* (environment) and the *disposition* (traits of the person). We are always trying to explain why people behave the way they do, and to do this, we must make assumptions. For example, imagine that you witness the following scene. A man arrives at a meeting one hour late. On entering, he drops his notes on the floor. While he is trying to pick them up, his glasses fall out of his coat pocket and break. Later, he spills coffee all over his tie. How would you explain these events? The chances are good that you would reach conclusions such as "This person is disorganized and clumsy." Are such attributions accurate? Perhaps. But it is also possible that the man was late because of unavoidable delays at the airport, dropped his notes because the paper was slick, and spilled his coffee because the cup was too hot to hold. Research shows that we are more likely to overestimate dispositional causes and underestimate situational causes of others' actions. This bias is referred to as the fundamental attribution error.[6] **Attribution error** occurs when we perceive others as acting as they do because they are "that kind of person" rather than because of any external factors that may have influenced their behavior.

Suppose, as actually happened during 1997 and 1998, a woman accuses the president of the United States of sexual harassment—for example, of making unwanted sexual advances toward her. Why would she do this? One possible reason is that she was very upset at the time and believed that it was her duty to call this inappropriate (and illegal) behavior by the president to public attention. But now suppose that soon after she made her claim, a reporter discovers that the woman had an affair with the president and was upset about being dumped by him. So another possible explanation for her action is revenge—perhaps she wanted retribution for what she perceived as mistreatment. After learning of this second potential cause, how would you view the first cause (her desire to do her duty and warn other women)? The chances are good that you will view it as a less likely or less important cause. Our tendency is to attribute dispositional causes to others' behaviors (she did it for revenge) and to attribute situational causes to our own behavior (I did it because I wanted to warn other women).

Now, in contrast, imagine the same situation involving the president with one difference: The woman makes her claim of sexual harassment even though she strongly supported the president and worked vigorously for his election in the past. What will you conclude about her claim now? You will probably believe that it is true and that it is motivated by the woman's desire to warn the public about the president's behavior. The difference in our perception of the woman depends on what we already know about the woman and what we attribute to her behavior.

■ **attribution** The complex process through which we attempt to understand the reasons behind others' behaviors.

■ **attribution error** Perceiving others as acting as they do because they are "that kind of person" rather than because of any external factors that may have influenced their behavior.

## ◼◼ Physical Characteristics

A person's weight, height, body shape, health, strength, and ability to use his or her five senses account for the way he or she takes in perceptual differences. For example, a person who is visually impaired experiences the world in ways that a sighted person finds difficult to comprehend or even imagine. Sighted people might not automatically take such differences into account, thus making communication more difficult.

Short people and tall people sometimes perceive events differently. Consider this situation: Two young boys were walking to a neighborhood store when two older boys threatened them with a knife and demanded their money. Afterward, the police asked the victims to describe their assailants. One boy gave the robbers' heights as about five feet six inches and five feet ten inches and estimated their ages to be about sixteen and twenty. The other boy described them as about five feet ten inches and six feet two inches and guessed their ages to be about twenty and twenty-seven. The first boy was nine years old and just over five feet tall; the other was six years old and four feet tall. Of course, the smaller boy perceived the robbers as much taller and older.[7]

In 2004, John Edwards, presidential candidate, was generally considered the best looking of the Democratic hopefuls, but he came in second among those running for the nomination. His only problem with respect to appearance was that he looked too young (the baby-face effect) to be president though not too young to be vice president. He turned fifty during the primary but his youthful appearance elicited perceptions about immaturity—both positive (trustworthy, honest) and negative (submissive and naïve) rather than mature, masculine ones.[8]

When we meet someone for the first time, we usually react to a variety of factors. Any observable cue, no matter how superficial, may affect our perception of them, resulting in emotional reactions that lead to a positive or negative image. One such factor is the clothing they are wearing. Beyond such factors as neatness or perceived cost, clothing color seems to have an effect on our perception. It seems that we make an automatic association between brightness and affect; specifically, bright is good, and dark equals bad.[9] Perceptions are also influenced by observable disabilities, the presence of eyeglasses, height, physique, and men's facial hair.[10] Once again, perceptions can lead to assumptions and those assumptions influence our communication.

## ◼◼ Psychological State

Another factor that can influence or alter our perceptions of people, events, and things is our state of mind. All information that we receive goes through various filters and screens that sort and color what we receive and how we perceive it. Obviously, when everything is going well and we are in a positive frame of mind, we view

THIS IS NOTHING. WHEN I WAS YOUR AGE THE SNOW WAS SO DEEP IT CAME UP TO MY CHIN.

The age and physical height differences between the son and the father clearly affect their perception of the snow depth. However, the father has not taken this difference into account in his communication. Reprinted by permission of the Marcus estate.

things, events, and people much more positively than when our mind-set is negative. When we are under a great deal of stress or if we have a poor self-image, these conditions will influence how we perceive the world around us. Sometimes this distortion is small and temporary and has no appreciable effect on communication. At other times, our state of mind can actually reverse meaning or alter a message, changing how we select, organize, and interpret it. It is undeniable that psychological disposition can color or alter perceptions and, ultimately, communication. Think about how you feel when you are upset, angry, or frustrated with someone or something and when you are not. How does your disposition affect your perception of that person or event? In the next chapter, the connections between self-concept and perception are discussed in more detail.

## ■■ Cultural Background

Cultural background can also affect the way in which people perceive other people, events, and things. There are well over a hundred different definitions of culture, each taking a different perspective. For our purposes, **culture** may be best defined as learned behaviors that are communicated from one generation to another to promote individual and social survival.[11] A culture evolves through communication, beliefs, artifacts, and a style of living that is shared among people. A group's culture usually includes similarities in religion, language, thinking, social rules, laws, perceptions, communicative style, and attitudes, all of which contribute to a group's identity as being different from other groups.

Take a moment and reflect about the cultural beliefs that you hold that influence how you perceive the world and interact in it. Your views on work, education, freedom, age, competitiveness, personal space, cleanliness and hygiene, gender, loyalty, death and mourning, etiquette, health, status differentiation, bodily adornment, courtship, family, art, music, technology, and the like all play a role in your cultural identity.

Cultural identity has little or nothing to do with physical features such as skin color, shape of eyes, or sex because these characteristics are passed on genetically and not by communication. Because people of a particular race or country are often taught similar beliefs, values, and attitudes, those similarities have created such labels as "African American," "Hispanic," "Native American," or "European American." Each of these labels by definition suggests that there are cultural differences among these groups, but the labels do not suggest that there may also be differences within the groups as well. Most of us have been conditioned to believe that people who are similar in race or nationality think and behave in the same way. This way of thinking, however, is likely to lead to misunderstandings and perceptual errors. For example, two Hispanic business owners, one in New York City and the other in rural

■ **culture** Learned behaviors that are communicated from one generation to another to promote individual and social survival.

Nebraska, while labeled "Hispanics," are likely to have different values, beliefs, and lifestyles because of where they live. Yet both are labeled Hispanics. Therefore, to assume that they think and act alike because of how they are labeled or because of their physical features is likely to be wrong. The competent communicator does not rely on physical characteristics to make assumptions about people's values, attitudes, beliefs, or behaviors. The competent communicator does, however, learn about others through communication and observations of others' behaviors.

Culture is an integral part of each of us and determines many of our individual characteristics. Culture identifies us as members of a particular group and shapes our values and biases. Much cultural influence occurs without our realizing it; typically, we are not conscious of the fact that much of our behavior is conditioned by our culture. The way we greet others, the way we use language, our opinions about what and when to eat, and many of our personal preferences are all culturally conditioned.[12]

The connection between culture and communication is crucial to understanding communication. In fact, it is because of culture that we learn to communicate, according to McDaniel, Samovar, and Porter. For example, a Korean, an Egyptian, or an American learns to communicate like other Koreans, Egyptians, or Americans. Each knows that certain behaviors convey certain meanings, because they are learned and shared in their respective cultures.[13] Just as they behave in a certain way, people also perceive and organize their thoughts, observations, and values according to the dictates of their culture. For example, in a purely scientific sense, the moon is a rocky sphere; yet when they look at the moon, many Americans see the "man in the moon." Some Native Americans view this same image as a rabbit, the Chinese interpret it as a lady fleeing her husband, and Samoans see in it the shape of a woman weaving.[14] These particular differences might not seem significant, but they point to the way that people from different cultures can view the same phenomenon quite differently. When cultural differences are apparent, it requires sensitivity, patience, and tolerance to avoid or reduce misunderstandings that can create barriers to effective communication and to relationship development.

Those who cannot appreciate ideas, customs, or beliefs that differ from those of their own cultural background and who automatically assume that their own view is superior to that of any other culture are ethnocentric. **Ethnocentric** individuals go beyond pride in their heritage or background to the conviction that they know more and are better than those of other cultures. Those who lack interaction or contact with other cultures may find it hard to understand that other cultures and their practices may be as acceptable as our own. Even if we know of weaknesses in our own culture (too competitive, too materialistic, too informal, and so on), we are unlikely to criticize our culture when comparing it to others.

## MAKING CONNECTIONS for Success

### Perceptions of Groups

Create a list of groups, such as Korean Americans, Midwesterners, athletes, Catholics, homosexuals, Muslims, ranchers, Protestants, and so on. You can use these groups if you wish, but you should try to add at least three to five of your own groups. Now select several of the groups, and list the traits most characteristic of each.

Would you find this a difficult task? Probably not. You likely will be able to construct a list of traits or characteristics of each group; moreover, you can do so even for those groups with whom you have had limited or no personal contact.

1. Why?
2. How do the characteristics you listed affect your perceptions?
3. In what ways would the list of characteristics you developed influence how you communicated about and with individuals in these groups?
4. Given the list you constructed and given what you have read about perception and communication, how would the list influence your communication with individuals from these groups?

■ **ethnocentric** A person whose pride in his or her heritage or background leads to the conviction that he or she knows more and is better than those of other countries.

Ethnocentrism is a learned belief that our own culture is superior to all others. This is not necessarily a bad thing, but it does alter our perceptions and often colors how we look at others who are different from us. We learn to behave through our culture, and the way we behave, most of us believe, is the way everyone else should behave. We use our culture and our cultural behaviors as a yardstick by which we judge all other cultures and people who are different from us. The difference between a person's own culture and other cultures is often judged on a superiority–inferiority scale. People often view cultures that are different from their own as inferior. The greater the differences, the more people perceive other cultures to be inferior to their own.

A form of ethnocentrism is **cultural myopia,** which not only refers to perceiving one's own culture as superior to other cultures but also means a very narrow or shortsighted view of other cultures. Like ethnocentrism, cultural myopia is not usually a conscious act; it is usually learned at the subconscious level. For example, most American schools teach American history, geography, literature, and government, which indirectly is teaching cultural myopia and ethnocentrism. Of course, this kind of myopia and ethnocentrism also occurs in other cultures.

When people take on a broader worldview and open their minds to different cultures as merely being different and not judging them as inferior because they are different, they are accepting the philosophy of **cultural relativism.** People who have a cultural relativistic attitude strive to understand differences rather than to judge them so that intercultural relations can develop. Cultural relativism is "we-oriented," whereas ethnocentrism is "me-oriented." Cultural relativists are willing to put themselves in the place of others who have a different culture in order to understand it without making judgments about it.

## ▬■ Gender

Another factor that affects the way we perceive our world is gender. Unlike biological sex, **gender** is a social construct related to masculine and feminine behaviors that are learned. Some theorists believe that women and men learn to understand the world around them differently, resulting in different ways of communicating.

It has been shown, in groups containing both females and males, that males tend to talk for longer periods of time, take more turns at speaking, exert more control over the topic of conversation, and interrupt females more frequently than females interrupt males. Also, what males say appears to be taken more seriously than what females say.[15] These communication differences may occur because of how females and males understand their roles and how the roles are defined by culture.

An interesting study on voice usage and perceived affection in initial interactions by Kory Floyd and George B. Bay, two communication scholars, found that men whose voices were higher-pitched were seen as weak or effeminate and would therefore not be seen by women as being a good relational fit.[16] However, with women, the opposite was found to be true. Women with higher-pitched voices were perceived to be more affectionate than women with lower-pitched voices. The researchers' conclusion is that men's voices are perceived to be friendlier and less dominant or aggressive when they are lower in pitch, whereas women's voices are perceived to be friendlier and less dominant when they are higher in pitch.[17]

There remains a great deal of uncertainty about what causes the differences in the roles of men and women in our society. We are told about "the gender gap" and that men and women don't understand each other or speak the same language. Men are often confused when women want to continue to talk about something that they think has been settled; women often find themselves frustrated when men don't

■ **cultural myopia**
Perceiving one's own culture as superior and having a very narrow or shortsighted view of cultures other than your own.

■ **cultural relativism**
Taking on a broader worldview and opening our minds to different cultures as merely being different and not judging them as inferior because they are different.

■ **gender** A social construct related to masculine and feminine behaviors that are learned.

seem to listen or respond to what they say. The perceptions that men and women have of each other and of themselves are not always clear, especially in this time of transition in which the roles of men and women are constantly changing. Most of us today believe that both men and women can pursue careers or can be involved in homemaking and child care. Americans, as a group, have to some extent enlarged their perspectives on the roles and abilities of both men and women.

## ▬ Media

Sometimes other people influence our perceptions deliberately. Advertisers, government leaders, political advocates, and many others attempt to shape our views. Advertisers have mastered techniques to encourage us to think and behave in ways that will benefit their clients.

Have you ever wondered how much the media influence our perceptions? In recent elections, candidates have hired people often referred to as "handlers" or "spin doctors." Their job is to create a positive image of the candidates and to protect them from any exposure that might create a negative image.

What about the shows we watch on television? Do they create or alter our perceptions? Although family sitcoms, for example, present families that are generally atypical, regardless of race or ethnic background, they still influence our image of families. Network news shows select events from all the reports they receive and present them to us in a half-hour broadcast, which, when the commercials are removed, amounts to approximately 24 minutes of actual news. The information we see is not only limited but also selected and edited for our consumption, affecting our perceptions of the world.

The influence of the media on our perceptions was no more evident than in the coverage of Operation Iraqi Freedom by the world's media. The media, whether supporting the Iraqi forces or supporting the allied forces, can create differing perceptions of who is winning or losing the war via what they say or what they show to their audiences. For example, Iraqi television showed captured and dead American soldiers to show that they were defeating the Americans. At the same time, American television, radio, and print media, while showing some of these same pictures, also showed thousands of Iraqi soldiers who had been captured or who had surrendered. The information sent by the media as to what was happening in the war depended greatly on what the media could and wanted to show its audiences.

### MAKING CONNECTIONS for Success

#### Advertising and Ethics

Bob, a photographer, is hired by a local motel owner to take pictures to make the motel appear attractive for a brochure and Internet site. When he gets to the motel location Bob notices right away that it is located in an undesirable part of the city, parking is difficult, and there are few attractions or restaurants nearby. Therefore, he does not take any photos that show the motel's surroundings. He does, however, photograph a model dressed to look like a successful businessperson approaching the newly remodeled entrance. He takes photos of a few attractive models in and around the pool. He takes a shot of one of the rooms using a wide-angle lens to give the illusion of spaciousness. Bob has created the impression that the motel attracts businesspeople, its customers are attractive, and its rooms are spacious.

1. What do you think of what Bob has done regarding the perceptions he has created through his photos?
2. Because there are no attractions or fine restaurants, Bob decides to take photos of attractions and fine restaurants that are in another part of the city and uses them in the brochure, giving the impression that they are close to the motel—is this ethical? Why or why not?
3. You are looking for a motel on an Internet site and you see photos that are similar to those that Bob has taken but for another motel—as a competent communicator is there anything that you might do to ensure that pictures are truthful?
4. Are advertisers obligated to present their products in a completely truthful way?

These examples show that the media mold our perceptions in powerful ways. You might believe that there is nothing wrong with this, but think about how we depend on the media for information and how literally many people accept what is presented to them. There can be a great deal of difference between reality and what is presented to us.

### ▬ Internet

As we come to depend more and more on the Internet for our information, it too has a tremendous influence on our perceptions of the world around us. Like the print and broadcast media, the Internet can be a valuable source of information that can provide both accurate and inaccurate perceptions. People who want to distort information or mislead us can easily do so via the Internet or in their email messages. Many who use email believe that their messages do not create perceptions or that, if they do, the perceptions are not interpretable. However, like anything that we communicate, our emails do create perceptions that are very interpretable. As senders of emails, we should always be aware that the messages we send are open to inferences and interpretations by those who receive them. Therefore, we need to be careful in what we write and how we write it. Those who receive our emails form impressions and make inferences based on the language we use, spelling accuracy, and the tone in which we write our messages.

We must also keep in mind that the information we receive via the Internet and email messages is only as good or as reliable as the sources of the websites or messages. What you see, hear, or read on the Internet or in your emails does affect your perceptions and ultimately your view of the world. The Internet is a powerful tool like the media, and like the media, the Internet cannot be assumed to be reliable information in and of itself. Competent communicators check the information they receive, especially when the source is unknown to them, to determine its truthfulness and accuracy.

## ▬ Improving Perception Competencies and Perception Checking

For us to be competent communicators, we must understand the impact that perceptions have on us, how we communicate with others, and what we accept as reality through the communication we receive. We tend to take the validity of our perceptions for granted and fail to look beneath the surface. But if we analyze specific personal experiences, we can begin to recognize and identify misperceptions that create communication problems for us. In this section, we first discuss ways to improve our competencies as perceivers of information, and then we discuss ways for us to check our perceptions for accuracy so that we can become more competent communicators.

### ▬ Become an Active Perceiver

*First, we must be active as perceivers.* We must be willing to seek out as much information as possible about a given person, subject, event, or situation. The more information we obtain, the deeper our understanding and the more accurate our perceptions will be. We must question our perceptions to determine how accurate they are. By considering the possibility that we may misinterpret information, we prompt ourselves to confirm facts and impressions before we draw conclusions. Taking the time to gather more information and to recheck the accuracy of our perceptions is well worth the effort.

## ■■ Recognize That Each Person's Frame of Reference Is Unique

*Second, we must recognize the uniqueness of our own frame of reference.* We must remember that our view of things may be only one of many views. Each of us has a unique window to the world, as well as a unique system of understanding and storing data. Some of us make judgments about people based on appearance, whereas others base their judgments on ability, income, education, gender, ethnicity, or other factors. This variety of approaches shows that all of us operate on different perceptual systems, and it is wrong to assume that one system is better than another.

## ■■ Distinguish Facts from Inferences

*A third way to improve our perceptions and interpretations is to distinguish facts from inferences or assumptions.* A fact is something put forth as objectively real that can be verified. For example, which building is the world's tallest, Gina has been late to class five times this semester, or Hilary received more votes than Bill. An inference is an interpretation that goes beyond what we know to be factual. For example, Bonnie is always late to group meetings, she always stares off into space, and generally does not give her opinion. The members of the group see her as lazy, unprepared, and rude. Saying that she is lazy, unprepared, and rude goes beyond the facts; she might be late because of other commitments, she might stare off into space because she feels unwanted in the group, and she might not give her opinion because she is extremely shy.

Because facts and inferences are often extremely difficult to distinguish, it is very easy to confuse them. We sometimes treat inferences as if they are facts. A statement such as "Bonnie is lazy" sounds factual, and we tend to accept those types of statements as truth rather than communicating to find out what is fact and what is inference. We need to label our statements as our inferences when we communicate them. For example, saying "Bonnie seems to be lazy" is much more tentative and is not stated as a fact or certainty. A next step might be to learn more about Bonnie—try to draw her out, and find out if there are things affecting her life at the moment.

### MAKING CONNECTIONS for Success

#### Just the Facts and Nothing But the Facts

Competent communicators can distinguish facts from inferences—can you?

1. The St. Louis Arch is as wide as it is tall—fact or inference?
2. Students who don't do their assignments are lazy—fact or inference?
3. Chapter 2 discusses perception and communication—fact or inference?
4. Maria scored 1400 on the GRE—fact or inference?
5. Religious leaders have high morals—fact or inference?
6. Athletes who use special equipment to enhance their performance are ethical—fact or inference?

For answers see page 52.

When making inferences, competent communicators qualify them by labeling them as such. How would you qualify the above statements that are not factual?

## ◾ Become Aware of the Role Perceptions Play in Communication

*A fourth way to improve our perceptions and interpretations is to be aware of the role that perceptions play in communication, take others' perceptions into account, and avoid the tendency to assume too much about what we perceive.* To make the most of the information that we receive, we must first evaluate it. We should check the source of the information and the context in which the information was acquired. We should make sure we are not reading too much into the information. To help ensure that our perceptions are accurate, we should ask questions and obtain feedback whenever possible. We cannot determine whether our perceptions are accurate without testing them.

## ◾ Keep an Open Mind

*A fifth way to improve our perceptions and interpretations is to keep an open mind and remind ourselves that our perceptions may not be complete or totally accurate.* Thus we must continue to make observations, seek out additional information, be willing to describe what we observe mentally and out loud, state what a given observation means to us, and put our perceptions into words to test their logic and soundness.

## ◾ Perception Checking: Being a Competent Communicator

To improve the accuracy of our perceptions and their interpretations we must learn to perception check. When it comes to interpreting perceptions, there are so many variables and possibilities for misunderstanding; therefore, the potential for jumping to conclusions without fully knowing all of the information is very easy to do. For example, a friend of mine and I exchange emails periodically, but if I don't respond within a day or so of receiving his email, he assumes that I am upset with him. Of course, I am not upset with him, but that is what he perceives when I don't email him almost immediately after receiving his message. Think about this example and of how many times others have jumped to inaccurate conclusions about your thoughts, feelings, or motives.

Developing the skill of perception checking should help prevent jumping to the wrong conclusions about others' thoughts, feelings, or motives. For example, a teacher whom you think likes you walks by, you say "Hi" and smile, but the teacher does not even acknowledge your presence though you believe she looked directly at you. It would be very easy to assume that the teacher ignored you because she doesn't think much of you or that you are simply unimportant to her. A competent communicator would employ perception-checking skills, which would include the following:

1. Describe the teacher's behavior, which was that she ignored your presence.

2. Provide at least two interpretations of the teacher's behavior—was she ignoring you because she doesn't think you are important enough or did she ignore you because her mind was preoccupied and she didn't hear or see you?

3. Finally, to verify your interpretation you might ask the teacher, "Why didn't you say hello to me when we passed in the hall, is there something wrong?" This would immediately clarify any possible misunderstandings.

## MAKING CONNECTIONS for Success

### Competent Communicators Check Their Perceptions for Accuracy

In this chapter we have discussed perception, its relationship to communication, and our competence as communicators. In order to check our perceptions we should (1) try to state what we observed as best we can, (2) recognize that what we observe is a possible explanation, (3) consider other possible explanations, and (4) ask or check on accuracy of the possible explanation(s).

**Example:** You saw Jason, an athlete friend, walking out of a clinic known for its distribution of steroids; Jason has shown a significant improvement in his athleticism over the past several months.

**Perception-checking steps:** I saw Jason, a good friend and athlete, coming out of a clinic that has been rumored to sell steroids [(1) what was observed—describe, don't infer]. Jason was there to buy steroids [(2) possible explanation]. Jason was at the clinic to get his sprained ankle checked out, to check on a friend who was hurt, or to get pain killers for his ankle sprain [(3) other possible explanations]. Which explanation is the correct one, if any [(4) check on the accuracy or qualify the observation by stating that "you don't know the reason Jason was coming out of the clinic"].

**Example for you to create your own perception-checking statements:** Debra, a friend of yours who has been struggling in her speech class with Cs on her speeches, borrows an outline of a speech for which you received an A grade last semester. You overhear her bragging to another friend that she received an A on her last speech.

1. How would you use the perception-checking steps in the above example?
2. What did you learn from the use of perception-checking steps?

By using perception checking as a means of verifying your perceptions, you are less likely to assume your first interpretation is the only one or the correct one. To prevent misunderstandings or misinterpretation of perceptions requires cooperation and willingness to communicate and being open-minded to the communication received.

## GUIDELINES Check Your Perceptions: Competent Communicators Do!

1. Separate facts from assumptions.
2. Remember that perceptions, especially first impressions, are not always accurate.
3. Recognize their personal biases.
4. Recognize that people from different cultural backgrounds do not always attach the same meanings to events, objects, and people.
5. Remember that perceptions are a function of the perceiver, the perceived, and the situation in which the perception occurs.
6. Aren't afraid to communicate to verify their perceptions. They ask questions and seek information rather than leave themselves open to misinterpretations and misunderstandings.
7. They are willing to admit their misperceptions and to change them when necessary.

# Summary

Perception is the process of selecting, organizing, and interpreting information in order to give it personal meaning. It lies at the heart of the communication process. It is a part of everything we do; therefore, it is important to understand how it influences our communication. For us to be perceptive about our surroundings, we must first be aware of them, cognitively process them, and finally classify them via our language.

Perception involves selecting, or deliberately choosing to experience or to avoid particular stimuli; to focus on some stimuli and ignore or downplay other stimuli; and to retrieve information that we have already selected, organized, and interpreted. Organization is the categorizing of stimuli so that we can make sense of them and interpretation is the assigning of meaning to stimuli. A common phenomenon that can distort our perception of reality is a perceptual set, a fixed, previously determined view of people, things, or events. Perception set is a form of stereotyping. Stereotyping and our desire to attribute causes to people's behavior can also lead to inaccuracies in our perception and ultimately our communication.

When the sender and receiver have different cultural backgrounds, their communication can become more complicated. People whose pride in their heritage or background leads to the conviction that they know more and are better than those who differ are ethnocentric. A form of ethnocentrism is cultural myopia, which is a very narrow or shortsighted view of cultures other than your own. The opposite of ethnocentrism is cultural relativism, which is when people take a broader worldview and open their minds to different cultures as merely being different and not judging them as inferior because of differences.

Communication between men and women is also shaped by culture. Because our communication is grounded in our experiences and because our experiences exist within a culture, people who come from different cultural backgrounds bring a variety of perspectives and worldviews to their interactions with others.

To improve our communication, we should constantly remember that perceptions are not always the same for everyone and that our perceptions are only one view of many that may be possible. It is always wise to check your perceptions, especially when you might not have all of the information or if you are uncertain of its accuracy.

# Answers

**Making Connections for Success**   1, 3, and 4 are facts and 2, 5, and 6 are inferences.

# Discussion Starters

1. Describe a person who is perceptively competent.
2. Explain the connection between perception and communication.
3. What effect does cognitive complexity have on our perception of the world around us?
4. Provide a personal experience that illustrates attribution error. How did the error affect communication?
5. Compare and contrast perceptual set with ethnocentrism.
6. What does it mean to take a position of cultural relativism?

**7.** Explain the role the Hollywood media have on our perceptions and ultimately how we perceive the world around us.

**8.** How do we form perceptions of people over the telephone and the decisions we make about them?

**9.** Are we more or less likely to make inferences about people if they send us an email message than if we see the individual in person?

## Notes

1. R. L. Scott, "On Viewing Rhetoric as Epistemic: Ten Years Later," *The Central States Speech Journal* (Winter 1976): 261.

2. W. V. Haney, *Communication and Organizational Behavior: Text and Cases,* 3rd ed. (Homewood, IL: Irwin, 1973), 289–408. The term "perceptual set" is similar to what W. V. Haney refers to as "programming" or "frozen evaluation" in his book *Communication and Interpersonal Relations: Text and Cases,* 5th ed. (Homewood, IL: Irwin, 1986), 205–206, 408–38.

3. M. Piattelli-Palmarini, *Inevitable Illusions: How Mistakes of Reason Rule Our Minds* (New York: Wiley, 1994), 17.

4. Ibid., 18–19.

5. C. Stewart and W. Cash, *Interviewing: Principles and Practices,* 10th ed. (New York: McGraw-Hill, 2003), 31.

6. S. Kassin, *Psychology* (Upper Saddle River, NJ: Prentice Hall, 1998); D. T. Gilbert and P. S. Malone, "The Correspondence Bias," *Psychological Bulletin* 117 (1995): 21–28; F. Van Overwalle, "Dispositional Attributions Require the Joint Application of the Methods of Difference and Agreement," *Personality and Social Psychology Bulletin* 23 (1997): 974–80; and E. E. Jones, "The Rocky Road from Acts to Dispositions," *American Psychologist* 34 (1979): 107–17.

7. J. Pearson and P. Nelson, *Understanding and Sharing: An Introduction to Speech Communication,* 3rd ed. (Dubuque, IA: Brown, 1985), 27.

8. M. Crowley, "Fresh Faced," *The New Republic* 42 (October 27, 2003); and L. A. Zebrowitz, J. M. Fellous, A. Mignault, and C. Andreoletti, "Trait Impressions as Overgeneralized Responses to Adaptively Significant Facial Qualities," *Personality and Social Psychology Review* 7 (2003): 194–215.

9. H. M. Cheverton and D. Byrne, "Development and Validation of the Primary Choice Clothing Questionnaire." Presented at the meeting of the Eastern Psychological Association, Boston (February, 1998); A. Jarrel, "Date That Calls for Judicious Attire," *New York Times* (October 4, 1998): 9-1–9-2; D. Mack and D. Rainey, "Female Applicants' Grooming and Personnel Selection," *Journal of Social Behavior and Personality* 5 (1990): 399–407; and B. P. Meier, M. D. Robinson and G. L. Clore, "Why Good Guys Wear White: Automatic Interferences About Stimulus Valence Based on Brightness," *Psychological Science* 15 (2004): 82–87.

10. C. S. Fichten and R. Amsel, "Trait Attribution about College Students with a Physical Disability: Circumplex Analysis and Methodological Issues," *Journal of Applied Social Psychology* 16 (1986): 410–427; S. J. McKelvie, "Stereotyping in Perception of Attractiveness, Age, and Gender in Schematic Faces," *Social Behavior and Personality* 21 (1993): 121–128; J. K. Lundberg and E. P. Sheehan, "The Effects of Glasses and Weight on Perceptions of Attractiveness and Intelligence," *Journal of Social Behavior and Personality* 9 (1994): 753–760; and M. L. Shannon and C. P. Stark, "The Influence of Physical Appearance on Personnel Selection," *Social Behavior and Personality* 31 (2003): 613–624.

11. The definition is based on the work found in L. A. Samovar and R. E. Porter, *Communication between Cultures,* 4th ed. (Belmont, CA: Wadsworth, 2001), 32–49 and E. R. McDaniel, L. A. Samovar, and R. E. Porter, "Understanding Intercultural Communication: An Overview," in *Intercultural Communication: A Reader,* 11th ed., eds. L. A. Samovar, R. E. Porter, and E. R. McDaniel (Belmont, CA: Thompson/Wadsworth, 2006), 6–15.

12. N. L. Gage and D. C. Berliner, *Educational Psychology,* 6th ed. (Boston: Houghton Mifflin, 1998), 152–53.

13. E. R. McDaniel, L. A. Samovar, and R. E. Porter, "Understanding Intercultural Communication: An Overview," in *Intercultural Communication: A Reader,* 11th ed., eds. L. A. Samovar, R. E. Porter, and E. R. McDaniel (Belmont, CA: Thompson/Wadsworth, 2006), 13.

14. N. Dresser, *Multicultural Manners* (New York: Wiley, 1996), 89–90.

15. L. P. Stewart, P. J. Cooper, A. D. Stewart, and S. A. Friedley, *Communication and Gender,* 4th ed. (Boston: Allyn and Bacon, 2003), 44–45.

16. K. L. Floyd and G. B. Ray, "Mapping the Affectionate Voice: Vocalic Predictors of Perceived Affection in Initial Interactions," *Western Journal of Communication* 67 (Winter 2003): 56–73.

17. Ibid., 68.

CHAPTER **3**

# Connecting Self and Communication

"There's only one corner
of the universe you can
be certain of improving,
and that's your own
self."

—ALDOUS HUXLEY

# This chapter will help you:

- **Make** the connection between self-concept and perception.
- **Understand** how your self-concept is developed.
- **See** how self-concept is connected to communication and communication apprehension.
- **Understand** how culture and gender affect self-concept.
- **Improve** your self-concept.

# Making everyday connections

### Comments that Influence Who We Are

"You're so talented. You do everything so well—I really enjoy working with you."

"Get outta here! I am sick of you."

"You are so ethical and honest."

"You're more trouble than you are worth. I wish you'd never been born."

"I enjoy having you around! Your smile makes me feel good!"

"You're so helpful and easy to work with, I am glad you are here."

"I am so glad I am on your team, you are such a good leader."

"You have a good head on your shoulders."

What others say about us determines in part how we perceive ourselves. These everyday connections ultimately become a part of us. Our perception of and relationships to those who make statements such as the ones listed above determine how we interpret the statements and give significance to the words. For example, if a person whom you admire makes one of the positive statements, it would most likely have a positive and reinforcing effect on your view of self. Conversely, if a person whom you admire makes one of the negative statements, it would most likely have a negative and damaging effect on your view of self. What others say to us in everyday statements can have a powerful influence on our self-concept. ■

**Questions to think about**

- Why do you think our self-concept is so affected by what others say and how they behave toward us?

- Why have self-esteem, self-image, and self-concept become so important, especially to those of us in the American culture?

- Describe how your view of self can affect your communication with others. Discuss both positive and negative effects.

- How can the understanding of self help you to become a more competent communicator?

A question that most of us have asked or at least thought about asking at one time or another is "who is the real me?" When college students are asked the question "who are you?" their answers typically consist of references to relationships (e.g., Melissa's boyfriend, son of Bill and Frances), social identities (e.g., a sophomore at Liberty University, a major in communication studies, a member of the swim team, Christian Student Fellowship, Nebraskans for Peace member, I belong to Sigma Lambda Chi, I am from Wahoo, Nebraska, I went to Central High School in Omaha), or personal traits (e.g., good student, organized, athletic, kind, friendly, sincere, trustworthy). But do these descriptions really tell who we are? We know from Chapter 2 that our perceptions of things and others are subjective as well as open to interpretation. We also learned in Chapter 2 that the accuracy of our perceptions is questionable because what we perceive of objects or others may not be the same as what others perceive of them.

In this chapter, we provide possible responses to the "who am I?" question. It is a question whose answer is often incomplete, and not entirely accurate or very satisfying for most of us. It's not because we don't want an answer to the question—it's just a very difficult question to answer accurately and completely.

Each of us is an extremely complex person. Early in life we begin to learn who we are—or at least who we think we are. We develop a social identity, or self-definition, that includes how we see and evaluate ourselves. Despite potential variability in how we answer the question, most of us manage to maintain a coherent image of our self, while recognizing that we define ourselves and behave differently in different situations. For example, when you are at home with your parents, your self-image as a responsible adult might at times come into question. You might not pick up things after yourself, or you might even expect that someone else will do your laundry, and so forth. However, when you are away at college, you perform these tasks competently and see yourself as a responsible adult. Despite such readily admitted pockets of irresponsibility, does this mean you will see yourself in this way? No, of course not! It depends on the situation and its importance to us as to how it affects our self-perception and ultimately our communication with others.

How others treat us and how they will treat us in the future have important implications for how we view ourselves. When it comes to self-perception, no person is truly an island. When we expect that others might reject us because of some aspect of ourselves, we can choose from a few different possible actions. To the extent that it is possible to change an aspect of the self and avoid being rejected by others, we could potentially choose to do that. In fact, we could choose to change only that particular feature when we anticipate being in the presence of others who will reject us

## MAKING Technology CONNECTIONS

### Who Then Are You?

Try to describe yourself. It's not easy for most of us to do this but we are often asked either directly or indirectly in personal conversations or interviews to do just that. Go to www.ablongman.com/seiler7e for a personal inventory questionnaire. This is a self-inventory in which you reflect on who you are and can describe various attributes that reflect how you see yourself. There are no right or wrong answers. It is, however, important that you seriously think about your responses, especially when they are asking for strengths and weaknesses. Another excellent website is www.queendom.com. This site provides a larger number of choices related to self-assessment and self-understanding. Each of the assessment tests or questionnaires has a nonmember test that is free and provides you with results and a brief interpretation of those results. The site has measures to assess both your self-esteem and your communication skills, which are particularly interesting to complete.

1. What did you learn about yourself in completing the inventory that you didn't know before?
2. What do you think about self-inventories or self-assessment tests? Is there value in doing them? Explain.
3. How can understanding "who you are" help you to improve your communication competencies?

because of it. In other words, people can attempt to hide some aspects of the self from disapproving others. To become competent communicators, we must understand that our image of self has a significant role in how we communicate and how others communicate with us. Therefore, we must try to understand what our self-concept is and its connection to our communication with others.

One of the most fundamental principles of the self is the social identity perspective,[1] when individuals can perceive themselves differently depending on where they are at a particular moment in time on what is referred to as the **personal-social identity continuum.** The personal identity end of this continuum refers to when we think of ourselves primarily as *individuals.* The social identity end refers to when we think of ourselves as members of specific *social groups.* Because it is impossible to experience all aspects of our self-concept simultaneously, the specific aspect of our identity that is prominent at any given moment will influence how we think about ourselves, and this, in turn, has consequences for our behavior. For example, when we think of ourselves as unique individuals, our personal identities are prominent, and this is likely to result in self-descriptions that emphasize how we are different from others.

At the other end of the personal-social identity continuum, we can perceive ourselves as members of a group, which means we emphasize the ways that we are similar to other group members. When we think of ourselves at the social identity level, we describe ourselves in terms of the attributes that members of our group share with each other as well as what differentiates "our group" from other groups. That is, descriptions of the self at the social identity level are intergroup in nature and usually involve contrasts between groups. For example, you may see yourself in terms of your social identity as a member of the school band, and describe yourself as musically talented and extroverted, attributes that you perceive to be shared with other members of the band, and as simultaneously differentiating the band group from other groups such as members of the debate team whom you see as more studious and scholarly than your group.

■ **personal-social identity continuum** Two distinct ways that the self can be categorized—at a personal level, which emphasizes the uniqueness of the individual, and at the social identity level in which the self is thought of as a member of a group.

On other occasions, you might think of yourself in terms of a different social identity, that of your gender group. For example, if you are a female, you might emphasize what you share with other women (e.g., warm and caring) and what you perceive as differentiating women from men. What's important to note is that when you think of yourself as an *individual,* the *content* of your self-description is likely to differ from when you are thinking of yourself as a member of a *category* that you share with others.

Of course most of us belong to a variety of groups (e.g., groups defined by age, religion, nationality, ethnicity, sexual orientation, occupation, sports), but all of these will not be prominent at the same time. When any particular social identity is prominent, people are likely to communicate in ways that reflect that aspect of their self-concept. Can we say that one of these "selves" is the "true" self—either the personal self or any one of a person's potential social identities? No, not really. Each view of self contributes to a larger general image of self, which is in essence who we are and what gives us an identity.

# ■ Understanding Self-Concept

Our **self-concept** or self-identity is our perceived self, which consists of an organized collection of beliefs and attitudes about self. Who we perceive ourselves to be is determined by our experiences and communication with others, the roles and values we have selected for ourselves, and how we believe others see us. Self-concept consists of two subcomponents: **self-image,** how we see ourselves or our mental picture of self (for example, I see myself as being a person, an athlete, student, worker, female, daughter, and mother), and **self-esteem,** our feelings and attitudes toward ourselves or how we evaluate ourselves (for example, I feel that I am an okay person, an average athlete, a good student, a hard worker, sexy, a loving daughter, and an average mother). Both self-image and self-esteem make up our self-concept.

■ **self-concept** A person's perceived self, which consists of an organized collection of beliefs and attitudes about self.

■ **self-image** A person's mental picture of himself or herself.

■ **self-esteem** A person's feelings and attitudes toward himself or herself.

■ **FIGURE 3.1** The Self-Concept

Self-concept is determined by our experiences and communication with others, the roles and values we have selected for ourselves, our perception of how others see us, and how we evaluate ourselves.

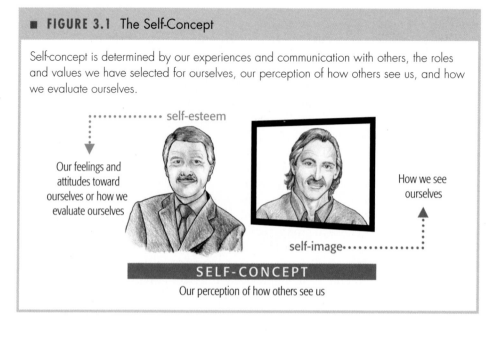

self-esteem

Our feelings and attitudes toward ourselves or how we evaluate ourselves

How we see ourselves

self-image

**SELF-CONCEPT**

Our perception of how others see us

Self-concept and perception are very closely related, so it is difficult to separate them. They constantly interact. For example, what you think about yourself shapes, and in many ways determines, what you do and say. What you think about yourself is influenced by the information you receive from others, which helps you create an image of who you are. If you think of yourself as a good speaker, you would take positive comments made about your communication as affirmation of your ability and skill. If someone made a disparaging comment, however, you probably would dismiss it as not reflecting your perception of how well you communicate. In fact, you might interpret the comment as a sign of jealousy or humor or simply feel that the person who made the comment doesn't know much about you.

The messages that we communicate, intentionally or unintentionally, relate directly to how we feel about and view ourselves. Who and what we perceive ourselves to be influence how we present ourselves to others. What and how we communicate with others and the reactions of others toward us help develop our self-image and self-esteem, both of which ultimately make up our self-concept. Each of us has a unique identity and a special sense of who we are.

Why is it important for us to understand the connection between communication and self-concept? Think about this, and read on to find an answer to the question.

## ▄▄ Self-Concept as a Process

Communication is a dynamic process because it has no beginning or end and is constantly changing. In the same sense, self-concept is also a process. Self-perceptions and the perception others have of us differ from time to time, from situation to situation, and from person to person. For example, your view of yourself may vary somewhat according to how you feel about yourself at a given time. If you receive a high grade on a difficult assignment, you might feel very good about yourself or at least about your effectiveness as a student. Your view of yourself might differ dramatically if you had received a low grade, especially if you had put a lot of effort into the assignment. In

In Papua New Guinea, two Huli children see themselves in an instant photograph. We see ourselves based on how we think we look and on how we think others see us. Our self-image and self-esteem are often based on these interactions.

addition, the perception you have of yourself as a student is likely different from the one you have as a co-worker, partner in a relationship, or family member.

The perceptions we believe others have of us affect how we receive their communication and influence our responses and vice versa. Equally, our view of ourselves influences how we communicate with others. Communication and self-concept are inseparable and both involve process—continuous change with no beginning or end.

## ◼ Development of Self-Concept

When we were children, our first communication involved sensing our environment—all the sights, sounds, tastes, and smells that surrounded us. We learned about ourselves as others touched us and spoke to us. Their responses to us helped to determine how we view ourselves. Parental communication, both verbal and nonverbal, generally has an extremely strong impact on the initial development of self-concept. For example, the clothes and toys that they provided and what and how they communicated to us affected who we have become in some way. As we age and expand our environment and relationships, the communication of others may reinforce or alter our perceptions of self. In her book *Old Is Not a Four-Letter Word: A Midlife Guide,* Anne Gerike writes that there are advantages to aging. For example, she says that aging brings increased self-confidence, a more reliable inner voice or "gut feeling," an acceptance of not being perfect, a sense of perspective that difficult situations get worked out, an acceptance that life isn't fair, and a willingness to accept responsibility instead of directing the blame elsewhere.[2] Assuming that Gerike's observations are correct, why do you think such developments occur with age?

Social psychologist Daryl J. Bem believes that sometimes we don't know our own attitudes, feelings, or emotions directly. We therefore focus on others to obtain such information.[3] Bem does, however, indicate that we learn a great deal about ourselves by observing our own behaviors. He suggests that what we do or how we act is a guide to what is happening inside us and how we feel about ourselves. Further, according to Bem, we draw inferences about ourselves in the same manner that we do about others. Thus the process through which we come to know ourselves is very similar to the process through which we come to know others.

Our self-concept, which develops through an extremely complex process, usually consists of many images that we place on a continuum, ranging from negative to positive. There is no way to predict which image will dominate because our view of ourselves is a composite of all the self-images, which is ever in a state of flux. Self-concept is affected not only by how we perceive ourselves, but also by how we perceive others, how others perceive us, and how we think others perceive us, as the cartoon on this page suggests.

"Gordon's got very low self esteem. Haven't you?
You bald headed four eyed twit."

We sometimes make insulting comments to be funny—especially at the expense of those we supposedly care about—not realizing the negative impact those comments may have on them.
www.CartoonStock.com

## MAKING CONNECTIONS for Success

### Values, Attitudes, and Beliefs about People with Disabilities

Be honest: Have you ever felt uneasy in the presence of a person with a physical disability? Words and phrases such as "Handicapped person confined to a wheelchair . . ." or "Young women stricken with cerebral palsy . . ." can shape incorrect perceptions of people with disabilities. The stigma or negative attitudes are often the greatest barrier that those with disabilities must overcome. People with disabilities are more similar to people without disabilities than most of us think. Most people with disabilities don't see their disability as a liability or limitation but see it as who they are. The problem for most of us is that we are strongly influenced by the visible characteristics and appearance of others. We might not be conscious of these reactions until they are pointed out. However, our actions, whether or not they are conscious, communicate our values and attitudes and ultimately affect our beliefs as well.

1. Why do phrases like those above form our values, attitudes, and beliefs about people with disabilities?

2. What are some of the values, attitudes, and beliefs that many people hold that make them see the disability first rather than the person first?

3. How might we use what we have learned here to help ensure that we communicate with sensitivity? Develop your own suggestions first, and then do an Internet search using the key words *interacting with people with disabilities* to see whether there are suggestions that you haven't thought about.

4. Provide a written example of a value, attitude, or belief of your own to share with your classmates.

An excellent resource on communicating with people with disabilities is the *Handbook of Communication and People with Disabilities Research and Application,* edited by Dawn O. Braithwaite and Teresa L. Thompson, New Jersey: Lawrence Erlbaum Associates. For a fascinating perspective regarding self-esteem, see an interview with Lucy Grealy, author of *Autobiography of a Face,* at www.findarticles.com/cf_0/m1285/n2_v26/18082720/p1/article.jhtml.

Self-concept is based on both past and present experiences, which affect how we will perceive ourselves in the future. Our self-concept is further determined by the values, attitudes, and beliefs we possess; how we attribute these qualities to others; and how they connect them to us.

**Values.**   General, relatively long-lasting ideals that guide our behavior are called **values.** Values can be classified into broad categories, such as aesthetic, religious, humanitarian, intellectual, and material. Each category determines our behavior as well as our communication and is reflected in our self-concept. For example, if material objects are important to us, we tend to judge ourselves by what we do or do not possess. A desire to have the finer things in life is not unusual, at least in our society, but the strength of the desire can greatly affect our behavior. Possessions can become so important to some people that they ignore other concerns. They may pursue high income at the expense of job satisfaction, family life, leisure time, and personal health. Thus values can have both positive and negative influences on how we behave and communicate.

> ■ **value** A general, relatively long-lasting ideal that guides behavior.

**Attitudes.**   Evaluative dispositions, feelings, or positions about oneself, others, events, ideas, or objects are called **attitudes.** Attitudes help determine self-concept, but unlike values, they are more narrowly defined. The relationship between values and attitudes is close because values are reflected in attitudes. For example, your attitude

> ■ **attitude** An evaluative disposition, feeling, or position about oneself, others, events, ideas, or objects.

## The Excuse?

Suppose that you are meeting a friend, and this person is late. In fact, after forty minutes, you begin to suspect that your friend will never arrive. Finally, your friend appears on the scene and says, "Sorry, our meeting just slipped my mind!" How would you react?

Imagine that your friend instead says, "I am really sorry for being late. There was a terrific accident, and there was a huge backup of traffic for miles." Now how would you react?

If this is the first time your friend has been late for an appointment or your friend has never used

this type of an excuse before, you may accept the explanation as true.

Now suppose that your friend is always late and has used similar excuses before. You might well be suspicious about whether this explanation is true.

1. On what will your reaction to this situation depend?
2. On what will your judgment regarding the real reason for your friend's lateness depend?
3. How will your communication be affected by the values, attitudes, and beliefs you hold regarding your friend?

might be that the university is spending too much money on athletics, especially at the expense of undergraduate academic programs. Your attitude says something about your value system; in other words, you value academics over athletics.

**Beliefs.** Closely related to attitudes are beliefs. A **belief** is a conviction or confidence in the truth of something that is not based on absolute proof. We have, for example, beliefs about history, religion, schools, events, people, and ourselves. We say, "Space exploration is helpful to humanity," "God is good to us," "Speech class is important," "We will win the homecoming game," "I know Sally loves me," or "I am going to get a high grade on my next speech." These statements and hundreds of similar statements that we make daily could begin with "I believe . . ." or "There is evidence that. . . ."

Our beliefs, like our attitudes and values, have a hierarchy of importance. That is, some are much more important to us than others. Our most important beliefs, such as those about religion, education, and family life, do not change easily, but our less important beliefs, such as those about today's weather or the outcome of a sports event, are only momentary in duration.

Making clear and absolute distinctions among values, attitudes, and beliefs is difficult because they are interrelated. Consider, for example, the close relationship among the following three statements:

*Value (ideal):* People should love one another.

*Attitude (feeling or position):* Love is good.

*Belief (conviction):* Love is important in our lives.

Attitudes differ from beliefs in that attitudes include an evaluation of whether someone or something is good or bad. Beliefs, in turn, reflect the perception of whether something is true or false. Your attitudes and beliefs about love may change as a result of your experiences, but the value you place on love endures. Table 3.1 provides definitions and examples of values, attitudes, and beliefs, with space for you to add your own examples.

■ **belief** A conviction or confidence in the truth of something that is not based on absolute proof.

■ **TABLE 3.1**  Values, Attitudes, and Beliefs

| TERM | DEFINITION | EXAMPLE | YOUR EXAMPLES |
|---|---|---|---|
| *Values* | Broad-based ideals that are relatively long-lasting | All Americans should support our millitary | |
| *Attitudes* | Evaluative dispositions, feelings, or positions about ourselves, other persons, events, ideas, or objects | Our fighting in Iraq and Afghanistan is too costly | |
| *Beliefs* | Convictions or confidence in the truth of something that lacks absolute proof | Even though its costs are high our military is the best in the world. | |

# ■ Communication and Self-Concept

A reciprocal connection seems to exist between self-concept and the way we communicate: Communication affects the self-concept, and self-concept affects how and what we communicate. A model developed by social psychologist John W. Kinch[4] demonstrates this relationship (see Figure 3.2). Our perceptions of how others respond to us (P) affect our self-concept (S). Our self-concept affects how we behave (B). Our behavior is directly related to how others react to our behavior (A). The actual responses of others relate to our perceptions of others' responses (P), and so we have come full circle.

■ **FIGURE 3.2**  Kinch's Model of the Connection between Self-Concept and Communication

Kinch illustrates the relationship between self-concept and communication. Our self-concept is based on our communication with others.

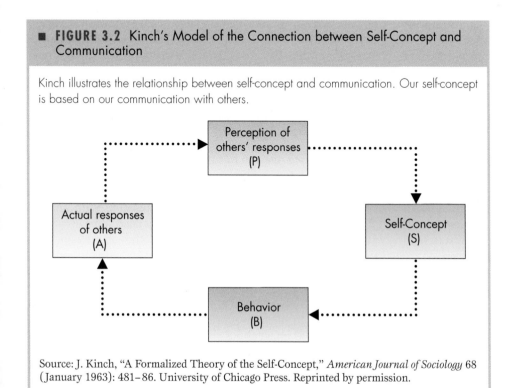

Source: J. Kinch, "A Formalized Theory of the Self-Concept," *American Journal of Sociology* 68 (January 1963): 481–86. University of Chicago Press. Reprinted by permission.

There is a connection between self-concept and the way we communicate—our communication affects our self-concept, and self-concept affects how and what we communicate. The way we perceive the communication we receive from others has a direct impact on our self-concept and our subsequent communication.

According to William W. Wilmot, a leading communication scholar, "each person's view of himself affects his as well as his partner's behavior."[5] This view of self is referred to as our *social self-concept*. It in turn consists of two components: one derived from interpersonal relationships and one derived from belonging to larger, less personal groupings such as race, ethnicity, or culture.

Personality theorists such as the late Carl Rogers believe that our self-concept is the single most important aspect of our personality. Our image of self determines our personality, which in turn determines our style of communication. For example, if you think of yourself as an outgoing, fun-loving person, you will likely be more dynamic and open in what you communicate to others. Also, if you receive reinforcement from others for being funny, entertaining, or empathic, this will likely influence how and what you communicate in the future as well. When interactions are considered with respect to self, it becomes necessary to take the context and the person or people with whom you are communicating into account. It is generally agreed that people with high social self-concepts function better in interpersonal situations than do those with low social self-concepts. The question here is not so much "Who are you?" but "Who are you when you are with your best friend, your mother, your father, both your mother and father, people you don't know, and so on?" In other words, our image of self determines our communication style as seen by others and internalized by us, which in turn affects how we communicate with others.

There is some evidence that how others see us relates to our style of communication, which in turn is a reflection of our self-concept. A study by Cynthia Stohl, a communication scholar, examining the connection between preschool children's style of communication and their physical attractiveness as perceived by their teachers and peers found that the higher children were rated on communication style, the more attractive they were to others. Those who were rated as less attractive were seen as having lower "communicator image," that is, were less "open, dramatic, contentious, animated, or impression leaving."[6]

**Communication Apprehension.**    Also relevant to a person's style of communication is the fear of communicating with others, known as communication apprehension, which relates directly to self-concept. **Communication apprehension** is "an anxiety syndrome associated with either real or anticipated communication with another person or persons."[7] There are few people who haven't experienced some apprehensiveness in talking with others and it's a fairly well-known fact that about 95 percent of Americans who have been surveyed have some fear of communicating in some situations.[8] A majority of the fear or anxiousness is related to public speaking, which survey results indicate is the number one fear most of us have.

■ **communication apprehension** Anxiety associated with real or anticipated communication with another person or persons.

Communication apprehension involves not only the fear of giving a speech to an audience or group, but also of any form of communication. Some highly apprehensive people will avoid talking to others as much as possible, but others may talk incessantly or inappropriately because of their nervousness or fear. The inability of those who suffer from communication apprehension to manage their fear of communicating with others is part of their self-concept and often has its beginnings in the person's childhood.

## MAKING Technology CONNECTIONS

### Communication Apprehension

If you are interested in learning more about communication apprehension and its effects on communication, search the Internet and you will find over three hundred thousand references related to it. There are also many sites that link communication apprehension to self-concept that you can explore.

We suggest that you do an analysis of your level of communication apprehension by going to www.rollins.edu/communication/wschmidt/apprehension.htm. This site will help you determine your apprehension level and how it compares to others.

1. How can knowing your level of communication apprehension help you to understand your interaction with others?
2. How can knowing about communication apprehension help you to be a more competent communicator?
3. If you suspect someone of being a high "communication apprehensive," what would you do to help them?
4. Why do you think so many people have high communication apprehension?

Those who have a high level of anxiety are often perceived as being unwilling to communicate, shy, withdrawn, less intelligent, less social, less attractive, less competitive, lower in self-esteem, lower in credibility, and so forth. These perceptions may not reflect reality. Having communication apprehension, however, can reinforce itself over time. If we expect ourselves to be anxious in a particular situation, we are likely to be anxious. For those who have little communication apprehension, the opposite would likely be true. To learn more about the effects of and ways to control or reduce communication apprehension, see Chapter 10.

## MAKING CONNECTIONS

### To Scholars

#### Cynthia Stohl
*University of California, Santa Barbara*

Cynthia Stohl's research and teaching are embodied in the title of her award-winning book, *Organizational Communication: Connectedness in Action.* Linking interpersonal and small-group communication processes to larger structural and cultural systems, Professor Stohl develops a global perspective on organizational communication. Building on her early work on the development of communicative competence and young children's social networks in daycare centers, Dr. Stohl's research explores the ways in which interpersonal, group, and organizational communication processes are embedded in overlapping networks of relationships that transcend personal and organizational

boundaries. Her recent work focuses specifically on NGOs and collective action.

In 1995, Dr. Stohl wrote, "It is through communication we evolve our culture, our social structure, our world views and shape our perceptions of what is and what could be. . . . To conceive of the world in terms of our communicative connections produces exciting possibilities and great responsibilities." Throughout her work, Dr. Stohl reminds us of the ethical dimensions of communication structures and practices.

Dr. Stohl is a Professor of Communication at the University of California, Santa Barbara. Before moving to Santa Barbara she was the Margaret Church Distinguished Professor of Communication at Purdue University. She is the recipient of several teaching and research awards, including the International Communication Association's "Top Paper" awards in 2005 and 2006 for her work on collective action in the contemporary media environment.

# ■ Self-Fulfilling Prophecy and Impression Management

In addition to values, attitudes, and beliefs, expectations determine how we behave, who we eventually become, and what we communicate to others and ourselves. Our own expectations and those of others influence our perceptions and behavior. Thus our self-concept is affected by our past experiences, our interactions with others, the expectations others have of us, and how we present ourselves to create an image.

## ■ Self-Fulfilling Prophecy

Expectations we have of ourselves or that others have of us help to create conditions that lead us to act in predictable ways. The expectation becomes a **self-fulfilling prophecy.**[9] The expectations that are placed on us by ourselves or others can be a powerful force for shaping our self-concept. A research study asked college students who were either characteristically optimistic or generally pessimistic to describe their future selves.[10] According to the research, both types of students could imagine a positive future, but the optimistic students had higher expectations about actually attaining a positive possible self than did those who were pessimistic. Thus we are more likely to succeed if we believe that we have the potential for success. By the same token, we are more likely to fail if we believe ourselves to be failures.

Self-esteem can have effects on the prophecies people make about themselves. It is a matter of attribution: People with positive high self-esteem confidently attribute their success to past successes; therefore they expect to succeed in the future. People with low self-esteem, however, attribute any success they might have had to luck and so predict that they will not necessarily succeed again unless they are lucky. How we describe ourselves is a powerful influence on our expectations. Our expectations therefore are a powerful force for shaping our self-concept.

Most of us want to set positive expectations for ourselves, and most of us manage to see ourselves favorably much of the time. The fact that most of us show the *above-average effect*—which is thinking we are better than the average person on almost every dimension imaginable—is strong evidence of our desire to see the self relatively positively.[11] Even when others communicate negative social feedback that contradicts our rosy view of ourselves, we often show evidence of forgetting such instances and communicate information that supports our positive self-perceptions.[12]

In contrast to our resistance to accepting responsibility for negative outcomes, we easily accept communication that suggests we are responsible for our successes. This is especially true for those of us with high self-esteem.[13] There are, however, culture-based limits on our willingness to "grab the credit." For the Chinese, for example, modesty is an important basis of their self-esteem.[14] Accordingly, Chinese students attribute their success in school to their teachers, whereas American students attribute it to their own skills and intelligence. Conversely, when it comes to failure, Chinese students are more likely to explain their failure as stemming from their own flaws, while Americans tend to explain their failures as being due to someone else's fault. Why do you think these differences exist in expectations?

You can probably think of many times when the expectations you had for a certain outcome didn't come to pass. Thus, the more we understand about the role of expectations in our lives and recognize their influences on our self-concept, the better we will be able to set realistic expectations not only for others, but for ourselves

■ **self-fulfilling prophecy** Expectations we have of ourselves or that others have of us that help to create the conditions that lead us to act in predictable ways.

as well. How can knowing the effects of expectations help us to communicate more effectively?

Self-fulfilling prophecies occur all the time, even though we might not label them as such. Here are a couple of examples: You predict that you are going to be nervous when you give an oral report in class, and you are. A good friend tells you that a teacher she had and one that you are about to have is a fantastic teacher, and she is. Another example is when parents tell a child over time that she can't do anything right. Ultimately, the child will incorporate the parents' prediction into her self-concept, and she will likely fail at many or most of the tasks she attempts. The opposite prediction could result in positive outcomes. The self-fulfilling prophecy is a communicative force that does influence self-concept; however, it cannot explain all outcomes. It is important that we communicate high expectations for others rather than place unnecessary limitations on them, but the expectations that we do communicate should be realistic and obtainable.

## ▰ Impression Management

Do you care about making a good first impression on others? You should, according to the research findings, because such impressions seem to exert strong and lasting effects on others' perceptions of us. A recent study of 10,526 participants in Hurry-Date sessions, in which men and women interact with each other for very short periods of time, usually less than three minutes, and then indicate whether they are interested in future interaction, found that individuals know if a person appeals to them when they see them—almost instantly. Men and women in the study assessed potential compatibility within moments of meeting. They based their compatibility on physically observable attributes such as age, height, attractiveness, and physique instead of harder-to-observe attributes such as education, religion, and income, which seemed to have little effect on their choices.[15] It is clear that the way others first perceive us strongly influences their behavior toward us and whether they want to interact with us.

So what, exactly, are first impressions? How are they formed? And what steps can we take to make sure that we make good first impressions on others? The desire to make a favorable impression on others is a strong one, so most of us do our best to "look good" to others when we meet them for the first time. The creation of a positive image of oneself in order to influence the perceptions of others is referred to as **impression management** (or self-presentation).

As your own experiences have probably suggested, impression management can take many forms. Most fall into two major categories: self-enhancement (efforts to boost your own image) and other-enhancement (efforts to make a target person feel good in your presence).

To better understand impression management, we have to know more about "self." Our *perceived self* is a reflection of our self-concept. This self is the person that we believe ourselves to be at any given moment of self-examination. There are many aspects of our perceived self that we keep private because we don't wish to tell others; for example, regarding appearance, we might see ourselves as being too fat even though everyone else tells us we are too thin, we might see ourselves as inept in social settings with people we don't know well, or we might see ourselves as smarter than everyone else.

Our *presenting self* is the public image or the way we want to appear to others. Most of us seek to create an image that is socially acceptable, that is, nice person,

■ **impression management** Creating a positive image of oneself in order to influence the perceptions of others.

### Self-Respect, Ethics, and Self-Image

We express our values and image in a thousand ways—when we submit our tax returns, when we vote, when we return money to the clerk who has made a mistake or a wallet to the stranger who lost it on the street, when we teach our children, and when we help our friends and families. Most of us try to "do the right thing" because we care about how others perceive us. This is especially true when it comes to our family, friends, fellow students, teachers, and co-workers.

1. What does it mean to have personal integrity? To be ethical?
2. How does personal integrity affect self-image and how others see us?
3. What image does an ethical person create and how does that image affect his or her communication with others?
4. In what ways does our culture or media influence our personal integrity?
5. How can we create an image or reputation of being a person of high integrity?

good student, articulate, hardworking, friendly, wild, ambitious, truthful, loyal friend, funny, competent, highly motivated, likeable, and so on. A research study asked college students to self-select fifteen adjectives from a list of 108 possible adjectives describing their perceived self and presenting selves. Males and females described themselves similarly in twelve of fifteen choices, differing in only three. Both males and females were most likely to select active, attractive, busy, capable, curious, faithful, friendly, generous, happy, independent, polite and responsible. Males also selected able, funny, and smart, whereas females also selected careful, sensible, and special.[16] When describing their most commonly presented characteristics, males and females were similar in the following characteristics: able, active, proud, and responsible. Males listed wild, strong, smart, brave, capable, and rough, whereas females more commonly presented the qualities of bright, funny, independent, sensible, and warm. How would you describe your presenting self?

Specific tactics when presenting self to others is referred to as facework. **Facework** is a term that was first used by Erving Goffman, a sociologist, to describe the verbal and nonverbal ways we act to maintain our own presenting image and the images of others.[17] Goffman says that each of us creates various roles or characters that we want others to believe about us. He suggests that we maintain face by putting on a front when we wish to impress others. The front consists of our choice of behaviors and what we communicate when we are around others that we want to impress. Think about the notion of facework for a moment and what you do differently when you are by yourself and when you are with others. How do you behave and communicate differently when at school, at home, at the library, at work, out on a first date, a job interview, and so on when you want to impress someone? How do facework behaviors reflect a person's self-concept?

# ■ Culture and Self-Concept

Culture has a broad, all-encompassing effect on each of us. Self-concept involves our perception of self, what we believe others perceive of us, our culture, our perception of our culture, and others' perception of our culture. The development of self-concept varies from one culture to another and is determined by a specific combination of cultural norms and behaviors.

Because our self-concept develops in a cultural context, one would expect differences across cultures. There are specific cultural factors that can influence the development of self-concept. For example, young Palestinians living in Jordanian refugee camps often have a low positive self-concept because they are raised in an autocratic

■ **facework** A term that is used to describe the verbal and nonverbal ways we act to maintain our own presenting image and the images of others.

setting of traditional Arab families and schools, giving them little independence and responsibility. However, among Chinese secondary school students, a cohesive, achieving family environment is found to be associated with a more positive self-concept and less depression.[18]

Much of the research related to cultural differences has focused on the effects of individualism versus collectivism on the self-concept. If you hold an **individualistic orientation,** you would tend to stress self or personal goals and achievements over group goals and "I" consciousness and a tendency to focus on individual accomplishments. Somewhat unique to the Western world are cultures that stress individualism with the norm of prescribing that self-interest is and ought to be a central determinant of one's behavior.[19] Individualist cultures have an "I" consciousness and a tendency to focus on individual accomplishments.

If you hold a **collectivistic orientation,** you are more likely to put aside your individual goals for the well-being of the group. Researchers have examined the influence of specific situational arrangements in which the participants were asked to describe themselves: in a group, with a faculty member, with a peer, and alone.[20] The investigators found self-concept variations as a function of culture, of the situation, and of the interaction of the two. The Japanese students were not only more self-critical, but also more affected by the situation than the American students were. American students were more likely than Japanese students to provide self-descriptions in terms of abstract, internal attributes, and they were more likely to make references to friends and family, for example, "I love my family." Japanese students tend to describe themselves in terms of physical attributes and appearance, activities, the immediate situation, and possessions, for example, "I am the youngest child in my family." Americans overall tended to generate more positive self-descriptions than did the Japanese. Why do you think Americans are more likely to give themselves positive self-descriptions?

Within a culture, social, institutional, and personal norms and beliefs related to self-concept are considered universal and not bound to a particular culture. This view is reinforced when two people from the same culture communicate within the context of their own culture. For instance, a white Anglo-Saxon Protestant in American society or a Japanese in Japanese society would have a stable self-concept with relatively few problems.

But when individuals are taken out of the context of their own culture and placed in a totally different society and culture, problems can arise. One's long-standing views and expectations no longer fit in the new culture. For example, if two people with different cultural backgrounds are communicating, each will have different expectations of the other. This situation can create a cultural conflict and may eventually lead to a redefining of self-concept, which then allows the person to function more comfortably in the new culture. Being able to communicate with individuals from different cultural backgrounds requires an understanding both of their culture and of culture's influence on self-concept and the ability to adapt communication to accommodate differences.

To succeed in such communication requires developing a way to sense when messages have been successfully conveyed. It might also require overcoming fear. One African American woman stated one reason why such communication is difficult: "If people don't share the same life experiences, they can't be expected to understand each other. If whites haven't been exposed to blacks, there will be a 'fear of the unknown.'"[21] This same fear or potential for misunderstanding can happen whenever people from different backgrounds or experiences come together. Interestingly,

■ **individualistic orientation** Tendency to stress self or personal goals and achievements over group goals and achievements.

■ **collectivistic orientation** Tendency to put aside your individual goals for the well-being of the group.

### It's Me, Me, All Me!

In North American culture, the individual occupies a very important place. If you listen to how people who were raised in North America communicate, you will hear the word *I* fairly often. Other cultures do not necessarily share this perception of the self as being at the center of the universe.

**1.** How often do you and those with whom you communicate use *I* in conversations? Keep a log over a one- or two-day period, and note the number of times you and others use this word in your conversations. Are your findings consistent with the statement that North Americans use *I* fairly often?

**2.** Talk to people from cultures different from your own to discover how much value they place on self.

**3.** In your discussions with people from other cultures, use the saying "the squeaky wheel gets the grease" (explain its meaning if you have to), and ask them whether this statement would hold true in their culture. Report your findings to the class.

To conclude this exercise, discuss in class what adjustments, if any, you should make when interacting with people from cultures that do not place such emphasis on the self.

in today's global village, our self-concept is in part established through social interaction with others both inside and outside of our culture. This ongoing trend may bode well for the future because it familiarizes us with those whose ways differ from our own. Contact with other cultures in the early development of self-concept might help us to avoid some of the communication problems that occur when people of different backgrounds get together.

# ■ Gender and Self-Concept

It seems that the most pervasive element of our personal identity is the aspect of social identity that is referred to as gender. That is, you might or might not pay much attention to your social class or ethnic identity, but it would be extremely rare for you to be unaware and unconcerned about being male or being female. In hundreds of ways, we are reminded each day of our gender by how we dress, how we act, and how others respond to us.

## ■ Sex and Gender

The terms *sex* and *gender* are often used interchangeably. We defined gender in Chapter 2 as a social construct related to learned masculine and feminine behaviors. **Sex** is defined in biological terms as the anatomical and physiological differences between males and females that are genetically determined.[22] Note, however, that these definitions are not universally accepted.

The origin of gender differences is sometimes a matter of dispute, but we are willing to assume that most gender attributes are based entirely on what one learns (such as an association between hairstyle and femininity), whereas other attributes may be based entirely on biological determinants (such as the presence of facial hair). Each of us has a gender identity: A key part of our self-concept is the label of "male" or "female." For the vast majority of people, biological sex and gender identity

■ **sex** The anatomical and physiological differences between males and females that are genetically determined.

coincide, though there is a relatively small proportion of the population in which gender identity differs from sex.

Some male and female differences may be explained by biological differences in brain structure and development. According to Julia T. Wood, a well-known communication scholar, research indicates that although both men and women use both lobes of the brain, each tends to specialize in one. Wood says that men generally exhibit greater development of the left lobe of the brain (the locus of mathematical abilities, analytical thought, and sequential information processing), whereas women manifest greater development of the right lobe of the brain (the locus of intuitive thought, imaginative and artistic activity, and some visual and spatial tasks). To support this theory, she states that research reported in 1995 suggests that women are more likely to use both sides of the brain to do language tasks, whereas men are more likely to depend on the left side of the brain. Women's brains, according to Wood, work less hard than men's to understand emotions.[23]

Gender identity occurs when gender becomes a part of one's self-concept. We develop a sense of self that includes maleness and femaleness,[24] and somewhere between the ages of four and seven, the concept of gender consistency (the sense that one is permanently male or female) develops. We begin to accept the principle that gender is a basic attribute of ourselves. As soon as these attributes become known to us and are firmly in place, our perceptions of self are affected by what we believe about gender.

From the moment of birth, no other characteristic of the self slants the treatment we receive more directly than our biological sex. Children's behavior begins to be shaped by their very first pink or blue blanket. It appears that these initial influences placed on children lead to gender stereotypes and expectations that strongly influence a person's self-concept.

## ▬ Gender Stereotypes

A research study found that when children (ages five to nine) and adolescents (age fifteen to college age) are shown videotapes of four nine-month-old infants, both age groups agree that the babies identified as female (named Karen or Sue) appear to be smaller, more beautiful, nicer, and softer than those identified as male (named William or Matthew).[25] Actually, the experimenters had assigned a male or female name to infants of both sexes. For example, each male baby was identified correctly as a boy for half the participants and incorrectly as a girl for the other half; similarly, each female baby was identified for half the participants as a girl and as a boy for the other half. The findings illustrate that gender stereotypes determined how the infants were perceived.

Even though our society has taken great strides to reduce stereotypical thinking about males and females, stereotypes and narrowly defined role expectations are still accepted by many in our culture and even more so in certain other cultures. These stereotypes affect communication behavior. There are many similarities in the communication behaviors of men and women. For example, there are soft-spoken men and verbally aggressive women; many men discuss their families and friends, and many women discuss sports and investments. It is, however, commonly accepted in our society that men and women communicate differently and prefer to discuss certain subjects. In addition, in some situations, men and women are expected to communicate differently because of imposed cultural norms.

Females have often been the objects of stronger and more persistent stereotypes than males. That is not to say that there are no stereotypes assigned to males; they, too, are perceived as being "all alike" in possessing certain traits. Female stereotypes, however, are often more negative in content than those applied to males. The positive stereotypes of feminine behaviors include characteristics such as nurturance, sensitivity, and personal warmth. These traits are believed by some to be less desirable and less suited for the valued roles of leadership and authority than are the gender stereotypes for males.[26]

This question is complex, because such gender differences, even if observed, may be more a reflection of our stereotyping and their self-confirming nature than actual differences between females and males.[27] Research and evidence, however, point to the following: There are some differences between males and females with respect to some aspects of each behavior, but in general, the magnitude of these differences is much smaller that prevailing gender stereotypes might suggest.[28]

## ■■ Gender Expectations

An overwhelming body of evidence demonstrates that sex differences in communication are the result of gender expectations. According to psycholinguist Deborah Tannen, men and women do see themselves as different, and as a result, they communicate differently. She says, "In this world [the man's] conversations are negotiations in which people try to achieve and maintain the upper hand if they can and protect themselves from others' attempts to put them down and push them around. Life, then, is a contest, a struggle to preserve independence and avoid failure." The man's world is a hierarchical social order in which people are either one-up or one-down. In the women's world, according to Tannen, "conversations are negotiations for closeness in which people try to seek and give confirmation and support and to reach consensus. They try to protect themselves from others' attempts to push them away. Life, then, is a community, a struggle to preserve intimacy and avoid isolation." The women's world is also hierarchical, but the order is related more to friendship than to power and accomplishment.[29] Are we really different?

According to one researcher's perspective, "the two sexes are essentially similar and . . . the differences linked to sexual functions are not related to psychological traits or social roles."[30] He further believes that most gender differences are relatively superficial and that differences that are perceived to exist are socially constructed in one's cultural upbringing. The differences between males and females, therefore, are more or less learned in and reinforced by culture.

When asked to describe themselves, males and females differ in their descriptions. Males tend to mention qualities such as ambition, energy, power, initiative, and control. They are likely to discuss their success in sports and with females. Females, however, typically list qualities such as generosity, sensitivity, consideration, and concern for others.[31] Males, it seems, are expected to be powerful and authoritative, whereas females are expected to be concerned with relationships and expressiveness.

## MAKING Technology CONNECTIONS

### Public and Private Selves: Our Image

A headline in the *Lincoln Journal Star* read, "DYING TO BE THIN." The newspaper ran a three-day series on the pressures of being thin in American culture. It is clear that there is a constant focus on weight and body image. The image of being thin is portrayed in our media, magazines, and store catalogues. Probably the most famous are Victoria's Secret swim summer catalogue or the *Sports Illustrated* Swimsuit issue.

1. Being physically attractive is important, but has it become too important?
2. Conduct an Internet search using the key words *self-concept and body image* or *self-esteem and body image*. Visit several of the sites that you locate to see whether they provide more insight or other answers related to question 1. Share what you learned with your class.

Despite some strides toward equality of the sexes, our society still has a cultural bias toward masculinity. But because communication behaviors are learned and are culturally defined, they can be unlearned and changed over time. To some extent, this has happened and continues to happen. For a long time in our society, women expected and were expected by others to stay home and rear children, whereas men were expected to be breadwinners. Now, however, according to the International Labor Organization report in 2003, women represent over 40 percent of the global labor force, approximately 70 percent in developed countries and 60 percent in developing countries. The report further states that women occupy between 30 and 60 percent of the professional jobs in a sample of countries in which data were available. In addition, women obtained 5.1 percent of the executive positions in the five hundred largest U.S. companies in 1999, compared to 2.4 percent in 1996. The report notes that when women hit the proverbial "glass ceiling" or encounter situations that make it difficult for them to balance work with their home

## MAKING CONNECTIONS
### for Success

### Getting Real About Our Image of Self

Our culture emphasizes perfectionism, which is an easy trap to fall into for many of us. We expect to be perfect in everything we do and that is a way that many of us set ourselves up for failure. For example, if we expect to be a perfect communicator in all situations, we have most likely set ourselves up to fail. It is much better to set a series of smaller goals that are realistic and obtainable. In other words, focus on one thing at a time and when you have succeeded on that, move on to another, and so on.

**1.** Set one specific self-improvement goal for yourself . . . I would like to:

_____

**2.** List or describe specific changes that you need to make in order to accomplish the goal:

_____

**3.** In order to ensure that I haven't set an unrealistic goal for myself, I will not ask myself to do the following:

_____

life, they often go out on their own. For example, in 1999, 38 percent of all firms in the United States were run by women. Other examples show that women in Australia accounted for 35 percent of the 1.3 million small-business owners in 1997, and the growth rate of female small-business owners from 1995 to 1997 was three times that for men. These data illustrate not only that more and more women are changing the expectations of what women can and are doing, but also that women around the world are taking part in this change. The expectations and accomplishment of women in the business world, as in many other areas, such as education, athletics, and careers, have influenced how women see themselves.[32]

# ■ Enhancing Self-Concept

Throughout this chapter, we discussed what self-concept is, how it's developed, and how it connects to communication. Most of us already have a pretty good image of ourselves, but most of us also have areas that we would like to improve or change. We are not naïve enough to believe that every one of our suggestions will automatically improve your self-concept, nor are we naïve enough to believe that everyone who reads our book will take our suggestions seriously. We do know that most of us have areas of ourselves that could be improved or altered, but improvement and change require effort and a willingness to accept that something needs to be done. We also believe that most everyone wants a positive self-image for themselves and to be seen by others as positively as possible. Building on what you have read on self-concept, we now explore possible ways that you can enhance or change your self-concept and grow as a communicator. The following guidelines help you begin the process:

| GUIDELINES | Improving Self |
|---|---|

1. *Decide what you would like to change or improve about yourself.* For change to occur, you must know or state what needs to be changed. Describe, as accurately, specifically, and completely as you can, what you would like to change or improve about yourself. If you are unhappy about something or you don't like something about yourself, identify what it is and state it, for example, "I don't want to be afraid when I speak in public," "I want to be taken seriously by my friends," or "I want to be better organized."

2. *Describe why you feel the way you do about yourself.* Is your problem or shortcoming brought on by yourself or by others? Many students, for example, do not want to be in college or to be in a certain major. They go to college or take a major because that is what their parents or friends expect or pressure them to do. Although many of these students would rather be doing something else, they are afraid to take a stand or to do what they really want to do. Before you can begin to feel better about yourself, you must recognize why you are unhappy and who is contributing to your problem. You might think you can't change majors, that you are not capable of earning good grades in a particular subject, or that you are too shy to make new friends. If you want to change something about yourself, you must first ask yourself why you feel that way. For example, are you living out a self-fulfilling prophecy?

3. *Make a commitment to improve or change.* Changing our self-concept or aspects of ourselves is not easy, especially if what we want changed has been with us for a long period. However, nothing ever changes by itself; thus to make a change we must begin with a concentrated effort and a strong commitment to change and a belief that a change can occur. For example, on the TV show the "The Biggest Loser," where people compete against each other to determine who will lose the most weight, the people on the show, in spite of external rewards, will not reach their goal unless they have made a personal commitment to do so. Wishing or thinking something should change may be the first step, but only wishing or thinking about a change won't make it happen—you have to commit to the change for it to have a chance to occur. It requires that you state what you want changed and decide that you are going to make a change.

4. *Set reasonable goals for yourself.* You must be reasonable in setting your goals. You may be able to change some things overnight, but other things may require a long-term effort. For example, you might decide that you are going to improve your grades by studying for several hours every night. You can begin your new study schedule immediately, but actually raising your grades could take much longer.

5. *Decide on the specific actions you are going to take.* Determine an action plan that will lead to the outcome that you want. Of course, any time you act, you run the risk of failure, but successful people learn that without risk, nothing can be accomplished. It is when you understand your shortcomings, learn how to deal with them, believe and commit yourself to making changes, and then take the appropriate actions that you will accomplish your goals. It is important to realize that changing your self-concept not only requires commitment and action, but it almost always takes time.

   If you feel unsure about or lack confidence in communicating with others, you might overcome or manage these feelings by approaching them in small steps. For example, you might feel hesitant to visit your professor in his or her office. Why not start by speaking briefly with your professor before or after class? You might begin by asking a question about your progress. Once you begin to feel more comfortable, ask for an appointment or stop in to visit during office hours. In order to start the conversation you might have a few questions prepared. If you continue such visits, you will gradually gain more confidence in yourself.

6. *Associate with positive people whenever possible.* Try to surround yourself with people you like and trust. This will make it much easier to discuss any problems that you have and to ask for support. When others know what you are trying to do and that you need help, they can provide support to help you make the changes you desire.

# ▪ Summary

Our self-concept, or self-identity, is our mental picture and evaluation of our physical, social, and psychological attributes. Like communication, self-concept is a process that has no beginning or end and is constantly changing. Competent communicators understand that our self-perception and other people's perceptions of us change from time to time, from situation to situation, and from person to person. Our self-concept is also based on our values, attitudes, and beliefs, which all play a significant role in who we are and how we communicate.

Part of our self-concept has to do with how we see ourselves as communicators. Competent communicators know that there is always some anxiety in communicating with others and therefore see it as a natural part of the communication process. Some people are overly anxious when confronted with real or anticipated communication with another person or people; this feeling is referred to as communication apprehension. This type of expectation can become self-fulfilling and ultimately determine how we behave, who we eventually become, and what we communicate to others and ourselves. The competent communicator knows how to use self-enhancement or other enhancement techniques to bolster his or her image in order to create a positive outcome in his or her communication with others.

Our cultural background and gender affect our development of our self-concept and how we communicate. Competent communicators know that communicating with people from different cultural backgrounds requires understanding of other cultures and an ability to adapt to them. They also know how gender stereotyping can affect the communication behavior of both males and females. People who understand gender roles are more likely to be successful in their interactions and careers than are those who do not.

Although it is not easy to alter self-concept, we can achieve progress through hard work, a desire to improve, and the belief that we are and will be successful. The following steps were discussed to help improve your self-concept: (1) decide what you would like to change or improve about yourself, (2) describe why you feel the way you do about yourself, (3) make a commitment to improving or changing yourself, (4) set reasonable goals for yourself, (5) decide on the specific actions you are going to take, and (6) associate with positive people whenever possible.

# Discussion Starters

1. What steps can you take to help others improve their self-concept?
2. Why is it important to understand the influence of self-concept on communication competency?
3. In what ways does your self-concept affect your communication effectiveness?
4. What do you need to know about self-concept and gender to become a more effective communicator?
5. Discuss the influence culture has on a person's self-concept.
6. What is the connection between self-concept and communication competency?
7. Discuss situations in which you use impression management techniques to improve your chance of reaching a goal.
8. What is the most useful information that you obtained in this chapter to aid you in becoming a more competent communicator?

# Notes

1. H. Tajfel and J. C. Turner, "The Social Identity Theory of Intergroup Behavior," in *The Social Psychology of Intergroup Relations,* 2nd ed., eds. S. Worchel and W. G. Austin (Monterey, CA: Brooks-Cole, 1986), 7–24.
2. A. Gerike, *Old Is Not a Four-Letter Word: A Midlife Guide* (Watsonville, CA: Papier Mâché Press, 1997).
3. D. J. Bem, "Self-Perception Theory," in *Advances in Experimental Social Psychology,* vol. 6, ed. L. Berkowitz (New York: Academic Press, 1972).
4. J. W. Kinch, "A Formalized Theory of Self-Concept," *American Journal of Sociology* 68 (January 1963): 481–86.
5. W. W. Wilmot, *Dyadic Communication,* 3rd ed. (New York: Random House, 1987), 61.
6. C. Stohl, "Perceptions of Social Attractiveness and Communicator Style: A Developmental Study of Preschool Children," *Communication Education* 30 (1981): 367–76.
7. J. C. McCroskey, "Classroom Consequences of Communication Apprehension," *Communication Education* 26 (1977): 27–28.
8. V. P. Richmond and J. C. McCroskey, *Communication: Apprehension, Avoidance, and Effectiveness,* 5th ed. (Boston, MA: Allyn and Bacon, 1998).
9. R. Rosenthal and L. Jacobson, *Pygmalion in the Classroom: Teacher Expectation and Pupils' Intellectual Development* (New York: Holt, Rinehart & Winston, 1968) vii; T. Good and J. Brophy, *Looking in Classrooms,* 4th ed. (New York: Harper & Row, 1987).
10. C. S. Carver, L. A. Kus, and M. F. Scheier, "Effects of Good Versus Bad Mood and Optimistic versus Pessimistic Outlook on Social Acceptance versus Rejection," *Journal of Social and Clinical Psychology* 13 (1994): 138–51.
11. M. D. Alicke, D. S. Vredenburg, M. Hiatt, and O. Govorun, "The Better Than Myself Effect," *Motivation and Emotion* 25 (2001): 7–22; Y. Klar, "Way Beyond Compare: The Nonselective Superiority and Inferiority Bias in Judging Randomly Assigned Group Members Relative to Their Peers," *Journal of Experimental Social Psychology* 38 (2002): 331–351.
12. R. B. Sanitioso and R. Wlodarski, "In Search of Information That Confirms a Desired Self-Perception: Motivation Processing of Social Feedback and Choice of Interactions," *Personality and Social Psychology Bulletin* 30 (2004): 412–422.
13. B. R. Schlenker, M. F. Weigold, and J. R. Hallam, "Self-Serving Attribution in Social Context," *Journal of Personality and Social Psychology* 58 (1990): 855–863.
14. M. H. Bond, "Chinese Values," in *The Handbook of Chinese Psychology,* ed. M. H. Bond (Oxford, England: Oxford University Press, 1996), 208–226.
15. R. Kurzban and J. Weeden, "HurryDate: Mate Preferences in Action," *Evolution and Human Behavior* 26 (2005): 227–244.
16. C. M. Shaw and R. Edwards, "Self-Concepts and Self-Presentations of Males and Females: Similarities and Differences," *Communication Reports* 10 (1997): 55–62.
17. E. Goffman, *The Presentation of Self in Everyday Life* (Garden City, NY: Doubleday, 1959).
18. S. Lau and L. K. Kwok, "Relationships of Family Environment to Adolescent's Depression and Self-Concept," *Social Behavior and Personality* 27 (2000): 41–50.
19. D. T. Miller, "The Norm of Self-Interest," *American Psychologist* 54 (1999): 1053–60.
20. C. Kanagawa, S. E. Cross, and H. R. Markus, "Who Am I? The Cultural Psychology of the Conceptual Self," *Journal of Personality and Social Psychology Bulletin* 27 (2001): 90–103.
21. S. A. Ribeau, J. R. Baldwin, and M. L. Hecht, "An African-American Communication Perspective," in *Intercultural Communication: A Reader,* ed.

L. A. Samovar and R. E. Porter (Belmont, Calif.: Wadsworth, 1994), 143. J. R. Baldwin and M. Hecht, "Unpacking Group-Based Intolerance: A Holographic Look at Identity and Intolerance," in *Intercultural Communication: A Reader,* 10th ed., eds. L. A. Samovar and R. E. Porter (Belmont, CA: Wadsworth, 2003), 358.

22. J. B. Beckwith, "Terminology and Social Relevance in Psychological Research on Gender," *Social Behavior and Personality* 22 (1994): 329–36.

23. J. T. Wood, *Gendered Lives: Communication, Gender and Culture,* 5th ed. (Belmont, CA: Wadsworth, 2003), 40.

24. N. Grieve, "Beyond Sexual Stereotypes. Androgyny: A Model or an Ideal?" in *Australian Women: Feminist Perspectives,* eds. N. Grieve and P. Grimshaw (Melbourne, Australia: Oxford University Press, 1980), 247–57.

25. D. A. Vogel, M. A. Lake, S. Evans, and K. H. Karraker, "Children's and Adults Sex-Stereotyped Perceptions of Infants," *Sex Roles* 24 (1991): 601–16.

26. M. E. Heilman, R. F. Martell, and M. C. Simon, "The Vagaries of Sex Bias: Conditions Regulating the Underevaluation, Equivaluation, and Overevaluation of Female Job Applicants," *Organizational Behavior and Human Decision Processes* 41 (1988): 98–110.

27. M. Chen and J. A. Bargh, "Nonconscious Behavioral Confirmation Processes: The Self-fulfilling Consequences of Automatic Stereotype Activation," *Journal of Experimental Psychology* 33 (1997): 541–560; T. Claire and S. T. Fiske, "A Systematic View of Behavioral Confirmation: Counterpoint to the Individualist View," in *Intergroup Cognition and Intergroup Behavior,* eds. C. Sedikides, J. Schopler, and C. A. Insko (Mahwah, NJ: Erlbaum 1998), 205–231.

28. B. A. Bettencourt and N. Miller, "Gender Differences in Aggression as a Function of Provocation: A Meta-Analysis," *Psychological Bulletin* 119 (1996): 422–447.

29. D. Tannen, *You Just Don't Understand: Women and Men in Conversation* (New York: Morrow, 1990), 24–25.

30. C. E. Epstein, *Deceptive Distinctions: Sex, Gender, and the Social Order* (New Haven, CT: Yale University Press, 1988), 25.

31. M. R. Gunnar-Von Gnechten, "Changing a Frightening Toy into a Pleasant Toy by Allowing the Infant to Control Its Actions," *Developmental Psychology* 14 (1978): 157–62; J. H. Block, "Differential Premises Arising from Differential Socialization of the Sexes: Some Conjectures," *Child Development* 54 (1983): 1335–54; J. T. Spence and R. L. Helmreich, *Masculinity and Femininity: Their Psychological Dimension and Antecedents* (Austin: University of Texas Press, 1978).

32. "U.S. Women Make More Progress in Management Than Women Abroad," www.womenof.com/Articles/cb71601.asp

# CHAPTER 4

# Connecting through Verbal Communication

"Language is used to

think as well as to speak."

—EVERETT ROGERS AND THOMAS

STEINFATT

# This chapter will help you:

- **Understand** how language helps you make connections with others.
- **Identify** examples of the power of language in communication events.
- **Provide** examples of language as a set of symbols in a system.
- **Demonstrate** that words and meaning depend on many variables.
- **Explain** how language is personal and how we all use language in unique ways.
- **Identify** the ways in which language influences perceptions, thought, culture, and views of reality.
- **Explain** the four elements of language.
- **Describe** language-based barriers to communication and suggest how they can be overcome.
- **Explain** how language choices can improve communication competence.

# Making everyday connections

Nermin Ferkic is a naturalized U.S. citizen who emigrated from Bosnia to the United States. He is fluent in five languages, and in his ten years in the United States, he has completed his B.A. and is working on a Master of Arts degree. When asked about how difficult it was to adapt to a new culture, Nermin laughed and said, "The toughest adjustment is the language!" Here's one of his accounts:

> When I was planning to come to the U.S., I had a language tutor from England, and he kept telling me, "I'm sorry! I cannot teach you how Americans speak." I laughed and thought: How could that be? English is English. I couldn't have been more wrong. In the first place, when you think of learning a new language, you think you'll use a dictionary. Wrong! Dictionary meanings got me into trouble. One place I worked there was a nice lady who talked all the time about her female dog. I wanted to be friendly and ask her about her dog, so, I looked up 'female dog' in the dictionary and the next day when she came in, I said, "Hey, Barb! How's your bitch?" The whole room was deathly quiet. And she said, "How dare you talk to me like that?" So, I explained. The dictionary says a female dog is a bitch. Isn't that right? After that, I used Spiderman cartoons to help me understand language.

*Reprinted by permission of Nermin Ferkic*

Language is how we communicate, how we make connections. But as Nermin has learned there's more to language than just what the dictionary tells us! ■

## Questions to think about

- Have you had similar language experiences to Nermin's?
- In what ways can we learn language and meaning?
- What can we learn about language use from Nermin's experiences?

According to the Educational Testing Service, college campuses will become increasingly diverse in the twenty-first century. During the next fifteen years, enrollment is projected to increase by 19 percent to sixteen million students enrolled in U.S. colleges and universities. Minority students are expected to account for 80 percent of the growth, with the proportion of African or African American students rising from 12.8 to 13.2 percent by 2015; the proportion of Hispanic students increasing from 10 to about 15 percent; and the proportion of Asian students increasing from 5.4 to 8.4 percent. The proportion of white students who attend college is expected to decline from about 71 percent to about 62 percent.[1]

Census Bureau figures released in March 2006 indicate a significant increase in the numbers of nonwhite voters in the 2004 presidential election. This further supports the fact that there is increasing diversity in the United States. Other nations, too, have become more diverse. In fact, communication scholars Samovar and Porter tell us that the significance of all this is that "[we] live in an age when all the inhabitants of earth are interconnected."[2]

English is increasingly *the* language of higher education around the world. This trend is enhanced by the spread of technology because much of the available computer software is written in English and because of the growth of the Internet where the English language prevails.[3] As technology grows, the world seems to shrink, and our careful use of language will become even more important than it was previously. As effective communicators, we must make appropriate language choices so that diverse groups of people can understand us.

The situation in Making Everyday Connections demonstrates that the words we use make a difference, and that it's not enough to know dictionary definitions. Nermin quickly learned that going strictly by the dictionary for his word choices could get him in trouble. Because the language we use is a message in itself, our use of language can convey a positive image of us, or it can damage and degrade us as well as others. The United States is primarily an English-speaking culture, and even though there are many cocultures within our society, educated people need to know which forms of English are expected and appropriate for different settings. In many college classrooms and in many business meetings and other workplace settings, standard English use is dominant and expected, whereas slang and informal language might be more suitable in other settings. Competent communicators must determine which form of language is appropriate for a particular situation and which is not.

Language is critically important to the communication process. In this chapter, we examine what language is, some common barriers to effective language use, the use of inclusive language, and the avoidance of stereotypes. We also provide suggestions about effective language use.

■ **language** A structured system of signs, sounds, gestures, and marks that is used and understood to express ideas and feelings among people within a community, nation, geographic area, or cultural tradition.

# ■ The Importance of Language

**Language** is a structured system of signs, sounds, gestures, or marks that is used and understood to express ideas and feelings among people within a community, nation, geographic area, or cultural tradition. In this chapter, we concentrate on spoken language; in the next chapter, we consider nonverbal communication. Without language, there would be little or no human communication as we now know it. Language allows us to encounter our world in meaningful ways because it allows us to share meaning with others. Can you imagine what it would be like to be unable to

## MAKING CONNECTIONS for Success

### Words and Meanings

Language choices and the way one communicates can create views of one's educational level, intelligence, social status, or economic status. When people mispronounce words, or use the wrong words in their interactions with others, it may be hard to change the negative perceptions others have. Numerous books have been published to help people use the appropriate words to communicate. Two such books are *100 Words Every High School Graduate Should Know* and *100 Words Almost Everyone Confuses & Misuses,* published by the American Heritage Dictionaries. Each provides information so that readers can "tell right from wrong or true errors from matters of taste."[4] Included in the lists of word pairs that are often used inappropriately are affect/effect, its/it's, and principal/principle. Check out the following words in a dictionary or thesaurus, or on Ask.com, Dictionary.com, or in one of the books noted above:

1. What's wrong with using "irregardless"?
2. What's a factoid?
3. What's the difference between infer and imply?
4. Incredible and incredulous are both adjectives. What does each mean? Are they interchangeable?
5. What's the difference between flaunt and flout?
6. Why does word choice make a difference?

tell someone what you know or think or feel? Language is a powerful tool! But it is only as effective and efficient as the people using it. Although we often believe that language is neutral, in actuality, it communicates much about what we are and what we think and therefore must be carefully used.

## ■■ Language Is Powerful

How many times have you walked through a crowd of strangers and momentarily paused when you thought you heard someone call your name? Why? Our names are not *just* names or words. Our names define who we are. "If any one thing is universal, it is a name. At every place and at every time, everyone has received a name. Names brand us with distinctive marks that separate us from the rest of the herd and, at the same time, make us a part of it."[7] Names are so important, for example, that people legally change them. In many cases, people change their names when the change better fits them or when their given names do not truly demonstrate their perceptions of themselves. Communication scholar Victoria De Francisco, for example, changed her paternal surname for her mother's surname. De Francisco and other feminist scholars suggest that naming has been a male-dominated power. They suggest that males do the naming and use "male" terms and that the world is viewed through a male perspective, leaving women in subordinate roles.[8] Name-calling can also affect individuals. If you have ever been told you were "stupid" or been called "sissy" or "weirdo," you know how name-calling can hurt.

Feminists raise issues about perspectives on language because they want an inclusive world. In a recent CRTNET (Communication Research and Theory Network) posting on the National Communication Association email list, communication scholar Anita Taylor pointed out how even Internet sources use language and images to perpetuate male perspectives.[9] Language can create biases for both men and women. When you hear the words "medical doctor" what image comes to mind?

## MAKING CONNECTIONS for Success

### The Power of Language

Arabs have a great appreciation of language. An ancient Arab proverb asserts, "A man's tongue is his sword." In the Arab culture, words used to describe events can become more significant than the events themselves. Communication scholars Samovar and Porter suggest that in Arabic, "Words are used more for their own sake than for what they are understood to mean. Whereas an American can adequately express an idea in ten words, the Arabic speaker may use one hundred."[5]

People in the Arab culture know that language is powerful. But, other countries, too, share that view. African cultures often use the spoken word over the written word, and proverbs are used to demonstrate issues. African Americans also place a high value on talk, conversation, and the oral storytelling tradition. An example from Kenya is: "Having a good discussion is like riches." This proverb demonstrates that both history and news are shared in the oral tradition.[6]

1. What are some of the things your parents, grandparents, or teachers have shared with you about the power of language?
2. Can you recall a time when you were rewarded for telling something? A time when you were punished for using the "wrong words"?
3. How will you share with others the message, "Language is powerful"?

What about a strong leader? When you hear "nurse" what is the image? We often think of leaders and medical doctors as men and nurses as women, but that's not always the case. In his poem, "New Kid on the Block," Jack Prelutsky shows us how wrong our images based on language can be. "The New Kid" is described by the narrator as tough, angry, and strong. The very last line of the poem surprises us when Prelutsky says, "I don't care for *her* at all." If you are a woman who hears a speech about heart disease, and the speaker always uses the word "he" when describing effects and symptoms, you might think "heart disease only affects men" and not concern yourself with the message when, in fact, heart disease is a major killer for both men and women. Inclusive language ensures that people at least perceive that they are included in the discussion.

### ■■ Language Affects Thought

The misuse of language involves more than misuse of words. Misused language affects our ability to think. Thought and language are inseparable. Most scholars agree that words help us to form thoughts. How many times have you found yourself struggling to find *the* word and without it, you could not express what you really meant. When you take the time to think a minute, however, the word usually appears. It is important to carefully consider language choices before we speak. We cannot erase what we said. We can correct or retract a statement and apologize for it, but we cannot eliminate the fact that we said it.

Those whose career success is profoundly affected by the ability to communicate expend great effort on evaluating the potential effects of using certain words. Musicians, for example, often search a long time for just the right word for their lyrics. Chuck D., cofounder of Public Enemy, in a speech on the campus of the University of Northern Iowa said, "Vocabulary is critical. It's critical to success in the world and it's critical to lyrics. Only those who know and use the language well will succeed."[10] The Dixie Chicks, too, learned the power of language. When lead singer Natalie

Politicians need to be careful about word choice when they speak and they must constantly assess how others might interpret their words. They know that failure to do so may place them in an awkward position, cost them an election, or even jeopardize national security.

Maines told a London audience, "We're ashamed the president of the United States is from Texas,"[11] the backlash in the United States was significant. Some radio stations stopped playing the group's songs, there was public outrage resulting in condemnation and the burning of their CDs, and those who were most offended offered to buy concert tickets so that no one would attend. Fans at the Academy of Country Music Awards even booed when the Chicks' name was mentioned. These two examples should reinforce what communication and language scholars have long maintained: Language is powerful, and what you say can either help you or hurt you. Communication scholar Cheris Kramerae suggests that people who do not have the power of "correct or appropriate" language have little voice in their worlds. Her **muted group theory** suggests that status and power are clearly linked.[12] Kramerae says that muted groups are often women and ethnic minorities or out-groups (people with disabilities, the elderly, and the poor). Communication scholar Marsha Houston reports that African American women **style-switch,** or move between dominant culture language and the language of their own coculture, to successfully operate in both the dominant society and their own coculture.[13]

When we communicate, we first form thoughts and then decide how we're going to express them. Competent communicators begin with clear thinking, followed by careful language choices that reflect an understanding of what language is, how it is used, and what effects it might have on listeners.

## ■ The Elements of Language

Language, talk, speech, and communication are four different but related phenomena. *Language,* as we noted earlier, is a structured system of signs, sounds, gestures, or marks (in other words, *symbols*) that allows people to express ideas and feelings to others; *talk* is what we do every day; *speech* is one vehicle used to transmit language; and *communication* involves the exchange of meanings. Language is one means by

■ **muted group theory** A theory suggesting that status and power are clearly linked and that women, ethnic minorities, and out-groups have little voice and people do not pay attention to them because they lack the power of appropriate language.

■ **style-switch** The process of moving between the language of one's own coculture and the language of the dominant culture to successfully operate in both.

## MAKING CONNECTIONS

### Karen Tracy
*University of Colorado*

Karen Tracy is fascinated with how the little stuff of everyday talk—selecting particular phrases, the shape of a story, changing a word midway in talk—can say so much about people and their relationships. She has been teaching a course about everyday talk for many years and in 2002 published the text, *Everyday Talk: Building and Reflecting Identities*. In her classes, students videotape a conversation of their own with classmates or friends, make a written record of it, and

## To Scholars

then analyze it in a number of different ways. Looking closely at talk, Dr. Tracy argues, enables people to arrive at interesting insights into communicative troubles; changing the little stuff can make workplace and intimate relationships function better.

Dr. Tracy is a communication professor at the University of Colorado in Boulder. She has published journal articles and books about communication problems between citizens and 911 call-takers, and the communicative challenges in group meetings of a variety of types, including contentious school boards and brown-bag research sessions. Outside of school she is a crime junky, reading mysteries and watching *Law and Order*.

which we communicate, and speech is one way in which we use language. The fact that we process language does not automatically mean that we communicate well, but we cannot verbally communicate without language, and language would be useless if it did not help us convey meanings. Of course, as you will see in Chapter 5, nonverbal communication also allows us to express ourselves. What is the relationship between language, speech, communication, and talk? Communication scholar Karen Tracy says,

> Language has always been part of the study of communication, but language only partly overlaps with talk. Language is an abstract code; talk is a, if not the, focal activity of ordinary life. Talking is how we express who we are and who we want to be; it is how we make relationships as well as relational problems; it is the instrument that creates, exacerbates, and—not quite as often as we'd like—solves problems.[14]

Tracy provides these distinctions: "**everyday talk** [includes] the ordinary kinds of communicating people do [in their lives from school to the workplace, and in relationships]. Who people are is what communication theorists call *identity*. Identity includes the most personal aspects of people . . . character, personality, [and] fixed characteristics."[15] In other words, we use language to create talk, to create ourselves, and to share ourselves and our views with others. Talking is what we do in our everyday lives, and communication is the process we engage in to be able to make sense of it all.

To more clearly differentiate these concepts, consider the fact that you can indicate an affirmative response to a question by nodding your head, thus using a gesture to communicate without speech. You can indicate the same response by writing the word *yes,* thus using writing instead of speech as the vehicle to transmit language. If you were traveling in a foreign country and said "yes," you might use language and speech without communicating your intentions.

■ **everyday talk** The ordinary kind of communicating people do in their lives.

The goal is to coordinate language and speech to produce effective communication, which is the transfer of meaning as intended. You can learn more about language by examining four of its key elements: sounds, words, grammar, and meaning.

## ■■ Sounds

Most of us learn to speak language before we learn to write it, and most of us are born with the physical mechanisms that enable us to make speech sounds. However, we do not all learn to produce the sounds in exactly the same way. Though using the same language, people of certain geographic regions or cultural groups may speak quite differently. Dialects and other speech patterns can complicate communication between people who speak the same language.

## ■■ Words

**Words** are symbols that stand for objects and concepts. A word can represent an object or an abstract concept: The word *desk* represents an actual piece of furniture, an object, while the word *love* represents a whole range of emotions associated with our feelings for those closest to us.

Words have meanings because communities and cultures give them meaning. People agree that certain sound combinations mean certain things to them. One of the intriguing things about languages is the **idioms,** or words whose meanings cannot be understood by the ordinary usage. I spent several months in Sweden and learned many Swedish words so that I could better communicate with my colleagues. Despite a Swedish–American English dictionary, I am still confused by the use of some terms. For example, we visited a KultureHus (Culture House) in one place, and I read about the KultureHuset (the Culture House) in another community. There is an agreed-upon meaning for the Swedes that my dictionary does not explain. But for understanding to occur, all parties in the communication event must agree on meanings.

## ■■ Grammar

Just as language has rules that govern how sounds may be joined into words, it also has rules that govern how words may be joined into phrases and sentences. This set of rules is called **grammar.** For example, the English grammar system requires that singular nouns take singular verb forms and plural nouns take plural verb forms *(friend is; friends are)*.

As we join sounds together to form words and join words together to form phrases, sentences, and paragraphs, we use language's sound and grammar systems simultaneously. The ability to use sounds and grammar correctly is crucial to competent communication. Grammar enables us to make complete sentences and to understand the sentences made by others.

Despite the many rules that govern language, there is virtually no limit to the number of different messages that can be created. It has been estimated that in the English language, it is possible to create ten quintillion twenty-word sentences.[16] This does not include sentences either shorter or longer than twenty words. Thus the number of possible sentences and messages is nearly infinite.

## ■■ Meaning

The study of meaning, or the association of words with ideas, feelings, and contexts, is called **semantics.** If language did not have meaning, it would serve little or no purpose. Because words and word patterns can be used to exchange meanings between people and even between generations, language is a useful tool for communication.

■ **word** A symbol that stands for the object or concept that it names.

■ **idioms** Words whose meanings cannot be understood by the ordinary usage.

■ **grammar** Rules that govern how words are put together to form phrases and sentences.

■ **semantics** The study of meaning, or the association of words with ideas, feelings, and contexts.

**Do Words Contain Meaning?**   We tend to associate language symbols (words) with specific meanings and to take that relationship for granted. But it is important to understand that, in fact, language by itself has no meaning.

This notion might seem to contradict our entire discussion so far. You might wonder how language can be a system involving rules and meanings, yet still have no meaning itself. Actually, it is entirely arbitrary that the word *cat* represents those four-legged felines that some of us love and some of us hate. There is nothing about the letters *c, a,* and *t* that is essentially related to the being of a cat. When we see or hear the symbol, we fill in the meaning.

Words are symbols that represent people, objects, concepts, and events; the word is not actually the person, object, concept, or event. For example, *computer, yellow, buildings, car, freedom,* and *tyranny* are only words, not the entities they symbolize. It is easy to miss this distinction. Even though words are symbols, try screaming "Snake!" in front of someone who dislikes snakes, and you will quickly see how words cause reactions—as if they were the actual thing!

The belief that words have meaning in themselves is widespread. During the past several years, we have asked students in beginning communication classes whether words have meaning. The data, though not scientifically collected, suggest that more than 75 percent of the students believe words do have meaning. But the simple fact is that words do *not* contain meanings by themselves. Words only acquire meaning through the context in which they are used and the fact that those who use them give them meaning. Figure 4.1 shows how two different people attach different meanings to the word *house.*

The following scene from Lewis Carroll's *Through the Looking Glass* illustrates this notion. Humpty Dumpty and Alice become involved in an argument about language and meaning:

> "I don't know what you mean by 'glory,'" Alice said.
>
> Humpty Dumpty smiled contemptuously. "Of course you don't—till I tell you. I meant there's a nice knock-down argument for you!"
>
> "But 'glory' doesn't mean 'a nice knock-down argument,'" Alice objected.
>
> "When I use a word," Humpty Dumpty said, in a rather scornful tone, "it means just what I choose it to mean—neither more nor less."
>
> "The question is," said Alice, "whether you can make words mean so many different things."
>
> "The question is," said Humpty Dumpty, "which is to be master—that's all."[17]

Who determines meaning? The answer is *you.* You control which words you use, the meaning you wish to give them, and, if you have mastered the art of communication, how people react to them. Although everyone has the ability to impart meaning to words, not everyone does so in the same way. Thus, a sender might intend one meaning for a message, but the receiver might either intentionally or unintentionally give the message a different meaning. Disparity between the meaning sent and the meaning received can be a greater problem when the sender and receiver have different cultural backgrounds or even different experiences and knowledge. For example, people who keep up with computers and technology often use specialized language that is unfamiliar to someone who doesn't have much knowledge about computers. Care in choosing words is especially important in such situations.

■ **denotation** The objective meaning of a word; the standard dictionary definition.

**Words Have Denotative and Connotative Meanings.**   **Denotation** is the common meaning associated with a word—its standard dictionary definition. Denotative meanings are usually readily understood. Many people use words as if they had only a denotative or specific meaning, but this is not the case. Although commonly

■ **FIGURE 4.1** Meanings Are Not in Words but in People

We cannot assume that using words that we consider appropriate and adequate to convey a particular message will succeed with every listener. As this figure illustrates, different people associate different meanings with even the simplest words. This is because words are symbols only—people fill in the meaning.

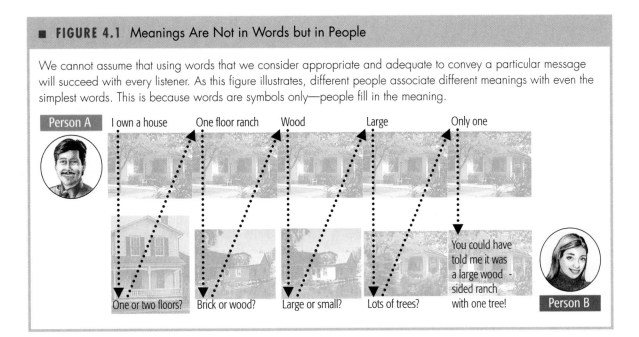

understood dictionary definitions (denotative meanings) do exist, when we communicate we usually use words connotatively. In the opening scenario, Nermin learned that dictionary definitions were anything but helpful, and did not facilitate effective communication.

**Connotation** is the subjective meaning of a word, what a word suggests because of feelings or associations it evokes. The connotative meaning is based on the context in which the word is used, how the meaning is expressed nonverbally (tone of voice, facial expression of the speaker, and so on), and the understanding of the person who is receiving it. The competent communicator can differentiate between denotative and connotative meanings and understands which is being used in a given situation. Connotative meanings may be generally accepted by most of the people who use the language, by people within a particular group, or by an individual. To someone who lives on either coast or throughout much of the South, the Midwest evokes images of farms as large fields of corn and farmsteads with chickens, pigs, and cows. To a midwesterner, a *farm* represents "home," or a place to live and work. Although not all midwestern farms have livestock, they still retain the denotative meaning, but not necessarily the connotative meaning held by those unfamiliar with farms.

**Words Can Be Concrete or Abstract.**   **Concrete words** are symbols for specific things that can be pointed to or physically experienced (seen, tasted, smelled, heard, or touched). For example, words such as *car, book, keys,* and *dog* are concrete words. They represent specific, tangible objects, and therefore their meanings are usually quite clear. We can be even more specific with *Buick, the Bible, my house keys,* and *cocker spaniel.* Consequently, communication based on concrete words leaves little room for misunderstanding, and any disagreement can typically be resolved by referring to the objects themselves.

**Abstract words,** however, are symbols for ideas, qualities, and relationships. Because they represent things that cannot be experienced through the senses, their meanings depend on the experiences and intentions of the persons using them. For instance, words such as *happiness, faith, freedom,* and *justice* stand for ideas that

■ **connotation** The subjective meaning of a word; what a word suggests because of feelings or associations it evokes.

■ **concrete word** A symbol for a specific thing that can be pointed to or physically experienced.

■ **abstract word** The symbol for an idea, quality, or relationship.

## MAKING CONNECTIONS
### for Success

### What *Do* Words Mean?

The conversation between Susan and John illustrates much more than the use of abstract or concrete words. Culture, educational background, social status, age, the nature of the relationship, and gender are only a few of the factors that influence language choice and word meanings. Numerous communication scholars have discussed gender and cultural differences in the way people use language to communicate. Psychologist Deborah Tannen became a pop culture phenomenon for her books and assertions that men and women are quite different in their communication styles and language choices. Think about language choice in the following situations:

1. Identify two specific instances in which you and a person of the opposite sex had different views of language. What was the result of each?

2. What are the differences in language that you've noticed between generations? Would you talk or write to your grandmother the same way you would to your best friend? Why or why not?

3. List the characteristics of language appropriate to writing a class paper or work report. Then, list the characteristics of language appropriate for making an oral presentation in class or at work.

4. Together with your classmates, compare and contrast the two lists. What are the similarities/differences?

5. How would making a presentation to a group of high school students versus a group of retired professionals affect your language choices?

mean different things to different people. Thus the use of abstract words can easily lead to misunderstandings and result in ineffective communication, as illustrated by the following conversation:

> *Susan:* John, you said "a few minutes" half an hour ago! If we're going out to eat, we need to go!
>
> *John:* That's not what I meant. Susan, I can't go out right now. This football game is so close. I need to see how it ends.
>
> *Susan:* Fine. How long will it be?
>
> *John:* Five minutes.
>
> *Susan:* How long is five minutes in your world?

There are problems in this conversation because Susan knows that time is measurable and John's responses "a few minutes" and "five minutes" are neither measured nor accurate. The result is likely to be, at the very least, a disagreement about their plans. Susan's "fine" probably means just the opposite! John needs to tell Susan how he feels about the game and explain why it's important. He should have told her how much time was left in the game before she started getting ready to go out. John's responses were vague and the lack of specificity and clarity led to unfulfilled expectations on Susan's part. It's always a good idea to explain, define, or illustrate any abstract words that may be misunderstood in our conversations.

The "ladder of abstraction" (Figure 4.2), first described by Alfred Korzybski in 1933 and expanded on by S. I. Hayakawa in 1964,[18] is still a good way to explain concrete and abstract words and meanings. Figure 4.2 illustrates the varying degrees of concreteness among related words. *Derek* is the most tangible word because it refers

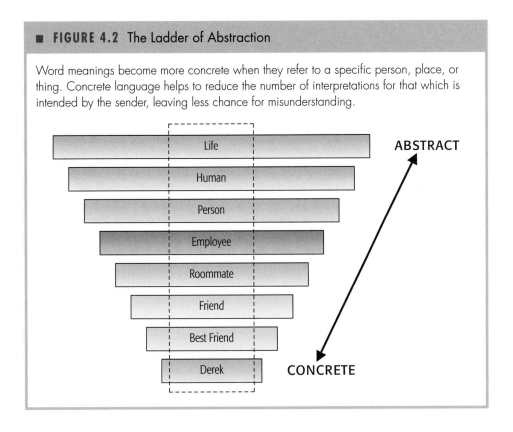

■ **FIGURE 4.2**  The Ladder of Abstraction

Word meanings become more concrete when they refer to a specific person, place, or thing. Concrete language helps to reduce the number of interpretations for that which is intended by the sender, leaving less chance for misunderstanding.

to a specific individual named Derek. You can see that as the words move from concrete to abstract, they become less specific.

**Meaning Depends on Commonalities.**   The more communicators have in common in terms of background, experience, and attitudes, the more likely they are to hold similar meanings for the words they exchange. However, competent communicators should not assume too much about how others will interpret their messages; they should continuously refine messages based on the feedback they receive. Individuals' personally held connotations can skew their interpretations of messages that are made up of words that seem straightforward and concrete. Consider the following situation:

> Deirdre and Karina are roommates. They have trouble budgeting for household expenses. Karina wants to buy the economy sizes of dish and laundry soap because they can save money over the semester. Deirdre becomes upset because she doesn't want to spend her entire budget the first week of the month. *Economy, budget,* and *careful spending* mean different things to the two, and stating those words usually causes a major conflict.

Instead of talking things through, each person goes her own way and spends the joint budget in ways she thinks best. The problem is that the roommates have never taken the time to try to understand the other's position. Their own backgrounds and experiences make a big difference in the way they choose and use language and meaning, and unless they can talk about it, they will not achieve a common understanding.

**Language Can Obscure Meanings.**   Words mean different things to different people, based on each person's experiences and the direct relationship of those experiences to particular words. For example, a medical doctor says, "Your mother has *myelodysplastic syndrome.*" You're already upset that your mother has been ill and doctors could not find out what was wrong, and now you're also confused. Because you have no frame of reference for those words, you're not even sure what questions to ask, so you likely ask for an explanation. *"Bone marrow failure"* isn't much better, but at least you have a basis for asking some questions to learn about your mother's illness. The medical team treating her all have a similar view of the seriousness of the illness. The family physician thinks about what procedures can help the patient. The oncologist is weighing the probability of which of the limited number of medications would be appropriate for your mother. You and your mother want to know if she will get well and what's involved in the treatment. The medical team realizes that approaching this discussion by talking about the *bone marrow failure* or *problems with blood cells* will make it easier for the family and patient to understand. Learning to choose more understandable words will help the family comprehend the nature of the disease as well as the treatment needed and reduce some of the frustration about lack of knowledge and information.

Also, the meanings of words, like words themselves, change from time to time and from place to place. It is easy to forget that the meaning we have for a word might not match the meaning held by others. For example, ask a person over age sixty the meanings of these words: *grass, geek, speed, pot, joint, gay, high,* or *stoned.* What words do we use now that might change in meaning over the next twenty years? We constantly add words to our language, especially technology-related words. How many new words have been added to the language because of these advances? Email, snail mail, fax, emoticons, text-messaging, IMing, wi-fi, tivo, spamming, googled, and netiquette are recent contributions.

Word meanings also vary from region to region. For example, in some regions of the United States, if you ask for pop at a store, the clerk will not understand you until you rephrase your question and ask for soda or a Coke. In Nebraska and Iowa, people get a drink of water from the drinking fountain, but in Wisconsin, people use a bubbler. Regional word use can lead to misunderstandings, and we must be sensitive to such potential differences. Also, cultures and cocultures hold differing meanings for certain words. For example, for most Americans *very dear* means something that is

Language, or jargon, used by a particular group or discipline may be too specialized or technical to be understood by the general public. In such a situation, one would need specific knowledge about the subject to understand what is being said.

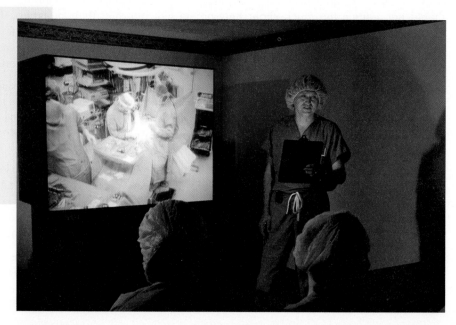

highly valued or loved, whereas in Ireland *very dear* means very expensive and has nothing to do with value or love.

Cocultures within a language community sometimes use words or phrases in ways that are unique to their group. Scientists, engineers, and health care providers use language that might be too specialized to be understood by the general public. This unique language use is referred to as **jargon.** Other cocultures, such as students, might use **slang** or words to communicate only with those who know the words, and the words and meanings change quickly. A car salesperson might use a slang term such as *flea* to identify a person looking for a bargain. Prisoners refer to a knife or to stab with a knife as *shank,* and a real estate agent might use the term *handyperson's special* to refer to a house in need of repair.[19] Professor Judi Sanders and her students in the Department of Communication at California State Polytechnic University in Pomona have a College Slang Project.[20] Since 1990, Sanders and her intercultural communication students have collected slang terms from academic institutions across the United States. Their website includes interesting information about slang terms (*da bomb* has been one of the most popular words for at least the last dozen years, and *cool* with differing meanings has been around since the 1940s). Here are some of the words from The Top 20 College Slang Project list, 2004:

*Bitch:* A very rude and mean person, usually female (20)

*Hella:* Very extremely, to a great amount (14)

*Homey/homie:* A friend or buddy (11)

*Cool:* neat, exciting, awesome (4)

*Chill/chill out:* to relax, rest, calm down (1)

Are these terms still commonly used? Have new slang words replaced them? Such words are constantly being discarded and new ones invented—sometimes just to make sure that people outside a particular group will not catch on to their meanings. All kinds of groups, including members of a given profession, college students, ethnic groups, and gangs, develop and use slang terms.[21]

Language is used to share meaning, but it also can be used to obscure, distort, or hide meaning. One way to obscure meaning is to use a euphemism. A **euphemism** is an inoffensive or mild expression given in place of one that may offend, cause embarrassment, or suggest something unpleasant. Our society also uses euphemisms to avoid taboo subjects or words that can trigger negative reactions. Employing euphemisms can defuse the emotional charge associated with controversial or difficult concepts. For example, when a person has died, we often use a euphemism such as "passed away" instead of blunter words. The phrase "passed away" seems to make a difficult, complex situation more approachable.

Euphemisms can also be used to enhance something, to make it seem a little more glamorous than it actually is. In our society, we have become so concerned with labels that we have renamed many things to give them a more positive connotation. For example, we rarely use the term *salesman* because, apart from being sexist, it also conjures up a negative image that is not exactly characterized by scrupulous business ethics. This unfavorable connotation has been fostered by the media and sometimes by personal experience. Thus referring to a person who sells merchandise as a sales associate, sales consultant, or sales representative sounds more positive. Sometimes the term *trash collector* or *garbage man* is recast as *sanitation engineer,* which makes the job seem more attractive.

Language can also be used to create deliberately ambiguous messages. William Lutz, a professor at Rutgers University, says that he can live with ordinary

■ **jargon** Language used by certain groups or specific disciplines that may be technical or too specialized to be understood by the general population.

■ **slang** Language used by groups to keep the meaning of the communication within the group. Slang words change frequently and are specific to specific regions or groups.

■ **euphemism** The use of an inoffensive or mild expression in place of one that might offend, cause embarrassment, or suggest something unpleasant.

euphemisms, but his teeth are set on edge when a worker is told he has been "dehired" because the firm is experiencing "negative employee retention." Actually, the employee has been fired in a layoff. But no one is willing to say so, laments Lutz, who wrote *Doublespeak,* a book denouncing the use of words to conceal meaning. **Doublespeak** is the deliberate misuse of language to distort meaning.

"It is going just too far," says Lutz, when the Pentagon refers to bombs that accidentally kill civilians as "incontinent ordinance" or when lawyers write off a plane crash as "the involuntary conversion of a 727." That, he says, is language "designed to distort reality and corrupt thought."[22] Lutz thinks the practice is disgraceful, dangerous to democracy, perverse, and pervasive. It's hard work, too. Doublespeak isn't just the natural work product of the bureaucratic mind; it is invented painstakingly by committees laboring to cloak meaning. Doublespeak is not a slip of the tongue or language used improperly because of ignorance. It is a tool that the powerful use to achieve their ends without clearly communicating with those who may be affected by their actions or who may foot the bill for them. According to Lutz and other scholars, doublespeak is particularly harmful when it makes something inappropriate or negative appear to be appropriate or positive.

As you can see, language and meaning are inseparable parts of communication. They mesh smoothly in successful communication. Unfortunately, a type of communication also occurs when a message is misunderstood.

## ■ Language-Based Barriers to Communication

Although it takes little physical effort to say something to someone, it does take mental effort to ensure that what we say conveys our intended meaning. Even if we create what we *think* is the perfect message, the possibility always exists that the receiver will misinterpret the message or find it ambiguous. Therefore the receiver must also make an effort to receive the intended message.

"There are over 300 different languages in everyday use in the United States. This number includes more than 200 Native American languages, the languages of the colonizers (English, French, and Spanish), languages of immigrants—both old and new—and a variety of dialects spoken in various regions of the country."[23] We must recognize that communication is a symbolic interaction rich in subtlety. It will never be strictly concrete or objective and thus always carries the potential for misunderstanding. Misunderstandings occur for numerous physical, mental, and cultural reasons. Ineffective use of language is one reason. Among the most common language-based barriers to effective communication are bypassing, indiscrimination, and polarization.[24]

### ■■ Meanings Can Be Misunderstood

What is *meant* by a speaker and what is *heard* and *understood* by the listener often differ. Such misunderstanding between a sender and a receiver is called **bypassing.** How many times have we said to someone, "But that's not what I meant"? Here is an illustration of bypassing:

> Your supervisor says, "Get the figures on how much space there is in the new office complex and give me a report as soon as you can." You find the information, make the calculations, make comparisons, identify advantages and disadvantages, and three days later take the supervisor your report. You're dismayed when you're told, "What took you so

■ **doublespeak** The deliberate misuse of language to distort meaning.

■ **bypassing** A misunderstanding that occurs between a sender and a receiver because of the symbolic nature of language.

## MAKING Technology CONNECTIONS

### Dictionary.com

Web searches on language can provide interesting information. Some sites help you understand the rules of grammar; others help you learn more about words, their usage, and their definitions. Dictionary .com is just what it says, a dictionary. When you key in a word on this site, the search engine provides the number of entries it finds and their sources so that you can compare meanings among the various online dictionaries. Try this to see what you learn.

1. Access www.dictionary.com.
2. Key in a word of your choice to see the number of entries and the different dictionaries that include your word. Try to find a word that is relatively unfamiliar to you—something someone said, or you read and didn't know. For example, when this author keyed in *syndrome,* Dictionary.com found

five entries: one from *The American Heritage Dictionary of the English Language,* 4th Edition (2000), one from *The American Heritage Stedman's Medical Dictionary* (2002), a third from *Merriam-Webster's Medical Dictionary* (2002), a fourth from WordNet 2.0, and a final one from the On-line Medical Dictionary, 1997–98 Academic Medical Publishing & CancerWEB.

3. If you can't think of a word, try one of these from this textbook: *intercultural, interpersonal, multicultural, panacea,* or *vivid.*
4. Compare the definitions—what are the similarities? The differences?
5. Compare your lists with others.
6. How can this source help you to become a more competent communicator?

long? I wanted that information two days ago. It's too late now." The supervisor never said the information was needed/wanted the next day, and you worked hard to get a polished report. Who's at fault? Was the supervisor not clear? Did you ask any questions?

Bypassing occurs in similar situations every day.

Bypassing usually results from the false belief that each word has only one meaning and that words have meaning in themselves. But a glimpse at our everyday language quickly illustrates that most words have multiple uses and meanings. If you access the Merriam-Webster's Online Dictionary and key in *house* you'll get 87 entries. Key in *bypass* and you'll find 183 entries, ranging from "trying to get around something" to "circumvent" to "a surgical treatment for coronary disease." Find a copy of the *Random House Dictionary of the English Language* and you'll find 96 definitions for the word *turn* and 60 different definitions for the word *call.* Words acquire many meanings because they change over time, are used and understood differently in various cultures and regions, and often reflect the knowledge and situation of the user. Therefore it is crucial that all of us as communicators, both senders and receivers, stay alert to the fact that words can be interpreted differently by different people.

The interpretation of words becomes even more complex when people from different cultures exchange everyday communication. The problem is magnified when someone uses common phrases that are unfamiliar to nonnative speakers of English. For example, consider this sentence: "Won't you have some tea?" The nonnative speaker of English listens to the literal meaning of the question and would answer no if he or she did in fact want tea. Because they use this wording so frequently, native English speakers forget that it contains a double negative. But a nonnative speaker might not know that, in practice, "Won't you have some tea?" and "Will you have some tea?" mean the same thing. In this situation, bypassing occurred because of cultural differences between the two speakers.[25]

## Language and Ethics in Public Life

Factoids are bits of information passed off to the unsuspecting as true, but actually having little or no basis in truth, or something that has been packaged and promoted as the truth for so long that people accept it as a fact. Politicians and marketing people have been known to say almost anything to get people to believe or accept their views or their products.

**1.** Is it ethical to say what you wish to get what you want? Do the ends justify the means?

**2.** Can we be evasive without breaking any rules or doing something wrong?

**3.** Recent U.S. presidents seem to have trouble with the truth. From Bill Clinton's statement that he did not have an affair with Ms. Lewinsky, to George W. Bush's insistence that Saddam Hussein had weapons of mass destruction he was ready to launch against us, we have had more prevarication than we need from our highest elected officials. But, they are not the only ones. With your classmates, brainstorm examples from the media of either euphemisms that go too far or double-speak that deliberately distorts.

Some speakers deliberately invite bypassing by using euphemisms or double-speak to soften or distort meanings. It is important to be aware of this. Politicians and advertisers sometimes will say one thing in order to get people to believe or accept something else. Listeners should critically examine what is being said. Both speaking and listening involve ethical considerations. Issues of conscience—what is right or wrong and what is beneficial or harmful—are everyone's responsibility.

**GUIDELINES** Reducing Bypassing[26]

**1.** *Be person-minded, not word-minded.* Think about words and their meanings, but also consider the persons using the words and the meanings they might give to them. Constantly question your own interpretation: "This is what the word means to me, but what does it mean to the others?"

**2.** *Query and paraphrase.* Ask questions and paraphrase your message or the meaning you've derived from others' messages, whenever there is a potential for misunderstanding. Differences in background, age, gender, occupation, culture, attitudes, knowledge, and perceptions may affect communication. If you are uncertain, ask others to explain. Restating a message in your own words gives you and the sender a chance to check that you received a similar message to what was sent. As the importance and complexity of a message increase, so do the need to ask questions and paraphrase.

**3.** *Be approachable.* Encourage open and free communication. The most frequent barrier to effective communication is an unwillingness to listen to others. Allow others to question and paraphrase your messages, and show respect for what they say. Being receptive is not always easy, but the effort will ensure a clear exchange of information.

**4.** *Be sensitive to contexts.* Consider the verbal and situational contexts in which communication occurs. The meaning of a word can be more precisely interpreted by considering the words, sentences, and paragraphs that precede and follow it and the setting in which communication takes place.

# ■■ Language Can Shape Our Attitudes

**Indiscrimination** is the neglect of individual differences and the overemphasis of similarities. Indiscrimination is a form of perceptual set (see Chapter 2) in which a person chooses to ignore differences and changes in events, things, and people. Language plays a significant role in our tendency to see similarities between things, even when they don't exist. Nouns that categorize people *(teenager, divorcé, student, professor, African American, southerner, liberal, friend, government official, politician, salesperson)* encourage us to focus on similarities. Statements such as "Politicians are crooks" and "Students cheat in school" may be interpreted to include all politicians and all students, instead of some politicians and some students. They fail to distinguish between individuals. Such categorization often results in stereotyping.

A stereotype, as defined in Chapter 2, is a categorizing of events, objects, and people without regard to unique individual characteristics and qualities. Stereotypes are often negative, but they may also be positive, for example, "All liberals are hardworking," "All conservatives want peace," "All teachers are dedicated professionals," "All environmentalists are concerned citizens." Whether the stereotype is negative or positive, the problem is the same: Individual qualities are ignored. Stereotyping is quick and easy to do because it does not require analysis, investigation, or thought. By precluding distinctions, stereotypes give us neat, oversimplified categories that facilitate our evaluation of people, situations, and events.

There are ways to reduce indiscrimination in our communication. **Indexing** points up differences that distinguish various members of a group and thus reduces indiscrimination. Indexing identifies the specific person, idea, event, or object to which a statement refers. When you hear someone say something that lumps people, ideas, events, or objects into a single category, such as, "All professional athletes are egotistical," "All professors are liberal," "Feminists don't care about family values," or "All politicians are corrupt," you need to immediately think and ask, "Which ones are you talking about?" Everyone is unique. None of us is all one thing or another and none of us is exactly like anyone else. Even though the media play up politicians who were greedy, or sold their votes or were otherwise influenced by Jack Abramoff or other lobbyists, each politician is different. The same is true of professional athletes, professors, and feminists. They may belong to a class or group with an identity and whose members have similarities, but the group is composed of unique individuals.

**Dating,** another technique for reducing indiscrimination, is a form of indexing that sorts people, ideas, events, and objects according to time. By telling when something occurred, we acknowledge that things change over time and add specificity to a statement. As an example of how important dating is, indicate the year in which you think each of the following news bulletins was probably made:

### Pope Condemns Use of New "Horror" Weapons

Vatican City—Prompted by widespread fears that new weapons of mass destruction might wipe out Western civilization, the Pope today issued a bulletin forbidding the use of these weapons by any Christian state against another, whatever the provocation.

### Moral Rot Endangers Land, Warns General

Boston—The head of the country's armed forces declared here today that if he had known the depth of America's moral decay, he would never have accepted his command. "Such a dearth of public spirit," he asserted, "and want of virtue, and fertility in all the low arts to obtain advantages of one kind or another, I never saw before and hope I may never be witness to again."[27]

■ **indiscrimination** The neglect of individual differences and overemphasis of similarities.

■ **indexing** A technique to reduce indiscrimination by identifying the specific persons, ideas, events, or objects a statement refers to.

■ **dating** A form of indexing that sorts people, events, ideas, and objects according to time.

The thoughts expressed in these two paragraphs could easily apply to what is happening today, but, in fact, the first paragraph pertains to a statement made by Pope Innocent II in 1139, and the second is a comment made by George Washington in 1775.

Did you think that these news bulletins referred to recent events? If so, you fell victim to indiscrimination. Why do such errors occur? How can we avoid or prevent them? The contexts of the statements in these news bulletins could be greatly clarified merely by adding dates: Vatican City, 1139, and Boston, 1775. Dating gives listeners valuable information that can increase their understanding of the intended message.

■ **polarization** The tendency to view things in terms of extremes.

■ **pendulum effect** Escalating conflict between two individuals or groups that results from their use of polar terms to describe and defend their perceptions of reality.

## ■■ Language Can Cause Polarization

**Polarization** is the tendency to view things in terms of extremes—rich or poor, beautiful or ugly, large or small, high or low, good or bad, intelligent or stupid—even though most things exist somewhere in between. This either–or, black-or-white way of thinking is aggravated by aspects of language.

Polarization can be destructive, escalating conflict to the point at which two parties simply cannot communicate. This escalation is referred to as the **pendulum effect.** The pendulum represents a person's perception of reality, which includes feelings, attitudes, opinions, and value judgments about the world. When the pendulum is hanging in the center, a person's perception is considered to be realistic, virtuous, intelligent, sane, honest, and honorable. Of course, most of us believe that our pendulums are at or near the center most of the time. When two individuals disagree in their perceptions of reality, their pendulums begin to move in opposite directions. The distance the pendulum swings represents their differences in opinion or conviction. As the conversation intensifies, each remark provokes a stronger reaction from the party to whom it is directed until both parties are driven to positions at opposite extremes. For example, when two roommates argue over whose turn it is to clean, one might begin by saying, "It's your turn. I did it the last time." The other is likely to respond, "No, I did it the last time. Now it's your turn." If the disagreement continues and no solution is found, both will become more entrenched in their positions, and their comments may turn into personal attacks: "You're always so messy and lazy." "And you're always so picky and critical." The situation can degenerate to the point at which one or the other threatens to move out. Such an extreme outcome is typical of a discussion driven by the pendulum effect. Emotions can eventually run so high that the differences between the parties seem insurmountable and a mutually agreeable settlement seems unattainable.

Speakers can avoid the dangers of polarization by recognizing the potential for misunderstanding and by making statements that do not represent unnuanced extremes. For example, a noncontroversial statement such as "Nebraska is hot in the summer" is not as meaningful as it could be because the word *hot* represents a generalized extreme. Further information will prevent misunderstanding: What is the basis of comparison (Florida or Minnesota)? Are Nebraska summers all the same, or do they vary from year to year? Is a Nebraska summer the same in all parts of the state, or does it vary from north to south? What is the average summer temperature? The problem of making an incorrectly

Polarization is the tendency to view things in terms of extremes—rich or poor, beautiful or ugly, large or small, high or low, good or bad, intelligent or stupid—even though most things exist somewhere in between. This either–or, black-or-white way of thinking is aggravated by aspects of language.

## MAKING Technology CONNECTIONS

### Grumpy Martha's Guide to Grammar and Usage

Want to learn more about language and grammar and how to use the correct word at the appropriate time and in the appropriate manner? Check out Grumpy Martha's Guide to Grammar and Usage on the Web at www.encarta.msn.com.

Here's a brief look at what she says:

*You may think, "Grammar, schmammar. Usage, schmusage," but when you use words incorrectly, you sound as funny as someone wearing underwear for a hat looks.*

*I'd like to spare you from this fate. You can sound smarter in just ten minutes with "Grumpy Martha's Guide to Grammar and Usage." This list isn't comprehensive, but it covers most of the frequent mistakes I hear. Plus, I give you a fat list of*

*links you can use to get more information and have a little more fun.*

1. Go to Grumpy Martha's website.
2. Check the explanations for "my, myself, and I."
3. Create a correct sentence for each term.
4. Then check "Be effective, not affected."
5. Create a sentence using each word correctly.
6. Check the remainder of Grumpy Martha's website for suggestions about correct grammar and usage.
7. Click on the Dictionary link on Grumpy Martha's web page, and look for the definitions of the word *language*. What is the core meaning of the word? From where does the word come?
8. How does this exercise connect to the content of this chapter?

overgeneralized and extreme statement is avoided here: "Nebraska summers can be hot. The average temperature is 85 degrees Fahrenheit, with lows around 74 degrees and highs around 105 degrees." Such clarification is especially important when the topic at hand is likely to provoke emotional, defensive, or unpredictable reactions.

## Language Can Be Sexist

There is a difference in how men and women may use language and converse with one another (as indicated in Chapter 3). Psychologist Deborah Tannen, for example, suggests that men tend to use language to assert status, whereas women use language to establish and maintain social relationships.[28] Tannen says that, rather than using language to dominate another, women tend to employ it to establish closeness and support. Men, by contrast, use language to dominate or compete. The result, according to Tannen, is that the game of communication for men and women is the same, but the rules are different. When men and women communicate with each other, there is the potential for clash and conflict because of different language use. The problem is magnified when sexist language is used either consciously or unconsciously. Our goal should be to use **gender-inclusive language**—language that does not discriminate against males or females.

Unfortunately, the English language is structured with an inherent bias in favor of men. There are, for example, no singular gender-neutral pronouns in the English language. Therefore, traditionally, the masculine pronouns *(he, him, his)* have been used to refer to people in general, even if the referent could be a male or female. Use of the masculine pronoun is not incorrect grammatically, but its use in generic situations is a social issue. Language sets expectations that at times discriminate against and stereotype people. According to traditional usage, the omnipresence of *he* and *him* and the general absence of *she* and *her* subtly but powerfully give the impression that men hold important roles but women do not. Thus our language creates the expectation that

■ **gender-inclusive language** Language that does not discriminate against males or females.

males are active and have important roles, whereas females are inactive and do not hold important roles. Furthermore, sexist language can be misleading. When a speaker constantly uses only female or only male pronouns such as "she can expect this," or "it is in his best interests," members of the excluded will believe the message has little or no relevance to them. When that happens, about 50 percent of the listeners may not pay attention to information that could be vitally important to them. If it's a medical situation, those who feel that it doesn't affect them might not heed the precautions and expose themselves to greater danger because "it doesn't apply."

Sexual stereotypes and the assumption that one gender is superior characterize **sexist language.**[29] In our society sexist language involves an attitude as much as the use of specific words. Words with a positive connotation are often used to describe males—*independent, logical, strong, confident, aggressive;* females are often associated with words having negative connotations—*dependent, illogical, weak, gullible, timid.* Sexist language suggests that one gender is more important than and superior to the other. Language that is used to discriminate can be quite subtle. Consider these statements: "She is president of the company, and she's a woman"; "Wanda got that position because she's a woman." They describe women who have risen to high authority positions, but they also imply that women do not typically hold these positions or that the only reason Wanda got the position was because she's a woman. In other words, they imply that women are less qualified than men.

Stereotypes do not occur in a social vacuum. On the contrary, they often exert powerful influence on the lives of those who are stereotyped. Gender stereotypes influence perceptions and behaviors of both men and women. Stereotypes of women affect both how they are treated in society and how they think of themselves. Language is one significant means of perpetuating these stereotypes. Avoiding sexist language and substituting gender-inclusive terms represent a positive step toward doing away with them.

Other stereotypes are reinforced in the use of homophobic language. When someone asks another to "tell me what to look for so I can recognize gays or lesbians and then avoid them," the speaker is demonstrating both insensitivity to individuals and a general negative categorization of a group of people, each of whom is unique.

Metaphors used in our culture to describe men and women are often sexist. A **metaphor** is a figure of speech that associates two things or ideas, not commonly linked, as a means of description. These stereotypical animal metaphors illustrate the use of sexist language: Men are likely to be described as aggressive *(wolf, tomcat, stud)* and women as harmless pets *(kitten, lamb, chick)* or as unattractive barnyard animals *(cow, pig, dog).* The effective communicator must avoid such negative metaphorical stereotyping, find more positive metaphors related to women, and use inclusive language in general.

■ **sexist language** Language that creates sexual stereotypes or implies that one gender is superior to another.

■ **metaphor** A figure of speech in which a word or phrase relates one object or idea to another object or idea that are not commonly linked together.

## GUIDELINES   Using Gender-Inclusive Language

1. Commit yourself to removing sexism from your communication.
2. Practice and reinforce nonsexist communication patterns until they become habitual. The ultimate goals are to use nonsexist language effortlessly in private conversation and to think in nonsexist terms.
3. Use familiar language whenever possible, but if you must choose between sexist language and an unfamiliar phrase, choose the unfamiliar phrase and practice it until it becomes familiar.

4. Do not arouse negative reactions in receivers by using awkward, cumbersome, highly repetitious, or unnecessary words. There are so many graceful and controlled ways to state your message inclusively that you need not use bland or offensive constructions.
5. Ascertain whether roots and meanings of words need to be changed before doing so.
6. Check every outgoing message—written, oral, nonverbal, and email—for sexism before sending it.[30]

It is important that the language we use be inclusive and not demeaning to any group of individuals. Language influences how we see others around us. Inappropriate language causes perceptual and social problems that should not be tolerated in our society.

## ■■ Culture Affects Language Use

Just as there are gender differences, there are also cultural differences in the ways people use language. As we saw in Making Everyday Connections, Nermin found that many words were confusing to him. Each language has its own grammatical rules, and some seem very strange to new speakers of a language. Anthropologist Edward T. Hall asserted that "all people are captives of the language they speak."[31] Intercultural communication scholars use the **Sapir-Whorf hypothesis** to help explain the connection of culture and language. This hypothesis suggests that language helps us think, and that culture and language are bound together. According to communication scholar Sarah Trenholm, this hypothesis involves two theories: **linguistic determinism** (the theory that language determines thought) and **linguistic relativity** (the theory that people from different language communities perceive the world differently).[32] In other words, language influences thought and thought influences language, and each are influenced by culture. Nermin had trouble with English because he first learned the British version and then came to the United States where he encountered a different form of English. The multiple meanings of words and the use of slang that may or may not sound like dictionary words are confusing. Add to that mixture a different culture and a different set of language rules as well as numerous new experiences, and it's easy to see why nonnative speakers of U.S. English have concerns about their language use. Together these two theories suggest that culture helps create variations in communication. In other words, according to the Sapir-Whorf hypothesis, language is more than simply attaching labels to the world around us. Language shapes our reality. We "know" the world only in terms of the language we have at our command, and that language determines our cultural reality. If we don't have the words to explain something, we don't really know it, and it doesn't exist. When we can use words to explain the concept, event, or idea, it takes on meaning that can be shared. Judith Martin and Thomas Nakayama suggest that the relationship between communication and culture can be viewed in three complementary ways: (1) Culture influences communication, (2) culture is enacted through communication, and (3) communication is a way of contesting and resisting the dominant culture.[33]

Further, anthropologist Edward T. Hall suggests that for some cultures the situation in which a particular communication occurs tells us a great deal about its meaning.[34] In a **high-context culture** the meaning of the communication act is inferred

■ **Sapir-Whorf hypothesis** An explanation of how thought influences our reality and how our thought process is influenced by our language.

■ **linguistic determinism** The theory that language determines thought.

■ **linguistic relativity** The theory that suggests that people from different language communities perceive the world differently.

■ **high-context culture** A culture in which the meaning of the communication act is inferred from the situation or location.

## Understanding the Difference between High- and Low-Context Cultures

Aleta is from China (a high-context culture). Her neighbor, Jennifer, is from the United States (a low-context culture). Jennifer's daughter is learning to play the piano and practices early in the morning, after school, and in the evening before bedtime.

One night at 9 P.M., Aleta knocked on Jennifer's door and said, "You must be so proud of your daughter. She practices the piano so much. You must plan to have her become a concert pianist."

"Why, no." Jennifer responded, "She's just beginning to play the piano."

"You must be proud that she practices early in the morning, after school, and into the night. She is certainly a dedicated student. She plays the piano so many hours." With that, Aleta turned around and went into her own apartment.

1. What is the difference between the language use in high- and low-context cultures?
2. What was the real message here?
3. Did Jennifer get the message?
4. If the neighbor had been another person from the United States, what do you suppose would have been said?

from the situation or location. In Japan (a high-context culture), for example, businesspeople do not conduct business in a social setting, although they might refer to their business interests. If one visits Japan on business and is invited out to dinner, there is no hidden agenda—the objective for the evening is to eat a meal together, not to conduct business. Business is saved for the office or the meeting place. Also, in a high-context culture, language is indirect, nonspecific, and not very assertive. In a **low-context culture** the meaning of the communication act is inferred from the messages being sent and not the location where the communication occurs. According to Hall, the United States is a low-context culture in which businesspeople are as likely to conduct business on the golf course, in a restaurant, or at a reception as they are in the workplace. People in a low-context culture typically are more assertive and more direct. They get immediately to the point. Because understanding such distinctions is essential to sending and receiving messages successfully, the competent communicator will learn as much about language and cultural differences as possible.

You should also be aware that there are cultures that have greater or lesser expectations for an individual's involvement in communication events. Students in Japan, Korea, China, Finland, and Thailand, for example, are expected to listen to their professors and not ask questions during class unless the professor gives them permission to become involved. These cultures seem to prefer low involvement on the part of the students. In Russia and the United States, however, students are expected to have high involvement in the learning process and are encouraged to ask questions and otherwise participate.

Media communication scholar Neil Postman once wrote that use of technology creates "a bargain with the devil." In *Technopoly*, he says that technology redefines culture through its control over and elevation of information and claims that for every good thing technology provides, it also gives us negatives or disadvantages. Postman is concerned that technology will take over the world, and remove too many of the face-to-face interactions that make us interacting social beings.[35] Given the rapid growth of technology, it is likely that some changes will occur simply because

■ **low-context culture** A culture in which the meaning of the communication act is inferred from the messages being sent and not the location where the communication occurs.

of the technological advances. Language, however, will still influence thought, and Martin and Nakayama's third point (communication is a way of contesting and resisting the dominant culture) might well be more needed than ever before.

# ■ How to Use Language Effectively

People of all ages, cultures, and educational levels use language every day. Nevertheless, the ability to use language efficiently and effectively requires years of practice and study. Although many variables influence the effectiveness of language use, five aspects of language merit special attention. They are accuracy, vividness, immediacy, appropriateness, and metaphor.

## ■■ Use Accurate Language

Using accurate language is as critical to a speaker as giving accurate navigational directions is to an air traffic controller. Choosing a wrong word can distort your intended message, misguide your receiver, and undermine your credibility. When you speak, your goal should be precision. Don't leave room for misinterpretation. You should constantly ask yourself, "What do I want to say?" and "What do I mean?" When necessary, consult a dictionary to be sure you have chosen the correct word to express your message.

The more words you can use accurately, the more likely it is that you will find the one you need to make your meaning clear. You must expand your vocabulary. Two of the best ways to do this are through listening to others and reading. Pay attention to words that you don't understand. Whenever you come across an unfamiliar word, determine the context in which it is used, and consult a dictionary to find its meaning. Once you have learned a new word, try to put it to use. Words that are not used are typically forgotten. Expanding your vocabulary takes effort and time, but with practice, it can become part of your daily routine.

## MAKING CONNECTIONS for Success

### Using Language Effectively

Compare the following two messages. The first was made by President Franklin D. Roosevelt. The second expresses a similar thought, though in a different way.

*I see one-third of a nation ill-housed, ill-clad, ill-nourished.*

*It is evident that a substantial number of persons within the continental boundaries of the United States have inadequate financial resources with which to purchase the products of agricultural communities and industrial establishments. It would appear that, for a considerable segment of the population, perhaps as much as 33.333 percent of the total, there are inadequate housing facilities, and an equally significant proportion is deprived of the proper types of clothing and nourishment.*

1. How would you describe the word choice in each message?
2. How does each message affect your emotions?
3. What impression do you have of each speaker?

One word of warning: As you develop your vocabulary, avoid the temptation to use long or little-known words when short or common words serve the purpose. Also be sure you know the shades of meaning and connotations of new words before you use them, and remember that words may have different meanings for different people.

Sometimes a message is unclear because it was not structured effectively. Poor sentence structure and word usage can wreak havoc on a statement's clarity. For example, classified ads in newspapers frequently are so condensed that their intended meaning becomes distorted or obscured. The result might be "1999 Cadillac hearse for sale—body in good condition" and "Wanted to rent—four-room apartment by careful couple; no children." Obviously, these advertisers knew what they intended to communicate, but their failure to phrase their messages accurately interfered with conveying their intended meaning.

When conversing, we can easily clear up misunderstandings caused by scrambled sentence structure or poor word choice. But to do so, we must first be aware of listeners' reactions to what we are saying. If they appear confused or ask a question, we should rephrase the message more clearly.

Effective speakers do not assume that what is clear to them will necessarily be clear to listeners. They are especially aware of this potential problem in situations such as public speeches, during which listeners might not be able to ask questions. To ensure comprehension, such speakers strive to make their meaning clear by, among other things, using familiar and concrete rather than abstract language and by being aware of the connotations associated with particular words.

## ▬▬ Use Vivid Language

■ **vividness** Active, direct, and fresh language that brings a sense of excitement, urgency, and forcefulness to a message.

To communicate effectively, make your message animated and interesting. Direct, fresh language given in the active voice can bring a sense of excitement, urgency, and forcefulness to what you say. Such **vividness** tells your audience that they had better listen because what you have to say is important.

For example, suppose an organization is trying to raise money for homeless people. It could take one of two approaches in seeking a donation from you: (1) present

To narrate this ceremony in a Vietnamese temple, the language should vividly and animatedly highlight the event, what people are wearing, the background ornamentation, and so forth. People tend to listen more completely when language is alive and remember more accurately when they are able to recall mental images.

## MAKING Technology CONNECTIONS

### Technology and Language Use

The language we use is important in initiating web searches. The way you use words to search and the specific search engine you use will affect the results of your search. You need to know whether to ask a question (such as on www.ask.com), put quotation marks around each separate word, or put *and, or,* or other joining words with the concepts for which you're searching. Here are some general guidelines to help you quickly find the information you are seeking.

1. When you use AltaVista (www.altavista.com), use quotation marks to separate words in the topic. This search engine considers each word independently unless you identify a group of words as a phrase within quotation marks. If you're looking for information on *lesson plans for health and nutrition,* you should enter the words as follows: + health + "lesson plans" + nutrition (or + nutri*, which tells the search engine that you will accept any form of the word that begins with the five letters *nutri*).

2. When you use Yahoo! (www.yahoo.com), you should set your options before you begin the search. The Yahoo! search engine gives you the option of restricting how far into the past you wish to search. To use this option you must make a selection from a drop-down menu from three years to one day. You can tell Yahoo! to handle the text you type into the search entry form as a group of single words or as a phrase. This is accomplished by using *or* or *and* as your connecting words.

3. If you use Google (www.google.com), type in a few descriptive words and hit the enter key (or click on the Google Search button for a list of relevant web pages). Google only returns web pages that contain all the words in your query. You should, therefore, refine or narrow your search. You can do this by adding more words to the search items you have already entered. Choose your key words carefully in order to get better results.

4. You can save yourself a great deal of time by checking the specific search engine to learn how to use words most effectively to search the Web.

5. If one word or term does not provide results, think of synonyms, key in those words, and search again. There is much information on the Web. You must choose your words carefully to get the most from your search.

statistics to illustrate the number of people who are believed to be homeless in our society or (2) present cases of actual individuals who are homeless, including children and their families. The first approach is rational, informative, abstract, and emotionally distant. The second approach is emotional, urgent, concrete, and forceful. The vividness of the second approach is likely at least to get your attention and perhaps influence you to contribute.

According to social psychologists, vivid language affects us in several ways. It is more persuasive than a flat, pallid presentation of information, because it is more memorable and has an emotional impact. Vivid messages are more likely to create readily retained and recalled mental images. Finally, people tend to listen more attentively to vivid messages than to uninspiring or uninteresting messages.[36]

Effective communicators use vivid language in all their interactions, whether it's one-to-one with friends or family, in small groups, or in the public arena. Use interesting words, try to include active verbs, and provide variety in the length of your sentences. Whenever possible, avoid clichés, and use slang appropriately, and with the appropriate audience. You are more likely to keep your listeners interested in what you have to say if you use fresh language to present your ideas in new and exciting ways.

## Use Immediate Language

**Verbal immediacy** identifies and projects the speaker's feelings and makes the message more relevant to the listener. Verbal immediacy draws listeners in and involves them in the subject at hand. The following statements illustrate different levels of verbal immediacy. The first sentence displays a high immediacy level, and the last displays a low immediacy level:

1. We will have a great time at the baseball game.
2. You and I will enjoy the baseball game.
3. I think you and I may enjoy baseball.
4. People often enjoy baseball games.

The first statement is directly related to the speaker, the listener, and the situation. It is assertive, and the speaker makes a connection with the listener by using the word *we*. In each successive statement, the speaker decreases the intensity of this association with the listener and the event. The language becomes less immediate, more distant in tone.

Verbal immediacy also makes the speaker appear relaxed, confident, competent, and effective. Also, receivers tend to view messages characterized by immediacy as similar to their own beliefs more readily than those cast in language unrelated to the speaker, topic, or receiver.[37]

## Use Appropriate Language

Each time you speak, your listeners have specific expectations about the kind of language you will use. Different kinds of language are appropriate to different situations. For example, the language you would use in addressing the president of your college or university would be much more formal than the language you would use when chatting with friends. You would be unlikely to call the president by a nickname, and you would be equally unlikely to call a friend Dr. or Mr. or Ms., except in jest.

Using language that is inappropriate for a given situation damages your credibility, and your message might be misinterpreted or disregarded. It is therefore crucial to assess each speaking situation and adjust your language accordingly. In public situations, profanity, improper grammar, and slang are always inappropriate.

## Use Metaphorical Language

According to some language scholars, our way of looking at the world around us is fundamentally metaphorical. Metaphors help us to structure what we think, how we perceive things, and what we do. Metaphorical language pervades our everyday language and our thoughts. A metaphor is a figure of speech in which a word or phrase relates one object or idea to another that is not commonly linked to it. A successful metaphor makes an object or idea more clear and vivid. Anna Levina used the following examples of metaphorical language in a presentation about her thesis:

> Twenty years ago, Postville, Iowa was the epitome of the "melting pot" of United States culture. Postville, located in Northeast Iowa, was for nearly 150 years an all-white, all-Christian farming community of 1000 residents, mostly of German and Norwegian ances-

■ **verbal immediacy**
Identifies and projects the speaker's feelings and makes the message more relevant to the listener.

## MAKING CONNECTIONS for Success

### Making Meaning with Metaphorical Language

Suzanne McCorkle, a communication scholar at Boise State University, has used metaphors to examine managing interpersonal conflict and to teach critical thinking and the ethical implications of language use.* She asks students to think about metaphorical language as a tool. In this activity, think about common terms and find new ways to explain them using metaphorical language. Complete the following:

1. College is . . . (fill in your metaphor) because . . . (give an explanation).
2. Communication is like the game of . . . because. . . .
3. Discuss your metaphorical choices with your classmates, family members, or friends.

4. Defend your choices.
5. What other metaphors or analogies might you have chosen?
6. Why did you choose these instead of the other ones?
7. Listen for others' use of analogies and metaphors. Write them down and bring them to class with you so that the whole group can discuss metaphorical ways of looking at things.

*S. M. McCorkle, "Metaphor in the Classroom: A Patchwork of Inconsistency," *Speech Communication Teacher* (Annandale, Va.: National Communication Association, summer 1999), 9–10.

try. Stephanie Simon, Los Angeles *Times,* 1999, described "the used-to-be" Postville as an "everyone-knows, live-and-die-here kind of town run by farmers of German and Norwegian stock."

In 1987 a Russian-born Jew, Aaron Rubashkin, a butcher from Brooklyn and a member of the ultra-orthodox Lubavitcher sect, bought a bankrupt slaughterhouse. He converted it to a kosher meat-packing plant and created new jobs. Three dozen rabbis and their families came to Postville. The plant brought jobs filled by people from Mexico, Guatemala, the Ukraine, Nigeria, Bosnia, the Czech Republic, Russia, and other places. Postville today is home to 20 different ethnicities. The packing plant is now the largest kosher plant in the world and Postville's population has increased by more than 54%.

Postville is no longer a melting pot. It is a tossed salad. The cultures have not melted together. Each new culture is unique, distinct, and retains its own traditions, dress, religious customs, and behaviors. And, the people seemingly get along quite well in this new milieu. When you visit the kosher deli, *Jacob's Table,* your eyes will be drawn to the row of brightly colored flags representing the native lands of Postville's residents. And, there's an array of wall clocks showing the time in places from Istanbul to Los Angeles. The "tossed salad" metaphor best describes this small town that has become a microcosm of the global society in which we live.[38]

Metaphorical language is culture bound, and most metaphors have meaning only within a specific language community. If your receivers cannot identify with a particular metaphor you use, it will be meaningless to them. Also, as we pointed out earlier in the chapter, avoid metaphors that negatively or unfairly categorize a specific person or group of people.

As a student, you probably can think of many metaphors that describe your college experiences. For example, some students have said that college life is like a rollercoaster ride. There are many ups and downs, as well as turns. What are some other metaphors that vividly express your college experience?

# Summary

Learning how to use language is important for effective communication in any situation. The ability to use language determines our success, makes communication personal, and allows us to translate our thoughts, feelings, and experiences into messages.

The misuse of language is more than simply a matter of misusing words; it also affects our ability to think. According to most scholars, thought and language are inseparable. When we cannot find the words to express a thought, perhaps our thinking is not clear. If our thoughts are not expressed clearly and accurately, misunderstanding is inevitable.

The elements of language help us to fashion our messages so that most people will be able to understand our meanings. Thus the ability to carefully choose the elements of language to construct and share messages effectively and efficiently helps us to become competent communicators.

The goal of communication is to exchange meanings. If language did not convey meaning, it would serve little or no purpose. We tend to associate specific words with specific meanings and to take that relationship for granted, but in reality, words have been arbitrarily paired with meanings. Words are not actual objects or ideas but symbols that represent objects or ideas. Meanings, therefore, are not in words but in people. As such, language can obscure, distort, or hide meaning and create barriers. The competent communicator will find ways to understand and be understood.

Language, culture, and thought are bound together. Effective communicators are aware of how to interact with people from other cultures. Competent communicators avoid unfamiliar words, seek to be sensitive toward another's culture and command of the language, and exercise patient effort to create and share understanding. The words and manner of speaking we choose to use can make our ideas clearer and more meaningful. Effective use of language requires practice and study.

# Discussion Starters

1. Provide two personal examples of the power of language.
2. How are language and thought related?
3. Why are language, communication, talk, and speech defined separately and not considered synonymous?
4. We say that language has rules, but we also say that language is arbitrary. Is that a contradiction in terms?
5. Why should we recognize and defend against the use of inappropriate language?
6. Why is "meanings are in people" an important concept?
7. Which of the language barriers discussed in this chapter is most likely to occur in your interactions?
8. How do indexing and dating affect communication efforts?
9. What words are common in your conversations that are the result of advances in technology?
10. How does language help us connect with others?

# Notes

1. Educational Testing Service Study on College Enrollment. Reported in *The Chronicle of Higher Education*, May 26, 2000: A35–A37.

2. L. A. Samovar and R. E. Porter, *Communication between Cultures*, 6th ed. (Belmont, CA: Wadsworth/ Thomson Learning, 2007), 2.

3. *The Chronicle of Higher Education,* September 8, 2000.

4. American Heritage Dictionaries, *100 Words Every High School Graduate Should Know.* (Boston: Houghton Mifflin, 2003), iii.

5. Samovar and Porter, 2007, op. cit. p. 151.

6. Helpful African Proverbs, compiled by Kane Mathis. www.kairarecords.com/kane/proverbs.htm. Last accessed June 29, 2006.

7. P. Le Rousic, *The Name Book* (Fairfield, IA: Sunstar, 1994).

8. V. De Francisco, personal conversations, March 24, 2003, and June 3, 2003. De Francisco writes about feminist perspectives on communication and wrote an article on the concept of naming.

9. A. Taylor, CRTNET postings, National Communication Association email list, June 3 and June 4, 2003.

10. Chuck D., cofounder of rap group Public Enemy, Hearst Lecture Series speech, University of Northern Iowa, January 2003.

11. "Country Music Fans Boo Dixie Chicks at Awards," *Waterloo/Cedar Falls Courier,* May 22, 2003, p. A10.

12. C. Kramerae, *Women and Men Speaking* (Rowley, MA: Newbury, 1981).

13. M. Houston, "Multiple Perspectives: African American Women Conceive Their Talk," *Women and Language* 23 (2002): 11–23.

14. K. Tracy, *Everyday Talk: Building and Reflecting Identities* (New York: Guilford Press, 2002), viii.

15. Ibid., pp. 8–9.

16. G. A. Miller, *The Psychology of Communication* (Baltimore: Penguin, 1967).

17. L. Carroll, *Alice's Adventures in Wonderland, Through the Looking Glass, and The Hunting of the Smark* (New York: Modern Library, 1925), 246–47.

18. A. Korzybski, *Science and Sanity: An Introduction to Non-Aristotelian Systems and General Semantics* (Lancaster, Pa.: Science Press Printing, 1933).

19. P. Dickson, *Slang!* (New York: Pocket Books, 1990).

20. J. Sanders, "College Slang Page," from the College Slang Research Project, Department of Communication, California State Polytechnic University, Pomona, www.csupomona.edu/~jasanders/slang. Professor Sanders may be contacted at jasanders@csupomona.edu (last retrieved May 13, 2006).

21. P. Dickson, *Slang!* (New York: Pocket Books, 1990).

22. W. Lutz, *Doublespeak: From "Revenue Enhancement" to "Terminal Living": How Government, Business, Advertisers, and Others Use Language to Deceive You.* (New York: Harper & Row, 1987), 3–4.

23. K. Cushner, A. McClelland, and P. Safford, *Human Diversity in Education: An Integrative Approach,* 3rd ed. (New York: McGraw-Hill, 2006), 159.

24. Adapted from W. V. Haney, *Communication and Organizational Behavior,* 3rd ed. (Homewood, IL: Irwin, 1973), 211–330; and *Communication and Interpersonal Relations,* 5th ed. (Homewood, IL: Irwin, 1986), 213–405.

25. L. M. Barna, "Stumbling Blocks in Intercultural Communication," in *Intercultural Communication: A Reader,* 7th ed., eds. L. A. Samovar and R. E. Porter (Belmont, CA: Wadsworth Publishing, 1994), 340.

26. Adapted from Haney, 232–33.

27. News bulletins from W. R. Espy, "Say When," *This Week,* 13 July 1952, quoted in W. V. Haney, *Communication and Organizational Behavior,* 396.

28. D. Tannen, *You Just Don't Understand* (New York: Morrow, 1990).

29. C. Miller and K. Swift, *The Handbook on Nonsexist Writing,* 2nd ed. (New York: Harper & Row, 1988).

30. Adapted from B. D. Sorrels, *Nonsexist Communicator: Solving the Problem of Gender and Awkwardness in Modern English* (Englewood Cliffs, NJ: Prentice-Hall, 1983), 17.

31. E. T. Hall, *The Hidden Dimension* (Garden City, NY: Doubleday, 1966).

32. S. Trenholm, *Thinking through Communication* (Boston: Allyn and Bacon, 2000), 87.

33. J. N. Martin and T. K. Nakayama, *Intercultural Communication in Contexts* (Mountain View, CA: Mayfield Publishing Co., 1997), 59.

34. Hall, 1966, op. cit.

35. N. Postman, *Technopoly* (New York: Alfred A. Knopf, 1992), 4.

36. S. T. Fiske and S. E. Taylor, *Social Cognition* (Reading, MA: Addison-Wesley, 1984), 190–94.

37. J. J. Bradac, J. W. Bowers, and J. A. Courtright, "Three Language Variables in Communication Research: Intensity, Immediacy, and Diversity," *Human Communication Research* 5 (1979): 257–69.

38. Adapted from remarks made in an oral defense of an unpublished thesis by Anna Levina, entitled, "Recent Jewish Immigrants' Communication in Postville, Iowa: A Case Study," University of Northern Iowa, June 3, 2003.

# CHAPTER 5

# Connecting through Nonverbal Communication

"There is no such thing as an empty space or an empty time. There is always something to see, something to hear. In fact, try as we may to make a silence, we cannot."

—JOHN CAGE

# This chapter will help you:

- **Explain** what nonverbal communication is.

- **Tell** why six key characteristics of nonverbal communication are crucial to using and interpreting it.

- **Know** the five common functions of nonverbal communication.

- **Describe** different types of nonverbal communication and their connection to cultural and gender uses.

- **Explain** why nonverbal communication is difficult to interpret and understand.

- **Improve** your interpretation of, and be a more competent user of, nonverbal communication.

## Making everyday connections

"Hi, did you see the game last night? I'm done—it's your turn to speak."

"No, but I did go to a movie with Lee. Your turn—I am done."

"Thanks, the game was really great. Dana was really hot. She must have made . . ."

"Do you mind? I'd like to say something."

"Okay. You want to talk about the movie some more—sure, go ahead."

"Yes I do, I rented *Crash* on DVD last night because I didn't see it when it first came out."

"Hey, can I say something?"

"Sure go ahead."

"You are first seeing *Crash* now? You can answer the question now."

"Okay, Yes. Did you want to say anything else?"

"Yes I do! It was out several years ago and you missed it? Okay, go ahead now and tell me about the movie."

"Thank you. I will continue about the movie. I saw it last night because my communication teacher recommended it to the class as an example of how perceptions influence our communication with others who are different from us. Did you want to say something before I go on?"

"No. Really, go ahead tell me more about what you thought about the movie."

Unusual conversation you say, but is it? ■

**Questions to think about**

- What would communication be like without unspoken cues?

- How does nonverbal communication make communication easier? More difficult?

- Why do you think we give little thought to our nonverbal communication and its role in our everyday communication?

- Which is more believable, our nonverbal or verbal communication?

- What role does nonverbal communication play in connecting or hooking up with others?

- Explain what nonverbal communication includes and what it does not.

# ■ What Is Nonverbal Communication?

**Nonverbal communication** includes all behaviors, attributes, or objects (except words) that communicate messages that have social meaning. Nonverbal communication includes tone of voice, facial expressions, posture, gestures, and appearance, all of which are used to communicate messages. Nonverbal communication supplements words, such as when tone of voice, volume, or facial expression adds emphasis to the meaning of a word. Unfortunately, nonverbal communication can also change the intended meaning of a message or make it confusing and unclear. Nonverbal communication can be intentional or unintentional, serving a variety of functions. Nonverbal communication does not, however, include gestures that represent words, such as American Sign Language (ASL), written words, or words transmitted electronically. To hearing persons, sign language is often seen as nonverbal communication. However, to persons who are hearing impaired, sign language is mostly verbal because the signs, body language, and facial expressions are signals for words, phrases, and emphasis.

The inclusion of nonverbal behavior in the study of communication is relatively recent. We tend to take nonverbal communication for granted because it is so basic, but its importance is unmistakable, and its connection to communication is undeniable. Research indicates that in most situations, we spend more of our time communicating nonverbally than verbally and that our nonverbal messages carry more meaning than our verbal messages.

A review of nonverbal research by Mark Knapp and Judith Hall concluded that some people depend more heavily on verbal messages, whereas others seem to rely more on nonverbal messages.[1] Another research study found that nonverbal behaviors were twelve to thirteen times more powerful in impact compared to the accompanying verbal message.[2] These findings indicate the importance and impact of nonverbal behaviors. Our communication must be viewed as a whole and not simply as verbal or nonverbal messages.

Without realizing it, we often use nonverbal communication as the basis for many daily decisions. Can you think of recent decisions you have made on the basis of the nonverbal communication of another person? For example, your professor's facial expression suggests that she is in a really good mood, so you decide that now is a good time to ask her whether you can miss next week's class to attend a friend's wedding.

■ **nonverbal communication** Behaviors, attributes, or objects (except words) that communicate messages that have social meaning.

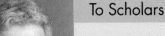

## MAKING CONNECTIONS

### Mark L. Knapp
*University of Texas*

Mark L. Knapp has always been fascinated by how two people affect each other's behavior in everyday interaction. He has been especially interested in the infrequent, subtle, indirect, and little noticed behavior that often seems to play a central role in important encounters. As a result, much of his work has focused on nonverbal behavior and communication in close relationships. Among other topics, he has studied compliments, appearance, greeting and good-bye rituals, play, relationship commitment, and communication with the dying. He is also known for developing a model of how communication changes as relationships go through different stages of coming together and coming apart (See

## To Scholars

Chapter 14 for details). His research and ideas on these topics can be found in the following books: *Interpersonal Communication and Human Relationships* (with A. L. Vangelisti) and *Nonverbal Communication in Human Interaction* (with J. A. Hall). In 1974, he conducted a ground-breaking study that examined the behavior of liars and truth tellers and he is currently working on a comprehensive book on the subject, tentatively titled: *Lying and Deception in Human Interaction.* He has an immense collection of rhino memorabilia and after he turned 60, he learned to tap dance and sky dive. He is currently a professor at the University of Texas and a member of the UT Academy of Distinguished Teachers. A former President of the International Communication Association and the National Communication Association, he also received the Distinguished Scholar Award from the NCA.

Even though our culture is verbally oriented, more and more scholars and teachers are recognizing the significant connection of nonverbal behavior to the communication process.

# ■ Characteristics of Nonverbal Communication

A question that students often ask is, "Why is it important that we study nonverbal communication?" There are many reasons for studying nonverbal communication, the primary one being its pervasive effects on what and how we communicate; we are always communicating something nonverbally, whether we intend to or not. Besides occurring constantly, nonverbal communication depends on context, is more believable than verbal communication, is a primary means of expression, is related to culture, and is ambiguous or easily misunderstood.

## ■■ Nonverbal Communication Occurs Constantly

When another person is present, you have to communicate. Whether you make eye contact, smile, frown, or try to totally ignore the other person, you are communicating something. Sometimes, what is said is less important than what is not said. For example, not attending a meeting at which you were expected, coming late to an employment interview, wearing jeans when you were expected to dress formally, wearing a suit when jeans were expected, talking about a sad situation with a smirk on your face, and speaking to someone but never looking him or her in the eye all convey strong messages. We all believe we can tell a great deal about people on the

What messages you send via your appearance, facial expressions, clothing, eye contact, body movements and posture about who you are may not always be clear or what you intended. What is perceived, however, is what is communicated whether its the intended message or not.

basis of their facial expression, appearance (sex, race, physique), clothing, willingness to make eye contact, body movements, and posture.

To illustrate that we are always communicating, whether intentionally or unintentionally, consider these two students pictured above: Sam is always dressed like a professional, perfectly groomed, and smells of expensive aftershave lotion. Olivia has punk-style hair, has tattoos on her arms and neck, wears piercing on her face and other parts of her body, and wears nontraditional clothes. By simply looking at them, we cannot tell what these two actually intend to communicate. Sam might simply be neat and uses aftershave lotion because it feels good, or he might really want to communicate that designer clothes and expensive aftershave lotion are important to him, or he wants to let everyone know he's got money. Olivia might simply like to show that she is not going to conform to everyone else, or she may be attempting to communicate that she disdains society's seeming obsession with outward appearances. Ultimately, it's not so much what Sam and Olivia intend to communicate as what others perceive. Both are communicating something about themselves through their appearance whether intended or not.

## ▬ Nonverbal Communication Depends on Context

The context in which nonverbal communication occurs plays a crucial role in its interpretation. Pounding on a table to make a point during a speech means something entirely different from pounding on the table in response to someone's calling you a liar. Direct eye contact with a stranger can mean something entirely different from direct eye contact with a close friend.

When you communicate, your nonverbal and verbal cues usually supplement and support each other. Your appearance, tone of voice, eye movement, posture, and facial expression provide cues about the communication relationship. For example, when you talk to a friend, your relaxed tone of voice, eye contact, and posture reveal much about your friendship. Your nonverbal cues can tell your friends how much you value them, how comfortable you feel, and how intimate your relationships have become. Such nonverbal communication is interpreted within the context of your friendships and is complemented by casual and personal conversations.

Without understanding the context in which communication occurs, it is almost impossible to tell what a specific nonverbal behavior may mean. In fact, misunderstandings can occur even when the context is fully understood. That is why we must think twice about our interpretation of others' nonverbal behavior and their possible interpretations of ours. When you see and hear nonverbal communication without a complete understanding of the context, you might not get the message that was intended. When you assume too much about a nonverbal message, further miscommunication and misunderstanding can result.

## Nonverbal Communication Is More Believable than Verbal Communication

Most of us tend to believe nonverbal communication, even when it contradicts the accompanying verbal message. Consider this conversation between a mother and her daughter regarding the daughter's husband:

"What's wrong? Are you upset with Chad?" asks Jess's mother.
(Stare and frown) "Whatever, I'm not upset, why should I be?" responds Jess.
"You seem to be in a funk, and you are avoiding talking to me. So what's wrong? Did you and Chad have a fight?" asks Jess's mother.
"I SAID NOTHING IS WRONG! LEAVE ME ALONE! EVERYTHING IS FINE!"

Throughout the conversation, Jess seems upset, snappy in tone, and to be sending a signal to her mother that she isn't telling the whole story. It seems clear from the interaction and the mother's intuition that Jess is hiding something, hence the second inquiry. Indeed, the real story is that Jess and her husband have not been getting along lately. They have been fighting over money, and the mother could sense that something was on Jess's mind. Nonverbal messages are much more difficult to control than verbal messages because nonverbal cues are more representative of our emotions, which are also more difficult to control.

Is the nonverbal or the verbal communication more likely to be truer? Verbal communication is more conscious; it involves more processing of thoughts and impulses into words. Although nonverbal messages can be conscious and deliberate, they often, as we have suggested, are unintentional and subconsciously generated. It is almost always easy to determine what you are going to say, but it is very difficult for most of us to control our voices, facial expressions, and other body movements when we are upset, hurt, or angry. Jess's mother interpreted her daughter's nonverbal communication as a more accurate reflection of Jess's feelings than her verbal communication.

## Nonverbal Communication Is a Primary Means of Expression

We can often detect other people's feelings of frustration, anger, sadness, resentment, or anxiety without their actually saying anything. We can detect others' emotions because nonverbal communication is so powerful. Almost all of our feelings and attitudes are expressed through our nonverbal behavior. For example, at a graduation party attended by many young children, one little girl entered with her parents and spotted a neighbor. She turned up her nose and walked away. Her mother, running after her, asked why she had suddenly left, to which the girl replied, "I don't like that

**MAKING** Technology

**CONNECTIONS**

### Emotion and Emphasis via Electronic Communication

The messages we communicate are given more meaning and emphasis through our nonverbal communication. But how can you use nonverbal expressions to illustrate emotions if you are communicating mainly via email with someone? When we write to others, we can put certain words in all capitals to emphasize their importance or to convey a strong meaning, such as frustration or anger. For instance, "CALL ME SOON!" illustrates a stronger message than simply "call me soon."

To emphasize that we are happy or sad about something, we sometimes use visual images, such as a happy smiling face or an unhappy sad face, on a letter or message to the make the point that we are pleased or displeased with something. Some symbols that convey a variety of emotions, which can be used when sending email messages, have become popular.

The most common emotions are conveyed by combining a colon, dash, and other symbols to relay nonverbal messages (they are referred to as *emoticons*). Here are some common ones.

| | | | |
|---|---|---|---|
| :-( | Depressed or upset by a remark | | |
| }{ | Face to face | :-l | Straight face |
| :) | Smile | :-o | Surprise |
| Q: | College graduate | | |

1. Locate or illustrate other symbols that convey emotions or feelings that might also be used when communicating electronically. Do a web search using the term emoticon.
2. What did you learn from your Internet search and investigation of nonverbal communication?
3. Do you accept these symbols as nonverbal communication? Why or why not?

girl over there." The nonverbal communication really didn't need much explanation; it was obvious what the little girl was saying through her actions, whether intentionally or unintentionally.

## ▪▪ Nonverbal Communication Is Related to Culture

Culture contributes significantly to differences in nonverbal behavior. Norms and rules that govern the management of behavior differ from culture to culture. Yet because human beings around the world share common biological and social functions, it should not be too surprising to also find areas of similarity in nonverbal communication. For example, studies comparing facial expressions have found that certain universal expressions, such as those indicating sadness and fear, are easily understood across varying cultures. Although much outward behavior is innate (such as smiling, touching, eye contact, moving), we are not born knowing what meanings such nonverbal messages communicate. Most scholars would agree that cultures formulate rules that dictate when, how, and with what consequences nonverbal expressions are exhibited. For instance, the way people sit can communicate different and important messages across cultures. In the United States, being casual and open is valued, thus people consciously or unconsciously, portray this value by the way they sit. Males in the United States often sit in a slumping and leaning back position as well as sprawl out so that they occupy a lot of space.[3] However, in other countries such as Germany and Sweden, where there is more formality, slouching is considered a sign of rudeness and poor manners. The manner in which your legs are positioned also has cultural meaning. For example, the innocent act of ankle-to-knee leg crossing, typical of many American males as they sit, could be taken as an insult in Saudi Arabia, Singapore, Thailand, or Egypt.[4] There also are many sexual connotations for gestures that are tied to culture as well. In the United States the middle

## MAKING CONNECTIONS for Success

### Body Language and Facial Expressions: It's All about Culture and Meaning

Examine the three photos and interpret what the gestures mean to you. Each gesture has a specific meaning in the United States and most other Western cultures.

1. What do the gestures mean?
2. Show photos to people from other cultures (especially non-Western cultures) to determine whether they interpret the gestures as you do.
3. What advice would you give to someone about nonverbal communication and traveling to different cultures?

finger is used to send an insulting obscene gesture. This sexual insult gesture, however, is not universal. In other cultures, the gesture that is used to represent the same insult is the forming of an O with the thumb and index finger, which means "A-Okay," or "good work" in American culture.

## ◼◼ Nonverbal Communication Is Ambiguous

Because nonverbal messages are always present, we must recognize their importance or impact yet also be very careful when interpreting them. Like verbal communication, nonverbal behavior can be ambiguous, abstract, and arbitrary. We cannot assume that nonverbal messages have only one meaning. For example, does crying always signify grief or sadness, or could it also express joy or pain? Interpreting nonverbal behavior requires understanding the context in which it takes place and the cultural norms governing it. Yet even when a person understands these dynamics, it is still very easy to misinterpret nonverbal behaviors. For example, does a fellow student's yawn signal boredom or fatigue? Does a speaker tremble because of nervousness or excitement? Most nonverbal behaviors have a multitude of possible meanings, and to assume automatically that you have grasped the only possible meaning could lead to a serious misunderstanding. There are no consistent rules for using nonverbal communication.

There are many reasons why you should study nonverbal communication. The following are some of the more important reasons. Nonverbal communication:

- carries most of the meaning of a message, particularly feelings and attitudes toward others.
- is a frequent source of misunderstandings.

- is not governed by a set of universal rules.
- is not a language.
- is multichanneled, complicated, and ever-changing.
- is context- and culture-bound.
- is more likely than verbal communication to be spontaneous and unintentional.
- is powerful and is more believable than verbal communication.
- is learned (not always consciously).
- is critical in relationship initiation, development, and termination.

# ■ Functions of Nonverbal Communication

Nonverbal communication adds life to our exchanges by complementing, repeating, regulating, and substituting for our words. Sometimes we even use it to deceive others (see Table 5.1).

## ■■ Complementing Verbal Behavior

Nonverbal cues can be used to complete, describe, or accent verbal cues. This use is called **complementing.** For example, after shooting a chip shot from about seventy-five yards, a golfer tells her partner that she missed the cup by inches and uses her thumb and index finger to show the distance. When saying hello to a friend, you show your genuine interest by displaying a warm smile, maintaining steady eye contact, and holding the friend's hand.

■ **complementing**
The use of nonverbal cues to complete, describe, or accent verbal cues.

We use complementary nonverbal cues to accent verbal behavior by emphasizing or punctuating our spoken words. For example, a mother trying to get her children to quiet down might say quietly, "Will you please keep it down." If that doesn't work and the noise is really bothering her, she might raise her voice to indicate that she wants quiet immediately.

**■ TABLE 5.1** Functions of Nonverbal Communication

| CATEGORY | CHARACTERISTIC | EXAMPLE |
|---|---|---|
| *Complementing* | Completes, describes, or accents a verbal message | A person needs help immediately, so he yells as loudly as he can. |
| *Repeating* | Expresses a message identical to the verbal one | A person says yes and nods her head up and down. |
| *Regulating* | Controls flow of communication | A person shakes his head up and down as a way of communicating, "I am interested in what you are saying," implying "tell me more." |
| *Substituting* | Replaces a verbal message with nonverbal signals to exchange thoughts | Two people use hand signals to communicate, because it is too loud to hear each other's voices. |
| *Deceiving* | Nonverbal cues that purposely disguise or mislead to create a false impression | A doctor examining a patient discovers a serious problem, but the doctor's facial expressions remain neutral so as not to alarm the patient. |

People who are excited or enthusiastic are more likely to use nonverbal cues for accenting their messages than are people who are restrained, having a difficult time expressing themselves, not paying attention, or not understanding what is being said. If used correctly in a public speech, that is, if accenting gestures and changes in tone of voice appear natural and flow smoothly with the message, they can be especially effective ways of making a point clearer to an audience.

## Repeating Verbal Behavior

Whereas complementing behaviors help to modify or elaborate verbal messages, repeating behavior expresses a message identical to the verbal one. For example, a father attempting to keep his child quiet at an adult gathering might place his index finger to his lips while saying, "Shush!" A speaker stating that she has two points to make might hold up two fingers. The actions of the father and the speaker are called **repeating** because they convey the same meaning as the verbal message.

Such repetition is especially common in sports. For instance, a referee on a basketball court shouts, "Traveling!" while rolling her arms in a circular motion, or a baseball umpire cries, "Strike!" while raising his right arm. These repeating nonverbal signals are deliberately planned so that all players and spectators will know the official's call. But most repeating messages are sent without much thought. They are simply a natural part of our communicative behavior.

## Regulating Verbal Behavior

As illustrated in the Making Everyday Connections example, nonverbal cues can also be used for controlling the flow of communication, a behavior known as **regulating.** For example, we frequently use nonverbal signals to indicate that we want to talk, to stop another person from interrupting us when we are talking, or to show that we are finished talking and that the other person may take a turn. When we are listening, we might nod our head rapidly to suggest that the speaker hurry up and finish, or we might nod slowly to show that we want to hear more.

Senders might not even realize that they are sending regulating cues, but receivers are usually aware of such signals. In class, for example, a professor receives a clear message when students put on their coats or close their notebooks to indicate that class is over. Although the students are merely recognizing that it is time for them to leave, the message the professor receives might be quite different.

## Substituting for Verbal Behavior

Using nonverbal messages in place of verbal messages is known as **substituting.** It is common when speaking is impossible, undesirable, or inappropriate. For example, ramp controllers at airports use hand signals to guide planes to their unloading positions, because the noise level is too high for spoken communication; friends often exchange knowing looks when they want to communicate something behind another person's back; some people with hearing impairments use a sophisticated formal sign language in place of the spoken word, as discussed at the beginning of this chapter.

## Deceiving

When we purposely mislead others by using nonverbal cues to create false impressions or to convey incorrect information, we are **deceiving.** Among the most common of such *deceiving* nonverbal behaviors is the poker face that some use when

**repeating** The use of nonverbal cues to convey the same meaning as the verbal message.

**regulating** The use of nonverbal cues to control the flow of communication.

**substituting** The use of nonverbal cues in place of verbal messages when speaking is impossible, undesirable, or inappropriate.

**deceiving** Purposely misleading others by using nonverbal cues to create false impressions or to convey incorrect information.

## MAKING CONNECTIONS for Success

### Telling the Truth: It's Not What You Say, It's How You Behave

There is a lot of guessing when it comes to people's honesty in relation to their nonverbal communication—are they telling the truth? Often, we make assumptions about the truthfulness of people based on the inconsistencies of their nonverbal and verbal messages.

**1.** Why is or isn't it ethical to make assumptions about others' truthfulness based on their nonverbal messages?

**2.** What can we do to prevent premature judgement about the truthfulness of others' nonverbal messages?

**3.** Why is it that we assume we know when people are lying or being deceptive from their nonverbal messages?

playing cards. Masking is a form of deceiving. We might try to appear calm when we are really nervous or upset, and we often act surprised, alert, or happy when in fact we are feeling quite the opposite. In addition, we consciously try to manage our nonverbal behavior when we give a speech or attend a job interview in order to disguise our true purpose and emotions.

Deception research has identified a set of nonverbal cues that people display when they are not telling the truth. In one study, it was found that people who lie make fewer hand movements and tend to look away from a person when they are not telling the truth. The research further found that liars' voices can also be a telling sign; there is a tendency to hesitate and to shift their pitch more often than those telling the truth.[5] Another study found that liars often try to control their voices, which often leads to sounding overcontrolled or undercontrolled, indicating anxiety or deception.[6] In spite of what we know about people's nonverbal behaviors when they are not telling the truth, very few of us are able to detect or interpret these

Detection of deception usually results from nonverbal cues such as facial expressions, eye contact, and body language that can help us decide whether a person is lying.

Nonverbal messages unrelated to the verbal message are sometimes helpful in identifying deception.
Used by permission of Mell Lazarus and of Creators Syndicate, Inc.

behaviors as signs of deception. People who can detect untruthfulness usually consider more than one nonverbal cue to determine whether someone is telling the truth. There is a very fine line between the nonverbal behaviors of someone who is legitimately anxious and someone who is not being truthful. Therefore there are no sure ways to confirm lying using nonverbal behaviors alone.

# ■ Types of Nonverbal Communication

When you dress in a suit for a meeting, smile at someone, sit in a specific seat in class, use your hands while talking, play with a pen or pencil while listening, dim the lights to create a romantic atmosphere, play music loudly, look someone directly in the eyes, or burn incense to create a pleasant odor, you are communicating nonverbally. Every day, we perform a wide range of nonverbal behaviors without even thinking about them, yet such behaviors can convey definite messages to others. Because nonverbal communication is so diverse, complex, common, and informative, we need to be sensitive to its many manifestations. In the following pages, we examine some of the more significant forms of nonverbal communication, such as kinesics (body movements, including gestures, facial expressions, and eye behavior), physical characteristics, haptics (touch), proxemics (space), chronemics (time), vocalics/paralanguage (use of voice), silence, olfactics (odors), artifacts, and environment.

## ■■ Facial Expressions and Body Movements

We use body movements—gestures, facial expressions, and eye behavior—to create an infinite number of nonverbal messages. For our purposes, we define **kinesics,** which is sometimes referred to as *body language,* as any movement of the face or body that communicates a message. Two particularly significant categories of kinesics are eye behavior and facial expressions. **Eye behavior** is a subcategory of facial expressions that includes any movement or behavior of the eyes and is also referred to as **oculesics,** which is the study of eye movement or eye behavior. The eyes, through eye contact with others, have the primary function of establishing relationships. **Facial expressions** include configurations of the face that can reflect, augment, contradict, or appear unrelated to a speaker's spoken message.

**Eye Behavior or Oculesics.**  According to some researchers, eye behavior is the first and primary characteristic people notice. The researchers found that during

■ **kinesics** Sometimes referred to as "body language"; any movement of the face or body that communicates a message.

■ **eye behavior** A category of kinesics and a subcategory of facial expressions that includes any movement or behavior of the eyes.

■ **oculesics** Study of eye movement or eye behavior.

■ **facial expression** Configuration of the face that can reflect, augment, contradict, or be unrelated to a speaker's vocal delivery.

## MAKING CONNECTIONS for Success

### The Eyes Have It

Try the following experiment. Go to a restaurant, elevator, a walkway on campus, the campus library, or some other place where people gather—the more people the better. Pick out two or three individuals, don't say anything, and then stare at them, making direct eye contact with them as long as you can. Watch their reactions!

1. What did you notice about people's behavior when you looked directly at them?
2. Describe any changes in the people's behavior.
3. How did you feel during the experiment?
4. Did you make contact with anyone who might have been from a different culture than yours and, if so, what did you notice?
5. What does this experiment tell you about oculesics (eye movement)?

interactions, people spend about 45 percent of the time looking at each other's eyes.[7] Through eye behavior, we establish relationships with others. Eyes also convey a variety of other important messages. We notice a speaker's eye contact, share mutual glances with friends, and feel uncomfortable when others stare at us. Eye behavior, according to Dale Leathers, a communication scholar, can serve one of six important communicative functions: (1) influence attitude change and persuasion; (2) indicate degree of attentiveness, interest, and arousal; (3) express emotions; (4) regulate interaction; (5) indicate power and status; and (6) form impressions in others.[8]

Eye gaze at the interpersonal level communicates sincerity, trustworthiness, and friendliness. Romantic partners are more likely to gaze into each other's eyes for prolonged periods when expressing their affection for one another.[9] Members of groups or teams use eye contact to build their relationships and to show unity or a sense of belonging to the group or team. In Chapter 10, we discuss the importance of eye contact between a speaker and an audience. In general, effective speakers use more frequent eye contact with their audiences than less effective speakers do. Eye contact is also important for those of us who are listeners, because looking at the speaker indicates our interest in what is being said and is a sign of respect for the speaker.

Have you ever had a conversation with someone who was wearing dark glasses? If you have, you know that it is a bit uncomfortable because you can't completely see how the other person is reacting to you. We do learn much about others' feelings and emotions from their eyes. For example, we associate a high level of gaze or indirect eye contact from another as a sign of liking or friendliness.[10] In contrast, if others avoid making eye contact with us, we are likely to conclude that they are unfriendly, don't like us, or are simply shy.[11] Although a high level of eye contact can be interpreted as positive, there are some exceptions to this rule. If people look at us continuously and maintain the eye contact regardless of actions we take, they are said to be staring. When confronted by unwanted staring, most of us tend to withdraw from the situation.[12] Generally, people find being stared at an unpleasant experience; it makes most of us nervous and tense.[13] This is especially true of what is referred to as a "cold stare," because it is a form of intimidation, and unwanted stares are often interpreted in our society as a sign of hostility and anger.[14] This is one reason experts on road rage—highly aggressive driving by motorists, sometimes followed by actual assaults—recommend that drivers avoid eye contact with people who are disobeying traffic laws and rules of the road.

**Facial Expressions.**   Facial expressions are windows to our emotions. They provide clues about our and others' emotional states, which at times can be very complex and difficult to interpret accurately. Alan Robinson of the Associated Press wrote, "If any NFL coach fits the description of a mad scientist, it's the unmistakable Bill Cowher (pictured), with his jutting jaw and angry eyes, his irrepressible intensity and spittle-flying sideline rages."[15] Coach Cowher's nickname is "Face," not only because he is an in-your-face coach but also because his distinctive facial expressions seem to tell his mood.

More than two thousand years ago, the Roman orator Cicero stated, "The face is the image of the soul." By this, he meant that human feelings and emotions are often reflected in our faces. Modern research suggests that Cicero and others who observed human behavior were correct: It is possible to learn much about others' current moods and feelings from their facial expressions. Researchers have found that our faces depict six different basic emotions clearly and from a rather early age: anger, fear, happiness, sadness, surprise, and disgust.[16] Other research suggests that contempt as an emotion may also be quite basic.[17] However, agreement on what specific facial expression represents contempt is less consistent than in the case of the other six emotions just mentioned.

It is important to realize that the relatively small number of basic facial expressions in no way implies that human beings can show only a small number of facial expressions. The human face is said to produce more than a thousand different expressions. Emotions often occur in many combinations (for example, joy tinged with sorrow, surprise combined with fear), and each of these reactions can vary greatly in emphasis. Thus, while there might be only a small number of basic themes in facial expressions, the number of variations on these themes is immense.

Our facial expressions typically display our emotions, but because of their complexity, these emotions can be difficult to interpret. Researchers have identified more than a thousand different expressions of the human face.

Facial expressions have an extremely powerful role in communication and relationships. Of all the body motions, facial expressions convey the most information. Researchers have examined the judgments we make regarding the facial expressions of others and have found that not only do we judge emotions but we also make judgments about personality, such as the tendency to be friendly or unfriendly, harsh or kind, based on facial expressions.[18] We perceive people who have relaxed facial expressions as having more power and being more in control than people whose facial expressions seem nervous.[19]

Overall, then, it seems safest to conclude that although facial expressions are not completely universal—cultural and contextual differences do exist with respect to their precise

## MAKING Technology CONNECTIONS

### Test Your Ability to Identify Emotions

How good do you think you are at recognizing emotions via facial expressions? Most of us think we are pretty good, but just how good are you? How good are you at interpreting culturally diverse facial expressions? Go to www.zzyx.ucsc.edu/~archer/intro.html and find out. This site allows you to test your ability at identifying emotions displayed on a variety of faces.

1. How well did you do?
2. How well did you do on those faces from cultural backgrounds different from your own?
3. What did you learn?

meaning—they generally need very little translation, compared to spoken language. However, despite cultural rules, our faces often communicate feelings and emotions spontaneously in reaction to a situation. For example, if you open the door to your house and a group of your friends hiding in the dark turn on the lights and yell, "Congratulations!" your face will probably automatically and unconsciously express surprise. If you open the door and they yell, "Boo!" your face will probably show fear or anxiety.

Although many facial expressions are unconscious and involuntary reactions to certain stimuli, researchers have found that facial cues may be only partially reliable in terms of what they express. Michael Motley, a communication researcher, in a study of facial expressions in everyday conversations, found that they are extremely difficult to interpret and may only be relevant as they relate to specific conversations or situations in which they occur.[20] This is in part due to the fact that most of us have learned to conceal our real feelings from others.[21] Most of us have learned how to control our facial muscles in order to hide inappropriate or unacceptable responses. Such controlling behaviors regarding our facial expressions are referred to as **facial management techniques.** Facial management techniques may be used to intensify, deintensify, neutralize, or mask a felt emotion[22] (see Table 5.2).

**Body Movements.** To make sense of thousands of different body movements, psychologists Paul Ekman and Wallace Friesen have devised a classification system based on the origins, functions, and coding of nonverbal behavior.[23] Their system divides body motions into five categories: emblems, illustrators, regulators, affect displays, and adaptors (see Table 5.3). Because there are so many body motions, many of which are interdependent, it is important to understand that the categories are not mutually exclusive. Some body motions may be classified under more than one category.

■ **facial management techniques**

Control of facial muscles to conceal inappropriate or unacceptable responses.

Finally, body movements and posture can reveal much about our physical states (vigor, age) and perhaps the extent to which we possess certain traits.[24] Evidence from several research studies supports these conclusions. For example, one study investigating males and females in four age groups (five to seven, thirteen to fourteen, twenty-six to twenty-eight, and seventy-five to eighty years old) had the partici-

■ **TABLE 5.2** Facial Management Techniques

| TECHNIQUE | DEFINITION | EXAMPLE |
|---|---|---|
| *Intensifying* | Exaggeration of expression to meet others' expectations | You receive a gift and try to look completely surprised, excited, and delighted. |
| *Deintensifying* | Understatement of reactions to meet others' expectations | You receive an A on a speech, a friend receives a C. You tone down your elation, just in case your friend feels bad about receiving a lower grade. |
| *Neutralizing* | Avoidance of any emotional expression in a situation—"poker face" shows no emotion | You show no fear or sadness when fear or sadness may be justified but you don't want to show your emotions. |
| *Masking* | Replacement of one expression with another considered more appropriate for the situation | Smiling when a friend wins a scholarship and you don't, even though you think you deserve it. |

■ **TABLE 5.3** Categories of Body Movements and Facial Expressions

| CATEGORY | CHARACTERISTICS | EXAMPLES |
|---|---|---|
| *Emblems* | Translate directly into words and are used for specific words or phrases. Meanings of emblems are like those of words—arbitrary, changeable with time, learned, and culturally determined | A hitchhiker's extended thumb, the thumb and circle sign for "OK," the peace sign |
| *Illustrators* | Accent, reinforce, or emphasize a verbal message | A child holding up his hands to indicate how tall he is while saying, "I'm a big boy"; an instructor underlining a word on a poster to emphasize it |
| *Regulators* | Control, monitor, or maintain interaction between or among speakers and listeners. Cues that tell us when to stop, continue, hurry, elaborate, make things more interesting, or let someone else speak. The dialogue at the beginning of the chapter is a good example of the need for regulators. | Eye contact, shift in posture, nod of the head, looking at a clock or wristwatch |
| *Affect displays* | Body movements that express emotions. Though your face is the primary means of displaying affect, your body may also be used. | Sad face, slouching, jumping up and down |
| *Adaptors* | Help one feel at ease in communication situations. Are difficult to interpret and require the most speculation. | Scratching, smoothing hair, playing with coins, smoking, hands in front of the face, moving closer to someone |

pants walk back and forth at a pace they felt was comfortable.[25] The walkers were videotaped and then shown to others who rated the walkers on various dimensions, such as gait, traits, age, and sex. By using adjustments and lighting techniques, the researchers were able to disguise the walkers so that the subjects saw only their gait.

The subjects made judgments about the walkers two different times. The first time, they rated the walkers' gait in terms of revealing certain traits (submissive or dominating, physically weak or physically strong, timid or bold, sad or happy, unsexy or sexy). The second time, they rated the walkers' gait in terms of several other characteristics (amount of hip sway, knee bending, forward or backward lean, slow or fast pace, stiff or loose jointed gait, short or long strides). In addition, the subjects were asked to estimate each walker's age and guess whether each was female or male.

The study's results were very interesting and clearly indicate that people's gaits provide important nonverbal cues about them. For example, as predicted, ratings of traits and gaits did vary according to age. Ratings of sexiness increased from children to adolescents and young adults but decreased for older adults. Further analysis revealed that possession of a youthful gait (one characterized by hip sway, knee bending, arm swing, loose-jointedness, and more steps per second) was strongly related to ratings of the walkers' happiness and power. Thus, persons with a youthful gait— regardless of their actual age—were rated more positively along several dimensions than persons with an older gait. Can you think of a situation or time when the way a person walked influenced what you thought of him/her? In what ways did the style of walking affect your perception?

## ■ Physical Characteristics

Whereas body movements and facial expressions change quickly and can be controlled to some extent, physical characteristics, such as body type, attractiveness, height, weight, and skin tone are fairly constant and more difficult to control, especially in the course of a single interaction. Physical appearance in our culture plays a significant role in communication and relationships. In recent years, segments of our society have become obsessed with physical appearance and general health, spending billions of dollars each year on modifying, preserving, and decorating their bodies. We might say that "beauty is only skin deep," but we are likely to respond positively to those who are attractive and negatively to those who are unattractive.[26]

Physical attractiveness has an extremely powerful influence on everyday communication. It appears that both males and females are strongly influenced by attractiveness, though males seem to be more responsive to appearance than are females.[27]

## MAKING CONNECTIONS for Success

### You Can't Judge People by Their Appearance or Can You?

Look at the young woman in the photographs above and think about what she might be like. Look at the before photo and respond to number 1 below, then look at the after photo in which she has had a makeover and respond to number 1 below, then respond to 2, 3 and 4.

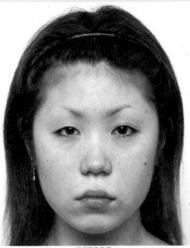

BEFORE      AFTER

1. Make a list of the physical characteristics that describe the person. Then based on those characteristics, describe the person in terms of her sociability, intelligence, poise, independence, masculinity or femininity, popularity, vanity, potential for success, integrity, concern for others, temperament, sexuality, and other features.
2. How do you think your or others' interactions with the person shown in the before photo might differ from the image of the person shown in the after photo?
3. Do you think men and women would differ in their responses to the questions above? Why or why not?
4. Based on the two photos, do you think any stereotypes might emerge and, if so, describe them?

Overall, though, an appealing physical appearance is perceived as a positive characteristic that influences interpersonal attraction (see Chapter 14 for more on interpersonal attraction) and interpersonal preferences. Numerous stereotypes are consistently associated with physical appearance, and it would not be surprising if you hold some of them yourself. Before continuing, take a look at the photos in the Making Connections for Success box and follow the instructions.

Numerous research studies have indicated that attractive people, when compared to unattractive people, are perceived to be more popular, successful, sociable, persuasive, sensual, and happy. One research study found that attractive students receive more interaction from their teachers,[28] unattractive defendants are less likely to be found innocent than attractive defendants in a court of law,[29] and attractiveness plays a predominant role in dating behaviors.[30] Attractiveness affects credibility and a person's ability to persuade others, to get a job, and to gain a higher salary. Handsome males are likely to be perceived as more masculine, whereas beautiful females are seen as more feminine, in comparison with those who are perceived as less attractive.[31]

In a few situations, attractiveness can be a disadvantage. Although attractiveness was found to be an asset for men throughout their executive careers, one research study found that being attractive could be a liability for women managers. Even when such women had reached top executive levels, their success was attributed to their looks rather than to their abilities, and they were consistently judged less capable than unattractive women managers.[32] Attractive females, in comparison to other women, are judged by some to be more vain, more materialistic, and less faithful to their husbands.[33] For both males and females, attractiveness is often considered the reason for their success, rather than their ability or hard work.[34]

We know that our society places a great deal of value on physical appearance, but do attractive individuals differ in behavior from others who are less attractive? The answer is no. In fact, attractive people do *not* seem to fit the stereotypes associated with them.[35] Surprisingly, self-esteem is not consistently high among those who are considered the most attractive. This could be because they believe that they are rewarded not for what they have done, but for how they look, thus diminishing their sense of self-worth.[36]

## MAKING CONNECTIONS for Success

### Whom Do You Touch?

A schoolteacher in Lincoln, Nebraska, loses her job for touching a student; a worker in Canton, Ohio, sues an employer for "improper" touching behavior; a person talks on the radio about touching behavior between male coaches and female athletes. Touching has many different meanings. When is it inappropriate, and when isn't it? Here are some situations to consider:

1. Does it mean the same thing when the boss places an arm around the secretary and when the secretary places an arm around the boss?

2. Does it mean the same thing when a teacher places a hand on a student's shoulder and when a student places a hand on a teacher's shoulder?

3. Does it mean the same thing when a doctor touches a patient and when a patient touches a doctor?

4. When is touch appropriate, and when isn't it?

5. How does the gender of the people affect your answers to these questions?

## ▪️ Touch

Touching is referred to as either tactile communication or **haptics.** Haptics is one of the most basic forms of communication. "Reach out and touch someone" is a slogan once used by a national phone company. Although the company's advertisement suggests touching in an abstract sense, the idea behind the advertisement is that touch is a personal and powerful means of communication. As one of our most primitive and yet sensitive ways of relating to others, touch is a critical aspect of communication. It plays a significant role in giving encouragement, expressing tenderness, and showing emotional support, and it can be more powerful than words. For example, when you have just received some bad news, a pat on the shoulder from a friend can be far more reassuring than any number of understanding words.

The kind and amount of touching that are appropriate vary according to the individuals, their relationship, and the situation. Some researchers have set up categories to describe these variations in touch. The categories are functional–professional, social–polite, friendship–warmth, love–intimacy, and sexual arousal.[37] Definitions and examples are given in Table 5.4.

The meaning of a particular touch depends on the type of touch, the situation in which the touch occurs, who is doing the touching, and the cultural background of those involved. Some cultures are more prone to touching behavior than others. Research has found that people in the United States are less touch-oriented when compared to persons in other cultures. For example, a study examining touching behavior during a one-hour period in a coffee shop found that people in San Juan, Puerto Rico,

▪️ **haptics** Tactile, or touch, communication; one of the most basic forms of communication.

### ▪️ TABLE 5.4 Touch/Haptics

| CATEGORIES OF TOUCH | DEFINITION/EXPLANATION | EXAMPLE |
| --- | --- | --- |
| *Functional–professional* | Unsympathetic, impersonal, cold, or businesslike touch. | A doctor touches a patient during a physical examination or a tailor touches a customer while measuring. |
| *Social–polite* | Acknowledges another person according to the norms or rules of a society. | Two people shake hands in our culture or kiss in other cultures to greet one another. |
| *Friendship–warmth* | Expresses an appreciation of the special attributes of another. Expresses warm feelings for another. The most misinterpreted type of touching behavior. | Two men or two women meet in an airport, hug, and walk off with their arms around each other. Athletes touch a shoulder or pat each other on their buttocks. |
| *Love–intimacy* | Occurs in romantic relationships between lovers and spouses. Highly communicative and usually requires consent between both parties even though one party might not reciprocate. | Two people hug, caress, embrace, kiss, and so on. |
| *Sexual arousal* | The most intimate level of personal contact with another. Expresses physical attraction between two consenting individuals. | Sexual touch behavior including foreplay and intercourse. |

touched 180 times in an hour; those in Paris, France, touched 110 times; and those in Gainesville, Florida, touched only two times.[38]

Gender differences in touching behavior are also interesting to note. Men tend to touch more than women do, women tend to be touched more often than men, and women seem to value touch more than men do. Gender differences in touching behavior may be partially attributed to men's sexual aggressiveness in our culture and their expression of power and dominance. According to Nancy Henley, men have access to women's bodies, but women do not have the same access to men's bodies. This, according to the research, may be a man's way of exerting power because touch represents an invasion of another's personal space.[39]

## ■■ Space

Statements such as "Give me some room to operate," signs that say "Keep Out," and the bumper sticker that reads "Keep Off My" followed by a picture of a donkey all are attempts to regulate the distance between people. Such behaviors are of special interest to researchers in **proxemics,** the study of how we use space and the distance we place between others and ourselves when communicating. Edward T. Hall, anthropologist and author of two classic books, *The Silent Language* and *The Hidden Dimension,* coined the term *proxemics.*[40] Hall was a pioneer in helping to explain how space is used in North American culture. In his study of proxemics, Hall identified four zones, which are illustrated in Figure 5.1. *Intimate space* is defined as the distance from no space between people to one-and-a-half feet between people. This zone is the most personal, and it is usually open only to those with whom we are well acquainted, unless such closeness is physically forced on us, such as in a crowded train or elevator.

The second zone is referred to as *personal space* and ranges from distances of one-and-a-half feet to four feet between people. It is not unusual for us to carry on conversations or other activities with close friends and relatives in this zone. If someone we don't know enters this zone, we are likely to feel uncomfortable or violated. The third zone is called *social space.* It ranges from four to twelve feet and is where most professional conversations occur, as well as group interactions, such as meetings. *Public space,* the fourth zone, includes twelve feet or more. This distance is not unusual for public speaking situations or other formal presentations. The actual distance or zone might be determined by the context and relationship of those involved in the interaction.

The need for us to identify certain amounts of space as our own is an aspect of proxemics called **territoriality.** We often position markers such as books, coats, pencils, papers, and other objects to declare our space. Some students become upset when someone else sits in a seat they usually occupy, even though seating is not assigned. This uneasiness stems from a strong desire to stake out and protect territory. Similar reactions occur when someone enters a room without knocking or tailgates when driving; it seems like an invasion of our territory.

■ **proxemics** The study of the use of space and of distance between individuals when they are communicating.

■ **territoriality** The need to identify certain areas of space as one's own.

**■ FIGURE 5.1** Edward T. Hall's Four Distance Zones

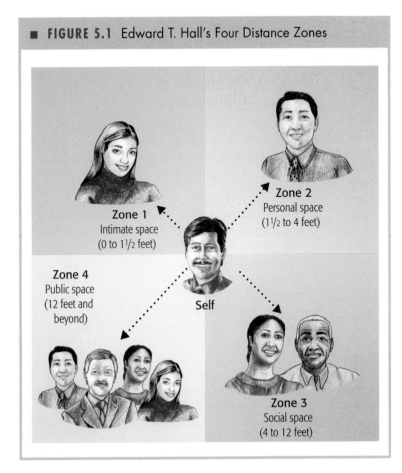

We usually give little conscious attention to the role of space in our communication, yet the way in which others use space gives strong clues to what they are thinking and how they are reacting to us. There are many variables that influence our use of space when communicating; status, sex, culture, and context are but a few.

Status affects the distance that is maintained between communicators. Research shows that people of different status levels tend to stay farther apart than do individuals of equal status. Furthermore, people of higher status tend to close the distance between themselves and people of lower status, but seldom do people of lower status move to close the distance between themselves and a person of higher status.

Men and women tend to differ in their proxemic patterns, but the differences in part hinge on whether the interaction is with someone of the same or opposite sex. In same-sex situations, men

## MAKING CONNECTIONS
### for Success

### Space: Who Needs It?

Let's have some fun. Keeping in mind the spatial zones that Hall identified, try the following experiments:

1. Go to the library, the student union, or some other place with a number of tables. Find a person sitting alone (someone of the other sex), and sit right next to the person. Notice the reaction and how the person looks at you. After a while—before the person leaves—tell him or her that you were doing an experiment for your communication class. Then ask what the person thought when you sat down close by and how he or she felt.

2. Now do the same thing with someone of your own sex. What happened? How did you feel?

3. If you feel uncomfortable doing the experiments in items 1 and 2, try this: When sitting with a friend or friends at a table where there are salt and pepper shakers or other items, slowly but surely start pushing the items toward a friend. Move them very slowly, and move as many items as you can—not all at once, but one at a time. Notice what happens. Discuss what the person was thinking as you kept moving items in his or her direction.

4. What do the results of these experiments tell you about how people treat space and its importance to them? Do men and women react to space considerations differently?

5. Do the results of your experiments match the findings of Hall? If not, why do you think your results were different?

prefer, expect, and usually establish greater conversational distance than women do. Opposite-sex distancing depends on how intimate the relationship is.

Culture creates a wealth of differences in the way individuals use distance for communication. For example, people from the United States tend to stand farther apart during conversations than do people from many European and Middle Eastern cultures. Arabs, for example, consider it polite to stand close to the person with whom they are communicating. There are as many culture-based differences as there are cultures, and it is not unusual for one group to be perceived as cold and unfriendly and another as pushy and forward as a result of their use of space. The important thing is to recognize that not all cultures view distance in the same way.

Context also influences the space that is maintained between individuals. For example, people in line at an automated teller machine usually stand back far enough to give the person who is using the machine the feeling that a transaction is not being observed. But passengers waiting to board a bus ordinarily stand close together to avoid losing their places.

## ▰ Time

**Chronemics** is the study of how people perceive, structure, and use time as communication.[41] People in our society are preoccupied with time. Everything seems to have a starting time and an ending time. We worry about how long we have to wait for something and how long it takes to do something. We even go so far as to say that time is money. Because we place such a high value on time, it plays a significant role in our nonverbal communication. We are particularly sensitive to people and events that waste our time or make exceptional demands on it. Consider your reaction, for instance, when your date keeps you waiting, when an instructor continues to lecture after the bell has signaled the end of class, or when you are given only one day's notice of an upcoming test. Your feelings might range from confusion to indignation to outrage, but you will almost certainly not be neutral. To some extent, your reaction will depend on who the other person is. You will probably be more tolerant if the offending party is a friend or someone who has great power over you. For example, if a blind date keeps you waiting too long, you might decide to leave, but if your professor is late for an office appointment, you will probably suffer in silence and continue to wait for his or her arrival.

We tend to have many expectations about how time should be used, and we often judge people by their use of time. For example, students are expected to be on time for class. Therefore, students who are punctual are more likely to create a positive impression, whereas those who are consistently late may be perceived as irresponsible, lazy, or uninterested. We must be constantly aware of the messages we send through our use (and misuse) of time.

Individuals can differ in their approaches to time. For example, some people are always looking to the future, others long for the past, and still others live for the moment. Each approach communicates something about people and the ways they use time to communicate who they are. Each culture teaches its members about time expectations, and these expectations vary. In some cultures, being punctual is expected; in others, being punctual is not important, and in fact it is expected that people will be late. In U.S. culture, for example, you are expected to be on time for a dinner party, but being up to twenty minutes late is socially accepted and still considered on time. In some European countries, arriving late for a dinner party is considered an insult. Our use of time communicates messages about us, and it is important that we adhere to the time-related norms of the culture in which we are communicating.

■ **chronemics** The study of how people perceive, structure, and use time as communication.

## ▬ Paralanguage/Vocalics

**Paralanguage/vocalics** is the way we vocalize, or say, the words we speak. Paralanguage includes not only speech sounds, but also speech rate, accents, articulation, pronunciation, and silence. Sounds such as groans, yawns, coughs, laughter, crying, and yelping, which are nonsymbolic but can communicate very specific messages, are also included. Expressions such as "um," "uh-huh," "ya know," "like," and "OK" are referred to as vocal fillers and are considered paralanguage. Vocal fillers are often sprinkled throughout conversations without forethought or a set order. They might reflect nervousness, speech patterns of a particular subculture, or a personal habit. In any case, the use of vocal fillers can influence our image positively or damage and degrade others and us.

The content of words is verbal communication, whereas the sound quality or volume that creates the words is a form of nonverbal communication. We rely more often on paralanguage than on the words themselves when interpreting another person's message. Note how the meaning of a sentence can vary according to the word that is emphasized:

1. *Jane's* taking Tom out for pizza tonight. (not Hilary or Dana)
2. Jane's taking *Tom* out for pizza tonight. (not Bill or Dave)
3. Jane's taking Tom *out* for pizza tonight. (not staying home)
4. Jane's taking Tom out for *pizza* tonight. (not seafood or hamburgers)
5. Jane's taking Tom out for pizza *tonight.* (not tomorrow or next weekend)[42]

■ **paralanguage/
vocalics** The way we
vocalize, or say, the
words we speak.

Even though the words in each sentence are identical, each creates an entirely different message solely because of the emphasis placed on specific words.

## MAKING CONNECTIONS
### for Success

### It's Not What You Say, But How You Say It!

"My professor is an easy grader."

Read the preceding statement aloud in four different ways: (1) with no expression at all, (2) as if your professor is really an easy grader, (3) as if your professor is anything but an easy grader, and (4) as if you are trying to convince someone that your professor is an easy grader. Note how you can change the meaning without changing the words.

1. What did you do to your voice to change the meaning of the sentence?
2. Did you notice anything else about your other nonverbal behavior while using your voice to change the meaning of the sentence?
3. What did you learn about vocal expression from this exercise?
4. How can vocal expression help you to become a more competent communicator?

Paralanguage includes pitch (how high or low the voice is), vocal force (intensity or loudness of the voice), rate (speed), quality (overall impression of the voice), and pauses or silence. The way we vary our voices conveys different meanings to receivers. For example, a person who speaks quickly may communicate a message that is different from a person who speaks slowly. Even when the words are the same, if the rate, force, pitch, and quality differ, the receiver's interpretations will differ. Researchers estimate that approximately 38 percent of the meaning of oral communication is affected by our use of voice, by *the way* in which something is said rather than by *what* is said.[43]

On the basis of paralanguage, we make many judgments about what is being said, the person saying it, the speaking and listening roles, and the credibility of the message. Of course, judgments about people based on paralanguage can be just as unreliable as judgments based on body type. We must therefore recognize the effect that paralanguage has on our communication and adjust our use of it accordingly.

## ▪▪ Silence

The sound of silence is a contradiction in terms; as hard as you try, it is almost impossible to have complete and absolute silence. Silence or vocal pauses are very communicative, very powerful messages that often say volumes, whether intended or not. **Vocal pauses** or hesitations are usually short in duration, whereas **silence** generally refers to extended periods of time without sound. Vocal pauses can be used to emphasize a word or thought or to make a point to get others' attention. For example, a speaker stands in front of an audience and gazes at the audience in the hope of gaining the audience's attention so that they will listen. A teacher pauses during a lecture to get students' attention. Sometimes, people use vocal pauses to gather their thoughts or to allow others time to think. Vocal pauses or prolonged periods of silence can create the perception that you are unsure of yourself, unprepared, or nervous. Regardless of why vocal pauses occur, they do send messages.

Silence sometimes seems very awkward in a conversation, especially when you are talking to someone whom you do not know well and who might be of higher status than you. Most of us in this situation feel or sense the pressure to say something to get the conversation going again. Silence can also be used to disconfirm or create discomfort in others. Have you ever said "hello" to someone you admire or respect and he or she didn't reply or acknowledge you? You likely felt slighted or less than important. It is not unusual to use silence to prevent communication with others. Silence can be used to prevent certain topics from surfacing or to prevent someone from saying something that he or she might later regret.

Silence is expected in certain contexts, for example, during a funeral or while listening to a speech presentation, or it can be self-imposed as a way of thinking or doing nothing at all. Silence has many possible meanings, none of which is easily interpreted. The next time a good friend says "Hi," try pausing for five to ten seconds before reacting. You will quickly learn the effect silence can have as a message. There are also cultural differences related to silence. What are some negative perceptions conveyed in our culture by silence at a business meeting or social gathering? In many cultures, silence is seen more positively. In Japan, for example, silence is considered more appropriate than speech in many situations.[44] The intercultural implications of silence are as diverse as those of other nonverbal cues.

## ▪▪ Smell

Smell communication, or **olfactics,** which is the study of smell or odors, is extremely important in our society. Billions of dollars are spent on perfumes, colognes, aftershave lotions, scented candles, deodorant, scented air sprays, soap, and other such products to enhance our surroundings and us. It is likely that when smells are pleasant, we feel better about ourselves.

Smell communicates very powerful messages, which can create a multitude of interpretations. In most developed parts of the world, people use an array of cosmetics to eliminate body odor or to replace it with other smells. Americans have the most smell-aversive culture in the world, according to Peter Andersen, a communication scholar.[45] We base many of our perceptions on smell; for example, when food smells good to us, we assume that it will taste good as well, and we are more attracted to others who have pleasant smells than those who do not. Many cultures consider natural odors to be normal; in fact, in some cultures, a person's smell is an extension of that person. As with all types of nonverbal communication, not knowing cultural variations in attitude toward smells can create misunderstandings and misperceptions, which ultimately can lead to incorrect assumptions.

▪ **vocal pause** A hesitation, usually short in duration.

▪ **silence** An extended period of time without sound.

▪ **olfactics** Study of smell or odors.

## ◼ Artifacts

**Artifacts** are personal adornments or possessions that communicate information about us. Such things as automobiles, eyeglasses, briefcases, grooming, clothing, hair color, body piercing, tattoos, makeup, and the many hundreds of other material perceptions that we create to communicate our age, gender, status, role, class, importance, group membership, personality, and relationship to others. For example, what are you telling people by the type and color of vehicle you drive? A silver SUV conveys a different message from a green sedan, a red car conveys a different message from a white car, a sports car conveys a much different message from a minivan, and a Cadillac Escalade conveys a different message from a Ford Escape. The number of cars you own also conveys messages about you.[46]

How do you react to people who have body piercing and tattoos? It depends, but what does it depend on? Effective communicators learn to adapt their use of artifacts to a specific situation and not to judge others by appearance alone. It is important that we use artifacts that are consistent with and reinforce our intended messages. If the messages that are conveyed are inconsistent, contradictory, and not reinforcing, it might be time to do a reality check on the messages others are receiving from the artifacts we use.

## ◼ Environment

Environment, as discussed in Chapter 1, is the psychological and physical surroundings in which communication occurs, including the furniture, architectural design, lighting conditions, temperature, smells, colors, and sounds of the location and the attitudes, feelings, perceptions, and relationships of the participants. The impact of the environment has a lot to do with the individuals, their backgrounds, and their perception of what is important to them at the time of the interaction. The best environment allows a speaker's intended message to be delivered accurately. Thus soft background music, dim lights, a log burning in a fireplace, a tray of hors d'oeuvres, and two candles would create the perfect environment for a romantic encounter but would fail to create the proper atmosphere for a pregame pep rally.

# ◼ Interpreting and Improving Nonverbal Communication

If nonverbal communication is so credible and powerful and if we can define, categorize, describe, and observe it, why do we still have difficulty interpreting it? There are at least three good reasons:

1. *Nonverbal cues have multiple meanings.* Nonverbal communication is difficult to understand because a single behavior can have many potential meanings. For example, a frown might indicate unhappiness, sadness, anger, pain, thought, aggressiveness, disapproval, dejection, fear, fatigue, discouragement, disapproval, or a combination of some of these. Unlike words, nonverbal cues lack dictionary definitions.

   Interpretations are unreliable because they depend so heavily on perceptions. Suppose, for example, that you have just walked out of a sad movie when you see a friend with tears in her eyes, talking to her sister. She might be reacting to the movie, or her crying could stem from breaking up with her boyfriend, hurting herself, or hearing about a death in the family. Her tears could even result from laugh-

**◼ artifact** A personal ornament or possession that communicates information about a person.

ing hard at something that occurred after the movie. Of course, some nonverbal behaviors, such as nodding the head for yes and shaking it for no (in U.S. society), are consistent in both their meaning and their interpretation. Unfortunately, such consistency is the exception rather than the rule.

2. *Nonverbal cues are interdependent.* The meaning of one nonverbal cue often depends on the correct interpretation of several other simultaneously occurring cues. For example, when we see someone enter a room, we begin to select certain cues about that person, such as gender, physical traits, facial expressions, voice characteristics, and clothing. Each cue intermeshes with the others and adds to the total picture. This interdependence of nonverbal behaviors and our inability to perceive all aspects of any one nonverbal communication make interpretation risky.

Looking for meaning by using more than one nonverbal message at a time is called the **functional approach.** The functional approach examines nonverbal behavior not by isolating nonverbal cues, but by seeing how each cue interacts and works with the others to perform various communicative functions.

3. *Nonverbal cues are subtle.* Many nonverbal behaviors are subtle and difficult to observe. A cue that one person notices immediately might be overlooked by another person; thus multiple interpretations may be made in the same situation. For example, a friend tells you that a person whom you are interested in getting to know has been looking at you, but you haven't noticed the glances or you see the eye contact as more accidental than a deliberate message of interest in you.

## MAKING CONNECTIONS for Success

### Impression Management: It's All in the Clothes You Wear—Or Is It?

We are told to dress to impress! There is nothing wrong with dressing nicely, but can there be potential ethical problems?

1. Think of an occasion when someone you know wore clothing that created a misperception of status or personal attributes. Describe the situation. What were the consequences?
2. Think of an occasion when you used clothing to create a positive or favorable image even though it was not accurate. Describe the situation. What were the consequences of this misleading impression that you created?
3. What are the ethical implications of this type of impression management?

## ▬▬ Improving Our Interpretation of Nonverbal Communication

Nonverbal communication is complex, but there are some things that you can do to interpret it better. First, be observant of and sensitive to the nonverbal messages that you receive. Second, verify nonverbal messages that you are not sure of or that are inconsistent with other cues. Assume, for example, that a friend who used to visit regularly hasn't come over in several weeks. It might seem logical to conclude that she doesn't want to see you anymore, but then again, she might have become wrapped up in her studies, taken a part-time job, or fallen ill. To accurately interpret her behavior, consider all the possibilities and avoid jumping to conclusions. Because it is so tempting to make inferences based on nonverbal behavior, it is important to remember not to go beyond actual observations.

One method to help verify the meaning of a nonverbal message is to use **descriptive feedback,** which is the stating of the interpretation of the message received back to the sender. The other person can then clarify an intended meaning. Descriptive feedback is not always necessary, but when a message seems inconsistent

■ **functional approach** Using more than one nonverbal message at a time to look for meaning.

■ **descriptive feedback** The stating of the interpretation of the message received back to the sender.

with the situation or other behaviors or when you're not sure you have accurately interpreted an important message, you should verify your perceptions with the other person. When using descriptive feedback, do not express agreement or disagreement or draw conclusions; simply describe the message you believe was communicated. For example, if you think someone's behavior seems to indicate that he is uncomfortable around you, but you're not sure, don't ask, "Why are you so nervous when I'm around?" Rather, describe the situation nonjudgmentally: "Jim, I get the impression that you may not be comfortable around me. Is that the case?" This allows the other person to explain without feeling defensive, and it enables you to avoid inaccurate interpretations.

## ■■ Improving the Nonverbal Communication We Send

■ **self-monitoring**
The willingness to change behavior to fit situations, awareness of effects on others, and the ability to regulate nonverbal cues and other factors to influence others' impressions.

We must be aware of the nonverbal messages we send to others. Fortunately, most of us do a good job of communicating nonverbally and thus do not need to make dramatic changes in the way we behave. Nonetheless, we cannot afford to ignore the effects of our nonverbal behavior or to allow the nonverbal messages that we send to go unexamined. If you find that others often misunderstand your intended meaning, you might want to consider how you communicate nonverbally. When you take action to show that you care about how others perceive your behavior, you are engaging in self-monitoring. **Self-monitoring** involves the willingness to change behavior to fit a given situation, an awareness of how we affect others, and the ability to regulate nonverbal cues and other factors to influence others' impressions. In Chapter 3, we discussed impression management techniques that can enhance a person's image. Self-monitoring is similar, but it goes beyond impression management. It entails both concern with projecting the desired image and the ability to assess the effects of it.

| GUIDELINES | Monitor Your Nonverbal Communication |
|---|---|

1. *Be aware of how people react to you.* If you notice that people react to you differently than you anticipate, you may be giving nonverbal messages that differ from your intentions.
2. *Ask friends or colleagues for their help.* It is very difficult to know whether you are sending nonverbal messages that are being misunderstood unless you seek feedback.
3. *Videotape yourself to see how you appear to others.* Then review the videotape by yourself, with a friend, or with your teacher to analyze your nonverbal behaviors.
4. *Adapt to the context or situation in which you find yourself.* As you carry out different roles or find yourself in different communicative contexts, your nonverbal behavior should conform, when appropriate, to the expectations and norms associated with the role or the context. To learn about expectations related to various contexts, observe how others behave in them. For example, if everyone is always on time for a meeting and you are always late, chances are you are violating an established norm. Thus you must make an effort to conform, or you will find that your nonverbal behaviors will be perceived in ways that you might not want them to be.

Our nonverbal messages greatly influence how others perceive us and our communication. For example, an extremely bright and talented student was constantly being turned down for jobs that he should have been getting. When I asked why he thought this was happening, he replied that he had no idea. To find out, friends videotaped a mock interview in which he was interviewed by another student. When he reviewed the tape, he immediately noticed that he never looked at the interviewer. Instead, his gaze wandered about the room. The lack of direct eye contact by the student gave the impression that he lacked confidence and that he might not be totally candid in what he was saying. Once he knew why he was being rejected, he could try to change his behavior. To help him practice, his friends videotaped another interview session. This time, he was reminded to look at the interviewer each time his gaze wandered. After several such sessions, he grew relaxed about looking at the interviewer and consequently appeared more confident and truthful in his communication.

Although changing your nonverbal behavior is not simple, it can be done with a little effort and desire. The key is to examine conscientiously how your nonverbal cues may be undermining your intended message. If you realize that you have distracting mannerisms, such as smirking, playing with coins, twisting your hair, shuffling your feet, or saying "you know" or "OK" too much, you can ask others to call your attention to these things. Then you can make a conscious effort to change.

## Summary

Nonverbal communication encompasses everything that we communicate to others without using words. It is not what we say, but how we say it with our tone of voice, body movements, appearance, use of space, touch, and time, all of which competent communicators understand.

We are always communicating something through our nonverbal behavior, regardless of whether we intend to. The interpretation of nonverbal cues depends on context. Nonverbal communication is more believable than verbal communication. It is our primary way of expressing our feelings and attitudes toward others, is related to culture, and is often ambiguous.

Nonverbal communication adds life to our exchanges by complementing, repeating, regulating, and substituting for what we have to say. It can also be used to deceive others. There are at least ten types of nonverbal communication, including kinesics or body language, physical characteristics, haptics or touch, proxemics or space, chronemics or time, paralanguage/vocalics or voice, silence, olfactics or smell, artifacts, and environment. All are interdependent and, together with verbal communication, contribute to the total communication process.

Competent communicators know that their nonverbal behavior may be interpreted differently by different people, because each cue has multiple meanings, the meaning of nonverbal cues often depends on the correct interpretation of several other simultaneous cues, and some nonverbal cues are so subtle that they might be difficult to detect. To avoid misinterpretation, competent communicators are observant of and sensitive to the nonverbal messages they receive, consider all their possible meanings, and avoid jumping to conclusions. They use descriptive feedback whenever possible to ensure that the message they received is the one that was intended.

Competent communicators are also aware of the nonverbal messages that they send to others. They can change their behavior to fit different situations, are aware of what they communicate nonverbally, and are able to regulate their nonverbal cues and other factors to influence others' impressions of them. They know that their nonverbal messages influence how others perceive them. They also are not afraid to ask others for help in changing any distracting nonverbal behaviors that they might have.

# Discussion Starters

1. Why do you think people don't take their nonverbal communication seriously?
2. In developing relationships with others, what role does nonverbal communication play?
3. Why is it important that we take our nonverbal communication seriously?
4. "You cannot not communicate." Describe situations in which you thought you weren't communicating anything but later you found out that you did.
5. Which nonverbal function do you think contributes the most to your understanding of a message? Why?

6. Explain what paralanguage is.
7. In what ways do we use vocal cues to make judgments about others?
8. Explain why you think nonverbal communication is more believable than verbal communication.
9. What is the most important lesson you learned about nonverbal communication from this chapter?

# Notes

1. M. L. Knapp and J. Hall, *Nonverbal Communication in Human Interaction,* 6th ed. (Belmont, CA: Wadsworth/Thomson Learning, 2006), 20–30.
2. M. Argyle, F. Alkema, and R. Gilmour, "The Communication of Friendly and Hostile Attitudes by Verbal and Nonverbal Signals," *European Journal of Social Psychology* 1 (1971): 385–402.
3. T. Novinger, *Intercultural Communication: A Practical Guide* (Austin, TX: University of Texas Press, 2001), 64.
4. M. S. Remland, *Nonverbal Communication in Everyday Life* (New York: Houghton Mifflin, 2000), 229.
5. T. H. Feeley and M. A. Turck, "The Behavioral Correlates of Sanctioned and Unsanctioned Deceptive Communication," *Journal of Nonverbal Behavior* 22 (1998): 189–204; and A. Vrij, L. Akehurst, and P. Morris, "Individual Differences in Hand Movemens During Deception," *Journal of Nonverbal Behavior* 21 (1997): 87–102.
6. L. Anolli and R. Ciceri, "The Voice of Deception: Vocal Strategies of Naïve and Able Liars," *Journal of Nonverbal Behavior* 21 (1997): 259–85.
7. S. W. Janik, A. R. Wellens, J. L. Goldberg, and L. F. Dell'osso, "Eyes as the Center of Focus in the Visual Examination of Human Faces," *Perceptual and Motor Skills* 4 (1978): 857–58.
8. D. Leathers, *Successful Nonverbal Communication: Principles and Applications* (New York: Macmillan, 1986).

9. P. Andersen, *Nonverbal Communication: Forms and Functions* (Mountain View, CA: Mayfield, 1999).
10. C. L. Kleinke, "Gaze and Eye Contact: A Research Review," *Psychological Review* 100 (1986): 78–100.
11. P. G. Zimbardo, *Shyness: What It Is, What to Do about It* (Reading, MA: Addison-Wesley, 1977).
12. P. Greenbaum and H. W. Rosenfield, "Patterns of Avoidance in Responses to Interpersonal Staring and Proximity: Effects of Bystanders on Drivers at a Traffic Intersection," *Journal of Personality and Social Psychology* 36 (1978): 575–87.
13. P. C. Ellsworth and J. M. Carlsmith, "Eye Contact and Gaze Aversion in Aggressive Encounter," *Journal of Personality and Social Psychology* 33 (1973): 117–22.
14. Ibid.
15. A. Robinson, "57 Varieties of a Coach," *Lincoln Journal Star,* September 8, 2002, 3D.
16. C. Izard, *The Psychology of Emotions* (New York: Plenum, 1991); and P. Rozin, L. Lowery, and R. Ebert, "Varieties of Disgust Faces and the Structure of Disgust," *Journal of Personality and Social Psychology* 66 (1994): 870–81.
17. P. Ekman and K. Heider, "The Universality of a Contempt Expression: A Replication," *Motivation and Emotion* 12 (1988): 303–308; and P. Ekman, "Are There Basic Emotions?" *Psychology Review* 99 (1992): 550–53.

18. B. Knutson, "Facial Expression of Emotions Influence Interpersonal Trait Inferences," *Journal of Nonverbal Behavior* 20 (1996): 165–82.

19. H. Aguinis, M. Simonsen, and C. Pierce, "Effects of Nonverbal Behavior on Perceptions of Power Bases," *Journal of Social Psychology* 138 (1998): 455–70.

20. M. T. Motley, "Facial Affect and Verbal Context in Conversation: Facial Expression as Interjection," *Human Communication Research* 20 (1993): 3–40.

21. M. Zukerman, D. T. Larrance, N. H. Spiegel, and R. Klorman, "Controlling Nonverbal Displays: Facial Expressions and Tone of Voice," *Journal of Experimental Social Psychology* 17 (1981): 506–24.

22. P. Ekman, W. V. Friesen, and P. Ellsworth, "Methodological Decisions," in *Emotion in the Human Face,* 2nd ed., ed. P. Ekman (Cambridge: Cambridge University Press, 1982), 7–21.

23. P. Ekman and W. V. Friesen, "The Repertoire of Nonverbal Behavior: Categories, Origins, Usage, and Coding," *Semiotica* 1 (1969): 49–98.

24. D. S. Berry and L. Zebrowitz-McAuthur, "Perceiving Character in Faces: The Impact of Age-Related Craniofacial Changes on Social Perception," *Psychological Bulletin* 100 (1986): 3–18.

25. J. M. Montepare and L. Zebrowitz-McAuthur, "Impressions of People Created by Age-Related Qualities of Their Gaits," *Journal of Personality and Social Psychology* 54 (1988): 547–56.

26. W. Wells and B. Siegel, "Stereotyped Somatypes," *Psychological Reports* 8 (1961): 77–78.

27. M. A. Collins and L. A. Zebrowitz, "The Contribution of Appearance to Occupational Outcomes in Civilian and Military Settings," *Journal of Applied Social Psychology* 71 (1995): 129–63.

28. V. P. Richmond and J. C. McCroskey, *Nonverbal Behavior in Interpersonal Relations,* 5th ed. (Boston: Allyn and Bacon, 2004).

29. M. G. Efran, "The Effect of Physical Appearance on the Judgment of Guilt, Interpersonal Attraction, and Severity of Recommended Punishment in a Simulated Jury Task," *Journal of Research in Personality* 8 (1974): 45–54.

30. E. H. Walster, E. Aronson, D. Abrahams, and L. Rohmann, "Importance of Physical Attractiveness in Dating Behavior," *Journal of Personality and Social Psychology* 4 (1966): 508–16.

31. B. Gillen, "Physical Attractiveness: A Determinant of Two Types of Goodness," *Personality and Social Psychology Bulletin* 7 (1981): 277–81.

32. "When Beauty Can Be Beastly," *Chicago Tribune,* 21 October 1986, 26a.

33. T. F. Cash and N. C. Duncan, "Physical Attractiveness Stereotyping among Black College Students," *Journal of Social Psychology* 122 (1984): 71–77.

34. S. M. Kalick, "Physical Attractiveness as a Status Cue," *Journal of Experimental Social Psychology* 24 (1988): 469–89.

35. A. Feingold, "Gender Differences in Effects of Physical Attractiveness on Romantic Attraction: A Comparison across Five Research Paradigms," *Journal of Personality and Social Psychology* 59 (1990): 981–93.

36. G. Maruyama and N. Miller, "Physical Attractiveness and Personality," in *Advances in Experimental Research in Personality,* ed. B. Maher (New York: Academic Press, 1981); B. Major, P. I. Carrington, and P. J. D. Carnevale, "Physical Attractiveness and Self-Esteem: Attributions for Praise from an Other-Sex Evaluator," *Personality and Social Psychology Bulletin* 10 (1984): 43–50.

37. R. Heslin and T. Alper, "Touch: A Bonding Gesture," in *Nonverbal Interaction,* eds. J. M. Wiemann and R. P. Harrison (Beverly Hills, CA: Sage, 1983), 47–75.

38. S. M. Jourard, *Disclosing Man to Himself* (Princeton, NJ: Van Nostrand, 1968).

39. N. Henley, "Power, Sex, and Nonverbal Communication," *Berkeley Journal of Sociology* 18 (1973–1974): 10–11.

40. E. T. Hall, *The Silent Language* (Greenwich, CT: Fawcett, 1959) and *The Hidden Dimension* (Garden City, NY: Doubleday, 1969).

41. J. K. Burgoon, D. B. Buller, and W. G. Woodall, *Nonverbal Communication: The Unspoken Dialogue,* 2nd ed. (New York: Harper & Row, 1996), 122.

42. B. E. Gronbeck, R. E. McKerrow, D. Ehninger, and A. H. Monroe, *Principles and Types of Speech Communication,* 11th ed. (Glenview, IL: Scott Foresman, 1990), 325.

43. M. L. Knapp, *Essentials of Nonverbal Communication* (New York: Holt, Rinehart and Winston, 1980), 7; M. L. Knapp and J. Hall, *Nonverbal Communication in Human Interaction,* 6th ed. (Belmont CA: Wadsworth/Thomson Learning, 2006).

44. E. R. McDaniel, "Japanese Nonverbal Communication: A Reflection of Cultural Themes," in *Intercultral Communication: A Reader* 11th ed., eds. L. A. Samovar and R. E. Porter (Belmont, CA: Wadsworth/Thomson, 2007), 270–271.

45. P. A. Andersen, "The Cognitive Valence Theory of Intimate Communication," in *Progress in Communication Sciences, Volume XIV: Mutual Influence in Interpersonal Communication: Theory and Research Cognition, Affect, and Behavior,* eds. M. T. Palmer and G. A. Barnett (Stamford, CT: Ablex, 1998), 39–72.

46. "You Are What You Drive: A Silver SUV Broadcasts a Very Different Message from a Green Sedan," *USA Weekend,* October, 2002, 20-1.

# Connecting Listening and Thinking in the Communication Process

**CHAPTER 6**

"Listening well is at the heart of intimacy and connection."

—HARRIET LERNER, THE DANCE OF CONNECTION

# This chapter will help you:

- **Recognize** the importance of listening so that you understand why you need to work at being a good listener.
- **Recognize** how listening helps you make connections with others in all aspects of your lives.
- **Distinguish** between hearing and listening.
- **Outline and explain** the complex nature of the listening process.
- **Explain** the role of feedback on communicators' ability to be effective.
- **Identify and explain** the functions of listening.
- **Identify** specific attitudes and behaviors to help you overcome the barriers to listening.
- **Identify** instances where you must be a critical listener.
- **Create** your own guidelines for listening improvement.
- **Use** technology to take better notes and organize your work.

## Making everyday connections

The following conversation takes place in a for-profit art gallery:

*Badreya (gallery owner):* We really need to change the opening display. The artist demands that we showcase her art in a more realistic setting. How do you think we ought to make that happen?

*Sara:* It seems to me we ought to make the area look like someone's living room. I heard the artist say she wanted to place her art in living rooms around the world. What if we were to create a typical east Indian living room to begin with, and then a typical German or French room, and finally, an American living room?

*Karina:* What a great idea! Just this morning I heard some of the people browsing through the exhibit question how any of those pieces would work in a home. Their unique sizes and shapes, they said, would not lend themselves to just any room in any home.

*Badreya:* Perfect! Why didn't I think of that?

Most of us have probably not worked in an art gallery and have not tried to set up displays that would meet the demands of the artist and the buying public, but we have been in situations in which our listening or failure to listen could have serious significance on the situation. ■

### Questions to think about

- What evidence do you find that the three women at the art gallery were listening to their clients and customers?
- Why would artists, art gallery managers, and art gallery or museum workers need to listen?

- Think of a job task or class assignment in which your failure to listen meant more work, embarrassment, or even a lower grade. What factors led you not to listen as well as you could have?

- What did you learn from that negative experience?

- Now think of a situation in which your good listening made a difference. How did that make you feel? Why were you a better listener in that situation?

Learners bring a variety of learning styles into the classroom; auditory, kinesthetic, and visual are among the most commonly known. Some of us are visual learners. We need to be able to see what is being discussed. Overheads, chalkboard text and drawings, or PowerPoint presentations help the visual learner. The kinesthetic learner experiences things. She or he needs to move around, touch things, watch things work, and take things apart or put them back together. The auditory learner, by contrast, listens to messages and processes information. This kind of learner doesn't need models or hands-on experiences as much as he or she needs to listen to and process information. **Listening** is defined as the active process of receiving, constructing meaning from, and responding to spoken or nonverbal messages. What kind of learner are you? What is the role of listening in your learning? How do you know? What kinds of activities help you learn? What kinds of activities help you listen?

Skills in listening, analyzing, processing, and recording information are often neglected during formal education. Have you ever had any formal training in listening? If you are a typical college student, you have completed course work in reading, writing, and speaking, but few students have ever enrolled in a listening course. Not only are there few opportunities for formal listening instruction, but informal listening training is not generally provided either. Yet as students, you are expected to listen approximately 50 percent of the time—listening is proportionately the most used language skill.[1] In Chapter 1, we discussed surveys from business executives who suggested that graduates need more work on communication skills; *listening* was high on all lists.[2] As of the late 1990s, 64 percent of organizations have provided some sort of listening training for their employees because they find that employees' listening skills are ineffective for today's work environment.[3] Listening has been identified as one of the top skills employers seek in entry-level employees as well as those being promoted, in numerous surveys and research projects.[4] Even though the research suggests that listening skills are critical, according to listening scholars Carolyn Coakley and Andrew Wolvin, it is the communication activity that receives the least instruction in school.[5] Even in the course that uses this textbook, it is likely that only about 7 percent of class and text time is spent on listening.[6] Inefficient listening is a prevalent (and expensive) problem in our lives, in terms of time wasted, poor customer relations, and the need to redo many tasks. The International Listening Association (ILA) is a professional organization comprising members dedicated to the study, application, and improvement of listening in all contexts. Visit the ILA website at www.listen.org for listening resources.

This chapter will help you become an effective listener and, as a result, an effective respondent. To enhance your listening competence, you will need to understand the importance of effective listening, the elements of listening, the functions of listening, and the most common barriers to listening. You need to analyze and evaluate what you listen to and make the connection between listening and thinking, which are separate but related processes. We will provide specific ideas to improve your listening.

■ **listening** The process of receiving, constructing meaning from, and responding to spoken or nonverbal messages.

## MAKING CONNECTIONS

### Andrew D. Wolvin
*University of Maryland*

Andrew D. Wolvin, a communication professor at the University of Maryland, says that the admonition, "Just listen," makes his skin crawl, much like the sound of a fingernail scratching a chalkboard. Listening, Wolvin argues, is a highly complex, probably the most complex, human behavior. Thus, it should not be dismissed so readily and so passively. But it's become too easy for people to let the speaker do all the work. We assume that if the speaker doesn't connect in some way through his or her style and/or message, then the communication hasn't been effective. Think, though, how the communication model assumes a coequal orientation. Listeners have to assume *at*

## To Scholars

*least* 50 percent of the responsibility for the outcome of the communication. Given the complexity of the process (receiving, attending, interpreting, responding) and the variables (listener age, gender, race, culture—just to name a few) that influence this process, it takes Herculean effort to communicate effectively through listening.

Through his research, writing, and teaching about listening, Professor Wolvin has reached thousands of people throughout the world. And, he has been identified as one of the most popular teachers on campus. His goal in life is to ensure that *listening* makes a difference in the way we communicate across cultures. We can reduce conflicts and we can care for our fragile planet by listening, understanding, and responding. So instead of "just" listening, communicators should truly engage as active participants.

# ■ The Importance of Effective Listening

Most misunderstandings that arise in our daily lives occur because of poor listening habits. Poor listening skills can create serious personal, professional, and financial problems. For students, poor listening can result in missed appointments, misunderstood directions, incorrect or incomplete assignments, lower grades, and lost job opportunities.

It might surprise you to realize how much of your waking day you spend listening; when you are not talking or reading, you are probably listening to something or someone. Many communication and listening scholars have found that college students spend 50 percent or more of their time listening, almost one-third in speaking, and less than one-third in reading and writing (see Figure 6.1).[7] In a German study, Imhof and Weinhard found that German primary school children are expected to listen for about two-thirds of classroom time.[8] An earlier U.S. Department of Labor report suggests that 55 percent of government managers' time is spent in listening.[9] Given these figures, it is easy to see how important listening is in our lives.

From the time we get up in the morning until we end the day, we are constantly listening to something. Yet most of us give little thought to the role that listening plays in our everyday experiences. Parents and children

## MAKING CONNECTIONS
### for Success

### Your View of Effective Listening

Think about someone whom you believe to be a good listener.

1. What behaviors does this person exhibit that make you think she or he is a good listener?
2. How do the things good listeners do and say make you aware of their effective listening?
3. How do you compare your own listening behaviors with those of the person whom you identified as a good listener?
4. How might you improve your own listening behaviors?

■ **FIGURE 6.1** Proportional Time Spent by College Students in Communication Activities

The graph indicates how typical college students spend their waking time. The proportions given in this graph are averages and, of course, can vary dramatically from person to person and situation to situation.

6% Email

10% Internet

8% Writing

6% Reading

50% Listening (all forms of listening: in-class, interpersonal, television, radio, CDs/tapes, and telephone)

20% Speaking

both complain, "They don't listen to me." A similar refrain may be heard from relationship partners, workers and bosses, teachers and students. You might even have heard a friend say to you, "You really ought to listen to yourself." As simple as listening appears to be, many of us are not efficient listeners.

Effective listening is important to our success in all aspects of our lives. It may surprise you to realize how much of your waking day you spend listening, but when you are not talking or reading, you are probably listening to something or someone.

According to a survey of executives by Office Team, a leading staffing service in Menlo Park, California, 14 percent of each work week is wasted because of poor communication between staff and managers—amounting to seven weeks per year.[10] Jim Presley, former vice president of professional services at SeeCommerce, a company that developed applications allowing customers to visualize supply chains and form collaborative groups, says that effective listening can improve sales by 30 to 40 percent.[11] Students, too, seem to have trouble as listeners. Informal surveys of our colleagues reveal that the instructors believe the "failure to listen" is one of the major problems in their students. There is little doubt that communicating, and in particular, listening, plays a significant role in society. Because we spend so much time as *consumers* of communication, we need to learn as much as we can about effective listening. In the global community in which we live and work, listening carefully to the messages conveyed by people of other cultures and backgrounds is a skill required to succeed in many areas of life.

Listening scholar Andrew D. Wolvin, author of *Listening in the Quality Organization* (1999), suggests that the individuals who make up organizations must be effective listeners. His book identifies the role of listening in the communication process and provides suggestions for how people can be more effective listeners. He concludes, "Quality listening, then is a benchmark for the quality organization of the twenty-first century. Some organizations have gotten there, while others are yet to develop a listening culture. . . . The challenge to get there is significant, but the rewards are tremendous. Indeed, our very economic, technological, political, and social lives depend on quality listening."[12]

# ■ Listening and Hearing: Is There a Difference?

Because most of us take listening for granted, we tend to think of it as a simple task. However, listening is actually quite complex. Scholars agree that listening, like communication in general, is a process and that it is closely linked to the thinking process. Wolvin and Coakley suggest that listening is a distinct behavior that is separate from other intellectual activities. They acknowledge, however, that much of the research closely links listening with reasoning, comprehension, and memory.[13] Listening scholars and teachers agree that hearing and listening are not the same. It is impossible to listen to sounds without first hearing them, but it is possible to hear sounds without listening to them. What distinguishes listening from hearing?

Communication scholars suggest that the major difference between listening and hearing is the difference between active and passive processes. Hearing is passive. If you have normal hearing, your ears receive sounds.[14] You don't have to work at hearing; it just happens. People can have excellent hearing and be terrible listeners. Listening, on the other hand, is active and requires energy and desire. The ILA defines listening as "the process of receiving, constructing meaning from, and responding to spoken or nonverbal messages."[15]

# ■ The Stages of Effective Listening

Listening is a highly complex behavior. Many people have tried to determine what happens when people listen. What is involved? What happens from the time someone makes sounds to the point where you make meaning from those words and the accompanying nonverbals? Listening scholar Judi Brownell works with people in the hotel and travel industry. She designed a behavioral approach to listening that incorporates the thinking and information processing that occurs when we listen effectively. Her explanation, the **HURIER model,** is what she uses to train businesspeople and students how to become more effective listeners. See Figure 6.2 for a visual representation of the six stages: hearing, understanding, remembering, interpreting, evaluating, and responding.

### ▥ Hearing

**Hearing** is the passive physiological process in which sound is received by the ear. Brownell suggests that accurate reception of sounds requires the listener to focus attention on the speaker, discriminate among sounds, and concentrate.[16] Given our discussion of the difference between hearing and listening, answer this question: When you play music while you study, do you *hear* the music or do you really *listen* to it? The sounds provide background that you hear; your hearing becomes listening only when you also carry out the remaining stages of the listening process.

### ▥ Understanding

**Understanding** might also be labeled *comprehension* and simply means that you assign meaning to the stimuli that you hear or otherwise perceive. Understanding involves the processing of information. The ability to accurately follow directions is one of the ways in which we can measure whether or not we understand what we hear. Students are often in situations in which understanding is critical. Another dif-

■ **HURIER model**
A six-stage model of the listening process involving hearing, understanding, remembering, interpreting, evaluating, and responding.

■ **hearing** A passive physiological process in which sound is received by the ear.

■ **understanding**
Assigning meaning to the stimuli that have been selected and attended to.

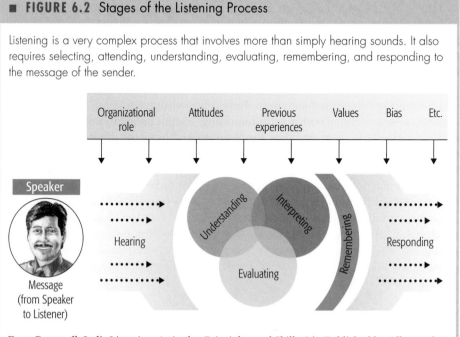

■ **FIGURE 6.2** Stages of the Listening Process

Listening is a very complex process that involves more than simply hearing sounds. It also requires selecting, attending, understanding, evaluating, remembering, and responding to the message of the sender.

From Brownell, Judi. *Listening: Attitudes, Principles, and Skills,* 2/e. Published by Allyn and Bacon, MA. Copyright © 2002 by Pearson Education. Reprinted by permission of the publisher.

ference between hearing and listening is understanding. Although there is no commonly accepted explanation of how understanding occurs, we know that past experience plays an important role and that you relate and compare new sounds and ideas to those you have previously heard. To learn statistics, for example, you must first learn algebra and other mathematical principles. However, if you are unprepared when you walk into your statistics class, you can attend to what the teacher is saying, but because you are unable to interpret the professor's message, you will not understand the material presented. This inability to understand reduces your listening effectiveness.

## Remembering

As a student, you are aware of the importance of **remembering,** or recalling something from stored memory. Most of your professors expect you to recall and apply what you have heard in lectures, discussions, assignments, and activities. Researchers suggest that working memory and long-term memory are both essential processes and that different aspects are required for different situations. Listening scholar Laura Janusik found that when people were presented with a series of unrelated sentences and asked to remember the last word of each sentence, they could remember, on average, 2.805 items. In a dynamic conversational listening task, in which people were asked to remember a series of related questions and respond to them, people could remember and respond to 2.946 items.[17] What this suggests is that if the topic seems more relevant, people will remember slightly more than they do if it seems irrelevant. As you'll recall from Chapter 2, the process of perception (selective perception and selective attention) can also account for the loss of information. We tend to remember only information that supports our own views. Other information is forgotten. Remembering helps you complete class assignments. Memory will also be very important in your work responsibilities when an employer expects you to acquire and apply knowledge, as well as in family and friendship situations.

## Interpreting

In the interpreting stage, the listener simply tries to make sense of the information received. Brownell says that there are two parts to the **interpreting** process: "[Y]ou take into account the total communication context so that you are better able to understand the meaning of what is said from the speaker's point of view,"[18] and you let the speaker know that you understand the message. This is when the specific situation and nonverbal aspects of communication come into play. An effective listener knows that facial expressions, posture, eye contact (or the lack of it), silence, and even paralanguage affect messages. Good listeners will work to develop greater sensitivity to these dimensions of communication.

## Evaluating

In the **evaluating** stage, the listener analyzes evidence, sorts fact from opinion, determines the intent of the speaker, judges the accuracy of the speaker's statements and conclusions, and judges the accuracy of personal conclusions. Once we begin to assess the message we received and understood, we might no longer hear and attend to other incoming messages. Later in the chapter, we further discuss analyzing and evaluating messages.

■ **remembering**
Recalling something from stored memory; thinking of something again.

■ **interpreting** The process of understanding the meaning of the message from the speaker's point of view and letting the speaker know that you understand.

■ **evaluating** The listener analyzes evidence, sorts fact from opinion, determines the intent of the speaker, judges the accuracy of the speaker's statements and conclusions, and judges the accuracy of his or her own decisions.

The main difference between hearing and listening is understanding. Once we have heard, selected, and attended to sounds, we must assign meaning to them for listening to be complete. We can enhance our listening by being open and receptive to what the speaker has to say.

- **responding** Overt verbal and nonverbal behavior by the listener indicating to the speaker what has and has not been received.

# ■ Responding: Sending Feedback

A receiver who has listened to a message can connect with the sender by verbally or nonverbally verifying the message's reception or indicating a lack of reception. This verification is referred to as responding or feedback. **Responding** is the listener's overt behavior that indicates to the speaker what has and has not been received. Examples of such behaviors are total silence (didn't hear the message, ignored the message, or was angry about what the message said), smiling or frowning (agreeing or disagreeing with the message), and asking for clarification of what was received.

Giving feedback is an important part of being an effective listener. Feedback was defined in Chapter 1 as the response to a message that a receiver sends back to a source. Feedback helps to ensure understanding and also helps speakers determine whether they have been successful in communicating. Feedback should be appropriate to the situation, deliberate, thoughtful, and clear. When it is important that you grasp every detail of a message, you should paraphrase or repeat the information for the sender to verify your reception, understanding, and recall of it. This also indicates to the sender that you are actively listening and are committed to receiving the intended message.

Students provide their instructors with feedback, both consciously and unconsciously. Some students, however, might not always be completely honest in their responses. For example, even though they might be totally confused, they might indicate through verbal and nonverbal cues that they are listening to, understanding, and agreeing with everything being said—even if the communication has made little sense to them. This behavior, unfortunately, can lead to more unclear messages and further confusion. When those who are confused admit their confusion, their instructors are more likely to improve their presentations. Active listeners always try to get the most out of the message by making sure that they have received it accurately and completely.

Listening is more than merely paying attention. Listening is an active, complex process. The HURIER model suggests that six

## MAKING CONNECTIONS
### for Success

### Listening Behaviors

A simple experiment illustrates what people tend to remember and for how long. For two or three minutes, read a newspaper or magazine article to a friend, and then ask the friend to repeat the key information. Do the same with several other friends. Most people will be able to report only about 50 percent of what they've heard. Then wait twenty-four hours and ask each person to repeat the information again.

1. Discuss with your friends what you learned from the exercise.
2. Did some people do better than others? If so, why do you think they did?

Tell someone what you learned about listening from doing this exercise.

## MAKING CONNECTIONS for Success

### Listening and Thinking

Andrew Wolvin in the Making Connections to Scholars box says that listening is probably one of the most complex of all human behaviors. So far in this chapter, we have talked about how much listening skills are valued and used, and what's involved in the listening process as well as references to thinking. Also, this chapter is titled "Connecting Listening and Thinking in the Communication Process." It's time to think about those connections. Margarete Imhof, a listening scholar from Germany, found that students report greater listening comprehension when they use active thinking strategies prior to and as they listen to something. Imhof suggests that students ask questions of themselves prior to the communication event, and then, during the communication, to work to find areas of interest and possible application. Try the following:

1. Pick a talk show or news broadcast on a television channel you don't normally watch.
2. Watch the show for 30 minutes without interruptions from other sources (shut off your cell phone, put the computer to sleep, stay in a room without other people).
3. Think about questions that you'll need to have answered during the program.
4. Tell yourself that you need to focus on the programming content.
5. At the end of the 30 minutes, check to see if your questions were answered.
6. Did a focus on the relevance of the material make a difference?
7. Could you see how the person(s) had views that were reasonable, even if you did not share their views?

interdependent stages are necessary for effective listening. A good listener knows that effective listening includes hearing, understanding, remembering, interpreting, evaluating, and responding.

Each of us has an optimal thinking style and we favor some listening styles over others as well. Listening scholars Barker and Watson found that the four primary listening styles are people oriented, time oriented, action oriented, and content oriented.[19] Which of the four best fits you? Critical thinking scholars have differing labels for optimum learning styles. Some of us are visual learners, while others are auditory. Some of us like things to be very linear and sequential, others don't really care about the order of messages and information. As competent listeners, we need to reflect on what works best for us, both as learners and as listeners. And, since there's a connection between listening and thinking, we need to think about how to use our "working memory" to better facilitate effectiveness as seen in Guidelines: Working Memory.

## Working Memory                                    GUIDELINES

Brownell and others suggest approaches to enhance your working memory. The following strategies will help you retain information long enough to use it.

1. *Repetition.* This is a strategy in which you repeat things to keep them in mind. When you have to go to the bookstore to get school supplies without a written list, you might constantly repeat your needs as you walk over: "PDA, stapler,

staples, index cards, special pen for art class, zip disks, book for listening class." Any kind of interference, however, can make you forget some or most of your list.

**2.** *Chunking.* When you have many things to remember, you might group them into categories so that you have fewer details to remember. Have you ever thought about why telephone numbers are created as they are? Researchers suggest that we can remember up to seven individual pieces of information. If you use chunking, you will keep your groupings in seven or fewer categories to retain information long enough to use it immediately, or help move it to long-term memory.

**3.** Identification of logical patterns. If you can identify patterns or themes in the information you hear, it is usually easier to remember, at least for a short time. Numbers in a sequence, or acronyms ("gee, I'm a tree" for remembering how to spell geometry or "every good boy does fine" and "face" for remembering the notes on the treble clef musical scale) are logical patterns that some of your earlier teachers may have provided to help you remember their subjects.

*Source:* Judi Brownell, *Listening: Attitudes, Principles, and Skills,* 3e. Published by Allyn and Bacon, Boston, MA, pp.151–52. Copyright © 2006 by Pearson Education. Reprinted by permission of the publisher.

If you want to keep information in working memory for future use, you have to find other strategies to process and put it into long-term memory. Judi Brownell suggests five techniques for storing things in memory so they can be used later.

- The first strategy is *association.* You probably already use this in some ways to connect something new to something you already know. Situations often provide the stimulus for associations. If you remember that Celine (as in Deon) is a choreographer whom you met in Charleston who always ordered a cafè latte and now lives in Chico, California, you have a number of cues that can help you remember Celine, where she is, and what she does.

- *Categorization* is a second strategy. When you organize information into categories, you can often remember better and longer. Plan your grocery shopping according to the aisles where the products are located. Remembering what categories there are helps you study for exams, what divisions to include in reports, and what tasks need to be accomplished. Categorization can increase your work efficiency because the logical order facilitates retrievable memory from storage.

- Meaningful information is much easier to retrieve. Unrelated pieces of data are harder to remember. *Mediation* works in the following ways. (1) form a meaningful word out of foreign words or meaningless syllables. This author went to Denmark to find relatives. The street name in Danish meant "church on the hill" so we looked for a church on a hill before we looked for Danish street signs and found the right place. (2) Words can be made out of the initial letters of the items presented. For example, ALS or Lou Gehrig's disease is much easier to remember than amyotrophic lateral sclerosis. Creating "words" can enhance your ability to recall information. (3) Another mediation technique is to create a word that links two or more words and ideas. If you need to remember *cat, ball,* and *pillow,* you might link them with the word *soft.* This can help you connect seemingly unrelated items.

- Most information is processed into your memory through one of two channels: the visual or the auditory. To tap into this, you can use *imagery,* by creating visual or mental images from the information presented. If you want to remember something, you create vivid mental images of that information in order to later recall and apply it.

- *Mnemonics* is the fifth technique. You create ways to make sense of the information presented and use visual imagery to make the impression vivid. By combining meaningful words and vivid images, you can recall information more quickly and accurately.[20]

Memory is only one aspect of the thinking process. The more we are able to remember, the better we will be able to analyze, evaluate, and apply concepts to the information we gain. We can use memory and thinking to be better listeners and better consumers of information.

# The Functions of Listening

You wake in the morning to the sound of an alarm clock, the noise your roommate makes moving around in the next room, or the ring of a telephone. While you dress, students talk outside your door, and a fire engine wails in the street. You turn on your radio. At breakfast, you join in a heated discussion about the proposed destruction of a historic building on your campus. Then you rush off to the last lecture before an upcoming exam. In the evening, you go to a concert. After the concert, you meet a good friend who is really upset over receiving a low grade on a test.

Throughout the day, you listened to many different people and things for a variety of purposes. You listened to the alarm clock to get up at the right time; you listened to your friends' opinions to evaluate the proposed removal of the oldest building on campus; you listened to your professor to get information about a subject; you listened to the concert for enjoyment; you listened to your troubled friend to understand his feelings. In each case, listening served a different function and involved different skills. Let's look at each of these functions in greater detail and the listening skills that each requires.

Empathic listening occurs when we listen to what someone else is experiencing and seek to understand that person's thoughts and feelings. When we empathize, we try to put ourselves in the other person's place to understand what is happening to him or her.

## Listening to Obtain Information

You probably spend great amounts of time **listening for information,** that is, listening to gain comprehension. You listen as your teacher discusses process, perception, nonverbal and verbal communication, famous speakers, and similar topics in order to learn about speech skills. Each day, you listen for information such as news, weather forecasts, sports scores, directions, orders, assignments, names, numbers, and locations.

## Listening to Evaluate

**Evaluative listening** is listening to judge or to analyze information. A car owner who hears a squeak coming from the front end rolls down the window and does some evaluative listening. The owner tries to pinpoint the exact location and cause of the bothersome noise. A teacher listens to students' speeches to discriminate between good and poor presentations and to assign grades. In most situations we all should listen critically. We should constantly judge evidence, arguments, facts, and values. We need to ask questions to be effective listeners. We are bombarded by messages asking us to believe, accept, or buy things. For our own protection, we must evaluate everything to which we listen.

## Listening with Empathy

**Empathic listening** occurs when you listen to what someone else is experiencing and seek to understand that person's thoughts and feelings. It is not sympathy, which means that you feel sorry for the other person. Empathy means that you try to put yourself in another person's place to try to understand what is happening to that person. We might find it difficult to avoid making judgments when we listen to someone else's problems, but that is exactly what we must do to listen with empathy. Listening empathically can be a healing and soothing process. Empathic listening indicates that we are aware, appreciative, and understanding of another person's feelings.

Caring about someone requires a great deal of sensitivity as well as the ability to communicate that sensitivity. It is not easy to listen; it is even more difficult to listen with empathy. If we fail to empathize with others, however, we also fail to understand them. (You will learn more about relationships and relational communication in Chapters 13 and 14.) Law enforcement and the medical profession are two examples of careers that require empathic listening.

## Listening for Enjoyment

When we listen purely for pleasure, personal satisfaction, and appreciation, we **listen for enjoyment.** We usually listen to music, for example, simply because we enjoy it. The same is true for most of us when we combine listening and viewing as we watch television or a movie.

Listening for enjoyment involves more than merely sitting back and letting sounds enter our ears. Listening for enjoyment also involves the thinking process. We evaluate what we hear and see to understand something or to learn more about it. As we listen to music, we try to find some personal value or relevance in the lyrics and the instrumentation. Even if we attend an opera for the first time and do not understand the language, we can enjoy the performance as we seek to understand it. In other words, listening for enjoyment uses the same process as other kinds of listening: We select, attend, understand, evaluate, and remember. We construct meaning from what we hear and respond to it in some way.

■ **listening for information** Listening to gain comprehension.

■ **evaluative listening** Listening to judge or analyze information.

■ **empathic listening** Listening to understand what another person is thinking and feeling.

■ **listening for enjoyment** Listening for pleasure, personal satisfaction, or appreciation.

# ■ Barriers to Effective Listening

Why are most people poor listeners? The answer to this question is surprisingly complex. The quality of our listening changes from time to time and from situation to situation. A number of barriers contribute to our ineffectiveness as listeners. The context of each communication will affect how important each barrier actually is, and some of the barriers that reduce our listening effectiveness are under our control whereas others are not. The following six barriers to effective listening were identified by Ralph Nichols, who is considered the "father of listening research."[21] Nichols and other researchers have replicated his research in subsequent studies and found the same results. Although these six barriers may not be the only ones, they are the most common. And remember, listening, like communication, is a learned behavior, so we *can learn* to overcome the obstacles that interfere with our listening effectiveness.

## ■ Considering the Topic or Speaker Uninteresting

The level of interest and the amount of importance we place on a subject or a speaker usually govern how much effort we put into listening. Deciding that a subject or person is uninteresting or boring often leads us to the conclusion that the information being presented is not important. However, this is not necessarily true. What appears to be dull or insignificant might very well be vital for passing an exam, doing an assignment correctly, learning something, following your supervisor's instructions, making a sale, or learning a new way of doing something on the job. In other words, a competent listener keeps an open mind.

## ■ Criticizing the Speaker Instead of the Message

How many times have you judged a speech by the number of "ahs" and "ums" the speaker used? How many times has a speaker's volume, mispronunciations, or accent influenced your opinion? Have you ever missed a message because you were focusing on a mismatched shirt and tie, bizarre earrings, or the speaker's facial expressions or nervous behaviors?

Of course, when possible, speakers should do everything in their power to eliminate personal quirks that may distract attention from their message, but listeners must also share responsibility for receiving the message. An effective listener must be able to overlook the superficial elements of a person's delivery style or appearance to concentrate on the substance of the presentation. In short, the listener must stay involved in the message, not the speaker or the speaker's attire or behaviors.

## ■ Concentrating on Details, Not Main Ideas

Many of us listen for specific facts such as dates, names, definitions, figures, and locations, assuming that they are the important things to know. But are they? Specific facts are needed in some situations, but we often focus too much on details. As a result, we walk away with disjointed details and no idea how they relate to each other and to the total picture.

Competent listeners focus on the main or most important ideas, not on every single word. All stages of the listening process are affected adversely when we forget that general ideas can be more significant than the details that surround them. Listen carefully to your professors or your supervisors for clues to what is most important and note when they ask you to carefully select what to write in your notes, or include in your work tasks.

## ◼ Avoiding Difficult Listening Situations

Most of us find it difficult to keep up with the vast amount and increasing technical complexity of the information that confronts us each day. At times, we might deal with complex listening situations by giving up and ignoring what is being presented.

Concentration and energy are needed to overcome the temptation to ignore or avoid what might seem difficult and confusing. When you are faced with a difficult listening situation, the best approach is usually to ask questions. For example, physicians often use complex medical terminology when talking to patients, but patients can take the responsibility for gaining understanding. They can ask the physician to explain terms, to review procedures, and to supply missing information. The same principles apply to the classroom or to the workplace. You should never hesitate to ask about something when you don't understand it, because without understanding, you cannot learn.

Sometimes, you might not listen to new and difficult information because you lack motivation, but once again, the responsibility falls on you to make the effort to listen. Try consciously and continually to listen to such communication. Each time you are successful at staying tuned in, you will acquire not only some information, but also improved confidence and ability.

## ◼ Tolerating or Failing to Adjust to Distractions

Distractions constantly disrupt our concentration. As listeners, we have the responsibility to adjust to, compensate for, or eliminate distractions and to focus on speakers and their messages.

We can control some distractions. If noise from another room competes with a speaker, for example, the listener can close the door, ask the person who is creating the noise to be quiet, move closer to the speaker, or ask the speaker to talk louder.

Some distractions must be overcome through mental rather than physical effort. A noise in the background can become a major distraction, or we can reduce it to a minor nuisance by forcing ourselves to listen more intently to the speaker. When distractions occur, we must consciously focus on selecting the appropriate messages and attending to them. We must take advantage of our ability to filter out extraneous noise and distractions and concentrate on the sounds that are important to us. If we cannot modify external noise, we must alter our internal listening behavior in order to understand the speaker's message.

## ◼ Faking Attention

At one time or another, everyone pretends to pay attention to something or someone. You appear to listen intently, but your mind is somewhere else. You might even smile in agreement when all you are really doing is maintaining eye contact. In class, you might pretend to take notes, although your mind might not be following what is being said.

Pretending to pay attention can become a habit. Without even realizing what you are doing, you might automatically tune out a speaker and let your mind wander. If, after a speech, you cannot recall the main purpose or the essential points presented by the speaker, you were probably faking attention. Although it might seem harmless, such deceptive behavior can lead to misunderstandings and cause people to question your credibility and sincerity.

■ **TABLE 6.1** Ineffective and Effective Listening Habits

| BAD LISTENER | GOOD LISTENER |
| --- | --- |
| Thinks that topic or speaker is of no interest | Finds areas of interest—keeps an open mind |
| Focuses on the speaker's appearance and delivery | Concentrates on the content of the presentation and overlooks speaker characteristics—stays involved |
| Listens only for details | Listens for ideas |
| Avoids difficult material | Exercises the mind—prepares to listen |
| Is easily distracted | Resists distractions |
| Fakes attention | Pays attention |

Table 6.1 summarizes the differences between ineffective and effective listening habits.

Competent listeners need to ask themselves, "Am I really paying attention?" When listeners realize they are distracted, they should make an effort to pay attention. Good listeners recognize when they are not listening well and do whatever it takes to return their attention to the speaker. While you may think, "What's in it for me?" when someone is sharing something that seems irrelevant to you, if you make use of your critical thinking and critical listening skills, you'll try to determine how it may be helpful at some point, even if it's not right now. Competent listeners demonstrate attitudes, behaviors, and thinking that allow them to focus on others. They know that listening is an active process that requires energy and effort.

# ■ Critical Listening and Critical Thinking: Analyzing and Evaluating Messages

As listeners, our goal is more than simply understanding a message; we also try to become critical listeners. Practicing **critical listening** involves analyzing and assessing the accuracy of the information presented, determining the reasonableness of its conclusions, and evaluating its presenter. In other words, we must ask ourselves questions about the message: Is the message true? Is it based on solid evidence? Is it complete? Is it logical? What motivates the speaker to present the message?

We are constantly confronted with choices and decisions. For example, we are exposed to numerous commercial messages each day in addition to the interpersonal messages we receive at school, home, work, and in recreational situations. We also live in an increasingly technological world. Web searches to find information for our college papers and presentations; to enhance a presentation at work; or even to learn more about a city, country, or company provide an infinite number of resources very quickly. (We discuss web searches for speeches in greater detail in Chapter 8.) Because we are limited in the amount of experience we can acquire on our own, we must depend on others to provide information and advice. Thus we must evaluate and assess that information in order to judge its value and utility. We do this through critical thinking. Critical thinking is integrally linked to critical listening, because they are

■ **critical listening**
Listening that judges the accuracy of the information presented, determines the reasonableness of its conclusions, and evaluates its presenter.

both a part of the process of gaining an understanding of our world. There are many definitions of critical thinking. One definition of **critical thinking** suggests that critical thinkers ask and answer the right questions to determine the appropriate responses to problems and issues.[22] In an earlier work, critical thinking scholar Robert Ennis defined critical thinking as the ability to analyze and assess information.[23] From these two definitions alone, you should be able to make the connection between listening and thinking. You must listen carefully and construct meaning from ideas, messages, and so forth if you are to make sense of the world around you. Critical thinking has become so important to academic institutions and to employers that more and more colleges and universities include courses or units in critical thinking in their curricula; some even provide a web page devoted to the characteristics of the critical thinker.[24] Bellevue Community College's web page identifies nine characteristics of a critical thinker and two implications and six aspects of critical thinking. Basically, you need to remember that the link between critical thinking and critical listening is that critical thinkers have specific attitudes and mental habits. They are intellectually curious, flexible, objective, persistent, systematic, honest, and decisive. They use their critical listening abilities to assess information and choose the best options from among those available. Critical thinkers are aware of the ways they learn best and capitalize on opportunities to expand their learning abilities. One goal of a liberal arts education is to encourage students to think critically. We hope that this text helps you develop "habits of mind" to enable you to become effective thinkers, listeners, and communicators.

Critical thinking and critical listening are closely linked. The critical thinker knows how to analyze and assess information. The critical listener knows how to make connections between messages and issues. The critical listener also uses the ability to analyze and evaluate messages to determine whether ideas are logically presented and whether the speaker is well informed and exhibits clear thinking. Critical listeners must be critical thinkers. Critical thinking and critical listening are closely related parts of a very complex process. Listening with a critical ear involves two phases: (1) assessing the speaker's values and intent and (2) judging the accuracy of the speaker's conclusions.[25]

### ■ Assessing the Speaker's Motivation

Assessing a speaker's motivation generally involves three stages of information processing: (1) making a judgment about the speaker's beliefs, (2) comparing our standards and those of the speaker, and (3) evaluating the worth of the message being presented.

Values are strongly held beliefs central to the communication process and to each individual's perceptual system. They affect our perception and interpretation of both the messages we send and the messages we receive. The first consideration in listening, therefore, is to examine the message to determine the speaker's values: We critically think about what the speaker is saying and how it compares to our own

■ **critical thinking**
The ability to analyze and assess information.

**cathy®**                                        **by Cathy Guisewite**

value system. Of course, we should not automatically dismiss a message merely
because the speaker's values conflict with our own. However, any time we are confronted with a message that differs from our own views—one that asks us to do
something, buy something, or behave in a certain way—we should be aware of the
purpose behind it.

The second consideration is to determine whether the message urges us to conform to or go against our principles or standards. Finally, we consider how to evaluate and respond to the messages. We use our critical thinking skills to recognize and
understand the motivation behind the messages we receive.

## ▬▬ Judging the Accuracy of the Speaker's Conclusions

To make accurate judgments and to think critically about important messages, ask
the following questions:

- Is the speaker qualified to draw the conclusion?
- Has the speaker actually observed the concept or issue about which he or she is
  talking?
- Does the speaker have a vested interest in the message?
- Is there adequate evidence presented to support the conclusion?
- Is the evidence relevant to the conclusion?
- Does contrary evidence exist that refutes what has been presented?
- Does the message contain invalid or inadequate reasoning?

# ▪ Improving Listening Competence

With appropriate knowledge and practice, all of us can become better listeners. First,
we must recognize the importance of listening effectively. Second, we must think of
listening as an *active* behavior that requires conscious participation. Third, we must
recognize that a willingness to work and a desire to improve are essential to increasing listening effectiveness.

In some situations, we need not listen with full attention. For example, if we listen
to a CD while conversing with a friend, we're not likely to create problems by attending closely to the friend and partially to the music. However, each listener must be able
to identify when total energy and involvement in the listening process are crucial.

## MAKING CONNECTIONS for Success

### How Do Others Rate You as a Listener?

How do you think the following people would rate you as a listener? Use a scale of 0 to 100, with 100 being the highest rating.

1. Your best friend
2. Your boss or a teacher
3. Your roommate or a co-worker
4. Your parents

After you rated yourself, go to each person and ask him or her to rate you (without disclosing your rating, of course). Compare the ratings. Were they the same? If not, why?

Effective listening often requires both energy and concentration; listeners need to constantly remind themselves that listening is vital to communication. People call on different listening skills, depending on whether their goal is to comprehend information, critique and evaluate messages, show empathy for others, or appreciate a performance. According to the National Communication Association, competent listeners demonstrate (1) knowledge and understanding of the listening process, (2) the ability to use appropriate and effective listening skills for a given communication situation and setting, and (3) the ability to identify and manage barriers to listening, all of which we have covered in this chapter.

Competent listeners work at listening. They are prepared to listen and know what they wish to gain from their listening experiences. Competent listeners also engage in appropriate listening behaviors. They realize that being a good listener is an active and complex process. They know that they must pay attention if they are to listen well. They do not interrupt others, they look at the speaker, they listen to ideas, and they concentrate on what is being said.

## GUIDELINES   Competent Listeners

1. Be prepared to listen. Learn to control internal and external distractions.
2. Behave like a good listener. Stop talking, and let others have their say. Do not interrupt. Concentrate on what is being said, not on who is saying it or what the speaker is doing. Good listeners maintain eye contact with speakers, ask questions at appropriate times, and maintain flexibility as they carefully listen to the speaker's views.
3. Take good notes. Listen for main ideas, and write down the most significant, most important points; don't attempt to write down every word. Good note taking helps listeners remember better and longer and provides a written indication of ideas to remember. Brevity is usually best so that you can carefully listen to the speaker and the speaker's intent. Write clearly to facilitate the review of your notes later. Review your notes as soon after the event as possible to help you recall them later. Finally, reorganize or rearrange your notes if necessary for clarity before filing them for future reference. Do not get so involved in note taking that effective listening is lost. Note taking should be used as an aid to listening, not as a replacement for it. All six stages of the listening process are brought into play when we listen effectively. Never concentrate so hard on writing everything down that you fail to think about what is said.
4. Ask questions to clarify information. Make sure you know what your supervisor or teacher requires.

## MAKING Technology CONNECTIONS

### Listening and the Internet

You probably spend a great deal of time on the Internet. Can we listen on the Internet? If we can, how do we do it? In today's job market, many of the early aspects of matching applicants and jobs are completed via the Internet. The responses the employer gets to questions posed in email communication often substitute for the telephone conference call or phone interview. Because transportation costs are so high, more and more of the "interviewing" of candidates occurs online, but employers often say they miss the listening aspect. Think about these questions and share your answers with a classmate.

1. How do you adapt to online information versus the old way of listening to and observing responses in person or by phone?

2. How do you think an employer adapts to Internet interview information, versus the traditional face-to-face interview?
3. Can you listen to what is not being said when you communicate online?
4. Does the Internet keep us from stereotyping people or does it make us more likely to stereotype? Why do you think as you do?
5. Can we overcome racial or cultural bias and prejudice because of the Internet? Why? Why not?
6. What, if anything, takes the place of observing nonverbal behavior or listening to tone of voice, pauses, and inflections?

## ■ Listening and Technology

Just as some people think that computers and technology will destroy families and relationships, some believe that computers, email, and the Internet will harm listening in all areas of our lives. What we and other communication scholars have found

Technology can be used to the listener's advantage if it helps the listener focus on the central point in a presentation.

Email conversations are similar to other communication, especially one-to-one interactions. Interactants should carefully "listen" to each other for meaning, and "eavesdroppers" are not appreciated!

in our communication classrooms, however, is that technology can be used to students' advantage if it is used as a tool. We suggested that taking notes helps us become better listeners, and appropriate technology as a delivery tool can also serve that function. Recent studies reported at ILA conventions indicate an increasing use of computer-enhanced presentations (such as PowerPoint) and an expanding student ability to take better notes help students perform better on exams when technology and note-taking instruction are provided early and reinforced throughout the semester.[26] Listeners must remember to think independently. The words on the screen cannot eliminate individual choices. It is too easy to let the screen images take priority. But, as we have pointed out in this chapter, listeners must listen with their eyes, their minds, their bodies, their hearts, and their ears. Students need to listen to determine where the instructor's emphases are and take notes accordingly.

Our students interviewed employers about their expectations of listening behaviors for employees. Many of the employers said that listening is more critical than ever and that electronic messages are harder to "listen to" because the nonverbal elements are missing. Interviewees suggested that technology and listening require people to ask clarifying questions.

# ■ Intercultural Listening

Research in intercultural listening is fairly new, so there is not a great deal of information available. What we do know, however, is that people in all cultures are required to listen. We also know that some cultures value listening much more than we do in the United States. Interviews with international students suggest that people in Asia, Mexico, and Venezuela especially value listening. In contrast, Northern European students report that listening is "just something we do" and "something that is expected of us. We aren't really taught to listen." Interviews with teachers in Europe indicate that they would like to know how to get their students to be better listeners.[27]

When asked how listening is taught in Eastern cultures, interviewees state that children are taught to listen to others in a respectful way. Much of the teaching in schools is done through examples and specific statements of expectations to be courteous and to attend to what others are saying. Students in Asia and in Mexico are taught to listen first and ask questions later. The Chinese symbol for the term *to listen* is made up of symbols for eyes, ears, and heart and corresponds with the Chinese view that people must listen with their entire beings: their eyes, their ears, and, most especially, their hearts (see Figure 6.3). The Chinese believe that listening is very important and that when one listens, nothing else should occur because listening should take one's entire attention and energy.[28]

■ **FIGURE 6.3** The Chinese Character for the Term *To Listen*

The elements of this character incorporate a person's entire being.

Although we don't have the answers to the similarities and differences in listening in every culture in the world, we do know that communicators need to be aware of both. In the United States, we think nothing of interrupting a speaker in conversation. According to the responses gained in interviews, in places such as Hong Kong, China, Taiwan, Japan, China, Mexico, and Venezuela, if you interrupt, you will be branded as a discourteous person, and the local residents will avoid speaking with you. The best advice for communicating with people from other cultures is to (1) respectfully ask questions and (2) be aware of cultural differences. The guidelines for competent listeners apply equally to intercultural listening and domestic listening experiences. Listening requires energy and commitment with whomever we communicate.

## Summary

The listening process is often taken for granted because people think that it "just happens." However, listening actually is a complex process crucial to effective communication. Hearing and listening are two different but related things; hearing is the first stage in the listening process. Unless you can accurately receive (hear) the sounds and messages that are sent, you will not be able to understand, remember, interpret, evaluate, or respond. The six stages of the HURIER model demonstrate the complexity of listening.

Students spend a great deal of time listening, and the function of that listening is often to gain information for future use. You also need to learn and apply thinking skills to evaluate the messages you receive. If you want to enhance your relationships, you will listen empathically to understand your family, friends, or partners. Most of us spend large amounts of time in pleasurable listening pursuits. All in all, you spend the majority of your waking hours in some kind of listening behavior. It is therefore important to understand the process and functions of listening.

To be competent, you must work at listening. I tell my students that the listener is 51 percent responsible for effective communication. This does not take away the responsibilities of the speaker; it merely emphasizes the importance of listening in the communication process. You can learn to be a better listener, overcome bad listening habits, and develop effective attitudes, behaviors, and mind-sets. The benefits might well be that you take better notes, follow assignments better, get higher grades, perform more effectively on the job, and receive pay raises and promotions because you took the time to learn effective listening behaviors. Technology should be used as a tool to enhance listening. In Asian cultures, listening is a very important skill. The Chinese symbol for the term *to listen* suggests that true listening comes from using the eyes, the ears, the heart, with undivided attention.

# Discussion Starters

1. Why do we take listening for granted?
2. How important is effective listening?
3. What are the characteristics of effective listening?
4. Why is listening more complex than hearing?
5. What is the role of memory in the listening process?
6. How are listening and thinking connected?
7. How can you improve your memory?
8. Why is it important to understand the different functions of listening?
9. What does it mean to listen with empathy?
10. On the basis of what you read in this chapter, how can technology help you take better notes?

# Notes

1. R. Bohlken, "Substantiating the Fact That Listening Is Proportionately Most Used Language Skill," *The Listening Post* 70 (1999): 5.
2. National Association of Colleges and Employers, Work Week, *Wall Street Journal,* February 8, 2000. Also, American Council on Education, *Spanning the Chasm: Corporate and Academic Cooperation to Improve Work-Force Preparation* (Washington, D.C.: American Council on Education, 1997).
3. What Employers Teach (1997, October). 1997 Industry Report. [Special issue]. *Training,* 33–75.
4. AICPA 2005. *Highlighted Responses from the Association for Accounting Marketing Survey. Creating the Future Agenda for the Profession—Managing Partner Perspective,* www.aicpa.org/pubs/tpcpa/feb2001.hilight .htm. Accessed on June 20, 2006. V. P. Goby and J. H. Lewis, "The Key Role of Listening in Business: A Study of the Singapore Insurance Industry," *Business Communication Quarterly* 63(2) (2000): 41–51; G. E. Hynes and V. Bhatia, "Graduate Business Students' Preferences for the Managerial Communication Course Curriculum," *Business Communication Quarterly* 59(2) (1996): 45–55; M. James, "Essential Topics and Subtopics of Business Communication: Are we Teaching What Employers Want?" *Business Education Forum* 46(4) (1992): 8–10: J. D. Maes, T. G. Weldy, and M. L. Icenogle, "A Managerial Perspective: Oral Communication Competency Is Most Important for Business Students in the Workplace," *The Journal of Business Communication* 34(1) (1997): 67–80; K. K. Waner, "Business Communication Competencies Needed by Employees as Perceived by Business Faculty and Business Professionals," *Business Communication Quarterly* 58(4) (1995): 51–56; S. C. Willmington, "Oral Communication Skills Necessary for Successful Teaching," *Educational Research Quarterly* 16(2) (1992): 5–17; J. L. Winsor, D. B. Curtis, and R. D. Stephens, "National Preferences in Business and Communication Education: A Survey Update," *JACA* 3 (1997): 170–179.
5. C. Coakley and A. Wolvin, "Listening in the Educational Environment," in eds. M. Purdy and D. Borisoff, *Listening in Everyday Life: A Personal and Professional Approach,* 2nd ed. (Lanham, MD: University Press of America, 1997) 179–212.
6. L. A. Janusik, "Teaching Listening. What Do We Know? What Should We Know?" *International Journal of Listening* 16 (2002): 5–39, and L. A. Janusik and A. D. Wolvin, "Listening Treatment in the Basic Communication Course Text," in ed. D. Sellnow, *Basic Communication Course Annual* (Boston: American Press, 2002).
7. L. A. Janusik and A. D. Wolvin, "24 hours in a Day. A Listening Update to the Time Studies," paper presented at the meeting of the International Listening Association, Salem, Oregon, 2006. Other studies that

show similar results are: R. Bohlken (1999), see Ref. 1; P. Rankin, "Listening Ability," *Proceedings of the Ohio State Educational Conference's Ninth Annual Session,* 1929; E. K. Werner, "A Study of Communication Time," unpublished Master's Thesis, University of Maryland, College Park; L. Barker, R. Edwards, C. Gaines, K. Gladney, and F. Holley, "An Investigation of Proportional Time Spent in Various Communication Activities by College Students," *Journal of Applied Communication Research* 8 (1980): 101–109; O. Hargie, C. Saunders, and D. Dickson, *Social Skills in Interpersonal Communication,* 3rd ed. (New York: Routledge, 1994).

8. M. Imhof and T. Weinhard, "What Did You Listen to in School Today?" Paper presented at the 25th annual convention of the International Listening Association, Fort Myers, Florida, April, 2004.

9. U.S. Department of Labor, *Skills and New Economy* (Washington, D.C.: U.S. Government Printing Office, 1991).

10. Office Team Survey, 2000, cited in *Sssh! Listen Up!* HighGain, Inc. Newsletter (June 2000): 4.

11. J. Presley, "Putting It into Practice," cited in *Sssh! Listen Up!* HighGain, Inc. Newsletter (June 2000): 3.

12. A. D. Wolvin, *Listening in the Quality Organization* (Ithaca, NY: Finger Lakes Press, 1999), 54.

13. A. Wolvin and C. Coakley, *Listening,* 5th ed. (Dubuque, IA: William C. Brown, 1998), 70.

14. E. C. Glenn, "A Content Analysis of Fifty Definitions of Listening," *Journal of the International Listening Association* 3 (1989): 21–31.

15. International Listening Association Definition, 1994, in A. Wolvin, "On Competent Listening," *Listening Post* 54 (July 1995), 1.

16. J. Brownell, *Listening: Attitudes, Principles and Skills,* 3rd ed. (Boston: Allyn and Bacon, 2006), 15.

17. L. A. Janusik, "Researching Listening from the Inside Out: The Relationship Between Conversational Listening Span and Perceived Communication Competence," *UMI Proquest: Digital Dissertations.* wwwlib .umi.com/dissertations.

18. Brownell, *Listening,* 15.

19. L. L. Barker and K. W. Watson, *Listen Up. How to Improve Relationships, Reduce Stress, and Be More Productive by Using the Power of Listening* (New York: St. Martin's Press, 2000.)

20. Brownell, *Listening,* 154–57.

21. R. Nichols, "Factors Accounting for Differences in Comprehension of Material Presented Orally in the Classroom" (Ph.D. diss., University of Iowa, 1948); R. O. Hirsch, *Listening: A Way to Process Information Aurally* (Dubuque, IA: Gorsuch, Scarisbrick, 1979), 36–41.

22. V. R. Rugierro, *Beyond Feelings: Critical Thinking,* 6th ed. (Belmont, CA: Mayfield Publishing, 2000).

23. R. H. Ennis, "A Concept of Critical Thinking," *Harvard Educational Review* 32 (1962): 83–84.

24. Bellevue Community College, www.ir.bcc.ctc.edu/ library/ilac/critdef.htm. Accessed on June 15, 2006.

25. E. D'Angelo, *The Teaching of Critical Thinking* (Amsterdam, The Netherlands: B. R. Gruner, 1971), 7; R. H. Ennis, "A Taxonomy of Critical Thinking Dispositions and Abilities," in *Teaching Thinking Skills: Theory and Practice,* eds. J. Baron and R. Sternberg (New York: Freeman, 1987).

26. P. E. Emmert and V. Emmert, ILA Convention Papers, 1997, 1998; M. L. Beall, ILA Convention Papers, 1997, 1998, 2001.

27. M. L. Beall, "Perspectives on Intercultural Listening," an unpublished paper presented at the National Communication Association Convention 2, New Orleans, Louisiana, November 2002.

28. M. L. Beall, "Asian Perspectives on Intercultural Listening," an unpublished paper presented at the World Communication Association Summer Conference, Lincoln, Nebraska, August 2002.

# Selecting a Topic and Connecting to the Audience

"Information is the coin of the realm in cyberspace."

—CHARLES RUBIN

# This chapter will help you:

- **Understand** the requirements for choosing a topic.
- **Describe** the options for choosing a topic.
- **Assess** the appropriateness of a topic for speaker, audience, and occasion.
- **Formulate** general purpose statements.
- **Create** specific purpose statements.
- **Apply** the process of audience analysis in selecting and modifying a topic.
- **Apply** the information you gain from your analysis to make better connections with the audience.
- **Evaluate** the suitability and relevance of the topic for the audience.

## Making everyday connections

One day soon your communication professor will say something such as, "Today we begin our discussion of the public communication process. You will soon present an informative speech to your class-mates. This speech will allow you to make connections among the chapters and concepts we've covered so far. In the next few weeks you will experience the entire range of activities for giving a speech: selecting a topic and connecting to the audience, gathering and using information, organizing and outlining your speech, speech delivery, dealing with anxiety, and informative and persuasive speaking. Your assignment for the week of October 16 is an informative speech on a concept. Generally, we present informative speeches to share information that is potentially relevant and useful for the listeners in some aspect of their lives."

As soon as you finish learning about this assignment and the components that go into putting a speech together, you need to begin thinking about the speech. It is never too early to start thinking about the speech situation, the topic, and how it will serve the needs of your listeners. Most of us are concerned that we don't have anything worthwhile to share. It is your task to make sure that you choose a topic your listeners can connect with and one that you'll enjoy learning more about and sharing with your classmates. ■

### Questions to think about

- How do you feel about making a speech in class?
- How many times in the past have you made formal presentations?
- What were your concerns, then, and now?

- How did you overcome your reservations or anxiety?

- What topics come to mind as things you'd enjoy sharing?

- What do you already know about your listeners that will help you select a topic that is relevant to them?

Students often tell us they plan to give very few speeches in their lives and they've been talking for 18 or more years, so they really don't need to have additional information about the public communication context. As we have suggested throughout this text, talking and communication are hardly the same thing. And although we don't want people to make cookie-cutter speeches, there are principles and guidelines of public communication that have been established to help people prepare for the numerous times they *will* give speeches. Although you might never be a public speaker, you can expect to give speeches on the job, in social organizations, in your place of worship, in the courtroom, or classroom. At some time, almost all of us are called on to "make a speech."

Surveys of bosses and recruiters from for-profit and not-for-profit organizations over the past thirty years indicate that organizations want employees who know how to make effective presentations. For example, a 2005 survey by the Association for Accounting Marketing identified "[making] presentations as one of the top three roles and responsibilities for marketers today." The survey also found that "Interpersonal Communication: ability to communicate one-to-one or to a large group of people, including listening and presentation skills" was the number one competency/skill for managers today and would remain a top three skill in the next three years.[1] In another area, research chemist John Borchardt wrote that while chemical knowledge would "remain a bedrock skill" for a chemist's career, the chemist's skill sets

## MAKING CONNECTIONS

### Judith S. Trent
*University of Cincinnati*

Judith S. Trent is a Professor of Communication at the University of Cincinnati where she directs the departmental graduate program and teaches undergraduate and graduate courses in presidential campaigns, women in politics, and rhetorical criticism. Dr. Trent's research is related to the campaign communication of women who run for elective office at local, state, and national levels, and to the early stages of presidential campaigns (the surfacing and primary periods). Since 1988 she and her colleagues have conducted field research in New Hampshire during the primary campaign, focusing on the image of presiden-

## To Scholars

tial hopefuls, media bias, and voter characteristics for a series of journal articles that discuss "the ideal candidate."

The author or editor of textbooks, book chapters, and academic journal articles, Dr. Trent is perhaps best known for the book *Political Campaign Communication: Principles and Practices,* which is coauthored with Robert Friedenberg and is now in its fifth edition. *Political Campaign Communication* was the first book-length study of election campaigns that utilized the principles and practices of speech communication to examine elective politics. This book has been characterized as a "classic" and as a "seminal work in the field."

Dr. Trent has served as the president of the Central States Communication Association and the National Communication Association.

include: "leadership skills/interpersonal skills, communication skills, computer literacy, problem-solving ability/initiative and follow-through."[2] Although making presentations is only one of the communication skills required for many careers, it is necessary for those who wish to achieve success. Judith Trent, a former National Communication Association President, has conducted research on the role of public communication in all walks of life and believes that communication will continue to play an important role in everything we do.[3]

People make many presentations in the classroom and beyond. Here are some typical examples:

- Germana will speak at the local Rotary Club International about her visit to Palestine and Israel.
- Martha is a member of the campus International Club. She will share with the group her experiences about growing up in Mexico City.
- Sergei just completed an internship in a Chicago public relations firm. He will discuss his experiences with the Marketing and Public Relations students on his campus.
- Darin will inform his co-workers at a local business about new technologies in the workplace.

In U.S. culture, the ability to communicate effectively is one of the most important skills a person can possess. In formal public speaking, in which the speaker is the central focus of an audience's attention, the presentation of a speech is usually prepared in advance.

These students are preparing for public speaking events, even though each event is labeled as a project or assignment. The ability to give effective presentations in classes, organizations, residence hall meetings, sports team meetings, government campaigns, political demonstrations, or other events on and off campus is critical. **Public speaking** is the presentation of a speech, usually prepared in advance. In such instances, the speaker is the central focus of an audience's attention. In Chapter 1, we stated that the ability to communicate is one of the most important skills a person can possess. Public speaking and listening are two vital and significant forms of communication. Beginning public speakers frequently express two concerns: fear of not having anything worthwhile to say and fear of speaking in front of others. Both of these concerns will be discussed in detail in this part of the text.

What you learn and apply about making effective presentations will help you in all your roles the rest of your life. The speech-making process will help you develop researching, organizing, listening, and thinking skills for both oral and written communication. In addition, these skills will also help you gain self-confidence.

# ■ Selecting a Speech Topic

Selecting a topic is the first step in preparing a speech. In these chapters on public communication, you will read about topics that were presented in a variety of classroom, business, and professional situations. The choice of topics is often prompted

**■ public speaking**
Presentation of a speech, usually prepared in advance, during which the speaker is the central focus of an audience's attention.

### Public Speaking and You

Sometime soon you will choose a topic, complete research, organize the information, prepare and practice, and present one or more speeches in front of your classmates and instructor. While this may seem to be almost frightening, it's a common experience for all of us, and this textbook and course are designed to help you through the process. Take a few minutes to reflect on public speaking in your life. If the opportunity presents itself, share your reflections with others.

1. What speeches/presentations have you heard that you found memorable?
2. What do you remember—content or presentation? Why?
3. What specific ideas do you remember?
4. What makes a presentation memorable for you? Enjoyable?
5. Was there anything special the speaker did to get you involved?

by the situation itself, the needs of others, and the position and qualifications of the speaker. Selecting a good topic for you and the speaking situation requires thought and a systematic approach.

## ■ Selecting an Appropriate Topic

Many factors contribute to an effective speech presentation, including research, organization, wording, and delivery, but none is more important than selecting an appropriate topic. The topic and your interest and motivation in developing and presenting it are vital to your success as a speaker. The best topic for you, your audience, and the assignment, isn't always easy to determine.

Some beginning speakers worry that they might not be able to think of something about which to talk. This concern is unwarranted. For example, if you read a newspaper or magazine or watch television, you will be exposed to a variety of stimulating and interesting topics ranging from military involvement in foreign lands to health care. When a topic isn't assigned by the instructor, the trick is to identify a topic that matches *your* interests and qualifications, the interests and existing knowledge of your audience, and the requirements of the situation in which the speech is to be presented. If you are vitally concerned about the topic and have enthusiasm for sharing it with others, your concerns can be drastically reduced.

Many factors contribute to an effective speech presentation, including research, organization, wording, and delivery, but none is more important than selecting an appropriate topic. The topic and your interest and motivation in developing and presenting it are vital to your success as a speaker.

| Selecting an Appropriate Topic | **GUIDELINES** |
| --- | --- |

1. *Choose a topic that is meaningful to you.* The more meaningful a topic, the more likely you are to put the necessary time and effort into researching and developing your speech. The stronger your commitment to a topic, the more enthusiastically you will present it. A speaker's commitment to a topic usually transfers to the audience members and gets them involved. The audience involvement in a topic can be an effective gauge of your success as a speaker. After all, the reason for giving a speech, besides completing the assignment, is to gain your listeners' attention, and this is more easily accomplished if you consider the topic to be important.

2. *Choose a topic that will allow you to convey an important thought to your audience.* The thought does not have to be a matter of extreme urgency, but it should at least be relevant to your audience's interests, have some direct effect on them, or be something that you believe the audience should know. Ask yourself the following questions:

   Will the audience want to learn more about the topic?
   Will the audience believe the topic is relevant?
   Will the audience be affected in some way by the topic, either now or in the future?
   Will the audience benefit from listening to a presentation on the topic?
   Will the audience believe you are a credible speaker on the topic?
   If you can answer yes to each of these questions about your topic, you are on your way to selecting an appropriate one.

3. *Choose a topic that is familiar and interesting to you.* This will make the development and delivery of your speech easier. It would be easier to begin your research and development of a talk on DVD technology if you had some knowledge of DVD and the principles on which it is based. Researching and developing a speech will be more enjoyable if you are interested in the topic. You may find it enjoyable to select a topic in which you are interested but about which you know little. For example, you are intrigued by the idea of in vitro fertilization (fertilization of an egg by a sperm in a test tube) but do not know the exact procedure or issues surrounding it. Choosing a topic that interests you can increase the likelihood of audience interest and speaker credibility. (We discuss speaker credibility in Chapter 12.)

4. *Think like a listener.* Evaluate your topic as if you will be the listener. If it seems to be a topic you would enjoy listening to, it probably will be more interesting for you to prepare and more interesting for your listeners. Focus your attention on what the audience will like and want to hear about this topic you know and enjoy, and you are well on your way to choosing an interesting, informative, relevant, and potentially useful topic.

## ▬ Techniques for Finding a Topic

If you have difficulty thinking of interesting subjects, there are some techniques that might help you: self-inventory; brainstorming; reviewing current magazines, newspapers, and television news programs; and conducting an Internet search. All four techniques will generate a wide range of possible topics from which you can then select the most appropriate.

**Self-Inventory.**   A **self-inventory** is a list of subjects that you know about and find interesting. The list might include books and newspaper articles you've read; television shows you watch; hobbies you enjoy; sports you participate in; and community, state, regional, national, or international issues that concern you. Here are some sources of topics that might spark your interest:

**Books, Articles, Web Sources**

*Lost and Found*
*Lapham Rising*
*What Should I Do with My Life?*
*Guests of the Ayatollah*
"Boost Your Immunity"
"Cool Tools for the Third World"
"Teaching Doctors to Care"

**Technology/Media**

iPod or MP3?
Financial Success on the Web
Impact of Sirius and XM
*Desperate Housewives*
*CSI: Miami*
Are Newspapers Dying?

**Campus/Community Issues**

The New Fraternity Image
The Drunk Bus
Community Service and Students
Binge Drinking on Campus
Campus-Cummunity Conections

**Regional, National, International**

The Environment
Alligator and Shark Attacks
Surviving Hurricanes and Tornadoes
Renewable Energy Sources
Outsourcing U.S. Jobs
Military/Government Cover-Ups

**Hobbies/Personal**

Backpacking Around the World
Exercise for Health, Fitness, Fun
Scrapbooking
Great Gifts for Grads

**Sports/Recreation**

Canine Disc
Disc Golf
*Sports Off-Center*

**Health Issues**

Safety of Medicines
Vitamins & You
Tanning & Skin Cancer
Food Health Connections

■ **self-inventory** A list of subjects that you know about and find interesting.

■ **brainstorming** A technique used to generate as many ideas as possible within a limited amount of time, which can be used during any phase of the group discussion process to produce topics, information, or solutions to problems.

Another self-inventory technique involves listing broad categories and then narrowing them down to specific examples. Here's one possibility:

Environmental Issues
Water and Your Environment
Water Consumption
Water Economy and You
How You Can Economize on Water Use to Save a Precious Resource

The category of Environmental Issues was narrowed to a specific area, How You Can Economize on Water Use to Save a Precious Resource.

**Brainstorming.**   Another topic selection technique that you might find useful is brainstorming. **Brainstorming** is a technique used to generate as many ideas as possible within a limited amount of time. Set aside a short period of time (four to six

## MAKING CONNECTIONS
### for Success

### Your Own Self-Inventory

On the previous page we suggested a self-inventory as a place to start thinking about the kinds of topics you might choose for your speeches. Supply as many items as you can for each of the categories in this self-inventory. Then, examine each item to determine whether it could be an appropriate speech for you, the audience, and the situation.

**Sports/Recreation**

_____

_____

**People**

_____

_____

**Media Sources**

_____

_____

**Activities**

_____

_____

**Hobbies/Interests**

_____

_____

**Objects**

_____

_____

**Books/Music/Movies**

_____

_____

**Problems to Solve**

_____

_____

**Events**

_____

_____

1. Which of the above categories most interests you? Why?
2. Which specific topics would you avoid?
3. What other categories would you like to pursue?

**Pet Peeves/Personal Causes**

_____

_____

Share in class what you learned about personal topics from this exercise.

minutes) for intensive concentration, and list all the ideas that come to mind as topics. To keep things simple, write key words or phrases only. Don't stop to think about whether the ideas are good or bad. The goal of brainstorming is to generate a lot of ideas, so every word or phrase is appropriate.

After listing as many thoughts as you can, select those that appeal to you. Then have a brainstorming session to list more ideas related to them. For example, the term _education_ could serve as the springboard for an entirely new list:

Distance education                        College education and the job search

Meeting affirmative action quotas          Experiential learning

Ethics in the classroom                    Private schools

## MAKING CONNECTIONS for Success

### Brainstorming

Brainstorming involves simply thinking about topics. It is an effective tool to help you find an appropriate topic for your speeches.

Use brainstorming to generate topics you might use for your next informative speech. Take five minutes, and write down whatever ideas come to mind, without stopping to evaluate them. At the end of five minutes, look over your list and select terms that appeal to you. Then brainstorm for another five minutes, listing topics related to them. Now look at your list and answer the following questions:

1. What criteria would you use to determine the *best* topic for your presentation?
2. Apply those criteria to the topics you've generated.
3. Using the criteria you have established, determine which topic you will use.

Compare and contrast the criteria you listed for selecting the best topic to the criteria provided in the chapter.

| | |
|---|---|
| Liberal arts core classes | Education trends |
| Tuition increases | Entrance exams |
| Online exams | Research projects |
| Public education | Evaluating teachers |
| Funding concerns | Use of textbooks |
| Online courses | Online texts |
| PowerPoint for presentations | Service learning |
| Assessment and technology | Home schooling |
| Classroom evaluation | |

With a little effort, brainstorming will help you generate a number of potential topics in a short time. And the process can be repeated over and over until a suitable topic is found.

**Reviewing the Current Media.**   A third way to generate topic ideas involves the popular media. The media are channels or means of communicating messages to the public, such as through newspapers, books, magazines, television, and movies. **Reviewing the current media** is an excellent way of developing a list of potential topics. *The Readers' Guide to Periodical Literature* is a source of hundreds of up-to-date topics. For example, you will find listings of articles on education, government, finance, marketing, terrorism, crime, air safety, health, television violence, technology, and entertainment. Specialized indexes, such as those in the fields of agriculture and natural resources, business, economics and statistics, biology and life sciences, computers, education, and history, can provide thousands of suggestions. The world is at your fingertips via newspapers, magazines, and Lexis-Nexis on the Web. You can scan headlines, the complete article, and even advertisements in any magazine or newspaper—*Time, Newsweek, U.S. News and World Report, Money, Consumer Reports, Business Week,* the *New York Times, USA Today,* regional or local newspapers. Other good sources are television documentaries, news specials, cable channel programs, and even regular programming.

■ **reviewing the current media** A technique for developing a list of possible topics by looking at current publications, television, movies, and other forms of public communication.

One caution should be noted about using the current media to generate speech topics. Some beginning speakers have a tendency to rely on one media source for the entire speech. A summary of an interesting article or movie is not acceptable for most classroom speaking assignments. The media are an excellent source for potential topics, but they are only a starting point from which to build. The content must be adapted to suit you and your specific audience, and most classroom assignments require a variety of sources. You should always bring something new to your topic— a fresh insight or an application that is suitable to the speaking situation.

**Surfing the Web.** The rapid development of technology, the ever-increasing number of websites, and the amount of new information on the Web provide unique opportunities for students in a speech communication class. Using one or more of the many search engines available can provide unique topics and sources of information on the topic for the careful student.[4] Because information is often not reviewed and accepted by experts or authorities on the subject before it is placed on a web page, and because anyone who knows how to put a web page together can put it online, students need to carefully evaluate both the information presented and its source. How do you evaluate a web source? Use the same process you use when evaluating other sources and information, asking questions like these:

1. Who is the author or producer? What are the author's credentials?
2. How reliable is the source? What is the authority or expertise of the individual or group that created this site?
3. Is the writer or producer biased? (For example, if you find information that cites a study conducted to determine whether a specific product is carcinogenic and learn that the company that commissioned the study is the top producer and marketer of that product and the study results indicate a safe product, think twice before accepting its report as a scientific study.)
4. How complete and accurate is the information?
5. For whom is the information intended?
6. Is the web page up to date?
7. Does the writing on the page follow basic rules of grammar, spelling, and usage? Is the language used appropriately?
8. Is the webmaster identified? Or is contact information for the author or producer provided so that you can seek additional information?
9. Check these websites for more information: "Evaluating Information Found on the Internet" at www.library.jhu.edu/researchhelp/general/evaluating/ and "Thinking Critically about Discipline-Based World Wide Web Resources" at www.library.ucla.edu/college/help/critical/discipline.htm. Last retrieved June 25, 2006.

We discuss Internet research further in Chapter 8.

How you find your topic is not the critical issue, but it is important that you begin looking as soon as possible. Over the years of talking with students who have succeeded in selecting appropriate topics, one common factor emerges: They start looking for a topic as soon as they receive the assignment. Students who delay almost always have more difficulty finding an appropriate topic. Whenever you come across something that you think might be a good idea, write it down. The more ideas you

## MAKING Technology CONNECTIONS

### Research on the Web

Surfing the Web has become a habit for many of us. When you plan trips, you can access Travelocity.com or individual airlines to find the least expensive fares. Or if travel times and dates are flexible and you are willing to wait, you might be able to find some really good airfares, car rentals, and hotels on Priceline.com. If you are driving to some new place, you can get door-to-door directions from sites such as MapQuest. If you're interested in genealogy, there are numerous sites to help you locate your ancestors, determine exactly when they entered the United States, and even on what specific ship.

We can use the Web not only to find information but also to help us choose topics for our presentations. Try the following exercise.

1. Take about a minute to brainstorm five to ten topics in which you have some interest, already know something about, or want to learn something more about.
2. Choose four or five items that seem most interesting to you.

3. Access a search engine that you have not used before or one that is relatively unfamiliar.
4. Click on the help area or the icon that will help you understand how to do the most effective search.
5. Key in the words of your first topic.
6. How many hits did you get? What does this number tell you?
7. Check the first ten hits by scrolling through the list and reading the responses.
8. Pick the one that seems most interesting to you. Carefully read and evaluate that site.
9. Does this topic seem like a good one? If so, pursue it further. If not, go back to the next most interesting topic and repeat the process.

This combination of personal brainstorming and web surfing can help you find topics with adequate information. This process uses the Web to help you choose a topic that your web research reveals has adequate information.

can accumulate, the easier your job of selecting a good topic will be. Also, the earlier you choose your topic, the more time you will have to research, prepare, and practice your speech.

## ■■ Assessing the Appropriateness of a Topic

Once you have identified a possible topic, the next step is to determine whether it is appropriate for you, your assignment, and your audience. Ask yourself these questions:

1. Does the topic merit the audience's attention?
2. Will the audience see a relationship between you and the topic and between the topic and themselves?
3. Will the topic meet the objectives of the assignment?
4. Does the audience have sufficient knowledge and background to understand the topic?
5. Can you make the topic understandable to everyone in the audience?
6. Is the topic of sufficient interest to you that you will be motivated to present it effectively?

**7.** Do you have adequate knowledge of the topic?

**8.** If you are not already familiar with the topic, will you be able to learn enough about it to give an informed speech?

**9.** Is the topic appropriate for the situation in which you will present it?

## ■■ Narrowing the Topic

Once you have determined that your topic is appropriate to your audience and yourself, the next step is to decide whether it is narrow enough to fit the time limit and accomplish the goal of the assignment. This step can save you much time and trouble because a topic that is well focused is much easier to research than one that is too general. For example, you could work for years on a speech called "The Problems with American Education" and still not cover all the information exhaustively. If you restrict the scope to problems with education in the United States during the past five years, you begin to focus your search for information. You could narrow the topic even further by choosing a single issue with U.S. education during the past five years. Each time you narrow your topic, you increase its potential depth.

The more abstract the topic, the more important it is to narrow it to meet the constraints of the speech situation. Let's say that you have an assignment for a ten-minute speech on a concept about something you wish to gain more information about for yourself and your listeners. You think the Muslim religion would be a good topic. Obviously, you cannot talk about everything in the religion in ten minutes. So you narrow the topic to "the teachings and practices of the Muslim religion." There is still an abundance of information, far too much to cover. You decide to focus on the principles of the Muslim religion in Indonesia, the single nation with the largest Muslim population. This continual narrowing of the topic allows you to focus your research and content development on a more clearly defined area of the topic. This will be helpful to you, the speaker, as well as to your listeners because you will have more substance on an important concept. Speakers can narrow the scope of a subject according to time limits, function, goals, location, and the requirements of a specific topic. Narrowing the topic is a skill critical to your success as a communicator not only in the classroom but also in the workplace and in the organizations of which you are a member and for which you may be called on to make a presentation.

## ■ Determining the General Purpose, Specific Purpose, and Thesis of a Speech

Once you have chosen and narrowed your topic, you need to begin thinking about how the final presentation will be structured. Speakers should begin their preparation with a clear idea of the general purpose, the specific purpose, and a specific thesis statement. In this section we briefly discuss each of these concepts. Chapter 11 provides in-depth coverage of informative speaking, and Chapter 12 is devoted to persuasive speaking.

## ■■ The General Purpose

The **general purpose,** or overall goal, of a speech is usually to perform one of three overlapping functions: to inform, to persuade, or to entertain. A speech rarely serves only one function. Even though most classroom speech assignments are intended to

■ **general purpose**
The overall goal of a speech, usually one of three overlapping functions: to inform, to persuade, or to entertain.

This speaker on drug and alcohol abuse has a specific purpose in his talk to high school students in upper New York state. He uses his ambulatory mike to make his points, to demonstrate face to face his concern and his message. The audience's reaction suggests he is being successful.

emphasize a single function, the speeches themselves may contain aspects of all three functions. For example, a speech about rappelling is meant to inform, but this does not mean that the speech cannot contain some persuasive and entertaining elements as well. If you are assigned an informative speech, however, you need to think carefully about how to organize and present those ideas to your listeners. If the general purpose is to inform your audience, your emphasis should be on presenting information about a new, interesting, and potentially useful and relevant topic.

For classroom speaking assignments, your general purpose is usually specified by the instructor, but for speeches outside the classroom, the occasion, what the audience knows or doesn't know about your topic, and how you want the audience to respond will determine whether you speak primarily to inform, to persuade, or to entertain.

The speaking goal is usually designed to affect the listeners in some purposeful way. The reaction of the listeners determines whether your speech has accomplished its purpose successfully.

**Speeches That Inform.**   When the general purpose of your speech is to inform, you are expected to convey your knowledge of a particular subject. An **informative speech** enhances an audience's knowledge and understanding by explaining what something means, how something works, or how something is done. Communication scholar David Zarefsky suggests that informative speeches do not specifically ask listeners to believe or do any particular thing.[5] The goal is to share information clearly and accurately while making the learning experience as enjoyable as possible for the audience. If you are assigned an informative speech, you need to think carefully about how to organize and present those ideas to your listeners. If the general pur-

■ **informative speech** A speech that enhances an audience's knowledge and understanding by explaining what something means, how something works, or how something is done.

pose is to inform your audience, your emphasis should be on presenting information about a new, interesting, and potentially useful and relevant topic.

Whether you describe how to protect yourself during an assault, discuss a proposed apartment complex development in a run-down neighborhood, explain the important uses of an electromagnetic field, report how the university uses its parking fees, or explain how the electoral college works, you should assume that most of your audience does not already know all the information you plan to present. The content of the speech depends heavily on what you think the audience knows and on how much you know or are able to learn about the topic. Your task as a speaker is to provide more information than the audience would normally get from reading a short article or listening to the news.

When a topic is controversial, for example, "stem cell research," speakers whose general purpose is to inform should not take sides; instead, they might choose to provide background on what is involved in stem cell research, how it is used, and for what. The informative speaker might identify the pros and cons, but will not take a stand. The speaker presents the information and lets the listeners draw their own conclusions.

## MAKING CONNECTIONS for Success

### Thinking about Informative Speeches

In the individual self-inventory chart there are examples of a variety of categories. Whether your instructor allows you to choose any topic, or identifies a specific type of informative speech (speech on a concept, speech on a person, speech on an event), you still are required to choose and work with a topic that will do well for you. Now it's your turn to think about possible topics for an informative speech.

1. Create an inventory where you identify at least three campus, community, state, or regional issues that are in the news or are a current topic of conversation.
2. Choose one and write a specific purpose statement for that topic that you could present to your classmates for the informative speech.
3. Share your topics in class, in small groups, or individually.
4. In your discussion, determine what topics have the greatest appeal.

**Speeches That Persuade.** A **persuasive speech** attempts to change listeners' beliefs, attitudes, or behaviors by advocating or trying to gain acceptance of an idea or point of view. When speakers try to convince audience members to eat breakfast, to endorse the building of a new athletic complex, to change the way we elect U.S. presidents, to become a volunteer, to ensure a safe campus or neighborhood, or to believe that ethical behavior in the United States is on the decline, they are attempting to persuade. Speakers must present evidence and arguments to justify their positions in order to win their audience over to their point of view.

The difference between informing and persuading is not always clear. You have a persuasive action goal when you try to persuade your parents to loan you money for a car. Your message contains the following: informing about the circumstances and need for a car and convincing them that you need the car and the money. They may accept your reasons and agree that you need the car but still might not loan you the money. In this example, the persuasive purpose is not only to inform and convince your parents that you need a car and the money to buy it but also for them to take action—to actually give you the money you need. Providing information is a necessary part of a persuasive speech, but its ultimate goal is action. Once your parents give you the money, you have achieved your purpose.

Whereas the focus of an informative speech is to convey information and understanding by explaining, reporting, or demonstrating your point of view, the purpose of a persuasive speech is to change beliefs or attitudes or motivate listeners to act in a

■ **persuasive speech** A speech that attempts to change listeners' attitudes or behaviors by advocating or trying to gain acceptance of the speaker's point of view.

specific manner. The action might be to think, to respond, or to behave in a certain way. The purpose might be to eat a healthy breakfast, to place greater personal and societal emphasis on ethics, to approve a proposal, or to join a group.

The important and necessary ingredient that makes persuasion different from information is the action (to think, to respond, to behave) taken by the listener as a result of the message presented. The informative speech provides more knowledge about a topic, whereas the persuasive speech provides information and a direction or course of action the listener is to take.

**Speeches That Entertain.** An **entertainment speech** provides enjoyment and amusement. Speeches that entertain may be dramatic or humorous in nature and often occur on special occasions, such as after a dinner or a "roast." A speech to entertain generally has three key qualities: It is light, original, and appropriate to the situation. An appropriate speech does not offend the sensibilities of the audience. The speaker may use humor but not at the expense of the audience's sense of values or ethics. Effective speakers do not use offensive language or potentially offensive jokes or situations. Audience members, unlike television viewers, are a captive audience and cannot click the remote to switch off offensive words or ideas. The speaker must use tasteful examples and stories that will not hurt anyone's feelings or violate their ethical principles.

In using humor, the speaker may create imaginative illustrations and figures of speech, twist meanings, tell amusing stories, create amusing character sketches, or tell jokes—all with the willing participation of the audience and in the spirit of the occasion. This does not mean, however, that an entertaining speech cannot be both informative and persuasive or that informative and persuasive speeches cannot be entertaining. What distinguishes these three kinds of speeches is the function (informing, persuading, or entertaining) on which the speaker places the most emphasis. The entertaining speech should, therefore, leave the audience members feeling entertained or amused.

## ■■ The Specific Purpose

The general purpose of a speech provides direction for its content. In the classroom, the general purpose is usually specified in the assignment. Outside the classroom, it may or may not be specified. When the general purpose is not identified, you must determine it for yourself. To be a successful speaker, you must know exactly what you plan to accomplish by speaking.

Once you have determined your general purpose (to inform, to persuade, or to entertain), you are ready to determine your specific purpose. A **specific purpose** is a single phrase that defines precisely what you intend to accomplish in your speech. Anneke chose videogames as her topic. Her specific purpose was "to inform my classmates about the three major effects of videogames on children." The clear and concise statement tells exactly what the speaker intends to do and what she wants her audience to know.

An effective specific purpose identifies (1) the general purpose of the speech, (2) the audience, and (3) the exact topic to be covered. These three pieces of information significantly help the speaker develop and deliver the speech. Note that in the videogames example, the speaker's specific purpose cites the general purpose of the speech, which is to inform. The specific purpose also identifies the audience, which is important, because different audiences may require different information. For exam-

■ **entertainment speech** A speech that provides enjoyment and amusement.

■ **specific purpose** Single phrase that defines precisely what is to be accomplished in a speech.

ple, if a speech is to be presented to children only, to adults only, or to both children and adults, the content will have to be adjusted to fit the group. Thus, even though the general and specific purposes are the same, the content of the speech will vary depending on the listeners' backgrounds, knowledge, and attitudes toward the topic.

The careful writing of a specific purpose is important to all aspects of planning and developing a successful speech. The following guidelines should help you write an effective specific purpose.

## Specific Purpose                                                    GUIDELINES

1. The specific purpose should include a verb form that describes the general purpose of the speech. The inclusion of the verb form clarifies the action the speaker hopes to accomplish.
   *Ineffective:*   Media violence and children
   *Effective:*     To inform my audience of the three effects of media violence on children aged five to ten

2. The specific purpose should be limited to one distinct thought or idea. The following ineffective statement is too long and contains more than one subject. An entire speech could be developed around either area. It is best to select only one idea and refine it as the purpose for the speech.
   *Ineffective:*   To inform the audience of the three effects of drugs and the four best ways to prevent binge drinking by college students
   *Effective:*     To inform the audience about the three most dangerous effects of drugs on college students
                    or
                    To inform the audience about the four best ways to prevent binge drinking by college students

3. The specific purpose should not be a question. Although a question may indicate the topic, it fails to specify the general purpose of the speech.
   *Ineffective:*   How does volunteerism create a sense of community?
   *Effective:*     To persuade the audience that increased rates of volunteerism have a positive effect on community building

4. The specific purpose should be concise and carefully worded. The ineffective statement given here tries to cover too much material, is too general, and does not state clearly what is to be achieved by the speech.
   *Ineffective:*   The effects of a permissive society can be extremely harmful to children and can also create a society that eventually becomes desensitized to reality
   *Effective:*     To persuade the audience that a permissive society limits children's views of reality

Formulating your general and specific purposes makes it easier to develop your speech. They will guide your thinking and planning. You should be ready to reconsider your specific purpose, however, throughout the development stages of the speech. As you research a topic, you might find information that leads you to revise your thinking. Or you might learn something about your audience members that will make you want to adjust your specific purpose to their needs.

## MAKING CONNECTIONS for Success

### Creating Specific Purpose Statements

Keep the guidelines for creating specific purpose statements in mind as you craft specific purpose statements for three of the broad topics listed.

1. Hybrid cars
2. Fraternities/sororities
3. Satellite radio
4. Entertainment
5. Disk golf
6. Global warming
7. Identity theft
8. Topic of your choice

What did you learn from this writing exercise? How will this help you identify and create specific purpose statements?

## ■■ The Thesis

The specific purpose of your speech states what you wish to accomplish or what effect you wish to have on your audience. It also serves as the foundation for the thesis of the speech. The **thesis** is a sentence that states specifically what is going to be discussed in a speech. For example, the specific purpose "to explain to my audience the four advantages of using computer-aided instruction" tells what the speaker wants to do but does not describe the content of the speech. A thesis concisely states the content: "Computer-aided instruction saves time, allows for self-pacing, provides practice, and is enjoyable." This clearly worded statement tells exactly what the four advantages of computer-aided instruction are.

If the specific purpose is "to persuade the audience to contribute to the performing arts center," the thesis might be "The new performing arts center will help the university attract Broadway shows, will generate increased ticket sales and thus more money for the university, and will create a renewed sense of community pride in our university." The thesis gives the three main ideas the speaker will discuss: (1) why the new performing arts center will attract Broadway shows, (2) why it will generate more money through ticket sales, and (3) why it will renew a sense of community pride in the university. The thesis should be expressed as a full sentence, should not be in the form of a question, and should be clearly and concisely worded.

Here are two examples to show the relationship of the topic to the general purpose, specific purpose, and thesis:

*Topic:* Inexpensive, renewable energy

*General purpose:* To inform

*Specific purpose:* To inform my audience about wind as an energy source

*Thesis:* Wind is an inexpensive, easily accessible, renewable energy source

*Topic:* Biological research

*General purpose:* To inform

*Specific purpose:* To inform my audience about the development and implications of biological research

*Thesis:* I will examine biological research by looking at the history of biological research, the research conducted, and the advances influencing future biological research

■ **thesis** A sentence that states specifically what is going to be discussed in a speech.

You can easily see in these examples how a broad topic area is narrowed as the speaker moves from the specific purpose to the thesis. This narrowing procedure is a crucial step in preparing a speech.

# ■ Connecting with the Listeners

Selecting a topic, narrowing it, choosing a specific purpose, and creating a clear thesis statement so that you can connect your speech to the specific listeners in your audience require careful thinking as well as knowledge and understanding of your audience. The development of ideas requires similar understanding and knowledge. Therefore the speaker needs specific information about the listeners. You have now spent several weeks with the people in your communication class. It is likely that you have each had a chance to respond to the activities and class discussions. What people say, how they act, and their nonverbal communication have all helped you to form impressions of your classmates. Those impressions are important, but you might need to get further information to do a good job of connecting with your audience. Because this is so critical to a speaker's success, the remainder of this chapter examines the audience's point of view, kinds of audience members, key information to gain about audiences, methods for researching audiences, and adapting your speech to an audience.

An audience is the collection of individuals who have come together to watch or listen to a speech. The more you know about your audience's past experiences, knowledge of the subject, relation to the subject, and reason for being there, the easier it will be for you to develop a speech that is meaningful to them.

**Audience analysis** is the collection and interpretation of data about characteristics, attitudes, values, and beliefs of an audience. Analyzing the audience is an essential step in developing and delivering a speech. An audience becomes actively involved in a speech and reacts to the speaker, to the subject, to what is said, to how it is said, to other audience members, and to the situation. The more speakers know about the audience, the better they can adapt their speeches to them.

## ◾◾ Understanding the Audience's Point of View

For our purposes, the **audience** refers to the collection of individuals who have come together to watch or listen to a speech. The individuals may become part of the audience for many different reasons. Each individual may have several reasons for being present, and the audience members may come from many different backgrounds. Students, for example, come to class to listen to lectures because attendance is required to obtain a passing grade.

The reason individuals come together to form an audience is an important point that every speaker should consider when planning a speech. If people join an audience because they wish to listen to a speech, it is reasonable to assume that they also want to hear something that is meaningful to them. Most individuals ask the same basic questions about their involvement in an audience. What's in this for me?

This question suggests that your audience will judge what they hear on the basis of their past experiences and the relevance of the information presented. The more you know about your audience's past experiences, knowledge of the subject, relationship to the subject, and reason for being there, the easier it will be for you to develop a speech that is meaningful to them. For example, imagine that you are an expert on reading and have been asked to give a speech entitled "How to Teach Children to Be More Effective Readers." You have spent many hours getting ready for the speech and are now prepared to present it. But are you really prepared? Have you thought about the members of your audience? Who are they? What do they know about reading? What is their attitude toward reading? Would you present the same information to professionals who teach reading, to parents who want their children to become better readers, to children who are indifferent about reading, or to a combination of all three groups? What results would you expect if you used the same approach for all three audiences? What results would you expect if you varied your approaches? Asking these questions and finding answers to them are essential preparation for an effective and successful presentation.

**◾ audience analysis**
The collection and interpretation of data about characteristics, attitudes, values, and beliefs of an audience.

**◾ audience** The collection of individuals who have come together to watch or listen to someone or something, such as to listen to a speech.

**◾ captive participant** A person who is required to hear a particular speech.

**◾ voluntary participant** A person who chooses to listen to a particular speech.

## ◾◾ Captive versus Voluntary Participants

Many kinds of people attend speeches for many reasons, but all are either captive or voluntary participants. Audience members required to listen to a particular speech are called **captive participants.** They may happen to want to hear the speech, but they have no choice but to attend. Some people may resist participation more than others.

Even though few circumstances force a person to be part of an audience, some situations demand attendance to avoid a penalty. For example, a teacher requires attendance during speech presentations, an employer requires employees to attend new product demonstrations, or a military leader orders troops to attend lectures on military maneuvers. In such situations, audience members cannot be absent and cannot leave without being noticed or penalized for doing so. To be effective, a speaker must recognize when he or she is dealing with captive participants.

In contrast to captive participants, **voluntary participants** choose to hear a particular speech because of interest or need. True volunteers attend only because of what they expect to hear. There is no other motivation or force behind their presence.

# Key Audience Information

You should gather two kinds of information about your prospective audience: demographic and psychological. The more you know about your audience members, the better able you will be to adjust to them and relate your topic to them.

**Demographic Analysis.**   **Demographic analysis** is the collection and interpretation of basic information such as age, gender, cultural or ethnic background, education, occupation, religion, socioeconomic status, geographic location, political affiliation, voting habits, family relationships, marital and parental status, and group memberships. The more similar the demographic characteristics of members of an audience, the easier it is for a speaker to adapt to their needs and interests.

*Age.*   Knowing that members of the audience differ in age can help the speaker select a range of appropriate examples and evidence. An age difference between the speaker and the audience can also alter what messages are presented and how they are expressed. For example, if an audience consists of only eighteen- and nineteen-year-olds, the speaker has only one age group with which to deal. If audience members range from fifteen to sixty-five years of age, the speaker will have to take into account several age groups and make language and content choices on the basis of that wide range of listener ages.

*Gender.*   Gender is an important demographic characteristic and can present challenges. The speaker should consider the attitudes of each sex toward the other as well as the attitudes of each sex toward itself. As we indicated in several places in this text, gender-based biases should be avoided. Speakers should be sensitive to potential gender-based biases, for example, referring to women as "passive" or providing examples of women only in certain careers, such as nursing or teaching. Although some topics may still be more appropriate for one sex than the other, clear-cut distinctions are becoming increasingly rare.

*Cultural or Ethnic Background.*   Cultural or ethnic background is often not considered as thoroughly as it should be, even though a tremendous diversity of backgrounds exists in our society. Speakers should be sensitive to the different groups that may be present. The following communication variables are culturally determined and influence interactions between and among members of different ethnic and racial backgrounds.

| | |
|---|---|
| Attitudes | Use of spatial relationships |
| Social status within the group | Meanings of words |
| Thought patterns | Time |
| Expected behaviors | Nonverbal expressions |
| Use of language | Beliefs |
| Values | Cooperation versus competition |
| Respect for age | Collectivism versus individualism |

Each of these variables determines and regulates how an individual creates and interprets messages. Although the list is not exhaustive, it points out some of the important cultural and ethnic factors to consider as you plan a speech. Culture is dynamic and extremely important; culture helps define who individuals are in relationship to

■ **demographic analysis** The collection and interpretation of characteristics (age, gender, religion, occupation, and so on) of individuals, excluding values, attitudes, and beliefs.

## MAKING CONNECTIONS for Success

### Culture and the Public Speaker

Pajaree and Dawn are discussing their upcoming assignment: a ten-minute informative speech on a topic demonstrating ethical principles. Pajaree says she wants to talk about the concept of "saving face," but Dawn does not understand what this expression means and how it is appropriate for the assignment. Pajaree explains that saving face is a concept in her native culture that means a person does not purposely do anything to make another lose credibility or status. Pajaree says that she often does not ask the other students questions because she is aware that the questions could cause people to lose face in their own minds or in the minds of others. According to Thai beliefs, ethical speakers and ethical listeners will not willingly cause another to lose face, nor will they willingly lose face by making a mistake. Dawn is fascinated and asks more questions to learn about Pajaree's culture.

Each of us should be aware of cultural perspectives and how they may affect speakers and listeners in a speaking situation. Think about the cultures (or cocultures) represented in your communication class, and then answer these questions:

1. What values do these other cultures promote?
2. How do the cultural values affect the way a person might respond to certain topics? Give some examples.
3. How can you increase your sensitivity and awareness of cultural perspectives?
4. What can you, as a speaker, do to adjust to different cultural values in your communication class?

the world around them. Speakers who do not take culture into account may embarrass and insult an audience, and ultimately, themselves. Speech content should not offend values, customs, or beliefs held by members of the audience.

*Education.*   Although it may be impossible to find out exactly what an audience knows and understands about a specific topic, it is often possible to ascertain their general education level. Knowing whether most listeners have completed high school, college, or graduate school can help you to gauge their intellectual level and experience and to adapt your speech accordingly.

*Occupation.*   Knowledge about audience members' occupations can also tell you something about possible interest in and familiarity with some subjects. For example, lawyers might be interested in topics related to the law or in legal aspects of some topics.

*Religion.*   Speakers must be as sensitive to religion as they are to ethnicity. That is, they must recognize issues that touch on religious beliefs and treat them carefully. If you plan to speak on an issue that may have religious ramifications, you should evaluate how your message will affect audience members. Otherwise, you run a risk of offending or losing the attention of some or all of your audience. For example, choosing a quotation to support your viewpoint might be more appropriately taken from the Koran than from the Bible if your audience is of the Islamic faith.

*Geographic Origins.*   Knowing your audience's geographic origins can help you adapt your speech to them. For example, people from rural communities are more likely to know and care more about agricultural topics than are people from large urban areas. People from the South might not be interested in information related to heating their homes in winter, but if they live in an oil-producing state, they might be interested in the price of a barrel of oil.

*Group Membership.* A **group** is a collection of individuals who have joined together for some common cause or purpose that may be social, professional, recreational, or charitable. Recognizing that individuals in your audience come from groups with special interests can help you relate your speech directly to their needs and concerns. Of course, it isn't always possible to reach every group in your audience, but by appealing to the largest group, you can create strong attention and interest. For example, a student who belonged to a sorority decided to inform her audience about sorority and fraternity functions other than social activities. Three-quarters of her student audience was not affiliated with a Greek group. Knowing this, she began her speech by talking about her thoughts on Greek organizations before she became a member. By first pointing out her reservations about such groups, she created a common understanding between herself and her listeners. Had her audience been three-quarters sorority and fraternity members, that kind of introduction would have been unnecessary.

*Other Demographic Factors.* We earlier identified marital status, family makeup, and socioeconomic status as other possible elements of demographic analysis. Knowledge of the listeners' marriage and family status provides information about their priorities and interests. An awareness of socioeconomic status will also provide information about the interests and abilities of audience members to grasp the ideas presented. All in all, more information about who the listeners are and what characteristics they share with us and with others will promote a better understanding of how to prepare the speech for the specific audience.

**Psychological Analysis.** **Psychological analysis** is the collection of data on audience members' values, attitudes, and beliefs. A psychological analysis seeks to determine how the audience will react to the speaker, the speaker's topic, and the surroundings in which the speech is presented. In addition to the items related to demographic analysis, a psychological analysis helps the speaker become aware of what motivates listeners to attend to the message of a particular speech. The size of the audience; the physical setting for the presentation; the knowledge level of the audience; and the attitude of the audience toward the speaker, the topic, and the situation all play vital roles in the planning, development, and delivery of a speech.

**Size of Audience.** The number of audience members has a considerable psychological effect on a speaking situation and strongly influences how a speech should be delivered. The larger the audience, the more difficult it is to use an informal, conversational speaking style. Size also affects the speaker's use of language, gestures, and visual aids. There is a difference between speaking to ten or thirty people, as in a typical classroom speech assignment, and speaking to several hundred people in an auditorium.

The size of an audience can also affect the psychological disposition of the audience members and their relationship to each other and the speaker. For example, each member of a small audience is aware of himself or herself as a unique member of the audience, and each feels a close, intimate relationship to the speaker. As the size of the audience increases, members lose their sense of identity as unique individuals and feel more distanced from the speaker. Effective speakers know this and plan their presentations to meet the requirements of each situation.

**Physical Setting.** In evaluating the physical setting, consider factors such as room size, ventilation, seating arrangement, lighting, speaker's platform, and potential for using visual aids. Some professional speakers require specific settings and will refuse to give presentations if their conditions can't be met. Unfortunately, you do not have that choice in a classroom assignment. You can, however, assess the physical setting and take full advantage of what is available to you.

■ **group** Collection of individuals who have joined together for some common cause or purpose that may be social, professional, recreational, or charitable.

■ **psychological analysis** The collection and interpretation of data about audience members' values, attitudes, and beliefs.

The seating arrangement of your audience is often predetermined, as it is in classroom settings, but sometimes a slight modification can make your presentation more effective. For example, a speech professor was asked to address a group of thirty police officers. He purposely arrived early so that he could see the room and assess the speaking conditions. The seats were arranged classroom-style: The chairs were placed in uniform rows directly in front of a raised speaker's podium, on which stood a large wooden lectern with a microphone. The professor believed that the setting was too formal and would inhibit his presentation, so he quickly rearranged the room by placing the chairs in a semicircle and moving the speaker's podium off to one side. These simple changes gave his presentation a more casual feeling and encouraged audience involvement.

The physical setting can also affect audience members' psychological disposition toward one another as well as toward the speaker. The more relaxed the physical setting, for example, the more open and comfortable audience members will feel in relation to one another and to the speaker. The proximity of audience members to one another can also have an effect. If, for example, the audience members are scattered throughout a large meeting room, they will not have the sense of inclusion that occurs in a physical setting in which the members are densely packed together. The close proximity of other people may create a feeling of belonging to the group and help the speaker reach the audience.

**Knowledge Level.**   The extent of an audience's knowledge about a topic has a tremendous effect on the outcome of a speech. If an audience has little or no background on a topic and the speaker does not realize this, both the audience and the speaker can become frustrated. When an audience isn't ready to receive information or when the information is too technical for them to understand, the speaker must present the material in terms everyone can understand.

A speaker must also adjust a presentation to reach a knowledgeable audience. A physician addressing a medical conference would not explain familiar medical terms. Even though people are apt to be more interested in subjects they know something about, an audience does not want a rehash of familiar information; they want to hear a new twist and add to their existing knowledge. For example, a student decided to present a five-minute informative speech about the lead pencil. After interviewing his classmates, the speaker noted that they all had a similar response: "What can you say about a lead pencil other than that it is made of lead and wood and is used for writing?" On the basis of his analysis, the student developed a creative, fascinating speech. Using a casual and entertaining style, he provided detailed information about the history of the lead pencil and its affect on society. The speech was a great success.

**Connecting with the Listeners.**   The listeners' knowledge of the speaker strongly influences how a speech should be developed and delivered. Even people well known in their own fields or famous media personalities know that they have to connect with their specific audiences. You've spent several weeks in this class; your instructor has provided numerous opportunities for all students to share ideas with each other, so from participation and observation, everyone in class already knows a great deal about each other. At the same time, your classmates probably do not know you extremely well. Here's how one student's first sentences helped her connect with her listeners. "Two years ago I was riding home from Prom with my three best friends. None of us had been drinking and we all had enjoyed a wonderful, memorable night. Little did I know how memorable that night would become. A drunk driver, traveling at excessive speed, slammed into our car as we were turning, with the light, to go into Perkins. My friend Lisa died upon impact. The rest of us were injured and taken by ambulance to the hospital but luckily, had few injuries. The pain of losing Lisa will never leave me. As a result of that Prom night accident, I have a new mission in life. Today, I want to share with you the reasons for the slogan, "If you drink, don't drive." The listeners were very quiet and attentive throughout the speech. As this example illustrates, sharing a personal experience helped the speaker connect with her listeners and in turn, held their attention. Listeners will always formulate some attitude toward a speaker. Help them form one that keeps them tuned in to your presentation.

This example also demonstrates how character (*ethos,* or ethical traits, discussed as an aspect of credibility more fully in Chapter 12) is derived from what the listeners know and believe about a speaker as well as how they perceive the speaker's use of both logical and emotional appeals. Effective speakers recognize that character, logic, and emotional appeals can affect their listeners' views of the speaker and the speech, and adjust their presentations accordingly.

**Attitudes and Values Related to the Topic.** The audience's attitude and values as they relate to the topic are as significant as their knowledge of the speaker. If audience members do not relate to a topic, the speaker will have a difficult time getting them to listen. For instance, a student chose to speak on individual retirement accounts for his persuasive speech. He researched the subject thoroughly, practiced his delivery, and presented the speech in an enthusiastic manner. His audience remained cool and uninvolved. The speaker had failed to consider the value the audience placed on the topic; the age of its members should have tipped off the speaker. Saving for retirement is not a high priority for most college students. The speaker could have made the speech more relevant by discussing young people's indifference to retirement saving and convincing them that they should become concerned now.

**Attitudes Related to the Situation.** The speaker must also examine the audience's relationship to the overall situation in which the speech is presented. Why has the audience gathered? Audience members' expectations influence their attitude toward the situation, which in turn reflects on the speaker and the topic. A speaker who talks about the need to further fund social security to a group of seventeen- to twenty-four-year-olds has chosen the wrong topic for an audience who cares little about retirement and social security, which is decades away for them. Listeners who believe a topic is not relevant to their own situations are less likely to listen to the speaker.

## Ways to Learn about the Audience

The three most common ways of gathering information about an audience are observation, survey interviews, and questionnaires.

**Observation.** Probably the easiest method of audience analysis is through observation. The speaker draws on accumulated experience with a particular audience and with similar groups. Through **observation,** the speaker watches audience members and notes their behaviors and characteristics. Although this approach relies strictly on the speaker's subjective impression, it can be useful.

No doubt you have already learned a great deal about your audience from classroom assignments. You already know the number of students, the number of males and females, and their approximate ages. Through introductions, general conversations, and other interactions, you have learned about their majors, group memberships, jobs, whether they commute or live on campus, and their interests. You have learned about your classmates' attitudes, interests, values, and knowledge. You know

■ **observation** A method of collecting information about an audience in which the speaker watches audience members and notes their behaviors and characteristics.

your instructor's views and expectations for your classroom performance. You also know the size of the classroom, the location of the lectern (if there is one), the seating arrangement, the availability of audiovisual equipment, and other physical features of the environment. You have obtained all of this information by observation.

**Survey Interviews.**   A **survey interview** is a carefully planned and executed person-to-person, question-and-answer session during which the speaker tries to discover specific information that will help in the preparation of a speech. Such interviews can be done in person or over the phone. The purpose of the survey is to establish a solid base of fact from which to draw conclusions, make interpretations, and determine future courses of action. This method of audience research can be highly productive. To be most useful, however, surveys require a great deal of planning and organization, which take time and energy. (Specific interviewing skills are discussed in more detail in the next chapter.)

**Questionnaires.**   A **questionnaire** is a set of written questions distributed to respondents to gather desired information. The same questioning techniques used in survey interviews are also used in questionnaires. In some cases, questionnaires are more practical and take less time than interviews. They can be administered to relatively large groups of people at the same time. One advantage is that the respondents can remain anonymous, which often leads to greater honesty and openness in answering questions. Although learning to develop good questionnaires takes time and practice, here are some simple guidelines to help you get started:

1. Decide exactly what information you want to gather.
2. Decide on the best method for making multiple copies of your questionnaire.
3. Decide when, where, and how to distribute the questionnaire.
4. Plan the introduction to the questionnaire. Will the respondent need specific instructions on how to answer it?
5. Make sure your questions are clear and understandable.
6. Limit the number of possible responses to each question.
7. Keep the questionnaire as brief as possible.

Figure 7.1 shows a typical questionnaire. Note that it provides simple instructions, it is brief, the questions are clear, and the number of possible responses is limited.

**Choosing the Best Information-Gathering Technique.**   The easiest way to find out about your audience is through observation. Your success with this method depends on the amount of experience you have with your audience and your ability to make accurate inferences. In most classroom situations, observation will yield adequate information for planning a speech, but if you seek more specific data, you may want to use a survey. A survey interview takes planning and time and is not very efficient, but it does provide an opportunity to get information in person and to probe for more data when necessary. If you are dealing with a large group of people, you may decide to gather information by using a questionnaire. Although good questionnaires take time to write, they can be administered more quickly than survey interviews and often yield more candid responses, especially to sensitive topics.

**Connecting with and Adapting to the Listeners.**   The goal of observing, survey interviewing, and administering questionnaires is to gather information so that you can relate and adapt your speech to those who make up your audience. Can you discern any patterns in the information you have gathered? What conclusions can you draw? How

■ **survey interview** A carefully planned and executed person-to-person, question-and-answer session during which the speaker tries to discover specific information that will help in the preparation of a speech.

■ **questionnaire** A set of written questions that is distributed to respondents to gather desired information.

---

■ **FIGURE 7.1** Sample Questionnaire

Questionnaires contain a set of written questions and are an excellent way to quickly gather information from large groups of people. If done effectively, they can be practical, take less time than interviews, and provide for the anonymity of the respondent.

**Check one:** _____ Female     _____ Male

**Directions:** Check the response that best indicates the strength of your agreement or disagreement with each statement.

1. Same-sex couples should be allowed to adopt children.

   _____ Strongly Agree

   _____ Agree

   _____ Undecided

   _____ Disagree

   _____ Strongly Disagree

2. Our society actively punishes gays, lesbians, and same-sex couples.

   _____ Strongly Agree

   _____ Agree

   _____ Undecided

   _____ Disagree

   _____ Strongly Disagree

3. Social support should be provided for same-sex couples who wish to adopt a child.

   _____ Strongly Agree

   _____ Agree

   _____ Undecided

   _____ Disagree

   _____ Strongly Disagree

4. The entire community should show more support for same-sex couples who have a child.

   _____ Strongly Agree

   _____ Agree

   _____ Undecided

   _____ Disagree

   _____ Strongly Disagree

---

certain can you be of them? How can you use what you have learned to improve your speech? Let's say that you survey fifty female and fifty male students on your campus, using the questionnaire in Figure 7.1. When you tally the results, you find 50 percent of the women and 25 percent of the men believe that same-sex couples should be allowed to adopt a child. How will that information help you prepare a speech to convince your listeners that same-sex couple adoptions ought to be allowed and supported?

To give the best results, a questionnaire must be completed by a group of people who represent a sample of the entire population. You also need to make sure you have enough responses to make reliable generalizations about the group you are surveying. If your analysis is thorough and correct, you should have a fairly good picture of your audience—their relevant demographics; interests; knowledge levels; and attitudes toward the topic, the speaker, and the general situation. Although your findings will rarely be uniform, you should be able to reach some general conclusions. For example, you may find that 70 percent of your audience members strongly disagree that capital punishment should be used in U.S. society, 15 percent have no opinion, and 15 percent strongly agree. If your purpose is to persuade them that capital punishment should be used in U.S. society, you will need to adjust your speech to this audience. How will you get those who oppose you to listen to what you have to say? What can you say to draw in those who have no opinion or who already strongly agree with you?

### Persuasive Speaking and You

In a persuasive speech, the speaker tries to convince listeners to think about something, accept a perspective as valid, or to take some kind of action. In government, speakers use persuasion to promote and pass specific bills. During 2006 many congressional members gave fiery speeches on one topic or another. The continuing war in Iraq became a divisive topic with some in Congress calling for more troops, and others calling for troop withdrawal. Hilary Rodham Clinton made such a speech on June 21, 2006. Read or view Senator Clinton's speech (or find one she made since this textbook was published) and try to identify strategies she used to connect with her listeners in the Senate and with public citizens who read/listened to her pre-

sentation. Her official news site may be found at: www.clinton.senate.gov.

1. What words did Clinton use to connect with both Democrats and Republicans?
2. What images come to mind as you read her words?
3. How do you know she feels strongly about the topic?
4. What does she say to try to overcome the differing views held by Democrats and Republicans?
5. Whether you agree or disagree with Clinton's politics, how would you rate her speech on a one-to-ten scale with ten being excellent? Were you persuaded to at least consider her view? Why or why not?

Although it is never easy to win over people who oppose your views, you can try to do so by discussing their views first and then discussing your views. You should also make use of credible, unbiased sources—people are more likely to accept information from them. In addition, you should acknowledge that your listeners' views have as much merit as yours but assert that your views will lead to a better outcome.

If your research indicates that your audience has little or no opinion about the information you are presenting, you need to provoke their interest. Begin by telling why they should listen to what you have to say and by showing how the topic relates to them personally. Focus on helping them recognize the benefits and importance of your topic, and remember that clearly communicating your own enthusiasm can help generate interest. Tell your listeners a memorable story using the information you gained.

Finally, when you are dealing with an audience that agrees with you and what you have to say or knows a lot about your topic, you need to acknowledge what you share with them. For example, if you and your audience agree that a new auditorium should be built, note your shared agreement and then go on to talk about what can be done to get the new facility built. In the process, you might try to strengthen their beliefs about the need for the auditorium.

No matter what your audience's position on your topic may be, your research will enable you to identify it in advance. You can use this information to pursue your specific purpose and to adjust your presentation to your audience. Of course, the more information you have, the better your ability to adapt your speech to your audience.

## Summary

One of the most important aspects of public speaking is choosing a topic. If a speaker has interest in and some degree of passion for the concept, the topic is more likely to be an excellent choice. In addition, speakers should choose topics that are interesting, relevant, and potentially useful to the listeners. Therefore the speaker should focus on the listener. "What's in it for me?" is a phrase I tell my students to remember as they choose topics, prepare, and present their speeches. Selecting a topic for class speeches need not be a difficult task. You can use personal inventories, brainstorming, web searches, or some combination of techniques to help you find an appropriate topic for you, your listeners, the situation, and the course requirements.

You need to narrow your topic so that it fits the assignment and time limits and still allows you to provide adequate information for your listeners. In addition, you need to think about the general and specific purposes and decide exactly what you want your listeners to walk away from the speech knowing or able to do.

Effective speakers have a focus on the listener. They realize that listeners vary in their interests, knowledge, motivation to listen, and ability to attend to messages. As a result, they will carefully analyze who the listeners are and what strategies might best allow the speaker to keep listeners interested. They will gather additional information about their listeners to help them develop a speech that will make listeners aware that the speaker really *is* interested in sharing something with the listeners and answers the question "What's in this for me?" Remember that effective speakers find ways to connect with their listeners. During all phases of the speech preparation process, you'll need to find ways to make those connections.

## Discussion Starters

1. What is the role of public communication in society?
2. How can effective public speaking help you connect with listeners?
3. Identify the criteria you would use to determine whether a topic is appropriate for this class.
4. Why should you formulate both a general purpose statement and a specific purpose statement?
5. Why do speakers need a thesis statement?
6. How can demographic analysis help you develop and deliver a speech?
7. How can a speaker reach a captive audience?
8. Why should you be concerned with your audience's attitudes toward you and your topic?
9. What web sources have you found useful in choosing topics?

## Notes

1. AICPA 2005. *Highlighted Responses from the Association for Accounting Marketing Survey. Creating the Future Agenda for the Profession—Managing Partner Perspective.* www.aicpa.org/pubs/tpcpa/feb2001.hilight.htm. Accessed on June 23, 2006.
2. J. W. Borchardt, "How Many Hats Can You Wear?" Workplace Perspectives, *Today's Chemist* 10 (7) (2001): 27–28, 20. www.pubs.acs.org/subscribe/journals/tcaw/10/i07/html/07work.html. Accessed on June 24, 2006.
3. J. S. Trent, Keynote Address, Central States Communication Association Convention, Omaha, NE, April 2003; and J. S. Trent (Ed), *Communication: Views from the Helm for the 21st Century* (Boston: Allyn and Bacon, 1998).
4. Students may wish to surf the Web to find topics. Keying in "Topics for Speeches" on Google netted nearly 34,000,000 hits in 0.25 seconds on June 24, 2006. This site also offered topics and help for choosing topics: www.faculty.cincinnatistate.edu/gesellsc/publicspeaking/topics.html.
5. D. Zarefsky, *Public Speaking: Strategies for Success,* 4th ed. (Boston: Allyn and Bacon, 2005), 352.

# Gathering and Using Information

> "Knowledge is of two kinds. We know a subject ourselves, or we know where we can find information upon it."
>
> —SAMUEL JOHNSON, *BOSWELL'S LIFE OF JOHNSON*, 1775

# This chapter will help you:

- **Identify** four principal sources of information for your speech topic.
- **Explain** how each source of information contributes to the research process.
- **Identify** appropriate sources for specific kinds of information.
- **Use** the library, electronic databases, and the World Wide Web to gather information.
- **Explain** how to evaluate information from various sources.
- **Cite** at least five guidelines that can make the research process more efficient.
- **Explain** how the various types of sources can be used to support and clarify a speaker's message and enhance the impact of a speech.
- **Describe** why a variety of sources is better.

## Making everyday connections

Two weeks and counting! Your communication professor reminds you that the informative speeches will begin in just over two weeks, you must have at least three different types of sources, and research is required. You have a topic but you're not really sure where to go next—you're uncertain what he means about "research" and "types of sources." You want to give a superb speech. What will you do? Where will you go? The library is a good place to start (either the building, or the materials that are accessible on the Internet). This chapter will answer those questions and help you make those decisions. Before reading on, reflect on and respond to the following questions. ▪

### Questions to think about
- Think about a really good presentation you've heard. What made it good? Why do you remember it? What, specifically, do you remember about it?
- Now, think about a poor presentation. What made it bad?
- What are three major differences between the memorable speech and the poor one?
- Did the kind of information that was presented have anything to do with your evaluation of the speech?

**W**hat impresses listeners? Professors, supervisors, colleagues, and audience members will have similar responses. Listeners are impressed with worthwhile, current information that is carefully constructed to tell a story. If you find an adequate amount of good, relevant, up-to-date information, you can create an impressive speech. Gathering information can be exciting and fun as well as a great learning experience. The information you gather becomes the backbone of the speech, which is only as good as your information. In this chapter, we focus on the research process and how to use the information you gather to support and clarify your message.

# ■ Gathering Information

College professors and professional speakers have said that every ten minutes of speaking time requires at least ten hours of research and preparation time. Each topic and speaking occasion will require a different amount of information, but there is no question that the more information you have, the better equipped you will be to design and develop your presentation and adapt it to your audience. Of course, quality of information matters more than quantity, especially when your time is limited. That is why it is important to develop your research skills. The more skilled you become at doing research, the better use you will make of your time.

## ▬■ Using Yourself as a Source of Information

If you want to make the best use of your time and gather the best information, where should you begin? Most often, with yourself. You are one of the most valuable sources of information available.

Your own experiences and knowledge can contribute to the content of your speech and give you authority to speak on a subject. Kent, for example, works in the Wellness and Recreation Center. In addition, he is a rock climber who spends every break rappelling and climbing. When Kent had to prepare a speech, he naturally thought first of his own personal passions and experiences. He knew he had lots of good information to share with his audience, and he also knew that there were sources of information that would enhance his own knowledge. Think about the effect of Kent's experiences as he related them in his informative speech:

> During spring break, three friends and I went to Colorado to climb mountains. We were pretty sure we could make it halfway to the top of Pike's Peak in one day. We learned a lesson in good equipment care when one of our climber's ropes broke and he fell a short distance. Luckily, he was not badly hurt, but his equipment failure and fall were good lessons for us. Today I'd like to explain a rock climber's equipment and its functions. I'll also explain how to care for that equipment so no one will have an accident similar to Tom's.

How does Kent's personal experience enhance the speech? What is added that would not be there if Kent were merely talking about something he had read?

Paulina, an international student, used her own experiences of growing up in Venezuela in her informative speech. She talked about her people and their music, clothing, and dances. She explained some of the unique differences between her country and the United States. You also have experiences that can be valuable sources for your speeches.

Probing your own knowledge of a subject can help you to organize your thoughts, develop a research plan and eventually move you more quickly through the research process.

## ▬▬ The Interview as a Source of Information

Of course, for most topics your firsthand experience and knowledge will not be sufficient. The interview can be a valuable tool for gathering **expert opinion** (ideas, testimony, conclusions, or judgments of witnesses or recognized authorities) and the most up-to-date information. A good interviewer can often discover information that could never be obtained through any other sources.

An interview is a carefully planned, person-to-person, question-and-answer session aimed at gathering information. An interview requires a constant exchange of questions and answers between two individuals. Both people speak and listen, as in a social conversation. In fact, social conversations constitute the most frequent interview situation because they are frequently a series of questions and answers. Let's look at the steps involved and some questions you need to ask in the interview process.

## ▬▬ Steps in the Interview Process

1. *Establish the purpose of the interview.* What do you want to know? What information will be most helpful? How can you learn what you need to know about the topic?

2. *Choose the interviewee.* From whom will you get the best, most up-to-date information? What are that person's credentials? Is the interviewee willing to openly and honestly provide that information? Is the interviewee accessible? How many people should be interviewed to get complete and accurate information?

3. *Conduct research prior to the interview.* You need to learn as much as you can before the interview on both the interviewee and your topic so that you can ask intelligent questions to gain the best, most important information.

4. *Record the interview.* You should either take notes or audiotape the interview in order to accurately recall information later. Choose the method that best allows good interaction. Use the Recording Interviews guidelines on the next page.

5. *Prepare questions.* Carefully prepare questions in advance. Be flexible enough to ask additional questions to get more information, to probe further, or to follow an unexpected opportunity the interviewee might provide.

6. *Organize the interview.* An interview, like a speech, usually has three identifiable segments: an opening, a body, and a closing. Organize your interview, and provide a template for the interviewee's responses.

7. *Other considerations.* Appropriate dress, punctuality, and attentive listening contribute to a successful interview. Always give the interviewee your complete, undivided attention during the interview. After you check your notes or listen to the tape, if anything is unclear, contact the interviewee for clarification as soon as possible after the interview.

Of course, for most topics your firsthand experience and knowledge alone will not be sufficient to develop an effective speech. The interview resource can be valuable for gathering expert opinion and the most up-to-date information.

■ **expert opinion**
Ideas, testimony, conclusions, or judgments of witnesses or recognized authorities.

## GUIDELINES  Recording Interviews

1. Ask permission to take notes or to tape the interview, and let interviewees know that they will have the opportunity to check the notes or that you will send a copy of the transcribed notes.
2. If you are using a tape recorder, be sure it is in good working order and test it prior to the interview. Make sure that you know how long your tape is and how the machine operates. Set the volume before you begin. The tape recorder should be positioned as inconspicuously as possible during the interview.
3. Maintain eye contact as much as possible.
4. Take notes throughout the interview.
5. Agree to follow any ground rules the interviewee establishes and offer the interviewee the opportunity to review the script of your speech prior to your presentation.
6. Review your notes or tape recording as soon after the interview as possible.
7. Remember to be courteous throughout the interview and to thank the interviewee for taking the time to speak with you.

## MAKING CONNECTIONS  for Success

### Thinking about the Interview

One of the ways to get the most up-to-date information available is by interviewing an expert or someone with firsthand knowledge of your topic. For the topics identified on the left, identify a person whom you could interview to get information about that topic. For each topic, identify at least two individuals who might give you unbiased information. Identify the person you would interview first and explain why. An example will get you started.

| TOPIC | INTERVIEWEE |
|---|---|
| The role of computers in the classroom | Campus technology office; computer salesperson; computer manufacturer |
| Stem cell research | _____ |
| Commonalities of types of music | _____ |
| An effective job portfolio | _____ |
| World religions | _____ |
| Avian flu precautions | _____ |

## ■ The Library as a Source of Information

Making use of the library requires some effort, but once you understand how the system works—and most libraries use essentially the same system—you will find that the library is a useful and beneficial resource for speech preparation. Libraries are very user friendly. Many libraries have invested great sums of money to install computerized systems to help researchers find materials quickly and easily.

If you do not know how to locate material, now is the time to learn. A little time invested now will save you a great deal of time later, and you will find that the library is a convenient and pleasant place to locate information. If you do not use the library, you will be at a disadvantage not only in your speech class but also in your other classes.

Start by attending one of the tours or orientation sessions that many libraries offer. Some also provide educational packages or Web-based tours with instructions on how to use the library. Principal sources of information in the library include: the librarian, library computer-assisted search programs, the electronic catalogues, and the reference department.

**The Library Computer Search.**    Most libraries have computer-assisted research systems. Each year these systems improve and become easier to use.

Many universities and colleges have network systems that allow you to enter the library indexes through home or campus computers. Once you learn the appropriate log-on procedures to access the library computer, menus guide you through the steps to find what you want. You will learn where the materials are located and whether they are available at your library.

**The Reference Department.**    Most library research begins in the reference department. Here you will find sources for specific subject areas such as dictionaries, almanacs, biographical aids, encyclopedias, yearbooks, atlases, bibliographies, indexes, and guides to periodical literature. If you are uncertain what to use or how to use them, ask the librarian.

There are specialized indexes for particular subjects, such as agriculture and natural resources, business and economics, statistics, biology and life sciences, computers, education, and history. An index widely used by beginning speech students is the *Readers' Guide to Periodical Literature.* This index lists articles from popular periodicals. Issues of the guide, published semimonthly or monthly, are bound separately for the latest publications and compiled in volumes for publications that are a year or more old.

Because magazines, research journals, and newspapers have the most recently available information on a subject, they are the most often used resources for speech writing. If you want to know the latest opinions and trends on almost any social, political, or economic issue, weekly magazines and newspapers will probably be your best resources. When you seek current research or classic studies, journals published by professional organizations (e.g., National Communication Association, American Psychological Association) will provide the best information.

Magazine and newspaper articles are usually brief and written for a general audience, so they are rich sources of basic information for speeches. Given their brevity, you can read several articles in order to gather different points of view. Libraries often have local, state, regional, and major national and international newspapers. Many academic libraries also have a subscription to LexisNexis, an online newspaper source with hundreds of newspapers from around the globe. Access to these sources will provide you with an even broader perspective and allow you to compare information among various sources.

If you do not know what your library has to offer, take time to learn about it. The search for knowledge is never easy, but thought and preparation will enable you to find ample information about almost any speech topic.

## ■■ Electronic Information Sources

Many libraries have access to an online database of current periodicals: newspapers, magazines, newsletters, transcripts, and wire information. LexisNexis provides the most current information available. In some cases, you can access LexisNexis at midnight your time and read the next morning's news from another part of the world. Many libraries have an ERIC (Educational Research Information Clearinghouse) database as well. ERIC provides access to reviewed convention papers, a source of the most up-to-date research findings as well as opinion pieces by experts in their fields. When searching an electronic database, you need to determine keywords and phrases to use in your search before you begin so you can maximize your time and effort. Check the options for each, but, generally, the word *and* is used as a connector between keywords. This allows the database to search the available materials for the information you need. Complete directions for carrying out searches are provided by your library or may be found on the screen where your search begins. Electronic databases provide valuable information.

Most colleges and universities have access to the **World Wide Web (WWW),** a global information system that allows users to access Internet information. Web searches can provide a great wealth of information quickly and easily. Remember that web information does not go through a review process, nor is it necessarily fact-checked in any way, so material on a web page is more suspect than that gathered from traditional sources. Critically weigh and verify the information you find, because much of it is unreliable. In Chapter 7, we reviewed ideas for evaluating web sources; review that section as you consider the information and the qualifications of the authors of your web sources.

To find information on the Web, conduct a search using one of the many available search engines. There are topic-based searches and site-based searches. The most common Internet search is the topic-based search. When you identify a general topic (computers, health issues, communication), you can access information about all aspects of that topic. You may, however, receive too many responses to your query and need to narrow your topic to find responses you can easily peruse to find information for your speech. Each search engine has a tutorial to help you get started. Among the more readily accessible are these:

| | |
|---|---|
| **Lycos** (www.lycos.com) | **Go.com** (www.go.com) |
| **AltaVista** (www.altavista.com) | **Google** (www.google.com) |
| **Yahoo!** (www.yahoo.com) | **Excite** (www.excite.com) |
| **Infoseek** (www.thefrontpage.com/search/infoseek.html) | **Ask** (www.ask.com) |

In addition, there are metasearch engines that search many sources for information. Among the useful metasearch engines are: "All the best search engines piled into one" **Dogpile** (www.dogpile.com) and **"the Mother of All Search Engines"**®, **Mamma.com** (www.mamma.com).

■ **World Wide Web (WWW)** A global information system that allows users to access information from the Internet.

When you find information on the Web, be sure to write down the specific bibliographic information (the URL [uniform resource locator or address], date accessed, page number, and author or producer), print the information, save it on a disk, or bookmark it. If you're using Netscape, for example, pull down the File menu to Page Setup. Click on each of the boxes so that a check mark appears in front of Document Title, Document Location, Page Number, Page Total, and Date Printed. If you create

Web searches can provide a wealth of information quickly and easily. Web information comes from a variety of sources. Some are reliable and credible, and others are not very useful, credible, relevant, or reliable. It is important that you check out your sources to ensure they are reliable and accurate.

a bookmark, you will also need to save it on the hard drive or on a disk. Many campus computer labs do not allow users to save information, or it may be saved only for a short period of time. In many cases, you will not be able to save the URL, so be sure to print at least the first page with the URL or write it down so you can find it later.

## ▄▄ Surfing the Web: The Internet as a Source of Information

Searching the Web can be interesting, entertaining, frustrating, addicting, and educational, and the Web facilitates access to a wealth of information in a relatively short period of time. Web information comes from a variety of sources. Some are reliable and credible, and others are neither useful, credible, relevant, nor reliable. Websites are not subject to the same evaluation and review as print sources are, so it is important that you assess not only the information on a website but also the people, or organizations responsible for the site. It is no accident that when you key in the words *critical thinking,* many responses will be suggestions for evaluating web sources. Several of the scores of critical thinking websites were actually titled "Thinking Critically about Web Sources." Three of our favorite guides for evaluating web sources (because of their thoroughness and because they are from respected university libraries) are provided by Esther Grassian at the UCLA library, Elizabeth Kirk of the Milton S. Eisenhower Library of the Johns Hopkins University, and Michael Engle, Cornell University. Each is different, yet all contain similarities. Each asks the surfer to consider specific questions about websites being accessed for information or research purposes.

Kirk (www.library.jhu.edu/elp/useit/evaluate/index.html), for example, offers four basic evaluative criteria:

1. *Author.* Who wrote the material? How do you know this person is qualified to write about this subject? Can you contact the author if you have questions?

2. *Publishing body.* Who "publishes" or sponsors the website? When you look at the web page, do you see a header or footer that shows a connection to a larger website? Is there a link on the page that takes you to the home page of the website? What can you learn from the Internet address (the URL)? Check the letters just to the left of the first backslash (/). Following are some abbreviations that provide some insight to a web source, which are used with URLs:

   | | |
   |---|---|
   | .edu | Refers to a college or university |
   | .cc(state)us | Refers to a community college |
   | .k12(state)us | Refers to a school for kindergarten through twelfth grade |
   | .com | Refers to a business or other commercial enterprise |
   | .org | Refers to a nonprofit organization or trade association |
   | .mil | Refers to a military site |
   | .gov | Refers to a government agency, official, or organization |
   | .net | Refers to a network administration organization |

   Look beyond the backslash. If you see a tilde ( ~ ) or if the URL includes terms such as "/users/" or "/people/," you may be looking at an individual's personal page within the official pages of a larger website. If it is a personal page, you have no way of knowing whether the information on the page represents the organization. However, if you know the author's identity and qualifications (say, a librarian at an educational site), you will be able to ascertain the credibility of the personal page.

3. *Currency.* How recently was the website published, created, or updated? This information should be at the bottom of the web page or home page of the website. Does the document contain data that must be recent? Is there a date connected to that information? (When the population of Hispanics is given with a 1990 date, for example, the information is not current.) Does the website have links to other sites that no longer work?

4. *Purpose.* Can you determine why the information is on the Web? Does the site provide information, give explanations, persuade, publicize, sell products, or entertain? Sometimes the URL will give you a clue. Part of the URL contains a function indicator, such as *gov* or *com,* that indicates the purpose of a website:

   | | |
   |---|---|
   | .edu or .gov | Provides factual information and explanations |
   | .com | Promotes and sells products, or provides current news and information |
   | .org | Influences public opinion and advocates for particular issues |
   | .net or .com | Entertains |
   | .info | Especially used to provide truly global general information; most current registrations are in the United States |
   | .biz | Specifically for businesses |
   | .name | Indicates the site is for individuals |

## MAKING Technology CONNECTIONS

### Thinking Critically about Websites

College libraries often provide criteria for you to check the accuracy and validity of websites. Check your school library's website to see if there is a set of criteria for evaluating websites. Then go to the following sites and compare and contrast all you find.

Evaluating Web Sites: Criteria and Tools (Michael Engle, Cornell University Library, Revised, October 28, 2005) (note especially, the Webliography provided on this page): www.library.cornell.edu/okuref/research/webeval.html.

UCLA College Library: Thinking Critically about WWW Resources (Esther Grassian): www.library.ucla.edu/libraries/college/help/critical.

1. How are the criteria similar? Different?
2. How do these sites compare with the information in the text from Elizabeth Kirk at the Johns Hopkins University Library?

| | |
|---|---|
| .pro | Indicates professionals; attorneys, dentists, or medical doctors, for example, register their sites for easy access. (For example, Janedoe.law.pro identifies a site belonging to attorney Jane Doe.) |
| .museums | Accredited museums worldwide |
| .aero | Globally recognized suffix for airlines, airports, computer reservation systems, and related industries |
| .coop | Identifies business cooperatives, such as credit unions and rural electric co-ops worldwide |

Finally, consider one more question: How does web information compare with other available resources? If there are discrepancies among sources, do some further checking to find the best sources of information you can. Remember, too, that websites change quickly. You might search a specific topic and find 20,000 hits and then return an hour later and find 35,799 hits. Websites are added rapidly and changed often. Also, a search engine may sample more or fewer individual sites at different times. The library websites in the Making Technology Connections box may have changed from the initial writing to the time this book is published. Sometimes you will automatically be redirected to another site. At other times, you will need to search further or find another source. This is another good reason for writing down URLs and bookmarking websites: You can go back to the exact site to get further information or direct others to a specific site.

# ■ Suggestions for Doing Research

There are no shortcuts to good research, but there are ways to make research more enjoyable and easier no matter what sources you choose to use. Here are several suggestions:

1. *State a clear purpose before starting your research.* Knowing what you want to find makes the job of searching easier. If the purpose of your speech is to persuade your audience that breakfast is the most important meal of the day, the key word

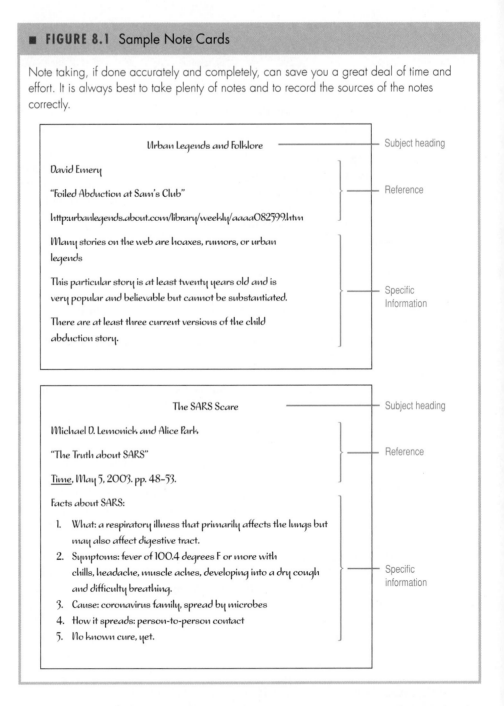

■ **FIGURE 8.1** Sample Note Cards

Note taking, if done accurately and completely, can save you a great deal of time and effort. It is always best to take plenty of notes and to record the sources of the notes correctly.

Urban Legends and Folklore —————— Subject heading

David Emery

"Foiled Abduction at Sam's Club" —————— Reference

http:urbanlegends.about.com/library/weekly/aaaa082599.htm

Many stories on the web are hoaxes, rumors, or urban legends

This particular story is at least twenty years old and is very popular and believable but cannot be substantiated. —————— Specific Information

There are at least three current versions of the child abduction story.

The SARS Scare —————— Subject heading

Michael D. Lemonick and Alice Park

"The Truth about SARS" —————— Reference

_Time_, May 5, 2003. pp. 48–53.

Facts about SARS:

1. What: a respiratory illness that primarily affects the lungs but may also affect digestive tract.
2. Symptoms: fever of 100.4 degrees F or more with chills, headache, muscle aches, developing into a dry cough and difficulty breathing. —————— Specific information
3. Cause: coronavirus family, spread by microbes
4. How it spreads: person-to-person contact
5. No known cure, yet.

would be _breakfast._ You will begin your search with that term but might also want to look at _health, nutrition,_ or _healthy lifestyles._ You need to consider all possible areas of research in advance to keep your research productive and efficient.

**2.** _Begin your research early._ Because finding appropriate materials takes time, you should start your research as soon as possible. If you wait until the last minute, you might discover that the materials you need are unavailable or that it takes longer to find them than you anticipated.

3. *Use computer searches when possible.* The computer is one of the simplest means of obtaining lists of sources on any topic. If you are unfamiliar with your library's computer system, ask for help. Librarians will gladly help you find what you need.

4. *Maintain a bibliography of sources.* As you find sources on the computer, electronic catalogues, in electronic databases, and in periodical guides, copy them in the same form onto a sheet of paper or index cards (3 x 5 inch or 4 x 6 inch) or into a computer file. The advantage of index cards is that you can sort them quickly, either alphabetically or by importance to the speech. List each item separately and make notes about its importance to the speech presentation. This may seem tedious and time-consuming, but if you fail to record something and need it later, it's much easier than starting all over because you cannot find the original. Keying and saving this information into computer files can also help you stay organized and save time in the long run. If you cannot save your files on the library computers, type the information into an email and send it to yourself.

5. *Take notes.* Efficient and accurate note taking is a must. Once you have located information, either record it by hand or photocopy it for later use. Whether you quote a statement verbatim, summarize it, or paraphrase it, record the original information accurately and completely. Take plenty of notes, and always make sure that the source is fully and accurately indicated, as in the sample note cards in Figure 8.1. Nothing is more frustrating than having information you cannot use because you don't know the source and cannot return to it for additional information. The more information you record, the better. You should always have more than you need to write your speech.

# ▪ Using Research to Support and Clarify Ideas

More than 2,000 years ago, Aristotle, a famous Greek scholar, wrote that there are essentially two parts to every speech: a statement and its proof. Aristotle's description is still valid today. How a speaker clarifies and supports ideas determines the quality of the speech. For example, consider the following statement:

> Today's students are much smarter than students of every earlier generation. The reason? Students have access to computer technology that gives them more available information than ever before.

On the surface, this statement might seem valid, but is it accurate, and will an audience accept it at face value? Does the statement offer any data to help you accept the first sentence as true? What proof is provided that students who have access to computer technology have advanced more quickly than those who do not? Careful analysis shows that we need to think carefully before we accept the statement as true.

Audiences generally accept information because of the perceived believability of the speaker or the information itself. Thus the statement would likely be more acceptable to audiences if it were made by a well-known educator and researcher than if it were made by a student. But regardless of the source, most listeners require some proof or specific data before they completely accept a statement. Consequently, effective speakers justify each main idea in their speeches with a variety of supporting and clarifying materials.

## Thinking about Traditional and Web Information Sources

There are many places to find information that will enhance your speeches. Using the library and the Internet and interviewing experts are several sources discussed in this chapter. Imagine that in two weeks, you will present an informative speech using presentational aids in your communication class. Your professor has indicated that the topic may be of your own choosing. Follow these steps as you begin your search for information:

1. Identify the general topic area for your speech.
2. Identify the general subject of your key word search.
3. Decide whether to use traditional library sources or electronic sources.
4. Decide when you will use library sources and when you will use web sources.
5. Identify five sites where you might find information on your topic.
6. Conduct a web search.
7. Refine your search, and narrow your topic in that search.
8. Determine what criteria you will use to evaluate your information.
9. Determine what guidelines you will use as you seek information on the Web.

Supporting and clarifying materials bring life to a speech. They can make the content of a speech appealing, vivid, exciting, meaningful, acceptable, and more useful to listeners. Compare these two paragraphs:

> Alzheimer's disease has a great impact on family life. Everyone is affected in differing ways when a family member suffers from this terrible disease.

> Who are the "real" victims of Alzheimer's disease? Although Alzheimer's obviously has an effect on all family members, it may be the teens who are left to care for a grandparent who suffer the most. "I wish my parents would have known the symptoms of Alzheimer's," said 13-year-old Ashley, whose grandmother has the disease. "I remember staying home alone with my grandma and she had this blank look on her face as if she was a zombie or something. Her disease has really affected me."[1]

Which paragraph do you find to be more meaningful? More interesting? Why?

Consider the following statement made in a speech by a student:

> Exercise is the best means of losing weight. Although many people consider exercise to be hard work, it doesn't have to be. In fact, there are a number of exercise programs that are easy, and you don't even have to sweat to lose pounds.

Too good to be true? Yes. And it's not very persuasive, either. Most of us want more proof. The speaker needs to present evidence before the audience will believe this.

The quantity and quality of a speaker's supporting and clarifying materials, plus the speaker's ability to use them correctly, make the difference between a mediocre speech and a good one. In this section, we focus on the basic kinds of supporting and clarifying materials used in speeches: testimony, examples, definitions, and statistics.

## ▬ Testimony

■ **testimony**

Opinions or conclusions of witnesses or recognized authorities.

The opinions or conclusions of witnesses or recognized authorities are referred to as **testimony.** Speakers use testimony to support or reinforce points they want their audiences to accept. The value of the testimony is related both to the listeners' opin-

## MAKING Technology CONNECTIONS

### Listening to Voices from the Past

Ever wondered how a past U.S. president sounded? Or why your parents and/or grandparents make such a big deal about some event? (How many times did you hear where they were when one of the Kennedy brothers was assassinated?) The History Channel website provides a vast amount of information from the past. Go to the Web and key in www.historychannel.com. To listen to the actual voices, you must have RealPlayer installed (the site allows you to download a free copy). When you get on the home page, click on Speeches and Video. (It may be slow to load, be patient!) Click on "Harry S. Truman removes General MacArthur from Korean command" and listen to the twenty-two seconds of

Truman's speech. Then, click on Historical Figures and browse the list. Click on "03/05/1946—Churchill coins 'Iron Curtain'." At the time this text was published, there were a total of fifty speeches and videos available. Choose two more brief speeches and listen to the words and delivery, then think about and answer the following:

1. Other than availability, why do you think these speeches were included?
2. What can we learn from speeches that have been labeled as being of historic significance?
3. What factors, other than voice and delivery, made these speeches significant?

ion of its acceptability and to the speaker who presents it. Consider this opening of a student's speech:

> What do you think when you see a person who has Down syndrome? If you're like most people, you feel pity. I'm here to tell you that you need not feel pity, because people with Down syndrome are some of the most loving, caring people in the world! Why do I say that? Because my son is a Down syndrome child, and he gives us more love and caring than I ever imagined anyone could possess.[2]

The young mother who gave this speech immediately captured our interest and attention. She expressed her own emotions and shared the wonderful things that had happened to her family because of her son. Her story moved every member of the audience.

The use of testimony usually adds trustworthiness to what a speaker says—a necessity for all speakers who are not yet established as experts on their chosen speech topic. The speaker's own experience can be an excellent form of testimony as in the previous example. When the speaker's reputation and experience are insufficient, the use of a recognized and trusted authority can be invaluable in gaining listeners' acceptance.

Testimony can either support or clarify material or both. Here is an example of testimony that does both:

> Civic engagement is the new catchphrase of many college and university student groups. Many student groups have joined the technology phenomenon and created websites to ensure action and exposure. One such group is The Get Informed: Raise Your Voice Student Action for Change. The group's website quotes The Task Force on Civic Engagement at the University of Minnesota's definition: "Civic Engagement means an institutional commitment to public purposes and responsibilities intended to strengthen a democratic way of life in the rapidly changing Information Age of the twenty-first century."[3]

The speaker uses testimony and a definition from a student action website to help make a point about the importance of students giving back to the community through civic engagement.

Testimony can be either quoted directly or paraphrased. Paraphrasing is an effective method of condensing a long text or clarifying a technical passage. Sometimes audience members tune out speakers who use long and complex quotations. Restating long quotations in your own words helps to make the source's words fit the tone of your speech. If you paraphrase, do not violate the meaning of the original statement.

Certain statements are so well phrased that they cannot be stated any better. An example is the forceful and unforgettable statement made by John F. Kennedy in his 1961 presidential inaugural address: "Ask not what your country can do for you; ask what you can do for your country." Always quote such statements word for word. Misquoting someone can be embarrassing, but even worse, it can destroy your credibility. Double-check every quotation for accuracy and source, and never use a quotation out of context.

Testimony should meet two essential tests: The person whose words are cited must be qualified by virtue of skills, training, expertise, recognition, and reputation; and the expert's opinion must be acceptable and believable to your listeners.

The person you quote should be a qualified authority on the subject. For example, an athlete's endorsement of tennis shoes and a movie star's endorsement of cosmetics are fairly believable because they use such products in their work. But when celebrities advertise products completely unrelated to their area of expertise, their

The value of testimony is related both to the listener's opinion of the acceptability of the message and to the credibility of the speaker who presents it. Tennis star Venus Williams is a credible spokesperson for Reebok, but she might not be a qualified authority on other subjects.

opinions becomes less believable. Avoid using names solely because someone is well known. The best testimony comes from a person whose knowledge and experience are related to the topic and who is recognized by your listeners.

For maximum credibility, testimony should also come from objective sources. The objectivity and neutrality of authorities are particularly important when your subject is controversial. For example, in trying to persuade an audience that today's automobiles are safer than those of a decade ago, it is more convincing to quote the American Automobile Association or the National Safety Council than the president of an automotive company. Listeners tend to be suspicious of opinions from a biased or self-interested source.

## Examples

An **example** is a simple, representative incident or model that clarifies a point. Examples are useful when you are presenting complex information to listeners who are unfamiliar with a topic and when your purpose is to inform or instruct. Brief examples, illustrations, and analogies are three kinds of examples that help make things clear for an audience.

**Brief Examples.**   A **brief example** is a specific instance used to introduce a topic, drive home a point, or create a desired impression. The following brief example was used to introduce a subtopic related to the main topic of outsourcing.

> Outsourcing has become an almost hated word and concept to many in the American workforce.

A series of brief examples can also be used to create a desired impression:

> "Outsourcing" has become an almost hated word and concept in the United States. To many, jobs they once had or hoped to attain are now outsourced to Mexico, India, or other highly populated areas where there are skilled workers who work for less than Americans. As a result, U.S. jobs are lost. Another result is that much of what used to be "local" now takes place far away in places such as Mexico City or Bombay (now Mumbai). While you may not be aware of this, if you lose your luggage on a flight, the phone call you make to determine where that piece of luggage might be located is as likely to be to Mumbai as it is to Chicago. The phone call you make to complain about your cell phone service may go to Calcutta where a woman who says her name is Mary answers your call. According to *Time*, June 26, 2006, "Every night, young radiologists in Bangalore [India] read CT scans emailed to them by emergency-room doctors in the U.S." Your bank may outsource its data processing to workers in New Delhi. The average per capita income in India in 2005, according to that same *Time* magazine article, was $3,300. By comparison, in China it was $6,800.[4] No matter where American companies send their outsourced jobs, the people work for less in those countries than here, so American companies can prosper while American workers are losing ground.

**Illustrations.**   An **illustration,** or extended example, is a narrative, case history, or anecdote that is striking and memorable. Illustrations often exemplify concepts, conditions, or circumstances, or they demonstrate findings. If an example refers to a single item or event, it is an illustration. Because illustrations go into more detail than brief examples, they are useful in establishing proof.

■ **example** A simple, representative incident or model that clarifies a point.

■ **brief example** A specific instance that is used to introduce a topic, drive home a point, or create a desired response.

■ **illustration** An extended example, narrative, case history, or anecdote that is striking and memorable.

Dr. Martin Luther King Jr., Nobel prize winner and leader of the Civil Rights movement, was a brilliant and mesmerizing speaker. In 1963, he gave his famous "I Have a Dream" speech to a crowd of thousands in Washington, D.C. His rhythmic repetition of the phrase "I have a dream" pinpointed his message and captivated the audience.

An illustration lends depth and explanation to the point a speaker is trying to make. It also gives the information more meaning. An illustration may be either factual or hypothetical. A **factual illustration** tells what has actually happened; a **hypothetical illustration** tells what could happen, given a specific set of circumstances.

A hypothetical illustration, because it is speculative, asks listeners to use their imaginations. Such examples are often short stories that relate to a general principle or concept. One instructor used the following hypothetical example to help her students envision how to use their voices when delivering an emotional speech:

> Imagine that an angry mob has accused your friend of a crime—a serious crime—and that they are going to hang him because they believe he is guilty, even though you know he isn't. Your only chance to save your friend is to persuade the unruly mob that he is innocent.

■ **factual illustration** A report of something that exists or actually happened.

■ **hypothetical illustration** A report of something that could happen, given a specific set of circumstances.

This hypothetical illustration demonstrates that people who are involved in serious situations must use their voices to make their point. The speech to the mob would have to be vivid, forceful, convincing, and highly emotional.

The use of a hypothetical illustration can be particularly effective when it involves the listeners. The illustration should create a vivid picture in the listeners' minds. The more realistic the situation, the more likely it is that the listeners will become involved. A speaker should always specify whether an illustration is factual or hypothetical.

**Analogies.**   An **analogy** is a comparison of two things that are similar in certain essential characteristics. Analogies explain or prove the unknown by comparing it to the known.

There are two kinds of analogies. A **figurative analogy** draws comparisons between things in different categories. For example, in her description of the immigration experience in Postville, Iowa (previously cited in Chapter 4), Anna said that in the past, Postville was a "melting pot" where the primarily German and Norwegian cultures had blended and melted together. The recent immigration experience, however, was a "tossed salad" in which the newcomers kept their own cultural practices and did not try to blend to become more like each other.[5] A **literal analogy** is a comparison of members of the same category and makes a simple comparison, for example, two majors (art and music), two search engines (Yahoo and Google), or two genres of literature (drama and poetry).

Most topics offer opportunities to use analogies. Figurative analogies make ideas vivid and clear, whereas literal analogies supply evidence to support points. Analogies are effective, efficient, and creative means of supporting and clarifying information.

**Restatements.**   Speakers can and should use a variety of strategies to make their speeches memorable. Effective speakers have often used both **restatement** and repetition to support and clarify their ideas. A restatement is the expression of the same idea using different words. It may take the form of a summary, synonym, or rephrasing.

Restatement does not provide evidence, but it often has a persuasive effect. A well-planned use of restatement can add clarity, meaning, and dramatic rhythm to a message. Martin Luther King Jr., in his famous "I Have a Dream" speech, used both repetition and restatement to make his point:

> I say to you today, my friends, so even though we face the difficulties of today and tomorrow, I still have a dream. It is a dream deeply rooted in the American dream.
>
> I have a dream that one day this nation will rise up and live out the true meaning of its creed, "We hold these truths to be self-evident, that all men are created equal."
>
> I have a dream that one day on the red hills of Georgia the sons of former slaves and sons of former slave owners will be able to sit down together at the table of brotherhood.[6]

■ **analogy** A comparison of two things that are similar in certain essential characteristics.

■ **figurative analogy** A comparison of things in different categories.

■ **literal analogy** A comparison of members of the same category.

■ **restatement** The expression of the same idea using different words.

## Using Examples: Some Tips

GUIDELINES

1. Use factual examples to add authenticity to your presentation. Factual examples build on the basic information presented and add credibility to both you and your speech.
2. Use realistic examples that relate directly to your discussion. If you try to generalize from unusual or rare situations, you risk undermining credibility.
3. Use authentic, accurate, and verifiable examples. Always give credit to the source so your listeners can verify it.

## ▪ Definitions

You must define all unfamiliar words and concepts, especially technical terms, if you want your listeners to understand and accept your speech. Nothing is more bothersome to listeners than a speaker who uses terminology they do not understand. In most cases, it is better to offer too much explanation than too little. However, do not patronize your audience by explaining the obvious. You can use several different kinds of definitions to keep your audience's attention. For example, "Calculus is defined as a system of calculation in advanced mathematics, especially a system using algebraic symbols to solve problems dealing with changing quantities."[7] The definition tells us what calculus is and separates it from other forms of mathematics.

A **logical definition,** the most common form used by speakers, usually contains two parts: a term's dictionary definition and the characteristics that distinguish the term from other items in the same category.

An **operational definition** explains how an object or concept works, gives the steps that make up a process, or states how conceptual terms are measured. Here are some examples:

> People who have communication apprehension are those who score a 90 or higher on the Personal Report of Communication Apprehension (PRCA) test.
>
> For our purposes, an A will be awarded to those who correctly identify 94 or more items in the exam.
>
> The average of the grades received in this class is the sum of all scores divided by the number of students in the class.

A **definition by example** clarifies a term not by describing it or giving its meaning but by mentioning or showing an example of it.

> When I talk about sexist language, I mean any words that do not include everyone in the room. If you say, "I think you guys ought to know this," you are using sexist language because usually at least half of the people in the class are female.

**▪ logical definition**
A definition consisting of a term's dictionary definition and the characteristics that distinguish the term from other members of the same category.

**▪ operational definition** A definition that explains how an object or concept works, or lists the steps that make up a process.

**▪ definition by example** Clarifying a term, not by describing it or giving its meaning, but by mentioning or showing an example of it.

---

## MAKING CONNECTIONS

### Carolyn Calloway-Thomas
*Indiana University*

Carolyn Calloway-Thomas, a former Fulbright and Carnegie scholar, is an associate professor at Indiana University. Calloway-Thomas examines how and why African Americans used the spoken word to talk their way to freedom in the United States. She probes such questions as: What is the nature of talk that leads to freedom? And under what conditions do black speakers succeed rhetorically and under what conditions do they fail? In her book *Dr. Martin Luther King, Jr. and the Sermonic Power of Public Discourse,* she argues that King changed the way in which politics is practiced in the United States today

## To Scholars

because of his ability to blend key Christian values with the democratic traditions of American society.

Dr. Calloway-Thomas also spells out what happens when human beings interact with others—both near and far. Using storytelling, cultural concepts, and fascinating historical examples across a range of cultures in both *Intercultural Communication: Roots and Routes* and *Intercultural Communication,* Calloway-Thomas tells us a great deal about a rapidly transforming world culturally and linguistically. According to Dr. Calloway-Thomas, we must "learn what it is like to live by someone else's light." Toward this end, she has traveled to many exciting places, including England, Estonia, Finland, France, Gambia, Germany, Italy, Japan, Nigeria, Russia, South Africa, Sweden, and Switzerland.

## Using Definitions: Some Tips

1. Define a term or concept whenever you suspect your audience might not understand what you mean or that multiple interpretations are possible.
2. Keep definitions short and to the point. Do not make your explanation more complex than necessary.
3. Use clear and concise language your audience can easily understand. Make your definitions come alive for your audience by providing examples.

## ■■ Statistics

We read that the earth's population is more than six billion, that there are more than 1.3 billion people in China alone, and that India has a population of more than one billion. Although statistics can be interesting or even compelling, they can also be confusing and difficult to interpret. Numerical data that show relationships or summarize or interpret many instances are known as **statistics.** Every day we are confronted with numerical analyses.

Statistics enable speakers to summarize a large amount of data rapidly, to analyze specific occurrences or instances, to isolate trends, and to calculate probabilities of future events. They are used to clarify and support a speaker's position. For example, consider these two statements.

> Wind is an increasingly important source of energy.

> According to the June 5, 2003, *New York Times,* wind energy now accounts for less than 1 percent of all electricity produced in the United States. But the American Wind Energy Association, the industry's trade group, predicts it will grow to 6 percent in 2020.

The first statement is broad and possibly misleading. The second cites specific numbers and predictions and gives listeners a clearer view of how much wind energy contributes to U.S. usage. The second statement also uses a current source to add credence to the data. Statistics can also be used to emphasize the magnitude of a problem as seen in the following example:

> Interestingly, a study of nearly 3,000 victims of Augusto Pinochet's violent 17-year regime in Chile showed that it was the lingering memories of torture that did the greatest psychological damage.[8]

Statistics can also be informative:

> Lung cancer is among the least curable cancers. For people diagnosed with the disease, the average five-year survival rate is only about 14 percent.[9]

**Making the Most of Statistics.** Following five simple guidelines will help you make the most of the statistics you've gathered.

1. *Make sure that the statistics you present in your speech are from reliable and neutral sources.* The motives of the source of any statistics must be carefully assessed. For example, if you heard two sets of data on fuel economy per gallon of gasoline—one prepared by the DaimlerChrysler Corporation and the other

■ **statistics** Numerical data that show relationships or summarize or interpret many instances.

by the Environmental Protection Agency—which would you expect to be more reliable? Although DaimlerChrysler's data may be perfectly accurate, listeners would tend to believe that their data are biased. It would be to a speaker's advantage, therefore, to use the more neutral source, in this case, the Environmental Protection Agency.

It can often be difficult to identify the most neutral source. For example, whose statistics would you use if you wished to inform your audience about the U.S. strength in nuclear weapons: the Department of Defense or the Americans for Peace? Here the choice is debatable unless you intend to take a position on the issue. Remember, statistics can be used in many different ways and can thus influence interpretations and outcomes.

2. *Take time to explain the statistics you are using.* Interpret and relate your statistics to your listeners. Consider the following use of statistics:

> The sun's radius (distance from its center to its surface) is about 432,000 miles (695,500 kilometers), approximately 109 times Earth's radius. The following example may help you picture the relative sizes of the sun and Earth and the distance between them: Suppose the radius of Earth were the width of an ordinary paper clip. The radius of the sun would be roughly the height of a desk, and the sun would be about 100 paces from Earth.[10]

This explanation makes use of analogy and provides meaningful statistics by clearly comparing the size of the sun to commonplace objects.

When using data that listeners may have difficulty understanding or visualizing, try to provide appropriate comparisons in order to make the data more meaningful.

3. *Use statistics sparingly.* Statistics are difficult to comprehend. If you use too many, you run a risk of boring or confusing your audience. Use statistics only when necessary, and make sure they are easy to understand. The following example would be difficult for even the most attentive listener to comprehend:

> If my new proposal is accepted, we will have at least a 20 percent increase in production efficiency and at least a 50 cent per unit cost reduction, according to our 2006 projections. This, I might add, means a 10 percent, or a minimum of 35 cents per unit, cost reduction over the next five to six years. What this all adds up to is a 15 percent increase over this time period and an eventual profit of $110,000 per year. That will also give us a 6 percent depreciation allowance.

It would be much easier to understand if the data were presented as follows:

> The new proposal, if accepted, will increase production efficiency by 20 percent or 50 cents per unit according to our 2006 projections. This would provide a minimum cost reduction of 35 cents per unit over the next five to six years and a $110,000 per year profit for a 15 percent increase over the time period.

4. *Round off large numbers when possible.* Listeners understand and remember uncomplicated figures better. For example, it is easier to remember nearly one billion than 999,999,900. And although you can say that the Washington Monument rises 555 feet, 5⅛ inches high or 169.29 meters high,[11] listeners will more easily remember 555 feet or 169 meters. Unless exact measurements are required (when people actually create something as you talk), round off most statistics to the nearest whole number.

**■ TABLE 8.1** UNICEF Uses Contributions to Save Children's Lives

| TIME FRAME | DAILY DEATHS | # WHO DIED BEFORE AGE 5 | CHILDREN NOT ATTENDING SCHOOL | IMMUNIZED |
|---|---|---|---|---|
| 1970–80 | 70,000 | 25% | 160 million | 10% |
| 2000–06 | 33,000 | 9.4% | 99 million | 75% |

5. *Use visual aids to present statistical information, if appropriate and possible.* Use of visual aids saves explanation time and also makes statistics easier to understand. Compare the following paragraph with Table 8.1. Note how everything in the paragraph is quickly summarized into five columns and two lines. Which one are you more likely to remember?

> UNICEF figures demonstrate that their work has saved thousands of lives. A generation ago, 70,000 children died daily. Today that number has been cut by more than half. Thirty years ago, 1 in 4 children died before the age of five. The number of children not attending primary or secondary school has dropped below 100 million for the first time in recent history. UNICEF further states that in 1980, only 10% of the world's children were immunized against six killer diseases. Today that number is up to 75 percent.[12]

Figure 8.2 represents another example of how complex data can be summarized and presented in an interesting way. Note how the graphics make it easier to understand the statistics presented. (Chapter 10 discusses presentational aids in greater detail.)

**■ FIGURE 8.2** Visualizing Statistical Data

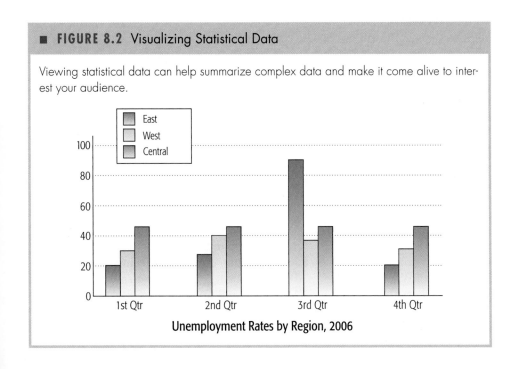

Viewing statistical data can help summarize complex data and make it come alive to interest your audience.

Unemployment Rates by Region, 2006

| GUIDELINES | Using Statistics: Some Tips |
|---|---|

1. Make sure your statistics come from reliable, neutral sources.
2. Use statistics sparingly.
3. Take the time to explain the statistics to your listeners.
4. Display statistics visually whenever possible. This saves explanation time.

# Summary

A key to effective speaking is the quality and currency of material you gather to support and clarify your ideas. Listeners appreciate worthwhile information that is presented so that they can remember the main ideas. Just as communication begins with you, an effective speech begins with you, your views, and experiences. You can also find a wide variety of useful information in the library. The reference section has a broad range of materials that can be helpful. In addition, there are numerous electronic databases (LexisNexis, ERIC, etc.) in which you can find up-to-date information on most topics. Interviews provide expert opinion, and the World Wide Web is an easily accessed source. Be sure to evaluate the information gained on the Web even more carefully than that from other, more traditional, sources, however, because Web-based material has not always undergone the same rigorous evaluation process. When you use Web-based materials, you should follow the assessment guidelines provided.

The research process can be both interesting and entertaining if you begin the process early, know what you need to look for, take careful notes, and write down all necessary information about your sources, including specific URLs, so that you and others can find the information later.

A good speaker knows that effective research that supports and clarifies main points can make the difference between a good and a poor speech. Testimony, examples, definitions, and statistics are the four basic types of supporting and clarifying materials. The materials you use will vary greatly depending on the topic and purpose. Your goal should always be to clarify your ideas so that your listeners will remember and even make use of it at some time, either now or in the future.

# Discussion Starters

1. What do you need to know about a topic before you consult with others or use the library?
2. When is an interview a particularly appropriate method?
3. What does one need to know and do to be an effective interviewer?
4. Your speech topic is "date rape." When you go to the library to do research, where should you begin?
5. Why is the reference section a good place to gather materials for a speech?
6. What role do supporting and clarifying materials play?
7. On what basis should you judge the effectiveness of a source of information in supporting a particular point of view?
8. As a listener, how do you feel when you hear someone using statistics in a speech?
9. When should we use electronic sources to find information?
10. How and why should we evaluate web sources?

# Notes

1. "Helping Teens Cope with Alzheimer's Disease," *Advances: The Alzheimer's Association Newsletter* (Spring 2001), 3.

2. Adapted from a speech by Samantha Burt, Oral Communication, University of Northern Iowa, October 2002. Used by permission.

3. Get Informed: Raise Your Voice. Student Action for Change, "What is civic engagement?" www.compact .org/scec/getinformed/civic-engagement.html. Accessed on June 27, 2006.

4. M. Elliott, "India Awakens," *Time,* June 26, 2006, 36–39.

5. Adapted from remarks made in an oral defense of an unpublished M.A. thesis by Anna Levina, entitled "Recent Jewish Immigrants' Communication in Postville, Iowa: A Case Study," University of Northern Iowa, June 3, 2003.

6. From "I Have a Dream" by Martin Luther King Jr., Copyright 1967, Martin Luther King Jr., copyright renewed 1995, Coretta Scott King. Reprinted by arrangement with the Estate of Martin Luther King Jr., c/o Writers House as agent for the proprietor, New York, NY.

7. "Calculus," World Book Multimedia Encyclopedia, Mac OS X Edition, Version 6.0.2, 2001.

8. M. Szegedy-Maszak, "Tyranny of Mind," *U.S. News & World Report* (May 12, 2003), 48.

9. "Should You Be Screened for Lung Cancer?" *Women's Health Reporter* 3(11) (2002): 1.

10. "Sun," World Book Multimedia Encyclopedia, Mac OS X Edition, Version 6.0.2, 2001.

11. "Washington Monument," World Book Multimedia Encyclopedia, Mac OS X Edition, Version 6.0.2, 2001.

12. UNICEF letter to contributors, May, 2006.

# CHAPTER 9

# Organizing and Outlining Your Speech

"The End of speech is
first to be understood,
and then to be believed."

—THOMAS FULLER

# This chapter will help you:

- **Identify** the purposes of the three main parts of speech.
- **Find** and use suitable content for the three main parts of the speech.
- **Describe** the main points of a speech.
- **Assess** the organizational patterns described and choose the best for your own speeches.
- **Use** transitions, signposts, internal previews, and internal summaries in your own speeches.
- **Complete** preliminary and presentational outlines for your speeches.
- **Use** websites to find examples of outlines and additional ideas for organizing speeches.

## Making everyday connections

We've probably all heard speakers who seemed to have good ideas but we had to struggle to understand exactly where they were going or what they were trying to tell us. And, we've also heard speakers who made us sit up and take notice. They had a message to share and they did it in such a way that we realized the topic was important, the content made sense, and that perhaps we should do something about the situation described. What's the difference in the two? Not the obvious ones—one person is organized and compelling, the other is not. Beyond that, what's the difference? Is it that they tell us what they're going to cover and cover it? Or, is it something more subtle than that? Before you read this chapter on speech organization and outlining, think about those two speeches and what makes one more successful and the other less so. ■

### Questions to think about

- What does it take to help you, as a listener, stay with the speaker?
- What strategies work for the effective speaker?
- Does a speaker need to state exactly where she or he is going in this speech? Why or why not?
- When you speak, what do you do to try to help your listeners follow along?

Y ou now have one of the toughest of the speaker's jobs completed: you've chosen a topic and gathered information. The next task is to organize the material into a sequence that others will understand. Organization is natural, right? No, it is a learned skill. One of the best places to learn and apply organizational skills is in the preparation of a speech. Although there are no prescriptions for success, there are guidelines that can be helpful. Most of your professors, especially communication professors, do not want you to have a cookie-cutter speech, but we do offer suggestions that are helpful in organizing your speeches. It is up to you, the speaker, to use some creative touches to help you get your points across to your listeners. Just as a construction worker building a house must start with the footings and the foundation and work up to the roof, there are steps in the organizational process that will help you to construct an organized speech.

**Organizing** your speech involves arranging its parts into a systematic and meaningful whole. Once you have thoroughly researched your topic, you can simplify your writing task by carefully organizing your material. All speeches are organized into three main parts: introduction, body, and conclusion. By this point, you have determined your speech's general and specific purposes and have begun to think about your thesis statement. This should help guide you in the organizing process. Because the body is the main part of any speech, containing most of its content, we recommend that students begin by working on the body and only later write the introduction and conclusion. Thus we examine the body first.

# ■ Organize the Body of Your Speech

The **body** of a speech presents the main content, and organizing it will help you formulate your thesis statement. To ensure that the body of your speech is well organized, your content must be divided into main points that are thoughtfully selected and stated; limited in number; and carefully ordered, connected, and supported.

## ■ Develop the Main Points

Well-developed **main points,** the principal subdivisions of a speech, are critical to defining your thesis statement. Let's assume your specific purpose is to convince your audience about the importance of the fine arts. To determine your main points and finalize your thesis, you must ask and answer two questions:

1. How do we define "fine arts"?
2. What impact do the fine arts have on us?

By asking these questions, *if* you have thoroughly researched your subject, you can determine the main points of your speech. The following is an example:

**Main Points**

   **I.** UNESCO defines art as "the embodiment of the human experience and goals."

  **II.** Research suggests that the human brain functions best when the analytical left side and the artistic right side work together.

The structure of the body of the speech will take shape around these two main points. The main points are derived from brain research. If the research or the topic

**■ organizing**
Arranging of ideas and elements into a systematic and meaningful whole.

**■ body** The main content of a speech that develops the speaker's general and specific purposes.

**■ main points** The principal subdivisions of a speech.

The thought and time you put into finding the most effective organization for your presentation will result in a speech that is interesting and makes sense to your audience.

you have chosen indicates that there are more than two main factors to brain function, each significant point would then be an additional main point.

Remember that every piece of information you have gathered does not constitute a main point. Main points are broad, overarching statements that help to organize the many particulars you have found through research. Statements such as "Interestingly, the separate sides of the brain are connected to each other" and "Art is the true medium of communication" are not main points.

**Relate Main Points, Specific Purpose, and Thesis.**     The main points serve as the basis for the thesis statement. Together, the specific purpose and the thesis will determine the direction of the speech. Here is the thesis resulting from the main points noted earlier:

> *Specific Purpose:* To persuade my audience of the importance of fine arts in our lives.
>
> *Thesis:* The fine arts help us keep a balanced life, help us use the whole brain, and also help us contribute to our society.

Here is another example of developing purpose, thesis, and main points. Let us say your specific purpose is to inform your listeners about the West Nile virus and how to get rid of the mosquitoes that spread the disease. Your thesis statement might then be something such as "We need to be aware of the causes, the symptoms, and how to combat the West Nile virus, a sometimes deadly mosquito-borne disease." This thesis statement establishes three main points: the causes of the West Nile virus, the symptoms of the disease, and the best ways to combat the mosquitoes that pass the disease along to humans. You will then develop these three points to create the body of your speech.

Or perhaps you are assigned to present a persuasive speech that will persuade your audience to act in some specific way. From your research on nutrition and healthy lifestyles, you know that breakfast is the most important meal of the day, so you decide to persuade your listeners to eat a good breakfast daily. There are

## Apply Your Knowledge of Purpose and Thesis Statements

Your instructor gives you an assignment to create and present an eight- to ten-minute informative speech on how some aspects of the arts benefit society. She says the topic should be one you find both important and relevant. She also suggests that you choose a topic on something that has had an effect on your family. As a practice, choose one of the following topics and write a general purpose, a specific purpose, and a thesis statement. Be prepared to share and justify your statements with your instructor and classmates.

1. A photography class helps you create memories.
2. Creating your own pottery can help reduce stress.
3. Involvement in community theatre is rewarding.
4. Dance keeps you healthy.
5. A topic of your own choice.

numerous approaches you can take, but remember, you ultimately want your listeners to either continue to eat a healthy breakfast or begin doing so. In this speech, you are not just reporting facts; you want your listeners to *do* something. You must make a compelling argument that will make them listen and act.

As you begin your research, you need to think about the general purpose: to persuade my listeners to begin eating or continue to eat breakfast. Then you need to ask yourself, "Why should my listeners eat breakfast?" As you generate answers, the main points of your speech will emerge. Eventually, you determine that a healthy breakfast gives the human body adequate fuel to energize one for the entire day, that "breaking the fast" will cause one's metabolism to kick in, and that when everything works smoothly, the body will burn calories more efficiently, which helps one to avoid midday slumps that lead to junk foods and unhealthy snacking. At this point, you are ready to refine your specific purpose and state your thesis and main points.

*Specific purpose:* To persuade my audience that eating breakfast can benefit them in three particular ways.

*Thesis:* Eating breakfast gives our bodies energy to begin and maintain our daily tasks, causes our metabolic processes to work efficiently, and provides enough energy to make it through the day without snacking.

*Main points:* (I) Breakfast is the meal that fuels our bodies so that we have the energy to complete our daily tasks. (II) Breakfast is the meal that makes our metabolic process begin its work. (III) Breakfast is the meal that helps our bodies function efficiently throughout the day.

**Present the Main Points.** Main points, like the specific purpose and thesis, should be carefully developed and written. They should also be specific, vivid, relevant, and parallel in structure. (We use Roman numerals to designate main points because, as you will see later, they eventually become the main elements in the speech outline.)

**Be Specific.** The more specific the main points, the less confusion they will create and the more meaningful they will be to an audience. It can be easy to misunderstand a speaker who makes vague, overgeneralized statements. Each main point in a speech should also be independent of the others and simple to understand. Compare the following:

**Ineffective Main Point**

   **I.** Volunteering is a worthwhile activity because it allows you to help others and it accomplishes things that might not otherwise be accomplished, and besides, it makes you feel good about something you have done.

**Effective Main Points**

   **I.** Volunteering is a worthwhile activity that allows you to help others.

  **II.** Volunteering is a worthwhile activity that allows you to accomplish something that might not otherwise be accomplished.

 **III.** Volunteering is a worthwhile activity that makes you feel good because you have done something to help someone else.

As you can see, the first example contains three ideas in one point, which makes it too complicated. The second example divides the three ideas into three separate points, thus making each one easier to understand.

    *Use Vivid Language.* In Chapter 4, we discussed the importance of language choice. When you listen to or present speeches, you become aware of language. The more vivid the main points, the more likely they are to create interest. Main points should be thought-provoking, attention-grabbing ideas that stand out from the supporting materials. It is more vivid to say "College student Brandi Russell says the proposed federal law requiring parental notification for birth control use would create a ludicrous situation for college students under age eighteen who are on their own" than to say "The proposed federal regulation requiring family planning clinics that receive federal funds to notify parents of anyone under the age of eighteen who wishes to use birth control devices would have a devastating effect on teenagers."

    Vivid phrasing should not, however, become overblown or exaggerated. Such language may hurt the speaker's credibility. The limits of good taste and ethical considerations should be taken into account.

    *Show Relevance.* Main points that are relevant to the audience's immediate interests encourage greater involvement and empathy. For instance, instead of saying, "Air pollution has reached high levels," say, "Air pollution in our city has reached high levels." Using direct references to the audience, whenever possible, increases the link between you, what you are saying, and your audience. Audience members like to know how the speaker's subject relates to them and why they should listen.

    *Create Parallel Structure.* Main points should be expressed in parallel structure, that is, using similar grammatical patterns and wording, when possible.

**Not Parallel**

   **I.** Fine arts help us use our whole brain.

  **II.** A balanced life results from participation in the fine arts.

 **III.** Contributions to society are the result of participation in the fine arts.

**Parallel**

  **I.** The fine arts help us use all areas of our brains.

  **II.** The fine arts help us keep a balanced life.

  **III.** The fine arts help us contribute to society.

Parallel structure of the main points makes material easier to develop and to remember. Audiences usually have only one opportunity to hear a speech; therefore anything you can do to make the main points stand out from the rest of the content is to your benefit. In addition, the speaker strengthens the bond with the audience by consistently using the phrase "the fine arts help us" in each of the three main points.

**Limit the Number of Main Points.**   The number of main points in your speech will depend on at least three considerations:

  **1.** The time available to deliver the speech

  **2.** The content to be covered in the speech, especially the amount and complexity of the supporting materials required for each point

  **3.** The amount of information that the audience can reasonably comprehend and remember

The time available for most classroom speeches is limited by practical considerations. As a result, most classroom speeches have no more than five main points, and the majority have two or three.

Try to balance the amount of time that you devote to each main point. For example, if you are assigned a five- to seven-minute speech, plan to allow about two minutes for the introduction and conclusion, distributing the remaining time equally among the main points. Of course, this is only a guideline. It isn't always possible to balance the main points exactly, nor should you. The nature of some speech topics requires that some main points be emphasized more than others.

An audience should be able to sort out and recall each main point. This recall is impossible if there are too many points. Common sense tells us that three points are easier to remember than five. Therefore, as a speaker, you must set reasonable expectations for both you and your listeners. If you have too many main points and a limited amount of time, you will be unable to develop each point thoroughly enough to make it clear, convincing, and memorable. Instructors are not arbitrary and capricious in their demand that you stay within the time limits for your assignments; they realize that all presentations inside and outside the classroom have time limits. You need to carefully consider and adhere to the time limits for classroom speeches, because most presentations you give in the workplace, in organizations of which you are a member, and in groups in your place of worship will have time limits.

## ▪▪ Order the Main Points

Once you have identified your main points, you must decide the order in which to present them. This takes serious analysis, because the order determines the structure and strategy of your speech. The most effective order of presentation depends on the topic, the purpose, and the audience. Several basic patterns of presentation have been recommended and used over the years: time sequence, spatial, topical, problem–solution, cause–effect (or effect–cause), and motivated sequence. Other cultures and cocultures, however, use alternative organizational patterns that are very effective. Many

Native Americans, African Americans, and women, for example, use mind-mapping and narratives or storytelling as a way of organizing their presentations. Many speakers effectively use a combination of one or more organizational patterns in a given speech. Until you're confident in your ability to organize your thoughts, you may wish to use one primary organizational pattern in any given speech.

Whatever organizational pattern you choose, you can make that pattern work for you when you make the speech compelling. In the paragraph above we noted **mind-mapping** as an organizational strategy. This is a strategy where you visually "map out" how the various ideas connect.[1] In a mind-map, one starts in the center with a word or symbol, and then writes down all the things that come to mind about that word/topic (see Figure 9.1). If you were mind-mapping the fine arts speech previously discussed, you might begin with a circle labeled "the fine arts" and then identify all the aspects of the fine arts that should be considered all around that circle. Another strategy identified above is the narrative or storytelling. A story in a speech doesn't have to be long and involved and need not follow the guidelines for traditional stories. Instead, it is an account that brings more enthusiasm, realism, or even passion to the topic. Think about a speech or class lecture you found enjoyable. What did the speaker do? Why was it enjoyable? This writer remembers a class in the religions of the world where note taking was easy, the content was memorable, and this listener was almost spellbound by the professor's compelling accounts. His

■ **Mind-mapping** A visual organizational strategy that uses words or symbols to identify the concepts and their connections to each other.

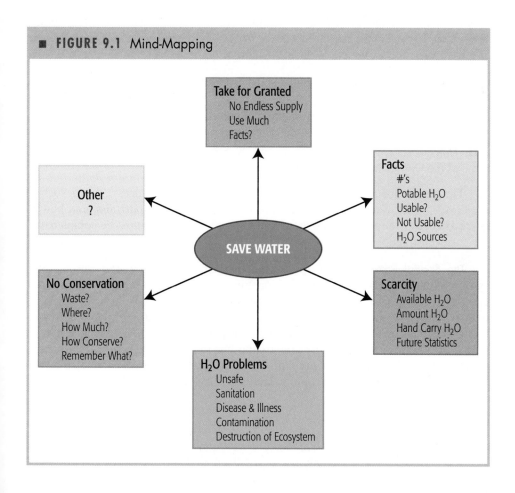

■ **FIGURE 9.1** Mind-Mapping

lectures may have been written on yellowed notebook paper, but the content was anything but dry and boring. (The professor only opened the notebook at the beginning of class, and never looked at it again until he picked up the notebook to leave the room.)

**The Time-Sequence Pattern.** In the **time-sequence pattern,** or chronological pattern, the presentation begins at a particular point in time and continues either forward or backward. The key is to follow a natural time sequence and avoid jumping haphazardly from one date to another. This pattern is especially useful for tracing the steps in a process, the relationships within a series of events, or the development of ideas. Topics such as the history of photographic technology, the steps in setting up an advertising display, and the development of the computer in today's society lend themselves to the time sequence. Here is an example of a time sequence that moves forward from a specific period of time.

**Main Points**

   **I.** To create the perfect speech, your first step is to choose a topic.

   **II.** To create the perfect speech, your second step is to gather information.

   **III.** To create the perfect speech, your third step is to organize the information.

   **IV.** To create the perfect speech, your fourth step is to prepare and practice.

A reverse-order sequence begins at a specific time period and works chronologically backward. For example, a speech discussing U.S. citizens' concerns, organized in reverse-order time sequence, could be as follows:

   **I.** In the twenty-first century, many U.S. citizens are concerned about environmental issues.

   **II.** In the late twentieth century, many U.S. citizens were concerned about the economy.

   **III.** In the early twentieth century, many U.S. citizens were concerned about the role of the United States in the world.

The time-sequence pattern can also be used to explain a process. Topics such as the development of a small business, how to create silhouette portraits, and how to administer the Heimlich maneuver all have specific steps that must be completed in the correct sequence for successful results.

■ **time-sequence (chronological) pattern** An order of presentation that begins at a particular point in time and continues either forward or backward.

■ **spatial pattern** An order of presentation in which the content of a speech is organized according to relationships in space.

***The Spatial Pattern.*** In a **spatial pattern** of presentation, the content of a speech is organized according to relationships in space. This method is especially appropriate for presentations describing distances, directions, or physical surroundings. For example, a spatial pattern might be used to describe how plants in each area of a garden can create a quiet retreat, the floor plan for an extended deck area on a house, or how to move from one area to another in an art gallery to get maximum effect of the different genre of art represented. A spatial pattern describes the relationships between all the main points. Here is an example of main points organized according to a spatial pattern:

**Main Points**

   **I.** When you visit the Hermitage in St. Petersburg, Russia, you'll find the historical background on the first floor, just inside the main foyer, and to the right.

**II.** The sculptures and statues may be found in the area behind the great hall.

**III.** The impressionist paintings may be found on the second floor, just above the sculptures and statues.

Both time-sequence and spatial patterns are well suited to informative speeches.

*The Topical Pattern.*    According to the **topical pattern,** the main topic is divided into a series of related subtopics. Each subtopic becomes a main point in the speech, and all main points are joined to form a coherent whole. In this way, the topical pattern is a unifying structure.

The topical pattern is most likely to be used when none of the other patterns of organization can be applied to the topic or purpose of a speech. Topics such as the health benefits of therapeutic massage, the advantages of taking a noncredit writing improvement course, or the guidelines for choosing language for your papers and speeches can easily utilize the topical pattern. Here is how the topical pattern could be used to organize the main points of a speech:

**Main Points**

**I.** The fine arts help us keep a balanced life.

**II.** The fine arts help us use all areas of our brains.

**III.** The fine arts help us contribute to society.

When the topical pattern is used correctly, each main point is parallel in structure and related to the others. Because the topical pattern is versatile, it can be adapted to most speech purposes and can effectively present material related to a variety of topics.

*The Problem–Solution Pattern.*    A speech that follows the **problem–solution pattern** usually has two main points: the problem and the suggested solution. The problem is defined as a need, doubt, uncertainty, or difficulty, and the suggested solution remedies or eliminates the problem without creating other problems. A problem–solution approach could be used to address topics such as the lack of daycare facilities in the workplace, the increased number of students per class because of the budget crisis, and the increased incidence of binge drinking on this campus.

The problem–solution pattern, correctly used, should do more than state a problem and a solution; it should help the audience understand both the problem and the solution and why the solution will work. For example, a speech advocating change in the university's policies toward on-campus drinking might follow this problem–solution pattern:

**Problem**

**I.** Each year, we hear about the significant increase in student binge drinking.

Lance Armstrong, cancer survivor and seven-time Tour de France winner, speaks on behalf of his foundation's Tour of Hope. Persuasive speakers of this type often use problem–solution, cause–effect, or the motivated sequence to organize their speeches.

■ **topical pattern** An order of presentation in which the main topic is divided into a series of related subtopics.

■ **problem–solution pattern** Order of presentation that first discusses a problem and then suggests solutions.

**Solution**

    **II.** Students must be taught about the dangers of binge drinking and taught to drink safely.

The problem–solution pattern usually includes three to five of the following:

1. *A definition and description of the problem,* including its symptoms and size
2. *A critical analysis of the problem,* including causes, current actions, and requirements for a solution
3. *Suggestions of possible solutions,* including a description of each solution's strengths and weaknesses
4. *A recommendation of the best solution,* including a thorough justification of its superiority over other proposed solutions
5. *A discussion of the best solution put into operation,* including a description of how the plan can be implemented

**The Cause–Effect Pattern.**   In the **cause–effect pattern,** the speaker explains the causes of an event, problem, or issue and discusses its consequences. Causes and effects may be presented in two different sequences. A speaker may either describe certain forces or factors and then show the results that follow from them or describe conditions or events and then point out the forces or factors that caused them.

Consider this example of using the cause–effect pattern to discuss the effects of computers on students' job placement. A speaker might begin by recounting recent developments in computer procedures that have led to a more accurate analysis of students' skills, and then show that, as a result, the number of students who have obtained first jobs in their chosen fields has increased dramatically. Or the speaker might reverse the process and first point out that the number of jobs that students are landing in their chosen fields is the result of more accurate computer analysis of their skills.

Regardless of the exact sequence, a speech organized by cause and effect has two main points: a description of the factors that are the *cause* and a prediction or identi-

■ **cause–effect pattern** An order of presentation in which the speaker first explains the causes of an event, problem, or issue and then discusses its consequences.

---

**MAKING Technology**

**CONNECTIONS**

### Organizing Your Presentations

A community group asks you to share information about your trip to help the survivors of Hurricane Katrina. Think about what we've covered in this chapter so far as you answer these questions:

1. What organizational patterns work for this kind of speech?
2. Check the steps for mind-mapping at "How to Make a Mind Map in 8 Steps" www.mapyourmind

.com/howto.htm (last accessed July 8, 2006) to see if this organizational pattern would work for you and your topic.

3. Which pattern will you choose? Why?
4. How will you try to make the content compelling for your listeners?

fication of the subsequent *effect,* or vice versa. Topics such as eating disorders in young adults, television violence, gaining the freshman fifteen, and new approaches to improving memory all lend themselves to the use of the cause–effect pattern.

Using the cause–effect pattern, a speech on the current budget crisis in our nation might be arranged in either of the following ways:

**Cause**

   **I.** Use of cell phones while driving creates a major lack of attention on the part of automobile drivers.

**Effect**

   **II.** The lack of attention to driving results in both major and minor automobile accidents.

   Or

**Effect**

   **I.** Hazardous traffic situations are often the result of a lack of preparation for sudden changes in traffic conditions.

**Cause**

   **II.** The distraction of a cell phone conversation makes drivers forget to watch for unique traffic situations.

Because the cause–effect pattern can be used in a variety of ways, it is a useful format for either informative or persuasive speeches. As long as the cause can be directly related to the effect that you are trying to prove, this pattern is an excellent choice for many different topics and a beneficial means of reaching your listeners.

**The Motivated Sequence Pattern.**    A widely used pattern of organization for the persuasive speech is the **motivated sequence,** developed by Professor Alan H. Monroe of Purdue University in the 1930s.[2] This pattern is specifically designed to help the speaker combine sound logic and practical psychology and is briefly mentioned again in Chapter 12. (We cover the idea in this chapter because it is an organizational strategy, but you may wish to refer back to this section as you read Chapter 12.) The motivated sequence is particularly effective because it follows the human thinking process and motivates listeners to take action. The sequence has five steps: attention, need, satisfaction, visualization, and action.

   **1.** *Attention.* In the first step, the persuader attempts to create an interest in the topic so that the audience will want to listen. This step takes place in the introduction and follows the guidelines for an effective presentation. The speaker is subtly saying, "Please pay attention. This is important to you."

   **2.** *Need.* In the second step, the persuader focuses on the problem by analyzing the things that are wrong and relating them to the audience's interests, wants, or desires. At this point the speaker is saying, "This is wrong, and we must do something about it."

   **3.** *Satisfaction.* In the third step, the persuader provides a solution or plan of action that will eliminate the problem and thus satisfy the audience's interests, wants,

■ **motivated sequence** A pattern of organization specifically developed for persuasive speaking that combines logic and practical psychology. Five steps are involved: attention, need, satisfaction, visualization, and action.

and desires. The speaker is saying, "What I have to offer is the way to solve the problem."

4. *Visualization.* In the fourth step, the persuader explains in detail how the solution will meet the audience's need. The speaker's message now becomes, "This is how my plan will work to solve the problem, and if you accept my solution, things will be much better."

5. *Action.* In the fifth and final step, the persuader asks the audience for a commitment to put the proposed solution to work. The speaker basically concludes by saying, "Take action!"

The following is an example of a motivated sequence outline:

*To persuade my audience to act now to prevent skin cancer* — Specific purpose

**Introduction**

I. Approximately 700,000 new cases of skin cancer are diagnosed every year. — Attention

**Body**

II. Prevention schemes are most important in dealing with skin cancer because treatment often requires painful, long-term follow-up. — Need

III. Frequent skin inspections and avoiding overexposure to the sun are two surefire ways to reduce the risk of skin cancer. — Satisfaction

IV. It is vital to do frequent (once every three months) self-exams on pre-existing skin markings to detect any changes. Also, one must avoid the dangerous ultraviolet rays (UVR) from the sun and artificial devices such as tanning booths. — Visualization

V. Minimize your exposure to the sun, avoid tanning salons, inspect your skin frequently, and use fresh, proper sunscreens to prevent skin cancer from claiming your life! — Action

The motivated sequence is most often used in persuasion. It is also commonly used by advertisers because it sells ideas.

**Choosing the Best Pattern.** We have emphasized the importance of matching the pattern of organization to your topic, specific purpose, and thesis. You must also consider another key factor: your audience. The wise speaker anticipates responses from the audience. Therefore if your audience analysis indicates that important questions or objections are likely to be raised, you should arrange your main points to meet those objections. For example, if you advocate that a statewide recycling effort be mandated and are certain that someone in your audience will object to mandates of any kind, you might structure your presentation as follows:

**Main Points**

I. Recycling is an easy way to create more space in our state.

II. Recycling is a good way to reduce and reuse many products.

III. Recycling is cost-efficient.

No matter what pattern you select, as a beginning speaker you should probably use only that pattern when sequencing your main points. As you become more proficient, you might wish to combine patterns.

## ■■ Connect the Main Points

A conversation can move from one unrelated topic to another without losing meaning or impact, but for a speaker to communicate effectively with an audience, the thoughts in the speech must be systematically connected. The four most common connecting devices that speakers use, singly or in combination, are transitions, signposts, internal previews, and internal summaries.

**Transitions.**   Phrases and words used to link ideas are called **transitions.** They form a bridge between what has already been presented and what will be presented next. Transitions are typically used between the introduction and the body of a speech, between main ideas, between supporting materials and visual aids, and between the body and the conclusion. A transition can review information that has already been presented, preview information to come, or summarize key thoughts. Here are some typical transition statements that might be made in a speech:

> Let me move on to my next point.
>
> Now that I have discussed the history of the Internet, I would like to talk about its uses.
>
> Turning now to . . .
>
> The final point I would like to make is . . .
>
> Another example might be . . .
>
> Keeping in mind these four items I discussed, we arrive at the following conclusion.

**Signposts.**   Just as a traffic sign warns drivers about travel conditions, **signposts** are words, phrases, and short statements that let the audience know what is ahead. Here are some typical signposts:

> Let me first illustrate . . .         As you look at my chart . . .
>
> My second point is . . .           Next . . .
>
> To recap . . .                       Finally . . .

Questions can also be used as signposts:

> How powerful is language?
>
> What happens next?
>
> How many people are affected by this plan?
>
> How can we responsibly respond to this issue?

Such questions draw the audience's attention to a forthcoming answer.

A signpost not only prepares an audience for what to expect next but also alerts the audience that the upcoming information is important. Some examples are as follows:

■ **transition** A phrase or word used to link ideas.

■ **signpost** A word, phrase, or short statement that indicates to an audience the direction a speaker will take next.

The most essential aspect of this is . . .

Let's look at possible solutions to . . .

The only thing you need to know is . . .

**Internal Previews.** Short statements called **internal previews** give advance warning, or a preview, of the point(s) to be covered. Here is an example: "Next we'll look at possible solutions to the problem of budget shortfalls."

**Internal Summaries.** An **internal summary** is a short review statement given at the end of a main point. For example:

> Let me briefly summarize what I have said so far. In a time of fewer dollars from the legislature, and rising costs, finances become very tight. For every percentage point of budget shortfall, we must raise tuition by 4 percent. We must convince the governor and the legislature to provide more funding for the university.

## Support the Main Points

Main points by themselves are nothing more than assertions. An audience needs supporting and clarifying material in order to accept what a speaker says. It is crucial that each main point be supported and that the support be relevant and logically organized. When supporting materials are included, the body of a speech expands to outline form, in which the main points are followed by subpoints, which in turn may be broken into further supporting points

I. Tobacco use causes thousands of cancer deaths.   ■ Main Point

   A. Tobacco causes 440,000 annual deaths in America.   ■ Support

      1. Lung cancer can result from either smoking or secondhand smoke.   ■ Clarifying Material

      2. Symptoms of lung cancer include coughing, shortness of breath, wheezing, chest pain, and loss of appetite.

      3. These deaths are preventable.

**■ internal preview**
Short statements that give advance warning, or preview, of the point(s) to be covered.

**■ internal summary**
A short review statement given at the end of a main point.

**■ introduction**
Opening statements that orient the audience to the subject and motivate them to listen.

Supporting materials should be clearly related to the specific purpose, thesis, and main points of the speech.

# ■ Organize the Introduction of Your Speech

Experienced speakers often develop their introductions after, not before, the body of the speech. An **introduction** includes opening statements that serve two important functions: motivating the audience to listen and orienting them to the subject. Therefore your introduction should prepare your audience for the main ideas of your speech by setting the stage for the topic.

Your introduction should be based on the information you gathered in your audience analysis. If your analysis was accurate and thorough, you should have a pretty

Nobel prize–winning author Toni Morrison is a world-renowned novelist who has many resources she can call on to arouse the interest of an audience. She might refer to the subject or occasion, tell stories, use personal and biographical information, present a startling statement, use humor, read passages from her work, or ask rhetorical questions to get her audience's attention.

good understanding of your audience's frame of reference and how it might differ from your own. Your introduction should meet these three goals:

1. Orient the audience to the topic
2. Motivate the audience to listen
3. Forecast (preview) the main points

## ▬ Orient the Audience to the Topic

Decide how much background information to provide based on what your audience knows or does not know about your subject. This is the appropriate time to gain attention, state your specific purpose and thesis statement, and define terms that are essential to understanding the speech.

Several approaches can be used to gain attention and arouse the interest of your audience, including referring to the subject or occasion, using personal references or narratives, asking rhetorical questions, presenting a startling statement, using humor, or using quotations. You should choose these devices carefully to fit the audience, occasion, and context. None is always effective, and each has limitations. For example, using humor to focus your listeners' attention on a serious topic such as disease would not be effective. Consider the overall speech as you choose your approach, because all parts of the speech must fit together well to achieve your desired purpose.

**Refer to the Subject or Occasion.**   You may be asked to speak on a special occasion such as a holiday, founders' day, graduation, or an anniversary. Here is a sample attention-getter related to an occasion:

> It is truly a privilege to speak at this convocation. I am honored to be a part of the celebration honoring you for completing all of the requirements leading up to your admission into the teacher education program.

**Use Personal References or Narratives.** Whenever you can relate your own experience to a speech, do so. Personal experiences make your speech more meaningful to your audience and show them that you know your subject. Here is how a speaker used a personal experience to introduce a speech on why she didn't drink milk:

> As a child, I was always forced to drink milk. I never wanted to drink it, and I never asked for milk at meals or for snacks. A few years ago I learned why I "didn't like milk"—I have a lactose intolerance. And people who have a lactose intolerance probably should not drink milk, unless it's soy or rice milk, instead of a dairy product.

**Ask Rhetorical Questions.** A rhetorical question is a question for which no answer is expected. Asking rhetorical questions in an introduction usually encourages an audience to become intellectually involved. (Asking real questions is also an effective way to get your audience interested in and involved in the speech, but it is important to let the audience know that you intend to get answers from them when asking this type of question.) Such questions can also be used to create suspense. Here is one example of rhetorical questions used to involve the audience.

> Does dining on prepared low-cal, low-fat fare help weight loss? What would you say if I told you that the Weight Watchers frozen dinners you've been nuking to help you maintain a lower calorie level may not be the right choice? Kathy K. Isoldi, MS, RD, coordinator of nutritional services at the Cornell Comprehensive Weight Control Center, points out that skimping on calories and protein can backfire, leaving you hungry in an hour or two and tempted to reach for less healthful snacks.[3]

**Present a Startling Statement.** A startling statement can be used when you want to shock or surprise your audience. Startling statements are extremely effective at getting attention, as shown by this example, "The harsh reality is this: Party time is over!" Startling stories can also be used to get your audience's attention:

> There may be a time bomb within your body. Really. It may be ticking away unmercifully, and unless you recognize the symptoms and change your lifestyle, that time bomb may cause you to have serious health problems and even affect the length of your life. The time bomb within is stress. "We're all under stress," according to Drs. Bruce McEwen and George Chrousos. And, when we're stressed, our bodies react with a "fight-or-flight" response. The body pumps out adrenaline, increasing heart rate and blood pressure (and readying us to fight), and sending more blood to our muscles (so we can flee).[4]

**Use Humor.** A funny story or relevant joke not only gains the attention of your audience but also relaxes them. Stories and jokes must be tied to the content of the speech and not offered simply for the sake of humor. One speaker began his talk as follows:

> The last time I gave a speech to this large a group, an audience member raised his hand in the back row and shouted, "I can't hear you." Immediately, a hand went up in the front row, and the person asked, "Can I move back there?" Now I know all of you want to hear me, so I'll try to speak loud enough so that you can understand what I have to say about becoming familiar with the room in which your speech will be made so that you know how to present your ideas.

**Use Quotations.** Sometimes a quotation can grab your audience's attention, and if cited accurately, it can also add to the credibility of your speech. A student talking about language started her speech as follows.

Lee Iacocca once said, "It's important to talk to people in their own language. If you do it well, they'll say, 'God, he said exactly what I was thinking.' And when they begin to respect you, they'll follow you to the death."[5] Today I want to talk with you about the power of language and how you can use it to help you be a competent communicator.

Whatever you choose to gain attention and maintain interest in your introduction, it should be relevant and orient the audience to the topic.

**State the Specific Purpose and Thesis.**   Once you have your audience's attention, you need to state the specific purpose and thesis statement of your speech. Both the specific purpose and thesis statement were discussed in detail earlier in this chapter. Sometimes the specific purpose and thesis statement are best stated together; sometimes it is appropriate to state the specific purpose at the beginning and the thesis toward the end of the introduction, where it serves as a preview of the speech. By stating the specific purpose and thesis, you are orienting your topic to the audience and giving them a clear indication of where you are headed with your speech. Also, this preview is essential in helping your audience recall what you said, because they have only one opportunity to hear your message.

## THE FAR SIDE® BY GARY LARSON

© 1990 FarWorks, Inc. All Rights Reserved/Dist. by Creators Syndicate

**The class was quietly doing its lesson when Russell, suffering from problems at home, prepared to employ an attention-getting device.**

The Far Side® by Gary Larson© 1990 FarWorks, Inc. All Rights Reserved. The Far Side® and the Larson® signature are registered trademarks of FarWorks, Inc. Used with permission.

## ■■ Motivate the Audience to Listen

Design your introductory comments to gain the attention and interest of your audience. You must hold their interest and attention throughout the entire presentation, but that task will be easier if you can capture them by making the topic significant and important to them and by establishing your credibility.

A standard way of making your topic relevant is simply to point out the reasons for presenting your speech. It is important that the audience find a reason to listen to the speech as early in the speech as possible. You should also consider whether it is necessary to establish your credibility in speaking on the topic you have selected.

**Credibility** refers to a speaker's believability based on the audience's evaluation of the speaker's competence, experience, and character. If, for example, Madonna, who is a singer, entertainer, and actor, were to speak on health care or violence in our society, she would have to establish her credibility on the subject by relating the subject to herself and by indicating how she became an expert on the topic.

■ **credibility** A speaker's believability, based on the audience's evaluation of the speaker's competence, experience, character, and charisma.

## ▄▄ Forecast the Main Points

Before you finish introducing your speech, let the audience know what you will cover in the speech itself. This is known as *forecasting,* and it affords listeners a "road map" so that they know where you will take them in the remainder of your speech. Forecasting helps your audience be better listeners.

Let's look at some sample introductions. The following portions show you how to orient and motivate your listeners and forecast the main points of your speech:

| | |
|---|---|
| "A Pentagon project to develop a digital super diary that records heartbeats, travel, Internet chats—everything a person does—also could provide private companies with powerful software to analyze behavior. . . . Known as LifeLog, the project aims to capture and analyze a multimedia record of everywhere a subject goes and everything he or she sees, hears, reads, says, and touches." This amazing statement from an AP wire service article on the front page of our newspaper details how the Defense Advanced Research Projects Agency, or DARPA, plans to have the digital diary in place in the next two years. | ■ Orienting material |
| Now I don't know about you, but I'm very concerned that the same military agency that brought us the Internet and the global positioning satellite system has bids out on a project that violates our privacy in this invasive manner. "Big Brother" will not only be watching us, but also *recording* everything we do! This is not even an antiterrorism tool. Instead, the agency calls LifeLog a tool to capture "one person's experience in and interactions with the world."[6] | ■ Motivating material |
| Although DARPA claims that this is a tool people will choose, we should be concerned about its potential uses. In my speech, I will explain how LifeLog operates and the applications DARPA envisions for its use. | ■ Forecasting of main point |

Can you label the specific parts of the previous introduction? Now look at the following example. The specific parts are labeled for you.

| | |
|---|---|
| Selena was walking toward the garden when she collapsed. She was rushed to the hospital and admitted for observation. After two days of testing, Selena was told that she was suffering from acute chronic stress and needed to change her lifestyle or she could face serious health problems. Now you might think, "This only happens to older people," but Selena is only 20 and is a full-time college student who works forty hours per week. Her stress is the kind of stress any of us could experience. | ■ Orienting material (attention-getter) |
| Stress is a part of our daily lives. Some of us even believe that it's what holds us together! And a certain amount of stress is actually good for you—it helps you focus and get things accomplished. | ■ Motivating material (significance of topic) |
| But chronic stress can cause depression and anxiety and even suppress the immune system.[7] | ■ (effects) |

The next introduction accomplishes several functions at one time: It gets attention, it relates the topic directly to the audience and to the speaker, it establishes the speaker's credibility on the topic, and it also notes the main points of the speech.

What do you fear most? Surveys conducted over the past twenty years suggest that Americans' greatest fears were death, accidents, and heights. Most, however, identify fear of public speaking as their absolute greatest fear. Most of us in this room would probably agree with this finding. Speaking is never easy, but the experiences I have had in the business world and in this class have made me more confident and a better speaker. Today I'd like to define speech anxiety, identify its causes and effects, and share ideas about how to control or reduce anxiety.

- Rhetorical question
- Citing research to establish credibility

- Relating topic to audience
- Establishing credibility

- Thesis and forecasting of main points

The following introduction incorporates background and an attention-getter; it provides listeners with a reason to listen, points up the significance of the topic, lets the listener know "what's in it for me," and states the specific purpose and thesis:

### A Sample Introduction

Six weeks ago, my friend purchased a prairie dog. Today my friend is covered with a rash and ugly pockmarks on his face, neck, trunk, hands, and arms. He's had severe fever and chills, and he's wishing he had never even seen a prairie dog. My friend contracted monkeypox, the latest example of how animals are making us sick.

- Background and attention-getter

Robert G. Webster, a leading virologist at the St. Jude Children's Research Hospital in Memphis, says, "There are probably hundreds if not thousands—maybe even millions of viruses out there . . . we don't even know they're there until we disturb them. SARS is probably just a gentle breeze of what one of these big ones is going to do someday."[8] Scientists agree that animals are transmitting viruses, bacteria, and parasites to humans more rapidly than ever before, spawning ailments known as zoonotic diseases.[9] Why do you need to know this? Because, according to Stephen S. Morse of Columbia University, "There are a multitude of factors that allow people to come in contact with what may once have been infections that were buried deeply into the ecology. With the global traffic of people and goods . . . there are many more pathways, or highways, for what I called some years ago, 'viral traffic.'"[10]

- Reason to listen

- Significance of topic

- Relevance

After hearing my speech, I hope you will have a better understanding of zoonotic disease. We'll first look at what zoonotic diseases are, how they develop and spread, and how best to avoid zoonotic disease.

- Specific purpose and thesis

## Develop Your Introduction

**GUIDELINES**

1. Keep the introduction relatively brief, making up only 5 to 10 percent of the speech's total content (thirty to fifty seconds).

2. Allow plenty of time to prepare the introduction carefully. Because it is critical to the success of your speech, it should not be rushed or written at the last minute.

3. Make the introduction creative and interesting. To accomplish this, think of several possible introductions, and choose the most effective one.

4. As you research your speech, watch for material to use in the introduction. Keep a notebook or file of interesting quotations, stories, humorous statements, and other items that might give your opening some dazzle. But remember: A successful introduction *must* be relevant to the speech topic.

5. Develop the introduction after you have completed the main part of your speech. Relevant introductions are easier to create after you have determined the content and direction of the body.

6. Write out the introduction, word for word. This section of the speech is too important to improvise or leave to chance. In addition, knowing exactly what you will say at the beginning of your speech will give you confidence and help you get off to a strong start. Then, practice delivering the introduction until you can present it conversationally, but flawlessly.

## MAKING CONNECTIONS for Success

### Introducing Your Speech

First impressions are very important. Think back to your first day of this class. You made some instantaneous judgments about the class, the professor, your classmates. Have those first impressions changed? Researchers and businesspersons tell us that speakers/interviewees/salespersons must get the listener's attention in the first fifteen seconds or risk losing them. Communication scholar David Zarefsky says, "The introduction to a speech powerfully affects the audience's first impressions of a speaker."[11] Analyze the introduction and answer the questions following:

*The surfboard was first used by men aboard Captain Cook's ship in March, 1779. Surfing is a difficult sport to learn. Today I'd like to share my experience in surfing, the history of surfing, and how to surf.*

1. Which of the guidelines for the introduction are not covered?

2. What could be done to improve this introduction?

## ■ Organize the Conclusion of Your Speech

■ **conclusion** Closing statements that focus the audience's thoughts on the specific purpose of a speech and bring the most important points together in a condensed and uniform way.

Your **conclusion** should focus your audience's thoughts on the specific purpose of your speech and bring your most important points together in a condensed and uniform way. Your conclusion should relate to your introduction, helping your audience make the connections between the various parts and points of the message. In persuasive speeches, you may also use your conclusion to spell out the action or policies you recommend to solve a problem. In every case, your conclusion should reinforce what you want your audience to remember.

Because your conclusion is as important as any other part of your presentation, you should give it the same amount of attention. Be especially careful to avoid adding new information in this part of the speech. Also, remember that you, as a speaker, have only one chance to get your message across to your audience. Repetition is an important strategy for helping listeners recall the important information you have presented. Your conclusion should

1. Let your listeners know that you are finishing the speech.
2. Make your thesis clear to your listeners.
3. Reinforce your purpose by reviewing your main points.
4. Leave your listeners with a memorable thought.
5. Tie everything together.

## Show That You Are Finishing the Speech

You need to prepare your listeners for the end of your speech; otherwise, they are left hanging and uncomfortable, sensing that something is missing. Do not bluntly state that you are finishing or even say, "In conclusion, . . ." Instead, you should carefully and creatively indicate that the speech is winding down. An example might be, "As you have seen in this speech, there are ways we can become better listeners."

## Make Your Thesis Clear

Repetition is important when you have only one chance for the listeners to hear your message. Be sure you creatively remind your listeners of your central idea; "You've already heard me tell you early in my speech that effective listening is a highly valued skill that can be learned."

## Review the Main Points

Repeating the main points of a speech is particularly helpful any time you want your audience to remember your main points. For example, the speaker who informed her audience about barriers to effective listening concluded her speech as follows:

> Let me review the barriers that have the most impact on our listening. They are language, factual, mental, and physical distractions. If you remember these and how they affect listening, you will be a more effective listener.

In addition to helping the audience remember your content, reviewing the speech reinforces both your purpose and the thesis statement.

## End with a Memorable Thought

A memorable thought may include referring back to an attention-getting device, citing a quotation, or issuing a challenge or appeal. Citing a memorable quotation can be a good way to leave a lasting impression on your audience. When it is relevant and reinforces your thesis statement, a quotation can give your speech additional authority and help to increase your credibility. It is crucial that you always cite the source of all quoted information or any information that is not your own. (The importance of citing sources and the responsibilities of a speaker to cite sources are discussed in Chapter 10.) A speech on zoonotic diseases might conclude as follows:

### Evaluating Conclusions

The conclusion lets your listeners know that you're wrapping up the speech, but it should also leave them with something to think about and remember. Steven Johnson, author of *Everything Bad Is Good for You,* concludes his book as follows:

> The cultural race to the bottom is a myth; we do not live in a fallen state of cheap pleasures that pale beside the intellectual riches of yesterday. And we are not innate slackers, drawn inexorably to the least offensive and least complicated entertainment available. All around us the world of mass entertainment grows more demanding and sophis-

ticated, and our brains happily gravitate to that newfound complexity. And by gravitating, they make the effect more pronounced. Dumbing down is not the natural state of popular culture over time—quite the opposite. The great unsung story of our culture today is how many welcome trends are going up.[13]

1. We say that effective conclusions leave the listener with something to think about and remember. Does Johnson do that in his writing?
2. What is Johnson's point about popular culture?
3. Do you agree or disagree with him? Why?

Monkeypox is just one of the numerous viral diseases carried by animals and is one of the least dangerous. Lassa fever is another that sparks epidemics in West Africa that kill as many as half of its victims and it is spread by a cute little rat. "Someone could decide to make cute pocket pets out of those critters," said Peter Jahrling, a senior scientific adviser to the U.S. Army Medical Research Institute of Infectious Diseases. "Then we'd have an outbreak of Lassa fever here to worry about."[12] We need to be aware of the dangers involved in keeping exotic pets if we value our lives and our health.

If your purpose is to persuade, the conclusion may also include a challenge or appeal to action. The following conclusion recaps the main points and asks the listeners to take action:

> Sleep researchers are just beginning to understand what we have lost when we lose sleep. Our bodies change drastically when we're sleep deprived and there are many health risks. Our hormone levels change to the point that our energy levels are very low when we awaken and are actually comparable to the low morning levels usually associated with the elderly. Furthermore, sleep deprivation may lead to obesity, a decline in immune function, fuzzy thinking, and even to cancer risks. You need to change your schedules! You need at least eight hours of sleep. Plan your work so that you can always get a good night's rest. If you do get behind, take a nap! A short nap works best—about forty-five minutes can improve your health, your attitude, and your thinking. I urge you to take charge of your life. Get some sleep![14]

**GUIDELINES** Develop Your Conclusion

1. The conclusion should be brief and should end with a definite summarizing statement. The conclusion should account for between 5 and 15 percent of the content of the speech (thirty to sixty seconds).
2. The conclusion should not contain information that was *not* already mentioned in either the introduction or the body of your speech.

3. The preparation of the conclusion should not be rushed. Allow plenty of time to develop it, and write it carefully.
4. Leave your audience with an impact that will make your speech memorable. Think of several possible endings, and choose the one that best serves the purpose of your speech.
5. Write out the conclusion word for word. Then learn it well so that you can end your speech smoothly, conversationally, and confidently.

Signal your audience that your speech is nearing its end by using phrases such as "Today, we have examined . . . ," "In the past minutes, we have examined . . . ," "Finally, let me say. . . ." Each prepares your audience for your concluding remarks. The following conclusion lets listeners know that the speech is nearly finished and it summarizes and synthesizes the major points covered. There is an appeal for action, and listeners are left with a memorable thought.

| | |
|---|---|
| Today I have shared with you some important points about skin cancer. | ■ Signal of speech's end |
| It is important to understand the three types of skin cancer including risk factors and recognition of the tumors. Even though Americans love to get a nice tan, it is one of the most dangerous things that you can do in relation to getting skin cancer. There are some very specific things you can do in order to prevent skin cancer. First, you must minimize sun exposure by avoiding tanning salons and using fresh sunscreen appropriate for your skin type and the length of time you're in the sun. You must also be able to recognize the changes in the skin that may indicate skin cancer when you conduct self-exams every three months. With early detection most skin cancers are very curable. With a little knowledge and a little effort you can prevent skin cancer from claiming your life! | ■ Summary of main points<br><br>■ Appeal for action<br><br><br><br>■ Memorable final thought |

# ■ Outline Your Speech

Outlining is one of the most difficult (and, therefore, mistakenly avoided) steps in preparing a speech. Outlining and organizing are similar terms. **Outlining** involves arranging the entire contents of a speech in a logical sequence and writing that sequence in a standardized form. The outline is often referred to as the blueprint or skeleton of a speech. Organizing is arranging ideas or elements in a systematic and meaningful way. To organize your speech, select one of the patterns of organization discussed earlier in the chapter. Both organizing and outlining involve arranging information to form a meaningful sequence, but outlining is a more rigorous written process. David Zarefsky, communication scholar and public speaking textbook author says, "Speakers depend on outlines at two stages: when they put the speech together and when they deliver it. Each stage requires a different kind of outline."[15]

Outlining is more detailed than organizing and helps to unify and clarify thinking, makes relationships clear, and provides the proper balance and emphasis for

■ **outlining** Arranging materials in a logical sequence, often referred to as the blueprint or skeleton of a speech, and writing out that sequence in a standardized form.

each point as it relates to the specific purpose of a speech or written paper. Outlining also helps to ensure that information is both accurate and relevant.

As you prepare your outline, you will gain an overview of your entire presentation. Developing an outline should help you gauge the amount of support you have for each of your main points and identify any points that need further development. The actual process of outlining usually requires three steps:

1. Create a preliminary outline that identifies the topic and the main points to be covered in the speech.
2. Expand the preliminary outline into a full-sentence outline that clearly and fully develops the speech's content.
3. Condense the full-sentence outline into a presentational outline to aid delivery.

## ▬▬ The Preliminary Outline

■ **preliminary out-
line** A list of all the main points that may be used in a speech.

A **preliminary outline** is a list of all the points that *may* be used in a speech. Suppose you are preparing an eight-to-ten minute persuasive speech on the importance of the fine arts.[16] Because of the limited amount of time, you know you cannot possibly cover everything related to the topic. And, because your general purpose is to persuade, you need to focus the content of your speech to influence your listeners. Thus,

## MAKING CONNECTIONS

### for Success

### Ordering Ideas in an Outline

For a speech entitled "Making Reading Your Hobby," rearrange the following sentences in proper outline form for the body. Make sure to arrange the content in a logical sequence. Place the number of each sentence in the proper place in the outline. (See page 251 to verify your answers.)

1. Low-cost rental libraries are numerous.
2. Reading is enjoyable.
3. It may lead to advancement in one's job.
4. Books contain exciting tales of love and adventure.
5. Many paperback books cost only $12.95 to $15.95.
6. People who read books are most successful socially.
7. Reading is profitable.
8. One meets many interesting characters in books.
9. Reading is inexpensive.

I. _____

   A. _____

   B. _____

II. _____

   A. _____

   B. _____

III. _____

   A. _____

   B. _____

you recall what you have already read about topic selection, audience analysis, and gathering information, and using supporting and clarifying materials, you determine your specific purpose: To persuade my audience of the importance of the fine arts in our lives. On the basis of this specific purpose, you can prepare a preliminary outline of possible main points as shown in the following sample preliminary outline. Once your possible main points are arranged in this way, you will find it easier to analyze your thoughts. You can then decide exactly which main thoughts to include in your speech and choose the best order for presenting them. Here is what your preliminary outline might look like:

---

**Sample Preliminary Outline for Persuasive Speech**

The Importance of the Fine Arts ■ Topic

To persuade ■ General purpose

To persuade my audience of the importance of the fine arts in our lives ■ Specific purpose

■ Possible main points

   I. What are the fine arts?

     A. Definition of "art"

     B. The importance of the fine arts in the mind

   II. The fine arts around us

     A. Why the fine arts are being left behind in today's society

   III. The Panther Prowl

     A. Use interviews

     B. What the Panther Prowl does for students

   IV. Results of the survey I conducted

     A. Reiterate the importance of the fine arts

     B. Emphasize what the university does for students

   V. Recap what the speech covered

   VI. Present the challenge to the audience to illustrate a new appreciation for the fine arts

---

## ■■ The Full-Sentence Outline

A **full-sentence outline** expands on the ideas you have decided to include in your speech. The preliminary outline identified possible topics. The full-sentence outline identifies the main points and subpoints you will cover, written as full sentences. Although you will not have every single word you'll utter included in a full-sentence outline, you will have a fairly detailed view of the speech. The full-sentence outline is one I require of my students as a final outline, turned in with their evaluation sheet prior to speaking. A good outline helps the speaker to stay on task and provides reminders of what comes next. The full-sentence outline should conclude with a bibliography or list of references identifying all sources you have used in your speech and helps you create a presentational outline that we will discuss in succeeding pages.

■ **full-sentence outline** An outline that expands on the ideas you have decided to include in your speech. It identifies the main points and subpoints you will cover, written as full sentences.

## Outlining

1. The preliminary outline should list the possible topics you might cover in the speech.
2. A good outline should identify the importance of the ideas you will present.
3. The outline should provide an overview of your content.
4. The outline should help you clarify your thinking; it gives you the ordering of ideas and the amount of supporting material you have for those ideas.
5. It is helpful to write out the entire introduction and conclusion in your outline so that you can make sure you have included everything you need.

## MAKING Technology CONNECTIONS

### Text and Web Outlines

Organizing and outlining are essential steps in the speech process. This web-based activity will give you practice in analyzing and evaluating others' outlines and speeches before you begin this step on your own.

1. Got to www.ask.com.
2. Ask the question, "How should I outline my speech?"
3. Check five of the responses. (Do not include anything such as "sample term paper outlines" or "term paper outlines.")
4. How many hits were there? What kinds of information did you find in the responses you received?

5. What are the similarities between what you found on the Web and what was covered in this chapter in your textbook? Who created the sites you visited? What are their qualifications?
6. Check "Narrow Your Search" in the right column. Are there more specific examples in that area?
7. Click on one of the "sample outline of an informative speech" responses, read the outline, and evaluate it using the criteria provided in this chapter.
8. Be prepared to discuss your analysis with classmates.

---

**Sample Full-Sentence Outline**

| | |
|---|---|
| The Importance of the Fine Arts | ■ Title |
| Fine arts | ■ Topic |
| To persuade | ■ General purpose |
| To persuade my audience of the importance of the fine arts in our lives | ■ Specific purpose |
| To convince my audience that the fine arts help us use the whole brain, help us keep a balanced life, and also help us contribute to our society | ■ Thesis |

**Introduction**

| | |
|---|---|
| What do you see? Seriously, what does this picture tell you? What if I show you the title? | ■ Attention-getting strategy |
| How does that change your interpretation of what is shown? | |
| The fine arts are very important to each individual. Whether you realize it or not, the fine arts are as much a part of your daily life as are the acts of waking up and going to bed. | ■ Motivation |

I hope to convince you that the fine arts are important in our everyday life because they help us use our whole brain, help us keep a balanced life, and help us contribute to society.

■ Thesis statement

■ Forecasting of main points

**Body**

I. According to www.viewzone.com/bicam.html., the human brain is split in two hemispheres, the "right" and the "left." It has been found that the left side of the brain is "analytical," and the right side is "artistic."

■ Main point

   A. Interestingly, the separate sides of the brain are connected to each other to work together, but can also work separately.

**Example**

   1. A brain patient once had a tumor that affected the brain in such a way that the brain hemispheres had to be disconnected from each other. The operation went well, until follow-up tests.

   2. It was then discovered that the man could not at the same time recognize and name the objects placed before him. He could either recognize or name, but not both together.

   B. The brain functions best when both sides are equally trained. The old saying of only using a small margin of our total brain is true, and by training both sides we increase our total brain usage.

■ Support

   C. When you looked at the picture, you allowed the right side of the brain to take over to figure out what I was trying to get you to see. As soon as I gave you a title your left brain took over and logic told you what the artist "wanted" you to see.

■ Matt ties in the Introductory Question here to maintain relevance and interest.

   D. Your goal should be to use as much of both sides of your brain as possible.

II. So what is art? UNESCO defines art as "the embodiment of the human experience and goal."

■ Second main point

**Definition**

   A. What does that mean? Art is the "true" medium of communication. It can illustrate better than words what we are really feeling or trying to explain.

   1. In fact, the truest form of art, the form that best illustrates human emotion, is music.

   2. Music can cause a person to feel happy, sad, content, etc. (UNESCO)

   B. Art, then, provides balance in our lives.

III. Artists create works to not only express themselves but also provide a means for helping society better itself. Unfortunately, especially in today's society, there are many distractions that prevent people from seeing this work and developing themselves further.

■ Third main point

   A. One of those distractions would be athletics.

■ Uses examples to illustrate meaning

1. Athletics can be logically traced back to primal times when the strongest of the species would survive (hunting for food or fighting enemies).

2. Obviously war is much more sophisticated these days, and while the need to be fit is still necessary to survive, there is little hand-to-hand battle. Sports serve as the "revival" of carnal needs and now instead of killing someone the games reflect who is the biggest, fastest, and strongest through competition. (Bradley Williams, MBA Business Administration)

B. Another distraction is technology.

1. Let's face it, we are a technology-bound society. It is easy to sit and watch TV or work on the computer.

2. How many of you try to do homework in your dorm, but find yourself turning on the TV or finding something else to do?

IV. The University of Northern Iowa knows the fine arts are important as well.

■ Main point to support value

A. UNI supports the College of Fine Arts and Humanities in every activity. It even helps choose the productions for the next season at Theatre UNI. (Chad Kolbe, Stagecraft lecture)

B. The Panther Prowl was begun this fall to increase student involvement on campus. Four of the six venues that are included in the "prowl" are fine arts or fine arts related. The "prowl" is sponsored by the venues and the Office of Financial Aid.

■ Relevance to specific listeners

1. The venues include: Theatre UNI, Thursdaze, School of Music, the Gallagher Bluedorn, WRC, and Athletics.

2. Five of the six venues are free with the other venue having student ticket prices at half price, with Student Rush tickets being $5.00. There is no other college in the state with rates that good for students.

C. I recently conducted a survey that sampled fifty percent of the students from the class. The results are as follows.

■ Use of listeners' responses to support the point made

**Statistics**

1. About 60 percent participating prefer athletics over the fine arts.

**Quotation**

2. The reasoning ranges from greater personal enjoyment in athletics to liking fine arts better because it "Does more for my mind. I can get totally involved in theatre, ballet, dance, opera, music, etc., but don't have the same total commitment to all sports."

3. What can be concluded from this survey?

■ Notice how Matt makes the figures relevant to the listeners in *subpoint a* by comparing the numbers and percentages from the class to the larger community.

**Statistics**

a. Assuming the class would be split similar to this sample, out of the twenty-five students, fifteen would prefer athletics. Apply this to Black Hawk Co. The reported population living in Black Hawk Co. in 1995 was 123,300 (www.co.black-hawk.ia.us/about.html). 73,980 would prefer athletics, compared with 49,320 who would prefer fine arts.

    b. According to the survey I conducted, three of twelve only participated in athletics. Of the 73,980 that means that only 18,495 participated in sports in high school. Using deduction, that means that 25 percent of the total population of Black Hawk County has not trained the right side of their brain much, if any! This may still sound small to you, but this means that 25 percent of the people of Black Hawk Co. are making "less intelligent" decisions because they haven't trained their brain equally. And what are the chances of you knowing one of those people? One in four!

V.  The statistics don't prove it yet? Here's some other interesting information to chew on.

    A.  A large number of athletes learn how to dance or play an instrument to be more nimble on their feet or to think more creatively. Have you ever wondered how many instructors from the College of HPELS go to fine arts events? I personally have seen several at the Gallagher for shows.

    B.  According to the Sarasota Florida Herald-Tribune, even the CIA recognizes the importance of the fine arts. The CIA has hired several graduates from the Ringling School of Art and Design because of their fine arts abilities. These people have been responsible for the creation of documents that the President personally looks at!

    C.  Some of the brightest individuals have recognized the importance of the fine arts. Albert Einstein played violin simply because he knew the importance of the duality of the brains! (UNESCO)

■ One more attempt to convince listeners

■ Examples to support

## Conclusion

As you can see, the fine arts are very important to daily life and functioning. Several sources agree. Scientists, universities, government organizations, and more are all aware of the importance of the fine arts to function with full capacity and the greatest amount of understanding of the world. Now that you understand the importance of the arts, I challenge you to apply this to your opportunities here at UNI. Unfortunately, an awesome production of Sueño has just closed at Theatre UNI, but there are still great shows this season, as well as many School of Music events you could attend. I challenge you to get out there and start utilizing the right side of your brain!

## ▬ The Presentational Outline

A **presentational outline** is a full-sentence outline in which detail is minimized and key words and phrases replace full sentences. This is the outline you will work from when you present your speech. The advantages of the presentational outline as a delivery aid are that it is concise, requires little space, and is comprehensible at a glance.

Your presentational outline should include your main points and sufficient clarifying and supporting material to aid you in making your presentation. The outline may also include your complete introduction and conclusion, although the choice is up to you. Key words and phrases are important to use in a presentational outline because they will remind you of the points you want to make. Some speakers use codes, symbols, or even colors to remind them of key points, vocal pauses, changes in speaking rate, and so on. But remember, if your presentational outline is too long, complex, or detailed, you can easily get too involved in your notes and lose contact with your audience. The following example on the importance of the fine arts shows a concise, condensed outline.

■ **presentational outline** A full-sentence outline in which detail is minimized and key words and phrases replace full sentences.

### Sample Presentational Outline

#### Introduction

POINT TO PRESENTATIONAL AID ■ Attention-getting strategy

What do you see? Seriously, what does this picture tell you? What if I show you the title?

How does that change your interpretation of what is shown? ■ Motivation

The fine arts are very important to each individual. Whether you realize it or not, the fine arts are as much of your daily life as are the acts of waking up and going to bed.

I hope to convince you that the fine arts are important in our everyday life because they help us use our whole brain, help us keep a balanced life, and help us contribute to society. ■ Thesis statement

■ Forecasting of main points

COVER DRAWING

#### Body

I. According to www.viewzone.com/bicam.html, the human brain is split in two hemispheres, the "right" and the "left." It has been found that the left side of the brain is "analytical" and the right side is "artistic."

A. Interestingly, the separate sides of the brain are connected to each other to work together, but can also work separately.

#### Example

1. A brain patient once had a tumor so that the brain hemispheres had to be disconnected from each other. The operation went well, until follow-up tests.

2. It was then discovered that the man could not at the same time recognize and name the objects placed before him. He could either recognize or name.

BREATHE

MOVE SLIGHTLY

B. The brain functions best when both sides are equally trained. By training both sides we increase our total brain usage.

C. When you looked at the picture, you allowed the right side of the brain to take over to figure out what I was trying to get you to see. As soon as I gave you a title your left brain took over and logic told you what the artist "wanted" you to see.

D. Your goal should be to use as much of both sides of your brain as possible.

PAUSE—SMILE—MOVE

II. So what is art? UNESCO defines art as "the embodiment of the human experience and goal."

**Definition**

A. What does that mean? Art is the "true" medium of communication. It can illustrate better than words what we are really feeling or trying to explain.

1. In fact, the truest form of art, the form that best illustrates human emotion, is music.

2. Music can cause a person to feel happy, sad, content, etc. (UNESCO)

B. Art, then, provides balance in our lives.

PAUSE

III. Artists create works to not only express themselves but also provide a means for helping society better itself. Unfortunately, especially in today's society, there are many distractions that prevent people from seeing this work and developing themselves further.

PAUSE

A. One of those distractions would be athletics.

1. Athletics can be logically traced back to primal times when the strongest of the species would survive (hunting for food or fighting enemies).

2. Obviously war is much more sophisticated these days, and while the need to be fit is still necessary to survive, there is little hand-to-hand battle. Sports serve as the "revival" of carnal needs and now instead of killing someone the games reflect who is the biggest, fastest, and strongest through competition. (Bradley Williams, MBA Business Administration)

B. Another distraction is technology.

1. Let's face it, we are a technology-bound society. It is easy to sit and watch TV or work on the computer.

2. How many of you try to do homework in your dorm, but find yourself turning on the TV or finding something else to do? Raise your hands.

SMILE—PAUSE—MOVE

IV. The University of Northern Iowa knows the fine arts are important as well.

A. UNI supports the College of Fine Arts and Humanities in every activity. It even helps choose the productions for the next season at Theatre UNI. (Chad Kolbe, Stagecraft lecture)

B. The Panther Prowl was begun this fall to increase student involvement on campus. Four of the six venues that are included in the "prowl" are fine arts or fine arts related. The "prowl" is sponsored by the venues and the Office of Financial Aid.

1. The venues include: Theatre UNI, Thursdaze, School of Music, the Gallagher Bluedorn, WRC, and Athletics.

2. Five of the six venues are free with the other venue having student ticket prices as half price, with Student Rush tickets being $5.00 There is no other college in the state with rates that good for students.

PAUSE BRIEFLY, LOOK AT EVERYONE AND TAKE ONE STEP CLOSER

C. I recently conducted a survey that sampled fifty percent of the students from the class. The results are as follows.

**Statistics**

1. About 60 percent participating prefer athletics over the fine arts.

**Quotation**

2. The reasoning ranges from greater personal enjoyment in athletics to liking fine arts better because it "Does more for my mind. I can get totally involved in theatre, ballet, dance, opera, music, etc., but don't have the same total commitment to all sports."

3. What can be concluded from this survey?

PAUSE

a. Assuming the class would be split similar to this sample, out of the twenty-five students, fifteen would prefer athletics. Apply this to Black Hawk Co. The reported population living in Black Hawk Co. in 1995 was 123,300 (www.co.black-hawk.ia.us/about.html). 73,980 would prefer athletics, compared with 49,320 who would prefer fine arts.

b. According to the survey I conducted, only three of twelve participated in athletics. Of the 73,980 that means that only 18,495 participated in sports in high school. Using deduction, that means that 25 percent of the total popu-

■ Information relevance

lation of Black Hawk County has not trained the right side of their brain much, if any! This may still sound small to you, but this means that 25 percent of the people of Black Hawk Co. are making "less intelligent" decisions because they haven't trained their brain equally. And what are the chances of you knowing one of those people? One in four!

PAUSE, LOOK AT EVERYONE

V. The statistics don't prove it yet? Here's some other interesting information to chew on.

MOVE WHILE LOOKING AT AUDIENCE

A. A large number of athletes learn how to dance or play an instrument to be more nimble on their feet or to think more creatively. Have you ever wondered how many instructors from the College of HPELS go to fine arts events? I personally have seen several at the Gallagher for shows.

B. According to the Sarasota Herald-Tribune of Florida, even the CIA recognizes the importance of the fine arts. The CIA has hired several graduates from the Ringling School of Art and Design because of their fine arts abilities. These people have been responsible for the creation of documents that the President personally looks at!

C. Some of the brightest individuals have recognized the importance of the fine arts. Albert Einstein played violin simply because he knew the importance of the duality of the brains! (UNESCO)

PAUSE, SMILE, TAKE A BREATH

SHOW PICTURE AGAIN

## Conclusion

As you can see, the fine arts are very important to daily life and functioning. Several sources agree. Scientists, universities, government organizations, and more are all aware of the importance of the fine arts to function with full capacity and the greatest amount of understanding of the world. Now that you understand the importance of the arts, I challenge you to apply this to your opportunities here at UNI. Unfortunately, an awesome production of Sueño has just closed at Theatre UNI, but there are still great shows this season, as well as many School of Music events you could attend. I challenge you to get out there and start utilizing the right side of your brain!

SMILE! PAUSE

MOVE TO TAKE DOWN DISPLAY

## Works Cited

*Arts and Man, The (1969).* UNESCO. New Jersey: Prentice-Hall Inc.

Cary, J. (1958). *Art and Reality: Ways of the Creative Process.* New Hampshire: Ayer Co.

Eden, D. "Left Brain: Right Brain." www.viewzone.com/bicam.html. Last accessed November 4, 2004.

Kolbe, C. November 2004. Class lecture, Theatre Arts I, University of Northern Iowa.

Sieren, M. Unpublished Drawing: "Luck." September, 2004.

Survey, 12:30 Oral Communication Class, October 26, 2004, University of Northern Iowa.

"Statistics about Black Hawk County." Created 1995. www.co .black-hawk.ia.us/about.html. Last accessed November 5, 2004.

"The art school; The Ringling School of Art and Design has educated the right brain in a left brained world for 73 years." *Sarasota Herald-Tribune* [Florida], October 3, 2004.

Williams, B. Personal Interview by Matthew Sieren, November 1, 2004.

## MAKING Technology CONNECTIONS

### Citing Sources

There are excellent sources on the Web to help you create your reference pages. (Some instructors will ask for a bibliography, others, a notes page, and some may want a Sources Cited page. All are acceptable, but be sure to ask your instructor for her/his preference.) The Modern Language Association Handbook for Writers of Research Papers, 6th edition, the Publication Manual of the American Psychological Association, 5th edition, and the Chicago Manual of Style, 15th edition, are all excellent sources for learning how to put your reference page together. Most can be found online through your own institution's library website. One very complete website is the Duke University Libraries.[17] Complete the following activity to help prepare you for the specific outline and reference page required by your instructor.

1. Go to www.library.duke.edu/research/citing/
2. Determine how to cite two different kinds of print sources.
3. Next, determine how to cite web sources.
4. Look again to see whether you can find examples of how to cite an email interview. If that site does not include personal or email interviews or conversations, search for another site to determine how to cite interviews.
5. Bookmark or print these sites so you have a handy reference for citing sources. (This will be useful when you create your reference page to turn in.)

The presentational outline can be easily transferred onto note cards. Some speakers prefer to use note cards, and in some classroom situations students are required to use them. Figure 9.2 illustrates note cards that might be used in presenting your speech. The number of note cards and their use should be kept to a minimum. Classroom assignments sometimes specify that you use only one side of two or

■ **FIGURE 9.2**  Sample Presentational Note Cards

Note cards should be easy to read. They help the speaker recall information and serve as a reminder of the speech's key ideas.

---

WHY SHOULD YOU AVOID DAIRY PRODUCTS?                                1

Get prepared—look at entire audience, take a deep breath

As a child, I never really liked milk or even ice cream. And, in fact, when either was offered, I often refused. No, I'm not crazy, and not abnormal, but I do have a lactose intolerance.

Lactose intolerance, according to the National Digestive Diseases Information Clearinghouse, is the inability to digest significant amounts of lactose, the predominant sugar of milk.

Lactose intolerance affects many people who are unaware that they have it. To enlighten you about its effects, I will share what lactose intolerance is, how it is diagnosed, how it is treated, and how to have a nutritionally balanced diet without dairy products.

---

Pause-slow                                                         2
   I.  What is lactose intolerance and how is it diagnosed?
       A.  Shortage of enzyme lactose
           1.  Distressing results (show Visual I)
           2.  Common symptoms
       B.  Causes of lactose intolerance
           1.  Born with LI
           2.  Develops over time (slow chart)
               a.  30–50 million Americans have LI
               b.  nearly 75% of African Americans and Native
                   Americans have LI [NDDIC]
               c.  90% of Asian Americans are LI
  II.  Treatment
       A.  Children
       B.  Adults

---

  III.  What to avoid, how to balance nutrition                    3
[look at audience, get A-V materials ready to show]
       A.  Avoid or limit these foods [show poster]
       B.  Include these calcium-rich foods [show chart]
       C.  Calcium needed [show calcium table]
[be sure to show visuals AND talk about them]
[Put American Dietetic Association (ADA) and International Foundation
for Functional Gastrointestinal Disorders (IFFGD) addresses on overhead]

---

All information in the note cards came from National Digestive Diseases Information (NDDK), National Institutes of Health, www.niddk.nih.gov/health/digest/pubs/lactose.htm, "Lactose Intolerance," accessed June 16, 2003.

three cards. When this is the case, you need to adjust the amount and type of information that you include to aid you in remembering key information. The advantage of using note cards is that they are easier to handle than full sheets of paper and usually require only one hand, thus freeing the hands for gestures.

| GUIDELINES | Using Presentational Note Cards |
|---|---|

1. Use only a few note cards (they are a help but cannot capture the whole speech).
2. Always number the note cards so that if they get out of order, you can reorder them quickly.
3. Write on only one side of the card.
4. Use abbreviations as much as possible.
5. Do not write out your speech—use an outline format.
6. If you prefer, write out the introduction and conclusion in their entirety.
7. List only the main points and subpoints on the cards.
8. If necessary, write out quotations, statistical data, and other information that must be cited accurately (see Figure 9.2 for sample note cards).

## Summary

Effective organization can help you present a speech that your audience will be able to follow, understand, and appreciate. There is an old anecdote that is often used by speech teachers and business consultants: If you want to get your audience to listen to you, you must tell them what you're going to tell them, tell them, and tell them what you just told them. In other words, you have to have an introduction, a body, and a conclusion. Good speech organization is a skill that carries over into writing papers, giving directions, and other school- and work-related tasks. The body of the speech is where you tell your audience about your topic. There are main points and subpoints, all of which should be constructed in such a way as to tell a logical, coherent, interesting "story." You'll want to make sure you have adequate research material to support and clarify your points.

You can utilize one of seven different patterns of organization in the body of the speech. The choice you make depends on your general and specific purposes and on how you wish to present your ideas. You will need to connect the main points and subpoints in your speech with special organizing strategies. And you need to be sure that you say everything you need to say about the topic in the time you have.

The introduction helps you orient your listeners to your speech content and provides them with reasons to listen. The conclusion summarizes and synthesizes your speech so that listeners remember it.

## Discussion Starters

1. How can organization help a speaker?
2. How does organization or the lack of it affect listeners?
3. How can you make your ideas more meaningful to your listeners?
4. Why should you learn about different patterns of organization?
5. What does the introduction accomplish?
6. Why is the conclusion important?
7. What do outlines accomplish?

# Answers and Explanations

**Making Connections: Ordering Ideas in an Outline (page 238)**
One set of possible answers: I. (2), A. (4), B. (8), II. (9), A. (1), B. (5), III. (7), A. (3), B. (6).

# Notes

1. Buzan, T., *Mind Maps at Work: How to Be the Best at Work and Still Have Time to Play* (New York: Harper-Collins, 2004). Also, "How to Make a Mind Map in 8 Steps" www.mapyourmind.com/howto .htm. Accessed July 8, 2006.
2. B. E. Gronbeck, R. E. McKerrow, D. Ehninger, and A. H. Monroe, *Principles and Types of Speech Communication,* 14th ed. (Glenview, Ill.: Scott, Foresman/ Little, Brown Higher Education, 1999), 180–203.
3. "Frozen 'Diet' Dinners," *Women's Health Reporter* 4(6) (2003), 1, 7.
4. M. Terletsky, "Strike Back at Stress," *Women's Health Reporter* 4(6) (2003), 4.
5. Lee Iacocca, cited in Glenn Van Ekeren, *Speaker's Sourcebook II* (Englewood Cliffs, NJ: Prentice Hall, 1994), 73.
6. "'Super Diary' Project Could Record Person's Every Move," from the AP Wire Service in (Waterloo-Cedar Falls) *Courier,* 3 June 2003, A1, A5.
7. M. Terletsky, op. cit.
8. "Infections More Widespread as Animals Pass Them On," from *The Washington Post,* in the (Waterloo-Cedar Falls) *Courier,* 16 June 2003, A5.
9. Ibid.
10. Ibid.
11. D. Zarefsky, *Public Speaking Strategies for Success* (4E) (Boston: Allyn and Bacon, 2006), 222.
12. "Infections More Widespread as Animals Pass Them On," op. cit.
13. Johnson, S., *Everything Bad Is Good for You* (New York: Riverhead Books, 2005), 198–99.
14. S. Brink, "Sleepless Society," *U.S. News and World Report,* October 16, 2000, 62.
15. Zarefsky, 252.
16. These outline examples are based on "The Importance of the Fine Arts," a speech presented by Matthew Sieren in Oral Communication, Fall 2004, University of Northern Iowa, and used with permission.
17. Kelley A. Lawton and Laura Cousineau, Duke University Libraries, and Van E. Hillard, The University Writing Program, Guide to Library Research, www.library.duke.edu/research/citing. Accessed July 8, 2006.

# CHAPTER 10

# Managing Anxiety and Delivering Your Speech

"You gain strength, courage, and confidence every time you look fear in the face."
—ELEANOR ROOSEVELT

# This chapter will help you:

- **Identify** the role of ethics in speech preparation and delivery and avoid plagiarism in your speeches and presentations.

- **Apply** the preparation process in creating your own speeches.

- **Create** effective oral footnotes and reference pages.

- **Manage** your speech anxiety.

- **Demonstrate** self-confidence in your presentations.

- **Describe** effective vocal and physical delivery factors.

- **Explain** the four methods of speech delivery and provide a rationale for how and when each might be used.

## Making everyday connections

Ten days and counting! Your speeches begin soon. How does that make you feel? If you're a typical student, no matter what your age or geographical area, those words send a chill down your spine. The fear of public speaking tops most people's list of phobias. Anxiety is a normal response to public speaking, and most of us have some degree of anxiety. Before you read the chapter to find suggestions that will help you manage your anxiety and help you deliver effective speeches, take a few minutes to think about and answer the following questions: ■

### Questions to think about

- What frightens you about giving a speech?

- Why?

- How have you dealt with your anxiety in the past?

- Were your strategies effective? If so, why? If not, why not?

Presenting speeches is fun. You might not believe that now, but if you have carefully completed all your work up to this point, you, too, may enjoy presenting your thoughts in front of the class. You have researched, organized, and arranged your ideas. Now you can focus on the delivery.

Every speaker should prepare for the speech presentation. If you can, rehearse in the classroom. If not, find a room comparable to the one where you'll give your speech, and practice out loud. If possible, get someone to listen to you and provide you with feedback about both content and delivery. What does this do for you? First, it allows you to know what the speech sounds like. The written word and the spoken word are not the same and do not have the same effect. Practice helps you hear that. Second, practicing in front of someone provides you with listener response, and you need that to help you make the right choices and to feel more confident about the speech.

# Qualities of Effective Speakers

By cultivating certain personal qualities, you can enhance the likelihood that your listeners will accept your message. The most effective speakers are ethical, knowledgeable, prepared, and self-confident.

## Ethics

Ethics, an individual's system of moral principles, plays a key role in communication. As speakers, we are responsible for what we tell others. We should always hold the highest ethical standards. We must communicate with honesty, sincerity, and integrity. In addition, a responsible, ethical speaker presents worthwhile and accurate information in a fair manner. Communication scholar David Zarefsky says, "Speech has tremendous power and the person who wields it bears great responsibility . . . both speakers and listeners should seek high standards of ethical conduct.[1]

Furthermore, ethical speakers do not distort or falsify evidence to misrepresent information, do not make unsupported attacks on opponents in order to discredit them, do not deceive an audience about their intention or objective in an attempt to persuade or take advantage, do not use irrelevant emotional appeals to sensationalize the message and divert attention from the facts, and do not pose as an authority when they are not.[2]

Ethical speakers always cite the sources of their information. Any time you use information and ideas that are not your own, you are obligated to cite the originator or source. The use of another person's information, language, or ideas without citing the originator or author, thus making it appear that you are the originator, is referred to as plagiarism. For example, it is unethical to use statistical data, direct quotations, or any information that you did not originate without giving credit to the originator. Most speeches, unless otherwise specified, require that you as the speaker be the originator of the speech's content. Of course, it is perfectly legitimate to use a reasonable amount of information and ideas from others, as long as you give them credit and cite your sources within the speech.

## GUIDELINES | Avoiding Plagiarism

1. Do not rely on a single article as the only source of information for a speech.
2. Avoid using other people's language and ideas.
3. Get information and ideas from a variety of sources, and integrate them into your own thoughts.
4. Cite sources prior to quoting such material—"Dr. Wilson, in her 2006 article on healthy living, stated 'The best. . . .'"
5. Always identify your sources—"*Newsweek* last week indicated that President Bush's tax plan is . . ." or "According to Robert Jones, a leading economist, in the May 29, 2006, *Wall Street Journal*, 'Our economy is. . . .'"
6. Give credit where credit is due—"According to Bill O'Hanlon in *Do One Thing Different,* 'the solution-oriented approach focuses on the present and the future and encourages people to take action and change their viewpoint.'"

Similarly, listeners are also responsible for determining the truth. We expect speakers to be ethical, but as listeners we must be willing to verify the information we receive to ensure that it is accurate and valid. Zarefsky states, "Above all, listeners have the responsibility to think critically about the speech. Do not reject or refuse to consider the speaker's message simply because it differs from what you already believe. . . . Assess the speech carefully to decide whether it merits your support."[3] (See Chapter 6 for a discussion of the responsibilities of the listener.)

## ■■ Knowledge

Knowledge is a speaker's greatest asset. Knowing your subject is essential if you plan to "reach" your listeners. Noted speakers are almost always avid readers. To enhance your understanding of events, people, and values, you must read and observe things around you. From experience, you know that it is easier to talk about things you are familiar with than those you are not. Many colleges, universities, and businesses have identified the characteristics of an "educated person." As an educated person, you should not only know about past international, national, regional, and local events, but also keep abreast of current events. You should read all kinds of books, at least one trade (professional) magazine, and one daily newspaper, in addition to listening to news broadcasts and documentaries.

In Chapter 8, we explained the importance of completing adequate research. You might have considerable knowledge about a topic, but you still need to complete careful research to add to that information base. Most instructors have minimum requirements for sources, both numbers and types. Sometimes students think they don't have to do much research. From many years of listening to speeches and receiving class members' responses, your authors can tell you that more research is always required! The more you do, the better your speech will be. Speeches require the same kind of diligent preparation as exams. If you want

## MAKING CONNECTIONS for Success

### An Ethical Dilemma

Christine's speech is about the religious symbolism in Mel Gibson's film, *The Passion of the Christ*. Early in her research, she found lots of background information about the gross revenue, the number of tickets sold, the number of people who attended, the names and numbers of groups who picketed, lists of a wide range of people who disagreed with Gibson, and the people who claimed that the film was anti-Semitic. But Christine cannot find the notes she made, and the information she found early in the research process does not show up when she does an Internet search to find exact numbers and sources. So, she looks to Wikipedia for her information. She remembers her professor saying that Internet sources had to meet the evaluation criteria, and that Wikipedia is not a reliable source. But she's desperate, and, after all, this is just background information, not the major part of her speech. She decides to use the information from Wikipedia but does not include Wikipedia as her source in her reference pages.

1. Is Christine being an ethical speaker? Why? Or why not?
2. What suggestions would you give Christine, if she were to ask you for advice?
3. What would happen to Christine if she were to do this in your communication class and get caught?

### David Zarefsky
*Northwestern University*

David Zarefsky is Owen L. Coon Professor of Argumentation and Debate and Professor of Communication Studies at Northwestern University. A star debater as an undergraduate at the school, Zarefsky joined the Northwestern faculty in 1968 and completed his graduate degrees while he rose through the faculty ranks. He headed Northwestern's nationally recognized forensics program from 1970 to 1975, chaired communication studies, and served as Associate Dean before becoming Dean in 1988, a post he held until 2000.

Zarefsky's research and teaching focuses on rhetorical history and criticism, argumentation and debate, and forensics. He has taught courses in the study of American public discourse, with a special

### To Scholars

focus on the pre-Civil War years and on the 1960s. He is also the author of *Public Speaking: Strategies for Success,* 4th edition. Professor Zarefsky is a prolific scholar and has won awards for two of his books: *President Johnson's War on Poverty: Rhetoric and History* and *Lincoln, Douglas, and Slavery: In the Crucible of Public Debate.* He currently is working on the controversy surrounding the annexation of Texas during the 1840s and on the legal and political dispute following the 2000 election and culminating in the U.S. Supreme Court decision in the case of Bush v. Gore.

His research and scholarship represent significant contributions to the communication discipline because his analysis of current and historical events also helps us to understand the current situation in political communication. Zarefsky and his wife, Nikki, are the parents of two grown children whom they enjoy visiting.

to establish yourself as a knowledgeable person, you will gather more information than you could possibly use in your speech. Why? So that you have a solid foundation for your speech and so that you can answer questions your listeners might ask. Effective speakers do not limit their research, nor do they present superficial speeches. Competent communicators make sure they have a strong knowledge base for all presentations.

## ■■ Preparation

People rarely make speeches without at least some preparation, and the most successful speakers are very well prepared. Poet Maya Angelou often makes speeches and gives poetry readings at colleges, universities, and other venues across the country. Angelou visited our respective campuses during September 2000. In her speech, she discussed her preparation for the presentation. Her remarks included references to planning and practicing the entire presentation well in advance of her scheduled appearance. She indicated that the prior preparation and practice allowed her to respond to the situation and the listeners much more freely than if she had not prepared in advance.

A successful speech is somewhat like a successful business meeting or athletic event—all require planning, preparation, and work. Preparation means more than practicing the speech ahead of time. It also means that speakers will think through the situation and possible snags or problems. In the example in the previous paragraph, we mentioned that Maya Angelou carefully prepared herself before her presentation. Her preparation included not only practice but also a process of thinking through all possible audience responses so that she could effectively handle questions.

## MAKING CONNECTIONS
### for Success

### Are You a Source?

WunJen Yan is an international student from Taiwan. Her professor assigned a speech on some aspect of intercultural communication for the informative speech. Yan was happy because she wanted to let others know more about her own country and its customs, and she wanted to share the similarities and differences between Taiwan and the United States. She was concerned, however, that she wouldn't meet the assignment criteria for the number of and type of sources required because so many of her ideas came from her personal experience.

1. What kind of experiences might Yan include in her speech?
2. Where else can she go for sources?
3. How will she know when to find outside sources?
4. How do you, as a listener, feel about presentations when the speaker includes stories or personal experiences?
5. How should speakers make listeners aware of their personal experiences?

---

Wil Linkugel, a retired professor of speech communication at the University of Kansas, told this story, which illustrates the importance of practice:

A student athlete was delivering a speech to the class. The student, speaking in a monotone voice, kept reading from a prepared script. Finally, Professor Linkugel interrupted the student.

*Professor:* Why don't you put down your notes and just tell us what your notes say?

*Student:* I can't do that. I'll never get it right.

*Professor:* Let's see what you can do.

The student tried speaking without his notes, but the result, although greatly improved, left much to be desired.

*Student:* I'll never do this right!

*Professor:* In football practice, if you were running a pass pattern and you didn't do it right, what would your coach make you do?

*Student:* We'd run it over again.

*Professor:* How many times would you run it over?

*Student:* As many times as it would take to get it right.

What message was Professor Linkugel trying to get across to the student? Is there a message in the story for you? Whether playing football or delivering a speech, for the beginner as well as the experienced speaker, preparation, practice, and knowledge of the fundamentals are important. Remember, however, that you don't want to practice so much that your speech sounds memorized or "canned." Effective speakers should sound conversational, not mechanical. Too much practice can make you lose the spark of spontaneity and reduce your effectiveness.

## Self-Confidence

Self-confidence, or the belief in oneself, is so essential to becoming an effective speaker that much of this book's content is aimed at helping you strengthen this quality. Refer back to the information in Chapter 3 to make the associations between self-image,

A good speech depends on good delivery, and good delivery almost always depends on practice. After organizing and writing a speech, present the speech out loud to a friend in an informal setting or in front of a mirror. Make changes, if necessary, to make the speech more effective.

self-concept, self-confidence, and a variety of communication situations. Because self-confidence is so strongly influenced by anxiety, we discuss this problem in detail.

## ■ Managing Speech Anxiety

The *World Book Encyclopedia/Dictionary* defines *anxiety* as "uneasy thoughts or fears about what may happen; troubled, worried, or uneasy feeling."[4] If you experience the fear of speaking before an audience—a condition known as **speech anxiety,** or stage fright—it might help to know that you are not alone. It is perfectly normal to encounter some anxiety before, during, and sometimes even after a speech. In fact, even the most experienced speakers confess to having some anxiety about speaking before a group. What should you know about stage fright? This question, for some teachers of public speaking, is controversial. If the subject is presented, will the mere mention of anxiety create unnecessary anxiety in the speaker? That is, will the dis-

■ **speech anxiety**
Fear of speaking before an audience.

cussion of stage fright bring out more anxiety in speakers than they would experience if it had never been mentioned at all? There is no evidence to suggest that discussing stage fright increases or decreases it, but it is commonly accepted that the more we know about stage fright and how to cope with it, the better able we are to *control* it.

Communication apprehension and speech anxiety are two of the most researched areas in communication. One of the reasons is that speaking in front of others is identified as people's greatest fear.[5] You should keep in mind that anxiety is normal. Most of us have some degree of anxiety when we speak in front of others. Anxiety is only a problem when we cannot control it or when we choose not to communicate because of it.

## ■■ Communication Apprehension

Communication apprehension, the most severe form of speech anxiety, was defined in Chapter 3 as anxiety syndrome associated with either real or anticipated communication with another person or persons.[6] Communication apprehension can be seen in individuals who either consciously or subconsciously have decided to remain silent. They perceive that their silence offers them greater advantages than speaking out, or that the disadvantages of communicating outweigh any potential gains they might receive. Communication apprehensive individuals fear speaking in all contexts, including one-on-one communication and small-group discussions. Among the fears of those with communication apprehension is that of speaking before a group. However, not everyone who fears speaking before a group necessarily suffers from communication apprehension. That term refers to the much deeper problem of virtually cutting oneself off from most, if not all, communication with others.

## ■■ Symptoms of Speech Anxiety

Speech anxiety refers more specifically to the fear of speaking before a group. Anxiety is a condition during which our bodies secrete hormones and adrenaline that eventually overload our physical and emotional responses. These chemical reactions

**MAKING** Technology **CONNECTIONS**

### Dealing with Anxiety

Sometimes people get "cotton-mouth" when they have to give a speech. Others have too much saliva, or they have cold, clammy hands. Some of us get flushed and every bit of visible skin is a bright red. Communication scholar James McCroskey and his colleagues have researched the phenomenon they label "communication apprehension." It may be of some comfort to know that most of us experience some degree of anxiety or fear when faced with real or imagined public speaking situations. And, those who teach special anxiety sections suggest that the first step in learning to manage your anxiety is to recognize it.

1. Do you have some anxiety about speaking in public?
2. What are your symptoms? (Dry mouth, sweating, etc.)
3. Have you found any strategies to help you deal with your anxiety? What are they? What others have you tried?
4. Have you tried deep breathing? Sometimes that can benefit you.
5. Access www.soyouwanna.com and see what suggestions they have for managing your fears.
6. Find another web source for dealing with your fear of public speaking and compare their suggestions with Soyouwanna.com.

■ **TABLE 10.1** Behaviors Associated with Speech Anxiety

| | |
|---|---|
| *Voice* | Quivering, too soft, monotonous, too fast, nonemphatic |
| *Fluency* | Stammering, halting, awkward pauses, hunting for words, speech blocks |
| *Mouth and throat* | Breathing heavily, clearing throat often, swallowing repeatedly |
| *Facial expressions* | No eye contact, rolling eyes, tense facial muscles, grimaces, twitches |
| *Arms and hands* | Rigid and tense, fidgeting, waving hands |
| *Body movement* | Swaying, pacing, shuffling feet, weight shifts |
| *Nonvisible symptoms* | Feeling too warm, too much saliva, dry mouth, butterflies in the stomach |

Adapted from A. Mulac and A. R. Sherman, "Behavior Assessment of Speech Anxiety," *Quarterly Journal of Speech* 60, 2 (April 1974): 138.

are the same as those you might experience when you are waiting to see a friend you haven't seen in years or going to your first job interview. Your heart begins to beat faster, and your blood pressure begins to rise. More sugar is pumped into your system, and your stomach might begin to churn. When you experience these reactions, you may feel as if your body is operating in high gear and that little or nothing can be done about it. You have to realize that some of these feelings are perfectly normal and, for most us, will not interfere with our speech performance.

Speakers who experience speech anxiety often display the visible signs listed in Table 10.1. These behaviors can occur separately or in any combination, depending on the degree of anxiety the speaker is experiencing.

Speakers who experience speech anxiety may also make telling statements. For example, they may offer self-critical excuses or apologies such as "I'm not any good at this anyway," "I didn't really prepare for this because I didn't have enough time," or "I never was able to say this correctly." Instead of improving the situation, these comments tend to draw more attention to speakers' nervousness and thus magnify the problem.

Speakers who have speech anxiety often overestimate how much the audience notices about their behavior. The audience, for their part, tends to underestimate a speaker's anxiety. For example, audiences cannot detect a speaker who is experiencing butterflies unless the butterflies cause an observable reaction or the speaker's voice sounds nervous.

## ■■ Causes of Speech Anxiety

Just as physicians can better treat an illness if they know its cause, people can better reduce and control speech anxiety if they can determine the underlying problem. Many people with speech anxiety treat only the symptoms and tend to ignore the causes, but trying to remove the symptoms without understanding the causes is usually a losing battle.

Severe speech anxiety begins at an early age as a result of negative feedback in the home. For example, children who are not encouraged to communicate or are punished for doing so are likely to learn that communicating is undesirable and that silence is beneficial. As these children avoid communicating, others may unknowingly contribute further to their fear by asking questions such as "Cat got your tongue?" or "You're afraid to talk, aren't you?" Such words can make the anxious children feel inadequate and thus perpetuate the fear and anxiety associated with communicating.

People may also develop speech anxiety if they constantly hear that speaking in front of others can be a terrible experience. Being told immediately before giving a speech, "Don't worry about it—you'll do fine," reinforces the notion that something can go wrong. If speakers believe that something can go wrong and that they might make fools of themselves, they are apt to lose confidence and develop speech anxiety.

In our society, success, winning, and "being number one" are too often considered all-important. When we can't be the most successful, we sometimes consider ourselves failures. No one likes to fail, therefore we are apt to feel that success brings rewards and failure brings punishment. If you are a winner, you are praised; if you are a loser, you are ridiculed. As a result, we place tremendous pressure on ourselves and others to be successful.

When we haven't been successful at something, we are often told to try again. But if the consequences of the failure are dramatic and the payoff for success doesn't seem worth the effort, we may prefer to avoid the situation. Avoidance may result in punishment, but we may perceive that as better than trying to do something and failing. Sometimes society is more lenient. For example, in a competition we assume that there will be a winner and a loser. No one likes to lose, but playing your best and losing is often acceptable. When someone makes a mistake in a speech, however, we may be more critical. Rather than acknowledging that the person is making an honest effort, we might perceive him or her as inadequate or unskilled. Consequently, the stress created by fear of making mistakes in front of others can be so great that it produces anxiety and sometimes complete avoidance of speaking situations. Among the other most common causes of speech anxiety are the following:

Fear of physical unattractiveness

Fear of social inadequacy

Fear of criticism

Fear of the unknown

Fear of speech anxiety

Conflicting emotions

Excitement from anticipation[7]

We learn to respond in specific ways when facing something that creates anxiety because we have become conditioned to do so. Each of these common reactions to a speech-making situation is *learned*. Because speech anxiety is a learned behavior, the only solution for its sufferers is to examine the potential reasons for the anxiety and learn how to use this knowledge to manage the discomfort.

## ■■ Speech Anxiety and Other Cultures

Each year there are increasing numbers of international students and Americans whose first language is not English who enter our institutions of higher learning. These students only ask to be treated the same as others. But, because of language and cultural differences, these students do have some anxieties that go beyond those of native speakers. In interviews with international students and their professors, Xiaofan Liao learned that most international students were concerned about talking in class: "I don't know your language as well as I should. I'm nervous about responding in class." They were afraid that they would not fully understand the assignment, that others would not understand them, and that they would "lose face" with their American professors and classmates.[8]

Some of the international students were concerned about translating from English to their own language and back again, and that the translation process would be slow and perhaps inaccurate. They also felt that they didn't really fit in; their "foreign" status often precluded their U.S. classmates from interacting with them. Some of them stated that the classroom situation was so different from what they were accustomed to, that it made them even more nervous. In each case, they felt that their "differences" translated to being perceived as in some way inferior to the native-speaking students, and called undue negative attention to them. Giving a speech in front of a group is difficult for most of us. There are additional stresses for those from different language and cultural backgrounds.

Native Americans represent another group who have more anxiety when speaking because of cultural differences. In the Native American culture, eye contact is limited. In speaking situations in the dominant culture, eye contact is expected. Native American students explain that they feel even more uncomfortable when they are reminded that eye contact is critical. Those from different cultural and language backgrounds want their situations to be understood.

## ■ Treating Speech Anxiety

Although speaking before a group can produce stress and anxiety, few people allow their nervousness to prevent them from trying and succeeding.[9] In fact, as mentioned earlier, even well-known speakers feel some nervousness before giving a speech, but they have learned to *control* it. The key to successful control of your anxiety is the desire to control it. To cope with speech anxiety, we must realize that the potential for failure always exists, but that we can't let it stop us from trying. If we allowed the possibility of failure to overwhelm us, we probably would never do or learn anything. A child beginning to walk is a prime example of how most of our learning occurs. At first, the child wobbles, takes a small step, and falls. But when the child falls, someone is usually there to offer help, support, and encouragement to continue. In addition, the child usually is determined to walk regardless of the difficulties. Speech making, like learning to walk, involves many of the same processes. Help, support, and encouragement are important, but the essential ingredient is determination to succeed.

Most successful people will tell you that before they were successful, they had some failures and moments of embarrassment. Their drive and self-confidence pushed them to try again. Some of our first speeches were not very good, and we were quite nervous about speaking in front of our classmates. However, it didn't take us long to realize that even the best speakers in the class felt the same way. The only difference was that they weren't afraid to make a mistake.

Many of us are too hard on ourselves. Some students, after giving a speech, will say that they were extremely nervous, though the audience detected no signs of nervousness. To the audience, the speaker appeared relaxed and in control.

There are no cures for speech anxiety—only ways to reduce, manage, or control it so that it does not interfere with your presentation. Experts suggest several guidelines to help you reduce your anxieties:

1.  *Select a topic you enjoy and know.* The more you know about a subject, the easier it will be for you to talk about it. According to one research study, people who are highly anxious tend to be more negative in their assessments of themselves and more concerned with what others think of them. In addition, they tend to choose unfamiliar speech topics, which compounds their problem.[10] Sometimes, however, it is not possible to choose your own topic. In business settings, for example, we are often required to report information for specific situations in which the topic is selected by the circumstances. In this case, the speaker must work harder to have adequate information and to focus on accomplishing what is necessary for that situation.

2.  *Be prepared.* Because anxious people are more negative in their self-assessments, they tend to spend less time preparing, convinced they are not going to succeed no matter what they do. Thus, they set themselves up for failure, which perpetuates the cycle of anxiety and failure. Preparation can break the cycle. Know your audience and become familiar with the physical surroundings in which you are going to speak (such as the room size, lighting, placement of microphone, and audiovisual equipment). This will help create confidence by reducing the unknown. In Chapter 9, we advised you that carefully organizing your speech will help you be more effective. The work you put into research, organization, and practice will also help you be more confident.

3.  *Be confident.* Confidence plays a key role in controlling anxiety. We are often amazed at how many students sell themselves short. We have heard many student speakers over the years, and each of them had the ability and potential skill to be an effective speaker. Students who didn't believe that they could be successful seemed to have the most difficulty giving speeches. We have also had students who were extremely quiet in class, but when it came to speaking, they were exceptional. One student who seldom talked in class was asked how she felt after her speech, and she indicated that she was surprised at how good she felt. The first minute or so, she was nervous, she said, but once she realized that she knew what she was talking about and the audience appeared to be listening, she completely forgot about her nervousness and concentrated on informing her audience. You only have to try. Even if you do not do as well as you would like, the instructor is there to help you and your classmates and wants you to do well.

4.  *Think positively.* Visualize yourself giving a successful speech. Some students tell us it is easy to think positively but it doesn't help them give a successful speech. We disagree. Positive thought does work. There is ample proof to suggest that those who think positively and visualize themselves doing well often surpass their own expectations. Thinking that you are going to do poorly, however, is a sure path to failure.

5.  *Practice.* The better you know the content of your speech and your delivery plan, the more comfortable you will feel about your presentation. Few things are done well without some practice. For example, the quarterback who executes a perfect touchdown pass, the gymnast who scores a 10 in floor exercise, the actor who presents a flawless performance, the student who draws beautiful pictures, the person who passes the road test for a driver's license, and the person who gives a

polished and interesting speech have spent hours—and sometimes years—in practice. Knowing that you don't have weeks, months, or years to practice your speech, you must practice as much as you can with the realization that you may not perfect all aspects of your speech. Remember that most of us are somewhat nervous before a speech and that nervousness is perfectly normal.

Giving a speech and completing a pass play in a football game are not the same thing, but both require similar preparation. The successful pass play requires research, organization, learning, observation, practice, willingness to work hard, ability to perform, confidence, knowing your opponent's defenses (or knowing your audience), and timing. A successful speech presentation requires all of the aforementioned factors in addition to selecting an appropriate topic.

## GUIDELINES      Controlling Speech Anxiety

1. You are not alone! Almost everyone has some anxiety about giving a speech or making a presentation.
2. Select a topic that you are familiar with and that you enjoy, if possible.
3. Know your audience and the surroundings in which your presentation will take place.
4. Think positively. Prepare yourself mentally for success. Believe that you are going to be successful, and you probably will be.
5. Practice, practice, and then practice more!
6. Ask your instructor for additional advice and other possible treatment programs that may be available.
7. Don't give up. Others want you to succeed, and you can if that is what you want.

If none of the strategies in the accompanying Guidelines feature help to reduce your anxiety, then you should probably seek professional help. Individuals who suffer from abnormal levels of speech anxiety should know that the negative feelings associated with communicating in front of others do not simply occur; they develop over a long period of time. Therefore these negative feelings do not always disappear easily. But speech anxiety is a problem that we can do something about with help. Most university settings have psychologists or counselors who are trained to reduce the fear of speaking in public. Some colleges offer special sections of the beginning communication course for those who are anxious about speaking in front of others.

**Systematic desensitization** is a relaxation technique designed to reduce the tenseness associated with anxiety.[11] The goal is to help you develop a new, relaxed response to the anxiety-provoking event. Try this. Imagine yourself standing in front of this class, ready to give your speech. Visualize the wonderful speech you will give. You confidently place your notes on the lectern, look at the audience, smile, take a deep breath, and begin speaking. Your audience smiles and nods throughout the speech, and you become more and more relaxed as you speak. When you finish, they applaud loudly. Someone says, "That was a wonderful speech!" Remember how if felt to be so relaxed. Go through this visualization process, and think about how relaxed you are. This kind of mental rehearsal helps you change negative thoughts to positive ones.

■ **systematic desensitization** A relaxation technique designed to reduce the tenseness associated with anxiety.

### Anxiety and You

Your anxieties can usually be controlled if you work at them. The first thing you have to do is recognize and acknowledge that you have some anxieties about speaking in front of others. The second thing you must do is learn to control your thoughts about anxiety. When he gave his speech on a communication concept, one of our students, Scott Gordon, included an original poem, "Ode to Nervousness." In the poem, Scott says that he is extremely anxious: his heart is beating rapidly, he is shaking, his voice quavers, and his palms are sweating. By the end of the poem, he feels good about himself and his speech and looks forward to the "next time." For Scott, acknowledging his nervousness was more than three-fourths of the battle.

1. Do a Google search: key in Dealing with Speech Anxiety.
2. Read three or four of the noncommercial entries (look for a college site that identifies strategies or tips, not a publisher's or consultant's site).
3. Compare and contrast the suggestions you find on the Web with what we've provided here in the textbook.

---

Overcoming anxiety in public speaking situations is not easy, but you must remember that some anxiety can be helpful and is a normal reaction to speaking in public. When we asked students how they dealt with their fear of speaking, they suggested the following:

1. Practice, and have your introduction, main points, and conclusion clear in your mind. Students believe that once they know their introductions, main points, and conclusions, it is a lot easier to remember the details.

2. Walk confidently to the speaking area. Students believe that this helps create confidence. If you're confident, it is likely you will feel relaxed. In other words, positive behavior results in positive outcomes.

3. Do not start your speech until you are ready. The students suggest that having everything under control before you start to speak makes it easier to relax and concentrate on the speech, rather than on yourself.

4. Look at your audience, and focus most of the time on friendly faces. Students believe that concentrating on those who are likely to give positive feedback will help to promote a good feeling about speaking.

These suggestions are probably not new, and they are not surprising, but they will help in your quest to become a successful speaker. The best thing you can do is continue to give speeches in class and take more classes that will afford opportunities to speak under the supervision of a trained instructor. You can reduce and control your fear of speaking, but you must make that happen by acting on the guidelines we have provided here.

## ■ Methods of Delivery

An effective delivery conveys the speaker's purpose and ideas clearly and interestingly so that the audience attends to and retains what was said as it was intended by the speaker. The effectiveness of a speech therefore depends both on what is said and how it is conveyed. No two speakers are alike. For example, it is unlikely that anyone could deliver the "I Have a Dream" speech as effectively as Martin Luther King, Jr., did. This speech, widely regarded as a masterpiece, was delivered on August 28, 1963, to more than 200,000 people gathered in Washington, D.C., to participate in a peaceful demonstration furthering the cause of equal rights for African Americans. If you have heard a recording of this speech, you know how King's delivery affected his audience. He had a rich baritone voice modulated by the cadences of a Southern Baptist preacher and the fervor of a crusader. Although the words of the speech can be repeated and King's style can be imitated, the setting, timing, and circumstances cannot be reconstructed. Therefore the effect that King had on that day can never be repeated.

A poorly written speech can be improved by effective delivery, and a well-written speech can be ruined by ineffective delivery. No set of rules will guarantee an effective delivery in every situation. The only consistent rule is that you must be yourself! Of course, as a beginning speaker, you probably have many questions about how to deliver a speech: How many notes should I use? Will I need a microphone? Where and how should I stand? Where or at whom should I look? How many and what kinds of gestures should I use? How and when should I use my visual aids? How loudly should I speak? How fast or slow should my speaking be?

Such questions are valid, but the answers will vary from person to person and from situation to situation. In the end, effective delivery comes from practice under the direction of a competent instructor. An awareness of self and knowledge of effective delivery also help to improve delivery. Although a speech may be delivered in many different ways, the four most common methods of delivery are impromptu, manuscript, memorized, and extemporaneous (see Table 10.2).

## ■■ Impromptu Delivery

The delivery of a speech with little or no formal planning or preparation (no research, no organization) is called **impromptu delivery.** You have used this method many times, perhaps without even realizing it. Whenever you speak without prior preparation, whether in response to a question in class, to a sudden request at a business meeting, or to a comment made by a friend, you are using the impromptu method of delivery. The more formal or demanding the situation, the more most speakers prefer to avoid this approach. At times, however, you have no choice. In such cases, muster your self-control, relax, and concentrate on what you wish to say. The lack of preparation time distinguishes the impromptu method from other methods of delivery and forces speakers to depend solely on their ability to think on their feet.

## ■■ Manuscript Delivery

■ **impromptu delivery** A delivery style in which a speaker delivers a speech with little or no planning or preparation.

■ **manuscript delivery** A delivery style in which a speaker writes the speech in its entirety and then reads it word for word.

Reading the speech word for word is known as **manuscript delivery.** Speakers who use this method are never at a loss for words. A speaker should use a manuscript for situations in which every word, phrase, and sentence must be stated precisely. Using a manuscript is not uncommon for politicians, clergy, teachers, and others who need to present information completely and accurately or who are likely to be quoted after their presentations. But in learning how to give a speech, manuscript delivery is often discouraged, because it invites the speaker to concentrate more on the script than the audience and reduces eye contact with the audience. Also, speakers who work from manuscripts are less able to adapt to the reactions of the audience and thus may sound mechanical. They are so busy concentrating on reading the speech that they may be unable to respond to their listeners.

■ **TABLE 10.2** Methods of Delivery: Advantages and Disadvantages

|  | ADVANTAGES | DISADVANTAGES |
|---|---|---|
| *Impromptu* | Spontaneous | No time for preparation |
|  | Flexible | Can be inaccurate |
|  | Conversational | Difficult to organize |
|  |  | Can be stressful |
| *Manuscript* | Good for material that is technical or detailed or that requires complete preciseness | No flexibility |
|  |  | Great amount of preparation time |
|  | High accuracy | Difficult to adapt to audience response |
|  | Can be timed to the second | May sound mechanical |
|  | Prepared | Lack of eye contact |
| *Memorized* | Good for short speeches | Inflexible |
|  | Speaker can concentrate on delivery | Requires practice and repetition |
|  | Easier to maintain eye contact | Speaker can forget or lose place |
|  | Prepared | Difficult to adapt to audience response |
|  |  | May sound mechanical |
| *Extemporaneous* | Organized | May be intimidating to inexperienced speakers |
|  | Flexible |  |
|  | Conversational |  |
|  | Prepared |  |
|  | Great amount of eye contact |  |

## Manuscript Delivery

**GUIDELINES**

1. *Write your manuscript for the ear.* There is a difference between content written to be read silently and that to be read aloud. The silent reader can go back to a previous sentence for reference and can reread a passage if it is unclear the first time, but a person listening to a speech cannot. Be listener oriented.
2. *Prepare your manuscript in an easy-to-read format.* Type it triple-spaced. Use special marks and comments to point out areas you plan to emphasize.
3. *Think about what you are saying.* The presence of a manuscript often tempts a speaker to read words instead of thoughts. Try to sound spontaneous and give meaning to the manuscript.
4. *Read with expression and vocal emphasis.* Remember that your voice can add meaning to the words. Thus the expressive use of your voice becomes an added dimension to the reading of the words.
5. *Practice reading out loud,* preferably with a tape recorder. The key to success is to sound as if the thoughts you are reading are fresh. The manuscript should be presented with enthusiasm, vigor, and interest.[12]

## ▬ Memorized Delivery

**Memorized delivery** requires that you memorize your speech in its entirety, usually from a word-for-word script. This kind of delivery is used for short presentations, such as toasts, acceptance speeches, and introductions, and is also commonly used by speakers in contests and on lecture circuits. Speakers frequently memorize certain parts of their speeches, including examples, short stories, statistics, quotations, and other materials that they can call up at the appropriate time. Politicians, salespeople, tour guides, and others often have a memorized pitch, or speech, to fit their needs.

Memorization has one advantage. You can concentrate less on what you have to say and focus more on your delivery. Of course, this is true only if you are extremely confident and have memorized your speech so completely that you don't need to think about each word. One disadvantage of memorized delivery is its lack of flexibility; it doesn't allow for much, if any, adaptation to your audience. Beginning speakers face another disadvantage: They might forget what they want to say and become embarrassed. In addition, it is difficult to deliver a memorized speech without sounding mechanical. Effective presentation of a memorized address requires a great deal of practice and confidence. The Guidelines feature about manuscript delivery applies equally to memorized delivery.

## ▬ Extemporaneous Delivery

In **extemporaneous delivery,** the speaker uses a carefully prepared and researched speech but delivers it from notes, with a high degree of spontaneity. Extemporaneous delivery is the method that is most commonly used in speech classrooms and in other public communication situations. When you give a report at work, for example, you will probably be expected to present your remarks extemporaneously. If you are a member of a problem-solving group at your place of worship and you have been selected to present the group's deliberations, you will also be expected to deliver your remarks in an extemporaneous manner. Instructors often require extemporaneous delivery in the communication classroom because it is the best style for most instances of public speaking.

Extemporaneous delivery is situated somewhere between memorized or manuscript delivery and impromptu delivery. Speakers depend on a brief presentational outline or notes and choose the actual wording of the speech at the time of delivery. (See Chapter 9 for a discussion of presentational outlines.) Speakers sometimes prefer to use a key word outline, which simply outlines the points and subpoints of the speech using key words. This helps keep the speaker organized and on track but does not allow the speaker to become too reliant on the outline or notes.

An extemporaneous speech might at first seem as difficult as an impromptu speech, but, in fact, it is much easier. Because it eliminates memorization and manuscript writing, it leaves more time for preparation and practice. Thus once you have prepared your outline, you can begin to practice your delivery. The goal of the extemporaneous method is a conversational and spontaneous quality. Conversationality and spontaneity are two hallmarks of speech delivery that listeners find appealing. It is much easier to listen to and attend to speakers who are conversational, lively, and spontaneous. Each time you practice your speech, the wording should be somewhat different, although the content remains the same. Your objective should always be to use delivery to help you share meaningful ideas with your audience.

These are the advantages of extemporaneous delivery: It gives you better control of your presentation than the impromptu method, it allows more spontaneity and

■ **memorized delivery** A delivery style in which a speaker memorizes a speech in its entirety from a word-for-word script.

■ **extemporaneous delivery** A delivery style in which the speaker carefully prepares the speech in advance but delivers it using only a few notes and with a high degree of spontaneity.

The speaker here is using an extemporaneous delivery, a carefully prepared and researched speech, but delivers it from notes with a high degree of spontaneity.

directness than the memorized and manuscript methods of delivery, and it is more adaptable to a variety of speaking situations than the other methods. Most teachers, as well as professional speakers, prefer to use the extemporaneous method because it allows them to adjust to the situation moment by moment. Extemporaneous delivery also allows audience members to become more involved in listening to the message.

# ■ Vocal and Physical Aspects of Delivery

Without solid content and valid sources, nothing is worth communicating; but without effective delivery, even the most compelling information cannot be clearly and vividly presented. Because the audience is the ultimate judge of effectiveness, you must deliver your speech well to involve them in your speech. Each audience member likes to feel as if he or she is being addressed personally. Try to think of your presentation as a conversation and your audience as your partners in dialogue. Then use your voice and body to create this impression.

## ■ Vocal Aspects

Many beginning speakers overlook the important role that voice plays in delivery. As you speak, your voice should be pleasant to listen to, relate easily and clearly to your thoughts, and express a range of emotions. Your voice should convey the meaning to your listeners that you wish to convey. The more natural, spontaneous, and effortless you appear to be, regardless of how hard you are working, the more your listener can focus on what you are saying rather than how you are saying it. Three aspects of voice that determine the effectiveness of delivery are vocal quality, intelligibility, and vocal variety.

**Vocal Quality.** The overall impression a speaker's voice makes on listeners is referred to as **vocal quality.** Voices may be harsh, nasal, thin, mellow, resonant, or full-bodied. Attitude can affect the quality of the voice and reveal to listeners whether the speaker is happy, confident, angry, fearful, or sad. Think about those times when you were extremely tired: How does your voice sound? Can you hide your tiredness from people listening to you? Probably not. Think about times when you were really excited about a topic. How do you think you sounded to your listeners? Generally, when we're really involved and interested in something, the voice carries energy and excitement that draws others into the conversation. Vocal quality is a highly accurate indicator of the presenter's sincerity. Also, listeners tend to believe that speakers whose vocal delivery is interesting and easy to listen to are more credible speakers and will probably be more willing to listen to speakers who use their voices effectively.

**Intelligibility.** A speaker's **intelligibility,** the degree to which an audience can hear and understand words, is determined by vocal volume; distinctiveness of sound; accuracy of pronunciation; articulation; and stress placed on syllables, words, and phrases. The keys to high intelligibility are self-awareness and consideration for listeners.

To determine the proper volume, consider the size of the room, and observe listeners' reactions. Do listeners look as if they're straining to hear you? Or is your voice too loud or booming for the size of the room?

We have all been known to mispronounce words. For example, a common word like *February* is often mispronounced as *Feb-u-ary.* Sometimes we mispronounce words out of habit, incorrect learning, or a regionalism. For example, many people pronounce *realtor* as *re-la-tor* instead of *real-tor.* When we mispronounce words, we lower our intelligibility and also run the risk of lowering our credibility. Speakers often drop off word endings, which makes it difficult to understand what is being said; the dropping of the *g* from words ending in *ing,* for example, makes it difficult for persons from other cultures to understand the words. Saying "I'm gonna tell you about . . ." instead of "I'm going to tell you about . . ." also may result in a loss of credibility. Effective speakers need to make sure that the words they use are clearly spoken, correctly used, and understandable. Always check a pronunciation dictionary for the most accurate pronunciations.

Grammatical correctness is an important consideration. Not only is the classroom teacher bothered by incorrect grammar and inappropriate use of words, but also in the world outside the classroom, we are judged by the way we present our ideas. This suggests that before we present a speech, we should practice it before a friend or colleague who might detect our errors, dropped sounds, grammatically incorrect words, and mispronunciations.

There is a difference, however, between mispronounced words and regional and ethnic dialects that affect pronunciation. The effect dialect has on an audience depends a great deal on the makeup of the audience and whether or not they understand the difference between dialect usage and standard pronunciation of words. Speakers should always strive to learn similarities and differences between their own dialects and those of others and adapt their messages to the situation. An African American student who uses Ebonics when speaking with friends, for example, needs to adjust language in the classroom and the workplace so that he or she can be easily understood by listeners.

Good articulation involves producing and saying words clearly and distinctly. Physical problems, such as cleft palate, difficulty in controlling the tongue, or a misaligned jaw, can create articulation problems that require specialized help, but most

■ **vocal quality** The overall impression a speaker's voice makes on his or her listeners.

■ **intelligibility** Speaker's vocal volume, distinctiveness of sound, clarity of pronunciation, articulation, and stress placed on syllables, words, and phrases.

articulation problems result from laziness. We sometimes chop, slur, or mumble words because we do not take the time to learn the words correctly. People say "gonna" instead of "going to," "didja" instead of "did you," or "dunno" instead of "don't know." Such articulation errors often result from habit and sloppiness rather than ignorance of what is correct.

Unfortunately, many people don't realize that their articulation is sloppy or incorrect unless someone tells them. Listen to what you say and how you sound. Concentrate on identifying and eliminating your most common articulation errors. Correcting articulation errors can be well worth the effort; you will sound more intelligent and more professional, and you will further establish your credibility as an educated person.

We need to make two more points about intelligibility. Avoid fillers and vocal pauses, which clutter speeches. Fillers such as "um," "uh," "ah," "and uh," "like," and, "you know" can become both distracting and irritating to your listeners. Most communication instructors will note (and probably reduce your grade)

## MAKING CONNECTIONS for Success

### Using Your Voice Effectively

Have you ever really stopped to listen to broadcast journalists? Take a few minutes to watch the local newscast and also one of the national broadcasts (NBC, ABC, CBS, CNN, FOX, ESPN, etc.). Television personalities and nationally syndicated radio announcers often have very clear vocal delivery. They don't drop word endings, they have naturally animated vocal patterns, and you rarely hear fillers and vocalized pauses such as "um," "uh," "and, uh," or "like."

1. Now, listen to your instructors and classmates. How many have "easy-to-listen-to" voices? What is the big difference between those who use their voices effectively and those who do not?
2. What effect do fillers such as those identified above have on you?
3. What other vocal characteristics distract you?
4. What vocal characteristics help you stay "tuned in" to the speaker?

when your speech has too many vocal fillers. The second point refers to the use of appropriate language. Adjust your language to suit the formal presentation. Just as you would not speak to your grandmother or a religious leader in the same way you speak with a group of your friends, you need to acknowledge the formality of the speaking situation by using appropriate language. Do not use slang terms or profanity, and do not use language and sentence structure that reduce your credibility. If you're not sure about what is and is not appropriate, check with your instructor.

**Vocal Variety.**   The combination of rate, force, and pitch variations that add to a speaker's overall vocal quality is called **vocal variety.** Such variety gives feeling to your delivery and adds emphasis to what you say. Your voice allows listeners to perceive subtle differences in the intent of your messages by altering rate, force, and pitch, promoting a genuine understanding between you and your audience.

**Rate** is the speed at which a speaker speaks—usually between 120 and 150 words per minute. Speaking at the appropriate rate requires self-awareness. A rate that is too fast, is too slow, or never changes can detract from the impact of your message. Sometimes when we're nervous, our speaking rate increases so much that we are practically unintelligible to our listeners. We must learn to control this rapid rate by breathing deeply before we begin speaking and by purposely using pauses to help us slow down and concentrate on the message.

Pauses are important. A pause can be an effective means of gaining attention, adding emphasis to an important point, and enabling listeners to follow shifts in ideas. Pauses punctuate and emphasize thoughts. Beginning speakers need to realize the important contribution of both rate and pauses to the overall effect of their presentations. Listen carefully to accomplished speakers. Notice how an effective

■ **vocal variety** Variations in rate, force, and pitch.

■ **rate** Speed at which a speaker speaks, normally between 120 and 150 words per minute.

## Use of Pauses

Read the following (aloud) without a pause.

*Adam said that he had a fear of public speaking and he said getting up in front of people is much more frightening than the thought of death or even taxes and he hoped he would be able to avoid giving speeches even though he had to take an oral communication class.*

Now read the same sentences and pause appropriately with periods and commas.

*Adam said that he had a fear of public speaking. He said, "Getting up in front of people is much more frightening than the thought of death, or even taxes." And he hoped he would be able to avoid giving speeches, even though he had to take an oral communication class.*

1. What difference do the pauses make in what you hear?
2. How did the use of verbal punctuation—your pauses—help to convey the meaning?

speaker varies rate and uses pauses to set off ideas, to prepare for the next point, and to provide silent emphasis for ideas. Again, accomplished speakers tend to do this within the context of a conversational style.

**Force** is the intensity and volume of the voice. You must choose a volume level that is comfortable for your audience. However, you can use force to communicate your ideas with confidence and vigor, to emphasize an important point, and to regain lagging interest. By learning how to use force, you can greatly increase your effectiveness as a speaker.

**Pitch** refers to how low or high the voice is on a tonal scale. Variety in pitch can eliminate monotony and add emphasis to key words. Variety in pitch contributes to greater conversationality and, thus, makes it easy for the listener to maintain interest in and attention to the speaker and message.

Obviously, any change in rate, force, or pitch makes a word, phrase, or sentence stand out. The greater the amount of change or the more sudden the change is, the more emphatic the word or statement will be. You can use such contrasts to make selected ideas seem more important than the material delivered without such variations.

## ▬▬ Physical Aspects

In Chapter 5, we discussed nonverbal communication in depth. You are encouraged to review that chapter, because much of the information about nonverbal communication will aid you in your speaking performances. Among the physical factors that can affect delivery are personal appearance, body movement, gestures, facial expressions, and eye contact. Each of these must be well coordinated and relevant to the purpose of your speech.

**Personal Appearance.** Personal appearance—what a speaker looks like and the way a speaker dresses, grooms, and presents himself or herself to others—is an extremely important consideration. Typical "student attire" is not always acceptable. As a general rule, you should use common sense in dressing for the occasion. For example, large, dangly earrings, "busy" printed T-shirts, and caps may distract your audience from what you are saying (and have a negative effect on the people evaluating your presentation). Most instructors frown on speakers wearing caps for a variety of other reasons as well: It is in questionable taste, and caps hide your facial expressions. First impressions are based mainly on appearance. Your audience may form quick and hard-to-change opinions about your attitude toward them and yourself. In this way, appearance can affect your credibility.

Research in nonverbal and relational communication suggests that personal appearance plays a role in communication. Appearance can have an impact on a

■ **force** The intensity and volume level of the voice.

■ **pitch** How low or high the voice is on a tonal scale.

speaker's self-image and thus affect how the speaker communicates with others.[13] Dress for a special occasion when you present your speech. When you look good, you feel good, and that positively affects your performance.

**Body Movement.** Body movement is closely related to personal appearance. It includes posture, which should be relaxed and natural; avoid slouching. Because an audience's attention instinctively follows moving objects, your motions should be easy and purposeful. The use of movement—stepping to the side, forward, or backward—can hold attention and help to communicate ideas. Movement can also serve as a nonverbal transition between points. Purposeful movement, along with posture, can indicate confidence and convey a positive self-image. Too much movement, or unmotivated, nervous movement, however, can distract your audience, make them think you are not poised and confident, and detract from your credibility.

**Gestures.** You can use **gestures**—movements of the head, arms, and hands—to help illustrate, emphasize, or clarify a point. Gestures should be spontaneous, not forced. For example, when you are talking to acquaintances about something you have strong feelings about, your gestures come naturally. If you are sad, angry, or happy, you automatically make gestures that express your emotions. To obtain equally natural gestures when giving a speech, you need to be equally involved in what you are saying. If you concentrate on getting your message across rather than on your gestures, you will find yourself moving more freely and naturally.

When you are first learning how to give a speech, using gestures might seem a bit uncomfortable, but not using gestures might also seem uncomfortable. To overcome this problem, practice the use of gestures in front of others who are willing to offer positive suggestions to help you improve. Be assured that as you give more and more speeches, you will find that gesturing becomes more natural and easier to do. Soon, without even thinking, you'll be using strong and smooth-flowing gestures that help to hold your audience's attention and add meaning to your message.

**Facial Expressions.** As defined in Chapter 5, facial expressions are configurations of the face that can reflect, augment, contradict, or be unrelated to a speaker's vocal delivery. They account for much of the emotional impact of a speaker's message. Your face is a very expressive part of your body. Facial expressions quickly and accurately tell your audience a lot about you. For example, whether you are serious, happy, worried, or angry, the audience will be able to "read" your face. Because your audience will infer a

---

## MAKING CONNECTIONS
### for Success

### Nonverbal Behavior and Effective Presentation of Information

Physical and vocal factors can play an important role in the effect of your presentation on your listeners. Your messages and your delivery can be enhanced or damaged by the way you present ideas. In an effort to analyze the behaviors of others in presenting information, take the next few days to observe professors, classmates, and others as they present information. Consider the messages (words, ideas) and the manner of presentation (physical and vocal factors of delivery). Take notes about the presenter and the presentation, and then answer these questions:

1. How did the speakers use their voices to communicate ideas?
2. How did speakers vary their rates? What was the effect?
3. How were pauses used? When? To what effect?
4. What positive factors of physical and vocal delivery did you observe? What effect did these positive aspects have on you, the listener?
5. What negative factors of physical and vocal delivery did you observe? What effect did these negatives have on you as the listener?
6. What will you remember about presentations from this activity?

---

■ **gesture** A movement of the head, arms, or hands that helps to illustrate, emphasize, or clarify an idea.

## MAKING Technology CONNECTIONS

### Technology and Speech Delivery

Technology has influenced every aspect of our lives, including the way teachers teach, students learn, and businesspeople make presentations. One of our communication colleagues, Dr. Lynn Disbrow of Sinclair Community College in Ohio, suggests that technology forces us all to be learners and that we all have to learn differently because of technology. How has technology affected the way speakers deliver their speeches? Let's Ask Jeeves.

1. Access your web browser.
2. Key in www.ask.com.
3. When you get Jeeves, phrase a question such as "How has technology affected speech delivery?"
4. Quickly look through the first few responses. Do they look like helpful answers? If so, read the responses. If not, ask another, similar question.
5. Read and compare the first ten new responses.
6. Answer the question, "How has technology affected speech delivery?"

great deal from your facial expression, it is important to look warm and friendly. Such an expression will inform your listeners that you are interested in them and in what you are saying. Of course, your topic, your purpose, the situation, and your audience will all determine exactly what facial expressions are appropriate as you progress through your speech.

**Eye Contact.** The extent to which a speaker looks *directly* at audience members, making **eye contact,** is associated with facial expression. Facial expressions indicate a speaker's feelings about the message, while eye contact seems more related to a speaker's feelings about the listeners. Eye contact is the most important physical aspect of delivery, as it indicates interest and concern for others and implies self-confidence. Most speech communication teachers recommend that you look at your audience while you are speaking, not over their heads or at a spot on the wall.

Looking at members of the audience establishes a communicative bond between your listeners and you. Failure to make eye contact is the quickest way to lose listeners. Speakers who ignore their audiences are often perceived as tentative, ill at ease, insincere, or dishonest.

Eye contact with your audience should be pleasant and personal. Give your listeners the feeling that you are talking to them as individuals in a casual conversation. When speaking to a small audience (five to thirty people), try to look at each individual for a few seconds at a time. To avoid looking shifty, move your eyes gradually and smoothly from one person to another. For larger groups, it is best to scan the audience and occasionally talk to a specific member or members. Do not look over people's heads, and avoid staring, which can give the impression that you're angry or hostile. Try not to make your listeners uncomfortable. We have students serve as peer listeners and evaluate speakers. They often comment on failure to establish eye contact and note when a speaker looks at a few and not the entire audience. If you look at only one or two people, others will feel left out, and those whom you "stared at" will feel uncomfortable.

Your eyes should convey that you are confident, sincere, and speaking with conviction. The message your audience should get from your eye contact is that you care about them and about what you are saying. At first, establishing eye contact with an audience may make you uncomfortable, but as you gain experience, you will begin to feel more at ease. You will soon find that making eye contact puts you in control of the situation and helps you to answer these questions: Can they hear me? Do they understand? Are they listening?

■ **eye contact** The extent to which a speaker looks directly at audience members.

Working to strengthen your use of positive vocal and physical behaviors and to reduce negative ones will greatly improve your delivery of a speech. Table 10.3 lists several behaviors that can detract from a speech's effectiveness. Observing yourself in front of a mirror or asking a supportive friend for feedback during a practice session will help you avoid these problems.

■ **TABLE 10.3** Distracting Speaker Behaviors

| *General Delivery* | *Eyes* | *Body* |
|---|---|---|
| Rapid speech | Rolling eyes | Tense, rigid |
| Speaking too slowly | Looking at the floor or ceiling | Sloppy posture |
| Sighing | | Swaying |
| Nervous laughter or smiles | Staring | Dancing |
| Choppiness | Lack of sustained eye contact | Hunched shoulders |
| Awkward pauses | | Leaning on lectern |
| *Face* | *Voice* | *Feet* |
| Scowls | Monotone | Shuffling |
| Listless look | Singsong patterns | Weight shifts |
| *Hands* | Nasal voice | Crossing legs |
| Waving | Mumbling | Leg/foot shakes |
| Playing with hair or object (such as notecards or a pen) | Too soft | |
| Hands in pocket | Too loud | |

# ■ Presentational Aids

Speeches and presentations can often be strengthened by the addition of materials to help audience members focus on and remember the topic. **Presentational aids,** also referred to as visual aids or audiovisual aids, are materials and equipment, such as diagrams, models, real objects, photographs, tables, charts, graphs, and computer-generated materials, that speakers may use to enhance the content of the speech as well as the delivery. Students often think that the only time they will be required to use presentational aids is in classroom speech assignments. In reality, speeches using visual materials are presented frequently, and many speeches depend on them. Imagine an architect explaining the floor plans for a new high-rise office building without a drawing, model, or photograph; a company executive explaining this year's annual profits and losses compared to last year's without a chart or graph; a coach explaining a play without a diagram; a teacher telling the class where Mauritius is located without a map or globe; or a salesperson selling a product without showing it.

Our world has become extremely information oriented. Because people are constantly bombarded with information from a variety of sources, it is important to present information in a way that captures the interest and attention of listeners. This is difficult when the audience is already experiencing information overload. Good aids can help.

Such presentational aids offer many advantages. If "a picture is worth a thousand words," then presentational aids are an excellent way to strengthen and reinforce the development and proof of a point. Such aids are a special form of supporting and clarifying materials, because they combine both verbal and visual

■ **presentational aids** Materials and equipment, such as diagrams, models, real objects, photographs, tables, charts, and graphs, that speakers may use to enhance the speech's content as well as their delivery.

modes of presentation. When carefully designed and used, presentational aids can help a speaker do the following:

Save time

Gain attention and hold interest

Clarify and support main points

Reinforce or emphasize main points

Improve retention of information

Research has shown that audiences remember information longer when it is accompanied by visual or presentational aids.[14] In many of today's businesses, employees are required to make presentations and to use the computer to enhance their presentations. Some company managers believe that unless the presenter uses the computer for audio, visual, or audiovisual aids, the speaker is not really performing well. Although classroom teachers do not always require the use of computer-generated or computer-assisted presentational materials, it is important to realize that they are common in the workplace. More and more, educators are required to make computer-aided presentations. Even medical doctors and dentists are creating multimedia presentational aids to help explain procedures, illnesses, and treatments to their patients. We'll next look at types of presentational aids and the methods of presenting them in speeches.

## ■■ Choosing and Using Presentational Aids

When planning to use presentational aids, keep the following guidelines in mind:

1. *Presentational aids should serve a need.* They should never be used just for the sake of using them. In some cases, visual aids are not appropriate, but in others, they can get a point across better than words alone. For example, it is easier to show an audience how to create PowerPoint slides than it is to tell them. Furthermore, it is easier to tell *and* to show them.

2. *Presentational aids should be planned and adapted to the audience and the situation.* For example, the size of the visual aid and the distance between you and your audience should be considered. The visual material should be kept simple and free from too much detail.

3. *Presentational aids should not dominate or take over a speaker's job.* They should supplement, but never replace, the speaker. Do not rely too heavily on visual aids; instead, use them to help elaborate or explain a point or idea or to create interest. In a speech, visual aids always require explanation by the speaker in order to make them meaningful.

4. *Presentational aids should look as professionally prepared as possible.* Accurate and neat materials will create a positive impression on the audience and reflect favorably on the competence of the speaker. Aids should be free from factual and spelling errors. They should also be bright, attractive, and easy to read from any spot in the audience. Audience members ought to be able to see, read, and understand the presentational aid once the speaker has carefully explained it.

5. *Presentational aids should be practical—easy to prepare, use, and transport.* Aids should not interfere with the speaker and presentation, and they should not call undue attention to themselves.

6. *Presentational aids that are not original or that contain information that is not yours require documentation.* Cite your source either directly on the aid where your audience can see it or in the context of your speech.

7. *Visuals should contain only one idea—one graph per poster, and so on.* Remember that presentational aids you provide are meant to clarify and strengthen your message. You want to limit yourself to one idea per poster, slide, chart, graph, or computer-ated screen so that your listeners can focus on that one idea at the time you are talking about that point or concept. Too much information distracts your listeners.

Using aids during a presentation requires planning and coordination. They should not distract the audience or interrupt the flow of the speech. See the Guidelines feature in the following section for ideas on using these aids.

## Kinds of Presentational Aids

There are many different kinds of visual aids. Those most frequently used include posters, real objects, models, photographs, diagrams, tables, and graphs. A special discussion of computer-generated graphics, scanned pictures, digitized pictures, and digitized video clips is included in a later section.

**Real Objects.**   A real object is any article related to the speech topic that a speaker displays or demonstrates, such as a musical instrument, piece of sporting equipment, or kind of food. Using a real object can make your topic more immediate and interesting, but it can also create problems if the object is too large, too small, or too impractical to show. Pets, for example, are often unpredictable and can be distracting before, during, and after a speech.

**Models.**   When displaying the actual article is not practical because of size or cost, a model should be considered. A model—or representation of a real object—allows a speaker to enlarge or shrink an object to a convenient size for display. It would be

A large-scale model, here a model sea horse, allows the speaker to clearly point the salient features to the audience.

impractical to show the actual circuitry of a computer microchip, which is no larger than a pinhead, or the inside of an actual space shuttle, which is enormous (not to mention inaccessible). Models are appropriate in such circumstances.

Models can also be life-size. Cardiopulmonary resuscitation (CPR) is a popular and important subject. To demonstrate this procedure, speakers often use life-size dummies of humans.

**Photographs and Prints.** When models are neither available nor practical, a photograph may be used. A photograph is an excellent device for explaining details and surroundings. One student, speaking on artistic style, brought prints of several paintings to illustrate their differences. A student who spoke on the construction of the Egyptian pyramids showed photos that she had taken on a vacation trip. She realized that the original photos were too small, so she had them enlarged for effective use in the classroom. The typical photograph is usually too small to be seen clearly unless the speaker moves through the audience or passes it around or scans it into a computer presentation. In both instances, the advantage of using photos is somewhat diminished because the audience tends to pay more attention to the pictures than to what is being said.

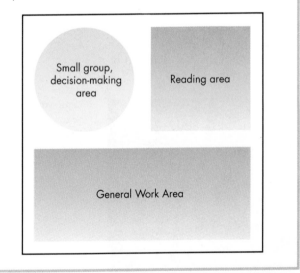

■ **FIGURE 10.1** Example of a Simple Line Drawing

Line drawings do not need to be elaborate or complex. In fact, line drawings, sketches, and diagrams can be rather simple.

**Drawings, Sketches, and Diagrams.** When photographs or prints are unavailable, are too small, or lack adequate detail, a drawing, sketch, or diagram may be used. Don't worry if you're not artistic, because most drawings used in classroom speeches are relatively simple. For example, Figure 10.1 is a line drawing used to describe a laboratory design. The diagram simply shows the division of the room for various functions and makes a professor's explanation of a seating arrangement much easier for students to comprehend.

Similarly, a speaker might use an architect's blueprint, a chart illustrating a company's organizational structure, a sketch of the basic positions of water-skiing, or a map of various segments of land. Virtually anything can be diagrammed or sketched.

**Tables and Graphs.** Tables and graphs are used mainly to display statistics. A table is an orderly arrangement of data in columns to highlight similarities and differences, as shown in Figure 10.2.

Tables conveniently display large amounts of data in a relatively small space, but remember that a complex or lengthy (and perhaps boring) table will require an equally complex and lengthy explanation. As with any visual aid you decide to use, a table must be concise, simple, and clear so that the important information is easy to spot. Complex data are often better illustrated by a graph.

Graphs help to make statistical data vivid and illustrate relationships in ways that are easy for the audience to grasp. Line graphs, as illustrated in Figure 10.3,

■ **FIGURE 10.2**  Example of Data Presented as a Table

Tables display large amounts of data in a relatively small space. The more complex the data, the more explanation required to make the table meaningful to your listeners.

### Popular Pharmaceuticals, Uses, Costs, and Effects

| DRUG | USES | COST | EFFECTS |
|---|---|---|---|
| Tylenol™<br>Over-the counter | Aches, Pains | $12.95 per 200 tabs | General pain relief; some side effects (minor) |
| Vioxx™<br>Prescription only | Arthritis, Pain | $192.00 per 50 tabs, 25 mg | Acute pains, osteoarthritis; Side effects may be serious—heart irregularities |
| Celebrex™<br>Prescription only | Joint pain | $195.00 per 50 tabs, 100 mg | Acute pain relief, Some side effects, Some major side effects |

Internet sites consulted for current prices.

*Annotations (right margin):*

Make sure the table title actually reflects content of the table.

Column heads should be simple, brief, and accurately identify the information in the table body.

Items in each column of the table should be parallel in structure.

If the table does not reflect your own data, be sure to give a complete source.

---

■ **FIGURE 10.3**  Example of Data Presented as a Line Graph

Line graphs are particularly helpful in clarifying comparative data over time. Cancer Survival Rates Keep Climbing!

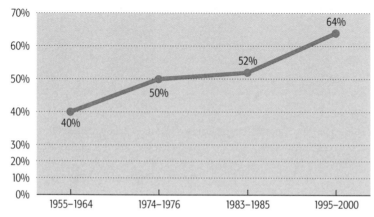

**Cancer Survival Rates Keep Climbing!**

(Line graph with y-axis from 0% to 70% and x-axis years: 1955–1964 at 40%, 1974–1976 at 50%, 1983–1985 at 52%, 1995–2000 at 64%.)

Data from the American Cancer Society Notes to Neighbors Campaign, 2006.

are particularly helpful for clarifying comparative data over time. Such graphs can help trace trends and show increases and decreases over a span of days, months, or years. Note in Figure 10.3 that cancer survival rates have increased from 40 percent in the decade between 1955 to 1964 to 50 percent just ten years later in a two-year time frame from 1974 to 1976. Then, cancer survivor rates increased another two percentage points to 52 percent between 1983 and 1985, and showed an even larger increase to a 64 percent survival rate in the five-year period from 1995 to 2000.

Bar graphs are another simple way to show comparisons. Note how much easier it is to compare the data depicted in the bar graph in Figure 10.4 than the data arranged in table form in Figure 10.2. Whenever possible, your visual aids should present only one or two basic relationships, so that your audience can quickly grasp your point.

Pie graphs are used to illustrate proportional divisions of a whole set of data. Each wedge of the pie represents a percentage of the whole. Pie graphs are often used to show distribution patterns and to illustrate national, state, or local budgets. Note in Figure 10.5 that the pie graph starts with a radius drawn vertically from the center to the twelve o'clock position. Each segment is then drawn in clockwise, beginning with the largest and continuing down to the smallest.

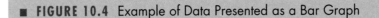

■ **FIGURE 10.4** Example of Data Presented as a Bar Graph

Bar graphs present comparative data much more clearly and vividly than does, for example, a table.

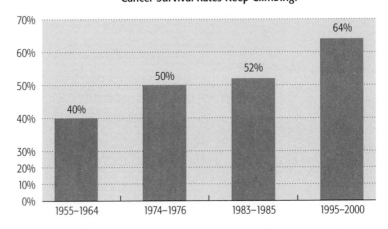

Data from the American Cancer Society Notes to Neighbors Campaign, 2006.

■ **FIGURE 10.5** Example of Data Presented as a Pie Graph

A pie graph illustrates proportions of a whole set of data. Each wedge represents a percentage of the whole.

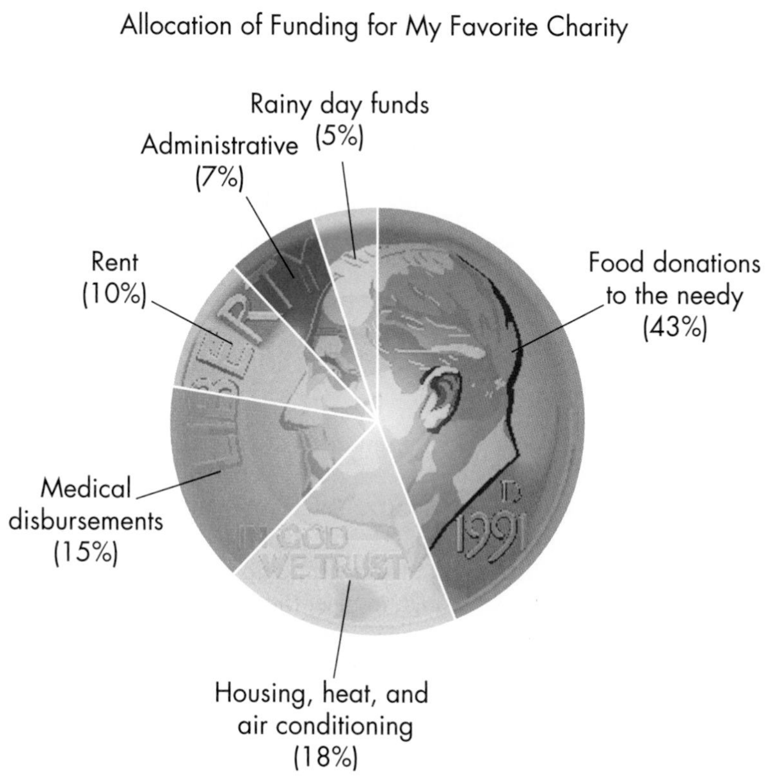

Allocation of Funding for My Favorite Charity

## Using Presentational Aids

1. Display visual materials only while you are using them. Do not distract your audience by showing your aids too early or by leaving them on display after you've finished talking about them. Even with a PowerPoint presentation, you can create a black, blank, or white screen in order not to distract your listeners.
2. Keep your presentational aids on display long enough to give everyone ample opportunity to absorb the information. Find the happy medium between "too long" and "not long enough."
3. Ensure that everyone can see your aids by making them neat, simple, large, bright, and readable. If you're using computer-generated text, the same guidelines apply. Depending on the size of the room, however, your font size should rarely be less than 36 points. For larger rooms, a 48-point or a 60-point font is desirable. The same thing applies to the television screen if you're in a distance learning classroom. Size, background, and color of text all become critical issues. For televised presentations, a blue background with either a white or yellow text

color is preferable. The opposite is true for yellow or white on overhead transparencies and many posters, charts, or graphs. Light colors fade and are virtually invisible on acetate and paper products. Red and black text work better for noncomputer presentational aids and often work better for computerized aids. Practice in the room with the equipment you'll use, well ahead of time.

4. Do not talk to your displayed objects or to the chalkboard. Discuss the content while maintaining eye contact with your audience.

5. Do not stand in front of your presentational aids. Determine where you will place or show your aids, and use a pointer or a laser to avoid blocking your audience's view.

6. Practice using your presentational aids until you feel comfortable with them. It becomes quite obvious to your listeners if you're uncomfortable and unfamiliar with the aids you've selected.

## ■■ Methods of Presentation

The most frequently used methods of presentation are posters, projected visuals, and handouts. Some instructors will allow you to use the chalkboard or whiteboard, others will not. These are readily available in most classrooms, but not always in other places. Both professors and listeners may believe that you didn't take the time to prepare a " real" visual if you hurriedly put something up on the board. They may also reason that it isn't "professional" enough to meet the criteria for effective visuals.

**Posters.**    Posters are a commonly used method of presenting information visually. The greatest advantage of posters is that they can be prepared in advance, which makes the speaker seem more efficient and professional. Here are three specific suggestions for using posters:

1. If an easel is not available, check to see whether there are clips on the board for hanging posters or whether you will need to use masking tape. If you must use masking tape, make large loops of tape and place them on the back of the poster in advance. Then, when you are ready to display the poster, merely place it on the board, pressing firmly on the tape loops to secure it. If you have more than one poster, you can place several of them on the board at once, or you can display each individually as you need it.

2. Make sure the poster is made of firm cardboard so that it will support itself if you have to stand it on a chalk tray or a table.

3. Posters should be displayed only when they are referred to in the speech. The rest of the time they should be turned over or covered so they don't distract the audience.

**Projected Visuals.**    The most common projected materials are slides, movies, overhead transparencies, and videotapes. The projection of such visuals requires planning and familiarity with the mechanical equipment. Each form has advantages and disadvantages, so knowing what each can and cannot do is vital. For example, showing slides and movies requires a darkened room, and the projectors may be noisy. Yet both enable you to show places and things that you could not show any other way. Films and videos add motion, color, and sound. But they can be costly and often tend to dominate a presentation by replacing the speaker for a period of time.

The most popular projected visual is the overhead transparency. These materials can be prepared in advance or created during a presentation, and whether prepared by the speaker or a professional, they are relatively inexpensive. In addition, overhead projectors are easy to use and do not require a darkened room.

When using a projector, consider the following:

1. Make sure the projector is focused correctly so that everyone in the room can read what is on the transparency.

2. Cover information on the transparency or surface until it is needed.

3. Use a pointer (pencil or pen) to direct the audience's attention to what is being discussed.

4. Practice using the overhead. Check it beforehand to make sure it is working correctly.

Mechanical devices, because of their potential for breakdown, require a backup method. It is a good idea to carry a spare bulb in case one burns out and to bring copies of visual aids in handout form.

**Handouts.**   Handouts can be a useful means of presenting information to your audience. If you are presenting a speech on organ donation, for example, you may want to hand out a copy of the form many states ask potential donors to carry. Or if your speech mentions helpful persons or related organizations, a handout may list these, together with addresses or websites, so that audience members may obtain additional information. Handouts are particularly helpful if you are unable to use any other method. Among their advantages are that they can be prepared in advance and that each audience member gets a personal copy. Their main disadvantage is that they can become a distraction. Passing them out can interrupt the flow of your presentation, and audience members may pay more attention to the handouts than to the speech itself. As a result, you should use handouts only when you have no other alternatives or when you have a creative reason for doing so. In addition, you should wait until the end of the presentation to use them, if possible.

## ■■ Computer-Generated Presentational Aids

Computer-generated materials have become *the* presentational tool for many. Many colleges, universities, and businesses require the use of computer-generated materials in a variety of presentations. There are problems with their use, as well. Unless presenters learn to use such tools effectively, the speaker is doing more harm than good.

Several excellent presentational software programs are available in college and university computer laboratories. Among the most popular is Microsoft's PowerPoint, which allows the presenter to select or create backgrounds, formats, layouts, colors, and tools to make a professional presentation (see Figure 10.6). Images and text can be animated to fade, dissolve, or move in from the top, the bottom, or either side of the slide. The presenter can scan in pictures, text, or other visuals (such as a brochure, a poster, a photograph), use a digital still camera, use a digital movie camera, use digitized clips from movies or other videos, and so on. The possibilities are almost endless. The kinds of materials we can create using the computer are limited only by the time, money, resources, and creativity at our disposal. The guidelines for use of other audiovisual aids apply to use of computer presentational materials, as well. There are, however, some additional suggestions you should consider if you are planning to use the computer to enhance your presentations. These are listed in the accompanying Guidelines feature.

■ **FIGURE 10.6** Example of a Computer-Generated Visual Aid

Clip art from a presentational software program such as PowerPoint can enhance your presentations.

Courses requiring
Computer-Generated
Materials in Presentations

| ARTS & HUMANITIES | NATURAL SCIENCES | SOCIAL SCIENCES | EDUCATION | BUSINESS |
|---|---|---|---|---|
| 15 | 17 | 19 | 30 | 30 |

**GUIDELINES** | **Using Computer-Generated Aids**

1. Don't overdo it! Just as you can have too many points in a speech and too many materials for traditional visual aids, you can present too much material on the computer. As a general rule, use a visual to support only 25 percent of your presentation. Select the materials carefully. Too many pictures, graphs, words, images, and animations can result in overload.

2. Make sure that the font size you use in your presentation is appropriate. Use nothing less than a 40-point font for a regular classroom. In a large lecture hall, use 60 points for headings and topics, and no less than 48 points for subpoints, quotations, and explanations.

3. Don't put too much on any given screen. It's easy to overdo it. If you put too many words or images on the "slides," people will not listen to what you have to say.

4. Remember that the computer visual is like any other visual: It is there to enhance the presentation, not to take the place of the speaker's words and ideas.

5. Practice using your computer visuals in the room in which you will present the speech, if possible, because what you see on the screen of your monitor and what people see on the screen in the presentation room may not be the same. Colors do not always enhance the material as well as they appear to on the small monitor screen. Sometimes the lighting can make a tremendous difference, and if you cannot dim the lights, you may want to change the background so that the materials are visible, clear, and easy to read anywhere in the audience. Check to see whether lighting and reflections will cause problems and whether there are decreased sight lines at certain angles in the room. Also, practice to make sure you do not lose eye contact with your audience while presenting these aids. Using the computer should not distract you from staying in touch with your audience.

# ▬ Thinking about PowerPoint

PowerPoint can be either an effective tool or something your intended listeners just tune out! We've all seen some really good uses of PowerPoint and some really bad uses. What's the difference? A good PowerPoint presentation emphasizes content, not the technology. An effective speaker knows that all presentational aids are supposed to *enhance* the presentation, not *become* (or replace) the presentation. So, it's important to make the right choices. The use of color, the type and size of the font, and the use of graphics and pictures are all important factors in effective presentations.

**Color.** Any psychology textbook or class will tell you that color is important and that certain colors are associated with certain things. If you want your PowerPoint presentations to connect with your audience and make your content memorable, you'll choose background colors and designs that are clear, clean, and not too busy. For the classroom, we encourage students to use blue or green backgrounds with little or no movement or sound. Blues and greens are calming, but also readable. Keep the material uncluttered. Use contrasting colors. Text colors should be black or white, and can sometimes be yellow in order to connect with the viewers. Red text may dance and waver and is very hard to read. Yellow is an attention-getting color, but too much can make words and images dance on the screen.

**Type and Size of Font.** Times New Roman, Times, and Courier are good fonts for your PowerPoint presentations. They are clean and easy to read. Too many curves and extras distract and are also hard to read. If you're in a typical classroom that seats twenty-five to forty people, the font size for headings should be about 44 points, and the text itself should be at least 36 points. If you're presenting in a large lecture hall, the font size increases as the size of the audience increases. Since you want everyone to see and read your presentation, keep the font size big enough that everyone in the room can read it easily. Be able to blank the screen when you don't need the image or when there's nothing for the audience to view. You can press the B key on the keyboard and the image is replaced with a black image. Press the B key again and the image is restored. In some classrooms, you can draw on the screen with your fingers, or you can use the Ctrl-P key combination to display a pen on the screen. You can then use the mouse to draw on the slide. Erase by pressing the E key, and get rid of the pen and drawing function by pressing the A key or the Ctrl-L key combination.

**Use of Graphics and Pictures.** Graphics and pictures help create and maintain interest. They should be used sparingly, however, in order to keep your listeners connected to your topic. A good rule of thumb is no more than twenty-five percent of your slides should have pictures or graphics on them. If you don't know how to import pictures or graphics, use the help function of your computer's program, or check with the technology department or division of your college. Many schools offer free PowerPoint, Word, Excel, and other workshops for students. If you don't feel comfortable using the computer, one of these free workshops would be most beneficial.

The best way to learn to use computer programs effectively is to take a class and then "play" with the program and materials. With time, you'll feel much more comfortable creating and using programs such as PowerPoint to enhance your presentations.

# ▬ Developing Presentational Aids

Today, many computer programs and technologies can help you develop presentational aids. If your university or college has a media center, and most do, check with the center or your instructor to learn about the most modern and easiest methods available for developing visuals. Certain programs and techniques will allow you to make graphics, charts, custom-made diagrams, and many other types of visual aids. Making professional-looking visual aids, whether computer-generated or traditional, is often quite simple and may require only that you become familiar with your school's offerings. Remember, too, that not every speech requires a high-tech application. In fact, many experts believe that we've gone too far in our use of graphics and images. Fewer images of higher quality, with more information, are preferable.

# ◼ Your Delivery

The best way to ensure effective delivery is to practice, practice, practice. Practice early and often until you feel comfortable with your speech content. Exactly how much practice you will need depends on a number of considerations, including how much experience you have had speaking before audiences, how familiar you are with your subject, and how long your speech is. There is no magic amount of time that will make your delivery perfect.

If your speech is not to be memorized, make sure to use slightly different wording in each run-through. When you memorize a speech, it is possible to master the words without mastering the content. Your goal should be to learn your speech, which will mean that you have mastered its ideas.

In practicing your delivery, it is important to start with small segments. For example, practice the introduction, then one main point at a time, and then the conclusion. After you have rehearsed each small segment several times in isolation, practice the entire speech until you have mastered the content and the ideas flow smoothly.

If possible, practice in the same room in which you will speak or under similar conditions. This helps you see how things look from the front of the class and to plan where you should place your visual aids. Your last practice session should leave you with a sense of confidence and a desire to present your speech.

Finally, concentrate on what you are saying and to whom you are saying it. Above all, be yourself.

# ◼ Summary

Competent communicators are prepared, knowledgeable, confident speakers who are ethical. Ethical speakers always provide oral footnotes within the speech, and they provide fair and accurate information.

Speakers who suffer from too much anxiety will have trouble giving speeches and keeping the audience's attention. The best way to overcome your anxiety is to understand it, control it, and be so well prepared that you are ready to share your ideas and know that you will do well. Students from other cultures and cocultures have added anxiety because of language concerns. If you are seriously anxious about communicating with others, you might have communication apprehension that will take special strategies to help you manage your fears.

Most communication professors say that an extemporaneous delivery is best. This means that you are fully prepared but present your speech in a conversational manner, using note cards to help you stay organized and on track.

Vocal and physical delivery should enhance your message. Although a speech is a formal presentation, you should not be rigid or mechanical, either vocally or physically. Instead, you should look and sound as if you really want to share your ideas with your listeners and you care about what they think. Effective speakers are listener oriented. They think about the content and the delivery well in advance and practice many times so that they can maintain eye contact with their listeners.

Presentational aids can help to make your content memorable. You can choose actual objects or some kind of medium such as posters or drawings. Because many employers require use of PowerPoint or other computer-generated presentations, it is good to incorporate technology whenever it helps you make your points better.

## ■ Discussion Starters

**1.** Why should we consider ethical behavior when we create and deliver speeches?

**2.** How does preparation help speakers?

**3.** Why do you think people have anxieties about giving speeches?

**4.** How can listeners help speakers to overcome their nervousness?

**5.** Why is vocal variety important?

**6.** What factors of physical delivery have made an impact on you as an audience member?

**7.** Think about an effective presentation. What vocal factors helped make that presentation effective?

**8.** Why do communication instructors recommend or require extemporaneous delivery?

**9.** Why should speakers be listener oriented?

**10.** What do presentational aids do for the audience?

**11.** When and how should presentational aids be used?

## ■ Notes

1. D. Zarefsky, *Public Speaking Strategies for Success,* 4th ed. (Boston: Allyn and Bacon, 2005), 29.

2. R. L. Johannesen, *Ethics in Human Communication* (Prospects Heights, IL: Waveland Press, 2002).

3. Zarefsky, *Public Speaking Strategies,* p. 29.

4. "Anxiety," *World Book Encyclopedia/Dictionary,* Mac OS X Edition, Version 6.0.2 multimedia edition, 2001.

5. Many sources identify "glossophobia" or "fear of public speaking" as one of our greatest fears. *The New Book of Lists,* 5th ed., (2006), by David Wallechinsky, Amy Wallace, Ira Basen, and Jane Farrow says that seventy-five percent of Americans identify "fear of public speaking" ahead of fear of spiders, snakes, and death. A Google search for "fear of public speaking" netted 43,700,000 responses on July 15, 2006. One site, www.soyouwanna.com, promises effective ways to manage your fears and give "a good speech."

6. J. C. McCroskey, "The Communication Apprehension Perspective," in *Avoiding Communication: Shyness, Reticence, and Communication Apprehension,* eds. J. A. Daly and J. C. McCroskey (Beverly Hills, CA: Sage, 1984), 13.

7. E. C. Buehler and W. Linkugel, *Speech: A First Course* (New York: HarperCollins, 1962).

8. X. Liao, "Effective Communication in Multicultural Classrooms: An Exploratory Study," unpublished Master of Arts thesis, University of Northern Iowa, May 2003.

9. D. W. Stacks and J. D. Stone, "An Examination of the Effect of Basic Speech Courses, Self-Concept, and Self-Disclosure on Communication Apprehension," *Communication Education* 33 (1984): 317–32; and R. S. Littlefield and T. L. Sellnow, "The Use of Self-Disclosure as a Means for Reducing Stage Fright in Beginning Speakers," *Communication Education* 36 (1987): 62–64.

10. J. A. Daly, A. L. Vangelisti, H. L. Neel, and P. D. Cavanaugh, "Pre-Performance Concerns Associated with Public Speaking Anxiety," *Communication Quarterly* 37 (1989): 39–53.

11. K. K. Dwyer, *Conquer Your Speechfright: Learn How to Overcome the Nervousness of Public Speaking* (Belmont, CA: Wadsworth Publishing, 1997). 73–83.

12. J. C. Humes, "Read a Speech Like a Pro," in *Talk Your Way to the Top* (New York: McGraw-Hill, 1980), 125–35; and J. Venlenti, *Speak Up with Confidence: How to Prepare, Learn, and Deliver Effective Speeches* (New York: Morrow, 1982), 23–26.

13. S. Chaiken, "Communicator Physical Attractiveness and Persuasion," *Journal of Personality and Social Psychology* 37 (1979): 1387–97.

14. E. P. Zayas-Baya, "Instructional Media in the Total Language Picture," *International Journal of Instructional Media* 5 (1977–78): 145–50.

# Informative Speaking

"Any piece of knowledge I acquire today has a value at this moment exactly proportioned to my skill to deal with it. Tomorrow, when I know more, I recall that piece of knowledge and use it better."

—MARK VAN DOREN

# This chapter will help you:

- **Understand** the power of information.
- **Choose** an appropriate topic for your informative speeches.
- **Create** a need to hear your information in your listeners.
- **Demonstrate** how to increase your listeners' knowledge of your topic through effective organization, careful use of language, and effective delivery.
- **Deliver** an informative speech that meets your professor's specific criteria.
- **Use** evaluation criteria to assess your own speeches prior to classroom presentation.

## Making everyday connections

One week and counting! Your first formal presentation is getting closer. What else do you need to know about preparing and presenting speeches? Much of our communication in the classroom, in the workplace, and in our various social and civic organizations is in the form of information. We create, share, and listen to information about something with/from our classmates and professor, colleagues, and co-workers. Even when we meet new people, we conduct "interviews" to learn about them. So, information and the search for it are powerful forces in our lives. The informative speech is but one example of how frequently we are called upon to create, share, and listen to information. Think about the role and power of information in your life. ■

### Questions to think about

- How many times a day do you send an informative message?
- How many times a day do you receive information you need to use, either now or, at some time in the future?
- What differences are there in the types of information you receive in the classroom as opposed to other areas of your life?

e've talked about the preparation process for all types of presentations in the last four chapters. It is now time to focus on the informative speech. Is there a reason that the informative speech is among the first formal speeches assigned in this class? Yes. Much of what we do in our lives involves information—someone asks for information and you provide it, or, you ask another for information, and then use what you heard. **Information,** according to the 2002 World Book Dictionary CD-ROM, is "knowledge given or received of some fact or circumstance."[1] WordNet®, 2003, says that information may also be "a message received and understood."[2] Even if this sounds pretty simple, think about telling someone how to build a deck, or telling someone who knows little about computers how to set up an email account (if they are not sitting at the computer with you beside them), or how to connect the electrical wires to a ceiling fan. If you've ever tried to explain something detailed and relatively complex to one who knows little about it, you know that it takes time and careful choice of language as well as demonstration of steps to accomplish your goal.

Teachers inform on a daily basis. So do people in many other jobs. If you lack the skills to carefully explain, both you and your listeners may be frustrated. To help you with this process, we discuss all aspects of the informative speech in this chapter, from choosing a topic to delivering the speech. Informative speaking is one of the most common types of speeches we present in all aspects of our lives. Learning what you need to know and to be able to do in informative speaking will help you in your personal, career, home, and family life. We believe that the informative speech provides the basis for every speaking situation we face; thus if you learn the fundamentals of informative speaking, you will be able to apply those concepts to all other presentations.

## MAKING CONNECTIONS for Success

### Presenting Information

Each of us has a favorite presentational style. Think about all your professors. Each of them, too, has a favored way. Some like to think linearly and lecture presenting things that you can follow and actually outline. Others will tell "stories" or provide personal examples. Some will use basic information on a PowerPoint slide and fill in the rest as they talk. Others will put things on a projector. You may think one style is better because it's easier for you to follow. Effectiveness depends on a number of factors. Observe how your different professors present information. Take notes and be prepared to discuss your observations with the rest of the class:

1. What do you think makes a presenter effective?
2. What specific behaviors help make that person effective?
3. Are there any of those behaviors that might help you be an effective speaker? What are they? Where and how might you use them?
4. What do speakers have to do to get *you* and your classmates to listen?

## ■ Information and Power

Information helps us in all aspects of our lives. In preceding centuries, it was the people who had the information or knowledge who ruled the world. Priests in the Church and members of royalty were the only ones who knew how to read. For them, and for us, information is power. When we need information, what do we do? We turn to those who have it. The greater one's desire to gain important information, the more valuable that information. Thus, people who have information you desire, in a sense, have power over you because they have what you seek.

The ability to communicate information is essential in our society and will play an increasingly important role in the future. Over the years, we have moved from an

■ **information**
Knowledge given or received about some fact or circumstance.

The informative speech is meant to increase knowledge, whereas the purpose of the persuasive speech is to alter attitudes and behavior. Often there is a fine distinction between informative and persuasive speeches because there are elements of persuasion in an informative speech and there is information in a persuasive speech.

economy based on agriculture and heavy industries, such as steel, machinery, and automobile manufacturing, to an economy based on knowledge industries, such as research, health services, banking, training, and communications. During the 1950s, only about 17 percent of our labor force held information-related jobs. This figure

## MAKING Technology CONNECTIONS

### Freedom Forum and Newseum.org

The Freedom Forum, based in Arlington, Virginia, is a nonpartisan, international foundation dedicated to free press, free speech, and free spirit for all people. The foundation focuses on three priorities: the Newseum, the First Amendment, and newsroom diversity. It also provides online resources. Newseum.org features more than four hundred newspaper front pages from around the world. Stories are grouped by subject: Newseum, First Amendment, free speech, podcast, free press, and professional journalism; the top story in each section is featured on the main page.

1. Access Freedom Forum online at www.freedom-forum.org.
2. Click on one of the top stories on the main page and read the whole story.
3. Then, click on the Newseum.org link and check one or two newspapers in your hometown or home geographical area. Are the top stories you read also on the front page of your "local" newspaper?
4. Be prepared to share what you read with others and determine what they learned. Compare similarities and differences.

has now increased to more than 75 percent. This demand puts even more emphasis on workers' needs for greater skills in producing, storing, and delivering information. Much of the information we send and receive is written, but most is spoken. For example, teachers, trainers, consultants, media specialists, salespeople, technicians, mechanics, artists, doctors, nurses, lawyers, elected officials, police officers, and managers all depend on oral communication to succeed in their work.

# ■ Distinctions between Informative and Persuasive Speaking

The general goal of informative speakers is to increase their listeners' knowledge. There is a fine distinction between informing and persuading. The informative speech is meant to increase knowledge, whereas the persuasive speech is meant to alter attitudes and behavior. Information can be presented without any attempt at persuasion, but persuasion cannot be accomplished without attempting to inform.

Two examples will illustrate the difference between information and persuasion. You go into an electronics store to look at a computer. The salesperson wants to sell one, so she will do her best to persuade you to buy a computer. She will share all kinds of information about the computer: its speed, its memory, its flexibility, the ease of maintenance, the modem, the firewall, an explanation of all features, the warranty, and the help available to you. She will provide you with ample information and then make comparisons with other computers or, at the very least, give you compelling reasons to buy that computer from her. She may give you knowledge and understanding (information) about the computer, and she tries to persuade you, but you do not purchase the computer. She still made a persuasive speech even though you did not buy, because her goal was persuasive: She wanted you to buy the computer.

Your humanities professor explains deductive and inductive reasoning. He wants students to understand how these two types of reasoning can be used to help solve problems. He does not want to persuade you how things should be done; instead, he wants to help you gain knowledge and understanding so that you can solve the problem on your own. He moves to persuasion only if he tries to convince you that one method is better than another for solving problems.

The key to understanding the difference between information and persuasion lies in recognizing that *although information may contain some elements of persuasion, all persuasion must provide information.* What separates an informative speech from a persuasive one is the goal of the speaker. Persuasion is discussed in more detail in the next chapter.

# ■ Topics for Informative Speeches

Surprisingly, some students believe that they have little information to share with others. In actuality, most students have a wealth of information and a vast list of potential topics based on what they have learned from classes, readings, and other experiences. For example, your wellness class probably gives you all kinds of useful, relevant health and wellness information. Think about topics mentioned or covered in other classes, such as agriculture, industrial technology, technology in the work-

## MAKING Technology CONNECTIONS

### Using the Web to Find Topics

Topics for speeches really are virtually limitless. That vast information source, the Web, can be an excellent source of ideas and information. Be sure to find additional information from a variety of sources, however, and be sure to meet your instructor's specific criteria and requirements. Here are some excellent sources of interesting informative possibilities:

1. Dogpile at www.dogpile.com is a metasearch engine billed as "All the best search engines piled into one." It may be helpful as you search for topics. Access Dogpile. Then, key in "topics for informative speeches." (Many of the results are companies where you may buy a list of topics and/or lists of guidelines or even speeches. Do not buy your speech! It's not ethical, and the speeches usually don't fit you or your audience anyway.) Click on a link for an educational institution such as www.hawaii.edu/mauispeechhtml (Topic Selection Helper for Informative Speeches). This list was last updated in 2002, but includes scores of topics ranging from "general subjects" to "personalities" and includes a list of "Topics Based on Students' Own Lives."

2. The Public Broadcasting System has a website highlighting various up-to-date programs at www.pbs.org. This is a good site to bookmark so you can come back to get more ideas or find additional information. On the main page, go to Explore and click on and choose the topic you think might yield good results (Arts & Drama, History, Home & Hobbies, Life & Culture, News & Views, Science & Nature). Once there, scroll through the list and read one of your choice. News & Views offered Business & Finance, Health, Military, Opinion & Analysis, World, Government & Politics, Law & Order, Newsmakers, and Social Issues when accessed on July 15, 2006.

3. Bartleby.com is a source for free online literature, verse, and reference works. Electronic versions of thirty-five works are available, including: *The Columbia Encyclopedia,* the *American Heritage Dictionary, Roget's II: The New Thesaurus, Simpson's Contemporary Quotations, World Orations, The New Dictionary of Cultural Literacy,* and the *American Heritage Book of English Usage.*

place, computers in the workplace, the Internet, working from home, biological discoveries to create better living, computers and agriculture, computers and mechanics, computers and art, changes in education, graphic design, photography, medical advances, alternative health care, global terrorism, gender issues in the twenty-first century, the impact of an elderly population on our governmental agencies, the need for philanthropy, civic engagement, new jobs in the music industry, spirituality and religion, and multiculturalism. The list is endless, and the potential for informative topics is almost limitless.

There are some guidelines (suggested in Chapter 7) for selecting a speech topic. They are as follows:

1. Choose a topic that will allow you to convey an important thought or action to your audience.
2. Choose a topic that is familiar and interesting to you.
3. Choose a topic that is important to you.
4. Choose a topic that will be or can be made interesting to your audience.
5. Choose a topic that can be well developed within the speech's time limit.

Connecting with others through communication is easier when they see the value in and uses for the information you share with them. Most of us want the information we receive to be important and useful. We often are thinking, "What's in it for me?" (WIIFM?). When you first select a topic that you like and know something about, then you need to think about your audience: is this potentially useful for/to my listeners? Some topics are givens—"Preparing for the Job Interview," "Classes to Help in the Job Search," or "Getting Along with Others." These are topics most college students might find useful, if not right now, at least at some point in the future. Topics with less evident personal value, such as "Genetically Engineered Crops" or "Environmental Awareness," might seem less interesting, so you will have to clearly answer the question, What's in it for me? If you are passionately interested in something, it is likely your passion alone that can help generate interest. Although you may doubt that you have a worthwhile topic, if you think about your special interests, past experiences, and special knowledge, you will likely discover that you, too, have a great deal to share.

Successful speakers next consider their audiences. They communicate information accurately and clearly, but most important, they make the information they present meaningful and interesting to their audience by providing new information or correcting misinformation.

Informative speech topics can be classified in many different ways. One scheme divides them into speeches about objects, processes, events, and concepts.[3]

## ■ Objects

Speeches about objects examine concrete subjects: people, animals, things, structures, and places. Here are some possibilities:

| | | |
|---|---|---|
| The iPod | *Survivor* | Bill & Melinda Gates Foundation |
| PC versus Mac | School Choice | Steroid Use in |
| Reality TV | Immigration | Major League Baseball |
| Stem Cell Research | America's War | Unrest in the Middle East |
| Drug Wars | on Marijuana | |
| Flag Burning | The Human Brain | |
| Global Dictators | Organ Farms | |
| The Teenage Brain | Oprah | |
| Marriage Laws | Bono | |
| *Desperate Housewives* | Condoleezza Rice | |

These topics are general and must be narrowed in order to meet the guidelines of most classroom speaking situations.

Here are some specific purpose statements for informative speeches about concrete subjects, following the guidelines suggested in Chapter 7:

■ To inform my audience why immigration laws are of concern to us

■ To inform my audience about how the human brain functions

- To inform my audience that the teen brain is a work in progress
- To share with my listeners the increasing similarities between PCs and Macs

Each of these purpose statements is appropriate for an informative speech.

## ▪▪ Processes

A process topic usually focuses on a demonstration in which the speaker explains how something is done or how it takes place. Here are a few sample specific purpose statements for informative speeches about processes:

- To inform my audience about the mental processes involved in thinking
- To explain how we can gain control of America's obesity epidemic
- To inform my listeners about how an ordinary citizen can affect the legislative process

Speeches about processes generally serve two purposes: to increase understanding and to teach someone *how to do something*. This could involve anything from how to do CPR to how to buy the right car.

Process speeches are usually organized in time-sequence (chronological) order, meaning that they proceed step by step from the beginning of the process to its end. For example, let's say your speech is on saving lives through the automated external defibrillator. You would walk your listeners through all the necessary steps and procedures so they would know exactly what to do if the occasion were to arise.

The demonstration of a process usually benefits from the use of a visual aid. Some processes may require an actual demonstration in order to be understood. For example, to inform listeners about how to fold napkins might require that you do the folding during the speech presentation.

## ▪▪ Events

Informative speeches about events discuss happenings or occasions. The many possible topics include the following:

| | |
|---|---|
| Israel-Hezbollah Attacks of 2006 | Election 2006 |
| Stem Cell Research Legislation Debates | Tour-de-France |
| Iran's Nuclear Arsenal and Testing | Wall Street Reform |
| The Asian Tsunami of 2005 (or, 2006) | Kim's Nuclear Gamble |
| The Aftermath of Election 2000 | The Impact of Enron |
| Katie Couric Changes CBS | Discovery's Safe Return |
| The Bikini Turns 60 | The Great Heat Wave of 2006 |

Appropriate specific purposes for some of these topics might include the following:

- To share with the audience the reasons for high medical costs
- To inform the audience about congressional bipartisan efforts on stem-cell research
- To explain how Wall Street is internally reforming itself

## ▪️ Concepts

Speeches about concepts deal with abstract topics such as beliefs, theories, ideas, and principles. The challenge is to make the subject matter concrete so that the audience can easily understand it. Concept-based topics include the following:

| | |
|---|---|
| Communication Apprehension | Nonverbal Communication |
| Justice | Theory of Relativity |
| Cyberwar | Biomedical Ethics |
| Media Campaigns | The Greenhouse Effect |

These topics are too vague to be meaningful. If you were to ask a dozen people what each term or phrase means, you would probably receive a dozen different answers. The speaker is responsible for narrowing and focusing the subject so that the audience understands the intended meaning. Here are specific purpose statements based on some of the general, abstract topics:

- ▪️ To inform my audience about U.S. vulnerability to attack from cyberspace
- ▪️ To share Schutz's Interpersonal Needs with my audience so they can be aware of why we need to be around people
- ▪️ To share the effects of global warming on the environment

Speeches about concepts take extra time and effort to develop because of their abstract nature. These topics require the use of concrete examples, definitions, and clear language.

Whether a speech is about an object, a process, an event, or a concept is not always clear because a subject may overlap these categories. Often the specific purpose that the speaker chooses to emphasize determines the category. It is important to decide your approach to the subject and then develop your speech accordingly. If you are unsure of which approach to take, review Chapter 7 for more specific information about topic selection and how to determine which topics may be best suited for you and your audience (see the appendix at the end of this chapter for more topics).

| GUIDELINES | Preparing the Informative Speech |
|---|---|

1. When preparing to present an informative speech, you should begin with yourself. What are your interests? What are you passionately concerned about?
2. Informative speeches should appeal to the audience and provide them with knowledge of something potentially useful or beneficial.
3. Your audience will listen to you if you make the speech compelling.

# ▪️ Preparing and Developing an Informative Speech

The previous chapters on public communication relate directly to the principles and skills of informative speaking. All aspects of topic selection; audience analysis; information gathering; preparation of supporting and clarifying materials; and organizing,

The Dalai Lama successfully speaks about abstract concepts, such as peace, humanity, and human dignity, by using concrete examples that his listeners can relate to.

outlining, and delivering a speech are crucial to the effectiveness and eventual success of your informative presentation. In addition, you should be familiar with strategies for competing with distractions and noises, such as students arriving late, an airplane flying overhead, a lawn mower outside the window, and whispering in the audience. Such interferences cannot be ignored if you want to be successful in transmitting information to others. To achieve your main goal of increasing the audience's knowledge, you must strive to attain two subgoals: gain their attention and increase their understanding.

## ■■ Gain and Maintain Audience Attention

Motivating the audience to pay attention is critical to the success of any speech (see Chapter 9 for more on motivating your audience to listen). To accomplish this, you should follow a strategy that will work well for your audience.

**Generate a Need for the Information.**   A student gave a speech on the benefits of seat belt use. After reading his peer evaluations and reflecting on his videotaped speech, he emailed to ask why people did not like the speech. When he was asked whether he had determined how many people in his class do not use seat belts, he did not have an answer. When asked if he knew what the Iowa average of seat belt use was, he did not have those statistics

## MAKING CONNECTIONS
### for Success

### The Informative Speech

The speech process entails time and effort as you plan, research, organize, create, and practice the speech. This exercise will give you some practical application for the actual speech.

1. Select one of the purpose statements from each category on the previous pages.
2. Indicate the organizational pattern you think will work for each statement.
3. Identify two presentational aids that might be useful and be prepared to provide a rationale as to why you think they would be beneficial.
4. Identify three forms of support that would help make your listeners attend to and remember this information.

either. When we told him the latest statistics from the Highway Patrol and the Department of Transportation suggest that 82 percent of Iowans use seat belts, he was surprised. That should tell you two reasons his listeners did not seem to like his speech: Most of them already knew the benefits of seat belt use and use them regularly; and he had not done enough research to go beyond what his listeners already knew. As a result, his audience did not feel motivated to listen. How could he have avoided choosing a topic his audience wasn't interested in? He might have done a survey to find out what they knew, or he might have looked carefully at Iowa statistics. Or he could have found a way to make the speech more relevant to his listeners in this way:

> I realize most of you already wear seat belts when you drive or ride in a vehicle, but did you know that even in Iowa, where seat belt usage is said to be at 82 percent, injuries resulting because a seat belt was not in use account for more than 25 percent of all traffic deaths? That means that six of us in this class could have life-threatening injuries if we were involved in an automobile accident and were not wearing a seat belt.

This opening acknowledges the high percentage of people in the state who use seat belts, and it also piques interest because it asks a rhetorical question to make the listener aware of the consequences of that failure. (Notice that the speaker also makes the percentages memorable by identifying the number of class members who could be affected.)

Let's look at other examples of rhetorical questions used to begin a speech:

- Are you aware that in a preparation exercise, "computer hackers" were able to break into the Pentagon's central computer system, infiltrate and take control of the Pacific command center computers, and take control of the power grids and 911 systems in nine major U.S. cities?
- Did you know that in the United States alone there are over 115 traffic fatalities per day?
- Did you know that *Pirates of the Caribbean: Dead Man's Chest* (summer 2006) took in $258.2 million in the first ten days after its opening?
- Americans make more donations than people in many other countries. Are you aware that about half of the $15-billion increase in donations from 2004 was given in response to three natural disasters: The Indonesian tsunamis, the Gulf Coast hurricanes, and the earthquake in Pakistan?

Speakers can also use questions meant to generate responses from the audience as a strategy to gain and maintain audience interest and attention.

**Create Information Relevance.** People are much more likely to pay attention when they believe a speech relates directly to them. A speaker who gives an audience a reason to listen by relating the topic to their needs and interests creates **information relevance.** Ask yourself whether the information you intend to present is relevant to your listeners. If it is not, think about how you might make it so. One student presented a speech on wind energy. It was apparent that she had done a lot of research because she cited numerous sources and had interesting visuals. The problem was that she talked only about wind energy in California and Denmark and never mentioned that it is a viable source of energy in her own state. Her listeners needed to know how this could affect them at home, not somewhere thousands of miles away.

■ **information relevance** Making information relevant to an audience to give them a reason to listen.

Another speaker talked about the contributions of space technology to our everyday lives. She held up several items of clothing with Velcro fasteners and pointed out how Velcro is familiar to us now but was originally developed for the space program. The audience recognized the relevance of her topic and paid closer attention.

**Provide a Fresh Perspective.** Information that is perceived as *new* also attracts the attention of an audience. But whenever this statement is mentioned in class, someone responds, "But there isn't anything new to present." Actually, discussing something new does not necessarily mean that you have to present something about which the audience has never heard. It does mean that you need to devise a new view or angle. There are subjects that we have heard discussed many times, such as AIDS, pollution, smoking, drugs, safe sex, and recycling. A speaker who provides a fresh perspective on a familiar topic makes it more interesting and thus increases the chances of holding the audience's attention. One speaker informed the audience about illegal drugs that are medically helpful in treating certain diseases. She began her speech in the following manner:

> You have read and heard so much about cocaine, crack, heroin, and other illegal drugs that you are probably sick of the subject, but these drugs are not all bad. You might at first think that I am too liberal, but my mother is on drugs and I am glad of it. You see, my mother is suffering from cancer, and the only relief she can get is from the small doses of heroin she receives each day to ease the pain. Today, I am going to inform you about illegal drugs that actually aid our sick and dying.

This approach is not necessarily new, but it is different. Rather than taking a stand either for or against the banning of illegal drugs, the speaker focused on certain instances in which the use of illegal drugs can be beneficial. This also helped her to stay within the guidelines of the informative speech.

**Focus on the Unusual.** Sometimes focusing on an unusual aspect of a topic helps a speaker maintain the attention of the audience. A speaker might begin the speech like this:

> You're all aware, I'm sure, that Thomas Jefferson is the acknowledged author of the Declaration of Independence. Did you know, however, that Jefferson had a very fine editor who made the words immortal?
>
> The Continental Congress of 1776 appointed a committee to draft a declaration of independence from Great Britain that explained the decision. The committee comprised Thomas Jefferson, Benjamin Franklin, John Adams, Roger Sherman, and Robert Livingston. Jefferson was the committee chair and the one who wrote the first draft. Jefferson and Franklin held similar views on what was needed in the document, but their writing styles were quite different. Jefferson was much more poetic and philosophical than Franklin. Jefferson was also acknowledged to be the person who should create this important rationale for the colonies to revolt from an unjust system. The book, *Benjamin Franklin: An American Life* by Walter Isaacson (2003), suggests that "Jefferson . . . borrowed freely from the phrasings of others, including the resounding Declaration of Rights in the new Virginia Constitution that had just been drafted by his fellow planter George Mason, in a manner that today might subject him to questions of plagiarism but back then was considered not only proper but learned."[4]
>
> According to Isaacson, Jefferson finished his draft and made some changes suggested by others and then asked, "Will Doctor Franklin be so good as to peruse it?"[5] Franklin

made only a few changes, but one is particularly compelling. Jefferson wrote, "We hold these truths to be sacred and undeniable," and Franklin changed that phrase to "We hold these truths to be self-evident." What a difference word choice makes! Isaacson says that Jefferson's words implied that the principle in question—the equality of people and their endowment by their creator with inalienable rights—was an assertion of religion. Franklin's edit turned it instead to an assertion of rationality.[6]

Later, the Congress formed into a committee of the whole to consider Jefferson's draft. Massive changes were made, but Franklin's immortal phrase "We hold these truths to be self-evident" has gained immortality.

So what were the other contributions of Benjamin Franklin to the United States of America? They were significant. Let me share with you today Franklin's contributions to foreign diplomacy as an ambassador to France and his other contributions to U.S. government as we now know it.

Gaining and maintaining the attention of the audience is extremely important in presenting information. Audience members must believe they will benefit from receiving the information, believe it is relevant to their lives, and find it interesting enough to want to listen. Achieving this can be quite challenging to the beginning speaker, but by making your audience the central focus of the speech and using a little creativity, you can easily gain and hold their attention.

## ■■ Increase Understanding of the Topic

Once you have gained your listeners' attention, you have created the opportunity to increase their understanding. Understanding is the ability to interpret, grasp, or assign meaning to an idea. You can increase your audience's understanding by organizing your presentation systematically, choosing appropriate language, and providing clear definitions.

**Organize Your Presentation.**   In a well-organized speech, ideas are managed in a clear and orderly sequence that makes the material easy to follow and understand. Effective organization helps increase the speaker's credibility and improves the audience's comprehension and retention of information. See Chapter 9 and review the two organizational techniques that aid listeners' understanding: planned repetition and advance organizers.

*Plan for Repetition.*   **Planned repetition** is the deliberate restating of a thought to increase the likelihood that the audience will understand and remember it. The repetition of information generally helps us remember things more completely. For example, if you call directory assistance to get a phone number and have nothing to write the number on until you call, you probably say the number over and over so that you can remember it long enough to dial it.

The power of repetition is so great that it is the guiding principle behind most television commercials. Although we might find it bothersome, the constant repetition of the same commercial reminds us of the product and thus increases the chances of our purchasing it. You can use this same principle in an informative speech to get your audience to remember key ideas. For example, you might say the following:

How vulnerable is the United States to attack from cyberspace? How imminent is the threat? Many experts believe the clock is already ticking, and that America is already fighting a cyberwar. In the aftermath of 9/11/2001, most U.S. intelligence shifted to find-

**■ planned repetition** The deliberate restating of a thought to increase the likelihood that the audience will understand and remember it.

ing Al Qaeda cells around the world, but one group at the White House decided to investigate a new threat—attacks from cyberspace, or cyberwar.

> The website for the Public Broadcasting System is www.pbs.org—that's www.pbs.org.

You could also put the Web URL on a computer slide presentation, on a poster, or up on the projector. Or, you could write it on the board for additional repetition and emphasis. Internal summaries and previews may also include repetition to help your listeners remember the points you made and help them focus on what is yet to come in the speech.

***Use Advance Organizers.*** **Advance organizers** are similar to signposts in that they signal what is coming, but they also warn that the information coming is significant. They signal the listener to pay attention.

> Two points are critical here.
> You will need to know this in order to be able to complete the task.
> The following information is essential.

These warnings get the attention of your audience and emphasize that the forthcoming information is both necessary and important. Teachers use advance organizers to make sure that students know what is essential. Examples include the following:

> You'll see this again.
> The next exam will require you to demonstrate your knowledge of this concept.
> If you understand these two points, you will be able to solve the problem.

Advance organizers also serve as previews of main points. Using advance organizers in an informative speech introduction helps your audience concentrate and focus on what is coming in the speech. For example, one speaker used the following

> ■ **advance organizer** A statement that warns the listener that significant information is coming.

Competent communicators know that they have to keep the listeners' attention focused on their topics. How can they do that? There are important organizational strategies to keep them listening. Advance organizers and planned repetition as well as careful use of language are three strategies to keep the listeners with you.

statement in her introduction to let the audience know what was coming and what was important to meet her specific purpose:

> You'll need to understand two critical points in order to make sense of the information: In a cyberwar you can't tell whether the enemy has good weapons until they use them, and there's a new set of warriors fighting on the new battlefield of cyberspace.

**Choose Language Carefully.**　It is extremely important to match your level of language to the knowledge your audience already has about your topic. If you are speaking with experts or with people who are familiar with your topic, you are free to use technical terms without explaining them, but if your audience is unfamiliar with your subject, you will need to choose your words carefully and define any special terms. In some cases, you should avoid technical terms altogether. This may be necessary when such terms would only confuse your audience or when your audience lacks the ability or background to understand them. Sometimes a speaker's use of too many technical terms will turn an audience off or even create hostility. A speaker should choose language carefully to avoid creating unnecessary problems. When possible, choose words that are concrete rather than words that are abstract, and use descriptions to make your points clearer.

*Use Concrete Words.*　To increase your audience's understanding, try to use as many concrete words as possible. In Chapter 4, we said that concrete words are symbols for specific things one can experience through the senses. Concrete words stand for specific things one can experience through the senses. Concrete words stand for specific people, places, things, or acts: Hugh Beall, Springfield, Massachusetts, iPod, or reading information at www.pbs.org. Familiar, concrete language allows your listeners to form mental images similar to yours. If you say that something is the size of a quarter, your listeners should form a fairly accurate picture of what you have in mind. Concrete words leave less room for misinterpretation and misunderstanding.

Abstract words refer to ideas, qualities, or relationships: truth, liberty, the pursuit of happiness, friendship. The meaning of these words relies on the experiences and intentions of the people who express them. If a speaker says, "The mass transit system is good," we don't know whether he means that it is cost effective, on time, or beneficial for riders. Abstract language is imprecise and often leaves listeners confused about the speaker's intent.

If a speaker says, "The grading system at this college is unfair," listeners might have so many questions that they fail to listen to the rest of the speech. A more precise statement would be "The grading system in this college is unfair for two reasons: First, grading here is heavily reliant on exams, and second, the scale is arbitrary because anything below a 70 percent is failing and it takes a 94 percent or higher to get an A." The second effort is much clearer and more forceful than the first and leaves no doubt in the listener's mind about the speaker's intent.

## MAKING CONNECTIONS
### for Success

### The "Right Words" Are Important

Concrete words are more easily understandable to listeners. If our words are too abstract, we are in danger of making the listener "tune out" or, ensuring that people really don't understand what we mean. Rewrite the following sentences to make them more concrete:

1. Cyberwar is a real threat to America.
2. The Boston Tunnel project was dangerous.
3. Our school has lots of programs to help students succeed.
4. Underage drinking and bingeing are massive problems on most campuses.

Be prepared to share your changes with the class.

## Make It Lively, Please!

Words can be dry and uninteresting. Or, they can grab our attention and become almost exciting when they make us want to listen to someone. Look at the six phrases below and see if you can bring them to life.

- Language is important
- Cyberwar threatens us
- Technology is necessary
- Healthy fast-food

- This school and campus
- Best jobs for college grads

1. Use definitions, concrete words, or descriptors to make the phrases more lively.
2. Compare your words with the original. What are the differences?
3. Was it easy to make the phrases more lively?
4. Compare your changes with those of your classmates. What were the similarities and differences?

**Use Description.**    To make something more concrete, a speaker might describe its size, quantity, shape, weight, composition, texture, color, age, strength, or fit. Words used to describe something are called **descriptors.** The more descriptors a speaker uses that relate to the listeners' experiences, the greater is the likelihood that the message will be understood. One speaker used these descriptors in talking about the threat of cyberwar:

> According to PBS, "Eligible Receiver" is the code name of a government simulation where a team of hackers was organized to infiltrate Pentagon systems. The team was only allowed to use publicly available computer equipment and hacking software. While the information is still classified, we know that the hackers were able to infiltrate and take control of the Pacific command center computers as well as power grids and 911 systems in nine major U.S. cities. This simulation demonstrated the real lack of consciousness about cyber warfare. During the first three days of the exercise, nobody believed we were under cyber attack. This whole exercise underscores America's reliance on information technology systems and their vulnerabilities to attack.

The speaker's explanations provide one specific example of what the team was able to accomplish with information technology at the Pentagon without raising concerns. The descriptors are a chilling reminder that, in modern warfare, the things we take for granted can be used against us.

**Use Definitions.**    One way to ensure your audience's understanding is to define all potentially unfamiliar and complex words. Consider the importance of definitions in the following situations: Louis talked about moon theory and drought; Sergei discussed the Sapir-Whorf Hypothesis; Sarina informed her audience that women are often members of *muted groups;* and MarCena spoke on *style switching.* In each of the above speeches, the speaker needed to explain basic terms in order to be understood. Louis explained that there is an 18- to 19-year crop cycle that explains widespread drought every 18.6 years. In his speech, he says that the 18.6-year cycle of drought and rainy weather coincides with the moon's orbit around the earth, and when the moon's path is at its northernmost track above the equator, as it is in 2006, the corn belt is due for a drought.[7] Sergei explained that *linguistic determinism* is a theory within the Sapir-Whorf hypothesis that helps to explain how thought and language

■ **descriptors** Words used to describe something.

are interconnected. *Linguistic determinism,* he said, is the theory that language shapes how we think. Sarina defined *muted groups* as people who lack the appropriate language and thus have reduced power and status. She explained that women and minorities often fit into muted groups. MarCena said that *style-switching* occurs when African American women need to move between the language of the dominant culture and the language of their own coculture. In order to succeed in both cultures, they have to use the language of both, thus, they *style-switch,* and use each language when it is appropriate.

The most common form of definition used by speakers, the logical definition, usually contains two parts: the dictionary definition and the characteristics that distinguish the term from other members of the same category. An operational definition explains how an object or concept works, and a definition by example explains a term or a concept by using examples, either verbal or actual, to illustrate a point. In addition, there are four other methods of clearly defining a term for your listeners: using contrast, synonyms, antonyms, and etymologies.

**Show Contrasts.** A **contrast definition** is used to show or emphasize differences. This type of definition is helpful when you want to distinguish between similar terms. For example, a speaker discussing communication apprehension and speech anxiety differentiated one term from the other by stating that communication apprehension is a trait or global anxiety, whereas speech anxiety is a state or situational anxiety. A person suffering from communication apprehension might also have speech anxiety, but a person with speech anxiety will not necessarily have communication apprehension. A contrast definition might also point out differences in causes and effects. Thus the speaker might point out that people with communication apprehension actively avoid all interaction with others, whereas people with speech anxiety merely feel a bit of controllable discomfort when addressing an audience.

**Use Synonyms.** The use of synonyms can also help clarify the meaning of a word. A **synonym** is a word, phrase, or concept that has exactly the same or nearly the same meaning as another word, term, or concept. In describing a communicative extrovert, a speaker used the phrases "willingness to talk openly," "uninhibited speech," and "ability to speak in any situation without reservation." Each phrase describes the behavior that might be exhibited by a person who is a communicative extrovert.

**Use Antonyms.** In contrast, an **antonym** is a word, phrase, or concept that has the opposite meaning of another word, phrase, or concept. For example, a communicative extrovert is the opposite of someone with communication apprehension. Such a person is not shy, reserved, unwilling to talk, or afraid to speak. The person greatly enjoys talking with others. Using an antonym helps the audience to compare differences and leaves the audience with a memorable definition of an unfamiliar term.

**Use Etymologies.** An **etymology** is a form of definition that traces the origin and development of a word. One student used etymology to explain how the Olympic Games got their name. In the Greek system of telling time, an Olympiad was the period of four years that elapsed between two successive celebrations of the Olympian. This method of figuring time became common in about 300 B.C., and all events were dated from 776 B.C., the beginning of the first known Olympic Games. Such a definition provides the audience with a novel way to remember key information. The *Oxford English Dictionary* or the *Etymological Dictionary of Modern English* are excellent sources of word etymologies.

■ **contrast definition** A definition that shows or emphasizes differences.

■ **synonym** A word, term, or concept that is the same or nearly the same in meaning as another word, term, or concept.

■ **antonym** A word, phrase, or concept that is opposite in meaning to another word, phrase, or concept.

■ **etymology** A form of definition that traces the origin and development of a word.

Whenever there is any possibility that your audience may not understand a term or concept, select the kind of definition that will provide the clearest explanation. In some instances, more than one kind of definition might be necessary. To err by overdefining is better than providing an inadequate definition that leaves your audience wondering what you are talking about.

## Hints for Effective Informative Speaking

Almost everything we have covered in the text up to this point is relevant to informative speaking and audience participation. Adhering to the following two additional guidelines should be particularly helpful in ensuring your success: Avoid assumptions, and personalize information.

**Avoid Assumptions.** A student began speaking on CPR by emphasizing how important it is in saving lives. However, she failed to explain that the acronym CPR stands for *cardiovascular pulmonary resuscitation;* she assumed that everyone already knew that. Most of the audience did understand, but a number of people did not. In addition, some knew what the acronym meant but did not know how the technique worked. Because at least half of the class was unfamiliar with the technique, they found the speaker's presentation confusing and frustrating. One mistaken assumption undercut all the work she had put into her speech. Follow these guidelines to avoid making assumptions:

1. Ask yourself whether your listeners already know what you are talking about. Audience analysis may be appropriate. If you are addressing your class, randomly select some of your classmates and ask them what they know about your topic and its related terminology.

2. If you believe that even one audience member might not understand, take the time to define and explain your topic.

3. If you believe that a majority of your audience already knows what you mean, say something like, "Many of you probably know what euthanasia is, but for those who don't, . . . ." In this way, you acknowledge those who already know and help those who do not.

4. Do not make the assumption that your audience needs introductory information, especially if you have any doubts about what they know. You can always move through your basic definitions and explanations quickly if your audience seems to understand, but it is difficult to regain their interest and attention once you start talking over their heads.

**Personalize Information.** When you relate your topic to your listeners so that they can see its relevance for them, you are personalizing information. Judy presented a speech about nutrition and the eating habits of people in the United States. It was an interesting speech, but the practice audience didn't understand what it had to do with them. In revising her speech, Judy surveyed students in her residence hall and class about their eating habits. Then she personalized the information for her audience as follows:

> Bad eating habits can cause problems that you may not be aware of. In a survey I took, I found that many college students like you fail to eat a variety of foods from the necessary basic food groups every day. In fact, my data indicate that 61 percent of you—that is more than half of you—do not eat balanced meals. Furthermore, I found that 50 percent of you skip breakfast at least five times a week.

What does this mean to you? According to nutrition experts, people who eat balanced meals are more motivated and less tired than people who don't eat balanced meals. In fact, those of you who drink a can of pop and eat a candy bar for breakfast—and you know who you are—are more likely to have high blood pressure, lack ambition, feel highly stressed, and be vulnerable to chronic diseases later in life.

Information that is personalized not only holds attention, but also attracts interest. For example, think of your most effective instructors. Chances are that they take ordinary material and personalize it into meaningful, interesting knowledge. Listening to a string of facts can be frustrating, but a speech comes to life when it contains personal illustrations.

Most of us are interested in others. If we were not, there would be no *People* magazine, no *National Enquirer,* no *Late Show with David Letterman,* no *Survivor,* no *Oprah,* and no *Dr. Phil.* Stories are much more likely to affect listeners than are statistics. Whenever possible, personalize your information and dramatize it in human terms.

One student began an informative speech about the Heimlich maneuver, a technique used to clear the throat of someone who is choking, by relating the story of a four-year-old boy who saved his three-year-old friend. The boy, who had watched a television show in which the maneuver was used to save the life of one of the main characters, simply reenacted what he saw. By using this dramatic, real-life episode, the student was able to grab his audience's attention and prepare them for his discussion of who developed the technique, how it works, and how many lives it has saved.

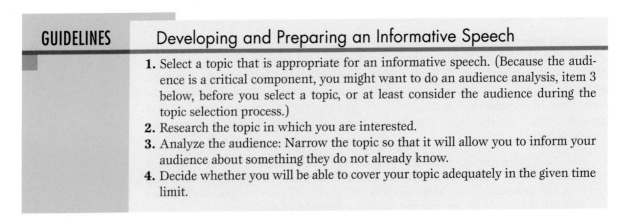

| GUIDELINES | Personalizing Information in Your Speeches |

1. Use examples and information that specifically relate to your audience.
2. Draw conclusions that your audience can identify with, and explain what the conclusions may mean for them.
3. Refer to people who are similar to your audience members, for example, single parents, nontraditional students, minority students, international students, computer science majors, commuters who must drive to campus.
4. Refer to topics and events that affect your listeners, such as campus activities, elections, state and local laws, social events, tax cuts or increases, cultural programs, and career decisions.

| GUIDELINES | Developing and Preparing an Informative Speech |

1. Select a topic that is appropriate for an informative speech. (Because the audience is a critical component, you might want to do an audience analysis, item 3 below, before you select a topic, or at least consider the audience during the topic selection process.)
2. Research the topic in which you are interested.
3. Analyze the audience: Narrow the topic so that it will allow you to inform your audience about something they do not already know.
4. Decide whether you will be able to cover your topic adequately in the given time limit.

5. Determine your specific purpose: Word it to ensure that it meets the objective of the informative speech.

6. Organize the speech: Select and word your main points so that they are clear and meet your specific purpose.

7. Develop clarifying and supporting materials to ensure that your audience will understand everything about which you are talking.

8. Check the organization of your speech against the guidelines of effective organization specified in Chapter 9.

9. Avoid assumptions.

10. Personalize information to your listeners as much as possible.

11. Practice the delivery.

12. After delivering your speech, analyze the effectiveness of it.

The successful informative speech always considers the listeners. The speaker carefully thinks about the following questions: What do I want my listeners to learn from my speech? What will be the best way to deliver my speech so my listeners will understand and retain the information? How will I know if I was successful in accomplishing my purpose?

# ■ Evaluating the Informative Speech

Every instructor uses specific criteria to evaluate a speaker's competence in creating and delivering a speech. The following are some common criteria used by instructors all across the world. Keep them in mind as you prepare your speech.

We have also included a speaker's self-evaluation form and a listener evaluation form (Figures 11.1 and 11.2) so that both speakers and audience members will be aware of their responsibilities to each other.

## ■ Topic

The selection of a topic should meet the following criteria:

■ The topic should merit your audience's attention.

■ The treatment of the topic should take into account the audience's level of knowledge of it.

■ The audience should be able to see the relationship between the topic and the speaker and between the topic and themselves.

■ The topic of the speech should be adequately covered in the time available. The topic should be narrow enough to be fully developed.

## ■ General Requirements

These general requirements hold for all informative speech presentations:

■ The speech's purpose should be clearly to inform and should be stated as such.

■ The speech should meet the time requirements set by the assignment.

> ■ **FIGURE 11.1**  Speaker's Self-Evaluation Form
>
> After you have completed an informative speech, take a few moments to think about your preparation and presentation. Complete the phrases on this form by stating what you would do similarly or differently, and why, if you were to give this same speech again.
>
> Title of speech: _____ .
> Date and place given: _____ .
> My topic was _____ .
> My research could be improved by _____ .
> The organizational pattern I chose was_____ .
> The introduction was _____ .
> The body of the speech needed _____ .
> My conclusion seemed to be _____ .
> My explanation of ideas should _____ .
> The support I provided for my ideas was _____ .
> My use of language might _____ .
> My visual delivery was _____ .
> My vocal delivery needed _____ .
> The ways I adapted my topic, ideas, and language to this audience were _____
> _____ .
> Things I would change are_____ ,
> because _____ .
> Things I would retain are_____ ,
> because _____ .

- The speaker should cite sources of information other than the speaker's own.
- The speech's purpose should be relevant to the assignment and relate to the audience.
- The speech should show evidence of careful preparation.

## ■■ Audience Analysis

The speaker must shape the speech to suit the audience, which often requires research (for example, determining the listeners' past experiences, beliefs, attitudes, values). The choices the speaker makes regarding content and the development of ideas should be customized for the listeners' benefit.

- The speech should reflect appropriate audience analysis.
- The speech should show the audience why the topic is important to them.
- At several points the speaker should make contact with the listeners by using familiar examples or showing knowledge of their preferences or experiences.

■ **FIGURE 11.2** Listener's Evaluation Form

This form can be used to evaluate speeches given by your classmates. Follow your instructor's directions for providing such feedback.

Speaker _____  Topic _____

Date _____

The appropriateness of the topic for this class, assignment, and context was _____
_____ .

One new or different perspective I gained was _____ .

The organization of the speech was _____ .

The reasons for my comments on organization are _____ .

I identified the speaker's purpose as _____ .

The speaker needed to explain _____ .

The types of supporting materials used _____ .

Presentational aids, if used, were _____ .

The speaker's language should have _____ .

The speaker could improve the physical aspects of delivery by_____ .

The one comment I wish to make about vocal delivery is_____ .

One aspect I especially liked was _____ .

One area that needs improvement in the future is_____ .

## Supporting Materials

Supporting materials supply documented evidence that the information conveyed in the speech is accurate and credible.

- The speech should be well documented.
- The sources should be cited completely and accurately.
- The research should be up to date.
- The speaker should use adequate and sufficient clarifying materials.
- Visual aids, if used, should be appropriate, add to the audience's understanding of the speech's content, and follow the guidelines established by the assignment.

## Organization

When judging the organization, the evaluator looks for a carefully planned, well-developed informative speech that takes a unified approach to the material being presented.

- The introduction should be properly developed.
  - It should orient the audience to the topic, gaining attention and arousing interest.
  - It should include a specific purpose and thesis statement.

A surfboard instructor explains surfboarding technique and body position to a group new to surfboarding. As she explains and demonstrates the concepts, she must be sure to cover all the important points and also make sure the listeners "get it" since their lives may depend on complete knowledge and understanding of those techniques and positions.

- It should define terms (if necessary).
- It should be relevant.
- It should establish credibility.
■ The organization of the body should be clear and easy to follow.
- The main points should be clear and parallel in structure.
- The main points should be related to the purpose of the speech.
- Transitions should provide appropriate links between ideas.
- The organizational pattern should be appropriate.
■ The conclusion should be properly developed.
- It should reinforce the purpose by reviewing the main points.
- It should end with a memorable thought.

## ■■ Delivery

The delivery techniques provide evidence that the speaker is aware of what the audience is interested in hearing, is involved in and enthusiastic about the topic, and is interested in sharing the material with the listeners.

■ The speaker's stance and posture should be appropriate.
■ The speaker's eye contact with the audience should be appropriate.
■ The speaker should follow the assignment in method of delivery (use of notes and number of note cards).
■ The speaker's facial expressions should help to convey and clarify thoughts.
■ The speaker's body movements should be appropriate and effective.
■ The speaker's vocal delivery should enhance the speech with appropriate volume and rate, conversational quality, enthusiastic tone, clear enunciation, appropriate pauses, and appropriate vocal variety.

## Language Choice

Language choice can enhance and clarify ideas considerably.

- Language choice should be appropriate to the assignment and audience.
- Word choice should be appropriate for the college level.
- Grammar should be appropriate and show college-level competence.
- Word pronunciations should be correct.

Speakers should always analyze their presentations. We are often called on to make reports or provide information in the workplace, in the groups of which we are members, and in classrooms (ours and others). Because speaking is so prevalent, it is important that the speaker step back and carefully and critically reflect on the speech, the situation, the audience, and the performance. If we hope to become effective communicators in public settings, we need to use reflective thinking to objectively analyze what happened and how successful we were. Figure 11.1 (earlier in this section) shows a sample speaker's self-evaluation form to facilitate this reflection process.

We spend a great deal more time listening to speeches than we do making speeches, and though the focus of this section may seem to be on making effective speeches, it is also important for each of us to be a critical consumer of speeches and other presentations. Figure 11.2 (earlier in this section) provides a sample listener evaluation form to help the listener directly respond to the speaker, in writing. It is helpful for the speaker to obtain listeners' perspectives on a speech. Honest and tactful feedback can be invaluable. But it is also a good idea to closely evaluate presentations for yourself, even when you will not be passing your comments on to the speaker. Listeners are encouraged to use Figure 11.2 as a basis for creating their own evaluations and applying their own criteria to presentations.

# A Sample Informative Speech with Commentary

The following speech (with our commentary) is an informative speech written and delivered by Dwayne Simnacher, a student at the University of Northern Iowa, in Oral Communication, Fall 2004.

General Purpose:  To explain small business ownership

Specific Purpose:  To share with my audience the benefits of becoming an entrepreneur and the satisfaction associated with it.

Thesis:  Being a small business owner can be very profitable and personally rewarding.

**Introduction**

Becoming a small business owner is not as difficult as it seems. To give you an idea of how successful it can be I will present some information to support those claims. By the end of my presentation I am sure you will better

- Here Dwayne gives the audience reasons to listen, provides direction, and defines entrepreneurship.

understand and be able to investigate entrepreneurial options for your own ideas in small business. Hirsch and Peters (1998, p. 9) define entrepreneurship as "the process of creating something new with value by devoting the necessary time and effort, assuming the accompanying financial psychic and social risks and receiving the resulting rewards for monetary and personal satisfaction and independence."

**Body**

I. There are several small businesses owned and operated by innovative people from diverse backgrounds all right here in Iowa.

    A. Nationally, small businesses generate half of U.S. non-farm private output and employment with 500 or fewer employees according to the U.S. Small Business Administration Office of Advocacy Small Business Profile, Iowa, 2004.

        1. The greatest activity the entrepreneurial sector has is between the ages of 24 to 44, which accounts for around 50 percent in the U.S. National Entrepreneurship Assessment (NEA) 2001, Executive Report 2001.

        2. Of those are U.S. males with a high school degree that have the highest entrepreneurial participation rate at 15.1 percent. Women with some college at 10.7 percent, NEA (2001).

        3. Entrepreneurship education in universities is on the rise. More than 1,500 four-year universities offer classes, in 1997 around 450 offered such courses, NEA (2001).

        4. Women-Owned Businesses account for 16 percent of small businesses, in 2003 representing 39 percent of self-employed persons in the state, U.S. Bus. Admin (2004).

        5. Minority-Owned Businesses account for 28 percent of self employed persons in the state, U.S. Bus. Admin (2004).

    B. So you can see from these figures that entrepreneurship is on the rise, even here in Iowa. It's a wide-open area with lots of room for anyone who wishes to work at it.

II. A business can be any size physically and be able to sell merchandise or function as a nonprofit company.

    A. DASCycle is a Custom motorcycle design and parts business that was started out of a *garage*.

        1. Retailing parts ranging from bolt on accessories to high performance power train components.

        2. The typical prices at retail for parts range from $10 to $25,000 for a completed motorcycle with optional custom finish.

        3. The majority of the parts are sold via the web address www.dascycle.com or online auction sources such as Ebay.com.

    B. Some entrepreneurships start out as a one-person company and become large corporations.

■ In the first main point in the body of the speech, Dwayne uses facts and figures from government sources as well as the National Entrepreneurship Assessment 2001 Executive Report to support his point that his listeners may find this information relevant and useful.

■ In his second main point, Dwayne talks about the logistics of company start-ups and provides examples of people and companies who have made a difference.

■ Dwayne uses PowerPoint slides to show his own business and the website. This serves as reinforcement for his words, but also gives the listeners something tangible to look at, as well as a website to check out.

1. Dell computer's Michael Dell began working with computers as a hobby and selling them out of his dorm room directly to the consumer, Kusher (2004).

2. In 1984, Dell founded the Dell Computer Corporation (DCC) with $1,000, Kusher (2004).

3. In just a little over 18 years, Dell has grown into a $31.2 billion company and it is the largest online commercial computer seller in the world, Kusher (2004).

C. Cedar Valley Greyhound Adoptions, Inc. (CVGA) is a nonprofit organization run by volunteers.

1. CVGA performs adoption preparation for each greyhound as it arrives from a breeding farm or a race track going directly into a foster home to be acclimated to urban life.

2. Mrs. E. Pruisman started three years ago and has placed almost fifty greyhounds that are between two and five years of age. "These creatures deserve a loving home, as they are very affectionate and gentle. Thousands of greyhounds are put to death when their racing days are over without adoption," E. Pruisman. (2004).

   ■ PowerPoint slides help reinforce this. Dwayne also includes this emotional appeal from the woman who started the greyhound adoptions in the area.

III. A number of small business resources are available at little or no cost to the operators to help develop your business foundation.

A. SCORE, Chapter 227, Cedar Rapids, Iowa

1. What is SCORE? score@scorecr.org SCORE is Service Corps of Retired Executives (SCORE)

2. An organization that offers business advice to new small businesses as a no-cost counseling service

   ■ In his third main point, Dwayne gives listeners information to help them research the possibilities as well as helpful advice and sources of advice.

B. In addition to the SCORE group there are many other online sources to help guide your business. The Small Business Administration (SBA).

1. SBA—Starting Your Business Start-Up Basics

   www.sba.gov

2. Small Business Information Center

   www.sbdcnet.utsa.edu

3. Small Home Business Start-Up Basics

   www.digits.com

4. Starting and Growing a Small Business

   www.entrepreneur.com

   ■ The following information is also on PowerPoint slides to help listeners remember it, or to be able to write down things that they found particularly relevant for them.

## Small business resources
## Other helpful organizations

- The Small Business Administration (SBA) http://www.sba.gov
- Small Business Information Center http://sbdcnet.utsa.edu
- Small Home Business Startup Basics http://www.digits.com
- Starting and Growing a Small Business http://www.entrepreneur.com/

IV. To have a successful small business you may also need financial assistance from agencies other than a traditional lending institution such as a bank.

A. Under the Federal and State Technology Partnership Program (FAST), funds now are available to help establish developing business clusters in smaller communities. U.S. Bus. Admin (2004)

   ■ Point IV in the speech provides additional resources, in terms of places to find financial support for one's plans.

B. "Partnerships with The Central Iowa Power Cooperative (CIPCO) can provide up to $10,000 per year to support students in entrepreneurial and business development with Iowa small based business," say Dennis Murdock CEO of CIPCO, as reported by McCue (2004, p. 1).

## Conclusion

In this presentation the items that make up a solid beginning for a small business have been shown. I have also pointed out that ideas don't need to be complex and the reward doesn't need to be material wealth to make business a success. Some of you will be interested in starting your own business; I hope my presentation has helped you to understand that it is possible to find a rewarding alternative in the world of work. Who knows? Maybe the next Michael Dell is among the students in this classroom.[8]

■ In his conclusion, Dwayne simply makes the case for what he's already told the audience in the speech. He has made ample use of statistics and examples throughout the speech, so he felt that the conclusion could simply sum up everything that had been presented.

## References

Hirsch, R.D. and M.P. Peters (1998) *Entrepreneurship,* 4th ed., New York: Irwin/McGraw-Hill.

Kusher, David (2004, September) Magic Man, *Fortune Small Business Magazine* p. 21.

McCue, Tim, NI News Writer, (2004, November, 9) "$10,000 gift to support student entrepreneurial endeavors," *The Northern Iowan,* p. 1.

National Entrepreneurship Assessment 2001 Executive Report. Retrieved November 9, 2004 from www.entreworld.org/usNEA2001.

Pruisman, E., team member Greyhound Adoption Agency, personal interview, (2004, November, 2).

SCORE, Chapter 227, Cedar Rapids, Iowa www.score@scorecr.org.

Simnacher, Dwayne Owner, DASCycle Personal Experience (2004, November, 2).

U.S. Small Business Administration, Office of Advocacy Small Business Profile: IOWA, p. 1 (2004).

## ■ Analysis and Evaluation

Dwayne Simnacher is a nontraditional student at the University of Northern Iowa. In addition to pursuing a bachelor's degree, he opened his own business because he wanted to find a better work environment. His speech in Oral Communication class (in 2004) gave his listeners a chance to understand the how's and why's of starting one's own business. Throughout the speech, Dwayne related the points back to his listeners. He used his own experience as well as the experiences of the well-known and the not-well-known entrepreneurs of the nation to illustrate how one can get started, the kinds of help they can get, and what to expect from owning one's own business.

Dwayne used examples, illustrations, statistics, and the personal experiences of people who started their own businesses to support his claim that owning one's own business provides both personal satisfaction and many benefits one could not attain in a "regular job." While he relates the topic to his listeners in Iowa, the supporting material he uses comes from across the nation and is as applicable to Ohio or to Texas or any other state, as it is to Iowa. He also makes sure to include the numbers of men and women and minorities who have started their own businesses, as well as some of the demographic information about them and their businesses.

His own experience and insights allowed his listeners to gain knowledge of things we might not otherwise have had the opportunity to learn. And, his shared experiences enhanced his credibility. Even if no one in class had ever considered opening a business of their own prior to that presentation, Dwayne's intimate knowledge of the process and the resources was insightful and might have provided a spark for others who want to find a unique career.

What did you learn by reading Dwayne's speech? Can just anyone start up their own business? Why or why not? What does it take to become an entrepreneur? Dwayne would assure you that anyone could find a rewarding alternative, if they're willing to work at creating the best business they can.

# Summary

The ability to present and receive information is vital in an information-oriented society. People who possess information and communicate it effectively possess power and command respect.

We are often asked to give informative speeches. The goal of an informative speech is to increase understanding. The goal of persuasive speaking is to change (alter) attitudes and/or behaviors. Information can be presented without attempting to persuade, but persuasion cannot be attempted without information.

Topics for informative speeches are almost limitless. You should choose something that interests you, that you already have some knowledge about, and that you can find additional information on through your research. Your topic should also be of interest and potentially useful for your listeners. Your specific purpose and the type of topic you choose will determine how you present the speech.

To increase your listeners' knowledge of the topic, you must gain their attention and increase their understanding of the topic. Listeners pay more attention to something that is meaningful to them and obviously important to the speaker. Listeners want novel ideas and want to know "what's in it for me?" The audience will listen if you give them reasons to listen.

Language choice and organization are both critical to audience understanding. The speaker must carefully plan the presentation. Language choice, as we discussed in Chapter 4, is very important in getting your message across and in helping listeners remember. Think about the ways your professors present information. Some of them are more interesting than others. What do the ones you label as "interesting" do that others do not? Did the chapter suggest some of the successful strategies you've noticed? Can you incorporate some of these effective strategies into your speeches?

The evaluation criteria should make you aware of the characteristics of an effective informative speech and speaker. Competent communicators analyze their listeners so they know their choices will work. They find ample sources from a variety of references, and they work to show their listeners the importance of the topic.

## Discussion Starters

1. What is the role of information in our lives?
2. Explain the concept "Information gives one power."
3. What are some examples of one who has the information holding the power?
4. What advice would you give someone about selecting a topic for an informative speech?
5. Where can we go to get information for our speeches?
6. Identify three topics that will work for an informative speech, and explain how you can make them interesting to and relevant for your audience.
7. What does it take to be an effective informative speaker?
8. Which of the criteria identified in the chapter mean the most to you as a listener?

## Notes

1. "Information," 2002 World Book Dictionary Media CD, Version 6.0.2, Mac OS X Edition.
2. *WordNet® 2.0, © 2003 Princeton University,* found at Dictionary.com, last accessed July 16, 2006.
3. This section is based on S. E. Lucas, *The Art of Public Speaking,* 6th ed. (Boston: McGraw-Hill, 1998), 343–52. The categories as cited in Lucas were described first by J. H. Bryns, *Speak for Yourself: An Introduction to Public Speaking* (New York: Random House, 1981), Chaps. 10–15.
4. W. Isaacson, *Benjamin Franklin: An American Life* (New York: Simon & Schuster, Inc., 2003).
5. Ibid.
6. Ibid.
7. Louis Thompson, retired soil scientist, Iowa State University, "Retired Scientist's Moon Theory Points to an Upcoming Drought," *Waterloo-Cedar Falls Courier,* July 16, 2006, D5.
8. Dwayne Simnacher, University of Northern Iowa student, speech presented in Oral Communication, Fall, 2004. Used with speaker's permission.

# Appendix

## Informative Speech Topics

Here are some possible topics for informative speeches. The items listed are not titles of specific speeches and need to be narrowed to fit specific purposes, time limits, or other requirements set by your instructor.

Religions of the World

Medical Breakthroughs

The Future of Space Exploration

Identity Theft

Beneficial Effects of Caffeine

New Treatments for Old Diseases

Disc Golf

Body Piercings

Ethics in America

Laser Technology Advancements

Body Rejuvenation without Plastic Surgery

The Ecosystem

Genetically Modified Organisms

The Never-Ending Conflict Between Nations

Fuel-Efficient Homes

Pharmaceutical Advances

High Cost of Health Care

What is Acupuncture?

Eradicating AIDS

Internet Security

Steroid Use in Sports

Great Statesmen & Stateswomen

World Terrorism

The Future of NASA

Memoirs: Fact or Fiction?

Global Warming

Technological Advances

Canine Disc

Tattoo Artistry

Financial Ethics After Enron

Voting Patterns in the U.S.A.

International Travel

Human Genetic Monitoring

Hybrid Cars

Fuel Conservation

Trouble for dot coms

Alternative Medicine

Juggling, the New Sport

What's the Fuss About Stem Cells?

Bioengineering

Organic Foods & Your Health

The North Pole is Moving

# CHAPTER 12

# Persuasive Speaking

"How the heart listened
while he pleading spoke!
While on the enlightened
mind, with winning art,
His gentle reason so
persuasive stole
That the charmed
hearer thought it was
his own."

—James Thompson

# This chapter will help you:

- **Identify** the goals of persuasion.
- **Choose** a topic suitable for you, your listeners, and the assignment.
- **Select** appropriate goals for your own persuasive speech.
- **Demonstrate** your credibility as a speaker.
- **Apply** evaluation criteria to your own speeches prior to presentation so you can make changes prior to the day you give the speech.
- **Reflect** on the presentation to prepare for future persuasive speeches.
- **Recognize** errors in your own thinking so that you can correct them.
- **Present** a persuasive speech that demonstrates your ability to construct and support your persuasive goals.

# Making everyday connections

Every day of our lives we are either creators or consumers of persuasion—usually both at various times of the day. Think about how many times you at least attempt to persuade someone. You ask your professor if you can have another hour after class to print out the paper that was due at the end of class today because your printer wasn't working and you didn't have time to go to the computer lab before class. You call and ask your parents for "a little money" to help pay your bills. You call the landlord and explain that while you've never been late with your rent payment before, you will get it paid, but you need one more day beyond the grace period. A co-worker asks to switch hours at work with you so he can study for an exam. Your friend or partner wants you to take some time off from all your study so you can go to a movie together. One member of your project group for your marketing class calls to ask you for a ride to and from the group meeting. ■

## Questions to think about

- How much persuasion is involved in each situation?
- What strategies, words, or approaches will make the difference between receiving an affirmative or a negative in each situation?
- What other situations in your everyday life involve persuasion?
- As a consumer of persuasion, what factors will make you say yes? Say no?

Ａs we saw in the opening Making Everyday Connections, persuasion is an everyday occurrence. If you aren't trying to persuade someone else, someone is trying to persuade you. Sometimes it's subtle, other times it's not. When someone recommends a specific movie, book, or video, asks you to vote for a specific candidate, or donate to a certain cause, you are a consumer of persuasion.

Because persuasion is such a vital part of our everyday lives, it is important to understand how to deal with persuasive situations effectively. In this chapter we'll discuss how to select a persuasive speech topic, how to enhance your credibility, and how to develop and prepare a persuasive message. In addition, we'll provide guidelines for persuading others and for being effective consumers of persuasion.

# ■ The Goal of Persuasive Speaking

**Persuasion** is a communication process, involving both verbal and nonverbal messages, that attempts to reinforce or change listeners' attitudes, beliefs, values, or behaviors. David Zarefsky, for example, says that "persuasive strategies aim not only to provide information but also to affect audience members' attitudes and behavior. They ask for a greater degree of commitment from listeners than informative strategies do."[1] Is it possible to change people's attitudes, beliefs, or values without changing their behaviors? The answer is yes. You might, for example, present your friend with reasons for attending one concert rather than another. Your friend might agree and still not buy a ticket. Were you persuasive? You might have been able to convince your friend that your ideas are valid but not to alter her behavior. Which is more important?

The ultimate goal of all persuasion is action or change. Successful persuasion reinforces existing beliefs, attitudes, or behaviors; changes existing beliefs, attitudes, or behaviors; or leads to new beliefs, attitudes, or behaviors. When you want to convince someone not to change, you try to reinforce the existing belief, attitude, or behavior. At other times, you may want a person to do something different. When a speaker's main goal is to achieve change or action, the speaker will pursue one of four subgoals: adoption, discontinuance, deterrence, or continuance of a particular behavior.[2]

Persuasion is usually not a one-shot deal; often, persuasion occurs over time, and the effect of a persuasive message on a listener is not apparent until some time after it has been received. In other words, the listener might think about the message for a long time and, with additional experiences, messages, and information, decide that a speaker was right. The listener might then decide to follow through on the speaker's request for action or change.

**Adoption** is an action subgoal that asks listeners to demonstrate their acceptance of an attitude, belief, or value by performing the behavior suggested by the speaker. One of your classmates might give a speech on becoming a Big Brother or Big Sister in your college community. If you had not previously even considered spending time with a young person but decide to do so after the speech and you become a Big Brother or Sister, you have displayed adoption. Your classmate has persuaded you. This adoption of the persuasive message might be only temporary, and you might not stay with the program throughout your college career or after, but you have responded positively to your classmate's initial persuasive message: to adopt a behavior.

Discontinuance is the opposite of adoption. **Discontinuance** is an action subgoal that asks listeners to demonstrate their acceptance of an attitude, belief, or value by avoiding certain behaviors. If your action subgoal is discontinuance, you want your listeners to stop doing something—going without breakfast, paying high rent,

■ **persuasion** A communication process, involving both verbal and nonverbal messages, that attempts to reinforce or change listeners' attitudes, beliefs, values, or behavior.

■ **adoption** An action subgoal that asks listeners to demonstrate their acceptance of attitudes, beliefs, or values by performing the behavior suggested by the speaker.

■ **discontinuance** An action subgoal that asks listeners to demonstrate their alteration of an attitude, belief, or value by stopping certain behaviors.

Not all persuasion leads to change. People may be persuaded by an argument in theory and still not want to take action. Most skateboarders know that wearing helmets, kneepads, and wrist and hand protectors is important for safety, but some choose not to use these protective devices.

or parking illegally. In these instances, you are trying to get your listeners to discontinue doing something negative.

**Deterrence** is an action subgoal that asks listeners to demonstrate their acceptance of an attitude, belief, or value by avoiding certain behaviors. Sample deterrent messages would be if you don't avoid breakfast, don't start avoiding it now; if you don't use illegal drugs, don't start now; if you are registered to vote, don't stop going to the polls. This action subgoal is similar to discontinuance in that you do not want a negative behavior to occur; but in deterrence, you are trying to *prevent* its occurrence rather than *end* its occurrence.

**Continuance** is an action subgoal that asks listeners to demonstrate their acceptance of an attitude, belief, or value by continuing to perform the behavior suggested by the speaker. For example, if you eat breakfast, don't stop; continue to volunteer as a Big Brother or Big Sister; purchase and consume more organic foods. This action subgoal is similar to adoption because you want a positive behavior to occur; but with continuance, you are trying to *keep* an existing behavior rather than *begin* a new behavior.

Note that the first two action subgoals, adoption and discontinuance, ask people to *change* their behavior, whereas the last two, deterrence and continuance, ask people *not to change,* but to continue doing what they are already doing or not change to something new.

Getting others to change or not to change their behaviors is not always easy. A speaker might have to settle for a change in attitudes, beliefs, or values, such as accepting the idea of wearing seat belts, is part of the persuasive process and must almost always occur before a change in behavior can take place. Not all persuasive speaking will lead to action, nor should persuasive speakers consider themselves failures if they do not obtain behavior change. Sometimes listeners will not immediately accept another's views, but after time and thought, the listener might decide

■ **deterrence** An action subgoal that asks listeners to demonstrate their acceptance of an attitude, belief, or value by avoiding certain behavior.

■ **continuance** An action goal that asks listeners to demonstrate their acceptance of an attitude, belief, or value by continuing to perform the behavior suggested by the speaker.

## MAKING Technology CONNECTIONS

### Persuasive Speech Ideas on the Web

Sometimes reading or listening to famous speeches from the past, or looking at lists of persuasive topics can be a motivation for our own persuasive topic choices. Three of the following sites provide a variety of speeches to stimulate your thought. (Each site was accurate as of July 20, 2006.) The fourth site provides a list of topics. Check each site to see if you can find topics of interest to you.

1. Professor Kay Smith at Valencia Community College has a webpage with more than 170 persuasive topics and questions. While the list is old (1999), it may stimulate your thinking about acceptable classroom topics. Check www.valencia.cc.fl.us/lrcwest/kaysmith.html.
2. The Gifts of Speech site at www.gos.sbc.edu offers (a) speeches of influential women from around the world; (b) Nobel Lectures by women;

and (c) the top 100 speeches of the twentieth century (according to the 137 leading scholars of American public address).
3. If you're interested in political debates, you can find the televised presidential debates from 1960 through 2000 at www.museum.tv/debateweb/html/history/1976/video.html. The site also has a link for curriculum resources on government and politics, history, debate, and communication. Each of these topics includes: topics, resources, glossary, classroom activities, and lines of inquiry.
4. A Google search can help you find all kinds of persuasive topics, including a list from Carla Gesell-Streeter, Instructor of Public Speaking at Cincinnati State Technical and Community College at www.faculty.cinstate.cc.oh.us/gesellc/publicspeaking/topics1.html.

that the persuasive message heard weeks ago was accurate and be influenced enough to change a belief, an attitude, or even a behavior. Persuasion usually occurs over time; and therefore the speaker might not always be aware of whether the message was truly persuasive. Often, listeners are persuaded only after they have heard similar messages from a variety of people, over a period of time. Especially as a beginner at persuasive speaking, you should not always expect to obtain a change in attitude, action, or behavior, but you should be able to get others to listen to what you have to say and to consider your point of view.

## ■ Topics for Persuasive Speeches

Some topics and themes lend themselves more readily to persuasive speaking than others do. Especially adaptable are current and controversial subjects. The list of topics in the appendix at the end of this chapter illustrates the variety of possibilities. You will increase your likelihood of success if you follow these suggestions:

1. Whenever possible, select a topic that you are interested in, know something about, want to speak about, need to speak about, or are personally concerned about. Remember, it is not always possible to choose your own topic; sometimes someone else chooses it for you. For example, a nursing supervisor might tell one of the nurses that he has to speak to a group of visitors about the importance of using sunblock to prevent skin cancer. Certainly, that might not be the first topic of choice for the nurse, but he does meet some of the other criteria for speaking on the subject: knowledge of the topic, awareness of the need, and a personal and professional concern about the topic.

2. Select a subject that is worthwhile and of potential concern to your audience.

3. Select a topic with a goal for influence or action. For example, the notion that exercise and eating well are good for your health might be a good persuasive theme, but if everyone in your audience is healthy and physically in good shape, could you find a strong persuasive strategy?

4. Select an issue that is current, but avoid one that is common knowledge or that has been discussed widely unless you plan to add a new perspective to it (see Chapter 7 on selecting a topic and the appendix at the end of this chapter for a list of persuasive topics).

Persuasive speeches are often, but not always, given on topics for which two or more opposing viewpoints exist and in situations in which the speaker's point of view differs from that of the audience. For example, the speaker might want the audience to support higher tuition because it will lead to more quality instruction, but most of the audience may believe that tuition is already too high. Especially when a speaker's goal is adoption or discontinuance, there must be some difference between the speaker's view and that of the audience, or there is no need for persuasion. However, when the speaker's goal is deterrence or avoidance, the speaker's and the audience's points of view might be more closely united. In such cases the speaker's goal is to reinforce beliefs, attitudes, or behaviors that are similar to those proposed in the speech.

Sometimes speakers want their listeners to think about something from a new perspective, and they try to influence the listeners to accept a specific point of view. The speaker's goal is to persuade the listeners that one point of view is sound, valid, or worthwhile, and the speaker wants to influence the listeners to accept that specific perspective. Such speeches typically address questions of fact, questions of value, questions of policy, or any combination of the three types of questions.

## ■■ Questions of Fact

A **question of fact** asks what is true and what is false. Consider these questions: Which building is the tallest in the world? Who is the richest person in the world? Which basketball player scored the most points last season? Which university was the first to be established? Who first developed the computer and for what uses? These questions can be answered with a fact that can be verified in reference books. Because they are so cut and dried, there can be little debate about them, thus making them weak topics for a persuasive speech.

In contrast, persuasive speeches may be built on predictions of future events that will eventually become matters of fact. Consider these: When will Americans elect a woman president? Which college football team will win the national championship next year? Will computers replace textbooks? Although none of these questions can be answered with certainty, a persuasive speaker could build an effective case predicting the answer to each.

Persuasive speeches can also be based on complicated answers to questions of fact or justifications for answers that are unclear. Why did so many tragic air disasters occur during the past decade? Was it because of drugs? Poorly trained air traffic controllers? Overworked controllers? Outdated equipment? Insufficient rules for the use of airspace near airports? Although no one answer covers the entire situation, a speaker could build a strong argument to show that one of these factors is the primary cause of air accidents.

Finally, some persuasive speeches may attempt to answer questions of fact that are not completely verifiable: Do unidentified flying objects really exist? Can

■ **question of fact** A question that asks what is true and what is false.

hypnotism enable a person to relive past lives? Is there intelligent life in outer space? A speech on why we should stop wasting water in our everyday lives might be planned this way:

| | |
|---|---|
| To persuade my listeners that we should stop wasting water | ■ Specific purpose |
| It is in our best interests to stop our everyday waste of water. | ■ Thesis |
|   I.  We often take water for granted. | ■ Main point |
|     A.  Distribution of the earth's water | ■ Subpoints |
|     B.  Water use per person | |
|   II.  Common ways to waste water | ■ Main point |
|     A.  Washing hands | ■ Subpoints |
|     B.  Brushing Teeth | |
|     C.  Showering | |
|     D.  Letting water run | |

On the surface, questions of fact may appear more appropriate for an informative speech than for a persuasive one, but if you consider the difficulty of persuading an audience that college athletics are big business, that a major fire will destroy much of Southern California, or that the pyramids of Egypt were designed by an intelligence far superior to ours today, you can see that questions of fact can offer rich possibilities for persuasion.

## ■■ Questions of Value

A **question of value** asks whether something is good or bad, desirable or undesirable. Value was defined in Chapter 3 as a general, relatively long-lasting ideal that guides behavior. A value requires a more judgmental response than a fact. Here are some typical questions of value: Who was the best president of this country? Who was the most influential world leader? Are international students better students? The answers to these questions are not based solely on fact, but on what each individual considers to be right or wrong, ethical or unethical, acceptable or unacceptable, or a good or a bad choice.

■ **question of value**
A question that asks whether something is good or bad, desirable or undesirable.

The answers to questions of value may seem to be based solely on personal opinion and subjectivity rather than on objective evidence, but this is not the case. Effective persuasive speakers will have evidence to support their positions and will be able to justify their opinions. For example, suppose a speaker says that bars should not target college students with their drink specials. He might plan his speech as follows:

| | |
|---|---|
| To persuade my listeners to support legislation banning alcohol specials such as two-fers or dollar draws | ■ Specific purpose |
| Bar owners target college students with their specials, thus encouraging underage drinking and excessive drinking. | ■ Thesis |

I. Bar owners' advertised drink specials encourage underage college students drinking.

    A. Underage college students interviewed by the campus newspaper stated that bar advertisements made them feel they needed to go there to drink.

    B. Underage college students are quoted as saying that the advertisements enticed them.

II. College students attribute bar specials as a cause of excessive drinking.

    A. Bar specials mean that cash-strapped students can get more drinks for their money.

    B. Once college students get to the bars and imbibe the specials, they forget to think about the dangers of excessive drinking.

■ Main point

■ Subpoints

■ Main point

■ Subpoints

Values vary dramatically from one person to the next. Person A might think that rap music is bad for society, and Person B might think that it is good for society; Person A might think that alcohol should be illegal on campus, and Person B might think it should be legal. When it comes to questions of value, one person's judgment is no better or worse than another's. People's values are usually complicated because they are rooted in emotion rather than reason. It is often extremely difficult to get people to change their values. A speaker's position on a question of value might be difficult to defend. You will need to gather a great deal of research and evidence and build a strong case to support one value over another—even though you know your values are right—because your listeners also believe that their values are right.

## ▬ Questions of Policy

A **question of policy** goes beyond seeking judgmental responses to seeking courses of action. Whereas a question of value asks whether something is right or wrong, a question of policy asks whether something should or should not be done. Should student parking on campus be more accessible? Should universities provide birth control to students? Should all students be tested for drugs before entering

■ **question of policy**
A question that asks what actions should be taken.

# Calvin and Hobbes     by Bill Watterson

Values are complicated. The cartoon illustrates the point that values are often based on emotion and personal views and, thus, are difficult to change.

college? Should the government provide basic health care for every U.S. citizen? Should everyone working in jobs that involve the safety of others be tested for drugs? Questions of policy involve both facts and values and are therefore never simple. And the answers to questions of policy are not agreed on by everyone in the same way.

Persuasive speakers can defend an existing policy, suggest modifications of an existing policy, suggest a new policy to replace an old one, or create a policy where none exists. If you defend an existing policy, you must persuade your listeners that what exists is best for the situation. If you want to modify or replace an existing policy, you must persuade your listeners that the old policy does not work and that your new one will. If you hope to create a new policy, you must persuade your audience that a policy is needed and that yours is the right one for the situation.

When discussing questions of policy, persuasive speakers usually focus on three considerations: need, plan, and suitability. If you believe that things are not fine as they are, then you must argue that there is a *need* for change. When you advocate change, you must provide a *plan,* or a solution. The plan tells the audience what you think should be done. Finally, you must defend your plan by explaining its *suitability* for the situation. Study the use of need, plan, and suitability in the following:

| | |
|---|---|
| To persuade my listeners that embryonic stem cell research should be unrestricted and have full government funding | ■ Specific purpose |
| Embryonic stem cell research is a new research area that has the potential for numerous treatments and cures for many disabling and terminal diseases and conditions. | ■ Thesis |
| I. According to the National Institutes of Health, there are 128 million people in the United States living with incurable or untreatable diseases or conditions. | ■ Need |
|   A. Stem cell research is most promising in treating these conditions. | |
|   B. Stem cell research is already helping people with Parkinson's disease and Alzheimer's disease. | |
| II. We must lobby Congress and our state legislatures to provide funding for embryonic stem cell research. | ■ Plan |
|   A. The first step is to educate policymakers on the benefits of embryonic stem cell research. | |
|   B. The second step is to lobby for the repeal of laws against stem cell research. | |
| III. Educational lobbying campaigns can help both the public and our policymakers learn about the true nature of embryonic stem cell research. | ■ Suitability |
|   A. Educational lobbying campaigns can educate people about the benefits of this research. | |
|   B. Once policymakers and the public are aware of the benefits, restrictions can be lifted to promote additional research.[3] | |

# ■ Persuasive Claims

When attempting to answer questions of fact, value, and policy, we cannot always develop a formal logical answer that will irrefutably counter the objections of others. Formal rules of argument do not always determine who is right and who is wrong. Even when you supply compelling evidence to support your view, most evidence is not 100 percent clear-cut and may be interpreted in different ways. These factors make persuasive speaking especially challenging.

Stephen Toulmin, a British philosopher, developed a model to help understand everyday persuasive arguments.[4] Although not everyone uses Toulmin's model for understanding and presenting arguments, a brief discussion of the model may be helpful, to both listeners and speakers, as a means of evaluating arguments. Toulmin's approach to supporting a persuasive position or argument involves three basic parts: claim, data, and warrant. The *claim* is what the persuader wants or hopes will be believed, accepted, or done (or, in terms of what we discussed in the previous section, whether it is a fact, a value, or a policy). Claims, however, require evidence, or what Toulmin refers to as *data*. Data are the supporting materials or evidence that should influence the listener to accept the claim as stated. Unfortunately, there is not always a clear or irrefutable relationship between the claim and the data. Thus the persuader must explain the relationship between the claim and the data. Toulmin refers to this as the *warrant*. Here is a possible application of Toulmin's model:

**Claim:** Americans waste thousands of gallons of water daily.

**Data:** According to the American Water Works Association, Americans consume about 100 gallons of water each day. Of that, 28 percent is used for toilets, 22 percent for clothes washers, 21 percent for showers (we each use about 20 gallons of water per shower), 12 percent from faucets, 9 percent from baths, 5 percent from toilet leaks, and 3 percent is used for washing dishes.

**Warrant:** Because we don't have to worry about the availability of water in the United States, we waste a great deal of water. And, because water is so plentiful, we think nothing about letting it run while we wash our hands, brush our teeth, or take a long, leisurely shower.

According to Toulmin's model, listeners can usually respond to the claims in three ways.

1. They can accept the claim at face value. This usually occurs when it is common knowledge that the claim is probably true. For example, a statement that U.S. educational programs need improvement is generally acceptable at face value.
2. They can reject the claim outright at face value. This usually happens when the claim is clearly false, such as the claim there is no pollution in U.S. lakes and streams. It also occurs when listeners are biased against the claim or see no relationship between the claim and themselves. For example, if a claim that U.S. forests are not being depleted is made to a group trying to preserve the environment, it is unlikely they would accept this claim because of their biased views.

### Everyday Acts of Persuasion

People often believe that persuasion only refers to situations where you change someone's mind and reverse a listener's beliefs. Actually, persuasion is broader than that. There is more to our views than a simple, "Yes, I believe that," or, "No, I disagree." Most of us have a range of commitment to any given idea. A persuasive speaker wants to move us one way or the other, along a continuum. David Zarefsky tells us that persuasion may involve: strengthening commitment, weakening commitment, converting, or inducing a specific action.[5] During the 2000 presidential campaign, Al Gore and Joseph Lieberman told audiences that the entertainment industry needed to more carefully market adult entertainment to children. Some members of their audiences accused Gore and Lieberman of undermining the First Amendment, while Gore and Lieberman said they were trying to weaken the industry's commitment to a position.

1. Can you think of examples where others have tried to weaken your position on something? How did they attempt to do so? What was the effect on you?
2. Identify one example in your own life of each of the above (strengthening, weakening, converting, or inducing an action). Be prepared to talk about its effect.
3. What types of action subgoals have you experienced in the last day or two?
4. How did the persuader attempt to persuade you? How successfully?

3. They can accept or reject the claim according to their evaluation of data and warrant. The person making the claim must provide evidence to support the claim or demonstrate that it is true.

When speakers provide evidence to support their claims, it is still up to listeners to accept the claim based on the evidence presented. Listeners essentially have three options:

1. They can accept the claim as supported by evidence.
2. They can reject the claim as not supported by the evidence.
3. They can request that the speaker provide more evidence to support the claim.

Competent speakers must develop arguments strong enough to make the claim and the supporting evidence stand on their own merits. They realize that not everyone will interpret the evidence in the same way they do, nor will everyone be convinced, even though the evidence they present may be, in their opinion, the best there is.

## ■ Establishing Credibility

The most valuable tool that you, as a persuasive speaker, can possess is credibility or believability based on the audience's evaluation of you as a speaker. At various points in this book, we have referrred to the speaker's credibility. Listeners will assess your competence, knowledge, and experience; your charisma and energy; and your character. The audience is the ultimate judge of credibility, but there is much you can do to influence their opinion. The key is to establish yourself as worthy of the listeners' attention right from the beginning of your speech.

## ▬ Competence

An audience will judge your competence by the amount of knowledge, degree of involvement, and extent of experience you display. The more expertise you show in your subject, the more likely it is that your audience will accept what you have to say. You can establish your expertise in several ways:

1. *Demonstrate involvement.* Martha is an international student from Mexico who spends her summers working on service projects in developing countries. In her visits, she has seen villagers travel three hours to get enough water for their families, and watched them carry water for a three-hour walking journey home. Although her visits did not in themselves make her an expert on the subject of scarce water, they established her credibility as a speaker because of her first-hand involvement.

2. *Relate experience.* One young man volunteered at the Red Cross and talked about the ever-increasing need for blood donors because of all the world calamities. He cited specific statistics about the amount of blood sent to the Gulf Coast after Hurricane Katrina and the blood and supplies sent to Indonesia after the tsunami. His own experience in helping get supplies ready to send made his listeners accept him as a knowledgeable person.

3. *Cite research.* Quoting information from written sources and interviews with experts can add weight and objectivity to your arguments. Mentioning sources that are respected by your listeners adds to your credibility and indicates that you are well read. Let's say you want to persuade your listeners that they can overcome communication apprehension. The following research may enhance your credibility on this topic:

According to James McCroskey, the communication professor who created the concept of communication apprehension, thousands of people in the United States alone suffer from some degree of communication apprehension. McCroskey has published hundreds of articles on the symptoms and effects of communication. McCroskey's website identifies him as the author, coauthor, or editor of forty-four books and two hundred journal articles. *The Quiet Ones: Communication Apprehension and Shyness,* deals with communication apprehension. You can visit his website at www.jamesmccroskey.com.[6]

## ▬ Character

An audience's judgment of your character is based on their perceptions of your trustworthiness and ethics. The best way to establish your character is to be honest and fair.

**Trustworthiness.** A speaker's **trustworthiness** is the audience's perception of the speaker's reliability and dependability. Others attribute trustworthiness to us based on their past experiences with us. For example, instructors may judge our reliability according to whether we come to class every time it meets. Friends may evaluate our dependability according to how we have followed through on our promises. People who have had positive experiences with us are more apt to believe we are trustworthy.

**Ethics.** In Chapter 1, we defined ethics as an individual's system of moral principles and stated that ethics play a key role in communication. Though this is certainly true in communication in general, it is especially true in persuasion. Persuasive speakers who are known to be unethical or dishonest are less likely to succeed in achieving their persuasive purpose than are people recognized as ethical and honest. You must earn your reputation as an ethical person through your actions. The best way to establish yourself as an ethical speaker is to do the following:

1. *Cite sources when information is not your own, and cite them accurately.* As you develop your speech, be sure you give credit to sources of information and to ideas that are not your own. If you do not mention the sources of your information, you are guilty of plagiarism. Provide the audience with an **oral footnote,** such as "the following was taken from . . ." or "the following is a quotation from. . . ." Be specific about from whom and where your information came.

2. *Do not falsify or distort information in order to make your point.* Never make up information, attribute information to a source who is not responsible for it, take quotations out of context, or distort information to meet your purpose.

3. *Show respect for your audience.* When audience members perceive that you are being respectful, even though they may not agree with your point of view, they are more likely to listen. And when they listen, you at least have a chance of persuading them. Do not try to trick audience members into accepting your point of view or to ridicule them for not agreeing with you.

## ▬ Charisma

As we stated earlier, other factors influence the way the audience perceives you. Among those is **charisma,** or the appeal or attractiveness that the audience perceives in the speaker contributing to the speaker's credibility. We often associate charisma with leaders who have special appeal for large numbers of people. Charismatic speak-

■ **trustworthiness**
The audience's perception of a speaker's reliability and dependability.

■ **oral footnote**
Providing within the speech the source that particular information comes from, such as "According to *Newsweek* magazine of July 24, 2006 . . ."

■ **charisma** The appeal or attractiveness that the audience perceives in the speaker, contributing to the speaker's credibility.

## for Success

### Persuasive Speakers

Have you ever noticed how the situation makes some speakers effective at one time and neither effective nor credible in others? If you've ever watched the news, C-Span, *The O'Reilly Factor,* or *Larry King Live* and seen such public figures as Diane Feinstein, Bill Frist, Ted Kennedy, John McCain, or Hilary Rodham Clinton in more than one of those shows, you may notice different people: they may seem more credible, effective, and persuasive when they're speaking one-on-one rather than speaking on a partisan issue in Congress. McCain and Kennedy, for example, have been known to "rant and rave" when speaking in a Senate committee, but come across as

much more mellow and contemplative when speaking with Larry King, or speaking to "regular" audiences. Think about public speakers (politicians, people in the news, media personalities, local officials, local "celebrities") whom you have heard, either in the media or in person.

1. Who were the credible ones?
2. Were they persuasive? How so?
3. What characteristics made them effective?
4. What can you learn about persuasion from the effective speakers?

ers seem to be sincerely interested in their listeners, speak with energy and enthusiasm, and generally seem attractive and likable. A credible speaker will take command of the speaking situation and engage the listeners so that they know that the message is honest, well prepared, and relevant. Charismatic speakers are able to get the audience involved in their messages.

Your audience's evaluation of your credibility will ultimately determine whether they accept or reject your persuasive goals. You should remember that credibility is earned, that it depends on others' perceptions, and that it is not permanent. Credibility changes from topic to topic, from situation to situation, and from audience to audience, and so you must establish your credibility each time you speak.

# ■ Becoming Effective Consumers of Persuasion

We spend a great deal of our lives listening to persuasive messages of one kind or another. It is important to think about what it means to be an effective consumer of those messages. (Refer to Chapter 6 to review the role of the listener in the persuasive process.)

As listeners, we have both the right and the responsibility to get accurate, reliable, and worthwhile information. Listen carefully to the message, and ask these questions:

How knowledgeable is the speaker?

What sources has the speaker used to gain additional information?

Are these sources reliable and unbiased?

Are there real advantages to accepting this position?

## MAKING CONNECTIONS for Success

### Using the Web to Find Supporting Materials

The Web provides a vast source of information for us all and can be a good place to find supporting materials. Check these helpful sites if you're still looking for a topic, or, if you're looking for additional data or material to support your claims.

1. Findarticles.com offers free access to "millions of articles from thousands of top publications." Topics are: Arts & Entertainment, Automotive, Business & Finance, Computers & Technology, Health & Fitness, Home & Garden, News & Society, Reference & Education, and Sports. You can search the database by keyword or subject category at www.findarticles.com/PI/index.jhtml.

2. Government websites may be found at www.firstgov.com. This URL links you to 20,000 government websites in a streamlined search-by-topic search engine.

3. Statistical data from over one hundred U.S. federal agencies in the areas of agriculture, crime, demographics, economics, education, energy, environment, health, income, labor, natural resources, safety, and transportation are available at www.fedstats.gov.

4. OnlineNewspapers.com is a metasite that indexes 10,000 online newspapers from around the world. These are offered by country, province, or state with links to the newspapers' homepages: www.onlineNewspapers.com.

5. Pub List offers a "database of over 150,000 magazines, journals, newsletters, and other periodicals." You can find "free in-depth information on familiar and hard-to-find publications from around the world, representing thousands of topics." The site is: www.publist.com.

Is the evidence presented in the argument worthwhile?

Can I believe the evidence?

Where can I get additional information?

Does the argument seem logical?

It pays to closely analyze and evaluate the information presented, whether you are listening to an advertisement, a telemarketer, a political candidate, a religious leader, or a financial planner. Use questions like these to evaluate information:

Is this *really* good information?

Is the information really relevant to me?

How can I learn more about this?

What additional questions should I ask to make sure that I get accurate and reliable information and sources?

Does the information really support the argument, or is it interesting but not essentially related?

Is there sufficient support for the claims and arguments?

Are there errors in the reasoning or the evidence?

Does the message basically make sense—and why or why not?

Also pay attention to the person delivering the message:

Is the speaker ethical and trustworthy? What is the evidence?

Is the speaker competent and knowledgeable? What is the evidence?

# ■ Preparing and Developing a Persuasive Speech

In a classroom situation, you typically will have only one opportunity to coax your audience to accept your persuasive purpose. Therefore it is important to set realistic persuasive goals and to give some special thought to what is covered in Chapters 7, 8, and 9 about researching, organizing, and gathering support for your speech. Review those chapters for a complete perspective. Much of this section reinforces these earlier chapters.

## ■■ Researching the Topic

Research for a persuasive speech must be especially thorough. You will need to gather as much information as possible about your topic, because the more you know, the better equipped you will be to support your position. When doing your research, look primarily for evidence that supports and clarifies your views. If, in the process, you discover information that contradicts your stand, make note of it and look for material that you can use to refute such information. Anticipating possible objections is especially helpful when your position is controversial and when your audience's opinions are likely to be split. If you know the arguments that could be used against you, you will be better able to support and defend your position.

## ■■ Organizing the Speech

A persuasive speech requires making several special decisions that will affect its organization. Here are decisions especially related to persuasive speaking:

1. *Should you present one side or both sides of an issue?* The answer to this question depends on your audience. If your listeners basically support your position, then presenting one side may be sufficient. If their views are divided or opposed to your position, it may be more effective to present both sides. This decision also depends on your audience's knowledge of the topic and their evaluation of your credibility. If audience members are well informed and educated, presenting both sides of an argument helps minimize the effect that counterarguments can have on your audience.

2. *When should you present your strongest arguments?* Presenting your strongest arguments at either the beginning or the end of your speech is more effective than presenting them in the middle. A good strategy is to state your strongest arguments early and then repeat them toward the end. Because audience attention is most likely to wander in the middle of a speech, that is a good time to present personal examples supporting your position.

3. *What is the best way to organize your persuasive speech?* The most effective sequence of presentation depends on your topic, specific purpose, and audience. Among the patterns of organization that work well for persuasive speeches are problem–solution, cause–effect, and Monroe's motivated sequence, which were discussed in Chapter 9.

## ▬ Supporting Materials

In persuasive speeches, speakers try to influence audience members through the impressiveness of their supporting materials. They choose their supporting materials carefully to build the kind of appeal that is most likely to sway their listeners. Based on the topic and their audience analysis, persuasive speakers try to appeal to their listeners' needs, to logic, or to emotions.

**Appeals to Needs.** **Appeals to needs** attempt to move people to action by calling on physical and psychological requirements and desires. Of course, different people have different needs, but most of us want to protect or enhance factors that affect our physical, safety, social, and self-esteem needs according to psychologist Abraham Maslow. According to Maslow's hierarchy of individual needs, our lower-order needs must be satisfied before higher-order needs.[7]

*Physical needs* are our most basic physiological requirements, such as food, water, sleep, sex, and other physical comforts. *Safety needs* pertain to our desires for stability, order, protection from violence, freedom from stress and disease, security, and structure. *Social needs* relate to our hopes to be loved and to belong, and our needs for affection from family and friends, for membership in groups, and for the acceptance and approval of others. *Self-esteem needs* reflect our desires for recognition, respect from others, and self-respect.

Speakers can appeal to any of these needs to motivate listeners to take action. For example, a speaker trying to sell individual retirement accounts would aim his appeal at our needs for security and stability; a speaker who hoped to persuade us to lose weight would call on our needs for physical comfort, acceptance by others, and self-esteem. Our readiness to accept ideas or to take action depends heavily on the speaker's ability to relate a message to our needs.

**Logical Appeals.** Attempts to move people to action through the use of evidence and proof are called **logical appeals.** When speakers lead their listeners to think "Yes, that's logical" or "That makes sense," they are building a case by calling on their audience's ability to reason. To accomplish this, competent persuasive speakers use evidence such as statistics, examples, testimony, and any other supporting materials that will sway their listeners.

A logical appeal requires an ability to argue for your point of view. When you argue in persuasive speaking, you usually make a claim or state an argument or *proposition,* which is what you want your listeners to believe after you have completed your speech. A claim or proposition usually assumes that there is more than one way to do things. For example, abortion should be illegal or abortion should be legal, the electoral process should or should not be changed. Speakers usually try to justify such a position with reason and evidence. The *justification,* or data, involves the use of all the supporting materials you can find to support your claim or proposition, including statistics, facts, examples, testimony, pictures, objects, and so on.

In presenting their evidence, persuasive speakers guide their listeners through a carefully planned sequence of thought that clearly leads to the desired conclusion. This train of logic may fall into one of four categories: deductive reasoning, inductive reasoning, causal reasoning, or reasoning by analogy.

**Deductive reasoning** is a sequence of thought that moves from general information to a specific conclusion. It presents a general premise (a generalization) and a minor premise (a specific instance) that leads to a precise deduction (a conclusion about the instance). One student set up his argument as follows:

■ **appeal to needs** An attempt to move people to action by calling on their physical and psychological requirements and desires.

■ **logical appeal** An attempt to move people to action through the use of evidence and proof.

■ **deductive reasoning** A sequence of thought that moves from general information to a specific conclusion; it consists of a general premise, a minor premise, and a conclusion.

| | |
|---|---|
| **General Premise:** | Americans consume too much sugar. |
| **Minor Premise:** | Sugar causes health problems. |
| **Conclusion:** | Americans who consume too much sugar will have health problems. |

Great care must be taken to ensure that the premises are accurate because faulty premises can lead only to a faulty conclusion. For example:

| | |
|---|---|
| **General Premise:** | Conservatives are radical in all their views. |
| **Minor Premise:** | Lowell Christensen is a conservative. |
| **Conclusion:** | Lowell Christensen is radical in all his views. |

The general premise must be both accurate and defensible before deductive reasoning can be used effectively as evidence to support a position.

**Inductive reasoning** is the opposite of deductive reasoning; it is a sequence of thought that moves from the specific to the general. An argument based on inductive reasoning usually progresses from a series of related facts or situations to a general conclusion. A student discussing the need to protect oneself from identity theft might lead her listeners through the following sequence of inductive reasoning:

| | |
|---|---|
| **Facts:** | **1.** Identity theft is a growing problem. |
| | **2.** Identity theft can create devastating results. |
| | **3.** It's a hassle to get your identity and your good credit back. |
| | **4.** Identity theft claims a new victim every 4.5 seconds. |
| | **5.** You can protect yourself against identity theft. |
| **Conclusion:** | You could be the next victim of identity theft unless you take steps to protect yourself. |

When your facts can be verified, when there are a sufficient number of facts, and when there are sufficient links between the facts and the conclusion, inductive reasoning can be an excellent way to persuade an audience of the validity of your argument.

Inductive reasoning can also be misused. How often have you heard general statements such as: all college professors are radical liberals; all car salespeople are dishonest; religiously devout people of all kinds are dangerous; all accounting majors are brilliant. Each of these generalizations is based on someone's past experience. The reality, however, is that limited past experience does not support the conclusion.

To avoid problems when using inductive reasoning, make sure your facts are accurate and that they support your conclusion. Also, make sure your conclusion does not extend beyond the facts you have presented. You will undermine your own case if your conclusion is so general that someone can easily point out exceptions to it.

**Causal reasoning** is a sequence of thought that links causes with effects. Thus it always implies or includes the word *because:* The earth's temperature is rising *because* the ozone layer is thinning. As in any form of reasoning, it is necessary to support the conclusion with evidence. In the example in this paragraph, the speaker would go on to cite scientific evidence linking thinning ozone to rising temperatures. The more verifiable and valid the evidence, the more defensible is the conclusion about the cause-and-effect relationship between ozone and temperature. Even though other factors may also be causes of the earth's warming, the

■ **inductive reasoning** A sequence of thought that moves from specific facts to a general conclusion.

■ **causal reasoning** A sequence of thought that links causes with effects; it either implies or explicitly states the word *because.*

speaker's argument can be considered reasonable if it is based on scientific evidence that supports the speaker's point of view.

**Reasoning by analogy** is a sequence of thought that compares similar things or circumstances in order to draw a conclusion. It says, in effect, that what holds true in one case will also hold true in a similar case. If you were to argue that we should make every effort to save the world's diminishing supply of water, you might use the following reasoning:

| | |
|---|---|
| **General Premise:** | Americans have an ample water supply and take it for granted that they will always have enough water for their needs. |
| **Minor Premise:** | In developing countries the water supply is limited, so people are very careful about their water use. |
| **Conclusion:** | People in the United States should save water as carefully as people in developing nations do in order to avoid reduced water supplies in the future. |

Analogies are useful reasoning tools when they are used wisely and with appropriate support for your conclusions. The relationship in the analogy must be valid, and the conclusion should be based on the assumption that all other factors are equal. For instance, our example is based on the assumption that people in developing nations are careful with the supply of water and that is seen as a positive action and Americans would do well to emulate the conservation of a diminishing natural resource. If the argument implied that there were other reasons for water conservation, other than that it's a diminishing natural resource, the argument would fail. To avoid problems when using analogies, it is crucial to consider any dissimilarities that might refute your point.

You might wish to base your speech on a single form of reasoning, or you might prefer a combination of types of reasoning. Whatever your choice, you must remember that your argument is only as good as the evidence you use to support it.

**Emotional Appeals.**   Attempts to move people to action by playing on their feelings—for example, by making them feel guilty, unhappy, afraid, happy, proud, sympathetic, or nostalgic—are known as **emotional appeals.** Because emotions are extremely strong motivators, this form of appeal can be highly effective. Note how the following introduction to a persuasive speech appeals to the emotions:

> My grandfather is a wonderful, caring person. He was always the person who would listen to me and lend me a shoulder to cry on. He is also one of the most intelligent people I've ever known. When I was growing up, Grandpa gave me suggestions to help me solve all kinds of problems, everything from completing my homework, to discussing why my friends were not friendly, to helping me find a summer job. Today, however, my grandfather doesn't know who I am, let alone my name, and he often doesn't even realize that I'm in the room with him. You see, Grandpa suffers from Alzheimer's disease. There is no cure, and we still don't know very much about it. What we do know, however, is that it takes the real person and their minds and leaves a hollow shell.

**■ reasoning by analogy** A sequence of thought that compares similar things or circumstances in order to draw a conclusion.

**■ emotional appeal** An attempt to move people to action by playing on their feelings.

Emotional appeals can be so powerful that they sway people to do things that might not be logical. A student's cheating on an exam, for example, can by no means be justified through logical thought, but the student may believe that she is justified from an emotional viewpoint because of parental pressure to get good grades. In fact, persuasive speakers often mix both logical and emotional appeals to achieve the

## MAKING CONNECTIONS for Success

### Consumers of Persuasion

We are constantly bombarded by attempts to persuade us to do something. Advertisers want you to take advantage of a credit card that will solve your financial problems (and likely create new ones); four or five direct mail advertisers send you offers for better cable and Internet services; another set of mailings wants you to donate to a worthy cause; a speaker wants you to donate blood to the local chapter of the Red Cross. Keep track of persuasive attempts for a two-day period. Identify and create a list of the number of times someone tries to persuade you, and then analyze the content so that you can share it with your class.

1. How many different persuasive attempts were made in that two-day period?
2. What kinds of reasoning were used by the persuader?
3. What strategies appealed to you? Which ones did not?
4. If any were successful, what made the persuasion a success?
5. Were the persuaders ethical? How so? Or, why not?

strongest effect. Persuasive speakers need to be aware of the issue of ethics discussed throughout this text. A speaker must present valid, reliable information in a way that will appeal to the listeners but will not violate their rights or their responsibilities. The speaker should be fair, accurate in presenting views, careful in presenting information, and attentive to the strategies used. An ethical speaker uses emotional appeals carefully and truthfully.

## Persuasive Strategies

Speakers need to use persuasive strategies to win over their listeners. First, the speaker needs to demonstrate *rhetorical sensitivity,* that is, the speaker needs to be aware of the audience and their needs, the situation, the time limits, and what listeners want and are willing to hear. The speaker is aware that listeners expect a strong, clear message to which the speaker is committed and in which the speaker believes. The speaker will also carefully adapt the message so that the listeners know that it is relevant and important to them. The audience expects the speaker to motivate them or make them want to hear the speech and learn more about the argument. The audience expects to understand the speaker's point. The audience expects the speaker to repeat and reinforce the message so that they are influenced to, at the very least, accept that the speaker has a point worth considering. All in all, the persuasive speaker will always keep the listener in mind while reinforcing the argument.

Speakers need to use persuasive strategies to win over their listeners. Bono is aware that listeners expect a strong, clear message to which he is committed and in which he believes.

# ■ Fallacies in Argument Development

As both creators and consumers of persuasive messages, all of us must be able to analyze and evaluate others' as well as our own use of reasoning to support persuasive messages (see Chapter 6). It is especially important to avoid causing listeners to question your credibility by presenting flawed arguments. Arguments that are flawed because they do not follow the rules of logic and, therefore, are not believable are called **fallacies.** Flawed reasoning occurs all the time, and often people do not realize that they have used flawed arguments. As a critical thinker, however, it is important that you understand what fallacies are, how to recognize them, and why you should not use them or let others use them in their communication.

Many different types of fallacies are used in communication, but only the commonly used or major errors are presented here. Let's look at basic fallacies in reasoning and evidence.

## ■ Fallacies of Reason

**Questionable Cause.**   **Questionable cause** is a common fallacy that occurs when a speaker asserts something that does not relate to or produce the outcome claimed in the argument. It is a part of our nature to want to know what has caused certain events to occur. If tuition is increasing, people want to know why; if the national deficit is increasing, we want to know why; if parking space on campus or at the shopping center is decreased or eliminated, we want answers! In a desire to know the cause of certain behaviors or events, we sometimes attribute what has happened to something that is not even related to the situation. For example, claiming that attendance at home athletic events has increased because there's nothing else to do on campus is a questionable cause, especially if there are the same number of activities on campus and in the community as in previous years.

**Ad Hominem.**   When someone attacks a person rather than the person's argument, he or she resorts to an **ad hominem** fallacy. This is also referred to as *name-calling.* If you call someone a geek, a klutz, or a jerk in response to an argument being made in order to diminish the relevance or significance of the argument, you are using name-calling as a refutation of the argument. This is merely a smoke screen; it shows an inability to provide good counterarguments or evidence to challenge what the other person is claiming. Name-calling, ridiculing, or personally attacking another person can diffuse an argument, but it usually results in a bad argument that side-steps the issue.

## ■ Fallacies of Evidence

**Fact versus Opinion.**   A major misuse of information involves the presentation of facts and opinions. Speakers who state opinions as if they are facts can be misleading and may be presenting a fallacious argument. For example, "our university's policy on drinking is too stringent" and "our university is short 250 parking spaces" are both statements of information. Which is fact, and which is opinion? The first statement is opinion, and the second is fact. How can you tell which is which? Facts can be verified; the lack of parking spaces can be verified, whereas the university's policy on drinking may be stringent or not, which is a matter of opinion.

Giving opinions can be helpful in persuasive speeches or arguments, but to treat an opinion as if it were fact or a fact as though it were an opinion is an error in criti-

■ **fallacy** An argument that is flawed because it does not follow the rules of logic.

■ **questionable cause** A fallacy that occurs when a speaker alleges something that does not relate to or produce the outcome claimed in the argument.

■ **ad hominem** A fallacy that attacks a person rather than the argument itself. This is also referred to as *name-calling.*

cal thinking. In either case, you will appear to claim too little or too much and raise questions about your competence and ethics.

**Red Herring.** Another misuse or avoidance of facts is the use of irrelevant information to divert attention from the real issue. This occurs when a speaker wishes to draw attention away from an issue that is being questioned or challenged. For example, have you ever questioned someone about something he or she did wrong, and the response you got didn't relate to the event to which you were referring? In fact, the person may change the subject or even attack your credibility to avoid discussing the issue. Irrelevant information used to divert attention away from the real issue is referred to as a **red herring** fallacy.

**Hasty Generalization.** As a common critical thinking fallacy, the **hasty generalization**

occurs when a speaker doesn't have sufficient data and therefore argues or reasons from a specific example. Conclusions are drawn from insufficient data or cases. It is not uncommon to find people making generalizations based on only one or only a few examples. For instance, to argue that male students think date rape is not a problem on their campus, a speaker might cite the opinions of two or three close friends. The speaker then states the following conclusion: "In surveying people I know, I have found that most students do not believe that date rape is a problem in our city." The argument that date rape is not a problem might sound impressive, but it does not represent a large or representative sample of students; therefore the claim is unjustified. The argument can be refuted as a hasty generalization.

When you develop or encounter arguments or reasoning that do not fit any of the fallacies described in the text but you doubt the argument's validity, put the argument to the following test: Can the argument be outlined? Do the data support the claim? Is there a solid relationship between the data and the claim? It is not important to know the name of a specific type of fallacy but to analyze how arguments are developed and used in order to determine whether they are valid.

■ **red herring** A fallacy that uses irrelevant information to divert attention away from the real issue.

■ **hasty generalization** A fallacy that occurs when a speaker does not have sufficient data and therefore argues or reasons from a specific example.

## Making Effective Persuasive Speeches — GUIDELINES

1. Be realistic in setting your persuasive goal and determining what you expect to achieve.
2. Conduct a thorough audience analysis to help you choose the most appropriate strategy for accomplishing your persuasive goal.
3. Clearly identify a need so that the audience recognizes that something should be done.
4. Be sure your solution is consistent with the audience's beliefs, attitudes, values, ethical standards, and experiences.

5. Make sure your solution is workable and practical so that your listeners can actually do or accept what you are asking of them.
6. Point out the advantages of what you offer and how those advantages will benefit your listeners. Remember that people are unlikely to accept your persuasive goal unless they see something in it for themselves.
7. Build your argument so any possible objections to your proposal by the audience will be clearly outweighed by the benefits the audience members will gain if they accept your proposal.
8. Use only valid and reliable evidence to support your persuasive goal.
9. Be ethical and fair in both content and tactics.
10. Practice until you are able to present your speech without having to read it word for word.
11. Deliver your speech with enthusiasm, sincerity, and confidence.

# ◾ Evaluating the Persuasive Speech

Here are some of the criteria used to evaluate the competence of the speaker and the effectiveness of a persuasive speech. Your instructor may consider these areas when evaluating your speech. You should be aware of them while preparing a persuasive speech presentation.

## ▄▄ Topic

The selection of topic should meet the following criteria:

- ◾ The topic should merit the audience's attention.
- ◾ The audience should be able to see the relationship between the topic and speaker and between the topic and themselves.
- ◾ The topic should be able to be adequately covered in the time available. The topic should have been narrowed enough to be fully developed.

## ▄▄ General Requirements

The following represent general requirements of most persuasive speech presentations:

- ◾ The purpose of the speech should be clearly to persuade and stated as such.
- ◾ The speech should meet the time requirements set by the assignment.
- ◾ The speaker should cite sources of information that are not his or her own.
- ◾ The speech purpose should be relevant to the assignment and related to the audience.
- ◾ The speech should show evidence of careful preparation.

## ▄▄ Audience Analysis

The speaker must shape the speech to suit the audience. This often requires research into the listeners' past experiences, beliefs, attitudes, and values. The choices the speaker makes regarding content and development of ideas should be tailored to the audience. (Chapter 7 provides details on audience analysis.)

- The speech should reflect appropriate audience analysis.
- The speaker should relate to and refer to audience members to get them involved and interested in the topic.
- The speech should include a goal, that is, the audience should be asked to think something, believe something, or take action.
- The speech should show the audience why the topic is important and relevant to them.

## Supporting Materials

Supporting materials supply documented evidence that the information conveyed in the speech is accurate and credible.

- The supporting materials help the audience to believe the information.
- The supporting materials should appeal to the audience's needs, logic, and emotions.
- The supporting materials should include a variety of factual statements, statistical data, personal experiences, analogies, contrasts, examples and illustrations, expert testimony, value appeals, and eyewitness accounts.
- Visual aids should be used where appropriate and helpful; they should follow guidelines established by the assignment.
- The supporting materials should be documented, cited correctly, and up to date.
- The supporting materials help the speaker to establish and maintain credibility.

## Organization

When judging the organization, the evaluator looks for a carefully planned, well-developed persuasive speech that takes a unified approach to the material being presented.

- The introduction should be properly developed.
  - It should orient the audience to the topic.
  - It should gain the audience's attention and arouse interest.
  - It should include a specific purpose and thesis statement.
  - It should define terms (if necessary).
  - It should motivate the audience to listen.
  - It should be relevant.
  - It should establish credibility.
- The organization of the body should be clear and easy to follow.
  - The main points should be clear and parallel in structure.
  - The main points should be related to the purpose of the speech.
  - Transitions should provide appropriate links between ideas.
  - The organizational pattern should be appropriate.
- The conclusion should be properly developed.
  - It should reinforce the purpose by reviewing the main points.
  - It should end with a memorable thought.
  - The audience should know what action is expected of them in response to the speech.

Poet and best-selling author Maya Angelou speaks with high energy and enthusiasm to an audience on the University of Northern Iowa's campus. She is able to get her audience involved in and enthusiastic about her topic, and the enthusiasm on both sides is infectious.

## Delivery

The delivery techniques provide evidence that the speaker is aware of what the audience is interested in hearing, is involved in and enthusiastic about the topic, and is interested in sharing the material with the listeners.

- The speaker should be enthusiastic.
- The speaker should convey a persuasive attitude through focus, energy, and appropriate vocal variety.
- Nonverbal communication (gestures, movements, eye contact, posture, facial expression) should enhance and clarify the verbal delivery.
- The speaker should be aware of the audience's presence and reactions and should adjust his or her delivery accordingly.
- The speaker should be confident and poised.
- The speaker should convey a sense of the topic's relevance and importance.
- The speaker's vocal delivery should enhance the speech with appropriate volume, appropriate rate, conversational quality, enthusiastic tone, clear enunciation, appropriate pauses, and appropriate vocal variety.

## Language Choice

As we discussed in Chapter 4, effective use of language is critical to communication. It is especially essential to use language carefully when crafting a persuasive message. Clear, vivid, specific, and acceptable language should be used to enhance and clarify ideas.

- The language choice should be appropriate to the assignment and audience.
- The language should be compelling.

- The word choice should be appropriate for the speaker, topic, situation, and audience.
- Grammar should be appropriate and show both competence and an awareness of the "formal" speaking situation.
- Word pronunciations should be correct.

Speakers should evaluate their own speeches and those of others. The forms in Figures 12.1 and 12.2 can help you analyze and reflect on the speeches you give and those to which you listen.

---

■ **FIGURE 12.1** Speaker's Self-Evaluation Form

On completing your persuasive speech, take a few moments to reflect on and think about all its elements. Using this form can help. Put yourself in the place of your listeners, and be specific in your comments on each aspect of the speech.

**Title of speech:** _____

**Date and place given:** _____

**Topic selection** _____

**Research** _____

**Appropriateness** *(to you, the classroom, the situation, the audience, the time limits)*

_____

**Organization** _____

**The introduction** _____

**The body** _____

**The conclusion** _____

**Explanation and clarity of ideas** _____

**Soundness of the claims or arguments presented** _____

**Support for ideas** *(Valid, worthwhile, ethical, sufficient number, clear?)*

_____

**Use of language** _____

**Visual delivery** *(movement, gestures, eye contact, posture)* _____

_____

**Vocal delivery** *(conversationality, sincerity, variety, ease of listening)*

_____

The ways I adapted this speech to this audience: _____

_____

If you made this speech again, what would you change? Why? _____

_____

What would you retain? Why? _____

_____

■ **FIGURE 12.2** Sample Listener Evaluation Form for Persuasive Speeches

Listeners are often called on to evaluate speakers. Some instructors have listeners complete an evaluation similar to this one. It provides the speaker with invaluable information. It is also a good critical thinking exercise for the listener.

Speaker _____ Topic _____ Date _____

1. What was the speaker's specific purpose? _____
2. What was the speaker's thesis? _____
3. Which arguments did you believe? Which arguments did you have a hard time believing? Were you convinced about the claim or argument the speaker presented? Why or why not?

_____

_____

4. What would it take to make you change your beliefs, attitudes, or behaviors about this topic? Do you think you might be influenced by this speaker and the stand taken in this speech? _____

_____

5. Did you hear any faulty reasoning in this speech? What kind? How could the reasoning be improved? _____

_____

6. Did the speaker provide support for arguments, statements, and claims? What types of evidence and support were provided? _____

_____

7. Was the speaker believable? Why or why not? What could the speaker do to be more believable? _____

_____

8. Was the speaker ethical? Fair? Accurate? _____
9. What kinds of appeals were used? _____
10. Was the speaker easy to follow? Was the organization clear? _____

_____

**GUIDELINES** | **Tips for Persuasive Speakers**

1. Establish yourself as an ethical communicator by employing good research, oral footnotes, and careful use of language and information.
2. Use repetition and restatement to help your listeners remember your speech.
3. Use appropriate organizational patterns.
4. Select appropriate supporting materials.
5. Use sound reasoning. Think about Toulmin's model and make your claim, support your claim with evidence (data), and show how the claim and date connect (warrant).

# ■ A Sample Persuasive Speech with Commentary

The following transcript was adapted from a speech by Martha Aragon, a student in Oral Communication Class at the University of Northern Iowa in 2004.

### It's Your Water: Don't Waste a Diminishing Natural Resource!

To persuade my audience to stop water waste in all daily activities.

■ Purpose

It's 8 a.m. I sit on the couch and my friend Tena turns on the shower to get ready to go to work. I look at the clock. It is now 8:20 a.m. and I can hear the water in the shower is still running. Twenty minutes later—the shower is still running. Finally, at 9 a.m., Tena turns off the shower and prepares for work. Think about that scene with me for a minute. Tena seems to take the availability of water for granted. She was lucky enough to be born in a country that can provide her with clean water to meet her daily necessities so she does not consider water as a life or death issue as it is considered in many other countries where people die because they have no access to water, not even to meet their most basic needs. It would be great if everyone could "use" as much water as they wanted without running the risk of facing life-threatening problems in the future. Unfortunately, that is not the case.

■ Introduction

■ Martha's opening narrative is something that many of us can agree with and understand. She makes us listen to her story and think about the effects.

I. Water is all around us and perhaps because of that, we often take it for granted.

■ Body

A. The distribution of the earth's water is as follows: 97.5% is salt water and only 2.5% is fresh water, but, 68% of the 2.5% of the fresh water available is frozen in the ice caps and 31% is located deep underground, so only 1% of fresh water is accessible.

■ In her first main point, Martha reminds us that water is all around us and something we take for granted. If we listen, carefully, however, we note that she reduces "all that water" to a very small percentage of usable water.

B. According to the American Water Works Association, the average person uses one hundred gallons of water a day. Most of the water is used in the bathroom: 28 percent to flush the toilet, 22 percent to wash clothes, 21 percent to take a shower, 12 percent is used by faucets, 9 percent to take baths, 5 percent for toilet leaks, and 3 percent for dishwashers.

■ The amount of water used, in percentages, for each activity should make us think about how much water we really use every day.

## ■ Earth's Water Distribution

| | |
|---|---|
| Salt Water | 97.5 % |
| ■ Fresh Water | 2.5 % |
| Ice caps | 68.0 % |
| Ground Water | 31.0 % |
| Accessible | 1.0 % |

Source: *The Atlantic Monthly*, July-August 2003

II. There are some common ways for us to waste our water.

    A. Hand washing. It is very normal for us to wash our hands without turning off the water faucet since we don't have to walk at least three hours to bring water home as many people around the world do.

    B. Teeth brushing. We let the water run while brushing our teeth. This seems to be the correct way to do it for many of us and we don't even bother to think that while we let the water run for no reason at all, women and children in some countries spend more than two hundred million hours just to walk to collect water for their use.

    C. Showering. Many of us like to take a shower without turning off the water, not even for a second. We don't take into account that we use approximately fifteen to twenty-five gallons of water in a five-minute shower, and that we are not the only ones who take a daily shower.

    D. Letting the water fountain run. Some people, once they have used the water fountain, are not careful to make sure it is off before they leave. They will sometimes let the drinking water go to waste, while some people in the world would be so thankful to have at least safe water to drink.

III. There are many water-related problems.

    A. There are water-related diseases.

        1. According to the Parliamentary Office of Science and Technology, one billion people do not have access to safe drinking water and four million people die from water-related diseases every year.

        2. In Bangladesh, about thirty million people from a population of more that 130 billion are likely to suffer arsenic-related diseases.

        3. Another water-related disease is Dracunculiasis, caused by the guinea worm. Its symptoms are: burning, itching in the affected areas, and often, fever, diarrhea, and vomiting. The adult female worm measures more than three meters in length and two millimeters in diameter, while the adults measure about twenty to thirty mm.

    B. The destruction of our ecosystem. Our activities affect the environment, too. Take a look at this picture of the Aral Sea. The Aral Sea was the fourth largest lake in the world prior to 1960. Now, the level of the water has dropped fifteen meters and it is going to keep decreasing if we don't do something about it.

    C. Statistics of the future.

        1. We all know that our population is growing very fast and according to the United Nations Population Fund, once we

■ Information relevance

■ Because we have a plentiful supply of water, we often do not think about those who live in countries where unsafe water causes illness and the result of our waste of a precious nonrenewable natural resource.

■ These numbers are compelling.

get to nine billion people, the water that will be available to us is going to be severely limited.

2. If people continue to use water at the same pace as people from developed countries now do, then 90 percent of all accessible water will be depleted by 2025.

IV. Things we can do to conserve water in our homes.

    A. When washing your face, brushing your teeth, or shaving, turn off the water faucet, and don't let it run the whole time.

    B. When showering and shampooing, turn off the shower for the time you're lathering.

    C. Use only the minimum amount of water necessary when doing things such as washing dishes.

    D. Promptly repair any leaking faucets.

I know many of us don't worry about water availability because we don't have to go through the entire struggle that many people go through. And, I know that we have faith that science is going to solve the water problem. Frank Moss, the author of *The Water Crisis*, says that we are not concerned because Americans have found the way to the moon, have created nuclear bombs to destroy the earth, and so forth, and that we already know how to desalinate seawater, but despite all these things, science cannot solve the political and legal problems that need to be solved first.

Finally, I know that many of you might think that if you do these things you are not going to make a big difference in a world with six billion people. But, we do have to begin somewhere, and soon! For, if you waste it now, it won't be available for you or anyone else later. Each of us can make a difference. We just have to start now, and spread the word. It's your water! Don't waste it. Water is life.[8]

■ Martha spent considerable time describing the extent of the problem. Now she's asking us to think about what we can do. "What's in it for me?" has been a recurring theme in her message. Here she tells us how we can make a difference.

■ Conclusion

■ Martha uses logic here and a reminder of information relevance to get people to understand the nature of the problem. She uses an author to remind us that not everything can be solved through science.

■ Martha's concluding statements repeat the relevance of the topic to each of us; and she uses emotion as well as logic to support her point. Her passionate delivery is also compelling.

## Bibliography

Addikson, Roy and Douglas Sellick. Running Dry. New York: Stein and Day, 1983. 29+.

American Water Works Association. "25 Facts About Water." 2004. 24 Nov. 2004 www.awwa.org/Advocacy/learn/info/425FactsAboutWater.cfm

Enviromental Situation. "Human Impacts on Lakes." 06 Nov. 2004 www.gep.iatp.org.ua/lake%20_pol.htm

Greeson, Phillip. Geological Survey Circular 848-D. "Infectious Water-borne Diseases." U.S Government Printing Office, 1981. 10.

Lawton Water Treatment Plant. "Facts About Water." 2003. 24 Nov. 2004 www.cityof.lawton.ok.us/waterplant/fact.htm.

Moss, Frank. The Water Crisis. New York: Frederick A. Praeger, 1967. 5.

National Wild & Scenic Rivers System. "River and Water Facts." 2004. 24 Nov. 2004 www.nps.gov/rivers/waterfacts.html.

Poe, Marshall and Jen Joynt. Waterworld: "The global scarcity of water is overblown. The real problem is sanitation. (The World in numbers)."(2003): 1-5. ASAP. Rod Library, University of Northern Iowa, Cedar Falls. 01 Nov. 2004 www.infotrac.galegroup.com/itw/infomark/502/340/57226379w6/purl=rc1_EAIM_0_A104210504&dyn=3!xrn_5_0_A104210504?sw_aep=uni_rodit.

Rogers, Peter. America's Water. Massachusetts: The Twenty Century Fund, 1993. 4.

The United Kingdom Parliament. "Access to Water in Developing Countries." 2002. 11 Nov. 2004 www.parliament.uk/index.cfm.

TVNZ. "The water that saves, the water that kills." 06 Nov. 2004 www.health.nzoom.com/health_detail/0,2811,219603-399-403,00.html.

United Nations Population Fund. "Water: A Critical Resource." 2002. 11 Nov. 2004 www.unfpa.org/issues/factsheets/pdfs/linking_water.pdf.

Water Partners International. "Water and Sanitation Facts." 2004. 11 Nov. 2004 www.water.org/assets/PDF/factsheet2003.PDF.

Welsh, Frank. How to create a Water Crisis. Boulder: Johnson, 1985. 3.

**Pictures taken from:**

www.efluids.com/efluids/gallery/splash.jpg

www.altoonashospital.org/fg/washing_hands.jpg

www.unicef.org/wes/950356e.jpg

www.dfait-maeci.gc.ca/canada-magazine/issue16/site/images/water2.jpg

www.lvwater.org/images/kidbrush.gif

www.missiontohaiti.org/Media/Clean-Water-Color-Mask.jpg

gbgm-umc.org/nwo/01ma/water.html

www.fotosearch.com/comp/phd/PHD243/46013.jpg

www.dermatologaldia.cl/images/pelocaida33.jpg

www.oxfamamerica.org/image/6692/well_sm.jpg

www.islamic-relief.com/projects/images/Bangladesh/IR-staff-teaching-women.gif

www.web.maynard.ma.us/history/schools/nms/nms9726.jpg

fmacu.wfuca.free.fr/eau_pour_la_vie.htm

www.clearwaterproject.org/images/bangladesh/Arsenic-s.jpg

www.health.nzoom.com/health_detail/0,2811,219603-399-403,00.html

www.asylumeclectica.com/malady/archives/dracun/cracun4.jpg

www.cns.miis.edu/pubs/dc/briefs/vozipres.htm

www.oemagazine.com/fromTheMagazine/sep02/images/dustfig2.gif

www.hgtv.ca/home/articles/article10.asp

www.askjuan.com/html/ppt/estructura/Sustainable%20Coffee%20Production%20Practices%20in%20Colombia/sld45.htm

## ◼◼ Evaluation and Analysis

This speech was one the speaker, Martha Aragon, felt passionately about—it was evident in her physical and vocal delivery that she'd chosen a topic that was meaningful to her. As such, it was easy for the audience to listen to her and hear her out. Several commented in the peer listener assignment that they had really never before thought about how much water we waste. The assignment was for a speech to convince—get the listeners to accept your ideas as worthy and valid. Action may be identified, but the big push was to convince the listeners that the ideas presented had merit.

In the speech and in the PowerPoint slides Martha presented, she made it clear that she had completed ample research and was well prepared to give the speech. The ideas flowed well and the slides emphasized the content. While Martha used many logical appeals, the pictures and the content also made use of emotional appeals. She got us to think, and perhaps to think about turning off the water while we're lathering our hair, and not letting the water run as much as we normally do.

What did you notice about this speech? Did the logic appeal to you? Had you given much thought to the ways we waste water before? Will this speech make you think about saving water the next time you take a shower?

## ◼ Summary

We need to be aware that persuasion affects us every day in almost every aspect of our lives. We attempt to persuade others just as others attempt to persuade us. Persuasion is an active, goal-oriented process. The subgoals of persuasion involve persuasive strategies to get people to act or believe in specific ways.

When you are assigned to present a persuasive speech in class or to a work group or for an organization of which you are a member, you need to think about your own interest in a topic and its value to your listeners. You should also consider whether or not it is a suitable action goal. You will answer questions of fact, values, or policies in your persuasive attempts. The Toulmin model can help you make clear arguments so that your listeners understand the claims, data, and warrants inherent within your persuasive attempt.

If you want your audience to listen to you and accept your views, you need to be perceived as a credible speaker who knows what she or he is talking about. Citing sources and providing oral footnotes can enhance your appeal to your listeners.

Effective persuasive speakers pay careful attention to research, organization, and supporting materials. Effective consumers of persuasion are concerned with good, reliable, relevant information from ethical sources and should carefully listen to, analyze, and evaluate all persuasive messages. Good speakers will avoid the fallacies of arguments and consider the criteria and strategies included in this chapter in order to be more persuasive.

## Discussion Starters

1. How does persuasion affect you?
2. What factors influence your view of an effective persuasive speaker?
3. Why do we suggest that behavioral change is the ultimate goal of persuasion?
4. What characteristics enhance your own evaluation of a speaker?
5. If speakers do not appear to be credible in your eyes, what can they do to gain or regain credibility?
6. What are the major differences between informative and persuasive speeches?
7. Are supporting materials used differently in a persuasive speech than they are in an informative speech? Explain your views.
8. How do you know whether a speaker is effective?
9. What factors are essential in an effective persuasive speech?

## Notes

1. D. Zarefsky, *Public Speaking: Strategies for Success,* 4th ed. (Boston: Allyn and Bacon, 2005), 410.
2. Adapted from W. Fotheringham, *Perspectives on Persuasion* (Boston: Allyn and Bacon, 1966), 33.
3. Adapted from a speech by Tim Schmidt, Oral Communication, University of Northern Iowa, Fall 2003, and used with permission.
4. S. Toulmin, *The Uses of Argument* (Cambridge: Cambridge University Press, 1969), 94–145.
5. Zarefsky, *Public Speaking,* 379.
6. J. McCroskey, www.jamescmccroskey.com. Last accessed July 20, 2006.
7. A. Maslow, *Motivation and Personality,* 2nd ed. (New York: Harper & Row, 1970). Maslow, in this edition, includes two additional desires or needs—the need to know and understand and an aesthetic desire—as higher stages of his hierarchy. These are often associated as subcategories of self-actualization, which is not included in this text.
8. This speech was presented by Martha Aragon, in November 2004, and is used here with her permission. Ms. Aragon was a student in Oral Communication at the University of Northern Iowa.

## Persuasive Speech Topics

Here are some possible topics for persuasive speeches. The items listed are not necessarily titles of specific speeches and might need to be narrowed to fit specific purposes, time limits, or other requirements set by your instructor.

Reduce Smoking—Live Longer

How to Reduce America's Obesity Problem

Congressional Term Limits

Stop Hate Speech!

Racial Profiling Is Wrong

FaceBook Should Be Monitored

Time Management Is Beneficial

Donating Blood Is Critical

Monitoring Adult Entertainment for Children

The Benefits of Acupuncture

Volunteer for Big Brothers/Big Sisters Today!

The Internet Must Be Censored!

The Internet Must NOT Be Censored!

Stop Elder Abuse

Stop Government Graft & Corruption

Say Yes to a Healthy Lifestyle!

Reorganize U.S. Education

Decrease Funding for Stem Cell Research

Increase Funding for Stem Cell Research

Requiring Internships without Pay

Affirmative Action Should Be Removed—
Its Goals Have Been Met

Drug Testing for Athletes

Drug Testing for Employees

Voter Apathy—What to Do?

Control Road Rage

Blogs Should Be Monitored

Baseball Must Control Steroids

Organizing Your Life Is Easy

Rain Forest Devastation

Choosing Alternative Medicine

Save the Environment!

Global Warming & the Environment

Dangers on the Internet

The Benefits of Massage Therapy

Environmental Awareness

Benefits of Chiropractic Medicine

Reduce Pharmaceutical Costs

Save Your Life—Avoid Tanning

Civic Engagement

Making a Difference

Why Students Should Be Required to
Participate in Service Learning Programs

# CHAPTER 13

# Interpersonal Communication

"You can make more friends in two months by becoming interested in other people than you can in two years by trying to get other people interested in you."

—DALE CARNEGIE

## This chapter will help you:

- **Improve** your interpersonal communication competence.
- **Become** familiar with interpersonal communication theories and frameworks.
- **Understand** the fundamental motivations related to our need for interpersonal interactions with others.
- **Know** the connection and differences between face-to-face and online interactions.
- **Improve** your small talk when attempting to initiate relationships.
- **Understand** self-disclosure and its role in our interactions with others.
- **Become** more competent in your use of self-disclosure.

## Making everyday connections

The following is taken from an essay titled "The Donut Shop Experiment," written by Jonathan Butler, a high school history teacher in Riverside, California. According to Mr. Butler, he and a group of his friends and relatives wanted to do something crazy on a Saturday night. They were tired of board games and television. So about ten of them, some under thirty and some over—brothers, a sister, a friend, in-laws, and parents—struck on an idea that the group of them would infiltrate a little café in twos and threes, at differing times, until all were seated around the counter. They would arrange themselves as couples chatting, an old man sitting alone, or three friends in a row. Their plan was to interrelate—"get acquainted"—as total strangers appearing to get to know one another. Their plan was to see how the others in the café would react.

They chose a doughnut shop with a truck-stop atmosphere . . . that lacked promise socially. Then one of them asked the cashier, "Say, do you use bleached flour in these donuts?" From that one question, conversation flowed and relationships began to form.

Butler writes, "The conversation ranged from food to politics to music to how strangers never talk in strange places like a café." The people in the café, according to Butler, reflected on what they were doing and laughed, realizing that an improbable conglomerate of people had formed some kind of community.

The group of ten left the café and arrived back at Butler's home dazed by the experience. Butler ends the story with: "How thin the walls that divide us from one another at ballparks and grocery stores and restaurants. How paper-thin."[1] ■

**Questions to think about**

- What do you think Butler means by his last statement?

- Why is it so easy to communicate with those we don't know via the Internet but not as easy when we are in face-to-face situations?

- What does Butler's café experiment tell us about communication and relationships?

- What does it mean to have "people skills"?

- How does having "people skills" differ from having interpersonal communication skills?

- Why do you think employers place so much importance on hiring people with interpersonal communication skills?

The title on the cover story of *Newsweek* (April 3, 2006) read "Putting the 'We' in Web." It appears that more and more of our time is spent communicating with others on the Web. Websites such as MySpace, Facebook, Xanga, Flickr, Myphotos, and YouTube are some of the latest in social networking. Facebook presently has the largest number of registered college students blogging each other, connecting with friends, and posting pictures of themselves in sometimes very revealing ways.[2] There is little or no question that the Internet is changing how we meet, interact, and form relationships with others.

The Internet is also changing how and what we communicate about ourselves to others and especially to those whom we don't know or know very well. It is not unusual for some students to place very personal information as well as photos on the Internet that they might not ever provide in a face-to-face meeting. Whether in a doughnut shop, chatroom, workplace, library, student union, dorm, athletic event, wedding, meeting, or on an airplane, train, website, or any place where people interact verbally and nonverbally, the success or effectiveness of their interactions will depend on their interpersonal communication skills. What does it mean to be a competent communicator in interpersonal situations? It is our purpose in this chapter and the following chapters in this section to provide you with an answer to this question and more.

## ■ Connecting with Others via Interpersonal Communication

Connecting with others and forming relationships is what interpersonal communication is all about. In Chapter 1, we defined interpersonal communication as creating and sharing meaning between persons who are in a relationship. This definition implies that interpersonal communication occurs between two or more people, can be casual, considered private, and reveals personal information. In addition, we stated in Chapter 1 that small groups and interviews also use various forms of interpersonal communication.

We know that not all of interpersonal communication is personal or private. Casual conversation or small talk is often very impersonal and can be very public; for example, Internet interactions, cell phone conversations, or other interactions that occur in public places can be overheard or viewed by others. Interviewing, which is a form of interpersonal communication, is dyadic by definition and includes casual or small talk, but is usually more formal, more highly structured, and usually private. Although there are many different types of interviews such as employment, information gathering, counseling, surveys, and so forth, the employment interview is for most of us one of the most important interpersonal communication interactions of our lives.

Interpersonal communication is often thought of as interaction that only occurs among those with whom we have close relationships. This, of course, is not always true; for example, there are individuals who will disclose the most personal information about themselves or others to complete strangers via the Internet or sitting next to someone on an airplane but not communicate that same information to a loved one. Thus, interpersonal communication occurs in a variety of contexts and situations and can be impersonal/superficial or personal/intimate, private or public, unstructured or highly structured. Our interpersonal competencies will likely differ not only from each other, but from situation to situation and from one person to another in how we are perceived by those with whom we interact. Competent interpersonal communicators know how to adjust and communicate effectively with a variety of people from diverse backgrounds in order to establish short or long-term relationships.

A **relationship** is an association between at least two people. It can be new or old, momentary or long lasting, superficial or involved, casual or intimate, friendly or unfriendly, relaxed or tense, hateful or loving, important or unimportant, good or bad, happy or unhappy, and so on. Relationships can also be described in terms of the level of intimacy or kinship, for example, girlfriend, boyfriend, lover, wife, husband, mother, father, child, uncle, cousin, stepparent, or stepchild. Sometimes relationships can be described on the basis of the roles people have in the relationship, for example, roommates, Internet friends, neighbors, boss and employee, co-workers, classmates, doctor and patient, ex-spouses, and so on. Relationships can be described in terms of time spent together, for example, "I knew her in high school" or "They just met him

■ **relationship** An association between at least two people, which may be described in terms of intimacy or kinship.

## MAKING Technology CONNECTIONS

### Proper Email and Email Etiquette

**To:** Smith@Yahoo.com
**From:** Stickittoya@hotmail.com
**Re:** _____

I am in your 2:30 class and I don't know what is expected of me on your next assignment—is it do on Tuesday or Thursday; your directions wasn't clear. I THINK THIS CLASS REQUIRES TOO MUCH WORK AND I DON'T HAVE THE TIME THIS WEEK TO GET IT DONE. I also need to be out of town next week so I am going to have to miss class. Will I miss anything when I am gone?

Grant ☺

1. What is the student's email message communicating?
2. How would you rewrite the above email?
3. What email etiquette rules did Grant violate in his email?
4. Can you recommend any websites, books, or articles to help you learn about proper email etiquette?
5. What are the rules that you should follow when sending email or text-messaging?

Most people who have physical disabilities will tell you that they don't want special treatment. Most prefer to be treated like any other person—as a person first.

the other day." Relationships may be based on shared activities or participation in events, for example, "We play volleyball together," "We go to the same yoga classes," "He is in my class," "She works with me," or "We both are from the same hometown."[3] Relationships are sometimes described in terms of situation or happenstance, for example, "We met on the Internet," "We met on the plane," "We sat at the same dinner table on the cruise ship," "We met at a bus stop," "We sat next to each other at the game," "We met over spring break in Florida," or "She takes her kids to the same daycare." However we describe them, we all have a need to enter relationships with others.

# ■ Motivation and Need to Form Relationships

Most of us want relationships in order to give our lives meaning and to fulfill a variety of social and psychological needs we have as human beings. Our motivations for staying in relationships are certainly varied and not always completely understood, as when people who have choices remain in abusive relationships. In this section, we discuss three different but related theories that help to explain why we have such a strong desire to interact, to form and keep relationships with others: uncertainty reduction theory, social exchange theory, and fundamental interpersonal relations orientation theory.

## ■ Uncertainty Reduction Theory

■ **uncertainty reduction theory** A theory suggesting that when we meet others to whom we are attracted, our need to know about them tends to make us draw inferences from observable physical data.

In the opening Making Everyday Connections scenario, the motivation of the group in the doughnut shop was to find out how others would react to their behavior. The desire to know about others and to understand how and why they behave as they do can be partially explained by uncertainty reduction theory.[4] **Uncertainty reduction theory,** developed by communication scholars Charles Berger and Richard Calabrese, suggests that when we meet others to whom we are attracted, our need to know about them tends to make us draw inferences initially from the physical data that we observe. An urge or desire to reduce our uncertainty about those individuals motivates our desire for further communication with them. The theory's core assumption is that when strangers meet, they seek to reduce uncertainty about each other. The more attracted we are to the other person, the stronger is the desire to know more about that person.

According to the theory, reducing uncertainty is necessary in relationship development, so as we increase our desire to develop a relationship with others, we utilize more uncertainty reduction behavior. There are three stages of initial interaction. During the *entry phase,* we learn information that is easily observed, for example physical appearance cues such as sex, age, height, skin color, physical attractiveness, and economic or social status. We can easily supplement these observations with additional information, which we can obtain either from others or via conversation during this phase of relationship development. When we first meet someone, however, our communication is usually controlled by social rules and norms. That is, it is usually considered improper in the entry phase to ask intimate personal questions of the other person. When people begin to share attitudes, beliefs and values, and more personal information, they have entered the *personal phase* of the relationship. During this phase, the communication is less constrained, and there is more openness to freely communicate. The third phase of initial interaction is the *exit phase.* It is in this phase that the future of the relationship is decided. Effective interpersonal communication is often the critical difference between termination or continuation of the relationship.

To illustrate the three phases consider the following example: Olivia sees Sam across a crowded room at a party and is interested in meeting him. She observes that he is standing by himself and thus assumes he came to the party by himself, but isn't sure. She knows nothing about Sam and doesn't know if he is dating anyone or if he is serious about someone, for that matter. Olivia's uncertainty is high, but so is her desire to find out more about him (entry phase). She learns from a friend that Sam is single, but doesn't know if he came with anyone to the party or not. Olivia's uncertainty has been somewhat reduced but certainly not eliminated. She decides that the only way to learn more about Sam is to be direct and talk with him. She does find out that he came by himself to the party and that he is not dating anyone at the present time (personal phase). The party ends and Olivia and Sam are still talking with each other and have truly enjoyed their time visiting, but now they must decide what will happen next with their relationship. After almost an hour of conversation, they decide to share phone numbers with the idea that they might continue their relationship (exit phase).

## ■■ Social Exchange Theory

Have you ever entered a relationship because of the benefits that you believed you would gain from it? Of course you have. We all have at one time or another entered relationships because we believed there would be benefits for us to do so. For example, you date someone because you are receiving—companionship, affection, love, and ego-gratification. Social psychologists John W. Thibaut and Harold H. Kelley originated the **social exchange theory,** which is based on the assumption that people consciously and deliberately weigh the costs and benefits associated with entering a relationship and seek out relationships that benefit them and avoid those that don't.[5] Thibaut and Kelley believe that most of us are motivated to enter and maintain relationships in terms of the exchange of benefits and costs. A **benefit** is anything that is perceived to improve our self-interest. It refers to things or relationships that bring us pleasure, satisfaction, or gratification. For example, outcomes such as good feelings, status, prestige, economic gain, or fulfillment of emotional needs are considered benefits. **Costs** are negative things or behaviors that we perceive to be not beneficial to our self-interest. For example, in order to enter or maintain a relationship it takes time, and physical and emotional energy, and there are almost always some economic costs as well, such as buying dinners or gifts.

■ **social exchange theory** A theory based on the assumption that people consciously and deliberately weigh the costs and rewards associated with a relationship or interaction.

■ **benefit** Anything that is perceived to improve our self-interest.

■ **costs** Negative things or behaviors that we perceive to be not beneficial to our self-interest.

According to the theory of social exchange, we are motivated out of self-interest to act or behave in certain ways. Social exchange theorists argue that we assess our relationships in terms of these costs and rewards. For instance, when we are with friends we are giving up our time to be with them, which is necessary to maintain a relationship, so in a sense the time spent is a cost. There are times, however, when friends may need us at an inopportune moment; then the costs of the relationship are higher. For example, you are trying to finish a term project that is due the next day and your best friend has just broken up with his girlfriend and needs to talk with you. You can see that the friendship is costing you time that you need to complete your term project. So in a sense, you must weigh the costs and benefits of the time you give to your friend.

The theory suggests that if the benefits we gain are greater than any potential costs we incur, then we likely would regard the relationship or interaction as pleasant and satisfying. But if the benefit gain (benefits minus costs) falls below a certain level, then we might find a relationship or interaction not worth the potential cost. The ratio between benefits and costs varies from person to person and from situation to situation. Thus, what is a desirable ratio of benefits and costs for one person may be different for another person. If a relationship is healthy and satisfying, there is probably equity or what is referred to as equality between benefits and costs. Equality is when people are engaged in a relationship in which both parties perceive a balance between benefits and costs that is "fair" or "equal" for each person in the relationship. It should be no surprise then that most relationships begin and prosper because those involved benefit in some way from it.

## ■■ Fundamental Interpersonal Relations Orientation Theory

Interpersonal communication literature consistently discusses the premise that each of us needs to include others in our activities and to be included in theirs, to exert control over others and have them control us, and to give affection to others as well as receive it from others. Will Schutz, a psychologist and one of the most respected leaders in the field of human relations, developed **fundamental interpersonal relations orientation theory,** which provides insight into our communication behaviors. Schutz's theory consists of three needs: affection, inclusion, and control.[6] Although many other needs exist, according to Schutz, most of our interpersonal behavior and motivation can be directly related to our need for affection, inclusion, and control. Although needs differ from person to person, from situation to situation, and from culture to culture, knowing and understanding our interpersonal needs should help us understand how they influence our interactions with others.

For most of us, our interpersonal needs do not remain static; desire and importance vary with circumstances. For instance, giving and receiving affection might be far more important in a relationship, especially as the relationship intensifies and moves toward bonding, whereas inclusion might be more significant when a relationship is coming apart. Awareness of personal needs and the needs of others also varies depending on the depth of a relationship, the timing, the context, and so forth. Let's look more carefully at each of the interpersonal needs and how they influence our interpersonal interactions.

**The Need for Affection.**  The need for affection is the need to feel likable or lovable. Every day we see people striving to fulfill this need; for example, people who join

■ **fundamental interpersonal relations orientation theory** A theory that provides insight into our motivation to communicate. This theory consists of three needs: affection, inclusion, and control.

## MAKING CONNECTIONS
### for Success

### It's Me That Counts

Brad and Paige have been dating for more than six months. They agree that they have a very close relationship. After a romantic dinner at their favorite restaurant, Brad and Paige go back to Paige's apartment and are in the middle of some serious kissing when Paige says, "Brad, I want you to stop. I don't want to go any further." Brad says, "Are you kidding me? Don't you love me? I mean, it's not like we haven't been going out for six months." Paige does not respond immediately; she seems to have been caught off guard. Finally, she says, "Brad, I do know how you feel about me, and I do trust you, but going all the way just isn't right for me. I also don't want to end up hav-

ing a kid before we are married." Brad quickly says, "But I thought you really cared about me. You know, Paige, I love you!" Paige replies, "I know, but I am not ready for sex, and I really don't want to until I am married—you have to understand that."

1. Is Brad's communication motivated more out of self-interest than interest in Paige? Explain.
2. How would you describe Brad and Paige's relationship based on their interaction with each other?
3. Describe the relationship in terms of social exchange theory.

---

social groups or dating services are seeking to fulfill their need for belonging and love. According to Schutz's theory, a person who seems to be liked by many and therefore has adequately fulfilled this need is referred to as *personal*. Someone who is unable to fulfill this need is labeled either *underpersonal* or *overpersonal*.

Underpersonal people avoid emotional commitments or involvement with others. If we examine these individuals, we often find that they are hiding their true selves because they fear that others will not like them as they are. These people, like all other human beings, have a need for affection, but they have learned to cover it by not letting others get close to them. Do you know someone who seems to fit this category? Why do you think this person is unwilling to get close to others?

Overpersonal individuals are the opposite of underpersonals. They need affection so badly that they often go to extremes to ensure acceptance by others. They frequently seek approval by being extremely intimate in what they communicate. These individuals may be possessive and get jealous when others talk to their friends.

Personal people tend to be poised, confident, mature, and able to deal with almost everyone with whom they come in contact. Personals want to be liked, but they do not consider being liked by everyone essential for happiness. They are easy to talk with and are at ease with themselves.

**The Need for Inclusion.** The interpersonal need for inclusion encompasses our needs to feel significant and worthwhile. Schutz describes individuals in terms of this need as *social, undersocial,* or *oversocial*. Undersocial people do not like being around other people because, like underpersonal individuals, they find communicating with others threatening. They tend to be shy and find initiating conversations with others difficult. Typically, undersocials find it difficult to speak out and generally avoid saying anything for fear of drawing attention to themselves.

Oversocial people cannot stop themselves from getting involved and communicating with others. They attempt to dominate conversations, often speak out of turn, and find it hard to keep quiet. They prefer situations in which they can take over relationships by dominating the flow of communication. The oversocial person fears

The need for affection and inclusion for most of us is a motivator to interact with others. However, there are many who isolate themselves from others for fear that they will not be accepted or liked for who they are or find interacting with others threatening.

being ignored by others. Can you think of people who have the tendency to be over-social? How do you react to them?

Social people have satisfied their needs for inclusion. They are capable of handling situations with or without others, and few, if any, situations make them feel uncomfortable. They have confidence in themselves and are assertive enough to speak when they feel it is necessary to do so.

**The Need for Control.**   Schutz's third need is for control, which is derived from responsibility and leadership. Almost all of us have some need to control others and our surroundings. However, some individuals wish to be controlled by others. The strength of this need and the way we manifest it determine whether we are *abdicrats, autocrats,* or *democrats,* according to Schutz.

Abdicrats are extremely submissive to others. They have little or no self-confidence, often perceive themselves as incompetent, take few risks, rarely make decisions on their own, and need much reinforcement to believe they are useful and capable.

Autocrats never have enough control. In a group, they are always willing to make the decisions or at least voice strong opinions about what decision ought to be made. Because autocrats have a strong need for power, they might not care whom they hurt in their search for control. And they show little, if any, respect for others.

Democrats have their control needs essentially satisfied. They are comfortable as either leaders or followers, do not exaggerate either the leader's or the follower's role, and are open minded and willing to accept others' suggestions for the good of the group. They like to get things done but not at the expense of someone else.

Schutz's theory of needs clearly illustrates the reasons that motivate us to communicate with others. We develop relationships with others for many reasons. The

## MAKING Technology CONNECTIONS

### Blogging on the Internet: Motivation and Need to Form Relationships

In a July 3, 2006 *Time* magazine article entitled "You Gotta Have Friends," author Robert Putnam writes that "Americans are more socially isolated today then we were barely two decades ago." People are searching for relationships and connections with others and in the process are turning to the Internet, which itself may be more of the problem than the solution. The information you provide about yourself on various websites as a means to "social network" with others can and has been used in investigations by universities, local police, employers, and other agencies. For example, students have been expelled or reprimanded for hate speech, posting indecent pictures, and for criticizing a teacher. Employers have searched websites for information on potential hires as well. Here are some questions that you should think about and others you might want to discuss in class before placing any information about yourself on a website:

1. Will you be anonymous about the information that you provide about yourself on the Internet?
2. Why do you think so many people are willing to reveal very personal information on the Web?
3. Which of the three theories just described illustrates best why people use such Internet sites as Facebook and MySpace?
4. What are some of the risks that you face when you place personal information on the Internet?

social needs we have discussed explain a great deal about our motivation to form relationships, but there are other reasons to develop relationships: to avoid or lessen feelings of loneliness, to learn more about ourselves, and to share our lives with others.

# Relationships: Getting to Know Others and Ourselves

One of the most interesting aspects of being a human being is the way we react to other people—making acquaintances, becoming friends with a few of those acquaintances, and sometimes actively disliking others. Each of us tends to evaluate others in positive and negative terms, and they, of course, evaluate us in return.[7]

Some very specific and generally predictable factors determine whom we will get to know and how well we will get to know them. Relationships can be based on love or hate or any of the possibilities in between. Of the more than five billion people living, any one of us will come into contact with only a few. Of this small percentage, there remain hundreds of potential friends, enemies, and lovers. We, however, tend to form meaningful relationships with a small number of individuals at any given time. Researchers have often asked how we decide which relationships will become meaningful and lasting. How would you answer this question?

## Learning about Others through Face-to-Face Relationships

Whether we get to know others might have little or nothing to do with their specific characteristics or ours. Usually, the likelihood of two people becoming acquainted has to do with contact through physical proximity and a positive rather than a negative experience at the time of the face-to-face contact. Often, the contact is not planned but occurs because of circumstances. For example, contact may take place with a person sitting next to you in an airplane, with a neighbor, a classmate, a co-worker, a member of your religious organization, a person standing next to you in line in the cafeteria, a player on your softball team, and so on. After you encounter a person several times and easily recognize him or her, you will likely become comfortable interacting with the person or at least making small talk.

**Small talk** is casual conversation that is often impersonal and superficial, including an exchange of hellos or comments about the weather, newsworthy events, or trivia. Most relationships begin with small talk and often depend on small talk to continue. Small talk provides an avenue for getting to know another person by talking about nonthreatening, impersonal subjects. Some people, however, believe that small talk is a waste of their time, because it is based on trivial, unimportant information.

In meeting people for the first time, opening lines play a crucial role in establishing relationships. Many prescriptions for good and bad opening lines are provided by the media, friends and acquaintances, and other sources. However, most do not identify the importance of the relationship of those communicating, the context, and the nonverbal cues of the communicators.[8] For example, people meeting in a professional business setting usually shake hands and introduce themselves, whereas meeting people on an airplane is much more informal and introductions often do not occur even though the conversation might become more than simply small talk.

Small talk or casual conversation is important in the development of social skills and relating to people. Casual conversation, one on one, is also a good way to learn how to establish the basis for communicating and responding.

■ **small talk** Casual conversation that is often impersonal and superficial, including greetings, comments about the weather, newsworthy events, or trivia.

Besides opening lines, small talk serves many functions and is a way of maintaining a sense of community or fellowship with others. We often use small talk to satisfy our need for inclusion because it requires individuals to communicate with one another. Small talk generally does not create disagreement or conflict. It does create supportiveness and affirmation, which are indispensable for people to form relationships. It generally serves as a proving ground for both new and established relationships. In this sense, it becomes an "audition for new relationships." A

Opening lines do create first impressions and play a crucial role in establishing or initiating relationships. It is usually safer to use innocuous lines—you're more likely to get a positive response.
DILBERT © Scott Adams/Dist. by United Features Syndicate, Inc.

research study examining types of conversations people engage in found that nearly half of all the conversations with acquaintances, friends, romantic partners, family members, and others consist of relatively informal, superficial talk.[10]

Small talk is a safe way for us to let others know something about us and at the same time let us begin to learn something about them. It is a way of buying time to determine what we wish to share with others. If something we share about ourselves isn't working, we can shift to something else about ourselves very quickly. Small talk allows us to reduce uncertainties about another person without revealing too much about ourselves. If everything seems to click in the small talk conversations, it is more likely that conversations will move from superficial to more self-revealing communication.

Small talk is also important because it can serve as an interpersonal buffer. Because it is usually nonthreatening, small talk can serve as a release, escape valve, or diversion from more serious talk that requires more conscious thought and effort.[11]

## MAKING CONNECTIONS for Success

### The Importance of Small Talk

Being able to connect with others through small talk can lead to big things, according to Debra Fine, author of "The Fine Art of Small Talk."[9] A former engineer, Fine recalls being so uncomfortable at networking events that she would hide in the restroom. Now a professional speaker, Fine says the ability to connect with people through small talk is an acquired skill. Successful people know how to use small talk effectively and know its importance in entering and maintaining relationships.

1. Do you find making small talk easy or difficult? Why?
2. What are the most difficult small talk situations you have encountered and what did you do to deal with them?
3. What role does small talk play in building and maintaining relationships? Explain.
4. Develop a set of tips that might improve your small talk and share them with each other for the following: general/social icebreakers and business/professional icebreakers.

## Suggestions for More Effective Small Talk                    GUIDELINES

Conversation with others is a two-way responsibility and you can't rely on the other person to carry the conversation for you—a monologue is not a conversation. In order to become effective at small talk you must be fully connected and actively try to ensure that the other person feels comfortable. Here are some suggestions to consider:

1. *Use the other person's name as much as possible as you talk with him or her.* There is a rule that many follow in order to remember a person's name—say it at least three times when first interacting with someone you just met. Have the person restate it or spell it for you if necessary. Knowing and recalling a person's name creates the impression that the person matters to you and helps make small talk a bit more comfortable.
2. *Look at the other person, but strive for balance and comfort in eye contact.* When you look at the other person, you are indicating that you are paying attention and are interested in him or her. It also indicates that you are confident in yourself.
3. *Be careful in your use of eye contact with people from different cultural or ethnic backgrounds than your own.* For example, Hispanic and Japanese cultures believe that staring at someone or looking into someone's eyes is disrespectful. When communicating with people from these cultures, you might focus on the face in general, but not directly on their eyes.

4. *Get the other person to talk about himself or herself.* People generally like to talk about themselves. It can be a strong motivator for continuing the conversation. Listen carefully, and ask questions such as "What are you planning to do after graduation?" "What did you like most about _____ (the play, the movie, the book, the game, etc.)?" "What does your work involve?" "What do you like to do in your spare time?" "What do you enjoy most about your work?" and "Tell me about yourself." Use follow-up questions to keep the person talking if necessary.

5. *Keep small talk casual, light, and positive.* Moving too quickly to disclose personal information can be threatening and a real conversation stopper. Also, no one likes negative people or whiners. If you come across as one, your likelihood of future interaction is reduced dramatically.

6. *Be confident in yourself and listen carefully to what is being said.* It is critical that you have confidence in yourself if you are going to make small talk. Confidence doesn't mean arrogance; it does mean that you are not afraid to enter into a conversation with others. It is likely that the other person may have similar reservations about chatting with you as you might have with them. If you show that you are interested it will also motivate the other person to continue the conversation rather than end it abruptly.

7. *Keep abreast of current events.* Know what is going on around you by watching the news, using the Internet, and reading current magazines and newspapers on a regular basis. This can be very helpful because current events are often the topics of small talk. Being aware of what is going on will help make small talk easy, plus it shows others that you are concerned about what is going on around you.

8. *Use small talk to help reduce the uncertainty between yourself and others.* By doing so, you will increase your chances of initiating and developing a more lasting relationship.

9. *Know when and how to end the conversation.* It is important to know when the conversation should end. Small talk isn't intended to last very long, and if it goes on too long you run the risk of it becoming tedious and uncomfortable. Even if the conversation is going well and you and the other person are enjoying talking, you might end it before it does becomes uncomfortable. Sometimes ending a conversation can be awkward or difficult, but if you have a few well-rehearsed exit lines, that can be your best strategy. Make sure you use the person's name when exiting, for example, "Debra, I better move on to other guests. I enjoyed visiting with you," or "Jim, I would like to get some food before it's gone. I enjoyed talking with you.[12]

## ■■ Connecting with Others Online

As you know, with only a few clicks of a computer mouse, we can interact with someone, any subject, at any time, and in any place in the world. Face-to-face interactions usually allow us to form impressions much more quickly than we can by using computer-mediated communication. The likelihood of connecting to others and interacting with strangers, however, increases dramatically online.

The computer has indeed changed our way of interacting and connecting to others. For example, in our local newspaper, the following was featured in the Life section: "Chatroom brought them together." In the article, it explains how Shelly Zoz and Brian Davis met for the first time. In her first message to Brian, Shelly wrote, "Is

## MAKING CONNECTIONS for Success

### Interpersonal Success and Failure

Take a clean sheet of paper and fold it in half lengthwise. You now have two columns. Label the column on your left "Person A: Likely to experience interpersonal failure," and label the column on your right "Person B: Likely to experience interpersonal success." In their respective columns, list the characteristics, behaviors, and strategies that you believe characterize Person A and Person B in a situation in which each approaches someone of the same sex for the first time. Then answer the following questions in class:

1. Which characteristics, behaviors, and strategies would be the same or different if Person A and

Person B were meeting someone of a different sex? Why?

2. Which characteristics, behaviors, and strategies would be the same or different if Person A and Person B were meeting someone from a sexual orientation or an ethnic or cultural background that differed from their own?

3. How might Person A and Person B approach others over the Internet? What behaviors and strategies might succeed or fail in this communication context?

4. What did you learn from this exercise about interpersonal communication?

## MAKING Technology CONNECTIONS

### Lee's Blurb on MySpace.Com

About me: I'm a cool guy. I went to college my senior year in high school. First at the University of Nebraska at Omaha, didn't like it. So, I transferred to University of Nebraska at Lincoln, where I'm studying Marketing. Dance is really a new passion for me as well as a second major. However, I have dropped out of college for a while and am trying to make a name for myself in New York or California (whichever one works out better). I am a newly certified PiYo instructor, and love to work out. Being active and healthy is a huge part of my life, because I want to live strong and long enough to play with my children and grandchildren. I love kids and can't wait to have my own. *Status:* Single, *Here for:* Networking, dating, serious relationships, friends, *Orientation:* Straight, *Hometown:* Fremont, *Body type:* 6'4"/Athletic, *Ethnicity:* White/Caucasian, *Religion:* Atheist, *Zodiac Sign:* Leo, *Smoke/Drink:* No/No, *Children:* Someday, *Education:* Some college, *Occupation:* Student

1. What does the information above tell you about Lee? What doesn't it tell you about him?

2. In Chapter 3 we discussed impression management and in this chapter self-presentation—how does Lee manage or strategize the impression he is trying to present of himself in his blurb?

3. Why do you think people are more comfortable self-disclosing online?

4. Do you think that using Internet sites such as MySpace and FaceBook requires much in the way of interpersonal communication skills? Why or why not?

5. What would you put in a blurb? Try writing your own to share with the class.

Information used in the above is an actual "blurb" that is on MySpace but altered slightly to protect the person's identity—it was given to us with permission to use.

Reprinted by permission of Terry Saunders.

Text messaging has made it possible for us to interact with people anywhere in the world with just a few clicks. But do you think an online relationship is as satisfying as a face-to-face relationship?

it true?" He responded, "Is what true?" Before the evening was over, according to the article, they had exchanged telephone numbers. Brian said, "It was amazing. Everything just clicked between us." Shelly was quoted in the article as saying, "A lot of people in these chat rooms will feed you full of stuff and expect you to believe it, but he seemed honest." She went on, "We talked and talked about our feelings, and we were really on the same wavelength." Their first online encounter was in March 1999; by May, they had decided to meet in person. Brian drove the 1,500 miles to Lincoln, Nebraska, to meet Shelly. They met and liked what they saw, and they plan to marry. "A lot of people think meeting someone through a chatroom is totally nuts," Shelly said, "People are shocked that it worked out."[13]

Although many online connections that occur between individuals and groups of individuals are limited because of the lack of proximity of the individuals involved, it is more and more common for these types of interactions to result in relationships. Malcolm Parks and Kory Floyd, communication scholars, surveyed twenty-four newsgroups and asked a random sample of the users whether they had formed new acquaintances, friendships, or other personal relationships as a result of their interaction online. Almost two-thirds of those responding to the survey said that a personal relationship resulted from someone they had met on the Internet.[14]

Women, it seems, are more likely to form relationships on the Internet than men are. Research has found that 72 percent of women and 55 percent of men surveyed who interact on the Internet have formed personal online relationships. Not surprisingly, the more time you spend online, the more likely you are to form more online relationships.[15]

Cell phones, Blackberries, and PDAs (personal digital assistants such as Handsprings and Palm Pilots) are also changing the way people flirt and connect with others. With its roots in emailing and instant messaging, text messaging via cell phones or PDAs has become another extremely popular way to communicate because people are willing to write things they might not normally say over the phone or in person. Many people are wired today, and almost anyone can be reached at any given time, so the lines of communication are more open than ever. This can create a new set of problems.[16]

There are advantages and disadvantages to interacting with people online. The advantages are that you can remain anonymous, it is generally safe because physical contact is possible only if you allow it to occur, and you can choose the time and place of that contact. On the Internet, you share personality or inner qualities only through the words you transmit, and this can be an advantage as well as a disadvantage. We know that a person's voice and appearance provide a lot of information about that person. Without hearing the other person's voice, without seeing the other person, and without being able to touch him or her (e.g., a handshake, a hug, a kiss), the relationship will remain a mediated relationship that allows two people to communicate.

Although chatrooms, email communication, text messaging, and Internet dating services are expedient ways to initiate conversations with strangers, they might not be the best way to develop relationships with others. In fact, they can be outright dangerous.

Kevin Koelling, a psychotherapist, says, "I've seen everything from marriages breaking down to people using the Internet as an escape from the problems they need to deal with in their marriage."[17] Deb Hope, a psychology professor at the University of Nebraska, said, "Chat rooms can be dangerous to people who may not have the best judgment about relationships anyway. You can end up getting involved with someone—maybe even agreeing to meet them—and really not know who they are at all."[18] People have been exploited, taken advantage of, or even victimized by someone they meet via the Internet.[19] Communication is the overriding factor that will determine the kind of relationship that develops, if any at all, and how long it will last.

Of course, through technology, we can hear and see images of the other person via telephone, microphones, pictures, and minivideo cameras without ever having actual face-to-face contact. It is our belief, however, that interaction via technology can never replace face-to-face interactions or fulfill interpersonal needs. In Chapter 14, we discuss more about relationship development over the Internet.

# Self-Disclosure in Relationships

Relationships are built on interaction. The more sincere, honest, and open the interactions, the stronger and more lasting the relationship is likely to be. Much of our interpersonal communication, however, is small talk. Such light conversation might not provide a means for us to learn who we are, to fulfill our interpersonal needs, or to grow in our relationships. Nonetheless, it does maintain an important opening to further interaction. Self-disclosure is one type of interaction that changes as a relationship becomes closer.

To reduce uncertainty as suggested by uncertainty reduction theory and to meet our physical and emotional needs, we must communicate who we are; we must disclose information about ourselves. **Self-disclosure,** or the voluntary sharing of information about ourselves that another person is not likely to know, can be as simple and nonthreatening as telling our name or as complex and threatening as revealing deep feelings.

When self-disclosure occurs in caring relationships, it usually results in greater self-understanding and self-improvement. In addition, our self-disclosure to others encourages them to reciprocate and creates an atmosphere that fosters interpersonal communication and meaningful relationships.

## MAKING CONNECTIONS for Success

### Just Friends

The following excerpt is from an article by Patty Beutler, "Just Friends: Having a Pal of the Opposite Sex Has Many Advantages."

*When Holly Pace played matchmaker last year for her girlfriend, she ended up with a best friend—her girlfriend's boyfriend. Tyler Fritz no longer goes out with that girl, but he's remained Holly's best buddy. "I love her to death," he said without reservation. He's not talking about the sort of love that makes his palms sweat or his heart pump wildly. Instead, it's a comfortable, say-anything relationship.*

1. What are the advantages to having a best friend (not a romantic relationship) of the opposite sex?
2. What are the disadvantages to having a best friend (not a romantic relationship) of the opposite sex?
3. How do your answers to these questions relate to what you have learned so far in this chapter?

■ **self-disclosure**
Voluntary sharing of information about the self that another person is not likely to know.

## ▪ Self-Disclosure: The Process

Our use of self-disclosure is not static, and it can move back and forth from expressing our social self-identity (including our roles as students, parents, friends, or sports fans) to very personal, intimate information about our private lives. In any relationship, there is always tension between the need for privacy and the need for intimacy or more personal disclosure. According to communication scholar William Rawlins and others, the dynamic between the need for privacy and the need for intimacy creates movement in relationships.[20] When we express our personal selves with another or others, the communication moves toward the intimate end of the continuum. When we wish to maintain our privacy by expressing only our social selves, the communication moves toward the social end of the continuum. To benefit from disclosure, we must realize that it is an ongoing process that is incorporated into our daily interaction with others. The process of self-disclosure is best illustrated via the Johari Window and the social penetration model.

### ▪ FIGURE 13.1 The Johari Window

The Johari Window illustrates four kinds of information: the open area, the blind area, the hidden area, and the unknown area. In a relationship, certain areas of information are available to and hidden from each person. What we know about others is gained primarily through self-disclosure and interpersonal communication.

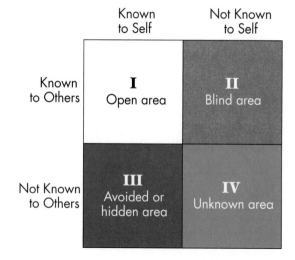

J. Luft, *Group Processes: An Introduction to Group Dynamics,* Palo Alto, Calif.: National Press, 1970. Reprinted by permission.

### ▪ Johari Window Model

One way to visualize and understand the dynamics of the self-disclosure process is to examine the **Johari Window** (see Figure 13.1), named after the first names of its creators, Joseph Luft and Harry Ingham.[21] It is one the most useful models describing human interaction because it depicts four different levels of knowledge that exist in our relationships with others. The lines dividing the four panes are like shades, which can move as interaction progresses and the relationship develops.

**Area I: The Open Area.** The open area contains information that is known both to the self and to others, because it is readily available through observation or willingness to share. For example, when people meet for the first time, they undoubtedly note each other's height, weight, skin color, and sex. They may freely share their names, hometowns, career fields, schools, majors, and courses they are taking.

During the first meeting, individuals usually disclose minimal information about themselves. At this point the open area is relatively small. But as people get to know each other through additional interactions, this area becomes much larger, as shown in Figure 13.2.

**Area II: The Blind Area.** The blind area includes information that others perceive about us but that we do not recognize or acknowledge about ourselves. For example,

▪ **Johari Window** A graphic model describing human interaction that is useful because it depicts four different levels of knowledge that exist in our relationships with others.

To reduce uncertainty and to meet our physical and emotional needs, we must communicate who we are; we must disclose information about ourselves. When self-disclosure occurs in caring relationships, it usually results in greater self-understanding and self-improvement.

instructors who show favoritism to certain students may not realize that their behavior is being interpreted in that way. In fact, when confronted with student evaluations that point out the problem, teachers often deny such behavior and argue that they treat everyone equally.

**Area III: The Hidden Area.** The hidden area includes personal and private information about ourselves that we choose not to disclose to others. Others cannot know personal information unless we choose to disclose it, and we are particularly selective about disclosing such private information. As a relationship grows, more and more private information is typically shared and the hidden area shrinks, but it is never completely eliminated.

**Area IV: The Unknown Area.** The fourth window is the unknown area, which contains information that is not known to us or to others. Simply because we are human, we may submerge or repress certain information in the subconscious—perhaps a difficult part of our

■ **FIGURE 13.2** Variation on the Johari Window

As self-disclosure increases in relationships, the *open area* becomes larger. The open area represents what is known about the self and others in a relationship.

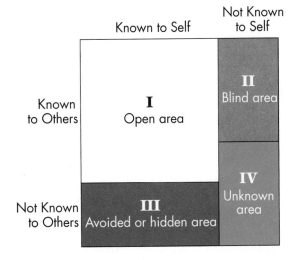

J. Luft, *Group Processes: An Introduction to Group Dynamics*, Palo Alto, Calif.: National Press, 1970. Reprinted by permission.

personality, a sexual preference, or the harm a drug is having on us physically or mentally. We may remain ignorant of these factors throughout life, or they may emerge through therapy, or through hypnosis or other consciousness-altering experiences. Another example of material in the unknown area might be an event that we seem to recall but cannot verify with certainty. Finally, we don't know about certain aspects of ourselves because they haven't had the opportunity to surface. For example, how would you handle a personal tragedy, especially if you never have had to deal with one? You might think that you can, but like most of us, you won't really know until something actually occurs.

Generally, the more guarded, or defensive you tend to be, the more likely you are to withhold information about yourself from others. Therefore in your relationships, the open area will tend to be smaller. The more willing you are to communicate and to encourage feedback, the larger your open area will be.

The Johari Window provides a helpful model of how the information we share with others shapes the overall relationship. It doesn't, however, explain why some people tend to disclose more than others. Researchers have found that women are more likely to disclose personal information than men are, although that is not true in all situations. For example, one research study suggests that women are likely to disclose more about themselves to intimate friends, whereas men are more likely than women to disclose personal information to strangers or casual acquaintances.[22] The choice of who will receive the disclosure is just as significant as the content of the disclosure.

## ▬▪ Social Penetration Model

The social penetration model, developed by social psychologists Irwin Altman and Dalmas Taylor, provides another view of how people connect with each other and how their communication moves from small talk to more intimate and self-revealing talk. **Social penetration** is the process of increasing disclosure and intimacy in a relationship.[23] Figure 13.3 illustrates the progression of our interactions as a relationship becomes more friendly or intimate.

According to the model, self-disclosure increases gradually as the relationship evolves. The model resembles a dartboard, with the outer ring representing superficial communication such as small talk, "Hi, I'm Bill from Lincoln, Nebraska," to the innermost circle, or bull's-eye, representing more intimacy and depth of interaction, such as "I love you with all my heart." So, as the relationship becomes more intimate, it will involve more personal information about self. The depth is represented on the model as penetration from external factual information (the outer ring) to inner feelings (the center of the circle or bull's-eye) revealing more private information about self.

## ▬▪ Why Do We Self-Disclose?

There are many abilities that differentiate human beings from other animals, one of which is to keep and share information about ourselves. We self-disclose for a variety of different reasons in order for others to better understand who we are, to gain sympathy, to see what others think, to gain trust, or to connect with others and establish relationships. Self-disclosure is essential if we are to form and maintain relationships. Here we will discuss three reasons why we self-disclose: self-presentation, relationship building, and catharsis.

■ **social penetration**
The process of increasing disclosure and intimacy in a relationship.

■ **FIGURE 13.3** Social Penetration Model

The social penetration model portrays relationship development as starting with factual information and small talk. But as the relationship develops, conversations become more personal, including feelings about self and values.

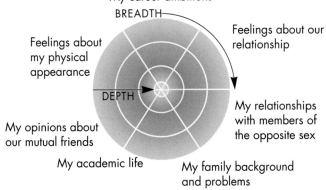

From *Social Penetration: The Development of Interpersonal Relationships.* Copyright © 1973 by Irwin Altman and Dalmas Taylor.

**Self-presentation.**    **Self-presentation** is an intentional self-disclosure tactic that we use to reveal certain aspects about ourselves for specific reasons. When you are asked in an employment interview, for example, to talk about yourself, you are often asked to discuss your background, experiences, and accomplishments. When you disclose information about yourself that may not be known to the interviewer you are engaged in self-presentation. The purpose of providing information about yourself is to emphasize that you are the person best suited for the job. For example, you tell the interviewer that you are a highly organized person with excellent communication skills or that you are team player and that you enjoy meeting and working with people from a variety of backgrounds. You might disclose, for example, that you come from a relatively poor background and that you have worked in order to help pay your tuition—you are implying by your statements that you are self-sufficient in hopes that the interviewer will judge you positively.

**Relationship Building.**    We self-disclose to start or maintain relationships. Self-disclosure via small talk or social conversation is one way we enter into relationships with others. The level of self-disclosure at some point can move to more intimate and self-revealing talk as the relationship develops. There are, of course, exceptions to this progression, and the depth and number of interactions can vary dramatically from one relationship to another. Also, moving from light social talk to more intimate and revealing talk does not necessarily imply that the relationship will automatically be a quality relationship.[24]

A relationship's location on the continuum between casual acquaintance and intimate confidant is determined by how people interact with each other and their specific communication behaviors. The way we communicate with another person reflects the nature and type of the relationship.

■ **self-presentation**
An intentional self-disclosure tactic that we use to reveal certain aspects about ourselves for specific reasons.

**Catharsis.**   Self-disclosing communication can be a form of communicative release or catharsis. This is especially true when we want to rid ourselves of information that is causing tension or guilt.[25] It is a way of getting something off our mind to reduce stress, such as telling your parents that you are in debt because you have been gambling or that you aren't doing as well in school as they think because you have been oversleeping. The benefit of this type of disclosure is that it allows us to rid ourselves of dealing with an issue or problem by ourselves in the hopes that we will receive sympathy or help.

## ■■ When Shouldn't We Self-Disclose Too Much?

Although full disclosure can be cleansing, it can also be harmful, risky, unwise, or insensitive as well as detrimental to a relationship. At one time or another, most of us have chosen not to say what was on our minds or not to tell others something about ourselves, themselves, or others because it might be hurtful. There are many reasons for withholding information, but it is usually to protect others, to avoid a potentially negative reaction, or to avoid hurting others or ourselves. Self-disclosure therefore is not always wise or appropriate.

The open and honest sharing of our feelings, thoughts, concerns, and secrets with others is at the heart of self-disclosure. This openness and honesty would be ideal, but it is not always practical or wise. Ultimately, self-disclosure must be based on personal judgment rather than rigid rules. The key should always be concern for both self and others.

---

**MAKING CONNECTIONS**
**for Success**

### Greeting Etiquette: Rules of Engagement

Discuss in class the appropriate ways to greet others:

1. Greeting others older or of higher status than yourself.
2. Greeting others from a different culture while in your own surroundings or in their surroundings.
3. Answering the phone in business and professional situations.
4. Voice mail greetings—what should you say and what shouldn't you?
5. How should you introduce friends to others?

There are many communicative situations that require a specific etiquette, for example, dinner table manners, walking into an office of an instructor, joining a conversation that others are having. We recommend that you learn more about appropriate etiquette and practice it as often as possible. The Internet can provide a vast amount of information about etiquette in a variety of situations.

---

## ■■ Self-Disclosure, Privacy, and Gender

How much is too much self-disclosure and when does it begin to invade or affect our privacy? **Privacy** is "the claim of individuals, groups, or institutions to determine for themselves when, how, and to what extent information about themselves is communicated to others."[26] These are not easy questions to answer because what might be appropriate for one situation may not be for another. Thus an important task for people in relationships is the negotiation of privacy boundaries.[27] Privacy boundaries work in a way very similar to personal space boundaries as discussed in Chapter 5. Just as we control and protect access to our physical self, for example, how close we allow others to come to us, in the same way we control and protect our privacy boundaries. Sandra Petronio, a communication scholar and expert in the area of privacy and how we manage our privacy boundaries, states

> Revealing private information is risky because there is a potential vulnerability when revealing aspects of the self. Receiving private information from another may also result in the need for protecting oneself. In order to manage disclosing and receiving privacy

■ **privacy** The claim of individuals, groups, or institutions to determine for themselves when, how, and to what extent information about themselves is communicated to others.

## MAKING CONNECTIONS

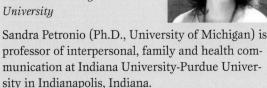

**To Scholars**

### Sandra Petronio
*Indiana University-Purdue University*

Sandra Petronio (Ph.D., University of Michigan) is professor of interpersonal, family and health communication at Indiana University-Purdue University in Indianapolis, Indiana.

Petronio developed one of the nation's first university courses in family communication twenty-two years ago and has built a long history of research in the field. Her book, *Boundaries of Privacy: Dialectics of Disclosure* (State University of New York Press), represents twenty years of

research on how people manage their privacy and offers a practical theory about why people make decisions about revealing and concealing private information. Her work examines the everyday problems in our personal relationships, our health concerns, and our work, to investigate the way we manage our private lives. Petronio argues that in addition to owning our private information, we also should take responsibility for guarding the privacy of others who have put their trust in us. If not, it could lead to betrayal, errors in judgment, deception, gossip, and privacy dilemmas. Her book serves as a guide to understanding why certain decisions about privacy succeed while others fail.

information, individuals erect a metaphoric boundary to reduce the possibility of losing face and as a means of protection. Also, people use a set of rules or criteria to control the boundary and regulate the flow of private information to and from others.[28]

The process of sharing more and more personal information about one's self with another person encourages further intrusion into one's privacy whether wanted or unwanted. It would seem to be common sense, but privacy boundaries are not always clear to either party in a relationship. For example, a man and a woman have been dating for several years and had been sexually intimate, but they are not married. The couple might try to control the privacy of their relationship, because revealing relational secrets could be embarrassing, or they could be fully open about their relationship. The determination of what should be kept private from each other and what should be kept private from others is usually negotiated by the mutual consent of the parties involved in the relationship.

When or if the boundaries of a relationship are violated or crossed, tensions may result, creating an imbalance in the relationship. Thus, negotiations between relationship partners often involve what can and should be shared and what is or should be off limits. Boundaries are erected to protect, control the flow of information, and regulate vulnerability. When one partner violates the privacy of the other, for example, attempts are made to reconstruct the privacy boundary by changing the topic or by avoiding the situation.

**Gender.**   As we learned in Chapter 2, using the terms *women* and *men* as identifiers to describe or distinguish communication between the sexes is troublesome. The terms imply sameness across all women and all men that might or might not be true. For example, to say "Women disclose their feelings more often than men do" is probably true, but it may not be true for all women or all men. Some men disclose more feelings than some women do, and vice versa. Thus, we must be careful to avoid stereotyping solely based on biological sex differences.[29]

Some research and some authors support the notion that men and women do communicate using different sets of rules and meanings. Deborah Tannen in her book *You Just Don't Understand: Women and Men in Conversation,* has reviewed many research studies and has taken the position that women's verbal and nonverbal behaviors are different from men's. For example, she has found that men talk less personally or inclusively when compared to women and that women tend to make more validating and confirming statements than men do.[30]

Women are more likely to talk about their relationships and disclose a deeper level of intimacy, but men often do not center their talk on relational closeness.[31] Concerning relationships, many men take the attitude that "If it ain't broke, why fix it?" Women may be more likely to express the attitude "If it's going well, how can we make it go better?"

In his study of 200 male and female college students, communication scholar Lawrence Rosenfeld found that males avoid self-disclosure in order to maintain control of a relationship and to avoid having to face things about themselves. Females, according to Rosenfeld, refrain from self-disclosure in order to avoid personal hurt and problems with their relationships.[32] All of us should have someone with whom we can share our feelings and thoughts, because it is generally good for our well-being and personal satisfaction. Self-disclosure is the most sensitive and beautiful form of communication that we can engage in, but it must be done with care.

It also appears that men and women differ in the defensive and protective strategies they use to reduce embarrassment and maintain privacy boundaries. Men's defensive strategies include blaming the incident on something else, laughing at their own behavior, or retreating from the situation, whereas women's defensive strategies often include blaming others and criticizing themselves. No matter how privacy is defined or explained, the means by which people regulate the release of private information is through disclosure.[33]

## ▄▀ Cultural Issues in Self-Disclosure

In general, people from different cultural backgrounds tend to follow similar patterns of self-disclosure. For example, people from various cultures are likely to begin relationships with small talk and progress to more intimate levels of interaction as the relationship continues. Of course, there are differences, especially in the initial contact stage, in some cultures; but in general, as people become friends, those differences seem to diminish.

Think about some of the characteristics that describe your cultural background, however, and how they might or might not influence your communication. Do you see yourself simply as an American, or identified with some other ethnic or racial group: African American, Filipino American, Latino, Vietnamese, Korean, German, or white? Do others view you the same way? How does your ethnicity affect your communication and with whom you choose to communicate? Do you use certain expressions that are understood only by members of your ethnic group? When you interact with people from a different ethnic group, how difficult is it for you to communicate? Thinking about the answers to these questions will help you to understand cultural differences and why interacting with people from diverse backgrounds is much more complex than simply exchanging information. It requires thought, a recognition of differences, and some adjustments for communication to be meaningful to both parties. Not everyone thinks and communicates in exactly the same way. This may be especially important to remember when we interact with people from cultures different from our own.

# Rhetorical Sensitivity

According to communication scholars Roderick Hart and Don Burks, **rhetorical sensitivity** is an alternative form of communication that can be applied to situations in which wide-open self-disclosure could be harmful. For example, you want to tell your friend to stop eating junk food because she is really putting on the weight and is getting extremely fat. Instead of telling her what you really think, you say, "Eating all that junk food can't be good for you," in the hopes that your friend will get the message. It represents a cautious approach to exchanging information while developing a relationship.[34] Rhetorically sensitive people can balance their self-interest with the interests of others. They can adjust their communication to take into account the beliefs, values, and mood of the other person. Considering the other person's views or feelings does not mean changing your own view or position, but it does mean finding an effective way to communicate your thoughts without offending or hurting the other person. Honest self-disclosure can be harmful if it is stated in a way that damages the relationship. Rhetorically sensitive individuals generally display the following attributes:

1. They accept personal complexity; they understand that every person is made up of many selves. For example, one person may be a mother, a daughter, a Republican, an Asian American, an abuse victim, a student, and a consumer.
2. They are flexible and avoid rigidity in communicating with others.
3. They do not change their own values, but they can communicate them in a variety of ways to avoid offending others.
4. They sense when it is appropriate to communicate something and when it is not.[35] Rhetorically sensitive people understand self-disclosure and know how to adapt their messages to a particular audience and situation.
5. They are aware of the language they choose, such as gender-inclusive nonsexist language; they do not use homophobic or racist language or inappropriate jokes that offend others.

# General Conclusions about Self-Disclosure

Research findings support these general conclusions about self-disclosure, whatever the interaction level obtained in a relationship:

1. Disclosure increases with increased relational intimacy.
2. Disclosure increases when rewarded—the reward outweighs the risk of disclosing.
3. Disclosure increases with the need to reduce uncertainty in a relationship.
4. Disclosure tends to be reciprocal—when one person in a relationship increases self-disclosure, the other person will typically follow suit.
5. Women tend to disclose personal information more often than men do.
6. Women seem to disclose more with those to whom they are close, whereas men seem to disclose more with those whom they trust.
7. Disclosure is culturally regulated by norms of appropriateness.
8. People will disclose themselves to people they like.
9. People will overestimate the amount of self-disclosure they actually permit.

■ **rhetorical sensitivity** A cautious approach to self-disclosure in which the situation and factors about the other person are considered before communication begins.

10. Self-disclosure does not automatically indicate attraction and, if inappropriate, can cause negative reactions.

11. Liking someone and wanting a relationship to continue can, in fact, discourage self-disclosure, because of the risk that self-disclosure might damage the relationship.[36]

The goal of self-disclosing is to match the amount and kind of self-disclosure to the situation. Thus, open and honest sharing of our feelings, concerns, and secrets with others is at the heart of self-disclosure. This does not mean, however, that we must disclose everything or that we cannot withhold information if it is likely to hurt us or someone else.

Ultimately, self-disclosure must be based on personal judgment rather than rigid rules. Self-disclosure should, if used properly, be the most sensitive and meaningful form of communication that we engage in as we enter and maintain relationships. There are many reasons we sometimes find it difficult to disclose to others. However, when based on mutual feelings and genuine communication, relationships cannot help but grow and mature.

## GUIDELINES | Suggestions for Appropriate Self-Disclosure

You should know there are no hard and fast rules when it comes to self-disclosure, but self-disclosing to others should be based on common sense and good judgment. Here are some suggestions that might help you to use self-disclosure appropriately and competently:

1. *Use reasoned self-disclosure.* Although open and honest relationships are desirable, it is important to recognize situational constraints. For example, as a youngster, you might have been caught shoplifting from a local store. You shoplifted only that one time and were required to do some community service. However, you are now running for public office, and you must decide whether to disclose the fact that you stole from a local store. To do so would more than likely hurt your chances of winning the election. Therefore, you choose not to bring up this error of judgment. This does not mean that you are being unethical or dishonest. In some situations and with certain individuals, not revealing a specific past behavior might be reasonable—particularly if it has little to do with the situation at hand. However, if you know that something that you did is going to come out, mentioning it before it comes out illustrates that you are not hiding anything.

2. *Make self-disclosure a two-way process.* Self-disclosure that is one-sided generally leads to relationships that are not very enduring, meaningful, or healthy. People are more likely to disclose information when they feel safe and when their communication is positively or warmly received. It therefore follows that each person who discloses to another will feel safer if both individuals are involved in the self-disclosure process. For example, once a mutual give-and-take is established, if one person self-discloses, the other person will usually follow suit. As trust increases between individuals, self-disclosure will likely expand and with continued self-disclosure, relationships will become stronger.

3. *Make self-disclosure appropriate to the situation and the person.* When we disclose personal information about ourselves, we run the risk of being hurt or rejected.

We can somewhat minimize the risk if we carefully match the disclosure to the person and the situation. Self-disclosure should be a slow process; rushing it like some have done on the Internet can increase vulnerability unnecessarily. In addition, it is safest to disclose only to truly caring people whom we trust. Disclosing too much too soon or disclosing to the wrong person or persons can lead to embarrassment and pain—and sometimes serious harm.

4. *Consider diversity.* The appropriateness and the level of self-disclosure vary by culture, group, and individual. The Japanese culture, for example, does not foster self-expression in the same way that U.S. or Korean cultures do. Even within the U.S. culture there are differences among groups, i.e., men and women. Consider these differences as you decide how much, to whom, and when to disclose personal information.

# Summary

Interpersonal communication is creating and sharing meaning between persons who are in a relationship. It is interpersonal communication that allows relationships to become established and to grow, satisfying our social needs. Because we have social needs and the desire to know others, uncertainty reduction theory is discussed as a motivator for interpersonal communication.

Many of the needs that we have as humans can be satisfied through communication. Two approaches that attempt to explain needs are Thibaut and Kelley's social exchange theory and Schutz's fundamental interpersonal relations orientation theory. Schutz's theory implies that we have three needs: the need for affection, the need for inclusion, and the need for control. Thibaut and Kelley's theory is based on the assumption that people consciously and deliberately consider the costs and rewards associated with a relationship or interaction and that they will seek out relationships that are rewarding and avoid those that are costly.

If we encounter people more than once and they become recognizable, we are more likely to be comfortable interacting with them or at least making small talk with them. Competent communicators know the importance of small talk as a social skill.

We develop relationships to avoid or reduce loneliness, to learn about ourselves, and to share. Lasting relationships are open, a feature that allows for relatively free self-disclosure. The more information we reveal about ourselves, the more likely we are to have relationships that will grow and mature into healthy and satisfying experiences.

The Johari Window is a graphic model that depicts four areas of information about each of us: the open area, the blind area, the hidden area, and the unknown area. These four areas expand and contract in relationships over time and from situation to situation.

The social penetration model is an example of how people enter relationships and how their communication moves from superficial levels of small talk to more intimate and self-revealing talk. We disclose information about ourselves because we recognize possible advantages that we gain from doing so. This approach of becoming known to others is called self-presentation. Privacy is our way of controlling what others know about us, and it should be up to us to determine when, how, and to what extent we provide information about ourselves to others. Rhetorical sensitivity is an alternative form of communication that competent communicators use when they know that too much self-disclosure could be harmful to those involved. Because frankness creates vulnerability, each participant must consider situational constraints when deciding what should or should not be disclosed.

# Discussion Starters

**1.** Discuss the theories presented in this chapter and decide which best explains our need to know others and to form relationships.

**2.** What are some inappropriate communicative behaviors that you have observed in interpersonal situations that really bug you? Why do you think these behaviors occur?

**3.** Describe rules or guidelines for proper or polite communication that you wish others knew.

**4.** What does it mean to be politically correct? Describe potential problems that occur when we use politically correct communication and when we don't.

**5.** Explain the difference between being rhetorically sensitive and honest in our self-disclosure.

**6.** Is honesty always the best policy when self-disclosing? Explain.

**7.** Describe the behaviors of a person who is interpersonally competent.

**8.** Explain the similarities and differences between the Johari Window and the social penetration model.

**9.** What advice would you give to someone to help them improve their conversational talk with others?

**10.** Develop a set of rules that you think should be applied when self-disclosing personal information to others.

# Notes

1. Adapted from an article written by Jonathan Butler entitled "The Donut Shop Experiment" in *The Front Porch Where People Share Life* published by The Front Porch, LLC, © 2002.

2. S. Levy and B. Stone, "The New Wisdom of the Web," *Newsweek,* April 3, 2006, 47; J. Rawe, "MYSPACE?" *Time,* July 3, 2006, 35–36; and R. Putnam, "You Gotta Have Friends," *Time,* July 3, 2006, 36.

3. M. L. Knapp and A. L. Vangelisti, *Interpersonal Communication and Human Relationships,* 5th ed. (Boston: Allyn and Bacon, 2005), 32.

4. C. R. Berger and R. J. Calabrese, "Some Explorations in Initial Interactions and Beyond: Toward a Developmental Theory of Interpersonal Communication," *Human Communication Research* 1 (1975): 98–112; and C. R. Berger, "Response—Uncertain Outcome Values in Predicted Relationships: Uncertainty Reduction Theory Then and Now," *Human Communication Research* 13 (1986): 34–38.

5. J. W. Thibaut and H. H. Kelley, *The Social Psychology of Groups,* 2nd ed. (New Brunswick, NJ: Transaction Books, 1986), 9–30; and E. Griffin, *A First Look at Communication Theory,* 6th ed. (New York: McGraw-Hill, 2006), 122–125.

6. W. C. Schutz, *The Interpersonal Underworld* (Palo Alto, CA: Science and Behavior Books, 1966), 13–20.

7. B. Park and C. Flink, "A Social Relations Analysis of Agreement in Liking Judgments," *Journal of Personality and Social Psychology* 56 (1989): 506–51.

8. M. Moore, "Nonverbal Courtship Patterns in Women! Context and Consequences," *Ethology and Sociobiology* 6 (1985): 237–47.

9. D. Fine, *The Fine Art of Small Talk* (New York: Hyperion, 2005).

10. D. J. Goldsmith and L. A. Baxter, "Constituting Relationship Talk: A Taxonomy of Speech Events in Social and Personal Relationships," *Human Communication Research* 18 (1996): 87–114.

11. J. Levin and A. Arluke, *Gossip: The Inside Scoop* (New York: Plenum, 1987), 28–29.

12. J. S. Caputo, H. C. Hazel, and C. McMahon, *Interpersonal Communication: Competency Through Critical Thinking* (Boston: Allyn and Bacon, 1994), 98–99.

13. B. Reeves, "Chat Room Brought Them Together," *Lincoln Journal Star,* 25 June 2000, sec. J, 1.

14. M. R. Parks and K. Floyd, "Making Friends in Cyberspace," *Journal of Communication* 46 (1996): 85.

15. M. Irvine, "Wireless Gadgets: Flirt-Friendly," *Lincoln Journal Star,* September 22, 2002, 9A.

16. Ibid.

17. B. Reeves, "Caught in the Net: Proceed with Caution, *Lincoln Journal Star,* 25 June 2000, sec. J, 1.

18. Ibid.

19. Ibid.

20. W. Rawlins, "Negotiating Close Friendships. The Dialectic of Conjunctive Freedoms," *Human Communication Research* 9 (1983): 255–66; and L. Baxter and B. Montgomery, *Relating: Dialogue and Dialects* (New York: Guilford, 1996), 133–39.

21. J. Luft, *Group Processes: An Introduction to Group Dynamics* (Palo Alto, CA: National Press, 1970), 11–14.

22. J. Stokes, A. Fuehrer, and L. Childs, "Gender Differences in Self-Disclosure to Various Target Persons," *Journal of Counseling Psychology* 27 (1980): 192–98.

23. I. Altman and D. Taylor, *Social Penetration: The Development of Interpersonal Relationships* (New York: Holt, Rinehart & Winston, 1973); and Knapp and Vangelisti, 14–20.

24. A. L. Sillars and M. D. Scott, "Interpersonal Perception Between Intimates: An Integrative Review," *Human Communication Research* 10 (1983): 153–76.

25. J. W. Pennebaker, *Opening Up: The Healing Power of Expressing Emotions* (New York: Guilford, 1990).

26. V. J. Derlega, S. Metts, S. Petronio, and S. T. Margulis, *Self-Disclosure* (Newbury Park, CA: Sage, 1993), 74.

27. S. Petronio, "The Boundries of Privacy: Praxis of Everyday Life," in *Balancing the Secrets of Private Disclosures,* ed. S. Petronio (Hillsdale, NJ: Erlbaum, 2000), 9–15.

28. S. Petronio, "Communication Boundary Management: A Theoretical Model of Managing Disclosure of Private Information Between Marital Couples," *Communication Theory* 1 (1991): 311.

29. J. T. Wood, *Gendered Lives: Communication, Gender, and Culture,* 6th ed. (Belmont, CA: Wadsworth, 2005).

30. D. Tannen, *You Just Don't Understand: Women and Men in Conversation* (New York: Ouill, 2001).

31. C. K. Riessman, *Divorce Talk: Women and Men Make Sense of Personal Relationships* (New Brunswick, NJ: Rutgers University Press, 1990).

32. L. B. Rosenfeld, "Self-Disclosure Avoidance: Why I Am Afraid to Tell You Who I Am," *Communication Monographs* 46 (1979): 63–74.

33. S. Petronio, "Communication Strategies to Reduce Embarrassment Differences Between Men and Women," *The Western Journal of Speech Communication* 48 (1984): 28–38.

34. R. P. Hart and D. M. Burks, "Rhetorical Sensitivity and Social Interaction," *Speech Monographs* 39 (1972): 75–91.

35. S. W. Littlejohn and K. Foss, *Theories of Human Communication,* 8th ed. (Belmont, CA: Wadsworth, 2005).

36. A. P. Bochner, "The Functions of Human Communicating in Interpersonal Bonding," in *Handbook of Rhetorical and Communication Theory,* eds. C. C. Arnold and J. W. Bowers (Boston: Allyn and Bacon, 1984), 554–621.

# CHAPTER 14

# Developing Relationships

"Some people come into our lives and quickly go. Some people move our souls to dance. They awaken us to understanding with the passing whisper of their wisdom. Some people make the sky more beautiful to gaze upon. They stay in our lives for awhile, leave footprints on our hearts."
—ANONYMOUS

# This chapter will help you:

- **Understand** the stages of relationship development and deterioration.
- **Know** how dialectical tensions push and pull on relationships.
- **Explain** what interpersonal conflict is and how to resolve it.
- **Determine** when a relationship is in trouble and how to use relational repair strategies.
- **Improve** your interpersonal communication skills and competencies in personal and professional relationships.

## Making everyday connections

Thursday—the free day Grant has during the week to do what he wants. He usually likes to spend part of the day relaxing, either by sleeping or playing hoops with his friends. Grant is a good student and is sure that he did well on his chemistry midterm test. Given that he has had a good night's sleep for a change, he decides to go to the courts to see if he can get in a pickup game of ball.

On his way, he picks up his mail and discovers that he has received an award for his excellent grades. He is so pleased that he begins to hum out loud as he continues to the basketball courts.

When he gets there, Grant notices a student from his chemistry class sitting outside the courts watching. He isn't sure of her name, but she smiles and says hello. "Hi," he says, "my name is Grant. You're in my chemistry class, aren't you?"

"Yes, I am and you're the guy that knows all the answers. By the way, my name is Ali. Are you here to play some basketball with those guys?"

Grant responds, "Yes." As he starts to walk away he looks back and Ali smiles. He thinks to himself, "I wonder if she is seeing anyone?" He then turns around and says, "Can I call you later?" Ali responds—"Sure." ■

### Questions to think about

- In what way or ways does our emotional state influence our communication?
- Describe in your own words what happens to communication during the various stages of relationship development, moving from being an acquaintance to being a friend or intimate friend.

- What role does small talk (discussed in Chapter 13) have in everyday interactions?

- Describe what occurs to communication when a relationship is coming apart or breaking up.

It is a human tendency to evaluate almost everything and everyone and to form attitudes about the people, objects, and events in our lives. As we encounter other individuals at school, work, or in our neighborhoods, we develop attitudes about each of them. These interpersonal evaluations fall along a dimension ranging from liking to disliking and also help to determine the type of relationship that may be formed—for example, friend, close acquaintance, superficial acquaintance, annoying acquaintance, or undesirable.

In Chapter 13, we stated that relationships have the potential to form any time two people make contact with each other, whether face to face or via some other medium such as the phone or the computer. Most contacts are made accidentally, depending on factors such as those described in the chapter opening scenario; they can also occur via classes you chose to take, seating arrangement in those classes, who happens to be in a chat room when you enter it, or the physical arrangements of a workplace, all of which increase the odds that you will come into repeated contact with people, while at the same time decreasing the odds that such contact will occur with others. As a result, although this might not seem all that surprising, physical proximity and timing are very often how people meet and begin relationships with each other.

## MAKING CONNECTIONS for Success

### The Dark Side of Interpersonal Relationships

Most of what we have discussed to this point about entering and maintaining relationships has been more-or-less positive. It has been our goal to discuss the positive aspects of relationships and how to be a successful communicator in interpersonal situations. However, we all know that relationships can at times have a painful and negative side. Consider this scenario:

Elissa and Josh met in a history course. He was athletic, good looking, sensitive, and had a great personality. They began dating and appeared to be the perfect couple. Elissa began spending more and more time with Josh and less time with her college girlfriends. Elissa felt that was a lot easier than responding to Josh's endless questions about her whereabouts and what she was doing every moment of the day.

Elissa's friends noticed a dramatic change in her personality. She seemed to have lost interest in the things she loved to do before she met Josh. She became distant and moody—just not her old self.

1. What do you think is going on?
2. What do you think happens to communication in an abusive relationship?
3. What are the warning signs that someone is in an abusive relationship?
4. Provide examples of verbal abuse.
5. Why is the phrase "If you loved me, you would . . ." a red flag and sign of potential abuse?
6. What can you do if you find yourself in an abusive relationship?

Chapter 13's opening Making Everyday Connections and the one in this chapter illustrate some ways in which relationships are formed. Whether a relationship evolves into any kind of ongoing or lasting one depends on many factors, such as attraction, motivation, and need—all of which were discussed in Chapter 13. Communication, however, is the overriding factor that determines and affects the type and depth of relationships that are formed and how long they last.

# ■ Forming and Dissolving Relationships

How we progress as individuals, survive, develop intimacy, and make sense of our world depends on how we relate to others. This chapter explores why some people are interpersonally attracted to others and the stages of growth and deterioration that most relationships go through, which are best exemplified by the theory of relationship stages and the theory of dissolution stages. The chapter also discusses interpersonal conflict, conflict management, and how to improve interpersonal communication competency.

## ■■ Interpersonal Attraction

Most of us develop relationships quite routinely, although the process is easier for some people than it is for others. Every day, we are enormously influenced by first impressions. **Interpersonal attraction** is the desire to interact with someone based on a variety of factors, including physical attractiveness, personality, rewards, proximity, or similarities. Although these are perhaps obvious referents, interpersonal attraction is a very complex phenomenon. Communication scholars James McCroskey and Thomas McCain identified three types of attraction: (1) social attraction ("He would fit into my circle of friends"), (2) physical attraction ("I think she's quite pretty"), and (3) task attraction ("My confidence in her ability to get the job done makes me want to work with her").[1] In other words, interpersonal attraction has a lot to do with evaluating other people.

Any given person (including you) is liked by some people, disliked by some, and seen as indifferent by many others. Why? This question is not easily answered, but, to some extent, differences in attraction depend on the person who is making the evaluation. Attraction also depends in part on the similarities and differences between the evaluator and the person being evaluated. As acquaintances evolve from first encounters to more engaged relationships, two additional factors come into play: the need to associate with someone and reactions to observable physical attributes.

What leads to attraction and eventual friendship? There are at least six billion people on our planet, and several thousand of them could conceivably become your friends. That is exceedingly unlikely to happen, however. Any one of us is likely to become aware of, interact with, and get to know only a small fraction of these individuals. Of those in this relatively small subgroup, only a few will become acquaintances, fewer still will become friends, and most will remain strangers. What determines awareness, interaction, and differential attraction?

Once two people come into contact and experience relatively positive effects, they begin a transition, the initiating stages of a possible relationship. They may simply remain superficial acquaintances who exchange friendly greetings whenever they happen to encounter one another but never interact otherwise. Or they may begin to talk, learn each other's names, and exchange bits and pieces of information. At this

■ **interpersonal attraction** The desire to interact with someone based on a variety of factors, including physical attractiveness, personality, rewards, proximity, or similarities.

**MAKING Technology CONNECTIONS**

## Soul Mate Online—Finding the Right One

Search the Internet by typing in any of these key terms—finding a date, finding a relationship, or finding a mate—and you will find over a million different sites. Here are some of their slogans:

"When you are ready to find the love of your life." "A marriage a day, a match every 17 minutes." "Genuine People, Real Love." "Over 100,000 current members searching for meaningful relationships." "Ever wish there was an easy way to find the person you were meant to be with?" "To create a deep and meaningful connection."

Internet sites such a Eharmony.com, Therightone .com, Perfectmatch.com, Mate1.com, Netmatching .com, Findadate.com, Facebook.com, Spacebook.com,

and hundreds more offer ways to meet others, to find a date, to get married, to be friends, to connect.

1. Why do you think that websites such as those listed above are so popular?
2. How would you describe the perfect mate?
3. How can you be sure you have found the perfect mate?
4. If you were to use the Internet to find a relationship, what criteria would you use to determine whether you would make a face-to-face connection with someone?
5. What, if any problems might you encounter with these types of services and putting information online for others to read?

point, they might be described as close acquaintances. Which of these two outcomes occurs depends on (1) the extent to which each person is motivated by the need to associate or the need for inclusion (discussed in Chapter 13) and (2) the way each person reacts to the observable physical attributes of the other.

## ▬ Physical Attributes

When we like—or dislike—some people at first sight, it is an indication that we have observed something about them that appears to provide information. For example, if a stranger reminds you of someone you know and like, your response to the person is extended by association.[2] You tend to like the stranger simply on the basis of a superficial resemblance to someone else. In other instances, the cue might not be related to a specific person in your past but to a subgroup of people to whom you respond positively—the stranger has a Wisconsin accent, for example, and you have a fondness for people from your home state. In a similar way, resemblance to a specific person you know and dislike or to a subgroup of people you dislike can cause you instantly to dislike or avoid a stranger. As we discussed in Chapters 2 and 5, stereotypes are poor predictors of behavior, but, nevertheless, we find ourselves reacting to other people on the basis of superficial characteristics.

Most of us have learned that "beauty is only skin deep," and we know that reacting to stereotypes on the basis of appearance is meaningless. However, people do in fact respond positively to those who are very attractive and negatively to those who are very unattractive.[3] This is especially true in the early stages of interpersonal contact with strangers. In U.S. society, we commonly accept or reject people on the basis of observable characteristics such as skin color, sexual orientation, height, weight, accent, and hair color. Physical attractiveness is a very powerful message and influences many types of interpersonal evaluations, but appearance is especially crucial with respect to attraction to members of the opposite sex.[4]

**Communication and Attraction.**   How does attractiveness affect relationships and interpersonal communication? Most people, according to one study, are afraid of being rejected by those who are more attractive than they are. Many people tend to reject others who are far less attractive than they believe themselves to be; in other words, they are saying, "I can do better than that." As a result, people tend to pair off, especially in romantic relationships, by selecting individuals whom they consider similar in attractiveness. "Mismatches" do occur, such as portrayed in the characters of Catherine (an attractive woman) and Vincent (unattractive disfigured man) in the story of "Beauty and the Beast." Why do these exceptions occur, and what explains them? If one person in a relationship is more attractive than another, for example, people tend to infer that the less attractive person in the relationship has an attribute that "balances" the mismatch, such as wealth, power, intelligence, sex appeal, or fame.

For example, in "Beauty and the Beast" Vincent's appearance is unattractive, but his kindness, gentleness, and bravery make Catherine's love for him believable. Whether we wish to accept it or not, physical appearance does play a role in determining relationships. Although this attractiveness might not always predict the outcome of a relationship, research has shown that physical attractiveness is important as an attention getter.[5]

**Chemistry and Attraction.**   Most of us are aware that sometimes our first impressions and reasons for being attracted to another are not completely rational. Sudden lust, love at first sight, or the intense dislike of someone with whom we have had no previous contact can seem inexplicable. Many social psychologists suggest that relationship development has a lot to do with the "chemistry" between the individuals in the relationship. Either the chemistry is right and the relationship develops, or it's a mismatch and the relationship never seems to move beyond the initial stages. The chemistry explanation probably holds some truth, but many other variables influence the development of a relationship.

We are most often attracted to individuals who support us and have similar interests, attitudes, likes, and dislikes. In fact, when asked to characterize their ideal friend, people often describe someone who is similar to their perceptions of themselves. For example, those who are religious tend to seek other religious people, those who like sports tend to seek other sports fans, and those who like children tend to seek others who like children. Of course, opposites sometimes do attract, but relationships in which there are significant differences in important attitudes or behaviors are often strained and more likely to deteriorate than are those that have no significant disparities.

The fairy tale "Beauty and the Beast" is an ancient story that continues to hold meaning. Its theme raises an interesting question: What is the basis of attraction between people? People usually select partners whom they perceive to be similarly physically attractive or more attractive than themselves. In what cases might there be an exception to this rule?

**Gender and Attraction.**   Another gender difference is exhibited in the personal ads placed by males and females who are seeking a romantic partner. It was generally found that women stress their appearance and men stress their material resources.[6] It could be, of course, that those who write ads are simply echoing widespread cultural beliefs about what people assume is most appealing to the opposite sex. One study investigated the number of replies that certain types of ad messages received.[7] In other words, do some factors in the ads attract more potential mates than others? Several interesting gender differences were found. For women, age as stated in their ads was negatively related to the number of replies; that is, the older a woman was, the fewer replies. For men, the opposite was true; the older a man was, the more replies he received. Also, the higher men's stated income and educational level, the more replies. For women, in contrast, these factors were unrelated to how many responses the ad generated. Thus a personal ad placed by a man was most effective if it indicated a mature, rich, educated individual. In ads placed by a woman, the only relevant ad content related to its effectiveness was age—the younger, the better. Interestingly, ads placed by gay men indicated a preference for younger males, and ads placed by heterosexual men indicated a preference for younger female partners. Whatever the reason, for both genders and for both heterosexuals and homosexuals, attractiveness is a positive characteristic, and numerous stereotypes are consistently associated with appearance.[8]

## Meeting on the Internet

In Chapter 13, we discussed how initial interaction on the Internet could result in relationships and the fact that the growth of those relationships is often limited for a variety of reasons. According to Malcolm Parks and Kory Floyd, two communication scholars whose research on Internet interaction was mentioned in Chapter 13, there are conflicting theories on interpersonal communication and relationship development. Because Internet interaction is limited by fewer social cues (i.e., nonverbal communication) and potential feedback delays can lead to uncertainty (and difficulty in reducing uncertainty about the other person), the development of personal relationships might be prevented, or at least retarded.[9]

Online interactions are generally assumed to lack many of the typical characteristics of face-to-face discussions that can aid in relationship development. An important question that researchers are asking is "Are the conditions that exist in face-to-face interactions necessary for a relationship to develop into something that is ongoing or lasting?" Thus proximity and other conditions that occur in face-to-face interactions may be helpful, but they are not required for a relationship to be rewarding or fulfilling; they are not necessary for interactants to develop feelings for each other and do not affect how cyberpartners treat each other.[10]

Parks and Floyd, in addition to finding that women are more likely to form relationships on the Internet than men are, also found that age and marital status were not related to the likelihood of developing a personal relationship online. People who were married and divorced, according to the survey results, were equally likely to form personal relationships over the Internet. In fact, of the 176 people Parks and Floyd surveyed, about 30 percent developed personal relationships. The more in-depth and personal an Internet relationship becomes, the more likely it is that communication will move beyond cyberspace to more private and direct channels such as the telephone, letters, or face-to-face communication.[11] As with all relationships, Internet relationships also go through stages of coming together and coming apart.

## Knapp and Vangelisti's Stages of Coming Together

Communication scholars such as Mark Knapp and Anita Vangelisti believe that for relationships to move beyond a brief encounter, they must go through various stages of growth and patterns of communication.[12] Although the relationship stages in

Knapp and Vangelisti's model are generally romantic in nature, they do not preclude or suggest that only romantic relationships or mixed-gendered relationships are included. In fact, Knapp and Vangelisti suggest that any and all kinds of relationships, including same-sex partners, can reach the highest level of commitment. It is interesting to note that David McWhirter and Andrew Mattison, research psychologists, found that when same-sex intimate relationships form, the same patterns or stages of development occur as with mixed-sex pairs.[13]

Knapp and Vangelisti strongly emphasize that the model simplifies a complex process. For example, in their model they show each stage adjacent to the next, seeming to suggest that when a communicating couple left one stage they entered the next. This is not their intention. Each stage actually contains behaviors from other stages, so that stage identification is a matter of emphasis.

Knapp and Vangelisti further their explanation of the model by stating that not all relationships go through the stages at the same rate, in the same way, or necessarily sequentially, and many relationships move in and out of the stages as they progress or regress. In describing the stages they say that we should resist the temptation to perceive stages of coming together as only "good" and those of coming apart as only "bad." In fact, they note that sometimes the termination of a relationship may be a good thing or conversely, that becoming more intimate with someone may not necessarily be a good thing. The stages are descriptive, according to Knapp and Vangelisti, of what seems to happen and not necessarily what happens. The coming-together sequence, however, often progresses from initiating to experimenting, intensifying, integrating, and ultimately bonding.[14]

**Initiating.**  Initiating is the stage during which individuals meet and interact for the first time. The initial interaction might consist of a brief exchange of words, either electronically or in person, or of eye contact during which the two individuals recognize each other's existence and potential interest to meet and converse. If conversation does not begin, the initiating stage may end, and the potential relationship might not progress any further. Whether the interaction continues depends on various assessments that the individuals make—for example, whether the other person is attractive or unattractive, approachable or unapproachable. A connection must be made to motivate one or both of the individuals to continue the interaction if a relationship is to develop. The decision to pursue the relationship also depends on whether the other person is open for the encounter. Is she or he in a hurry, too busy, or too involved with others?

During the initiating stage, we mentally process many impressions that lead to a key decision: "Yes, I do want to meet you" or "No, I am not interested in you." It might take less than fifteen seconds to determine whether a relationship will progress. At this stage, most of us feel extreme vulnerability and caution, even though there is considerable variance in people's initiating behaviors. The Internet seemingly is playing a larger and larger role in how people from all over the world meet and interact. People of all ages are using cyberspace to develop friendships as well as romantic relationships.

**Experimenting.**  Experimenting is the stage of coming together that requires risk taking because little is known as yet about the other person. You attempt to answer the question "Who is this person?" This stage can be extremely awkward, consisting mainly of small talk: "What's your name?" "Where are you from?" "What's your major?" "Do you know so-and-so?" Such conversation serves several important

## MAKING CONNECTIONS for Success

### Relationships and Decisions

Scott and Dionne have been going together for a few years now, but Scott cannot make any decisions on his own nor does he want to take responsibility for making them. He seems to just accept whatever Dionne wants to do. This is okay with Dionne, but then she never seems to know what Scott thinks, feels, or wants to do. The problem is that Dionne thinks that she is perceived to be controlling Scott's life and she doesn't like this because all of Scott's friends tell him that he is a wimp. Dionne has tried the silent approach—just not saying anything with the hope that Scott will take the initiative, but instead nothing is ever decided.

1. What does this tell you about Scott and Dionne's relationship?
2. Why do you think Scott is unable to make decisions on his own?
3. What can Dionne do so that Scott will start making decisions?
4. How does the above relate to needs and motivation discussed in Chapter 13?

functions in the development of a relationship: (1) It uncovers similarities and interests that might lead to deeper conversation, (2) it serves as an audition for the potential friend, (3) it lets the other person know who you are and provides clues as to how he or she can get to know you better, and (4) it establishes the common ground you share with the other person.

Relationships that are in the experimenting stage are "generally pleasant, relaxed, overtly uncritical, and casual."[15] Most relationships, according to Knapp and Vangelisti, do not progress very far beyond the experimenting stage. However, relationships that remain at the experimental level can become satisfying friendships or acquaintances.

**Intensifying.** The intensifying stage marks an increase in the participants' commitment and involvement in the relationship. Simply put, the two people become close friends. The commitment is typified by an increased sharing of more personal and private information, or self-disclosure (see Chapter 13), about oneself and one's family. For example, at this stage, it would not be unusual to share confidences such as "My mother and father are affectionate people," "I love you," "I am a sensitive person," "I once cheated on an exam," "My father is having another relationship," "I was promoted," "I drink too heavily," and "I don't use drugs."

Although the relationship deepens at this stage, there is still a sense of caution and testing to gain approval before continuing. In typical romantic relationships, we see much testing of commitment—sitting close, for instance, may occur before holding hands, hugging, or kissing. As the relationship matures, the participants become more sensitive to each other's needs. During this phase, many things happen verbally:

1. Forms of address become informal—a first name, nickname, or a term of endearment is used.

2. Use of the first-person plural becomes more common—"We should do this" or "Let's do this."

3. Private symbols begin to develop—special slang or jargon or conventional language forms with mutually understood, private meanings.

4. Verbal shortcuts built on a backlog of accumulated and shared assumptions, knowledge, and experiences appear. For instance, your friend needs to be told that he or she is loved; you say that the person is important to you but never say that you love him or her.

5. More direct expressions of commitment may appear—"We really have a good thing going" or "I don't know who I'd talk to if you weren't around." Sometimes such expressions receive an echo—"I really like you a lot" or "I really like you, too, Dion."

**6.** Each partner acts increasingly as a helper in the other's daily process of understanding what he or she is all about—"In other words, you mean you're . . ." or "But yesterday you said you were. . . ."

**Integrating.** When integrating occurs, the relationship has a sense of togetherness. Others expect to see the individuals together, and when they do not, they often ask about the other person. The two people have established a deep commitment, and the relationship has become extremely important to them. Many assumptions take place between the individuals. For example, sharing is expected, and borrowing from the other person usually needs no formal request because it is assumed to be all right.

Although a strong mutual commitment characterizes this stage of a relationship, it does not mean a total giving of oneself to the other. The verbal and nonverbal expressions of the integrating stage take many forms. For example, some individuals believe their relationship is something special or unique. Some share rings, pins, pictures, and other artifacts to illustrate to themselves and others their commitment to each other. The two may begin to behave in similar ways. Still others indicate their sense of togetherness through word choice—*our* account, *our* apartment, *our* stereo, *our* car.

**Bonding.** The final stage in a relationship's development and growth is bonding, the public announcement of the commitment—as when a couple announces that they are engaged or getting married. Bonding involves the understanding that the commitment has progressed from private knowledge to public knowledge, thus making a breakup of the relationship more difficult.

The relationship at this stage is contractual in nature, even though a formal contract, such as a marriage license, is not required. Both parties must understand, however, that a relationship exists, which entails explicit and implicit agreements to hold it together. The commitment implies that the relationship is "for better or for worse" and is defined according to established norms, policies, or laws of the culture and society in which it exists.

The integrating stage of relationship development conveys a sense of togetherness. The two people have established a deep commitment, and the relationship has become extremely important to them.

## ■■ Knapp and Vangelisti's Stages of Coming Apart

In U.S. culture, there are no guarantees that a commitment will create a lasting relationship. When a relationship stops growing and differences begin to emerge, the coming-apart process begins. Some relationships go through some or all of the stages in this process and emerge stronger than before, but when the forces that pull a relationship apart are stronger than the forces that hold it together, the alliance will end. Like the coming-together process, Knapp and Vangelisti's coming-apart stages do not flow necessarily in a sequential order, and it is likely that relationships often move into and out of the stages. The coming-apart process has five stages: differentiating, circumscribing, stagnating, avoiding, and terminating.[16]

**Differentiating.** In differentiating, the first stage of coming apart, the differences between the individuals are highlighted and become forces that slow or limit the growth of the relationship. The pair's communication tends to focus on how each differs from the other, and there is less tolerance of these differences. Indeed, differences that were once overlooked or negotiated now become the center of attention, putting stress on the relationship and its existence. Typically, things that were once described as "ours" now become "mine": "This is my apartment," "These are my books," and "They are my friends."

Conversations often move from mild disagreement to heated anger: "Do I have to do all the work around here? You don't do a darn thing." "Why is it that your so-called friends never clean up after themselves?" "I pay the phone bill, but you're the one who uses it the most." Conflict begins to overshadow the more positive aspects of the relationship and might lead to abuse of one or both parties in the relationship.

**Circumscribing.** In the circumscribing stage, information exchange is reduced, and some areas of difference are completely avoided because conversation would only lead to a deepening of the conflict. Comments during this stage might include the following: "I don't want to talk about it." "Can't you see that I'm busy?" "Why do you keep bringing up the past?" "Let's just be friends and forget it." Communication loses some of its personal qualities, is less spontaneous, and becomes increasingly superficial as the relationship becomes more strained. Interactions, in their amount and depth of disclosure, resemble those of the initiating and experimenting stages of coming together: "Have you eaten?" "Did I get any calls today?" "I saw Joe, and he said to say hi."

People in the circumscribing stage often conceal their faltering relationship in public. For example, driving to a party, a couple might sit in cold silence, staring stonily into space. But once they arrive at their destination, they put on their party personalities—smiling, telling jokes, and not disagreeing with one another. When they return to the privacy of their car, they resume their cold behavior.

**Stagnating.** The relationship reaches a standstill at the stagnating stage. The participants avoid interaction and take care to sidestep controversy. Some people believe this is the "boring" stage of a relationship, yet they do not do anything about it. Little hope remains for the relationship once it has deteriorated to this stage, yet one of the participants might still want it to be revived.

During stagnation, both verbal and nonverbal communication tend to be thoroughly

## MAKING CONNECTIONS
### for Success

### Just Want a Relationship

Knapp and Vangelisti's stages of relational coming together and apart seem to apply best to traditional romantic relationships. This, according to some critics, leaves out a variety of other same-sex or mixed-sex relationships that are equally important in our lives. What do you think?

1. How well do the stages explain other types of relationships besides romantic? For example, you could test the model with good or best friends, parent and child, grandparent and grandchild, co-workers, and others.
2. What changes do you think need to be made to make the stages more in line with what you described above? Create your own stages if you wish.

thought out, and the partners plan what to say, making interactions stylized and cold. Both parties are apt to reflect unhappiness and to act as if each is a stranger to the other.

Often the stagnation stage is relatively brief, but sometimes it is extended because of complications. For example, some people are seriously distressed by the loss of their relationship even though they know that parting is the right decision. Other people may count on the survival of the relationship, such as children, making the breakup more difficult. Others may prolong the situation in fear of experiencing additional pain and in hope of getting the relationship back on track or in an attempt to punish the other person.

**Avoiding.**  Up to this point, the participants in the relationship are still seeing each other or sharing the same living quarters. But the fourth stage, the avoiding stage, is marked by physical or emotional distancing and eventual separation. The basic message is "I am not interested in being with you anymore." As far as the participants are concerned, the relationship is over, and they have no interest in reestablishing it.

At times, the interaction in this stage is brief, direct, unfriendly, and even antagonistic: "I really don't care to see you." "Don't call me—we have nothing to discuss." "I'm busy tonight. For that matter, I'm going to be busy for quite some time."

**Terminating.**  The last stage in the breaking up of a relationship occurs when the individuals take the necessary steps to end it. Termination can be early, that is, when the relationship has barely begun, or it can occur after many years. For relationships that break up in the early stages of development, such as initiating or experimenting, the feelings of parting are usually not complex or lasting.

The interaction during this stage is self-centered and seeks to justify the termination: "I need to do something for myself—I've always put more into the relationship than I've gotten out of it." "We just have too many differences that I didn't know existed until now." "I found out that we just weren't meant for each other." When both individuals know that the relationship is ending, they say good-bye to each other in three ways: in a summary statement, in behaviors signaling the termination or limited contact, and in comments about what the relationship will be like in the future, if there is to be any relationship at all.[17]

Summary statements review the relationship and provide a rationale for its termination: "Although our love used to be very special, we both have changed over the years. We are not the same couple that we were when we first met." Ending behaviors reflect new rules of contact: "It would be good for both of us not to see so much of each other." "I wish you would stop coming over all the time." Finally, when the relationship is over, the participants state their preferences for dealing with each other in the future: "I don't want to see you anymore." "We can get together once in a while, but I only want us to be friends and nothing more." See Table 14.1 for dialogue that represents each stage of relationship development.

**The Process of Coming Together and Coming Apart.**  The stages of coming together and coming apart are complex and continuous as we move into, through, and out of relationships. Knapp and Vangelisti acknowledge that not all relationships move through each of the escalating and deescalating stages at the same pace or always in sequential order, but they state that most relationships do go through the interaction stages systematically and sequentially. They also suggest that it is possible for people

■ **TABLE 14.1** Knapp and Vangelisti's Stages of Relationship Development

| PROCESS | STAGE | REPRESENTATIVE DIALOGUE |
|---|---|---|
| *Coming together* | Initiating | "Hi, how ya doin'"? <br> "Fine. You?" |
| | Experimenting | "Oh, so you like to ski . . . so do I." <br> "You do? Great. Where do you go?" |
| | Intensifying | "I . . . I think I love you." <br> "I love you too." |
| | Integrating | "I feel so much a part of you." <br> "Yeah, we are like one person." <br> "What happens to you happens to me." |
| | Bonding | "I want to be with you always." <br> "Let's get married." |
| *Coming apart* | Differentiating | "I just don't like big social gatherings." <br> "Sometimes I don't understand you. This is one area where I'm certainly not like you at all." |
| | Circumscribing | "Did you have a good time on your trip?" <br> "What time will dinner be ready?" |
| | Stagnating | "What's there to talk about?" <br> "Right. I know what you're going to say, and you know what I'm going to say." |
| | Avoiding | "I'm so busy, I don't know when I'll be able to see you." <br> "If I'm not around, you'll understand." |
| | Terminating | "I'm leaving you . . . and don't bother trying to contact me." <br> "Don't worry." |

From Mark L. Knapp and Anita L. Vangelisti, *Interpersonal Communication and Human Relationships,* 5e. Published by Allyn and Bacon, Boston, MA. Copyright © 2005 by Pearson Education. Reprinted by permission of the publisher.

to skip steps during both the growth process of a relationship and the deterioration of a relationship. You might have had or heard of relationships that go from the initiating stage—"Hi, my name is"—to "Let's go to your place so that we can get to know each other better." These relationships move from the initiating step right to the intensifying step. Termination may occur suddenly and without warning in this situation, thus violating or skipping all the steps of coming apart. For example, in *Runaway Bride,* a popular movie in the late 1990s, Julia Roberts portrays a character who fell in love with several different men, but in each case, she left them standing at the altar because she did not believe the relationship was right.

Knapp and Vangelisti also suggest that relationships can move forward and backward from one stage to the next. The direction a relationship takes depends on how one evaluates the various benefits and costs (social exchange theory—see Chapter 13) and whether benefits outweigh the costs or vice versa, thus moving the relationship either forward or backward. Relationships are not static; therefore it is natural for all relationships, including the most stable, to experience periods of insta-

## MAKING CONNECTIONS
### for Success

### Retracing a Relationship's Progress

Clearly, no two relationships are alike, nor do they all evolve in the same way. Consider a relationship that is important to you, and then complete the following steps:

1. Record the significant developments in the relationship, from the time of the first meeting to the present. Label these developments according to Knapp and Vangelisti's stages.
2. After you have completed the labeling, imagine that your relationship is a book, and each stage or period in the relationship's history is a chapter. Create a title for each chapter, capturing that essence of the relationship during that period. You can have as many chapters as you find necessary to describe the relationship.

3. After you have titled each chapter, write a brief synopsis of what each title means. Do the chapters follow any particular pattern of development?
4. What are the similarities and differences between the stages of your relationship and Knapp and Vangelisti's stages?

Adapted from Leslie A. Baxter, "Dialectical Contradictions in Relationships Development," *Journal of Social and Personal Relationships* (1990) 7: 69–88. Reprinted in *Contemporary Perspectives on Interpersonal Communication*, eds. Sandra Petronio, Jess K. Alberts, Michael L. Hecht, and Jerry Buley (Dubuque, Iowa: Brown & Benchmark, 1993), 92–93.

bility. Each stage can also create its own movement, and like most things, the stages themselves have a beginning, middle, and end.

There are at least three reasons why relationships move through the stages sequentially: (1) Each stage provides information that allows movement to the next, (2) each stage enables the participants to predict what might or might not occur in the next stage, and (3) skipping a stage creates risk and uncertainty in the relationship.[18] Relationships that are happy and satisfying last because the participants have learned to satisfy each other through their communication.

## ▬ Signs That Show a Relationship Is in Trouble

Before we concede that a relationship is over, certain warning signs as well as some possible repair strategies might help to prevent its dissolution.

**Aggressive Behavior.** A preliminary warning sign that a relationship is heading toward trouble is when one of the parties becomes a little too aggressive by aiming hurtful communication at the other party. All of us, at one time or another, say something that we wished we hadn't said to someone about whom we care. However, whether intentionally or not, when people communicate hurtful statements to one another with increasing frequency, it is a possible sign that their relationship is in trouble.

**Lies.** Another warning sign that a relationship is in trouble is when one person deceives another by lying about something. Whether the lie is significant or trivial, it weakens the relationship's foundation, which is trust. Most of the time acts of deception have consequences that people don't fully consider when justifying their reasons for lying. You can probably think of many such consequences not only for the person being deceived but also for the deceiver. A relationship built on deceit is not likely to succeed for very long.

**Betrayal.** Another warning sign that a relationship is in trouble is betrayal. Betrayal can happen when someone trusts another person and, in one way or another, that trust is broken. For example, if you tell a friend a personal secret and especially ask for complete confidentiality and the friend then spreads the story to others, you have been betrayed. Deception and betrayal are similar; in fact, they are almost synonymous. The difference is that betrayal violates a confidence and an agreed-on expectation. Some common examples of betrayal include extramarital affairs, gossip, and harmful criticism behind someone's back.

Relationships that are injured by deception and betrayal are often not repairable because of the amount of hurt such breaches of trust cause. However, situations such as arguments that have gotten out of hand or misunderstandings can often be corrected or resolved. In these cases, competent communication can help repair and possibly save the relationship.

## ◾◾ Duck's Phases of Dissolution

Communication scholar Steve Duck theorizes that dissolving relationships go through a rather complex decision-making process that does not always follow a specific order of stages, in contrast to Knapp and Vangelisti's coming-apart stages. According to Duck, relationship breakups often occur sporadically, inconsistently, and with uncertainty over a period of time, but in deciding what to do about a potential breakup, a person proceeds through the following four phases: intrapyschic, dyadic, social, and grave-dressing. The termination of the relationship is strongly affected by the partners' social networks, and the influence of others outside the relationship is often reflected in any or all of the phases of a breakup. The uncertainty, or "on again, off again" approach that some relationships take as they dissolve defines the phases of Duck's approach.[19]

**The Intrapsychic Phase.** During the intrapsychic phase, people begin to internally assess their dissatisfaction with a relationship. This phase involves perception, assessments, and decision making about what to do about the relationship. In this phase, communication may actually decrease at times, and each of the partners might seek comfort from others outside the relationship. The intrapsychic phase is similar in some respects to the differentiating stage in which differences between the individuals become noticeable to at least one of the individuals in the relationship. Communication may decrease or become more self-centered and thus lead to more conflict and argument rather than negotiation.

**The Dyadic Phase.** In the dyadic phase, the people in the relationship discuss the status of their relationship. The interactions vary from cooperative to uncooperative in discussing the partners' unsatisfying traits or behaviors and whether to solve the problem or to separate. There is much negotiation, persuasion, and argument during this period; each person is trying to get the other person to comply or change in some fashion. Sometimes the dyadic phase ends with an agreement to repair the relationship, but if it doesn't, the relationship may eventually move on to the next phase. The dyadic phase would be consistent with what may occur as a relationship moves through the differentiating stage to the circumscribing stage. In this phase, it is likely that there is more conflict and less negotiation; the partners might also avoid subjects that may inflame the interaction. Thus when interaction occurs during this phase in the relationship breakup, it moves toward more impersonal or formalized conversations as illustrated in the circumscribing stage.

**The Social Phase.** In the social phase, the relationship difficulties become more public within the context of family, friends, co-workers, or other acquaintances. Most relationships that break up, except possibly secret love affairs, do not stand completely alone and usually have an impact on others outside the dissolving relationship. For example, there is usually an effect on the children if parents separate. During this phase, the opinions and feelings of others often have an impact on what a couple eventually does. For example, children of a married couple might influence the couple to stay together in spite of their differences. The concern might become, "What kind of relationship should be continued, if any? How should it be presented to others?" Other issues include where to place blame, how to save face, how to explain what has happened, and who should be sought out for support or to provide approval for the decision.

The social phase includes most aspects of the remaining three stages of Knapp and Vangelisti's coming-apart process: stagnating, avoiding, and termination. It is clear that the relationship has reached what appears to be an impasse, and therefore continuing it is most unlikely. However, the major difference between the two approaches is that Duck emphasized the impact the breakup of the relationship will have on others as well as the influence others will have on the relationship. Knapp and Vangelisti's stages do not address this issue directly. According to Duck, the individuals will seek out the approval of others, whereas Knapp and Vangelisti are more concerned with how the individuals justify the breakup to themselves.

**The Grave-Dressing Phase.** Duck names the final phase *grave-dressing* because after the breakup, each partner gives an account of why the relationship ended. This phase includes some similarities to the termination stage, because it is in this stage, according to Knapp and Vangelisti, that individuals begin to justify to others why the relationship had to end. These explanations aid in the healing process, in coping, and in the recovery from the breakup itself. It is not unusual for one or both individuals in the relationship to explain to others why the relationship dissolved. For example, if the relationship ended on friendly terms, you might hear statements such as "It just didn't work—we were too different" or "We needed time to grow, so we decided not to see each other for a while." If the relationship ended on unfriendly terms, however, you might hear explanations such as "He always wanted things for himself—he was selfish" or "She never seemed to be satisfied with what I'd do for her." Men and women handle relationship failures differently. Women, for example, tend to confide in their friends, whereas men tend to start a new relationship as quickly as possible.[20]

Not all relationships, however, end with mutual agreement that the relationship should be terminated. You are probably aware of situations in which one partner did not want to lose the other, but the person ending the relationship simply saw no reason to continue it. In such a case, the grave-dressing phase is usually one-sided; the person ending the relationship might say, "It just wasn't working" or "I have found someone new." Meanwhile, the person who does not want the relationship to end looks for a way to keep it going and cannot face the fact it is over. The person tries to justify to himself or herself and others that the termination is only temporary and that the other person will come to his or her senses and return.

Each phase poses certain communication challenges that Duck refers to as "social management problems." For example, in the intrapsychic phase, one must have the ability to discuss the perceived differences with one's partner. In the social phase, one must be able to discuss the breakup with others outside of the relationship. Clearly, as relationships move into and out of various phases, communication plays a significant role.

The research of Leslie Baxter, a communication scholar, supports some of Duck's explanations regarding dissolving relationships. Baxter believes that disengagement often involves repeated attempts to limit or end relationships. They are cyclical in nature and involve different communication strategies. Moreover, the communication strategies used during the breakup of relationships involve varying degrees of directness and concern for the other person.[21] The direct strategies are explicit statements describing the desire to end the relationship, whereas the indirect strategies are more subtle in design. For example, an indirect strategy for breaking up might involve using excuses such as "I have too much work to do," implying "I cannot see you now."

Someone with concern for the other person is more likely to use the indirect approach; the direct approach is much more expedient and may show little or no concern for hurting the other person. Baxter implies that strategies used in ending a relationship depend greatly on whether the breakup is one-sided or agreed on by both parties. As suggested earlier, agreed-on breakups usually involve some negotiation and face saving on behalf of both parties involved. All relationships, however, move through various stages and often move between various levels of tension or conflict.

To put it simply, relationships can be messy at times. This is true for even the best and most stable relationships because of the tensions that all relationships encounter from time to time. In fact, most romantic partners converse with each other less than a few hours a day, rarely self-disclose, often fight, on occasion become verbally and even physically violent, are rude to each other, and are more concerned with themselves than with sharing intimacies.[22] It is therefore not unusual that relationships don't measure up to the ideal, because most relationships—whether romantic, family, close friendship, or work-related—encounter difficult contradictions almost every day. These tensions and the conflicts that emerge from them are discussed in the following section.

## ■■ Dialectical Theory: Push and Pull

Relationships as well as individuals confront many contradictions or tensions, which push and pull us in many different directions at the same time. For example, as an individual you might want to be out with your friends for the evening but you have an important paper due in a few days that you haven't started. Thus, you have to decide between being with your friends or beginning your paper. Or you might want your best friend to spend more time with you, but when your friend does, you decide that you want more time to yourself. This might lead to your friend saying, "I thought you wanted to spend more time together, and now that we can, you're never around. So what do you want?" This illustrates the contradictory impulses or **dialectic** that push and pull us in conflicting directions with others. By contradic-

■ **dialectic**
Contradictory impulses that push and pull us in conflicting directions with others.

■ **TABLE 14.2** Dialectical Theory: Push and Pull

| TENSIONS | PUSH | PULL |
|---|---|---|
| Connection–autonomy | Dependent | Independent |
| | Together | Alone |
| Openness–closedness | Reveal | Conceal |
| | Public | Private |
| Novelty–predictability | Ambivalence | Certainty |
| | Different | Same |

tory impulses, we mean that each person is having two opposing and interacting desires, which push and pull the relationship in different directions. There are three commonly identified dialectical tensions described in the research: connected–autonomy, openness–closedness, and novelty–predictability (see Table 14.2).[23]

**Connection–Autonomy.**   Relationships require both the desire to connect to another person and the desire to retain autonomy as an individual. We want to connect to others, such as partners, friends, parents, siblings, or co-workers, but we also want to retain some control and independence or autonomy over our lives. There is a desire for our close relationships to be defined as "us," but this does not mean that we want to sacrifice our individuality or control over who we are.

When there is too much emphasis on connection or integration in a relationship, it can lead to the feeling of being smothered or consumed by a partner, friend, parent, or co-worker, such that we feel entrapped and controlled by the relationship, thus leaving us with no life of our own. Intimacy at its highest level does require a bonding that connects us with another person emotionally, intellectually, and physically, but it does not mean or require a complete loss of self. In healthy relationships, there is a reasonable balance of being connected and maintaining autonomy. Relationships that move too far in one direction or the other in terms of control versus autonomy are usually relationships that are extremely unstable and potentially destructive.

**Openness–Closedness.**   The second dialectic tension is the desire to be open and expressive on the one hand and closed and private on the other. In U.S. culture, we are encouraged to be open and honest with others because we are a society that admires those who are open and truthful. But even at the beginning of new relationships, when we are seeking as much information as we can about the other person, there is a counterforce that cautions against revealing too much too soon about ourselves. This tension between self-disclosing and keeping our privacy continues throughout the various stages of relationship development. We know that open expression is a necessary prerequisite in order for us to reach intimacy and bonding with another person. We also know that when we reveal ourselves to another individual, we make our relationship and ourselves more vulnerable. As discussed in Chapter 13, privacy is important for a relationship to survive. All of us therefore face the dilemma of how much self-disclosure or honesty we should allow there to be with

## MAKING CONNECTIONS for Success

### Temptation: Cheating to Trade Up

In early 2000, there was a reality show, *Temptation Island,* that had as its premise the idea of provoking committed but unmarried couples into promiscuous behavior by cheating on their partners. The basic assumption of *Temptation Island* was that participants should be ready to trade a current partner if a more attractive one came along. The theme of the show was "just go with the flow."

1. Is resisting the deliberate temptation of another attractive person an effective way to prove that a relationship is strong? Explain.
2. How might dialectical theory explain this show's impact on participants' relationships? On viewers' relationships?
3. Discuss the ethical implications of this show and how they would affect the communication in a relationship?

friends, relatives, and romantic partners and how much will be too much. Too much self-disclosure, as you learned in Chapter 13, can lead to strains on a relationship and is a sign of not being a competent, or, at the very least, a thoughtful, communicator. Relationships grow on the strength of the trust that is established between partners. When the trust that exists between partners is violated by revealing private information or by telling a partner something he or she is not prepared to hear, the relationship is at risk for deterioration or termination.

**Novelty–Predictability.**   To develop and build healthy relationships, a certain amount of predictability is needed. Without some stability or constancy, there is too much potential for uncertainty and ambivalence for a long-term relationship to survive. Therefore we need relationships in which we know that we can count on a certain amount of predictability. Families are a central stabilizing force in most people's lives and provide an anchor for security in a very unpredictable world. Predictability is a comfort to most of us because we know what to expect. Too much predictability in some aspects of a relationship, however, may make the relationship routine and boring, thus requiring a call for something unique or different. The dialectical tension created by the desire for predictability and consistency versus novelty and uncertainty in a relationship requires communication competence in order to relieve the tension and to prevent destructive conflict from occurring. Pushes and pulls, or dialectic tensions, will always be part of every relationship, and how we communicate will likely determine whether the relationship grows, stagnates, or terminates.

## ■■ Managing Relational Tensions

How we deal with the tensions in our lives creates some interesting communication challenges for each of us. It is also important to understand that relationships have both private and public dimensions and that relationships do not exist in a vacuum. There are many tensions or pushes and pulls from outside of a relationship as well as inside that can directly or indirectly affect how the parties in a relationship deal with or manage their dialectical tensions. Communication scholars Leslie Baxter and Barbara Montgomery suggest a number of approaches to enable us to manage our dialectical tensions.[24] The least helpful in dealing with tensions is *denial* that tension exits. How many times have you heard someone who is facing stress or tension say, "Everything is fine—there's no problem." The denial strategy is avoidance or cover-up, which often leads to lying or deception, if not to yourself, then most certainly to others. The dialectical tension does not disappear by denying its existence; it must be dealt with through communication.

Baxter, in a 1990 study, suggests that most people utilize a variety of strategies to manage their dialectical tensions.[25] The most often chosen are selection, segmentation, reframing, moderation, and reaffirmation. The strategy of *selection* is a strategy in which one end of the dialectical tension is chosen over the other. For example, a married couple finding themselves in a dilemma with their in-laws might choose to go along with the in-laws rather than do what they want to do so as not to create hardships or more distancing between themselves and the in-laws. In other words, they are choosing predictability over novelty.

The strategy of *segmentation* is a tactic in which a couple compartmentalizes different aspects of their relationship. For example, a couple might manage the tension between being open and being closed with each other by deciding to share information about their mutual friends but not to discuss their past romantic encounters with each other because that might be too hurtful or too insensitive. Thus some things are agreed to be open for discussion, and others are closed.

*Reframing* is a strategy that allows tensions to be redefined so as to dilute the tension, make it less obvious, or even make it disappear. Couples who have long-distance relationships, for example, might say that being apart has brought more intimacy and closeness to their relationship. Even though there is a great deal of stress in the relationship due to their physical separation, the couple have reframed it to mean that distance allows for great intimacy and closeness.

The strategy of *moderation* is characterized by compromises in which deals are struck to help reduce tensions. For example, a parent wants to know everything about your private life and is constantly asking you questions about personal things that you really do not want to share. You choose to answer some of the less private questions but ignore the most personal ones, thus reducing some of the tension created by the questions.

*Reaffirmation* is the strategy in which individuals recognize that dialectical tensions will always be present and therefore we should accept them and even embrace the challenges they produce. We should not ignore them or deny them, but we should consider dialectical tension as part of being human. Relationships are always going through pushes and pulls, and to grow and obtain a lasting relationship, the parties must manage and control the tensions through communication. The result of not managing and controlling tensions will likely be conflict.

## ■ Interpersonal Conflict

Conflict, like dialectic tensions in relationships, can occur for a variety of reasons, most of which are actions taken to block or interfere with others' interests because of perceptions of incompatible interests.

**Conflict,** according to communication scholars William Wilmot and Joyce Hocker, "is an expressed struggle between at least two interdependent parties who perceive incompatible goals, scarce resources, and interference from others in achieving their goals."[26] The key terms in the definition are *expressed struggle, interdependent parties, incompatible goals, scarce resources,* and *interference from others.* For example, suppose you want to go to a dance on Friday evening and your friend wants to go to a movie. Both of you explain your desire about what you would like to do (expressed struggle), neither of you wants to go out alone on Friday evening (interdependent parties), you cannot go to both the dance and the movie in the same

■ **conflict** An expressed struggle between at least two interdependence parties who perceive incompatible goals, scarce resources, and interference in achieving their goals.

evening (incompatible goals), neither of you can afford to do both because of time and money (scarce resources), and your friend will not consider going to the dance (interference). You have incompatible goals, and it seems one person must lose for the other to win.

The word *conflict* almost automatically brings to mind such things as fight, abuse, aggressiveness, violence, mistreatment, argument, disagreement, quarrel, clash, and differences. Not one of these words has a positive tone or gives us any reason to believe anything good can come from conflict. Wilmot and Hocker suggest that words such as exiting, strengthening, helpful, clarifying, growth producing, creative, courageous, enriching, intimate, opportune, and energizing could also be associated with conflict but most likely are not.[27] Why?

It seems that we sometimes exert a lot of energy to avoid conflict when in fact disagreements and differences of opinion can lead ultimately to compromise and solutions that might be far better for everyone. Conflict plays such a major role in U.S. culture that we need to understand its causes, why it is often destructive, and how we can better manage it or at least control it.

## What Causes Conflict?

Suppose you asked a large number of people to describe the major factor that contributes to conflict in interpersonal relationships. How do you think they would answer? The number one answer you would likely receive is poor or inadequate communication. However, if you asked the same people what is the best way to

## MAKING CONNECTIONS

### To Scholars

**Bill Wilmot**
*The Collaboration Institute*

Bill Wilmot has focused on personal relationships, interpersonal conflict, and mediation during his academic career. His teaching and research, in addition to conceptual development, have stressed application, making sure the academic work has some practical benefit. Of his numerous books, his best known are *Dyadic Communication* and *Interpersonal Conflict,* now in its 7th edition. While his earlier work on dyads helped chart the study of two-person relationships, his later work on conflict brought the study and practice of conflict management into the college classroom.

One outlet for fusing his academic and applied work is when Bill serves as a professional mediator. He is one of a handful of workplace "advanced practitioners" listed by the Association for Conflict Resolution. He has entered into over three hundred

disputes, and uses these experiences to enrich his books. All of his work is driven by a passion to make a difference in people's lives.

Bill has recently completed with coauthor Curtis R. Carlson, CEO of SRI International, a new book—*Innovation: The 5 Disciplines for Creating What Customers Want.* This ground-breaking book demonstrates how all types of organizations can thrive in these turbulent times by showing specific techniques for them to use.

Bill is Director of the Collaboration Institute (www.collaborationinstitute.com), a consortium of communication professionals dedicated to helping others. He has received awards for teaching and was also recognized by the Western States Communication Association with its highest honor—The Distinguished Service Award. He is Professor Emeritus at the University of Montana, still active in training and consultation work. When he is not traveling, he and his partner, Melanie Trost, live at their mountaintop home in Montana with their dog Rosie.

resolve or eliminate conflict, they would more than likely also say communication. Isn't it interesting that communication is cited as both a cause of conflict and solution for resolving it? What does this tell you? It should tell you that we often attribute the causes for and the resolution of conflict to "communication" and not ourselves. In other words, we don't take responsibility for conflict, but rather blame communication. If we use communication effectively and carefully, we can reduce or at least manage conflict more readily.

Our definition of conflict emphasizes the existence as well as the recognition of incompatible goals. Indeed, incompatible interests are the defining features of conflict. Yet conflicts can fail to develop, even though there are incompatible interests; in other situations, conflicts may occur when opposing interests do not exist but are believed to exist.[28] Clearly, then, conflict involves much more than opposing views of interest. In fact, a growing body of research suggests that social factors play a role that is as strong as, or even stronger than, incompatible interests in initiating conflicts; these social factors include faulty communication, faulty attributions, faulty perceptions, including stereotypes or prejudices, and personal traits or characteristics.

Faulty communication is a social factor that can lead to conflict. This is evident by the fact that individuals communicate in ways that anger or annoy others even though it might not be the communicator's intention to do so. Have you ever been harshly criticized in a way that you believed was unjustified, insensitive, unfair, and not the least bit helpful? If you have, you know that this type of perceived criticism leaves you feeling upset, angry, and ready to attack, thus setting the stage for conflict even though the criticism might not have been a result of incompatible goals.

Faulty attributions, such as errors concerning the causes behind others' behaviors, is one social factor that may lead to conflict.[29] When individuals believe that

Faulty communication is a social factor that may lead to conflict. This is evident when people communicate in ways that anger or annoy each other.

their goals or interests have been thwarted, they generally try to determine why. Was it poor planning on their part? Was it simply a case of bad luck? Was it a lack of the appropriate resources to reach the goal? Or was it because of someone's intentional interference? If it is concluded that the latter is the reason, then the seeds for conflict may be planted, even if the other person actually had nothing to do with the situation.

Another cause of conflict is faulty perceptions and our tendency to perceive our own views as objective and reflecting reality but to perceive others' views as biased or lacking in reality. As a result, stereotyping or prejudices create conflicting views by magnifying differences between our views and those of others, especially others whom we believe are different from us. Differences may be magnified for many of us when we confront cultures different from our own.

Finally, personal traits or characteristics can lead to conflict. This is especially true of Type A individuals: those who are highly competitive, like to win, are always in a hurry, and are relatively irritable when others interfere with the reaching of goals. Type A individuals, because of their nature, are more likely to get into conflicts than Type B individuals, who are calmer and less irritable about events around them.

So what causes conflict? Conflict does not stem solely from incompatible goals. On the contrary, conflict often results from social factors such as long-standing grudges or resentment, the desire for revenge, inaccurate social perceptions, ineffective communication, and similar factors. Although the major cause of conflict may be incompatible goals, the social and cognitive causes of conflict are also factors to consider.

## ■■ Does Conflict Have to Be Destructive?

Conflict does *not* have to be destructive. It becomes so when the parties involved are unwilling to negotiate their differences and instead engage in tactics that are harmful and hurtful—a win-at-any-cost approach. Here are some ways in which conflict can or may be destructive:

- When the resolution of the conflict ends with a winner and a loser
- When the individuals involved act too aggressively, when they withdraw from each other, when they withhold their feelings from each other, or when they accuse each other of causing their problems
- When it prevents us from doing our work or feeling good about ourselves
- When it forces us to do things that we do not want to do
- When the outcome is more important than the relationship

Of course not all relationship breakups are the result of conflict, nor are all relationship breakups necessarily destructive or harmful. However, when conflict results in the termination of relationships and leaves one or both of the parties feeling foolish, inadequate, or angry, it is usually destructive.

## ■■ When Is Conflict Beneficial?

There is little doubt that most of us see more destructiveness than benefits in conflict. However, not all conflict is that way. Many societies, including our own, see conflict as contradictory in that it can be sometimes good and sometimes bad. When is it appropriate to engage in conflict? The answer to this is confusing to most of us because of the contradictions as to when engaging in conflict can be helpful and when it should be avoided. For example, it is okay to have conflicts over ideas, but to attack someone personally for his or her ideas is not okay. In other words, it is good to have disagreements or conflicting views about ideas, but it is not good to attack individuals for their ideas because that is what becomes destructive.

Here are some benefits of conflict:

- It can bring out problems that need to be solved.
- It can bring people together to clarify their goals and to look for new ways to do things.
- It can eliminate resentments and help people to understand each other.
- It can bring out creativity in solving our differences.
- It can produce acceptable solutions that allow people to live more in harmony with each other.
- It can help people pay attention to other points of view.
- It can bring new life into a relationship and strengthen it.

Constructive conflict is characterized by a we-orientation, cooperation, and flexibility.[30] When and if possible, it is good to reach a solution that is agreeable to all. This does not mean that we have to feel warm and fuzzy while the differences are worked out, but it does mean that conflicting parties must be willing to negotiate, respect the other party's differences, and cooperate to resolve differences. Constructive conflict can be frustrating and difficult as well as contentious, and it does require competent communicators who are knowledgeable, skillful, sensitive, committed, and ethical in resolving their differences.

## ▬ What Are Useful Strategies for Conflict Management or Resolution in Interpersonal Relationships?

Because most interpersonal conflicts can be costly in terms of time, stress, energy, and other resources, people who are experiencing conflict generally choose to resolve their differences as quickly as possible especially if they are able to do so. Of course, there are situations in which conflicts are not confronted, and there are also times when conflicts go on for an indefinite period of time, but generally speaking, these are not beneficial to a relationship's growth. Therefore we need to learn how to deal with conflict in ways that will benefit our relationships and us. How we deal with disagreements or conflict can either strengthen a relationship or split it apart. In other words, conflict can be managed well, or it can be managed poorly.

There are many different ways to resolve conflicts. The conflict literature refers mainly to five options: withdrawing, accommodating, forcing, negotiating, and collaboration.[31] Each strategy involves a different outcome, which can be either positive, negative, or both in its effect on relationships that are involved in conflict.

**Withdrawing.**   When we choose to avoid further conflict by either psychologically or physically removing ourselves from the situation, we are withdrawing. Withdrawing can be done in a number of ways, such as changing the topic, cracking jokes, ignoring, or leaving the situation altogether. Usually, when a withdrawal strategy is used, the conflict is temporarily avoided, but it really doesn't go away. Withdrawal is a temporary escape from the conflict, but both parties know that it has not been resolved.

Stonewalling is a powerful form of avoiding conflict.[32] When people exhibit stony silence, refuse to discuss problems, or physically remove themselves from another person who is complaining, disagreeing, or attacking, they are said to be stonewalling. Consider the following discussion:

> *Melissa:* We need to discuss your unwillingness to set a budget. Your use of the credit card is going to bankrupt your father and me.
>
> *Tiff:* It isn't a problem, and there is nothing to talk about.
>
> *Melissa:* We have got to talk about it because you are ruining our credit.
>
> *Tiff:* Get a life, I am not ruining anything. I'll pay you back. [leaves the house]

Tiff is stonewalling by withdrawing from the conflict and claiming that she has everything under control. She believes that to discuss her use of the credit card will only make the conflict between her and her mother worse. Her mother is likely becoming frustrated with Tiff's stonewalling about the use of the credit card. Stonewalling by Tiff can also communicate her disapproval, self-righteousness, indifference, and defensiveness toward her mother.

Research indicates that avoidance is a frequently used way to manage conflict. Many of us want to avoid conflict whenever we can. For example, one research study found that 50 percent of the time, college students used avoiding or withdrawing strategies to keep conflict from escalating.[33] Other research studies have found that when facing conflict men use stonewalling more often than women do because of their fear that they won't be able to control themselves.[34]

An advantage to withdrawal is that it gives time for one or both individuals involved in the conflict to think about it and to calm down before again trying to deal with the conflict. The disadvantage is that it can create more hostility and ultimately make dealing with the conflict more difficult in the long run. So withdrawal can be a useful strategy, but it is also limited in its ability to resolve the conflict itself.

**Accommodating.** A person who uses accommodating as a means for managing or resolving conflicts does not assert his or her own needs but rather prefers to go along to get along. This form of conflict management requires that one person yields or gives in to another person's needs and desires. The accommodator is setting aside his or her concerns in favor of pleasing the other person because holding the relationship together is more important than continuing the conflict. In some situations, when someone accommodates to another to resolve a conflict, the accommodating person gives up because the conflict just isn't worth the stress and the destruction of the relationship, so in a sense it is a win–win situation. Of course, if one person is always accommodating another in a committed relationship, then there is winning and losing.

Accommodation tactics according to Alan Sillars and Bill Wilmot, communication scholars, include giving up or giving in, disengagement, denial of needs, or a desire to get along.[35] When a person *gives up or gives in* to the other person, he or she is basically saying, "Have it your way," "I don't want to fight about this," or "Whatever." If the person *disengages,* he or she is saying, "I don't care," "I don't want any part of it," or "I don't have the time to fight about this." If the person *denies* his or her own needs, the person is saying, "I am okay, you go without me" or "I can take care of it, even if I have to stay longer." Finally, if the person is motivated by *desire to get along,* he or she is saying, "It's more important to work together than it is for me to get what I want" or "I am unhappy and miserable when we fight. Let's let this go and start over again. I don't even know what we are fighting about."

From an individual satisfaction standpoint, the accommodating strategy requires one person to give up something, whereas the other person achieves something. Although the strategy is appropriate in certain conflict situations, such as whether to go to a basketball game or to the theater, it should be used sparingly because it can have negative effects both on the individuals and on the relationship itself. This is especially true if one side always tends to accommodate the other side to avoid or reduce conflict. When this happens, it is a clear sign that there is a power imbalance in the relationship, which means that the other person is saying, "I have little or no choice." When this occurs, it is a sign of an unhealthy relationship or a relationship that is one-sided.

**Forcing.** Forcing is a strategy in which one person has power and dominance over another person. It can result in aggression that could include threats, criticisms, hostile remarks and jokes, ridicule, sarcasm, intimidation, fault finding, coercion, or manipulation. Extreme cases of forcing include date rape, child abuse, and sexual harassment. This is a lose–lose situation. The person with the power can claim the victory, and the other person loses. However, in this situation, the competition is unfair because one individual has more control and power over the other, which ensures a victory regardless of the virtue of the other person's position.

Consider a relationship in which one person has power or control over the other. It is a relationship that is unequal and can lead to abuse. Of course, there are times when the dominance of one person could serve the relationship, such as in an emergency situation in which a decision has to be made quickly. The essence of force is to pressure others to agree with something so that we get what we want. The more force we use to get others to do what we want or to agree with us, the more likely it is that resentment will increase, leading to more destructive types of conflicts.

**Negotiating.** Negotiating usually involves a give-and-take process and leads to each party having some satisfaction and some dissatisfaction with the outcome. In other words, "Give a little and get a little." Some people interpret this to be a lose–lose style of conflict management.

In U.S. culture, many of us are led to believe that compromise or negotiation is a good way for both parties in a conflict to resolve their differences. We are told that it is fair for both because it means that both parties win something and both lose something. Thus compromise appears on the surface to be a reasonable approach to conflict and is extremely popular among many individuals, although there are potential problems with it. The most obvious problem is that the quality of the solution might be reduced. This is especially true if one of the parties in the conflict actually had a better solution that had to be compromised in order to reach agreement. Compromise can become an easy way out and might prevent creative new solutions from emerging. In addition, the compromise approach is often not the first choice in personal relationships because it often requires that one or both parties have to give in or give up on what they want.

## Conflict Online

Conflict can occur just as easily online as it does in face-to-face communication. Some people believe that there is a tendency to communicate more forcefully and directly via the computer than in face-to-face interactions. Thus, rather than resolving conflicts or differences, the conflicts tend to escalate more readily over the computer.

1. Why do you think conflict occurs so easily online?
2. What can you do to reduce online conflicts?
3. Create a guide to improving online communication etiquette. What advice would you give in your guide to others to reduce or prevent online conflicts?

For help, do an Internet search using the key words "online etiquette."

Despite the negative aspects of negotiating or compromising, it might be the only possible way to approach a conflict. This is most likely true when the parties involved have equal power, if no other alternative is available, if the outcome is not critical, if essential values are not undermined, or if the settlement is only a temporary one until a better solution can be found.

**Collaboration.** Collaboration is a strategy of conflict management that requires cooperation and mutual respect. It usually involves a problem-solving approach that addresses all the concerns of both parties to arrive at a solution that is mutually satisfying. It is a "we" rather than a "me" approach to negotiation. It might require extra effort by both parties because more resources and considerations of new options that meet the approval of both parties might be needed.

For collaboration to work as a strategy, both parties must recognize that there is a conflict, and they must want to find creative ways to resolve their differences. When both parties recognize that a conflict exists, they usually engage in some sort of confrontation, which is the opposite of avoidance. There are different degrees of confrontation, ranging from the very violent (often depicted in the media) to the respectful. For collaboration to be successful, both parties must be willing to resolve their differences, treat each other as equals, be honest and open in their differences, be empathetic toward each other, and be willing to listen to each other's points of view.

## Deception in a Relationship

I (Darin) have always been a little concerned about Olivia—she is such a charmer. She told me that she was through with Aaron, her old boyfriend. We began sleeping together, spending a couple of nights plus weekends together at each other's places. Then a friend of mine told me that she saw Olivia with her "ex," and it didn't look as if they had parted ways. My friend also said that Olivia and her "ex" appeared to be intensely involved with each other. I saw Olivia today, and she didn't act differently. In fact, she acted as if everything was the same.

1. What do you think you would do in this situation?
2. What would you tell Darin to do?
3. What does a situation like this one do to a relationship?
4. Is there anything that Olivia can do to explain her behavior to Darin?
5. Are there any considerations that Darin should take into account before he jumps to conclusions?

The collaboration strategy is usually considered a win–win situation for both sides in the conflict. Both sides believe that they have accomplished or gained something from the solution because of their willingness to listen to each other concerning the issues. In addition, when both parties believe that they have had the opportunity to voice their opinions and they have agreed in good faith to settle the dispute, it truly is a win–win situation. The collaboration strategy to manage conflict is the best strategy for a relationship, because it shows that each party cares about the other's well-being and interests. According to Wilmot and Hocker, collaborating, as a conflict management style, produces consistently positive outcomes that leave the participants satisfied with their decisions, the process, and the growth that occurs in their interpersonal relationship.[36]

Many scholars agree that conflict is inevitable in all relationships and that conflict need not be destructive. Conflict often produces stronger and more durable relationships. Conflict in itself should be considered neither negative nor destructive but a natural part of any relationship.

## Relational Repair Strategies

For situations in which both parties want to preserve the relationship, Duck has suggested the following repair tactics:

- Engage in more open and honest communication, and exhibit a willingness to listen to the other person with an open mind.
- Be willing to bring out the other person's positive side.
- Evaluate the potential rewards and costs for keeping the relationship together versus the rewards and costs for changing or ending it.
- Seek out the support of others to help keep the relationship together.
- Both parties must be willing to focus on the positive aspects of their relationship.
- Both parties must be willing to reinterpret the other's behaviors as positive and well intentioned.
- Both parties have to be willing to reduce negativity and try to keep a balanced perspective.[37]

Repairing relationships requires cooperation and mutual agreement; both parties must want to keep the relationship together in order to solve their differences. It also requires effective interpersonal communication.

# Improving Communication Competence in Relationships

The goal of this book is to encourage readers to become competent communicators. Communication scholars Brent Burleson and Wendy Samter describe the following interpersonal skills as important in developing and maintaining relationships: *conversational skill* (the ability to initiate, maintain, and terminate enjoyable casual conversations), *referential skill* (the ability to convey information clearly and unambiguously), *ego supportive skill* (the ability to make another person feel good about himself or herself), *comforting skill* (the ability to make others feel better when depressed, sad, or upset), *persuasive skill* (the ability to get people to modify their thoughts and behaviors), *narrative skill* (the ability to entertain through jokes, gossip, stories, etc.), and *regulations* (the ability to help someone who has violated a norm to fix the mistake effectively).[38] How would you rate yourself on each of the above communication skills? Most of us would likely rate ourselves as pretty good at using most of skills, but we would also likely say that we could be better at each of them.

In the remainder of this chapter, we are going to provide you with some suggestions that should help you to become a more competent communicator. By this point, you probably agree that effective communicators share the following characteristics:

1. Effective communicators address issues clearly and try to avoid ambiguous or abstract statements.

2. Effective communicators are likely to treat others with respect and therefore would not deliberately yell abuses or throw temper tantrums.

3. Effective communicators know that the use of praise, making the other person feel special, and telling them what they want to hear will most likely produce desired responses.[39]

At first glance, these statements make a lot of sense. However, each of us can probably think of times when being a little abstract or ambiguous was better than being too clear or direct in our communication. In certain situations, getting angry or throwing a tantrum might be appropriate to get across a point. It sometimes boils down to the difference between being honest and being brutally frank—being brutal never facilitates communication. Finally, you can probably also think of situations in which too much praise or too much agreement can lead to mistrust. Interpersonal situations often require a variety of communication strategies, some of which may violate expected norms. Although we are not endorsing unethical behaviors, disrespect, or rudeness, some situations demand unusual strategies.

The following section offers a variety of behaviors and actions that can improve interpersonal communication.

## ▬▪ Establish Supportive and Caring Relationships

Establishing supportive and caring relationships is important to our well-being, and this process is generally easier when communication is both positive and supportive.[40] One research study discusses romantic actions and verbal and nonverbal assurances that may affect commitment and satisfaction in relationships.[41] Positive strategies for romantic exchanges include the following:

1. Act cheerful and positive when talking to the other.

2. Do favors for the other, or help with tasks.

3. Initiate celebrations of special events from your shared past, such as the first time you met.

4. Do things to surprise the other person.

5. Suggest that you go out to eat together at a favorite or special restaurant.

6. Create a romantic environment, perhaps with candlelight and flowers.
7. Give the other person items of sentimental value, such as gifts or cards.
8. Suggest ways to spend time doing things together.

Assurances include the following verbal and nonverbal actions:

1. Physically display affection through kisses and hugs.
2. Express aloud to the other person what it would be like without him or her.
3. Reminisce aloud with the other about good times you have had together in the past.
4. Say "I love you."
5. Express long-term commitment to the relationship.
6. Act in playful ways toward the other person.

The research findings suggest that engaging in behaviors such as these do increase relationship commitment and satisfaction. However, it is interesting that females were more likely than males to report use of assurance and romance strategies, which suggests that females tend to undertake more relationship maintenance activity than their male partners do.

## ▬ Nurture a Supportive Environment

Positive and supportive communication occurs in environments that are caring, open, flexible, warm, animated, and receptive. In such environments, communication is constructive and centers on the individuals and their relationship. Here are some descriptions of how people feel when constructive communication is at the center of their relationship.[42]

I feel that I can talk and that there is someone who will listen to me.
I feel accepted and supported.
I feel there is a willingness to see my point of view.
I don't feel a need or pressure to change—I am accepted for who I am.
I don't feel that I am constantly being judged or evaluated.
I feel that I am trusted.
I feel that I am treated with respect as a person.
I feel that I am treated fairly.
I feel good about myself and about us.
I feel like a responsible person.
I feel that I have control over myself.
I feel that someone is interested in me and cares about me.
I don't feel as if I have to justify everything that I do.

One of the most effective and constructive means of demonstrating care and support for someone is to invite more communication.

## ▪▪ Invite More Communication

Many of us listen to others express their feelings and then immediately express our own. This gives the impression that we do not even acknowledge the other person's existence, let alone what he or she has said. In contrast, skilled and caring communicators usually do not respond immediately with ideas, judgments, or feelings that express their own views. Instead, they invite others to express more of their thoughts by responding with noncommittal responses such as these:

> Interesting.
>
> Uh-huh.
>
> You did, huh.
>
> I see.
>
> Oh.
>
> Really?

Or they might be more direct in asking the other person to continue, saying, for example,

> That's interesting. Go on.
>
> Tell me about it.
>
> Let's discuss it.
>
> Tell me everything.
>
> I understand. What else happened?

Such invitations to talk can contribute much to the development of a meaningful relationship. The willingness to listen and reserve judgment creates a positive and supportive environment that, in effect, tells people they are valuable, they are loved, and they have control over their own behavior.

## ▪ Summary

In our everyday lives, we are enormously influenced by first impressions and often tend to make snap judgments about people and form instant likes and dislikes. Interpersonal attraction, which includes physical attractiveness, personality, rewards, proximity, and similarities, plays a significant role in our desire to interact with others. Relationships, whether existing for a moment or for a lifetime, go through a series of stages of development and deterioration. According to communication scholars, there are five stages of coming together and five stages of coming apart. All relationships move through at least some of these stages but might not move through them in the same order or with the same intensity. There are signs that show a relationship is in trouble. They include aggressive behavior, deception, and betrayal.

There are three reasons for the complex and continuous process of coming together and coming apart: Each stage provides information for the next, each stage helps to predict what might or might not occur in the next stage, and skipping a stage can create risk and uncertainty in a relationship. The phases of dissolving a relationship involve a complex decision-making process that does not always follow a specific series of stages. Breakups often occur sporadically, inconsistently, and with uncertainty over a period of time.

Relationships are often messy, and even the most stable seem to go through various pushes and pulls, which can create tensions between partners. There are three dialectical tensions commonly mentioned in the research that describes the pushes and pulls: connection–autonomy, openness–closedness, and novelty–predictability.

Conflict is inevitable in all relationships. It is an expressed struggle between incompatible goals, scarce resources, and interference from others in achieving goals. Conflict is also caused by social factors that include faulty attributions and faulty communication. Managing conflict is not easy; in fact, resolving conflicts requires the use of a variety of strategies, including withdrawing, accommodating, forcing, negotiating, and collaboration.

To help repair and possibly save relationships, competent communicators know how to use repair strategies and effective interpersonal communication. In a positive and supportive environment, communication between individuals usually reflects caring, openness, flexibility, warmth, animation, and receptivity. The best way to develop and maintain relationships is to invite more communication.

## Discussion Starters

1. In your opinion, what elements play the strongest role in the development of relationships? Explain.
2. What did you agree with and disagree with in the explanation of the stages of relationship development?
3. Compare and contrast Knapp and Vangelisti's coming-apart stages with Duck's dissolution stages.
4. Describe what it takes to have a lasting relationship.
5. What happens when a relationship begins to come apart?
6. In what ways can conflict be constructive? Destructive?
7. What advice would you give to someone who wanted to improve his or her interpersonal communication?
8. What does it mean to be a competent interpersonal communicator?

## Notes

1. J. C. McCroskey and T. A. McCain, "The Measurement of Interpersonal Attraction," *Speech Monographs* 41 (1974): 261–66.
2. S. M. Andersen and A. Baum, "Transference in Interpersonal Relations: Influences and Affect Based on Significant Representations," *Journal of Personality* 62 (1994): 459–97.
3. M. A. Collins and L. A. Zebrowitz, "The Contributions of Appearance to Occupational Outcomes in Civilian and Military Settings," *Journal of Applied Social Psychology* 25 (1995): 129–63.
4. S. Sprecher and S. W. Duck, "Sweet Talk: The Importance of Perceived Communication for Romantic and Friendship Attraction Experienced during a Get-Acquainted Date," *Personality and Social Psychology Bulletin* 20 (1994): 391–400.
5. W. M. Bernstein, B. O. Stephenson, M. L. Snyder, and R. A. Wicklund, "Causal Ambiguity and Heterosexual Affiliation," *Journal of Experimental Social Psychology* 19 (1983): 78–92; K. H. Price and S. G. Vandenberg, "Matching for Physical Attractiveness in Married Couples," *Personality and Social Psychology* 5 (1979): 398–400; and M. Lea, "Factors Underlying Friendship: An Analysis of Responses on the Acquaintance Description Form in Relation to Wright's Friendship Model," *Journal of Social and Personal Relationships* 6 (1989): 275–92.

6. K. Deaux and R. Hanna, "Courtship in the Personal Column: The Influence of Gender and Sexual Orientation," *Sex Roles* 11 (1984): 363–75.

7. H. R. Baize Jr. and J. E. Schroeder, "Personality and Mate Selection in Personal Ads: Evolutionary Preferences in a Public Mate Selection Process," *Journal of Social Behavior and Personality* 10 (1995): 517–36.

8. L. Mealey, "Bulking Up: The Roles of Sex and Sexual Orientation on Attempts to Manipulate Physical Attractiveness," *Journal of Sex Research* 34 (1997): 223–28.

9. M. R. Parks and K. Floyd, "Making Friends in Cyberspace," *Journal of Communication* 45 (1996): 84; and J. B. Walther and M. R. Parks, "Cues Filtered Out, Cues Filtered In: Computer-Mediated Communication and Relationships," in *Handbook of Interpersonal Communication,* 3rd ed., eds. M. L. Knapp and J. A. Daly (Thousand Oaks, CA: Sage, 2002) 529–563.

10. M. R. Parks and K. Floyd, "Making Friends," 84.

11. Ibid., 85

12. M. Knapp, *Social Intercourse: From Greeting to Good-Bye* (Boston: Allyn and Bacon, 1978), 3–28, and M. L. Knapp and A. L. Vangelisti, *Interpersonal Communication and Human Relationship,* 5th ed. (Boston: Allyn and Bacon, 2005), 36.

13. D. P. McWhirter and A. M. Mattison, *The Male Couple* (Englewood Cliffs, NJ: Prentice-Hall, 1984).

14. Knapp and Vangelisti, 37–42.

15. Ibid., 39.

16. Ibid., 43–47.

17. M. L. Knapp, R. P. Hart, G. W. Friedrich, and G. M. Shulman, "The Rhetoric of Goodbye: Verbal and Nonverbal Correlates of Human Leave-Taking," *Speech Monographs* 40 (1973): 182–98.

18. Knapp and Vangelisti, 47–51.

19. S. W. Duck, ed., *Personal Relationships 4: Dissolving Personal Relationships* (London: Academic Press, 1982); L. A. Baxter, "Accomplishing Relationship Disengagement," in *Understanding Personal Relationships: An Interdisciplinary Approach,* eds. S. W. Duck and D. Perlman (Beverly Hills, CA: Sage, 1985), 243–66; S. W. Duck, *Human Relationships: An Introduction to Social Psychology* (Beverly Hills, CA: Sage, 1986); and S. Duck, "A Topography of Relationships Disengagement and Dissolution," in *Personal Relationships,* ed. S. Duck (London: Academic Press, 1982), 1–30.

20. K. A. Sorenson, S. M. Russel, D. J. Harkness, and J. H. Harvey, "Account-Making, Confiding, and Coping with the Ending of a Close Relationship," *Journal of Social Behavior and Personality* 8 (1993): 73–86.

21. L. A. Baxter, "Trajectories of Relationships Disengagement," *Journal of Social and Personal Relationship* 1 (1984): 29–48; and L. A. Baxter, "Strategies for Ending Relationship: Two Studies," *Western Journal of Speech Communication* 46 (1982): 223–41.

22. L. A. Baxter and B. Montgomery, *Relation: Dialogues and Dialect* (New York: Guilford, 1996).

23. J. T. Wood, "Dialectical Theory," in *Making Connections: Readings in Relational Communication,* 2nd ed., eds. K. M. Galvin and P. J. Cooper (Los Angeles, CA: Roxbury, 2000), 132–38; L. A. Baxter, "Dialectical Contradictions in Relationship Development," *Journal of Social and Personal Relationships* 7 (1990): 69–88; and L. A. Baxter, "Thinking Dialogically About Communication in Interpersonal Relationships," in *Structure in Human Communication,* ed. R. Conville (Westport, CT: Greenwood, 1994).

24. Baxter and Montgomery, 185–206.

25. L. A. Baxter, "Dialectical Contradictions in Relationship Development," *Journal of Social and Personal Relationships* 7 (1990): 69–88.

26. W. Wilmot and J. Hocker, *Interpersonal Conflict,* 7th ed. (New York: McGraw-Hill, 2007), 49.

27. Ibid., 14.

28. C. K. W. DeDreu and P. A. M. Van Lang, "Impact of Social Value Orientation on Negotiator Cognition and Behavior," *Personality and Social Psychology Bulletin* 21 (1995): 1178–88; and D. Tjosvold and C. DeDreu, "Managing Conflict in Dutch Organizations: A Test of the Relevance of Deutsch's Cooperation Theory," *Journal of Applied Social Psychology* 27 (1997): 2213–27.

29. R. A. Baron, "Attributions and Organizational Conflict," in *Attribution Theory: Applications to Achievement, Mental Health, and Interpersonal Conflict,* eds. S. Graha and V. Folkes (Hillsdale, NJ: Erlbaum, 1990), 185–204; and R. Cropanzano, ed., *Justice in the Workplace* (Hillsdale, NJ: Erlbaum, 1993), 79–103.

30. W. Wilmot and J. Hocker (2007), 55.

31. A. C. Filley, *Interpersonal Conflict Resolution* (Glenview, IL: Scott, Foresman, 1975); D. D. Cahn, "Intimate in Conflict: A Research Review," in *Intimates in Conflict: A Communication Perspective,* ed. D. D. Cahn (Hillsdale, NJ: Erlbaum, 1990), 1–24; W. W. Cupach and D. J. Canary, *Competence in Interpersonal Conflict* (New York: McGraw-Hill, 1997); and R. Blake and J. Mouton, *The Managerial Grid* (Houston: Gulf Publishing, 1964).

32. A. L. Sillars, S. G. Coletti, D. Parry, and M. A. Rogers, "Coding Verbal Conflict Tactics: Nonverbal and Perceptual Correlates of the 'Avoidance–Distributive–Integrative' Distinction," *Human Communication Research* 9 (1982): 83–95.

33. J. Gottman and S. Carrere, "Why Can't Men and Women Get Along? Developmental Notes and Marital Inequities," in *Communication Relational Mainte-*

*nance,* eds. D. Canary and L. Stafford (New York: Academic Press, 1994).

34. J. Gottman, *Why Marriages Succeed and Fail: And How You Can Make Yours Last* (New York: Simon and Schuster, 1994); and J. Gottman, *The Marriage Clinic: A Scientifically Based Marital Therapy* (New York: Norton, 1999).

35. A. L. Sillars and W. W. Wilmot, "Communication Strategies in Conflict and Mediation," in *Communicating Strategically: Strategies in Interpersonal Communication,* eds. J. Wiemann and J. A. Daly (Hillsdale, NJ: Erlbaum, 1994), 163–190.

36. W. Wilmot and J. Hocker (2007), 162–163.

37. S. W. Duck, "A Perspective on the Repair of Personal Relationships: Repair of What, When?" in *Personal Relationships 5: Repairing Personal Relationships,* ed. S. W. Duck (New York: Macmillan, 1984).

38. B. R. Burleson and W. Samter, "Effects of Cognitive Complexity on the Perceived Importance of Communication Skills in Friends," *Communication Research* 17 (1990): 165–82; W. Samter and B. R. Burleson, "Evaluations of Communication Skills as Predictors of Peer Acceptance in a Group Living Situation," *Communication Studies* 41 (1990): 311–26; B. R. Burleson, J. G. Delia, and J. L. Applegate, "The Socialization of Person-Centered Communication: Parent's Contributions to Their Children's' Social-Cognitive and Communication Skills," in *Explaining Family Interactions,* eds. M. A. Fitzpatrick and A. L. Vangelisti (Thousand Oaks, CA: Sage, 1995), 34–76.

39. Knapp and Vangelisti, (2005), 403.

40. J. M. Reisman, "Friendliness and Its Correlates," *Journal of Social and Clinical Psychology* 2 (1984): 143–55.

41. E. P. Simon and L. A. Baxter, "Attachment-Style Differences in Relationship Maintenance Strategies," *Western Journal of Communication* 57 (Fall 1993): 416–30.

42. Ideas for this section are derived from a Parent Effectiveness Training workshop and from T. Gordon, *Parent Effectiveness Training* (New York: Wyden, 1970).

# Group and Team Communication

"Never doubt that a small group of thoughtful, committed citizens can change the world; indeed, it's the only thing that ever does."

—MARGARET MEAD

# This chapter will help you:

- **Make** the connection between group communication and other types of communication discussed in previous chapters.

- **Explain** what a group is and what it is not and understand the importance of groups in our lives.

- **Distinguish** between primary and secondary groups and their purposes.

- **Learn** to perform more effectively in special types of groups, such as project teams, work teams, and focus groups.

- **Avoid** the disadvantages and limitations of group communication.

- **Ensure** that members of groups that you participate in are ethical.

- **Utilize** technology to communicate effectively in groups.

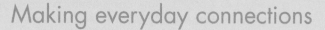

## Making everyday connections

The class assignment is over, and the group consisting of Bob, Shelley, Kyle, Louise, and Hanna arrived at several solutions to the campus parking problem, one of which they were particularly pleased about because it really had potential to solve the problem of not enough parking spaces on campus for students. Each group member came prepared to discuss the issue and had done their research on the topic. It immediately became clear Hanna was their leader and she made sure that there was an agenda for each group meeting and a nice place to meet. She also brought snacks for the group. They felt that they had established a good working relationship with one another, and each of the five times they met outside of class they left the meeting feeling that they had accomplished a great deal. In addition to getting the assignment done on time, they became friends and enjoyed each others' company. In fact, they had a good time trying to solve this campus problem.

Another group with Melissa, Ben, Joe, Shayna, and Diana tackled the same problem of campus parking for its assignment. This group, on the other hand, never could come to any agreement about which solution was best and felt that their group meetings never accomplished much. It wasn't unusual for Joe not to show up to the meetings and when he did he was often ten or fifteen minutes late. Melissa said very little and always appeared to be intimidated by Ben's domination of the group. Ben appeared to be the leader, but he didn't seem to provide much direction as to what the group was supposed to be doing. In fact, the group left most meetings feeling they were a big waste of time. Diana just wanted to finish the assignment and really didn't care much about what was going on as long as she got a good grade. The end result was dissatisfaction with each other and a solution to the problem that no one really accepted. ∎

**Questions to think about**

■ Besides the obvious differences in the two groups, what behaviors would you describe as making the difference between the two groups' outcomes?

■ If you were in group #2, what would you do to make the group more effective and efficient?

■ Group #2—Ben, Joe, and Diana all seem to have behavior problems according to their descriptions. What can be done in order to make each of these three more responsible and more effective contributors to the group?

■ What, in your opinion, are the differences between groups that are enjoyable, efficient, and effective and those that are not?

■ On a 1 to 7 scale, with 1 being adequate and 7 being excellent, assess your group communication skills. Assess your leadership skills. What are your strengths and what are the areas in which you need to improve?

The answers to the above questions illustrate that many variables contribute to a group's success or failure. No two groups will produce identical results, because no two groups are identical in makeup. Furthermore, prior success cannot guarantee that a group will produce similarly successful results. Nonetheless, understanding key principles and factors along with improving your competencies as a group member or group leader can increase the chances for achieving personal satisfaction and group success.

This chapter explains how group members communicate, what a small group is, the different purposes that groups can serve, the characteristics that are common to small groups, the disadvantages of groups, how gender differences affect group communication, the importance of ethical behavior in groups, and how groups can use technology effectively. Chapter 16 explores leadership, member participation, problem solving and decision making, conflict management, and group performance evaluation.

# ■ Small-Group Communication: Making the Connection

Effective communication is one of the major factors that influence whether a group experience is successful and satisfying. Small-group communication does differ from other types of communication in that it requires a variety of communication skills and must include at least three interacting people. By contrast, interviewing and interpersonal communication usually involve only two people interacting, whereas public speaking involves one person speaking and many listeners. However, interviewing, interpersonal communication, and presentational skills are all necessary for effective group communication to occur, whatever the size of the group. For example,

for Success

### Group Satisfaction

Your task is to list two or three groups that you have participated in recently or that you have observed in action. Then answer the following:

1. How did each group encourage member participation and satisfaction?
2. What were the strengths and weaknesses of each group's communication behaviors?

3. What did you notice about individual members' contributions to the group's goal?
4. In your most recent group participation experience, what did you like about it? What didn't you like about it?
5. Describe the communicative behaviors of the ideal group member and the ideal group leader.

the ability to ask effective questions, to listen, deal with interpersonal relationships, resolve conflicts, and present one's ideas are important in communicating with groups. In addition, constructive group communication requires that the group members respect one another, speak clearly, provide credible information, support each other, foster a positive climate, challenge each others' ideas and positions, persuade each other, and hold high ethical standards.

If each of us would stop to list the times we have participated in groups during the past month, we would have evidence of how common our group participation is in our lives. The family is probably the predominant small group. However, if you are like most, you have participated in many groups, some small and some large, during the past month alone. When we associate with other people and discuss common issues or problems, we are involved in group communication.

Small-group communication involves the exchange of information among a relatively small number of people, ideally five to seven, who share a common purpose, such as solving a problem, making a decision, or sharing information. Effective group communication requires a communication style that is honest, flexible, assertive, enthusiastic, and tolerant of others. Effective group members recognize the importance of all group members' input and want to ensure that everyone has an opportunity to participate. They are not only willing to listen to others, but also are willing to discuss ideas and issues whether they agree or disagree with them. Our primary focus in this chapter and the next is small groups, so we will not include much information about large public discussion group presentations such as symposiums, which are not discussions but a series of brief speeches related to a central topic, or panels, which are discussions involving specialists or well-informed people who share their views on a common topic for the benefit of an audience. Nor will we include the comprehensive study of group dynamics.

# What Is a Group?

A group is not simply a collection of people gathered in the same place. To qualify as a group, the people must be related in six ways:

1. *Perceptions:* Do the members make an impression on one another?
2. *Motivation:* Are there rewards for being together?

3. *Goals:* Do the members have a common purpose?

4. *Organization:* Does each person have some role or task?

5. *Interdependence:* Must each person depend on the others for his or her efforts to be successful?

6. *Interaction:* Is the number of persons small enough so that each person can communicate with every other person?[1]

For our purposes, we define a **group** as a collection of individuals who influence one another, have a common purpose, take on roles, are interdependent, and interact together. If any element is not included, what exists is a collection of independent people, not a group. People standing at a corner waiting for a bus, for example, meet some of the criteria of a group. They have a common purpose (transportation), they may interact, and they may make an impression on one another. But they do not constitute a group according to our definition because they are not interdependent, and they do not take on roles. They do share certain basic goals, such as getting to a destination safely. But they don't expect to interact in the future and usually don't perceive themselves as part of a group—unless some type of emergency occurred, which would change their status radically. Deciding whether a collection of persons constitutes a true group is a complex matter.

It appears that true groups are those high in **entiativity**—the extent to which a group is perceived to be a coherent entity. So what determines whether, and to what extent, we perceive several persons as forming a group? This question has received much attention from researchers in recent years, and a clear answer is beginning to emerge. It appears that true groups—ones high in entiativity—show the following characteristics: (1) Members interact with one another often, (2) the group is important to its members, (3) members share common goals and outcomes, and (4) the members are similar to one another in important ways. The higher groups are on these characteristics, the more they are seen by their members as forming coherent

■ **group** A collection of individuals who influence one another, have a common purpose, take on roles, are interdependent, and interact together.

■ **entiativity** The extent to which a group is perceived as being a coherent entity.

The photo on the left shows a collection of persons who happen to be in the same place at the same time; they are not part of a *group*. The photo on the right shows a true group: The people in this group interact with one another and have shared goals and outcomes. Moreover, they feel that they are, in fact, part of a group.

entities—groups to which they choose to belong. In sum, entiativity is a key characteristic that helps us understand precisely what constitutes a group and how being part of a group can influence our behavior.[2]

# ■ Group Formation: Why We Join . . . and Why We Leave

Take a moment to think about all the groups to which you belong: student organizations, clubs, religious groups, social groups, work groups, informal groups of friends. Why did you join them in the first place? It doesn't take a scholar to tell you that people join groups for many reasons, and your reasons are probably similar to those that motivate others to join groups. Paul Paulus, a social psychologist, suggests that at least five common reasons explain why people join groups:

1. Groups help to satisfy important psychological and social needs, such as the need for attention and affection or the need to belong. Imagine what it would be like to be absolutely alone, in total isolation from others. Very few of us find such a prospect appealing.

2. Group membership helps people achieve goals that otherwise might not be accomplished. Groups make it easier to perform certain tasks, solve difficult problems, and make complex decisions that might overwhelm one individual.

3. Group membership can provide multiple sources of information and knowledge that might not be available to one individual.

4. Groups can help to meet the need for security. The old saying that there is safety in numbers rings true in many situations; belonging to groups can provide protection and security against common enemies. For example, people join neighborhood watch groups to protect themselves from criminal activity.

5. Group membership can also contribute to an individual's positive social identity—it becomes part of a person's self-concept (see Chapter 3). Of course, the more prestigious and restrictive the groups are to which a person is admitted, the more the self-concept is bolstered.[3]

Cultural factors such as individualistic or collective orientations can have a profound effect on how people perceive groups and group activities. All cultures vary in the degree to which they emphasize individualism and collectivism. If you hold an individualistic orientation, you tend to stress self or personal goals and achievements over group goals and achievements.[4] Individualist cultures have an "I" consciousness and a tendency to focus on individual accomplishments.[5] That is, they are more likely to depend on themselves and have less commitment to group membership. For example, most North Americans value self-help, self-sufficiency, self-actualization, and personal achievements. According to communication scholars Carolyn Calloway-Thomas, Pamela Cooper, and Cecil Blake, the United States, Canada, Australia, the Netherlands, and New Zealand are nations that tend to foster and celebrate individual accomplishments.[6] Generally, people who have individualistic perspectives find working in groups more challenging and often frustrating because they have trouble putting their own goals after those of the group.

If you hold a collectivistic orientation, which is more predominant in Asian and Latin American countries such as Japan, China, Taiwan, Pakistan, Colombia, Guatemala, and Panama, you are more likely to put aside your individual goals for the well-being of the group.[7] Collectivist cultures have a "we" consciousness and a tendency to focus on group or team accomplishments. They also have a propensity toward working in groups and find group work to be very rewarding and satisfying. For example, American companies often are financially oriented, and value individual leadership and autonomy. Employees' roles are clearly defined and they are responsible for meeting specific goals. Each employee makes decisions in his or her realm of authority or expertise and the company defines who can make which decisions and about what. In contrast, Japanese companies tend to take a more intuitive approach to management. Employees' roles are not as defined and they are expected to work as teams to meet group goals. Decision-making is a group process, with large numbers of people involved in each decision. No culture, however, is entirely individualist or collectivist. All cultures comprise a mix of individualism and collectivism, but usually one or the other dominates.[8]

How you contribute to a group may depend on whether you have an individualistic or collectivistic orientation. These two perspectives have implications for group formation and collaboration. See Table 15.1 for a comparison of individualistic and collectivistic approaches to joining and working in groups or teams.

Another force that brings people together to form groups is a *common goal.* Examples of common goals include protesting a change in dormitory visitation rules, fighting a road expansion into a neighborhood, lobbying for a safer community, supporting a charity, or working for equal campus access for physically impaired stu-

■ **TABLE 15.1** Individualist and Collectivist Orientations: A Comparison of Small Groups

| INDIVIDUALIST ASSUMPTIONS | COLLECTIVISTIC ASSUMPTIONS |
| --- | --- |
| Individuals make better decisions than groups do. | The group's decision should supersede individual decisions. |
| Leaders and not the group members should do the planning. | The group should do the planning. |
| Individuals should be rewarded for their performance. | Reward and recognition should be shared among group members. |
| Competition among individual group members is good. | Teamwork is more important than competition. |
| The best way to get things done is to work with individuals as opposed to an entire group. | The group is the best way to accomplish goals. |
| Groups or teams are often perceived as a waste of time. | The commitment to the group is strongest when the group reaches consensus. |

Adapted from S. A. Beebe and J. M. Masterson, *Communicating in Small Groups,* 8th ed. (Boston: Allyn and Bacon, 2006), 18; and J. Mole, *Mind Your Manner: Managing Business Cultures in Europe* (London: Nicholas Brealey Publishing Limited, 1995).

dents. The goal itself draws people into a group, even though their approaches to the goal may differ.

Unfortunately, there are few, if any, unmixed blessings in life. Almost everything—no matter how helpful—can have a downside. And this is also true of group membership. Although we pointed out the reasons we join groups, groups also impose certain costs. Here we will cover some of the general costs to joining groups and later in the chapter we discuss specific disadvantages to groups.

Group membership can restrict personal freedom. Members of various groups may be expected to behave in specific ways, i.e., to follow the group's rules or to comply with requirements of their group roles. If the members don't comply, the group may impose sanctions on them or expel them.

Sometimes groups make demands on members' time, energy, and resources, and if the members do not meet the demands, they may be required to surrender their membership. For example, some honorary groups require dues or a specific grade point average and if you don't meet the requirements you are automatically dropped from membership. Some churches, for instance, require that their members donate a certain percent of their income to the church. Persons wishing to remain in these groups must comply—or face expulsion. Finally, groups sometimes adopt positions or policies of which some members disapprove. This may force dissenting members to remain silent, speak out and run the risk of strong sanctions, or withdraw. So group membership is not always beneficial; there are some real downsides hidden among the benefits, and members must often consider these carefully as they weigh the costs of group membership against its benefits.

People also avoid joining groups at times. Groups are sometimes perceived as ineffective and time-consuming; they require much work yet accomplish little. The most frequent complaint from students regarding groups is that groups are a waste of time. It is our hope that this chapter and the next will reduce the effect of negative experiences you might have had in the past and encourage you to participate actively in future group situations.

# ■ Types and Purposes of Small Groups

So far, you have read about what a group is and is not and why people join groups, as well as the role communication plays in groups. It is also important to understand the types of groups and why they are formed. There are two major categories of small groups: *primary* and *secondary*. Each serves different human needs, but characteristics of each are found in almost every group in which we participate.

## ■ Primary Groups

**Primary groups** focus on social or interpersonal relationships among members and exist primarily to satisfy what are labeled primary needs such as those we discussed in Chapter 13: the need for inclusion (belonging) and affection (esteem, likeability, love). Primary groups are usually long-term and include family, roommates, friends who meet to socialize, co-workers sharing time off together, and other groups of friends who might share vacations, card games, and so on. The groups might at times make decisions, solve problems, or take on a particular task, but their main purpose is to socialize, support one another, chat about a variety of topics, let off steam, and enjoy each other's company.

■ **primary group** A group that focuses on social and interpersonal relationships.

Communication scholars Robert Harnack, Thorrel Fest, and Barbara Jones have identified two main categories of social reasons for participating in primary groups outside of the family group: socialization and catharsis.[9]

**Socialization.** We often engage in small-group communication when socializing with others, such as at parties or at any event where people share time and conversation. When we gather in small groups for social purposes, our goals are to strengthen our interpersonal relationships and to promote our own well-being. Such groups fulfill our interpersonal needs for inclusion and affection.

**Catharsis.** Small-group communication allows us to vent our emotions, including frustrations, fears, and gripes, as well as hopes and desires. When we have a chance to let others know how we feel about something, we often experience catharsis, or a release from tension. This purpose is usually accomplished in the supportive atmosphere of bull sessions or family discussions, where self-disclosure is appropriate. Cathartic group communication tends to focus on personal problems rather than on interpersonal needs.

Primary groups are at the heart of interpersonal communication, and they are important to understanding small-group communication in general.[10] The main purpose of the primary group is member enjoyment and one another's companionship and support. Primary groups are not the main focus of this and the next chapter; typically, primary groups are studied in sociology, psychology, and interpersonal communication courses.

## ▪▪ Secondary Groups

**Secondary groups,** which will be the main focus of this and the next chapter, exist to accomplish tasks or achieve goals. They are formed for the purpose of doing work such as a class assignment, solving a problem, or making a decision. Members join together to enable themselves to exert power over their situation and others. The main reason for secondary groups is to get something done, but they can also help members achieve their primary needs for socialization and affection. Secondary groups include a variety of types of groups: decision making, problem solving, committees, learning and information sharing, and therapy or personal growth (see Table 15.2).[11]

**Decision Making.** People come together in groups to make decisions on issues such as deciding what to do for homecoming house decorations, where to hold a dance, which play to stage, or which computer is the most practical for their needs. It is not unusual for groups to vote on such issues to determine the group's decision. Voting is done especially when there is no clear agreement as to which decision is most acceptable to the group members. When voting, groups usually accept the majority's position. Discussing alternatives with others helps people to decide which choice is the best not only for themselves but for the group as a whole. In addition, when everyone in the group participates in the decision-making process, all are more likely to accept the final outcome and to help carry it out. Most of us resent being told what to do; we are more tolerant of a decision if we helped to shape it.

A classic research study demonstrated the value of group decision making. The study focused on a garment factory where managers had always made decisions without seeking input from their workers. The managers decided to update some of their production techniques, but the workers were resisting the changes. To analyze

■ **secondary group**
A group that exists to accomplish tasks or achieve goals.

■ **TABLE 15.2** Types and Purposes of Small Groups

| GROUP TYPE | GROUP PURPOSE | EXAMPLES |
|---|---|---|
| *Primary* | To fill basic needs of inclusion and affection with others | Family |
| | | Close friends |
| | | Co-workers |
| | | Neighbors |
| *Secondary* | To accomplish a task or achieve a goal | Decision making |
| | | Problem solving |
| | | Committee |
| | | Learning group |
| | | Therapy group |

the problem, an experiment was set up in which workers were divided into groups using three different procedures: (1) a no-participation procedure, which reflected the way things had always been done—employees had no voice in planning and change; (2) a participation-through-representation procedure, in which a few employees were involved in the decision-making process; and (3) a total-participation procedure, in which all the employees were involved. In each case, whether the workers contributed or not, the final decision belonged to management. The results revealed that

1. The no-participation group continued to resist changes.
2. Both the participation groups relearned their jobs significantly faster and surpassed the previous average production levels much sooner.
3. The total-participation group performed slightly better than the participation-through-representation group.[12]

What conclusion can you draw from these results regarding decision making in groups?

**Problem Solving.**   Small groups can also excel at solving problems. People form problem-solving groups in almost every imaginable context: in the workplace, in government, in school, and at home. The problems they attempt to solve include how to improve health care, how to make a better product, how to perform a task more effectively or efficiently, how to stop violence, how to resolve the parking problem on campus, and how to improve the image of fraternities on campus.

As you can see, groups can serve a variety of purposes and often serve multiple purposes at the same time. For example, a group can solve problems while at the same time serving as a learning, social, cathartic, or therapeutic outlet for its members. It was customary in the early and middle years of the twentieth century for most people to work relatively independently of one another. Even in large organizations, people had individual responsibilities and coordinated with others only when it was necessary to do so. Recently, the value of having people work in groups has been recognized, and a group approach has been implemented in many settings, including the workplace and the classroom.

**Committees.**   Committees are groups that are either appointed or elected and have been assigned a specific task by a larger group or person with authority, such as a teacher, supervisor, or leader. Committees are usually formed to solve problems, make decisions, or gather information for another group or larger group so that it can make decisions or solve problems. Committee work is often seen as time consuming, and many people react negatively to committee work. This is unfortunate and is more likely due to the people in the committee or the lack of defined goals assigned to the committee. If properly assigned and led, committees can investigate and report findings; recommend a course of action; formulate policies, principles, or guidelines for carrying out actions, and can also derive satisfaction from working together.

**Learning and Information Sharing.**   The most common reason people join small groups is to share information and to learn from one another. The sharing of information occurs in all kinds of group settings; the most familiar ones are corporations, schools, religious organizations, families, and service or social clubs. The underlying purpose of learning or information-sharing groups is to educate, inform, or improve understanding related to specific issues or areas of concern.

**Therapy or Personal Growth.**   Therapeutic group sessions primarily help people alter their attitudes, feelings, or behaviors about some aspect of their personal life. For example, a therapeutic group might include people who have drinking, drug, or other problems, such as coping with the loss of a loved one. Usually, the therapeutic group is led by a professional who is trained in group psychotherapy or counseling.

As with most communication contexts, groups are not purely primary or secondary. Small groups that you will be involved in are likely to include elements of all the groups described: social, task, decision making, problem solving, personal growth, and learning. Throughout this book, especially in the remainder of this chapter and the next, we hope to provide you with the necessary communication skills to become a competent group participant.

# ■ Project or Work Teams

Because they are so common in our society and in the classroom, we have chosen to discuss groups known as project teams or work teams. Many scholars who study groups believe that there is a distinction between group involvement and team involvement.[13] A **team** is a special form of group, characterized by close-knit relationships among people with different and complementary abilities and by a strong sense of identity. Similar to groups, teams involve interaction, interdependence, common goals, personality, commitment, cohesiveness, and rules. Teams do differ from groups, however, in three ways:

■ **team** A special form of group that is characterized by a close-knit relationship among people with different and complementary abilities and by a strong sense of identity.

1. Teams are more likely to consist of people with diverse abilities. For example, a surgical team performing an operation might include several surgeons, an anesthetist, and several nurses, each contributing a different skill or perspective to the task at hand. A group consists of several people, each contributing to the common goal of the group, whereas a team consists of people who have a specialization in and different perspectives on a common situation.

The work team is ideally suited for solving workplace problems. Each person brings his or her own special expertise to the table and coordinates efforts with others on a common solution.

2. Teams usually develop more interdependence. A sports team, for example, usually cannot succeed unless all the players believe they are part of a unit.

3. Members of teams have a high degree of group identity and are more likely to identify themselves as team members than as individuals who happen to be on a team.[14]

Thus all teams consist of groups, but not all groups are teams.

Project or work teams have existed for years in almost every type of organization. Typically, project or work teams consist of a variety of individuals who get together to solve problems or make decisions. In a **project team,** these individuals are usually specialists assigned to coordinate the successful completion of an assigned task (such as finding adequate and accessible parking for all who need it). Project teams in general work quickly to determine what needs to be done, and then they do it. They also often possess little history, usually work under a deadline, and may have difficulty establishing mutually agreed-on relationships.

A **work team** is a group of people responsible for an entire work process or segment of the process that delivers a product or service to an internal or external customer. For example, a university department would be considered a work team. Their goal is to deliver instruction in a certain subject area to students as effectively and efficiently as possible. Usually university departments have a history, they entail mutually agreed-on relationships, and the members work as a group to serve its own and the university's missions. Work teams often are subdivisions of a larger

■ **project team**
Individuals representing different specialties who are assigned to coordinate the successful completion of an assigned task.

■ **work team** A group of people responsible for an entire work process or a segment of the process that delivers a product or service to an internal or external customer.

## MAKING CONNECTIONS for Success

### Lessons from Geese

Each of the following facts about geese contains a lesson about working in groups. Read each fact and note what its particular lesson might be. The first one has been completed for you.

*Fact 1:* As each goose flaps its wings, it creates an "uplift" for the birds that follow. By flying in a V formation, the whole flock adds 71 percent greater flying range than could be achieved if each bird flew alone.

*Lesson:* People who share a common direction and a sense of the group's goal can usually accomplish it more quickly and easily. Mutual support makes everyone more efficient.

*Fact 2:* When a goose falls out of formation, it suddenly feels the drag and resistance of flying alone. It quickly moves back into formation to take advantage of the lifting power of the bird immediately in front of it.

*Lesson:* _____

_____

*Fact 3:* When the goose tires, it rotates back into formation, and another goose flies to the front position.

*Lesson:* _____

_____

*Fact 4:* The geese flying in formation honk to encourage those up front to keep up their speed.

*Lesson:* _____

_____

*Fact 5:* When a goose gets sick or wounded or is shot down, two geese drop out of the formation and follow it down to help and protect it. They stay with it until it dies or is able to fly again. Then they launch out with another formation or catch up with the flock.

*Lesson:* _____

_____

The "Lessons from Geese" facts were obtained at a religious retreat. The source was listed as Anonymous.

---

organization and can exist for an indefinite period of time or until a specific project is completed. Work teams also serve many purposes, including solving problems, making decisions, socializing, and learning.

The **focus group,** a special form of work team, tries to find out what its members think about specific ideas, issues, or people. A focus group usually consists of a manageable number of participants and a facilitator or leader. The facilitator runs the meeting, typically using a prepared list of questions and probes to encourage participants to contribute their ideas, beliefs, feelings, and perceptions related to the assigned topic.[15] The facilitator does not offer personal opinions or judgments but guides group members as they express themselves. The information that is gathered in the focus group sessions is analyzed and then used in decision making.

Following are sample questions that might be asked of a focus group: What do college students think of binge drinking? How do nontraditional students feel about returning to the classroom? Is the government responding to the needs of Native Americans? Focus groups have been used by advertising agencies to determine which ads might appeal to certain markets and by political campaign planners to determine what issues are important for candidates to address in speeches.

■ **focus group** A special form of work team that ascertains what its members think about specific ideas, issues, or people.

# ■ Characteristics of Small Groups

Small groups have a number of characteristics in common, including interdependence, commitment, cohesiveness, group size, norms, and group culture, that make each group unique. These characteristics also determine who will join the group, how well the group will function and achieve its goals, and how the members will interact.

## ■■ Interdependence

Probably the most essential characteristic of a small group is **interdependence**—the fact that group members are mutually dependent. Interdependence is reflected in all the other group characteristics, for without it there would be no group. Interdependence is built on each member's willingness to subordinate his or her individual desires and goals in order to accomplish the group's goal.

Groups function best and are most satisfying for their members when each individual recognizes and respects the crucial role that interdependence plays in group processes. A group's success is indeed based on each member's cooperation and willingness to work toward a common goal.

## ■■ Commitment

Another important characteristic of a group is commitment—to the task, to the group, and to the other individuals in the group. **Commitment** is the desire of group members to work together to complete their task to the satisfaction of the entire group. Members' commitment stems from interpersonal attraction; commonality of attitudes, beliefs, and values; the fulfillment of interpersonal needs; and the rewards that the group can offer.

Commitment is important to a group's effectiveness and ultimate success. For example, how often have you been in a group in which one or two members did the work and the others did little or nothing? Those who do little or nothing lack commitment and ultimately affect the group's cohesiveness and effectiveness. Working to accomplish a difficult task even when other group members slack off reflects commitment. For a group to be truly effective, all of its members must be committed to the group, its members, and the successful completion of its task. Commitment shows that the members' desire to remain in the group is greater than the desire to leave it.

## ■■ Cohesiveness

As an extension of commitment, **cohesiveness** refers to the attraction that group members feel for one another and their willingness to stick together. Consider two groups. In the first, members like one another very much, strongly desire the goals the group is seeking, and believe that they could not find another group that would better satisfy their needs. In the second, the opposite is true: Members don't care for one another, they do not share common goals, and they are actively seeking other groups to join that might offer them more rewards. Which group would exert a stronger pull on its members? The answer should be obvious: the first. The rewards for being in the first group outweigh those of leaving the group. Cohesiveness is

■ **interdependence** Mutual dependence of group members on one another.

■ **commitment** The desire of group members to work together to complete a task to the satisfaction of the entire group.

■ **cohesiveness** The attraction that group members feel for each other and willingness to stick together; a form of loyalty.

based on each member's need to remain in the group and the group's ability to provide members with rewards, making it worthwhile to give time and energy to the group. In a sense, cohesiveness is a form of loyalty or commitment.

However, cohesiveness in a group does not automatically ensure success, and when there is too much cohesiveness, it can lead to problems. It can lead to conformity or an unwillingness to change an unsuccessful decision or policy. Cohesiveness is a positive force when it attracts members of the group toward one another and increases effective group interaction, but it can become a negative influence if group members "go along simply to get along" or lose the ability to question group decisions.

## ▪▬ Group Size

Group size relates to the number of participants involved in a given small group and has important ramifications for the group's effectiveness. Although there is no perfect number of members for a group, groups of certain sizes seem appropriate for certain kinds of tasks. For example, five-member groups are the most effective for dealing with intellectual tasks; coordinating, analyzing, and evaluating information; and making administrative decisions. Many small-group experts recommend that groups have no fewer than three and no more than nine members. It is also recommended that for some decision-making and problem-solving groups, an odd number of participants, for example five, seven, or nine, helps to ensure that there are fewer stalemates because in voting on issues, it is likely there will be a tie unless someone abstains or doesn't vote.

A group that is too small can limit the information and ideas generated, whereas a group that is too large can limit the contribution that each person can make. As a group increases in size, the number of possible interactions increases dramatically (see Table 15.3). They include all the possible interactions between individual members and combinations of members. For example, in a three-person group, person A could interact with B and C separately or with B and C simultaneously. Both B and C have similar interaction possibilities, thus resulting in nine possible interactions.[16]

An important consideration in deciding on group size is that the larger the group is, the greater is the variety of skills and information that will be possessed by its members. However, the advantages gained when a group has more than seven members seem to be outweighed by potential disadvantages. For example, in a certain sense, ten opinions are superior to five and twenty opinions are superior to ten. But having twice as many opinions can create twice as much potential for conflict and make consensus at least twice as difficult to reach.

In addition, some consideration should be given to the number of men and women in the group. As was indicated earlier, stereotypical differences between men and women do exist in our society: Therefore, when possible, it is best to form groups with an equal number of men and women or groups in which women form the majority. These two combinations tend to reduce stereotypical behavior and create a more balanced group perspective. When deciding on the most effective size for a group, remember the following points:

▪ **TABLE 15.3** Group Size and Potential Interactions

| NUMBER IN GROUP | POSSIBLE INTERACTIONS |
|---|---|
| 2 | 2 |
| 3 | 9 |
| 4 | 28 |
| 5 | 75 |
| 6 | 186 |
| 7 | 411 |
| 8 | 1,056 |

1. Large groups reduce the time and amount of individual interaction.

2. Large groups provide a greater opportunity for aggressive members to assert their dominance. As a result, less assertive members might feel isolated and might withdraw from the group altogether.

3. Large groups make it difficult to follow a set agenda. It is easy for someone in a large group to switch topics or introduce subjects that are not related to the group's original priorities.

## ▰ Group Norms

The expected and shared ways in which group members behave are called **norms.** Both informal and formal guidelines determine which behaviors are acceptable and which are not. In most group situations, the norms are informal and unwritten. In your communication class, for example, certain behaviors are expected of you. At a minimum, it is assumed that you will read your assignments, respect others' rights to speak, do your own work, and be on time for class. However, there may also be formal written rules, such as specific dates for the completion of assignments, attendance requirements, and guidelines for achieving specific grades.

For a group to function effectively, its members must agree on how things are to be done. Therefore no matter what their size or task, groups establish norms. This is done for a variety of reasons; the strongest one is that shared ways of behaving enable members to attain group goals and to satisfy interpersonal needs. Without guidelines for behavior, most groups would be ineffective and disorganized.

Norms also help to give structure to a group. If members know what is expected of them, they are more likely to act accordingly and function more efficiently. Norms can be as simple as getting the task done or as involved as participating in complex rituals and ceremonies that must be respected if a member is to remain in the group.

In more formal situations, to increase efficiency and order, many groups use preestablished rules to guide their interaction. *Robert's Rules of Order* is the most widely used authority on conducting social, business, and government meetings. Such formal rules specify the roles of members, how meetings are to be conducted, and how topics for discussion are to be introduced, discussed, and accepted or rejected by the group's members. When it is important to maintain formal order, a group may appoint a parliamentarian to ensure that rules are correctly interpreted and followed.

## ▰ Group Culture

Just like societies, organizations, and other large groups, small groups develop unique cultures. **Group culture** is "the pattern of values, beliefs, norms, and behaviors that is shared by group members and that shape a group's individual 'personality.' "[17] Group culture is created by many factors, including the interaction patterns of group members, the roles members are assigned, the purpose for the group, the mixture of people included in the group, members' behaviors, and norms and rules that the group follows.

The group's culture underlies all of its actions and behaviors. The culture of a group is not static; it is constantly changing and developing as it adapts to each new situation or event it confronts and to the needs of the group and its members. A group's culture is expressed in behaviors such as how its members organize it, who begins the interactions, how much interaction is allowed by any one member, who

■ **norms** Expected and shared ways in which group members behave.

■ **group culture** The pattern of values, beliefs, norms, and behaviors that is shared by group members and that shapes a group's individual personality.

### The Rules Have It!

We all know that some groups can be a waste of time and, in general, never seem to accomplish much. It's not unusual for some group members to talk out of turn, interrupt each other, not listen to each other, come late, come unprepared, and to not speak at all or speak way too much. Can rules solve these problems?

1. What has to happen for rules to mean something to group members?

2. Describe a group situation you've witnessed or read about where a lack of rules prevented or made it difficult for the group to accomplish its goals.

3. Describe when a problem, decision, or topic may not be suitable for groups.

4. How would you describe your group behavior?

5. How can group members help to establish and uphold group rules?

Group culture is created by many factors, including the interaction patterns of the group's members, the roles members are assigned, the group's purpose, the mixture of people included in the group, members' behaviors, and norms and rules that the group follows.

interacts with whom, how formally or informally people behave, how much or how little conflict is allowed, how much or how little socializing takes place, and how much or how little tolerance the group allows for ambiguity. These factors, as well as others, weave together to create each group's unique culture.

## ■ Gender Differences in Group Communication

The differences between the way men and women communicate in groups are not clear, and the results of research are not always accurate or fair to one gender or the other. We could probably agree that most men are physically stronger than most women, but some women are stronger than some men. To say that men on average are physically stronger than women is a reasonable statement. But to say that all men are stronger than all women is not accurate, and it is not fair. Much of the research examining women and men is done by comparing averages. Thus specific individual behaviors are usually not accounted for, leaving only averages for our consideration.

Research shows that groups consisting of both men and women are more likely to be dominated by men talking than by women talking. Men tend to demonstrate more task-related behavior than do women; that is, men tend to be more goal oriented than women and can be more impatient about moving on to the next issue or problem. Women tend to offer positive responses to others' comments and, in general, tend to express their subjective opinions more readily than men. Men tend to be more objective in their comments than women.[18]

Because of stereotypical beliefs that exist in U.S. culture, women are sometimes perceived to be less competent than men in solving problems or making decisions. However, little if any difference has been found by researchers between men and women in their problem-solving abilities. The research does suggest that men appear to be better at certain kinds of problem-solving tasks than women, but that difference is reduced or eliminated when men and women work together and when all are highly motivated to solve the problem.[19]

When groups compete, it appears that, on average, women are more cooperative with their opponents than men are. Women are more likely to share resources with their opponents and are interested in fairness more than in winning. Men, on average, are more willing to engage in aggressive behavior and gain advantage through deception and deceit than women are. Also, men are more likely to be antisocial, using revenge, verbal aggression, and even physical violence, whereas women are more likely to use socially acceptable behavior such as reasoning and understanding to solve conflict.[20]

When groups are small, women prefer to work with other women, whereas men don't seem to have a gender preference. It is much more difficult for men to achieve cohesiveness in all-male groups than in mixed-sex groups. As U.S. culture continues to evolve, our stereotypes of men and women will change, together with the roles they play in groups. When comparing the research on men and women based on gender rather than biological sex, we are beginning to find that differences are based less on biological sex than on masculine and feminine traits. That is, individuals who have masculine traits, whether they are male or female, are more likely to be competitive and attempt to dominate and control interactions. More feminine individuals—of either sex—are less likely to display those behaviors.[21] It is important that both men and women understand the stereotypes that exist and make sure that each person who participates in a group is provided equal opportunities to participate.

# ■ Ethical Behavior in Group Communication

For groups to perform effectively, leaders and members must be ethical. There are behavioral assumptions that all people in civilized societies are expected to follow—laws, rules, standards, or agreed-on norms of a general culture. Individualism is a belief in the dignity and sacredness of the individual over the community or group. Cultures that stress individualism emphasize that people should think, make decisions, and speak for themselves and live on their own, whereas collectivist societies make clear distinctions between in-groups and out-groups and place more value on the other than on the self. Collectivist societies place a greater value on community, groupness, harmony, and maintaining face.[22]

It is important to realize that groups, by their very nature, take on a collectivist value in that the group must be more important than the individual if the group is to succeed. This can raise ethical considerations as to the commitment one has toward other group members and the group's goal. This does not mean that individuals should condone unethical behaviors, but it does mean that the success of individuals can be accomplished only through the success of the group as a whole. These expectations apply especially to behaviors within groups and raise some special ethical concerns that all groups and group members should consider when participating in group-related activities.

1. *All group members should have the right to state an opinion or a unique perspective.* No one should be prevented from speaking openly, even when expressing unpopular views. Of course, group members must also be sensitive and responsible in making sure that their honest statements do not violate someone else's civil rights. Similarly, it is inappropriate to ridicule or belittle members of the group in private or public, because they may disagree with a certain point of view. There is nothing wrong with disagreeing with another person's ideas; it is wrong, however, to attack the person instead of the idea.

2. *Group members should be willing to share all legitimate information that might benefit the group in reaching its goal.* Deliberately withholding information that might benefit the group is a violation of the group's trust and is unethical. Yes, there might be times when withholding information to protect the group or specific group members is appropriate. If a group member or members have a vested interest outside of the group that results in introducing false, faulty, or misleading information or in withholding information, however, it is the obligation of that member or members to notify the group or excuse themselves from the group.

3. *All group members should conduct themselves with honesty and integrity.* Members of a group should not deliberately deceive or present information that is false or untruthful. It is unacceptable to present inaccurate information in an attempt to persuade others to accept a particular viewpoint. The same principle would hold for the group itself: It would be wrong for the group to present to others results based on misrepresentation of facts. It is deceitful to persuade others to accept conclusions that are supported by misinformation. Integrity of group members individually and together as a group include other dimensions. For example, when a group makes a decision based on fair and ethical procedures, everyone should support the decision. Individual members should be willing to place the good of the group ahead of their own individual goals. The bottom line is that group members should ultimately do everything they can to benefit the group's goals.

4. *Confidential information shared in the group should remain confidential.* It is extremely unethical to share information outside of the group that members agree to keep private.

5. *Group members must use information ethically.* Members should give credit to the source of the information, should not falsify data or information, and should present all relevant information and all points of view to prevent bias. Ethical use of information helps produce effective, sound results, whatever the task.

## ■ Virtual Groups and Teams

The use of technology to make connections among group and team members has taken hold not only in the United States, but throughout the world. Group communication and teamwork used to take place primarily in same-place face-to-face settings.

However, in recent years, technology, including phone and computer conferencing, as well as online communication, has allowed groups to connect regardless of location. The choice of many of the world's Fortune 1000 companies is web collaboration, an easy-to-use, face-to-face online way of interacting with others over the Internet, because it allows a virtual workplace in which employees can quickly get information they need. It extends the possibilities globally by allowing team members to interact from distant sites—whether in neighboring cities or halfway around the world.

Have you ever had a problem or question that you couldn't answer or one about which you were unsure of the best answer? Did you think there must be others who know the answer or who are interested in the same issues that interest you? If so, the Internet could be your answer. A quick web search allows you to find groups of people who are interested in discussing almost any issue. If the topic that you are interested in isn't already on the Internet, then you can easily create your own website. One type of groups that are formed to discuss a particular topic on the Internet are referred to as newsgroups. A **newsgroup** is an online bulletin board where people can read and post messages about the topics of their choice. Once you post a message to a newsgroup, everyone who visits that newsgroup can read your comments and respond if they wish to do so. Newsgroups provide a vehicle whereby email messages are systematically made available to large groups of people.

The newsgroup, in a sense, resembles a gathering place similar to the local town meeting hall or restaurant where people come together to discuss subjects of mutual interest. With newsgroups, however, the communication occurs over the Internet and is electronically written, not orally discussed, as in the typical face-to-face small group arena. Like small groups, newsgroups revolve around specific topics, such as computers, social issues, literature and science, entertainment, hobbies, or current issues. Newsgroups provide easy access for meeting and communicating with people who share your interests from all over the world without having to leave their computers.

■ **newsgroup** An online bulletin board where people can read and post messages about topics of their choice.

## MAKING Technology CONNECTIONS

### Entering and Participating in an International Virtual Group

It's your turn to either join or create your own virtual group, if you haven't already done so. Those of you who already participate in an international virtual group skip the following and proceed to the questions listed below. For those of you who aren't in a virtual group, go to www.groups.yahoo.com. There are groups for almost everything and anything, or you can create your own group. You will need to participate in a virtual group in order to answer the questions below. It is easy to connect with people who share your interests to discuss sports, health, relationships, school, and news, and to communicate with a variety of individuals.

1. What differences in the interactions do you notice when communicating online versus communicating in face-to-face groups?
2. Are there aspects of the online group that make it more interesting and exciting than in face-to-face groups?
3. What are some of the problems you have encountered in online groups and how have you dealt with them?
4. Is one form of interaction better than the other? Why?

When members of formalized and established groups cannot meet in person, other forms of technology may provide a solution. Because of the cost and inconvenience of bringing people together, more and more organizations are opting to use such technologies as teleconferencing, videoconferencing, or interactive computer conferencing to hold meetings. **Teleconferencing** uses telephones and speakerphones to connect people in different locations. Speakerphones enable people in different locations to interact at one given location. Although extremely cost-effective, teleconferencing is limited because you cannot see those at the other locations. **Videoconferencing** is an extension of teleconferencing that includes picture and sound. It eliminates one limitation of teleconferencing in that it allows people at different locations to see each other via television. Disadvantages of videoconferencing include its cost and the need for special equipment to allow both picture and sound to be transmitted. Videoconferencing, is also much more vulnerable to extremely frustrating equipment failures than teleconferencing.

**Interactive computer conferencing** is similar to videoconferencing except that the interaction occurs via computer. Although interactive computer conferencing requires special equipment and software for both sound and picture, it is far more cost effective than videoconferencing. The advantages of interactive computer conferencing include convenience, in that interaction can occur from almost any location, and the fact that only a computer and connected video camera are required. In addition, interactive computer conferencing usually does not require technicians to operate the equipment once it is installed. Its disadvantages are similar to those of videoconferencing in that equipment failures can occur and getting online is not always easy.

Ultimately, the success of any technology for group sharing depends on two factors: accessibility and use. We use technology to communicate within groups if the technology is readily available and if all members know how to use it effectively.

■ **teleconferencing**
Use of telephones and speakerphones to connect people in different locations.

■ **videoconferencing** An extension of teleconferencing that includes picture and sound.

■ **interactive computer conferencing** Similar to videoconferencing except that the interaction occurs via computer.

Today more and more group interaction is occurring via videoconferencing where a group in one location can easily interact with other groups in multiple locations throughout the world.

When technologies are available, group members must agree on which technologies they will use, how often they will use them, and for what purposes.

In addition, if the technologies are to be empowering and useful, group members must agree on mutual expectations and rules that will guide the use of each technology. If an individual fails to check messages regularly, comes poorly prepared to teleconferences, or is not included in the exchanges by the other group members, the group will likely not be very successful. Groups that have used technology to communicate are aware that different types of technologies affect the richness and speed of their communication. Clearly, training and experience in the appropriate application of electronic communication technologies are critical to success.

# ■ Disadvantages of Small Groups

Most of what we have said so far about groups has been positive, and it is true that there are many advantages to groups over individuals working alone. But there are also limitations related to groups that can lead to less effective and less satisfying outcomes.

## ■ Going Along to Get Along

Too much cohesiveness can lead to conformity and blind loyalty to a group even when it is not in the individual group member's best interest to do so. Groups can become too cohesive or committed, resulting in **groupthink**—a dysfunction in which group members see the harmony of the group as being more important than considering new ideas, critically examining their own assumptions, changing their own flawed decisions, or allowing new members to participate.[23] The following situation illustrates groupthink. Students are asked to choose one of three solutions to a certain social problem. One group is formed for each solution. Each group is asked to defend its solution and to persuade the instructor that its solution is the best. As an incentive for preparing a sound argument, students are told that the instructor will accept only one group solution as the best.

As the groups begin to organize, their members make a modest effort to pull together. Each group selects a representative to present its argument. After hearing each representative, the instructor announces that he or she is undecided as to which group offered the best solution. Therefore all groups have one more chance to develop their arguments. The instructor also announces that students who did not like their group's solution are welcome to join another group. No one switches groups, even though some are tempted to do so after hearing presentations by other group representatives.

To raise the stakes, the instructor states that the groups with the second- and third-best solutions will be assigned a research project over the weekend, whereas the winning group will be exempt from this assignment. In response, the intensity within each group builds. Members pull their chairs closer together and talk more forcibly about their solution. They support one another's views more openly. The common objective has become clear and compelling: The students are motivated to persuade their instructor in order to avoid the research project. Oddly enough, this particular type of motivation can be hazardous. Groupthink is more likely to occur when a group's cohesiveness and commitment are too high and when the group is

■ **groupthink** A dysfunction in which group members value the harmony of the group more than new ideas, fail to critically examine ideas, hesitate to change flawed decisions, or lack willingness to allow new members to participate.

under pressure to achieve consensus at the expense of doing the best possible work. Once this collective state of mind develops, it seems that groups become unwilling and perhaps unable to change a decision, even if they realize that it is a poor one.

Research on groupthink indicates that it is a real and pervasive phenomenon that can explain some of the disastrous decisions made by groups.[24] One such outcome of groupthink occurred when a group of IBM executives in 1980 refused to consider the purchase of Microsoft's operating system from Bill Gates, cofounder, chairman, and chief software architect of Microsoft Corporation. The executives' decision resulted in a loss of revenues worth billions of dollars and, eventually, the emergence of a gargantuan competitor in the computer industry. In this case, the IBM executives were unwilling to consider new information. They simply thought the Microsoft operating system wouldn't work. Not one member of the executive committee was willing to go against the thinking of the group as a whole. We all now know that Bill Gates is one of the richest people in the world.

According to Irving Janis, a specialist in organizational behavior, eight symptoms lead to groupthink. They fall into three categories:

1. Overestimation of the group's power and morality
   - An illusion that the group is invulnerable, which creates excessive optimism and encourages taking extreme risks
   - A belief that the group will not be judged on the basis of the ethical or moral consequences of its decisions

2. Closed-mindedness
   - A tendency to rationalize or discount negative information that might lead members to reconsider their assumptions before making a decision
   - Stereotypical views of other groups as too weak and stupid to warrant genuine attempts to negotiate differences

3. Pressures toward uniformity
   - Individual self-censorship of differences that deviate from the group (that is, members are inclined to minimize their uniqueness and doubt the importance of their individual contributions).
   - A shared illusion of unanimity that pushes members to conform to the majority view as a result of self-censorship and the assumption that silence means consent
   - Pressure on group members who express arguments that differ from the majority to conform by making it clear that dissent is contrary to what is expected of all loyal members
   - The setting of "mindguards" against threatening information in order to protect the group members from adverse information that might shatter their shared complacency regarding their decisions[25]

Procedures can be used to minimize the possibility of groupthink. Here are some examples:

- Assign one group member to be a "devil's advocate" who intentionally questions and criticizes the group's actions.
- Set a guideline to prevent leaders from expressing their preferences first.

- Ensure that every group member has an opportunity to voice an opinion.
- Encourage individuals to express disagreement without being chastised by the group for doing so.
- Use computer technology to encourage thorough problem solving.
- Invite outside experts to participate or review conclusions to ensure all views have been considered.[26]

## Time Consuming

A second disadvantage of groups is that the decision-making or problem-solving process can be time consuming. It almost always takes longer to accomplish something when a group does it. The more members there are in a group, the more time it takes to accomplish the group's objectives. Individuals can almost always complete a task in a shorter amount of time than a group. For example, if you were to take a math problem-solving test, you would probably read each problem silently to yourself, write notes to yourself on scratch paper, and then attempt to solve the problems. If you were in a group, you would first have to discuss each problem, decide how the problem should be solved, and then work out the solution to the problem. In other words, group work is different from individual work because there must be interaction between and among the members. How can you ensure that groups use their time wisely and effectively?

## Varying Communication Styles

A third disadvantage is that in most groups it is not possible for all members to contribute equally. One reason for this is time, but also because each member has a different communication style and comfort level with the group, members contribute unequally. Some members might dominate and overwhelm conversations, whereas other members might not contribute at all. Also, the most verbally aggressive and dominant person in the group might not have the best ideas. In Chapter 16, we discuss in more detail self-centered behaviors of group members and how to control those behaviors that hinder a group's effectiveness. What can be done to ensure that everyone has an equal opportunity to participate and contribute to the group?

## Unfair Workloads

A fourth disadvantage of groups is that members believe the workload is unfair in the group. The most frequent complaint we hear from students about working on group projects is that they believe that some group members lack motivation and do not do their fair share of the work. This is referred to as social loafing. **Social loafing** is the tendency for individuals to lower their work effort after they join a group.[27] For example, suppose that you and several people are helping a friend move. To lift the heaviest pieces, you all pitch in. Will all the people helping exert equal effort? Probably not. Some will lift as much as they can, whereas others will simply hang on, perhaps even grunting loudly in order to seem as if they are helping more than they are. Social loafers can also be irresponsible by not showing up on time or not showing up at all because they believe others will do the work for them.

- **social loafing**
Tendency for individuals to lower their work effort after they join a group.

### Effective Groups

Imagine that you are part of a group within your school that is in charge of coming up with new ways to recruit more students to your school. The group is made up of a variety of students all selected by the Dean of Student Affairs. Everything seems perfect except for one member who recently had a personal crisis and is very distracted, which has affected the group's ability to focus on the problem at hand.

1. How would you deal with the situation?
2. What would you say to the group member who is going through the crisis?
3. What would you say to other group members?

Lack of motivation seems to be the central reason for social loafing. Although there is no magical list of procedures or behaviors that will reduce social loafing, here are a few suggestions: Make outputs individually identifiable, increase commitment to the task and the sense of task importance, make sure that each person's contribution is unique—not identical—to those of others, and build group cohesiveness. If these suggestions do not work, and if it is possible or reasonable, eliminate noncontributors from the group.

### Pressure to Fail

A fifth disadvantage is that sometimes groups may not meet their potential, because the majority of group members place pressure on the most capable members not to excel. The implication is that the weaker group members control the outcome and therefore require others who might want to excel to do only the minimum necessary to get the job done and no more. In fact, members who do not cooperate and do excel beyond other group members might find themselves teased, chastised, or worse for breaking the group's norm. This phenomenon occurs when groups decide to meet the minimum expectations; it is very similar to groupthink. How can this type of situation be avoided?

### Grouphate Phenomenon

Finally, people who have had only negative experiences with groups or those who do not have the communication skills to be effective in groups dislike group work. This dislike for groups has been termed the **grouphate phenomenon.**[28] For some people, group work is so distasteful that they avoid group situations whenever possible. In our experience, those who hate participating in groups the most are those who have little or no skill or lack training in how to communicate in groups. What can people do to eliminate or reduce their dislike of groups?

People who are not skilled communicators usually find group work overwhelming and unsatisfactory because they don't know how to use communication to benefit them in solving problems, resolving conflicts, or expressing themselves.

## Summary

■ **grouphate phenomenon** Dislike for groups.

Almost everyone participates in small-group communication on a regular basis either at school, at work, or in some other context. Small-group communication is the exchange of information that occurs among a relatively small number of people, ideally five to seven, who share a common purpose such as doing a job, learning, or solving a problem. Groups are collections of individuals who influence one another, have a common purpose, take on roles, are interdependent, and interact with one another.

People join groups for a variety of reasons. Groups help to meet both psychological and social needs, allow individuals to reach goals that they might not otherwise be able to attain, provide multiple sources of information and ideas, provide security, and can contribute to a positive social identity. Cultural orientation also determines, to some extent, our predisposition to join groups and helps to form our perception of the value of groups. Cultures that have individualistic orientations stress the self or personal goals, whereas collectivistic orientations stress putting aside individual goals for the well-being of the group. A major force in bringing people together to form groups is that they have a common goal.

There are primary groups, which focus on social or interpersonal relationships, and secondary groups, which exist to accomplish tasks or achieve goals. There are special forms of groups, such as teams, project teams, work teams, and focus groups. Each type of group or team has various characteristics that make small groups a unique context for communication. They involve interdependence, commitment, cohesiveness, size, and culture. Sometimes group members lose their individual identity and give up the individual right to free thought even when it is not in their best interest to do so. This is referred to as groupthink.

There are many advantages to groups; these include better decisions and solutions to problems, but there are also disadvantages, including the feeling that groups take too much time, not everyone contributes equally, some members don't take their responsibilities seriously and do their fair share of the work, referred to as social loafing, and some individuals simply dislike groups because of bad experiences they had with them; this is called the grouphate phenomenon.

Technology is playing a larger and larger role in group interaction. There are online bulletin boards where people discuss popular and controversial issues. One type of such groups are referred to as newsgroups. More and more businesses because of travel expenses and convenience are using methods such as teleconferencing, videoconferencing, and interactive computer conferencing to allow groups of employees to discuss problems and issues and make decisions.

# Discussion Starters

1. What do you like most about working in groups? What do you like least about working in groups?

2. What causes groups to be inefficient? What can be done to make them more efficient?

3. Which group characteristic (interdependence, commitment, cohesiveness, group size, or group culture) do you think is the most important for a group to succeed? Why?

4. What is it that competent group communicators do that others do not?

5. Discuss two norms that exist in your class that could be applied to a group.

6. Can you think of a recent event in which groupthink came into play? What happened?

7. Explain what you think are the differences that women and men might bring to a group discussion.

8. Explain how technology can help groups to accomplish their goals.

9. What does it mean to you to be an ethical group member?

10. How does a social loafer affect a group's climate, motivation, and productivity?

# Notes

1. M. E. Shaw, *Group Dynamics: The Psychology of Small Group Behavior,* 2nd ed. (New York: McGraw-Hill, 1976), 6–10.
2. B. Lickel, D. L. Hamilton, G. Wieczorkowski, A. Lewis, S. J. Sherman, and A. N. Uhles, "Varieties of Groups and the Perception of Group Entiativity," *Journal of Personality and Social Pyschology,* 78 (2000): 223–246.
3. P. B. Paulus, ed., *Psychology of Group Influence,* 2nd ed. (Hillsdale, NJ: Erlbaum, 1989).
4. B. B. Haslett and J. Ruebus, "What Differences Do Individual Differences in Groups Make?" in *The Handbook of Group Theory and Research,* 2nd ed., eds. L. R. Frey, D. S. Gouran, and M. S. Poole (Thousand Oaks, CA: Sage, 1999), 115–38; and C. H. Hui and H. C. Trandis, "Individualism–Collectivism: A Study of Cross-Cultural Research," *Journal of Cross-Cultural Psychology* 17 (1986): 225–48.
5. H. C. Triandis, *Individualism and Collectiveness* (Boulder, CO: Westview Press, 1995).
6. C. Calloway-Thomas, P. J. Cooper, and C. Blake, *Intercultural Communication Roots and Routes* (Boston: Allyn and Bacon, 1999), 113–14.
7. Ibid., 114.
8. H. C. Triandis, "Cross-Cultural Studies of Individualism and Collectiveness," in *Cross-Cultural Perspective,* ed. J. Berman (Lincoln: University of Nebraska Press, 1990); and G. Hofstede, *Cultures and Organizations: Software of the Mind* (New York: McGraw-Hill, 1991).
9. R. V. Harnack, T. B. Fest, and B. S. Jones, *Group Discussion Theory and Technique,* 2nd ed. (Englewood Cliffs, NJ: Prentice-Hall, 1977), 25–28.
10. K. Adams and G. J. Galanes, *Effective Group Discussion,* 6th ed. (New York: McGraw-Hill, 2006), 15–16.
11. Ibid., 16.
12. L. Coch and J. R. P. French Jr., "Overcoming Resistance to Change," in *Group Dynamics: Research and Theory,* 2nd ed., eds. D. Cartwright and A. Zander (Evanston, IL: Row Peterson, 1960), 319–41.
13. S. A. Beebe and J. T. Masterson, *Communicating in Small Groups: Principles and Practices,* 8th ed. (Boston: Allyn and Bacon, 2006), 6–12.
14. G. Lumsden, D. Lumsden, and S. Ketrow, *Communicating in Groups and Teams,* 4th ed. (Belmont, CA: Wadsworth, 2004).
15. L. C. Lederman, "Assessing Educational Effectiveness: The Focus Group Interview as a Technique for Data Collection," *Communication Education* 39 (1990): 117–27.
16. R. Bostrum, "Patterns of Communicative Interaction in Small Groups," *Speech Monographs* 37 (1970): 257–63.
17. Beebe and Masterson, "Communication in Small Groups," 102.
18. L. P. Stewart, P. J. Cooper, A. D. Stewart, and S. H. Friedley, *Communication and Gender,* 4th ed. (Boston: Allyn and Bacon, 2003), 44–50; D. N. Maltz and R. A. Borker, "A Cultural Approach to Male–Female Miscommunication," in *Language and Social Identity,* ed. J. J. Gumperz (Cambridge: Cambridge University Press, 1982), 195–216; and E. Baird, "Sex Differences in Group Communication: A Review of Relevant Research," *Quarterly Journal of Speech* 62 (1976): 179–92.
19. B. F. Meeker and P. A. Weitzel-O'Neil, "Sex Roles and Interpersonal Behavior in Task-Oriented Groups," *American Sociological Review* 42 (1977): 91–105; R. L. Hoffman and N. K. V. Maier, "Quality and Acceptance of Problem Solutions by Members of Homogeneous and Heterogeneous Groups," *Journal of Abnormal and Social Psychology* 62 (1961): 401–7.
20. J. C. McCroskey, V. P. Richmond, and R. A. Stewart, *One on One: The Foundations of Interpersonal Communication* (Englewood Cliffs, NJ: Prentice-Hall, 1986), 244–47; M. E. Roloff, "The Impact of Socialization on Sex Differences in Conflict Resolution" (paper presented at the annual convention of the International Communication Association, Acapulco, Mexico, May 1980); E. A. Mabry, "Some Theoretical Implications of Female and Male Interaction in Unstructured Small Groups," *Small Group Behavior* 20 (1989): 536–50; and W. E. Jurma and B. C. Wright, "Follower Reactions to Male and Female Leaders Who Maintain or Lose Reward Power," *Small Group Research* 21 (1990): 97–112.
21. J. Bond and W. Vinacke, "Coalition in Mixed Sex Triads," *Sociometry* 24 (1961): 61–65; B. A. Fisher, "Differential Effects of Sexual Composition Interaction Patterns in Dyads," *Human Communication Research* 9 (1983): 225–38; Jurma and Wright, "Follower Reactions," 97–112; and D. J. Canary and B. H. Spitzberg, "Appropriateness and Effectiveness Perceptions of Conflict Strategies," *Human Communication Research* 14 (1987): 93–118.
22. C. Calloway-Thomas et al., 113–14.
23. I. L. Janis, *Groupthink: Psychological Studies of Policy Decisions and Fiascoes,* 2nd ed. (Boston: Houghton Mifflin, 1983).
24. P. E. Tetlock, R. S. Peterson, C. McGuire, S. Change, and P. Feld, "Assessing Political Group Dynamics: A

Test of the Group Think Model," *Journal of Personality and Social Psychology* 63 (1992): 403–25.

25. Janis, *Groupthink.*

26. Adams and Galanes, *Effective Group Discussion,* 230–33.

27. S. J. Karau and K. D. Williams, "Social Loafing: A Meta-Analytic Review and Theoretical Integration," *Journal of Personality and Social Psychology* 65 (1993): 681–706; B. K. Latané and S. Harkins, "Many Hands Make Light the Work: The Causes and Consequences of Social-Loafing," *Journal of Personality and Social Psychology* 37 (1979): 822–32; and B. G. Schultz, "Improving Group Communication Performance," in *The Handbook of Group Communication Theory and Research,* eds. L. R. Frey, D. S. Gouran, and M. S. Poole (Thousand Oaks, CA: Sage, 1999), 371–94.

28. S. Sorensen, "Grouphate" (paper presented at the International Communication Association, Minneapolis, Minn., May 1981).

# Participating in Groups and Teams

"Teamwork is the ability to work together toward a common vision. The ability to direct individual accomplishments toward organizational objectives. It is the fuel that allows common people to attain uncommon results."

—ANDREW CARNEGIE

# This chapter will help you:

- **Recognize** why team building is important in groups.
- **Know** the roles and responsibilities of group leaders.
- **Explain** differences in men's and women's leadership styles.
- **Specify** the responsibilities of group participants.
- **Recognize and understand** group task roles, group building and maintenance roles, and self-centered roles.
- **Conduct** efficient and effective group meetings.
- **Use** effective problem-solving and decision-making steps.
- **Manage and use** conflict strategies to ensure positive outcomes.
- **Develop and use** criteria for evaluating groups.

# Making everyday connections

Deborah, who works as an account executive for the IPS Corporation in Omaha, a large international advertising and marketing company, is part of a marketing team that includes two research assistants and two design coordinators. Her day starts with a 7:30 a.m. videoconference with her counterparts in Tokyo, Milan, and Chicago to discuss the implementation and development of a survey for a major international client. At 9:30 a.m. she meets with her team to discuss how to design the survey; at 11:00 she is off to meet with the production staff of a local client to discuss the findings of another survey; at noon she has a luncheon meeting with members of the Omaha Community Foundation to plan a fund-raiser for a new soccer field for kids. She now has time to get some of her work done on another project, knowing that at 4:30 p.m. she has a meeting with her husband, a builder, and an architect to make the final decisions regarding the construction of their new home. After dinner, at 7:30 p.m., she will join the neighborhood association, which is meeting to discuss the neighborhood summer picnic. Meetings, meetings, meetings . . . ■

## Questions to think about

- Why the need for all of the meetings?
- What are the benefits of these types of meetings?
- In your opinion, what has to happen for meetings such as these to be efficient, productive, and rewarding?
- How will the meetings with clients differ from the neighborhood association meeting?
- What challenges does the format of the videoconference meeting pose?

Meetings and group discussions have been the brunt of many jokes and often have led to frustration, but working in groups can be a wonderful experience and can lead to outcomes that are far better than those provided by individuals. If you are like most people, you have likely been in meetings in which great interaction took place, time was used wisely, good progress was made toward a particular goal or accomplishing a task, lots of good ideas were shared, respect for each person's contributions was shown even though disagreement and conflict sometimes occurred, differences were resolved by open discussion, and decisions were supported by everyone. People leave such meetings with a real sense of accomplishment.

What is the difference between an effective and an ineffective group meeting? To answer this question, this chapter explores seven crucial aspects of small group communication: team building, leadership, conducting a meeting, member participation, methods of group problem solving and decision making, conflict management, and evaluation.

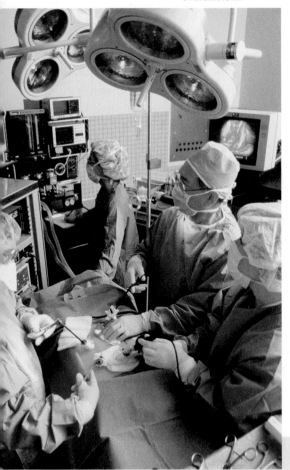

Members of an operating room team have a strong sense of identity with the group, and they cooperate fully because each has a specific role to play. This is a very effective group form.

# Team Building

Not all groups will become teams or work as teams, but it is important to understand that the more a group acts like or becomes a team, the more likely it is that the group will be successful. A team is likely to be more successful or effective because when people know they are part of a team, they tend to cooperate more fully; they form a close-knit relationship and a strong sense of identity as discussed in Chapter 15. As with any group or organization, a team needs a purpose and goals. For groups to establish a team approach, they must first set very clear and specific goals as well as determine roles.

## Setting Goals

It is unusual when participating in a group to find that all members participate with the same amount of enthusiasm or motivation. Unfortunately, the levels of enthusiasm and motivation differ in most group situations. One way to avoid this problem is to establish goals that are not only clear and specific, but also challenging and worthwhile for each group member.[1] If group members believe that the goals are trivial and unimportant, they will likely not participate, or if they do participate, it will be with little or no motivation. If the group members understand that their work effort and decisions will result in rewards, be appreciated, and be considered worthwhile, however, they are more likely to take ownership of their actions and behaviors as well as be motivated to accomplish their goals.

How can a group effectively determine whether its goals are clear and specific? If a group's goal is stated vaguely, the group will likely find it difficult to organize itself and to know when it has arrived at a solution or conclusion. For example, if a group discusses a topic such as "crime is on the rise," this topic provides little or no direction as to what needs to be done. However, if the topic is restated as "What specific actions should be taken by the community to help reduce the crime rate by the end of the year?" this tells the group exactly what it needs to accomplish: specific actions for reducing crime. If the group also believes that the specific actions they propose could be actually used to reduce crime, that would even be more of an incentive for the group to accomplish its goal. It would also give them a reason to take ownership of what they discuss.

## Determining Roles

Once the group has established and understands its goal, it must determine the roles of its members. Everyone in the group must be responsible for something, and everyone must be held accountable for what they are responsible to provide to the group. For example, a football team requires a head coach (a leader), assistant coaches (a subgroup within the larger group), players who have the talent and desire to fill the positions necessary to play the game, public relations people to promote the team, and so on. Everyone on the team has roles and assigned duties to accomplish. Football players cannot function as a team if there is no structure or if the coaches and players are uncertain of the roles they are supposed to fulfill. The same is true of any group; if the members are uncertain of their roles and there is no structure, the group will not be able to function effectively.

# Leadership

**Leadership** is an influence process that includes any behavior that helps to clarify a group's purpose or guide a group to achieve its goals. A **leader** is a person who is assigned or selected, or who emerges from a group, to guide or provide direction toward reaching the group's goals. In most cases, only one person has the title of leader, although there are times when the assigned or appointed leader does not show leadership even though he or she has the title of leader. It is also true that sometimes two or more people may emerge and share the leader responsibilities via their leadership behaviors. In other words, a leader is a role or title held in a group, whereas leadership is the behavior that influences or facilitates group members to achieve the group's goal or goals.

## Leading a Group

A leader is the person at the center of a group's attention or the person to whom the group members address their messages. For example, in business meetings, the boss is usually the leader, and the employees focus their attention on the boss, addressing their communications to him or her. At times, employees may address messages to other employees, or one employee might hold the attention of the group, but in neither situation does an employee actually become the leader of the meeting.

Another way to identify a leader is by the behaviors that he or she displays in guiding a group to its specific goal. If a person communicates a direction and the group members follow that direction to reach the goal, that person is demonstrating leadership.

Finally, a leader can be identified by his or her position or title, such as police chief, mayor, council president, chairperson of a committee, boss, teacher, coach,

**leadership** An influence process that includes any behavior that helps clarify a group's purpose or guides the group to achieve its goals.

**leader** A person who is assigned or selected, or who emerges from a group, to guide or provide direction toward reaching the group's goals.

## MAKING CONNECTIONS
### for Success

### What Makes a Leader?

Develop a list of names of leaders that you know, for example, political leaders, campus leaders, sports leaders, business leaders, community leaders, or friends who hold leadership positions.

1. Describe the leadership qualities or skills of each. What communication skills do the people on your list have in common?
2. How do people acquire the type of leadership characteristics and skills you have identified?
3. Of the qualities and skills you listed above, which is the most important? Why?
4. What role, if any, do ethics or morals have in leadership behavior?

captain, father, mother, and so on. But this method of identification requires caution. Even though a title signifies that a person is the stated leader, it does not mean that that person has leadership skills.

In most cases, a leader's ability to lead determines the success or failure of a group. Granted, not all successes or failures can be traced directly to the person in charge because the participants, the nature of the task to be accomplished, and the information available for completing the task also contribute to the outcome. The role of the leader in small-group projects is to get the task done. To do this, the leader must be objective enough to determine how the group is functioning and whether it is progressing toward its goal. This requires, at times, the ability to "step back" and examine the group objectively.

Leaders must help address two sets of needs found in all groups. **Task needs** are related to the content of the task and all behaviors that lead to the completion of the task, including defining and assessing the task, gathering information, studying the problem, and solving the problem. **Maintenance needs** are related to organizing and developing a group such that members realize personal satisfaction from working together. Maintenance needs pertain to intangibles such as atmosphere, structure, role responsibility, praise, and social–emotional control. To meet both task and maintenance needs, leaders in small groups must perform a number of functions:

- ■ **task needs** Needs related to the content of a task and all behaviors that lead to the completion of it.

- ■ **maintenance needs** Needs related to organizing and developing a group so that the members can realize personal satisfaction from working together.

- ■ **initiating structure** A dimension of leadership that focuses on getting the job done.

- ■ **consideration** A dimension of leadership that focuses on establishing good interpersonal relationships and on being liked by group members.

*Initiating*—preparing members for the discussion

*Organizing*—keeping members on track

*Maintaining effective interaction*—encouraging participation

*Ensuring member satisfaction*—promoting interpersonal relationships

*Facilitating understanding*—encouraging effective listening

*Stimulating creativity and critical thinking*—encouraging evaluation and improvement

## ■■ Leadership Styles and Behavior

All leaders are definitely not alike. They may share certain characteristics or qualities to a degree but more than likely they differ in personal, behavioral, or leadership style. Although there are as many different leadership styles as there are leaders, research on leader behavior suggests that most leaders can be described as **initiating structure** (or task-oriented leaders) and **consideration** (or relationship-oriented leaders).[2] Leaders who lead by initiating structure tend to focus on getting the job done. They engage in actions such as organizing work, making sure rules are followed, setting goals, and making sure that everyone knows who is in charge. For example Marissa Mayer, vice president at Google in charge of finding talented workers, thrives at her position by being extremely particular in hiring, a fanatical user of social networking, and apolitical when critiquing new ideas.[3] You may have experienced leaders like this, and in some group situations, this style can get the job done or the problem solved, but leaders who employ this style tend to sacrifice relationship development unless doing so will help get the task done more quickly.

Leaders who do not focus on task completion are more likely to be less organized, less goal oriented, and are less likely to be concerned about their own recognition as a leader.

Leaders who lead by consideration tend to focus on interpersonal relationships and being liked by group members. They engage in such actions as doing favors for group members, taking time to explain things to them, and watching out for their well-being. Leaders who do not focus on consideration usually don't care about the group members or whether the group members like them or not. (See Figure 16.1 for an overview of the two styles).

Is either of these styles superior? Probably not! Both offer a mix of advantages and disadvantages. Leaders who show concern for others generally foster stronger morale, but such leaders often avoid telling others what to do or offering critical feedback to improve group members. This could result in inefficiency and not getting things done in a timely manner. In contrast, when leaders solely focus on getting the job done, efficiency may be good, but group members feel no commitment to the outcome or to the leader. It appears that leaders who are able to use a blend of both styles are likely to have groups that are highly productive, committed, and enjoy working together to get the task done. In other words, leaders who can balance the two styles are often considered superior leaders.

Leadership may also be classified according to how much or how little power the leader assigns to the group members. Researchers have identified three primary styles of leadership: autocratic, democratic, and laissez-faire,[4] each having a very distinctive approach to the communication that occurs within the group (see Table 16.1). However, many leaders cannot be easily classified in one of the three styles exclusively. Often, effective leaders use a combination of styles or blends of the styles, which may change from one situation to the next.

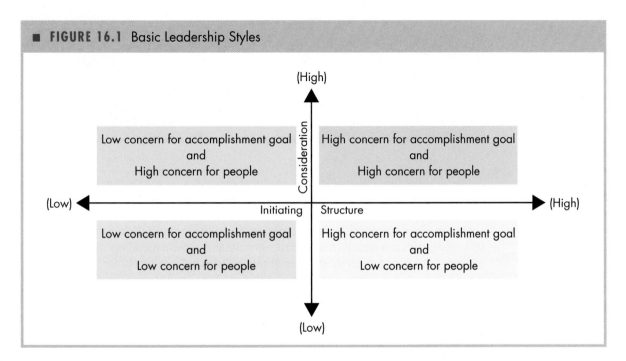

■ **FIGURE 16.1** Basic Leadership Styles

■ **TABLE 16.1** Leadership Styles: A Comparison

| AUTOCRATIC | DEMOCRATIC | LAISSEZ-FAIRE |
|---|---|---|
| Keeps complete control | Shares control | Gives up control |
| Sets policy and makes all decisions for the group | Involves members in setting policy and making decisions; does not make any decisions without consulting group members | Gives total freedom to group members to make policies and decisions; gets involved only when called on |
| Defines tasks and assigns them to members | May guide task assignment to be sure work is accomplished, but allows members to divide work | Completely avoids participation |

Leadership style is classified by how much or how little power the leader assigns to group members. Democratic leaders, for example, guide and direct the group and, though committed to being open to all points of view, they represent only a majority or plurality of points of view of the group.

■ **autocratic leader**
A leader who has complete control.

■ **democratic leader**
A leader who shares control.

■ **laissez—faire leader** A leader who gives up control.

In theory, the differences among the three styles of leadership are clear. The **autocratic leader** has complete control, the **democratic leader** shares control, and the **laissez-faire leader** gives up control. In practice, though, the three styles are not always so clear-cut. Most leaders do not use the same style all the time but vary their style to match each situation. Certain circumstances, group members, and group purposes call for direct control, whereas others require little or no control. For example, a military leader in combat and a doctor in a medical emergency will undoubtedly be autocratic leaders. Such situations require immediate action, and putting decisions to a vote could create problems. Autocratic leaders can have a negative impact on a group, for example, a jury foreman who imposes her opinion or rushes the decision so that other jurists agree with her.

## MAKING CONNECTIONS for Success

### Choosing a Leadership Style

Tia was elected chairperson of her church's administrative council. She was very pleased that others saw her as a leader, given that she was the youngest person and the only African American who had run for the position.

The committee was made up of seven members and, besides Tia, there was only one other female member. Even though this was only her third year on the church council (most members had served for longer periods), Tia felt ready to take charge but also knew that her assignment was not going to be easy.

A tremendous amount of work had to be done in a short time, and controversial issues were involved. Despite having less experience than most members, she was confident and knew that she could do the job.

1. What advice would you give to Tia regarding her choice of leadership style?
2. What other concerns should Tia have, if any?
3. Would these concerns be different if Tia were a male? If so, why?

The democratic leadership style is most often used when a leader is elected. For example, the president of the student government and the chair of a committee would probably use a democratic style. This style is most common when the leader is both a representative and a member of the group. The laissez-faire leadership style is often used when group members do not want or need a rigid structure to accomplish their goal, such as a group conducting a study session. If such a group decided that they needed a leader, they would take appropriate action, but in most cases, the group does not desire or require any assistance, and so it remains leaderless.

Leaders are not always free to follow the leadership style they prefer. For example, people who would rather be democratic or laissez-faire leaders might discover that pressures from others, the need to get things done in a certain way, or the desire to save time and energy require them to be more autocratic than they would like to be. On other occasions, when it is important for members to agree with a decision, leaders are more likely to use a democratic style. No single leadership style is perfect in all situations.

Researchers have concluded that skilled leaders have the ability to understand a situation and adapt their behaviors to meet its particular constraints.[5] Leadership entails the ability to determine the most appropriate style and behaviors for given situations. Here are some sample situations to which effective leadership is able to adapt:

- When group members are not committed or are unwilling to accept responsibility for implementing a decision, effective leaders use an autocratic style of leadership. For example, if a small group of neighbors gets together to discuss the new road next to their homes and its effects on the neighborhood, but only one of the residents has knowledge of the issues and comes to the meeting prepared with information, an autocratic style would be appropriate.

- If group members are highly committed and willing to accept responsibility for implementing a decision, effective leaders use a democratic style of leadership. For example, if a small group of neighbors gets together to discuss the new road next to their homes and its effects on the neighborhood and all of them are committed and prepared to discuss the issues, a democratic style of leadership would be appropriate.

■ If group members are highly motivated to complete a task and have the knowledge and expertise to accomplish the task, effective leaders realize that they should delegate the task to the group members and use a laissez-faire style of leadership. For example, if a small group of neighbors gets together to discuss the new road next to their homes and its effects on the neighborhood and all of them are highly talented, independent, and knowledgeable about the issues, a laissez-faire style would be appropriate.

Effective leaders examine situations, understand the groups they are leading, and determine what actions need to be taken to accomplish a given task. Although it is impossible to say exactly which styles work best in certain situations, common sense indicates that a leader needs to be flexible to promote productivity and satisfaction in a given group.

Research, although not conclusive, suggests that the democratic leadership style is superior to the autocratic style in getting a task done and at the same time satisfies group members.[6] Autocratic leaders are likely to get more done, but member satisfaction is considerably lower. Probably the most significant research finding is that autocratic leaders generate more hostility and aggression among group members, whereas democratic leaders produce more originality, individuality, and independence. Groups with laissez-faire leaders accomplish less, produce work of lower quality, and waste more time.

## ▬▬ Leadership and Gender Differences

Women continue to make great strides in assuming leadership roles such as elected offices (e.g., governors, mayors, and legislatures). They have also been appointed to the Supreme Court and cabinet positions, hold high rank in the military, and head major corporations. Women are also the leaders in creating and building a culture of creativity in organizations. In fact, 70 percent of a new breed of leaders called "Innovation Champions" are women. They are the ones stimulating people's minds by constantly pushing and creating new trends and ideas.[7]

Early research on small group leadership found that men usually emerged as leaders but today it seems that biological sex is irrelevant, although psychological gender is not. It now appears that task oriented women emerge as leaders as often as men who are task oriented. A study of groups of women found that those who emerged as leaders combined intelligence with masculinity or androgyny (exhibiting both masculine and feminine characteristics.)[8] A study examining groups consisting of both males and females found that regardless of sex, masculine and androgynous members emerged more often than feminine members.[9] It appears that leaders today are not chosen based on biological sex but based on performance. The research related to gender and leadership shows that men and women lead equally well, and group members are equally satisfied with both.[10] It is clear that women have made great strides in recent years and have proven to be effective leaders in a variety of settings and situations.

Do male leaders and female leaders differ in their style or approach to leadership? What do you think? Marilyn Loden, in her book *Feminine Leadership or How to Succeed in Business Without Being One of the Boys,* contends that the sexes do indeed differ in terms of leadership style.[11] Loden believes that female leaders often adopt a style that emphasizes cooperation and indirect means of management, whereas males tend to exhibit an "I'm in charge" directive strategy. But research on male and female leadership done by social scientists has generally found no consistent or significant difference between the sexes in terms of leadership style. The question is "Who is right?"

Because of the complexity of the subject, finding the answer to this question is not simple. In a review of 150 research studies, Alice Eagly and Blair Johnson found that potential differences between male and female leadership styles had been examined on two dimensions: (1) task accomplishment versus maintenance of interpersonal relationships and (2) participative (democratic) versus directive (autocratic) leadership style.[12] Sex-role stereotypes suggest that female leaders might show more concern for interpersonal relations and tend to be more democratic in their leadership style than male leaders are. Results of Eagly and Johnson's study, however, did not support these stereotypes. Their results suggest that no evidence supports any substantial difference between males and females regarding the first dimension (task

## MAKING CONNECTIONS
### for Success

### Are Women Better Leaders?

According to an article in *U.S. News & World Report* (January 29, 2001), more women are taking on leadership roles in government and business. The article stated that women have a greater tendency to take a holistic, contextual view of issues, whereas men tend to compartmentalize and assess the cause and effect of issues in a linear fashion. On the basis of what this article appears to say, women are therefore better leaders.

1. Defend or refute the article's contention that women are better leaders.
2. What does it mean to be holistic, and why would that make a person a better leader?
3. When considering the traits we generally associate with leadership, are they more likely to be masculine or feminine? Explain.
4. Who do you think is a very effective female leader? A very effective male leader? What do they have in common? What are their differences?

accomplishment versus maintenance of interpersonal relationships). There is, however, a significant difference between males and females regarding the second dimension (participative versus directive leadership style). Eagly and Johnson found that females were more democratic, or participative, in style than males were. What do you think accounts for this difference?

According to Eagly and Johnson, the difference in leadership style might exist because, as evidence suggests, women generally possess better interpersonal skills than men do. However, this cause-and-effect connection is only speculative. Much more research must be done before a definitive conclusion can be drawn about gender differences in leadership style and whether (and in what situations) those differences might be to a leader's advantage or disadvantage.[13]

# ■ Conducting a Meeting

When a group meets for the first time, the members usually begin by introducing themselves and briefly telling their reasons for joining the group or what they hope to accomplish as members.

After introductions, and depending on the nature of the group and its assigned task, members may appoint or elect a recording secretary. This person keeps a written account of the meeting's discussions that may be consulted later if necessary.

To ensure efficiency, procedures must be established, and meetings must be conducted according to a well-organized plan. The best way to accomplish this is by producing an **agenda,** a list of all topics to be discussed during a meeting. The leader usually determines the agenda, either alone or in consultation with the

■ **agenda** A list of all topics to be discussed during a meeting.

group members before each meeting. Sometimes, at the end of one meeting, the agenda for the next meeting is established. A typical meeting agenda might look like the following:

1. Call to order
2. Introduction of new members
3. Reading, correction, and approval of minutes from previous meeting
4. Unfinished business
5. New business
6. Announcements
7. Adjournment

Not all meetings operate in exactly the same way, but having an agenda should make any meeting run smoothly. Classroom groups might not follow a formal structure, but in general, they need a sense of organization and an informal agenda.

---

**GUIDELINES**

## Planning and Managing a Meeting

1. Identify a purpose, plan an agenda, and distribute the agenda in advance.
2. Invite only people who need to be there (*not* everyone who might have an opinion on the topic).
3. Establish start, break, and stop times, and stick to them.
4. Assign a moderator (leader) to keep the discussion on track.
5. Decide what follow-up actions are needed after the meeting, and set deadlines for their completion.
6. Avoid holding unnecessary meetings.
7. Don't let people drone on, dominate, or avoid participation during discussions.
8. Don't allow conversations to wander off the subject.
9. Follow up to make sure that members act on decisions made at the meeting.

From Harrison Conference Services, Business Schools at the University of Georgia and Georgia State University.

---

# ■ Member Participation

For a group to be successful, all of its members must be actively involved. Just like leaders, members of groups have certain responsibilities. The more members know about their leader's role and each other's roles, the better equipped they will be to perform. Furthermore, leaders change from time to time, so members should be ready to assume greater responsibility if doing so will benefit the group.

## ■■ Roles of Group Members

Successful group outcomes depend on group members assuming various roles that are constructive and beneficial to the group's outcome. There are many roles that group members can play. Group scholars Kenneth Benne and Paul Sheats developed a comprehensive list of roles that group members can assume.[14] Benne and Sheats classified the roles into three categories: group task, group building and maintenance, and self-centered roles.

Group task roles help the group to accomplish its task or objective. They are behaviors that orient the group to the task, allow for the exchange of ideas and opinions, and motivate the group to complete the task.

Group building and maintenance roles help to define a group's social atmosphere. These roles include behaviors that function to maintain a positive interpersonal climate within the group. A person who tries to maintain a peaceful, harmonious climate by mediating disagreements and resolving conflicts performs a maintenance function.

Individuals may adopt self-centered roles, which are generally counterproductive or destructive to a group, that tend to hinder group progress. In most groups, members are eager to make constructive contributions. From time to time, however, you will encounter individuals whose attitudes are not so positive. For the good of the group, it is important to recognize such people and learn how to cope with them. See Table 16.2 for various roles of group members.

## ■■ Contributions of Group Members

Recognizing and handling counterproductive contributions are the responsibilities not only of the leader but also of each group member. Sometimes the best approach to these situations is to discuss them openly: "John, you sure have been quiet about this problem. What do you think?" "Sally, your jokes seem to indicate that you don't believe the issue is very serious. Why?" Sometimes conflict needs to be resolved with a vote by the group. This lets members know the position of the majority so that discussion can continue.

**Comments That Are Open to Evaluation.** One of the greatest anxieties group members face is presenting their ideas for the group's evaluation. Group discussion can lead to the best possible information and the best possible decision, but this will happen only if members offer their comments for evaluation. Criticism should not be ignored or avoided. At the same time, members must remember that evaluations can be constructive only when they focus on the contribution and not on the person who originated it. It is one thing to find fault with specific data; it is quite another thing to find fault with the person who presented the data. Criticism should be based on what is said, not on who said it. To give effective criticism, members should describe and clarify their thoughts on the topic rather than simply finding fault.

**Provocative Comments.** Comments should be made not only to bring the group closer to its goal, but also to fuel thought for further contributions. This is worthwhile even if it makes for a somewhat longer meeting. If an idea has not been fully discussed and evaluated, appropriate decisions cannot be made. Asking questions (even ones that seem trivial), challenging assumptions, presenting bold new ideas (even if they seem unusual), and disagreeing can be valuable as long as these contributions are focused on making the final group product the best one possible.

Group participants need to study the meeting's agenda in advance so that they will be prepared to contribute. Meaningful input often calls for research, so each participant should be willing to spend time and energy on advanced preparation. Probably one of the greatest weaknesses of beginning group participants is their tendency to arrive at meetings unprepared. The group must then either spend time helping them catch up or do without their contributions. Either way, valuable time, effort, and input are lost. Also, successful group outcomes depend on group-centered attitudes and behaviors, which enhance participation and member satisfaction; they include open-mindedness, a positive attitude, the ability to listen, a willingness to contribute, and preparation.

■ **TABLE 16.2** Roles Group Members Can Play

| GROUP TASK ROLES | BEHAVIORS |
| --- | --- |
| Initiator–contributor | Provides direction and guidance, proposes new ideas, suggests solutions, or approaches to the problem |
| Information seeker | Sees the need for more information, asks for clarification of ideas and relevance |
| Information giver | Provides information, including facts, examples, statistics, and other evidence |
| Opinion seeker | Asks about people's feelings and views related to the task |
| Opinion giver | Provides personal beliefs, opinions, or judgments about ideas being considered by the group |
| Elaborator | Extends information and clarifies viewpoints, ideas, and solutions |
| Coordinator | Clarifies and notes relationships among ideas, viewpoints, and suggestions |
| Orienter | Attempts to summarize what has occurred |
| Evaluator/critic | Makes an effort to evaluate the evidence and conclusions |
| Energizer | Tries to motivate the group to take action |
| Recorder | Records the discussion for future reference |
| Tester of agreements | Determines how close the group is to reaching agreement |

| GROUP BUILDING AND MAINTENANCE ROLES | BEHAVIORS |
| --- | --- |
| Encourager | Offers praise by recognizing others' contributions |
| Harmonizer | Mediates disagreements, attempts to maintain positive interpersonal climate |
| Compromiser | Attempts to resolve conflicts by trying to find acceptable solutions to disagreements |
| Gatekeeper | Manages and directs the flow of communication |
| Standard setter | Articulates standards and goals that the group is to achieve |
| Follower | Goes along with the ideas and views of other group members |
| Feeling expresser | Highlights for the group its feelings, emotions, and attitudes |

| SELF-CENTERED ROLES | BEHAVIORS |
| --- | --- |
| Aggressor | Deflates the status of others to make themselves look better |
| Blocker | Resists, disagrees with, and opposes issues beyond reasonableness |
| Recognition seeker | Must be the center of attention, otherwise dissatisfied |
| Self-confessor | Contributes irrelevant information about self |
| Buffoon | Constantly jokes or engages in other kinds of horseplay |
| Dominator | Wants to be in charge of everything (autocrat) |
| Help seeker | Joins groups to satisfy personal needs |
| Withdrawer | Prefers not to participate at all |

Adapted from K. D. Benne and P. Sheats, "Functional Roles of Group Members," *Journal of Social Issues* 4 (1948): 41–49.

### The Buffoon

Jessica has always been fun to be around. She loves to kid and play practical jokes. Her design group has been fairly tolerant of her antics and at times has really had a good laugh, actually helping to reduce the group's stress level. But her recent behavior has really gotten out of control. In fact, her jokes are no longer appreciated, cause disruption, and show insensitivity to other members of the group.

No one has been willing to say anything to Jessica because they don't want to hurt her feelings. Besides, her other contributions have been excellent, and she has indispensable information regarding the problem the group is trying to solve. The situation is even more delicate because she is very sensitive and somewhat of a hothead. Members fear that if someone tells her to stop her unproductive behavior, she will leave the group.

You believe that Jessica doesn't think much of you as a leader. However, the group's morale has been steadily declining because of her, and if you don't say something to Jessica, other members might leave the group.

1. What should you do about this situation?
2. Are any ethical considerations involved in handling this problem?

# Problem Solving and Decision Making

Although the goal of some discussions, such as those in classrooms, is to share information, the goal of most discussions is to solve problems and make decisions: How can we raise more money for new computers? Who should be held responsible for date rape? What can be done to eliminate unethical behavior in our organization? How can we streamline production? How can we get the Hollywood media to reduce sex and violence in films and TV programs?

When solving problems and making decisions, groups must consider the alternatives and arrive at joint conclusions. To do this most effectively, they must take an organized and thorough approach to determine the exact nature of the problem and discuss its many aspects and potential solutions.

## Determining the Problem

Groups are usually formed because a task needs to be accomplished. As groups are being formed, members already have an idea of their purposes and goals. In the classroom, groups are often formed to discuss particular topics in order to learn something. In communication classrooms, for example, small groups sometimes discuss subjects related to communication and sometimes simply allow students to learn about small-group communication by experiencing it.

Unless your instructor assigns a topic, the first step of your group effort is to select a problem or topic. This is not always easy; after all, the topic has to be both important and interesting to everyone in the group to ensure a good discussion. A starting place might be areas that need improvement on your campus: What should be the role of athletics on the campus? Should better protection be provided for students who attend evening classes? The surrounding community is also a source for discussion topics: What can be done about public parking in the downtown area? What can the business community do to help college students get better jobs?

State, regional, and national issues can provide a broader base for topics: Can the state provide sufficient funding to the university? What should be the role of the federal government in providing loans to students? Selecting from thousands of topics and problems takes time. However, if the group does its homework, picking a topic that is agreeable to all members should not be difficult.

After a topic or problem is selected, it should be stated in the form of a question. There are four types of discussion questions: questions of fact, interpretation, value, and policy. A question of fact asks whether something is true or false; its answer can be verified: What is the current cost of tuition? How many people voted in the last election? A **question of interpretation** asks for the meaning or explanation of something: How does the state's economy affect education? How can exercise contribute to better health? A question of value asks whether something is good or bad, desirable or undesirable: Which college offers the best education for its students? Do coeducational dormitories provide satisfactory living conditions? A question of policy asks what actions should be taken: What restrictions should be placed on alcohol consumption on campus? What security measures should be instituted to make the Internet safe for kids?

Questions of fact leave little room for discussion. The answer can usually be found through research, and unless there are discrepancies in the data, no discussion is required. In contrast, questions of interpretation, value, and policy are not easily answered and thus make for good discussions. When phrasing discussion questions, whether for a classroom learning experience or another context, keep the following guidelines in mind:

1. The wording should reflect the discussion purpose or task at hand.
2. The wording should focus attention on the real problem.
3. The wording should specify whose behavior is subject to change.
4. The wording should not suggest possible solutions.
5. The wording should avoid emotional language.[15]

## ■ Discussing the Problem

In group situations, whether in the classroom or another context, it is important to determine a plan for carrying out the task or assignment. The agenda for discussing a problem, for example, usually includes the following five specific steps developed by the philosopher John Dewey: definition of the problem, analysis of the problem, suggestions of possible solutions, selection of the best solution, and putting the best solution into operation.[16] The steps developed by Dewey are referred to as "reflective thinking" steps because they provide a logical, rational way of structuring group interaction. Here is an outline of a typical problem-solving discussion:

I. Definition of the problem
   A. *Symptoms.* How does the problem show itself, or what are the difficulties?
   B. *Size.* How large is the problem? Is it increasing or decreasing? What results can be expected if the problem is not solved?
   C. *Goal.* What general state of affairs is desired (in contrast to the present unsatisfactory one)?

■ **question of interpretation** A question that asks for the meaning or explanation of something.

II. Analysis of the problem
  A. *Causes of the problem.* What causes or conditions underlie the difficulties?
  B. *Present efforts to solve the problem.* What is being done now to deal with the problem? In what ways are these efforts unsuccessful? What hints do they provide for further attacks on the problem?
  C. *Requirements of a solution*
    1. *Direction.* Where shall we attack the problem?
      a. Would an attack on some outstanding symptom be the most fruitful approach?
      b. Is there a cause that would be worthwhile to attack? It would need these two essential characteristics:
        (1) Would its removal substantially eliminate or greatly modify the problem?
        (2) Could its removal be accomplished with facilities—personnel, equipment, finances—that are (or can be made) available?
    2. *Boundaries.* What other values—social customs, laws, institutions— must not be harmed in attempting to solve this problem?

III. Suggestions of possible solutions
  A. *One possible solution*
    1. *Nature.* What, specifically, is the plan?
    2. *Strengths.* In what ways would this plan effectively fulfill the requirements or criteria of a solution, that is, make notable progress in the direction and stay satisfactorily within the boundaries of a solution?
    3. *Weaknesses.* In what ways would this plan fall short of effectively fulfilling these requirements or criteria?
  B. *Another possible solution*
  C. *Another possible solution*
  D. *Another possible solution*

IV. Selection of the best solution
  A. *Best solution (or solution with modifications).* How is this solution better than the others?
  B. *Part of problem unsolved.* If the solution leaves any part unsolved, why is it still considered the best?

V. Putting the best solution into operation
  A. *Major difficulties to be faced*
  B. *Possible ways of overcoming difficulties*
  C. *Best way to overcome difficulties*

## ▪▪ Applying Reflective Thinking to Problem Solving and Decision Making

In solving problems and making decisions, it is always wise to incorporate a reflective thinking process that follows a plan such as the one suggested by John Dewey. The Dewey reflective thinking steps should be used as a guide to decision making, not an exact formula in approaching every problem that needs to be solved. Randy Hirokawa, a communication scholar, concluded that a systematic approach to group problem solving and decision making is better than no organized approach at all.[17] We also believe that organization and direction are important in group problem-solving interaction, but inflexible, lock-step organizations can stifle or reduce a group's ability to arrive at the best solutions.

| GUIDELINES | Applying Reflective Thinking to Problem Solving |

1. *Clearly identify the problem you are trying to solve.* The discussion of a topic can be a good exercise, but if the discussion is not focused clearly or goals are not clearly defined as suggested earlier in the chapter, the discussion might wander without direction. For example, a group that decides to discuss the quality of public education but does not define what its purpose is for discussing the topic will likely not come to any conclusion. The group should focus on a clearly identified issue or problem, such as "How can public education be improved with limited resources?"

2. *Phrase the problem as a question to help guide the discussion.* Stating the problem or issue in the form of a question helps the group focus and direct the discussion more easily. See the list of suggestions in the section Determining the Problem for the best way to phrase a question.

3. *Do not start suggesting solutions until you have fully analyzed the problem.* Most group scholars generally agree that problems should be thoroughly researched to arrive at the best solutions. This will help you avoid thinking of solutions prematurely or before you have a complete understanding of the causes, effects, and symptoms of the problem under discussion.

4. *In the definition and analysis steps of reflective thinking, do not confuse the causes of the problem with its symptoms.* Perspiration is a symptom that a person is warm or nervous. The cause for the perspiration, however, might be a stressful situation such as having to give a speech, not dressing appropriately for weather conditions, or any number of other reasons. The key to successful problem solving is reflective thinking that examines the symptoms in search of the causes.

5. *Appoint at least one member of the group to remind others to follow the reflective thinking steps.* Although the reflective thinking steps were designed sequentially and should be followed as such, it is not unusual for groups to deviate from the order. Thus it is a good idea to assign some members to monitor the procedures to ensure that the group does not deviate too far from its structure.

From S. A. Beebe and J. T. Masterson, *Communicating in Small Groups,* 8th ed. (Boston: Allyn & Bacon, 2006), 272.

Roger Firestein, a small-group scholar, recommends that all members, whether leaders or participants, should help to keep the group on track and periodically ask the following questions:[18]

1. Do we have sufficient evidence to support our solution?
2. Have we examined a reasonable number of alternatives?
3. Did we reexamine discarded solutions to ensure they should be discarded?
4. Have we come to closure too quickly?
5. Were we open-minded in our thinking?

## Brainstorming

Sometimes groups find themselves unable to generate new ideas or to be creative in solving a particular aspect of a problem. In such cases, they may find brainstorming (also discussed in Chapter 7) helpful. Brainstorming, a technique used to generate as many ideas as possible within a limited amount of time, can be used during any phase of the group discussion process to produce topics, information, or solutions to problems. During the brainstorming session, group members suggest as many ideas as possible pertaining to the topic, no matter how far-fetched they might seem. One person records the ideas for later analysis. The leader lets the comments flow freely and may prompt the group by suggesting extensions of ideas that have been generated.

## Productive Brainstorming — GUIDELINES

1. Don't criticize any idea, either verbally or nonverbally.
2. No idea is too wild—encourage creativity.
3. Quantity is important—the more ideas, the better.
4. Seize opportunities to improve on or to add to ideas suggested by others.
5. Record all ideas generated by the group.
6. At the end of a specified time, evaluate ideas and determine which is the best.
7. Don't set too short a time limit.
8. Make brainstorming part of the group's strategy.

From A. Osborn, *Applied Imagination: Principles and Procedures of Creative Thinking* (New York: Scribner, 1953), 300–301.

The leader of a brainstorming group should create an open atmosphere that encourages creativity and spontaneity. Therefore it is important that the leader be a person of high energy who responds enthusiastically to new ideas. The leader should provide reinforcement and support to all members and encourage the members to keep contributing if they hit a dry spell. For example, the leader can use prompts such as these: "Let's generate at least two more ideas." "We've done great up to now—let's try one more time to generate some really innovative ideas."

Group members, as well as the leader, must not express disapproval (communicated by comments or looks) of any items until all ideas have been generated. Once the group has run out of ideas or time, the results should be evaluated. During this stage, members should work together to appraise each and every idea. The goal is to determine which idea or ideas merit more attention. It is appropriate to discard ideas that are unfeasible or weak, to improve undeveloped ideas, to consolidate related ideas, and to discuss further the most promising ones.

## Brainstorming via Technology

In Chapter 15, we discussed ways newsgroups allow groups of individuals to communicate with each other over the Internet to share and obtain information on a variety of subjects. Similarly, groups can use electronic brainstorming, in which a group generates ideas, solutions, or strategies and inputs their thoughts onto the computer, displaying them either via a liquid crystal display (LCD) projector on a large screen to the entire group or to individual computer screens in a lab, in separate rooms, or at another location. This high-tech approach uses the same principles that face-to-face brainstorming uses except all the ideas are input on a computer instead of being written on a chalkboard or notepad. Advantages of this method include the speed of recording and the ability for group members to send their ideas simultaneously.

Another advantage according to the research is that electronic brainstorming generates more ideas than traditional brainstorming approaches.[19] It has been speculated that the increase in ideas and contributions by group members is because of

## MAKING CONNECTIONS for Success

### Stormin' with the Brain

To begin this activity, the instructor should divide the class into groups of four to six students each. Each group should select one of the following four topics:

Ways to increase diversity on campus

Incorporating technology into the classroom

Ideas to improve local parks

Ways to improve Internet safety for underage users

Before the group discusses the agreed-on topic, each individual group member should create a list of ideas. Then the group as a whole should spend approximately ten minutes generating a list of ideas on the same topic. Make sure the group adheres to the accompanying guidelines for productive brainstorming.

1. After the group has finished the brainstorming session, discuss the value of brainstorming.
2. What did you learn about brainstorming?

---

the anonymity of the person who is generating the idea.[20] Group members feel less pressure and less embarrassment about ideas that are later rejected. The ideas that are generated are considered not on the basis of who suggested them but solely on their merit and quality. Like traditional brainstorming, electronic brainstorming encourages group interaction by allowing individual group members to build on the ideas of others.

## ■■ Reaching Group Consensus

The goal of most groups is to arrive at decisions or solutions that are agreed on and acceptable to at least most of the group members, if not all of them. The process of reaching consensus assumes that all group members have been able to express how they feel and think about the alternatives and have been given equitable opportunities to influence the outcome. However, it is important that consensus should not come too quickly; if it does, the group is likely a victim of groupthink as introduced in Chapter 15. Consensus on controversial issues usually does not come easily. It requires a certain amount of patience and a willingness to look for areas of agreement. This, of course, can be very time consuming.

Is the time it takes to reach consensus worth the effort? It has been proven time after time that groups that use effective group discussion methods, such as open communication, come prepared to discuss, are willing to challenge ideas and evidence, and almost always arrive at better-quality decisions than individuals alone.[21] It has also been shown that groups that reach agreement regardless of the time it takes are more likely to take ownership of their decisions and maintain their agreement longer.[22]

Communication scholars Steven Beebe and John Masterson provide three recommendations for reaching consensus in groups:

1. Groups have a tendency to change topics and to get off track, so members should try to keep themselves oriented toward the group's goal. The reason groups often don't reach consensus is because they engage in discussing issues that are irrelevant to their goal.

2. Members should be other-oriented and sensitive to all ideas. Listen and do not constantly interrupt one another. Make a good faith effort to set aside your views and seek to understand others.

3. Promote group member interaction and dialogue. It is important that everyone feel that his or her voice is heard and that no one is withholding their views even when they disagree with others.[23]

# Managing Group Conflict

When you hear the word *conflict*, what comes to mind? For most people, it conjures up terms such as *argument, dislike, fight, stress, hate, competition, disagreement, hostility, discord, friction, disunity,* and so on. All of these words do relate to conflict. However, they illustrate only the negative side of the concept. After all, in U.S. society, most people value and stress the importance of agreement and getting along with others. However, our society also loves competition. Sayings such as "All's fair in love and war" or "Stick to your guns" are often cited as the American way. But the desires to get along with others and yet to beat them in competition contradict each other. The idea that if one person wins, another must lose is implanted in almost every American's mind early in life.

On the one hand, we would like to avoid conflict and preserve unity. On the other hand, we cannot experience the thrill of winning unless we enter into conflict. Is there any middle ground between these two polarities? Can conflict be resolved only by forcing someone to lose? Must conflict always hurt someone?

Whenever people come together to communicate, there is bound to be conflict. But conflict does not always have to be harmful. In fact, it can be productive and, if properly managed, can result in better decisions and solutions to problems.

## Conflict and Group Communication

Communication scholars William Wilmot and Joyce Hocker suggest that communication and conflict are related in the following ways: Communication behavior often *creates* conflict, communication behavior *reflects* conflict, and communication is the *vehicle* for the productive or destructive management of conflict.[24] *Conflict* was defined by Wilmot and Hocker in Chapter 14 as "an expressed struggle between at least two interdependent parties who perceive incompatible goals, scarce resources, and interference from others in achieving their goals."[25]

Effective group decision making and problem solving often depend on conflict and open disagreement. The benefits of group conflict, when it is understood and controlled, include a better understanding of group members and issues, better involvement and increased motivation, better decisions, and greater group cohesiveness. These benefits are more likely to occur when groups accept collaboration and compromise.

Of course, too much conflict can create unmanageable tension and heighten disagreement, resulting in personal attacks on individual group members. If personal attacks come to dominate meetings, they produce no benefits and usually lead to hurt feelings, withdrawal, and eventually the disbanding of the group.

In collaboration, negotiating and problem solving are used to find a solution that fully meets the needs of all parties involved in a group conflict. In other words, each party achieves its desired results. For example, suppose you are serving on a college curriculum committee in which the student members think that the general education course should be practical, whereas the faculty believes it should be theoretical. There is much discussion, but both sides eventually see the benefits of each view and agree that all the general education courses should include both practice and theory. The result is an ideal solution in which both students and faculty members win. The collaboration between the students and faculty generated by the conflict has resulted in a superior, integrated general education curriculum.

Compromise is a shared outcome. Compromise means that conflicting parties are willing to give up part of their position to arrive at an alternative that includes parts of both parties' original positions. Compromise implies giving up something to gain something more important, so both parties involved gain from the compromise. For example, a grading appeals committee made up of two students and four faculty members has been presented with an appeal. A student believes that he should have received an A, and the professor of the course insists that the student got what he earned—a C. After hearing both sides, one student and two faculty members on the committee believe that the student appealing should have received an A, whereas the other student and the other two faculty members believe that the C was appropriate. A deadlock must be resolved. Through compromise, the conflicting parties agree that the student should receive a B. Neither party got exactly what it wanted, but both can agree to the compromise. The positive outcomes of conflict, according to Gloria Galanes and Katherine Adams, are as follows:

1. Conflict can produce better understanding of both issues and people.
2. Conflict can increase member motivation.
3. Conflict can produce better decisions.
4. Conflict can produce greater cohesiveness among group members.[26]

## Managing Conflict

For groups to be successful, conflict must be perceived as beneficial. It should not be avoided. In fact, we suggest that it be encouraged as long as it is created in order to produce better group decisions.

One of the primary reasons for having small groups in the first place is the notion that two heads are better than one. We also know that when people get together to discuss issues, there is bound to be conflict. If conflict is inevitable and we know that it can be beneficial as well as harmful, how can we ensure that it will facilitate rather than inhibit? The answer is the use of conflict management strategies.

**Principled negotiation** is a procedure that helps group members negotiate consensus by collaboration through the expression of each different need and a search for alternatives to meet those needs.[27] It is referred to as "principled" because the procedure is based on ethical principles that encourage participants to be respectful and civilized toward one another. In other words, exchanging information by asking questions instead of making demands or taking a rigid position on differences will aid in producing an agreed-on outcome. Participants must take into account other participants' views and consider them in the way they'd like their own views to be considered.

A committee consisting of management and labor discusses a benefit issue in a conference setting. To gain consensus, members who are not in agreement negotiate until agreement is reached. They do this by identifying different needs and searching for alternatives to meet those needs.

Of course, not every disagreement can be resolved, and at times other approaches might have to be taken. To resolve conflict, participants must be willing to communicate about their differences and must want to find a resolution to their differences.

## Ethical Behavior and Conflict

Galanes and Adams suggest that using ethical behaviors during a conflict situation creates a better understanding of the issues and increased cohesiveness while at the same time minimizing destructive outcomes, such as hurt feelings and personal attacks.[28] They have listed a number of helpful suggestions to aid individuals on how to behave ethically during conflicts:

1. Express disagreements openly and honestly. It is important to get disagreements on the table for discussion.

■ **principled negotiation** A procedure that helps group members negotiate consensus by collaboration through the expression of each differing need and a search for alternatives to meet those needs.

2. Stick to the issues. Be direct, and get to the point.

3. Use rhetorical sensitivity when presenting your disagreements. Don't simply put down others' ideas or views.

4. Criticize the idea and not the person.

5. Base disagreements on solid evidence and good reasoning, not on rumor, emotions, or unsubstantiated information.

6. Be receptive to disagreements. Don't become defensive simply because someone disagrees with you. Keep an open mind and listen carefully.

7. Always remain calm even if someone attacks you. Take a reasoned approach, and do not take the attack personally.

8. Look for ways to integrate ideas and to negotiate differences whenever possible.

# ■ Evaluating Small-Group Performance

It is important that groups and group members understand that they are responsible for their successes and their failures. It is the responsibility of the group to fix its own problems or at least attempt to fix them. Of course, when a group cannot resolve a problem or if there is a split in the group, sometimes an outside negotiator is necessary, but that should occur only after all other efforts have failed.

To ensure success, every group must periodically evaluate its effectiveness. The evaluation can take place at any time or at the end of one task and before another begins.

Evaluation is also important in classroom exercises. As students learn about group communication, they need their instructor's feedback and also to evaluate themselves. Such self-evaluation should consider the following questions:

1. Are we using our time efficiently? If not, why not?

2. Does everyone have an opportunity to participate?

3. Are some people dominating the discussion?

4. Are people listening to what others are saying?

5. Is each person bringing adequate information and research to the discussion?

6. Is the atmosphere free from personal conflict?

7. Does the group communication stay within the agenda?

8. Are the members happy about what is taking place in the discussion? If not, why not?

9. Do we set realistic goals for our meetings?

10. Do we get things accomplished? If not, why not?

For an evaluation to produce results, its findings must be made known to all members of the group. A crucial requirement for such sharing is a nonthreatening atmosphere. The leader and all the members must be willing to examine the situation without becoming defensive. The group's success is related to each member's willingness to work and cooperate with the others. If the group is not getting its job done, or if its members are unhappy, corrective steps must be taken. Otherwise, people will lose interest in the group, and it may disintegrate or become unproductive and dysfunctional.

# Summary

Leadership is the process of influencing behavior that clarifies a group's purpose or guides a group to achieve its goals. A person who is assigned or selected or who emerges from a group to guide or provide direction toward reaching a group's goal is a leader. Leaders are responsible for getting the group to accomplish its task and to ensure that group members find personal satisfaction in working together.

Successful groups depend on group members performing a variety of roles, for example, group task roles such as initiator–contributor, information seeker, information giver, opinion seeker, opinion giver, elaborator, coordinator, orienter, evaluator/critic, energizer, recorder, and tester of agreements. Group building and maintenance roles help to develop a group's social atmosphere and include encouragers, harmonizers, compromisers, gatekeepers, standard setters, followers, and feeling expressers. Sometimes, group members display self-centered roles such as aggressors, blockers, recognition seekers, self-confessors, buffoons, dominators, help seekers, and withdrawers, all of which can be counterproductive and destructive behaviors.

The process of planning and conducting meetings is an important step in reaching a successful outcome for any group. Most groups should use an agenda or list of topics to be discussed to ensure order and to save time. The first step in the process of decision making is to determine the problem or topic, which then should be stated in one of four types of questions: question of fact, question of interpretation, question of value, or question of policy.

When a group hits a snag or becomes bogged down, it might try brainstorming, which is a technique that if used correctly can help the group to generate new ideas and produce creative approaches that they might not ordinarily produce. Groups can create conflicts, as is true any time two or more people come together. However, groups that are competently trained know how to use principled negotiation, a procedure that helps group members negotiate consensus by collaboration in order to look for alternatives to meet differing needs. To ensure continuous success and progress, groups should do a periodic self-analysis and look for areas in which to improve.

# Discussion Starters

1. Describe a competent leader.
2. Who make better leaders: men or women? Explain.
3. Describe a competent group member.
4. How would you handle a group member who was acting the role of a buffoon?
5. How would you get withdrawn group members back into a discussion without embarrassing them?
6. Set up your organizational strategy for solving the following problem: What should be the role and responsibility of the university in monitoring cultural discrimination?
7. Describe a situation in which use of brainstorming would be appropriate.
8. Determine the criteria that you think would effectively evaluate a group's behavior.

# Notes

1. C. Larson and M. LaFasto, *Teamwork: What Must Go Right, What Can Go Wrong* (Newbury Park, CA: Sage, 1989).

2. F. E. Fiedler, *A Theory of Leadership Effectiveness* (New York: McGraw-Hill, 1967); and P. Weissenberg and M. H. Kavanagh, "The Independence of Initiating Structure and Consideration: A Review of the Evidence," *Personnel Psychology* 25 (1972): 119–30.

3. M. Conlin, "Champions of Innovation," *Business Week,* June, 2006, 19–26.

4. R. K. White and R. Lippitt, *Autocracy and Democracy: An Experimental Inquiry* (New York: Harper & Row, 1960), 26–27.

5. L. G. Bolman and T. E. Deal, *Reframing Organizations: Artistry, Choice, and Leadership,* 2nd ed. (San Francisco: Jossey-Bass, 1997); and G. Morgan, *Images of Organization,* 2nd ed. (Thousand Oaks, CA: Sage, 1997).

6. R. K. White and R. Lippitt, "Leader Behavior and Member Reaction in Three 'Social Climates,'" in *Group Dynamics: Research and Theory,* 2nd ed., eds. D. Cartwright and A. Zander (New York: Harper & Row, 1960), 527–53; L. P. Bradford and R. Lippitt, "Building a Democratic Work Group," *Personnel* 22 (1945): 142–52; and W. M. Fox, "Group Reaction to Two Types of Conference Leadership," *Human Relations* 10 (1957): 279–89.

7. M. Conlin, "Champions of Innovation," 20.

8. A. B. Gershenoff and R. J. Foti, "Leader Emergence and Gender Roles in All-Female Groups: A Critical Examination," *Small Group Research* 34 (April 2003), 170–96.

9. J. A. Kolb, "Are We Still Stereotyping Leadership? A Look at Gender and Other Predictors of Leader Emergence," *Small Group Research* 28 (August 1997), 370–93.

10. S. B. Shimanoff and M. M. Jenkins, "Leadership and Gender: Challenging Assumptions and Recognizing Resources," in *Small Group Communication: Theory and Practice,* 8th ed., eds. R. Y. Hirokawa, R. S. Cathcart, L. A. Samovar, and L. Henman (Los Angeles: Roxbury, 2003), 184–98.

11. M. Loden, *Feminine Leadership or How to Succeed in Business Without Being One of the Boys* (New York: Times Books, 1985).

12. A. H. Eagly and B. T. Johnson, "Gender and Leadership Style: A Meta-Analysis," *Psychological Bulletin* 108 (1990): 233–56.

13. D. Forsyth, M. Heiney, and S. Wright, "Biases in Appraisal of Women Leaders," *Group Dynamics: Theory, Research, and Practices* 1 (1997): 98–103; S. Shackelford, W. Wood, and S. Worchel, "Behavioral Styles and the Influence of Women in Mixed-Sex Groups," *Social Psychology* 59 (1996): 284–93; and A. Eagly, S. Karau, and M. Makhijani, "Gender and the Effectiveness of Leaders: A Meta-Analysis," *Journal of Personality and Social Psychology* 117 (1995): 125–45.

14. K. D. Benne and P. Sheats, "Functional Roles of Group Members," *Journal of Social Issues* 4 (1948): 41–49.

15. R. V. Harnack, T. B. Fest, and B. S. Jones, *Group Discussion: Theory and Technique,* 2nd ed. (Englewood Cliffs, NJ: Prentice-Hall, 1997), 153–54.

16. J. Dewey, *How We Think* (Lexington, MA: Heath, 1933).

17. R. Y. Hirokawa, "Consensus Group Decision-Making, Quality of Decision and Group Satisfaction: An Attempt to Sort 'Fact' from 'Fiction,' " *Central States Speech Journal* 33 (1982): 407–15; and "Why Informed Groups Make Faulty Decisions: An Investigation of Possible Interaction-Based Explanation," *Small Group Behavior* 18 (1987): 3–29.

18. R. L. Firestein, "Effects of Creative Problem-Solving Training on Communication Behavior in Small Groups," *Small Group Research* 21 (November, 1990): 507–21.

19. M. C. Roy, S. Gauvin, and M. Limayem, "Electronic Group Brainstorming: The Role of Feedback on Productivity," *Small Group Research* 27 (1996): 215–47.

20. J. J. Sosik, B. J. Avolio, and S. S. Kahai, "Inspiring Group Creativity: Comparing Anonymous and Identified Electronic Brainstorming," *Small Group Research* 29 (1998) 3–31; and W. H. Cooper, R. B. Gallupe, S. Pollard, and J. Cadsby, "Some Liberating Effects of Anonymous Electronic Brainstorming," *Small Group Research* 29 (1998): 147–77.

21. R. Y. Hirokawa, "Consensus Group," 407–15.

22. R. S. DeStephen and R. Y. Hirokawa, "Small Group Consensus: Stability of Group Support of the Decision, Task Process, and Group Relationships," *Small Group Behavior* 19 (1988): 227–39.

23. S. A. Beebe and J. T. Masterson, *Communicating in Small Groups,* 8th ed. (Boston: Allyn and Bacon, 2006), 193.

24. W. Wilmot and J. Hocker, *Interpersonal Conflict,* 7th ed. (New York: McGraw-Hill, 2007).

25. Ibid.

26. G. J. Galanes and K. Adams, *Effective Group Communication Theory and Practice,* 12th ed. (New York: McGraw-Hill, 2007), 360–61.

27. R. Fisher and W. Ury, *Getting to Yes: Negotiating Agreement without Giving In* (Boston: Houghton Mifflin, 1981).

28. G. J. Galanes and K. Adams, *Effective Groups Communication,* 377–379.

# Employment Interviewing: Preparing for Your Future

"You never get a second chance to make a first impression."

# This appendix will help you:

- **Know** what you should be doing to prepare before the employment interview.

- **Use** the Internet to locate jobs, send your résumé, research organizations, provide yourself with interview advice, locate job openings, and get a job.

- **Describe** the qualities that you possess that employers seek in applicants.

- **Develop** a résumé that will highlight or illustrate your competencies and experiences for prospective employers.

- **Interview** effectively and competently to ensure that you convey to potential employers your talents and skills and why they should hire you.

## Making everyday connections

Rachelle, a mother of two children, started college before having children, but she and her husband decided that she should put her college education on hold in order to raise their children. The children are now in junior and senior high school, and Rachelle has gone back to college and is about to complete her degree in communication studies. Because she doesn't know about all the job opportunities that are available for communication majors, she turns to the Internet for help.

Bill, who is graduating in May, is looking for a public relations position with a major corporation. He has called Mr. Muller, the personnel director of S & S Enterprises, to discuss his chances of being hired by that firm.

Liz is looking for an internship in marketing in order to get some experience before she begins the real job hunt. She has contacted several different marketing firms through her university internship office and is ready to be interviewed.

Sam needs to earn a few dollars in order to make it through college. He decides to get a part-time job and is scheduled to interview with a local clothing store. ■

### Questions to think about

- Which of the individuals above comes closest to representing you and your employment future?

- When should you start preparing for your career? Now? In your junior year? In your senior year?

- What is the value in doing an internship?

T he students in the above examples will participate in interviews that will affect the rest of their lives. It is never too early to prepare for your future, whether you are a first-year student or a senior who is about to graduate. The important part of preparing for your future is getting started, and those who start thinking and preparing for their future early will likely be the best prepared. In this appendix, we examine what you need to do to prepare for the employment interview—what you can expect to encounter and how you can make the best impression in the interview.[1]

# ■ Preparing for Your Career

The purpose of this book is to help you with the following skills: speaking, organizing, critical thinking, researching, persuading, informing, listening, discussing, making decisions, solving problems, and using nonverbal and verbal communication. Another purpose is to help you develop your leadership and interpersonal skills. After you have completed this course, it will then be up to you to continue developing each skill throughout your education and your lifetime. Because employment interviews are among the most important interpersonal communication events of your life, we have devoted this appendix to them.

Most of you taking this course are probably just beginning your college education. Whether you are a recent high school graduate or have returned to school after pursuing other interests like Rachelle, the following pages on employment interviews will give you important information that will aid you in preparing for your future after graduation. Although graduation and hunting for a full-time job may seem far away, your preparation for them should begin immediately. Don't wait until your senior year; that could be too late. You can begin by attending your university, college, or community's career day programs. Such programs bring together undergraduates, graduate students, and alumni with employers from government, private enterprise, and nonprofit organizations. It is a time for everyone—even first-year students—to

## MAKING CONNECTIONS for Success

### Thinking about Your Future

Refer back to the opening examples, and think about what each person must be able to demonstrate in order to land a job. SKILLS! That one word means a lot to your future. The recurring theme among the experts we surveyed is an emphasis on skills and competencies, rather than on completing specific studies.

Your major alone might not make a decisive difference in your future, but the skills you master and the way you communicate them to others can carry you through a lifetime of careers.

1. What is the message in the statements?
2. What advice would you give to Rachelle, Bill, Liz, and Sam as they prepare themselves for their interviews?

Some exceptional sources that you might consider to help you answer the above questions and prepare for your job interview are: P. Klaus, *Brag: The Art of Tooting Your Own Horn Without Blowing It* (New York: Warner Books, 2003), D. Bolles, *What Color Is Your Parachute?* (Berkeley, CA: Ten Speed Press, 2006), and Bolles also has a website you should consider: www.jobhuntersbible.com.

find out what organizations are looking for in potential employees. If you haven't already started to prepare for your career or first interview, you should begin now.

# ■ Career Research on the Internet

One of the most valuable tools available in preparing for the employment interview is the Internet. The Internet will allow you to research every aspect of the employment interview. For example, you can learn how to prepare for the interview, write a résumé, create an electronic résumé, research organizations, find job opportunities, find out what questions are commonly asked in interviews, and even get advice on what to wear to an interview. Most colleges and universities have a career and placement center that you can visit in person or contact through their home page. The career or placement center's home page can be an extremely valuable source of information. The University of Nebraska's (UNL) Career Services, for example, has one of the most up-to-date home pages on the Internet (see Figure A.1). Its Internet address is www.unl.edu/careers, and it provides information pertaining to almost every aspect of careers and the employment interview. You can click any of the boxed items to explore services and resources. For example, the Job Search Preparation area leads to information on how to search for a job on the Internet, job search strategies, résumé tips and a sample résumé, how to write cover letters and sample cover letters, whom to give as references, how to create a portfolio, information on organizations, and interviewing tips. The Internet is an incredibly valuable tool in preparing for your future career.

You should check with your college or university's career and placement center for its Internet address. You can also access a search engine and type in the word *jobs,*

## ■ FIGURE A.1  The University of Nebraska's Career Services Web Page

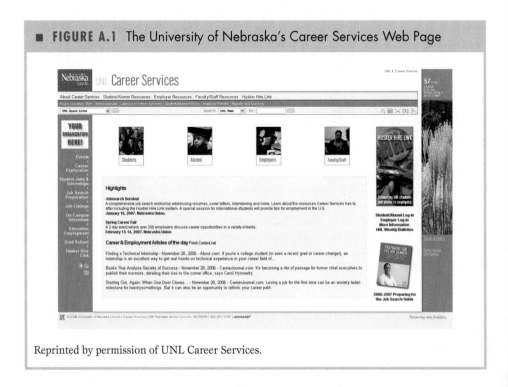

Reprinted by permission of UNL Career Services.

*career,* or *employment.* With the click of a mouse, you will find a vast array of information about employers, job opportunities, and almost anything else you want to know about getting a job or starting your career.

# ■ Choosing a Career

Choosing a career might be the most important decision you will ever make. An estimated 10,000 days of your life are at stake; that's about how much time the average person spends on the job. According to some experts, there are a minimum of 42,000 career options from which college graduates can choose. Every October, *U.S. News & World Report* describes "Best Jobs for the Future." This is a must-see resource for every college student.

Studying this section will not guarantee you the perfect job after graduation, but it should help improve your chances of getting one. There are approximately 150 million employment interviews conducted in the United States each year resulting in hundreds of thousands of jobs filled. To compete successfully for available jobs requires planning and preparation. Getting an early start will allow you to take advantage of all the opportunities your college or university provides in the way of extracurricular activities, which will help you develop a strong, diverse background for meeting your career objectives.

# ■ Qualities Employers Seek

Demographics of the U.S. workplace are changing more rapidly than ever as we move into the twenty-first century. Cultural diversity is more prevalent for most organizations because we have become a global economy. Women now make up more than 50 percent of the workforce, and there has been rapid growth in the Hispanic and Asian American populations as well. Today, the workforce in many organizations consists of women and men of diverse cultures, languages, and ethnic backgrounds.

During the past few decades, many organizations eliminated millions of middle-management positions. Thus advancement positions in many organizations are limited and difficult to get. In the past, college graduates who started on the ground level of an organization were almost guaranteed that working hard would move them up the organizational ladder to higher management positions. Now the higher management jobs are fewer, and those that are available are very competitive.

Charles Stewart and William Cash, Jr., communication scholars and authors of a top-selling interviewing text, suggest ten universal skills and attitudes that are essential to work in the twenty-first century:

1. You will need to be able to deal comfortably with numbers.
2. You will need to be computer literate.
3. You will need to be customer- and quality-oriented.
4. You will need to have a global and diverse perspective.
5. You will need to speak a second language.
6. You will need strong interpersonal skills.
7. You will need to deal with change and job ambiguity.

**8.** You will need to nourish a willingness to learn.

**9.** You will need to take on a team perspective.

**10.** You will need to be a problem solver.[2]

Dr. Larry Routh (email address: lrouth1@unl.edu), Director of Career Services at the University of Nebraska at Lincoln, suggests that students get as much experience in team building and working in teams as possible.[3] According to Routh, companies are no longer looking exclusively for people with supervisory skills as much as they are looking for individuals who can work with others. One company recruiter asks students the following question: "When you work as a part of a team, what unique role do you play?" Routh said, "Hiring people who are team players is important to many companies who have downsized and have fewer management positions, because they are much more team oriented." For example, one senior student answered the question by indicating that she was the person who brought the group back to task by clarifying and pulling the group ideas to the objective. Dr. Routh suggested that his own strength when working on a team was the ability to brainstorm ideas. Routh's strength is quite different from the senior student's, but both are important to team success. What is your role when working with others? Is it leading, organizing, brainstorming, or something else? You need to know what your strengths are.

Internships are also important. Dr. Routh suggests that students get involved in internships that are related to the jobs they will seek after graduation. In fact, in the most recent interview with him, he re-emphasized the value and importance of internships in today's job market. He says that students who have had internships can say that they have done the job or similar work, thus giving them a better chance at getting a job than those with no experience.

Almost every career requires skills such as writing, speaking, reading, listening, decision making, researching, reasoning, creativity, persuasion, leadership, interpersonal communication, and organization. In addition, a number of characteristics may be important for specific jobs: achievement, ambition, assertiveness, competitiveness, dependability, initiative, listening, motivation, oral communication, people orientation, responsibility, and responsiveness.[4] The way you acquire these skills and behaviors is, to a great extent, up to you. Without them, no matter how bright and knowledgeable you might be, landing a job will be extremely difficult if not impossible. The most likely way to obtain these skills and behaviors is through courses, reading, internships, part-time or full-time employment, extracurricular activities, and participation in communication functions. Acquiring most of them requires training and practice under a qualified instructor.

Knowing what an employer is looking for in a potential employee can help an applicant to prepare for an interview. Most employers that we have talked with emphasize the ability to communicate. Can the applicants speak clearly? Can they articulate what kind of person they believe themselves to be? In what kinds of work situations do they perform well? What are their strengths and weaknesses? Employers want to know about the personal qualities of the individual, so they ask questions to draw the applicant out and reveal whether the applicant has a sense of self. They look for an ability to verbalize an idea in clear, simple, understandable language. They also look for the ability to listen attentively and then the ability to respond to an idea or thought.

They also look for creativity. Is the applicant spontaneous? Some recruiters will ask "off the wall" questions just to see if this "throws" an applicant. How does an

## MAKING Technology CONNECTIONS

### Applying for a Job Online!

Most companies now require all applicants to apply online. Many companies or organizations will not interview until an online application is completed. You have two tasks: (1) Go to Riley Guide at www.rileyguide.com/eresume.html. There you will find many excellent suggestions for applying online; (2) Search at least one major corporation, for example, Newell Rubbermaid, Google, Xerox, Microsoft, Proctor & Gamble, General Electric, or any other company or organization that interests you to determine how they want you to apply for a job. Go to their website and look for their career link. There you will find all kinds of information as well as application forms.

1. What did you learn about seeking employment, preparing and submitting a résumé, a cover letter, or following online application instructions?
2. Did most companies want your résumé electronically or do you have to fill out information about your education and experience online?
3. What questions did you find on the company or organization site that you were required to answer?

---

applicant respond in these tough situations? Can the applicant be creative with the answers? This is very important to most employers, because in business situations with customers, employees often have to respond to sudden changes and unfamiliar problems. Employers need to know whether an applicant can handle such situations. What employers look for most in applicants are personal qualities such as assertiveness, self-motivation, ambition, and a competitive instinct. Applicants should be high achievers and have a willingness to work hard. Employers say that they can usually learn whether applicants have these qualities by how they present themselves and by the types of activities or jobs they have held while in school. Much of this information is found on the job application and résumé.

# ■ Preparation for an Interview

Preparation for a job interview takes planning and some thought about what will be expected of you as an applicant. Initial job interviews average only twenty to thirty minutes in length—a short time in comparison to the time you have spent earning a college degree. Yet these are probably the most important minutes you will spend in determining your job future. You would be surprised to learn how many applicants fail to plan adequately. Instead, they enter the interview saying essentially, "Here I am. Now what?" This gives the impression that they are indifferent, an impression that is seldom dispelled in the course of the interview. Ensuring that an impression of indifference isn't left with the employer is up to you. Make sure that you are prepared and that you present a positive picture of yourself.

## ■■ Writing a Résumé

A **résumé** (sometimes referred to as a vita) is a written document that briefly and accurately describes an individual's personal, educational, and professional qualifications and experiences. A well-written résumé increases a person's chances of making

■ **résumé** A written document that briefly and accurately describes an individual's personal, educational, and professional qualifications and experiences.

## What Every College Student Should Know to Prepare for the Job Interview

To learn firsthand what corporations are looking for today when they hire a college graduate, Seiler interviewed Gary Danek, who retired as an account executive with Procter & Gamble (P&G), a Fortune 500 corporation (www.pg.com). Before retiring, Danek had been with P&G for more than thirty-five years and had interviewed hundreds of college students. The Seiler and Danek interview is available on our website at www.ablongman.com/seiler7e.

1. On the basis of what you have read in the interview transcript, what could you do to make yourself a better candidate for a job?
2. If you were to give one piece of advice to someone based on the Danek interview, what would that advice be?
3. If you could ask Mr. Danek a question about what you could do to better prepare yourself for the job interview, what would that question be? Email your question to Bill Seiler (bseiler@unl.edu), and he will forward it to Mr. Danek for his response. Your question will be answered as soon as possible.

a good impression. A poorly written résumé can seriously jeopardize a person's chances, even though he or she may be well qualified. The résumé should clearly detail the experiences the applicant has had and demonstrate that he or she is an individual who takes action. For example, an assertive person might say, "I can do these things" and "I decided on this course of action," whereas a more passive person might say, "These are the experiences I have had." Employers are looking for people who can demonstrate that they are active and that they can get things done.

Many companies are now requesting that résumés be written so they can be scanned into a computer database. This means that résumés must include key words that describe your competencies and skills. The employer is then able quickly and efficiently to search thousands of résumés for certain key words that describe and narrow down a long list of potentially qualified applicants for a specific job. So that a résumé can be scanned, it must be typed neatly on high-quality white bond paper. You cannot use boldface type, underlining, or bullets if a résumé is to be scanned.

The personal résumé may highlight work experience (see Figure A.2) or skills (see Figure A.3). Many companies also require applicants to complete an application form, which requests personal data (name, address, phone number, social security number, citizenship, and whether you have ever been convicted of a felony), job interests (position desired, data available, and salary desired), educational training (high school, college, or graduate school), references (name, occupation, phone number, and address), employment history (name, address, dates of employment, salary, positions held, and reason for leaving), and possibly voluntary information (sex, race, or ethnic identification; military service record, if you are a veteran or disabled veteran; whether you have a disability).

A résumé is an extremely powerful form of communication. Because it represents an applicant, it must be accurate, complete, and neat. The contents and layouts of résumés vary as widely as the number of individuals who apply for jobs. A general rule, and the safest, is to *keep it simple, limit it to one or two pages, and list items within each section beginning with the most current one.* Employers are busy and do not have time to read lengthy, involved reports.

Most résumés include the following sections: introductory information, career objective, educational training, work experiences, extracurricular activities, and references, which is an optional section. The *introductory information* section should include the applicant's name, address, phone number, and email address. As an applicant, you are not required to provide information that might be used in a discriminatory way. This includes your age, sex, marital status, race, religion, and other

**■ FIGURE A.2** Self-Prepared or Personal Résumé
Emphasizing Work Experience

This figure illustrates a résumé format that many students use. The résumé layout is fairly standard, but it may vary depending on the work experiences of the individual.

**Jo Ann Doe**
712 Garfield Street, Apt.2-A
Lincoln, Nebraska 00000
402/555-9797
jdoe@yahoo.com

**OBJECTIVE**

An administrative assistant position in a federal, state, or city government agency where I can utilize my public relations skills.

**EXPERIENCE**

*Assistant Campaign Manager:* Senator Sally Jones, Lincoln, Nebraska
(July 2005–November 2006)
   Directed and coordinated all public activities.
   Arranged and scheduled personal appearances, debtes, and media releases.
   Purchased, designed, and supervised the development of campaign materials.
   Recruited, trained, and supervised community volunteer groups.
   Supervised a staff of 16 community volunteers.

*Staff Assistant as an Intern:* United Volunteer Agency, Lincoln, Nebraska
(December 2002–June 2005)
   Communicated the scope of Agency programs to Lincoln area businesses and
       community groups.
   Prepared Agency filmstrips, brochures, and news releases.
   Conducted public relations information sessions.

*Legislative Assistant:* Nebraska Legislative Session, Lincoln, Nebraska
(July 2000 to December 2001)
   Collected, compiled, and released information briefs and legislative action
       profiles to public news media.
   Typed and edited legislative bills.

**EDUCATION**

The University of Nebraska, Lincoln, Nebraska (2002–2006)
Bachelor of Arts Degree. Communication Studies and Journalism,
   Grade Point Average: 3.75/4.00.

**EDUCATIONAL HIGHLIGHTS**

Outstanding Senior Award, Creative Writing Award, Communication Club Secretary,
Phi Delta Kappa Vice President.

**Related Course Work**

Public Relations and Publicity          Survey of Mass Media
Social Political Communication          Interviewing
Public Speaking                         Advertising Principles
Federal Grant Development               Public Opinion

Available Immediately

References: Upon request (This is optional and may or may not be included.)

■ **FIGURE A.3** Self-Prepared or Personal Résumé Emphasizing Skills

This figure illustrates a résumé that emphasizes a person's skills. The résumé layout is fairly standard, but it may vary depending on the work experiences and skills of the individual.

**Robert L. Smith**
1525 East Center Street
Los Angeles, California 00000
213/555-9797
rsmith@hotmail.com

| | |
|---|---|
| **OBJECTIVE** | To help a retail company provide high customer satisfaction while managing merchandise efficiently in an entry-level management position. |
| **Skills** | • Resolved customer problems in retail merchandising<br>• Organized product floor for customer convenience<br>• Successfully dealt with wholesalers<br>• Organized and maintained inventories<br>• Completed college courses in management, personnel, finance, statistics, and marketing |
| **EDUCATION** | University of Southern California, Los Angles, California, Bachelor of Science Degree: Business, May 2006, Management |
| **HONORS** | Academic Scholarships, Delta Mu Delta (Business Honorary) |
| **ACTIVITIES and MEMBERSHIPS** | President of Delta Mu Delta; Student Senator; Youth Leader of 30 member church youth group |
| **EXPERIENCE** | B.C. PRINTING, Los Angeles *Graphic Arts*–Delivery Person<br>• Mastered all aspects of prepress operations<br>• Effectively dealt with and resolved conflicts<br>• Oversaw various camera procedures including working with numerous types of film and preparing press plates |
| **January 97–98** | QUALITY PRESS, IMC., Los Angeles, *Internship Graphic Arts–Delivery Person*<br>• Demonstrated ability to serve and communicate with customers in a diverse office supply operation<br>• Organized and maintained product floor and inventory |
| **Additional Information** | Paid 100% of college expenses<br>Worked to support wife and child while attending college<br>Computer training includes Basic, Cobol, Assembler, and Pascal |
| **Available** | Immediately |
| **Reference** | Available on request (optional) |

data as set forth by the Title VII Equal Employment Opportunity Act of 1972 and other affirmative action laws. The inclusion of such facts in a résumé is up to the applicant, but it is generally advised that they be omitted.

Many employment counselors recommend that a brief *career objective* be stated on the résumé immediately following the introductory information. The objective should be as specific as possible. For example:

> My long-term objective is to become a public relations director in either a major corporation or agency. My immediate goal is to obtain experience in sales, advertising, or marketing related to that long-term objective.

Such a statement can help a potential employer understand the applicant's goals and assess whether those goals relate to a particular job opening or company.

In the *educational training* section of the résumé, the applicant should list colleges and universities attended, degrees conferred, dates of degrees, majors, minors, and special major subjects. Scholarships should be listed, and some statement about grade achievement may be included, although it is not required.

The *work experience* section should include paid and unpaid jobs held, the dates they were held, and their locations. If the applicant has held numerous part-time jobs, only a few of the most important, most recent, and most relevant jobs should be listed. Other job experience can always be discussed at the interview if it is appropriate to do so.

In the *extracurricular activities* section, the applicant should list all offices held, all social and professional organizations that he or she was involved in, and any athletic participation. This section demonstrates the applicant's outside interests; well-roundedness; and social, leadership, and organizational skills. Such information is less important for experienced or older applicants who have demonstrated similar skills in other areas.

The *reference* section is optional and should simply state that the applicant will provide references on request. In preparation, you might make a list of people who are familiar with your work experience and professors in your major field or with whom you have taken several courses. Even though you might not be planning to apply for a job now, it is wise to get to know your professors and to make sure

## MAKING CONNECTIONS for Success

### References

Make a written list of at least three people who could write a letter of recommendation for you. Do not include relatives or friends. After each name on your list, answer the following questions:

**1.** Why is this person an appropriate reference for me?
**2.** What does this person know about me, my competencies, and my ability to succeed?

Share your completed list of references and information with your teacher, a career counselor, or a person who could advise you as to the appropriateness of your choices.

## MAKING Technology CONNECTIONS

### Find Résumé Guidelines on the Internet

**www.rileyguide.com/letters.html**
The Riley Guide: Résumés and Cover Letters is an extremely helpful guide that discusses the myths about résumés, tells why an Internet résumé is useful, helps you prepare your résumé for the Internet, gives suggestions about posting your résumé, and provide resources for writing your résumé.

**www.provenresumes.com**
This site provides free résumés and job search workshops; it also includes a quiz to rate your résumé.

**www.unl.edu/careers/prepare/resumes.html**
Tips and guidelines are provided by the University of Nebraska's Career Services.

Other sites to consider are: www.careerbuilders.com, www.hotjobs.com, www.flipdog.com, www.careerlab.com, and www.joboptions.com.

that they get to know you. Find appropriate times (office hours, perhaps) and reasons (discussion of a paper or an assignment) to visit with your professors so they become acquainted with you. Most professors enjoy meeting their students. Use common sense, and don't overstay your visits. Professors will find it easier to write a letter of recommendation for you if they know who you are, and the letter will be more personal and believable.

Never put a person's name on a reference list unless you have his or her permission to do so. When asking individuals to write references for you, be prepared to hand them a copy of your résumé and to tell them what kind of job you are seeking. Contacting people to write letters of recommendation should be done as professionally and efficiently as possible. Remember that you are requesting someone to take time to help you. Because most people enjoy helping others, you should never be afraid to ask for a reference.

After you write your résumé, proofread it carefully for errors and omissions. Then ask a counselor in the career and placement office or a professor to suggest improvements. If you follow these simple steps, your completed résumé should be acceptable.

## ◼◼ Emailing Your Résumé to the Employer

Here are some suggestions for when you email your résumé to a company or organization and you are not using their online application process.

1. Whenever possible send your résumé to a specific person. Determining to whom to send your résumé might require some research, but the effort of locating a specific individual is well worth it, because you will more likely get a response than if you address it to the company's personnel office or human resource department.

2. Your email message should introduce yourself and explain why you are sending your résumé. The email in this case would be similar to what you would write in a cover letter sent via the post office. It should be brief, usually no more than three or four short paragraphs, and never more than one page. It should be neat, contain no spelling or grammatical errors, be professional in appearance, and easy to read. There are many excellent websites that provide help and suggestions for preparing and developing cover letters and résumés that are listed in the Making Technology Connections box in the previous section.

3. According to *The Riley Guide* you have 15 to 20 seconds to get someone's attention using email. In that time, you have to convince the recipient to (1) open your email, (2) read your message, and (3) not delete your email. Do this incorrectly, get in the wrong mailbox, or make someone's job difficult, and even the best résumé in the world from the most qualified individual will be trashed.

4. Remember it takes very little effort to delete an email message. Don't give someone a reason to trash you! Make sure you double-check everything before you send it.

## ◼◼ Searching the Job Market

Getting a job requires motivation, energy, hard work, and preparation. Even an applicant with superb qualifications faces tremendous competition for the best positions. According to placement service records, the average applicant spends only about three to ten hours a week searching for employment, but the person who is highly motivated will treat the search as if it were a job itself. The more time a person spends searching, the sooner and more likely he or she will be hired.

Newspaper want ads, professional magazines, placement services, former teachers, and people working in jobs you are interested in can all be good sources of job leads. However, the most productive approach to locating jobs is networking. **Networking** is the systematic contacting of people who can provide information about available jobs or who can offer jobs. Relatives, friends, classmates, colleagues, and people at social and professional gatherings are all potential sources of information. If someone does not know of any job openings himself or herself, ask if he or she knows of anyone who might. Then contact that person. In this way, your network expands from one person to another, and you gain information from each new contact. The more people you know, the better your chances are of being interviewed and the greater your opportunity for employment.

Career fairs have become very popular in recent years as a means for college students and others to learn about jobs and about the companies who are offering them. Most college campuses or the communities in which colleges and universities are located hold career fairs. They are excellent for networking as well as for making contacts with organizations for internships. Contact your career services office at your college or university and ask when the next career fair will be in your area. You should attend as many career fairs as time permits and you should begin going to them as soon as possible. You don't have to wait until your senior year to attend a career fair. By making contact with a company early in your education, you can establish a relationship with that company as well as be in the best position for getting an internship or a job after graduation.

## Researching the Company via the Internet

Before arriving for an interview, you should know the full name of the company; background information on the company's history; where its headquarters, plants, offices, or stores are located; what products or services it offers; and what its economic growth has been and how its future prospects look. Such knowledge demonstrates your initiative and interest to the interviewer and can serve as a springboard for discussion. This also shows you have an interest in the company, rather than giving the impression you're settling for whatever job you can find.

It used to be that if you wanted to learn anything about a company, you would have to write to the company for its annual report or for recruiting materials. You could also go to the library and look through publications and special directories for information related to a given company. Today, however, the Internet is the best source of company information, and although you can still go to the library or a career services office and find information, it requires much more work than a few clicks of a mouse. For example, if you wanted to learn about Google, all you need to do is search the Internet for "Google" and you will find the following address: www.google.com. Click on the link "About Google" and you will find almost anything you'll ever want to know about the company (see Figure A.4). The same search process should get you information on almost any company in the world.

## Developing Questions to Ask the Interviewer

In preparation for your meeting, think about possible questions to ask the interviewer. Sometimes an interviewer might choose to say little or to stop talking altogether, in which case it becomes your responsibility to carry the conversation by

**■ networking** The systematic contacting of people who can provide information about available jobs or who can offer jobs.

■ **FIGURE A.4** Google's Home Page on the World Wide Web

Reprinted by permission of Google Inc.

asking questions and continuing to emphasize your qualifications for the job. Regardless of whether the interviewer stops talking, you should have a list of questions to ask. This does not mean coming to the interview with a written list of questions, but it does mean coming prepared to ask questions such as these: What are the duties and responsibilities of the job? Does the company provide training programs? How much traveling is involved in the job? What's the next step up from the starting position? Would I be able to continue my education?

## ■■ How to Dress for an Interview

Your primary goal in dressing for an interview is to feel great about the way you look while projecting an image that matches the requirements of the job and the company. Go for perfection. Wear professionally pressed clothing in natural fabrics. Although casual clothing in many settings is acceptable today, it is still wise to be conservative

## MAKING Technology CONNECTIONS

### Learning about the Organization

Following are the names of several companies for you to research. For each one, there is a question or questions to which you should be able to find the answers to by doing a search on the Internet. Report your answers to the class if requested to do so.

1. Ford Motor Company—Approximately how many people work for the Ford Motor Company worldwide?

2. Lowes—Where is its main headquarters?

3. General Electric—When was the company started? Who is its present CEO?

4. Strong Investments Inc.—Approximately what is the amount of assets that Strong manages in billions of dollars? When was the company founded and where?

in what you wear to an interview. This is especially true if you do not know the culture of the organization or business. The interview is usually not the time to make a personal statement of nonconformity or disagreement with society's concept of professional image.[5] There are many excellent websites that address the issue of what is appropriate to wear to a job interview. We suggest that you do a search using the key words "dress for job interview." You will find many sites that provide guidelines for what to wear.

# ■ The Interview

Much of the responsibility for a successful interview rests with the interviewer, but this doesn't mean that you can merely relax and let things happen. On the contrary, research suggests that most interviewers develop a strong opinion about a job applicant in the first thirty seconds. If you do poorly at the opening, your chances of getting the job are slim, no matter how brilliantly you handle the rest of the interview. It might seem unfair or superficial, but people do judge others on the basis of first impressions, and such impressions can be long-lasting. By all means, be on time for the interview.

## GUIDELINES

### Telephone Interview: Some Tips

Today, it is likely that your preliminary interview will be over the phone. According to Carol Kleiman, columnist for Chicago Tribune Newspaper, many firms screen out candidates who do not demonstrate minimal levels of enthusiasm or communication skills. She cites David Stiefel, consultant with PeopleScout, a Chicago-based firm, who says that about 65 percent of all job candidates are screened out for those reasons. He goes on to suggest that you can successfully obtain an on-site interview on the phone by speaking in a clear, concise voice and by sounding enthusiastic about the job. Here are some specific tips for the phone interview from Connor Cunneen, president of Grow Foodservice Profit, a consulting firm, also cited by Kleiman:

1. Keep yourself motivated.
2. Stand up when taking the call. This will project confidence.
3. Put a mirror in front of you, and check your reflection. By looking positive, you will you sound positive.
4. Dress as if you were actually going to the interview in person.
5. Smile. This might seem like strange advice, but when you smile, you project a positive image that can often be detected even on the phone.[6]

## ■ Frequently Asked Questions

One expert states that most applicants make two devastating mistakes when they are being questioned. First, they fail to listen to the question and answer a question that was not asked or give superfluous information. Second, they attempt to answer questions with virtually no preparation. Lack of preparation will reduce the chances of success even for skillful communicators. You should always take a moment to think about your answer before you respond to each question unless it is something that you have already thought through. Here are some of the most common questions interviewers ask and some possible responses to them.

1. *"What can you tell me about yourself?"* This is not an invitation to give your life history. The interviewer is looking for clues about your character, qualifications, ambitions, and motivations. The following is a good example of a positive response. "In high school, I was involved in competitive sports, and I always tried to improve in each sport in which I participated. As a college student, I worked in a clothing store part time and found that I could sell things easily. The sale was important, but for me, it was even more important to make sure that the customer was satisfied. It wasn't long before customers came back to the store and specifically asked for me to help them. I'm very competitive, and it means a lot to me to be the best."

2. *"Why do you want to work for us?"* This is an obvious question, and if you have done research on the company, you should be able to give a good reason. Organize your reasons into several short sentences that clearly spell out your interest. "You are a leader in the field of electronics. Your company is a Fortune 500 company. Your management is very progressive."

3. *"Why should I hire you?"* Once again, you should not be long-winded, but you should provide a summary of your qualifications. Be positive, and show that you are capable of doing the job. "Based on the internships that I have participated in and the related part-time experiences I have had, I can do the job."

The employee interview is a key communication event for most people. The applicant should be prepared to discuss goals and skills and be able to clearly answer questions pertaining to why he or she is right for the job.

4. *"How do you feel about your progress to date?"* Never apologize for what you have done. "I think I did well in school. In fact, in a number of courses I received the highest exam scores in the class." "As an intern for the X Company, I received some of the highest evaluations that had been given in years." "Considering that I played on the university's volleyball team and worked part time, I think you'll agree that I accomplished quite a bit during my four years in school."

5. *"What would you like to be doing five years from now?"* Know what you can realistically accomplish. You can find out by talking to others about what they accomplished in their first five years with a particular company. "I hope to be the best I can be at my job, and because many in this line of work are promoted to area manager, I am planning on that also."

6. *"What is your greatest weakness?"* You cannot avoid this question by saying that you do not have any; everyone has weaknesses. The best approach is to admit your weakness but show that you are working on it and have a plan to overcome it. If possible, cite a weakness that will work to the company's advantage. "I'm not very good at detail work, but I have been working on it, and I've improved dramatically over the past several years." "I'm such a perfectionist that I won't stop until a report is written just right."

7. *"What is your greatest strength?"* This is a real opportunity to "toot your own horn." Do not brag or get too egotistical, but let the employer know that you believe in yourself and that you know your strengths. "I believe that my strongest asset is my ability to stick to things to get them done. I feel a real sense of accomplishment when I finish a job and it turns out just as I'd planned. I've set some high goals for myself. For example, I want to graduate with highest distinction. And even though I had a slow start in my first year, I made up for it by doing an honor's thesis."

8. *"What goals have you set, and how did you meet them?"* This question examines your ability to plan ahead and meet your plan with specific actions. "Last year, during a magazine drive to raise money for our band trip, I set my goal at raising 20 percent more than I had the year before. I knew the drive was going to begin in September, so I started contacting people in August. I asked each of my customers from last year to give me the name of one or two new people who might also buy a magazine. I not only met my goal but I also was the top salesperson on the drive."

Interviews are now using more questions similar to this last question, based on the premise that the best predictor of future performance is past performance. This type of questioning is referred to as **behavioral-based interview questions,** which are questions that ask directly about a particular skill or trait (to which most interviewees would probably answer "yes"). The interviewer would then follow up by asking for an example of a situation in which the interviewee could demonstrate the skill or trait that would demonstrate and support the "yes" answer they gave to the initial question. For example, to determine whether a person had decision-making skills, an interviewer might ask, "Have you had to make many difficult decisions?" The interviewee would likely respond, "Yes." The follow-up question by the interviewer would attempt to solicit an example of a difficult decision the person had to make by saying something such as "Describe a situation in which you had to make a difficult decision under pressure or when there were time limitations." For

■ **behavioral-based interview questions** Questions that ask directly about a particular skill or trait.

more examples of behavioral-based interview questions, go to www.unl.edu/careers/prepare/behavioral.htm.

Here are a few other questions that are commonly asked in the employment interview:

What is your dream job?

What type of supervisors do you do your best work for?

What kind of legacy did you leave in college?

What are the differences between a leader and a manager?

What motivates you to get up in the morning?

Do you consider yourself to be a risk taker?

What was the last risk you took?

What five characteristics would make you a great salesperson?

If an interviewer were to ask you any of the eight most frequently asked questions, do you know how you would answer them? The key is to understand why a question is being asked. Remember, the purpose of the employment interview is to hire the best-qualified person for the job. The more often you can demonstrate through your responses to questions that you are the best qualified, the more likely you will be to get the job offer.

No matter what question you are asked, answer it honestly and succinctly. Most interviewers are looking for positive statements, well-expressed ideas, persuasiveness, and clear thinking under pressure.

If you are asked a question that violates the affirmative action laws, you can decline to answer. You might say, "I'm sorry, but I don't find that question relevant to the position being offered, and it is against affirmative action laws to ask it." You might simply ask the interviewer why he or she is asking you that question. Make sure that you are tactful, but be firm in letting the interviewer know that he or she is doing something illegal.

## MAKING CONNECTIONS
### for Success

### Knowing Your Strengths

Call to mind your experiences. If you can respond to the following with good-quality answers, you have a good understanding of who you are and what your strengths are:

1. Describe your greatest accomplishment.
2. Describe a situation in which you influenced a group to support an idea that was important to you.
3. Give an example of a time when you went above and beyond the call of duty to accomplish a task or goal.
4. Describe a situation in which you worked independently on a complex project and achieved good results.
5. Describe a situation in which you were confronted with and solved a difficult problem.
6. Describe a situation in which you took a leadership role in a group.
7. Write a statement that describes you.

## ■ Other Considerations

As a job applicant, you are expected to show good judgment and common sense about appearance, assertiveness, being on time, and being at the right place. Always maintain eye contact with the interviewer. Show that you are confident by looking straight at the speaker. Eye contact might not get you the job, but lack of eye contact can reduce your chances dramatically.

Most interviewers greet the applicant with a handshake. Make sure that your clasp is firm. Being jittery about the interview can result in cold, clammy hands, which create a negative impression. Therefore try to make sure your hands are warm and dry. If this is not possible, a firm handshake will at least show confidence.

When the interviewer asks you to sit down, if you have a choice, take the chair beside the desk rather than the one in front. This helps to eliminate any barriers between you and the interviewer and also makes you a little more equal, for which the interviewer will unconsciously respect you.

Before leaving, try to find out exactly what action will follow the interview and when it will happen. Shake hands as you say goodbye, and thank the interviewer for spending time with you. If you plan ahead and follow these simple suggestions, you should be able to avoid any serious problems.

# ■ Factors Leading to Rejection

Rejection is difficult for all of us to accept, but you should never give up. Being rejected by employers eight or nine times before receiving a job offer is not unusual in the present job market.[7]

Employers from numerous companies were asked, "What negative factors most often lead to the rejection of an applicant?" Here are their responses in order of frequency:

1. Negative personality or poor impression—more specifically, lack of motivation, ambition, maturity, aggressiveness, or enthusiasm
2. Inability to communicate; poor communication skills
3. Lack of competence; inadequate training
4. Low grades; poor grades in major field
5. Lack of specific goals
6. Unrealistic expectations
7. Lack of interest in type of work
8. Unwillingness to travel or relocate
9. Poor preparation for the interview
10. Lack of experience[8]

You must realize that rejection or not receiving a job offer has a lot to do with the number of people seeking jobs and the number of jobs available. You can of course enhance your chances of getting job offers by being prepared and presenting yourself in a positive and energetic way.

# ■ Factors Leading to Job Offers

An applicant who is well rounded and has good grades, some relevant work experience, a variety of extracurricular activities, an all-around pleasant personality, and effective written and oral communication skills is more likely to get job offers than are those who do not possess these qualities, according to Jason Meyers of *Collegiate Employment Institute Newsletter*.[9] Meyers says, "Sounds too good to be true? Perhaps it is, but a candidate who strives to attain these qualities and who comes across as a hard-working, mature individual should have a promising career outlook."[10]

A research study cited by Meyers in his article asked recruiters to describe what they believed to be the qualities of a well-rounded individual. They listed maturity, ability to be part of a team, good work ethic, good decision-making skills, superior work habits, and good judgment. Another study cited by Meyers found that the most popular characteristics that recruiters sought in job applicants fit two categories: (1) quantifiable characteristics, such as grade point average, education, and work experience, and (2) interpersonal characteristics, such as communication skills, personality, and career and management skills. The study suggests that a balance of the quantifiable characteristics and interpersonal characteristics is what makes an ideal job candidate.[11]

It seems that those who are well prepared; have effective communication skills; are mature, motivated, hard-working, team players; and can make good decisions will always be in demand. You must ask yourself how you match up to these qualities now and try to improve in those areas in which you are not as strong. You must also be able to demonstrate that you actually possess these qualities through the actions you have taken.

## Summary

Choosing a career is one of the most important decisions a person can make, and a successful job interview is a crucial step in achieving that end. Planning and preparation are critical to a successful employment interview. The Internet is one the most valuable tools available in preparing for the employment interview. On the Internet, you can learn how to prepare for the interview, write a résumé, research an organization, find job opportunities, know what questions are most frequently asked, and even what to wear to the interview. Applicants must know their strengths and weaknesses and be able to communicate effectively with the interviewer. Getting a job requires motivation, energy, hard work, and research, plus knowing where to look and whom to contact to obtain the necessary information.

## Discussion Starters

1. How can the Internet help you prepare for an employment interview?
2. What can you do to increase your chances of getting the best job?
3. If you were an employer, what would you look for in a job applicant?
4. What advice would you give fellow students about writing résumés?
5. Why should personal data such as age, gender, marital status, and religion be omitted from a résumé?
6. How should you go about getting references? Who should you ask?
7. What advice would you give regarding the best methods of doing a job search?
8. What should you know about a company before you are interviewed?
9. Why is it important for an applicant to ask questions of the interviewer?
10. If you were to interview someone for a job with your company, what would be some of the questions that you would ask an applicant? Why?
11. What can someone do to reduce the chances of being rejected?

# Making Team Decisions Systematically

*Vigilance* is a key word for good decision making. The degree to which members are vigilant about the quality of their decisions determines the degree to which they will be successful. Vigilant critical thinking and analysis proceed through a series of smaller decisions at four stages: examining the problem, clarifying objectives, developing available choices, and examining potential consequences (Gouran & Hirokawa, 1983; Hirokawa & Scheerhorn, 1986).

For our discussion, we have combined these decision stages with Simon's four-stage decision-making process (intelligence, design, choice, review) and the reflective thinking stages John Dewey (1910) developed years ago. The result is seven task activities to guide your decision making. These activities are useful in three ways: as strategies for work plans, as items for meeting agendas, and as reminders of essential elements so you don't miss important angles when thinking through decision-making tasks.

1   Analyze the problem.

2   Establish criteria for solutions.

3   List possible solutions.

4   Evaluate possible solutions.

5   Decide on the most appropriate solution(s).

6   Implement the decision.

7   Evaluate the effectiveness of the decision.

These tasks may provide the agenda for a single meeting if the problem to be solved is relatively simple, or they may guide a team's work over a period of months or even years. Because problem solving is so detailed, however, and because the team decision making does not always occur in this order, agendas may be modified considerably as meetings move along. Teams often overlap the tasks, loop back, and jump forward in vigilant analysis and achievement.

A systematic plan doesn't guarantee clear thinking. As you move through the decision-making tasks, you might use **brainstorming** to create multiple

*All decisions are made about imaginary worlds.*

Kenneth Boulding, 20th-century philosopher

**Brainstorming** Process of generating solutions by thinking of as many ideas as possible without constraint

perspectives and options. Brainstorming helps produce more ideas to improve your chances of making the highest-quality choices.

The best way to brainstorm is with a group, so you get a lot of ideas from diverse sources, but you can use the same process alone. The goal is to think of as many ideas as you can. Reach to the outer limits for wild and crazy thoughts. Look at the problem from every angle. Here are some guidelines:

1   Appoint someone to facilitate if you're in a group.

2   Don't stop to evaluate ideas.

3   Keep the flow of ideas moving fast.

4   Write down as many ideas as you can.

5   Do not "own" ideas, good or bad—keep egos out.

6   "Piggyback" or "hitchhike" ideas onto previous thoughts.

7   Sweat out silences and plateaus; sit quietly and let your brain incubate until something emerges.

8   After many ideas are on the list, analyze and winnow them down.

9   Start serious selection from the remaining possibilities.

Try it. You'll discover ideas you didn't dream you could have.

## Analyzing Problems

Dewey (1910) states that when people "feel difficulties," they have taken the first step in problem exploration. They sense that something is wrong, such as when students complain about their choices of classes or the final exam schedule. Sometimes, there are as many explanations of the problems as there are students lamenting.

The first task is to move from intuitions about difficulties to identification of the nature and scope of the specific problems. The team must ask questions, gather information, and think analytically, critically, and creatively to identify the problems and to find their causes and effects.

**Problem Identification**   Identifying problems is not as easy as it sounds. From "feeling the difficulty," you move to exploring the general area of concern to find trouble spots. Then you start isolating problems by tracking them. You analyze how things presently *are* functioning and compare that with the ways things *should* work.

Assume you have been appointed to a college task force charged with improving registration procedures. First, your team might track the registration process as staff and students actually experience it. To track through the issues, you could create a step-by-step flowchart to help clarify the team's thinking and identify the problem spots. A flowchart can be used at any stage of information sharing or problem solving, but it is particularly useful for identifying problems. Figure 11.2 shows a flowchart that might illustrate the registration process.

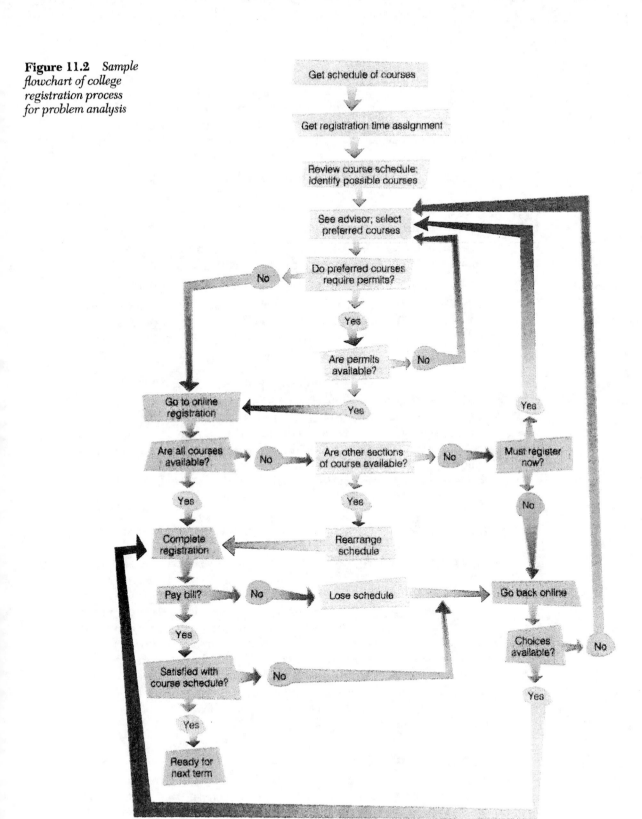

**Figure 11.2** *Sample flowchart of college registration process for problem analysis*

Next, compare your flowchart to registration procedures as described by established policies. Your task force can use the comparison to identify possible problem areas in the process and to isolate the policies that need more careful examination. Your analysis can begin by seeking answers to some of these questions:

- What difficulties are people experiencing? Where are the bottlenecks? At what points are many people encountering obstacles?

- What harms are being done? What is the scope of the problem? How many people are affected? How seriously?

- What conditions are relevant to the difficulties? Are the policies, procedures, objectives, or criteria missing or inappropriately applied?

As you start to analyze the registration problems, your task force may detect some patterns. One difficulty may be lack of sufficient classes at times convenient for students. The negative results are clear: Students can't get into classes or must take them at inconvenient times; they may have trouble completing requirements or getting course prerequisites.

**Causes and Effects** Tracking problems helps you see possible causes for them. Analysis of causes and effects makes or breaks problem solving. If you don't have the correct causes, you're not going to solve the problem—and you may create new ones. It can be difficult to determine whether one factor causes a problem or just happens to occur at the same time, possibly as another symptom rather than the cause. Chapter 3 develops guidelines for logical cause-effect reasoning, and those principles should be applied in your team's problem analysis.

A fishbone diagram, created on a flipchart or large board with all members participating, assists you in identifying, tracking, analyzing, and visualizing multiple cause-effect relationships (Ishikawa, 1982). See Figure 11.3 for an example.

You construct a fishbone by drawing a long line—vertical or horizontal—to represent the problem on which you're working. You then draw diagonal lines—like the ribs of a fish—off the problem line, labeled with the issues that the team identifies as related to the problem. For example, as shown in Figure 11.3, your registration fishbone could list students, departments, resources, and methods as potential components of the registration problem. Next, you might draw shorter horizontal lines off the diagonal lines, labeled with subordinate issues or categories that affect the larger problems. Now you have a diagram showing relationships among issues pertaining to the problem. The fishbone doesn't solve the problems or even prove the causes, but it does make the relationships among the issues much clearer.

## Establishing Criteria

To make quality choices from many options, you have to know the requirements of the solution. Criteria are those standards by which you will judge potential solutions to determine if you are selecting wisely. You can't assume you'll "know

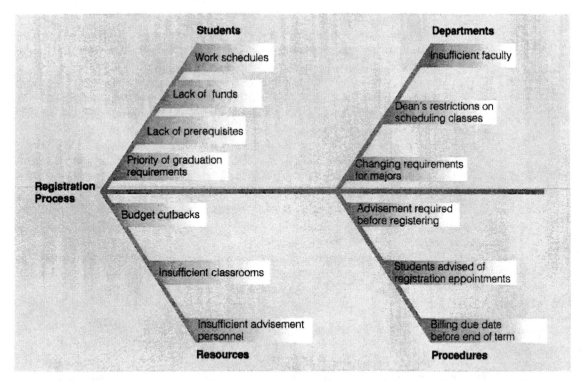

**Figure 11.3** *Sample fishbone analysis of registration process to identify problems' causes and effects*

it when you see it." You might not. Establishing clear criteria is extremely important to your success.

To set criteria, first brainstorm a list of what conditions would be like if you had the perfect solution. If your task is to create a class project, for example, your criteria will include meeting the objectives of the assignment, the objectives for learning and grades, and the conditions that you, as a team, have decided to include in your project. For example, suppose you're on a creative team for a film-making class. Your criteria for an "ideal" project could look like this:

- Be original and unique.
- Involve each member in a specific role.
- Deal with a controversial or timely topic.
- Demonstrate skill in each area listed on the syllabus.
- Write a good script.
- Use graphics effectively.
- Cut and edit smoothly.
- Achieve demonstration quality for each member's portfolio.
- Have fun.
- Earn an "A" for each member.

As you might surmise, some of these criteria are dictated by the assignment, but some are the product of the team's thinking about what will make a good film. Probably, this team would add and subtract criteria according to the possible projects they might do.

Once you've drafted your criteria, try to *visualize* what things would be like with a solution that meets those criteria. All members need to understand the team vision of their work—a mental picture of what that final result will be like, how it will feel, what it will provide. As you visualize and discuss the ideal solution together, you clarify any misunderstandings or assumptions that could cause problems later on. Further, the vision you hold in common motivates members to achieve it.

For any potential solution, you'll want to consider four issues in particular: (1) applicability, (2) practicality, (3) advantages versus disadvantages and risks, and (4) desirability and ethicality. We'll develop these in more detail later in this chapter.

Finally, and very importantly, *record your criteria*. The criteria should be written clearly and unambiguously and posted—possibly in big print on a flipchart—so you can check potential solutions against your criteria.

## Generating Possible Solutions

After carefully documenting a problem's causes, describing the effects, and noting the seriousness of their impact on people and operations, it's time to consider solutions. Generating possible solutions requires time, energy, and dedication. You need teamwork and creative thinking from all members to gather every imaginable solution. Use idea-generating approaches such as brainstorming to enlarge your list. Hold off judgment and criticism until you get as many ideas as possible on the table. Don't be afraid to get silly. You want quantity now; later, you'll evaluate the quality of the ideas.

When your team has a list of possible solutions and criteria, you're ready to make some decisions. It's easier to select the most appropriate solution when you use charting methods to visualize how each proposal measures on each of several critical issues. One useful technique is to prepare large charts of both the solution options and the criteria—on flipcharts, the blackboard, or taped-up butcher's paper.

**Analysis Tools**  Two approaches to analyzing possible solutions can help your team work through these tasks together.

*T-chart.*  One simple and effective way to keep everyone focused on the comparison is a T-chart. On a large sheet of paper or the blackboard, draw a T and label one side "Pros" and the other "Cons." As members make their observations about the merits of a solution, record them in the appropriate column. Figure 11.4 shows a sample T-chart for one possible solution for registration problems.

**Figure 11.4** *Sample T-chart for analysis of one solution to registration problems*

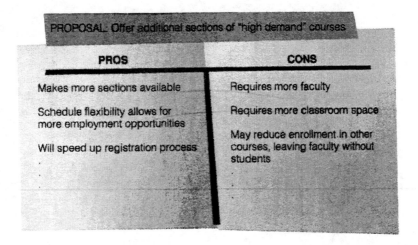

PROPOSAL: Offer additional sections of "high demand" courses

| PROS | CONS |
|---|---|
| Makes more sections available | Requires more faculty |
| Schedule flexibility allows for more employment opportunities | Requires more classroom space |
| Will speed up registration process | May reduce enrollment in other courses, leaving faculty without students |

*Decision matrix.* When you're comparing the merits of several solutions, a decision matrix lays out the information and jogs members' memories. As Figure 11.5 shows, a decision matrix is simply a large grid. Across the top, you label each column with one criterion from your list for the ideal solution. Down the left-hand side, you label each row with a designation for one possible solution. Then, as a team, you fill in the cells with notes as to how each plan meets each criterion. When you've completed the grid, you have a concise, easily comprehended set of comparisons for the proposals.

Once criteria are clearly established and visualized, your team can start examining critical issues. You need to focus on four areas: applicability, practicality, advantages versus disadvantages and risks, and desirability or ethicality.

*Applicability* How well a solution meets the criteria for solving a problem

**Applicability**  Different solutions have varying levels of **applicability**—how well they may meet your criteria for solving the problem. For each possible choice, you want to predict the outcome against each criterion. You could consider:

- Will the proposed step solve the entire problem?
- If a proposal solves only part of the problem, how significant is that part?
- How does the idea compare to others on goal achievement?

Suppose your sorority wants to send the officers to a national meeting and needs to raise $5,000. Your brainstorming list of solutions includes a bake sale. Somebody will have to bake a lot of cookies for that solution to solve your problem. At this point, some proposals will clearly be inadequate and therefore be eliminated or at least combined with other possibilities.

*Practicality* The likelihood that a solution to a problem can be implemented successfully

**Practicality**  Every possible solution can raise sticky issues of **practicality** that could keep them from being implemented successfully. These issues center on several areas:

**Figure 11.5** *Decision matrix for comparing possible solutions*

| Possible Solutions | Criterion #1: Reduce waiting | Criterion #2: Use classroom space efficiently | Criterion #3: Have students get classes when needed |
|---|---|---|---|
| Register by phone | Shorten wait Etc. | No effect Etc. | Immediate confirmation Etc. |
| Register online | No waiting Etc. | Yes—rooms assigned after all requests in Etc. | Little control over 2nd and 3rd choices Etc. |
| Register without advisors | Less wait, but reduces personal attention Etc. | No effect Etc. | Negative impact— may take wrong courses Etc. |

- How much time and money will be required, and will they be available?
- What kinds of support from others (teams, agencies, parent organizations, individuals) will be necessary?
- What kinds of barriers will have to be overcome?
- Will it be possible to sell the idea to those who will implement it?

If any of these issues are significant barriers, then the idea can't be implemented. Sometimes, however, you see ways to adapt a proposal to solve practical issues. In these cases, evaluate whether the adapted proposal weakens the effectiveness of the plan and whether it is still superior to other plans.

***Advantages*** Positive effects of a solution to a problem

***Disadvantages*** Negative consequences of a solution to a problem

**Advantages, Disadvantages, and Risks**  Aside from simply solving the problem, implementing a solution may bring with it extra advantages, disadvantages, or risks. A proposal may solve the immediate problem but also have other positive or negative consequences. To identify both **advantages** and **disadvantages,** consider what could occur if the project were implemented. Some questions you could think about include:

- What effects would the implemented proposal have on individuals or groups other than those it is intended to affect?
- Would the advantages flow automatically from implementing the idea or require some other action?
- Would some minor modification eliminate some disadvantages?
- How do the advantages and disadvantages weigh against each other?
- How do the advantages and disadvantages weigh against those of other proposed solutions?

***Risk*** Potential gains of solving a problem weighted against potential losses

These questions clarify the advantages and disadvantages, as well as perhaps revealing some previously unconsidered risks in the proposal. **Risk** refers to the potential gains achieved in solving the problem weighed against the possible adverse consequences, such as costly or damaging results or even failure. Any innovative and potentially successful idea involves some risk. By definition, the new idea isn't proven by long experience, so it necessarily carries the possibility of failure. Without risk taking, therefore, there would be no new ideas, no progress, no exciting possibilities. The reality, however, is that people have to weigh the risks and make the most informed choices they can.

**Desirability**   No matter how perfect a proposed solution may appear to be in terms of applicability, practicality, and so on, it may rise or fall depending on its desirability. **Desirability** judgments are based on the character of the proposal and the value systems of the team members involved. That is, you examine the relative worth of probable outcomes and the values and ethical choices that affect the decision. Here, values and goals come into play, as the decision makers debate how valuable and how worthwhile the goals are in terms of what it takes to implement a given plan.

*Desirability* The relative worth of a solution to a problem

A few years ago, an automobile manufacturer had considered, and rejected, a proposal to recall cars because the number of people *killed* due to its safety defect was not enough to justify the expense of recalling the cars. Management had weighed the number of deaths and the cost of possible lawsuits against the cost of recall and human lives lost. One may wonder how many lives would have been needed to tip the scale.

As your team looks at its proposals, ask some of these questions:

- How desirable are the probable effects of the proposal?
- Will the implemented proposal serve the team's vision?
- Will the proposal harm anyone spiritually, psychologically, physically, economically, and/or socially?
- Is any team member uncomfortable with the ethics of the proposal?

As you discuss ethical issues, you will find that some answers are easy. "No, that's against our values," or, "Yes, that's ethically defensible." Some issues, however, are not simple at all; they may present a dilemma when choices are among competing people and competing values (Toffler, 1986, pp. 21–22). You have an ethical dilemma, for example, when one team member believes a specific solution is unethical while another's values are violated by the only other practical alternative. How do you handle these competing values? First, team members must recognize that a dilemma exists by listening to and analyzing one anothers' ideas. Then, they must discuss the ethical issues and the relevant values and try to reach a consensus. Sometimes, resolving dilemmas requires a more objective outsider to facilitate the discussion.

As a team, consider in what ways alternative responses to the dilemma can be justified, and examine each set of reasons in the context of both individual and social codes of ethics. Jaksa and Pritchard (1994) point out that "seeking exact points of difference can help solve disagreements by eliminating false distinctions and evasions" (p. 17). Above all, don't brush the dilemma off with "Everyone's entitled to an opinion," or, "Value judgments are subjective." Such statements tend to bring a discussion to a quick end. Although these statements seem to express an attitude of tolerance, they also suggest that you do not have much to learn from one another.

Gouran (1982) suggests five questions that help a team examine the ethics of both its decisions and the processes by which it made them:

1   Did we show proper concern for those who will be affected by our decision?

2   Did we explore the discussion question as responsibly as we were capable of doing?

3   Did we misrepresent any position or misuse any source of information?

4   Did we say or do anything that might have unnecessarily diminished any participant's sense of self-worth?

5   Was everyone in the team shown the respect due him or her?

## Decision Modes

Although a team could go on analyzing alternatives indefinitely, at some point it has to make some decisions. Take time to be sure everyone's clear on the merits and characteristics of each proposal and to clarify questions. This lets you get second thoughts out in the open and check whether everyone's in agreement.

Your method of deciding affects the fairness of the decision and members' satisfaction with it, so your team needs to consider your approach. All too often, teams fall into making "twofer" decisions: two people speak for a decision and the silence of other members is interpreted as consent. Twofer decisions lead to disgruntlement and lack of commitment. Better modes include decision by consensus, voting, and even decision by authority.

# Notes

1. K. B. Barbour, F. B. Berg, M. Eannace, J. Greene, M. Hessig, M. Papworth, C. Radin, E. Rezny, and J. Suarez, *The Quest: A Guide to the Job Interview* (Dubuque, IA: Kendall/Hunt, 1991), 47.

2. C. J. Stewart and W. B. Cash Jr., *Interviewing Principles and Practices,* 10th ed. (New York: McGraw-Hill, 2006), 158.

3. Interview with Dr. Larry Routh, Director of Career Services (University of Nebraska, Lincoln, September 2000, March 10, 2003, and June 12, 2006).

4. Stewart and Cash, 164.

5. J. LaFevre, "How You Really Get Hired," *CPC Annual 1990/91,* 34th ed. (Bethlehem, PA: College Placement Council).

6. C. Kleiman, "Candidates Making Early Interviews Can Have Lasting Impact," *Lincoln Journal Star,* July 14, 2003, 4A.

7. Routh.

8. *The Endicott Report: Trends in the Employment of College and University Graduates in Business and Industry* (Evanston, IL: The Placement Center, Northwestern University, 1980), 8. In the June 12, 2006 interview, Dr. Routh said that the rejection reasons companies give today are not different from what they were in 1980.

9. J. Meyers, "The Ideal Job Candidate," *Collegiate Employment Institute Newsletter,* 15 July, 1989, 6.

10. Ibid.

11. Ibid.

# Index

# Photo Credits

| # | Speech Evaluation Form | NA | Excellent (4) | Good (3) | Average (2) | Poor (1) | Overall Score | Mean Score |
|---|---|---|---|---|---|---|---|---|
| 1 | Gained favorable attention | | | | | | | |
| 2 | Established relevance to audience | | | | | | | |
| 3 | Provided clear preview and thesis | | | | | | | |
| | **Body** | NA | E (4) | G (3) | A (2) | P (1) | Overall | Mean |
| 4 | Cleary organized main points | | | | | | | |
| 5 | Properly cited credible sources | | | | | | | |
| 6 | Used varied and multiple kinds of support | | | | | | | |
| 7 | Used transitions effectively | | | | | | | |
| 8 | Multisided persuasive strategy | | | | | | | |
| | **Conclusion** | NA | E (4) | G (3) | A (2) | P (1) | Overall | Mean |
| 9 | Summarized main points. Provided closure. | | | | | | | |
| | **Physical Delivery** | NA | E (4) | G (3) | A (2) | P (1) | Overall | Mean |
| 10 | Maintained good eye contact | | | | | | | |
| 11 | Effective use of gestures, posture, movement | | | | | | | |
| | **Vocal Delivery** | NA | E (4) | G (3) | A (2) | P (1) | Overall | Mean |
| 12 | Used appropriate vocalistics & enthusiasm | | | | | | | |
| 13 | Avoided vocal fillers (uhs, ums, you know) | | | | | | | |
| 14 | Appropriate use of note cards/not read | | | | | | | |
| | **Language Usage** | NA | E (4) | G (3) | A (2) | P (1) | Overall | Mean |
| 15 | Appropriate and correct grammar | | | | | | | |
| 16 | Clearly defined terms. Avoided cliches & jargon. | | | | | | | |
| 17 | Concrete and vivid language. | | | | | | | |
| | **Preparation** | NA | E (4) | G (3) | A (2) | P (1) | Overall | Mean |
| 18 | Bibliography | | | | | | | |
| 19 | Outline | | | | | | | |
| 20 | Topic choice | | | | | | | |
| 21 | Time | | | | | | | |
| 22 | Visual Aids | | | | | | | |
| | **Final Grade** | NA | E (4) | G (3) | A (2) | P (1) | Overall | Mean |
| 23 | Speech accomplished its purpose | | | | | | | |

Student Name

_____

Student ID #

_____

Section #

_____

Type of Speech

_____

Comments

_____
_____
_____
_____
_____
_____
_____
_____
_____
_____
_____
_____
_____
_____
_____
_____
_____
_____
_____
_____
_____
_____
_____
_____